Best Places to Raise an LDS Family

361 Communities Evaluated

From a Latter-day Saint Perspective

Michael D. Call

Copyright © 2010 by Michael D. Call

All rights reserved. Except for brief quotations in a review, this book, or any part thereof, may not be reproduced, stored in or introduced into a retrieval system, or transmitted, in any form or through any means, electronic, mechanical, photocopying, recording, or otherwise, through any system or process now known or yet to be invented, without the prior written consent of the publisher.

ISBN: 978-0-9828092-0-4

Library of Congress Control Number: 2010908998

Published by Civicus
5069 Edgemere Court, Suite 24
Roscoe, IL 61073

10 9 8 7 6 5 4 3 2 1

> **Leave your own comments and ratings for these communities at our website.**
>
> **BestLDSPlaces.com**

www.CivicusBooks.com

Contents

Chapter 1: The *Whys* and the *Hows* 5
    Table 1: Metropolitan Statistical Areas and 2009 Population 13
Chapter 2: The Categories 31
Chapter 3: Community Data 33
    Table 2.1: Communities in Order of Ranking 34
    Table 2.2: Communities in Alphabetical Order 41
    Tables 3.1 and 3.2: Best and Worst Communities for LDS Culture 48
    Tables 4.1 and 4.2: Best and Worst Communities for Education 49
    Tables 5.1 and 5.2: Best and Worst Communities for Crime 50
    Tables 6.1 and 6.2: Best and Worst Communities for Economic Environment 51
    Tables 7.1 and 7.2: Best and Worst Communities for Health 52
    Tables 8.1 and 8.2: Best and Worst Communities for Household Characteristics 53
    Tables 9.1 and 9.2: Best and Worst Communities for Housing 54
    Table 10: One-way Commute Times 55
    Table 11.1: Communities with Shortest Commute Times 62
    Table 11.2: Communities with Longest Commute Times 63
    Table 12.1: Most College-Educated Communities 64
    Table 12.2: Least College-Educated Communities 65
    Table 13.1: Communities with Lowest Property Crime 66
    Table 13.2: Communities with the Highest Property Crime 67
    Table 14.1: Communities with the Lowest Violent Crime 68
    Table 14.2: Bottom 25 Communities with the Highest Violent Crime 69
    Table 15.1: Communities with Most Families Earning the Most Income 70
    Table 15.2: Communities with Most Families Earning the Least Income 71
    Table 16.1: Communities with the Lowest Unemployment Rate 72
    Table 16.2: Communities with the Highest Unemployment Rate 73
    Table 17.1: Communities with Most Children Living with Married Parents 74
    Table 17.2: Communities with Least Children Living with Married Parents 75
    Table 18.1: Communities with Most Stay-at-Home Mothers 76
    Table 18.2: Communities with Fewest Stay-at-Home Mothers 77
    Tables 19.1 and 19.2: Best and Worst Communities for Ratio of Positive to Negative Establishments .. 78

Chapter 4: Community Data 79

About the Author

Michael D. Call has been studying and working with communities for nearly 25 years. Prior to opening his own consulting firm, he worked as the CEO of a major nonprofit organization in Illinois for nearly eight years. In that role he was able to work with community leaders, including elected officials, business, civic, and nonprofit leaders, community volunteers, and educators to help improve the quality of life in local communities. He also worked professionally for nearly seven years in state government, having received a gubernatorial appointment to lead a statewide commission to improve communities through volunteer and community service efforts. Accredited by the Public Relations Society of America and a Certified Fund Raising Executive, Michael earned a Bachelor of Arts degree in Communications from Brigham Young University. He was awarded a Master of Science in Management degree from the University of St. Francis in Joliet, Illinois, and is currently pursuing a PhD in Organizational Leadership from IndianaTech.

He is the principal of Civicus Consulting Group (www.CivicusConsulting.com), a firm that specializes in assisting nonprofit organizations and governments in their efforts to become more effective, efficient, and strategic in their operations. He is married to the former Shannon Brown of Logan, Utah. They are the parents of five children.

Chapter 1: The *Whys* and the *Hows*
Or, *What this Book Is and What it Is Not*

This book's beginnings date back to 1995 when my family and I were living in Orem, Utah. A family with five or six children—the oldest being about 13 or 14—moved to our neighborhood from another state, and I had an interesting conversation with the father of the family:

"So, you came here from out of state?"

"Yep."

"Were you transferred here for work?"

"Nope."

"Family in the area?"

"Nope."

"Cougar fan?"

"Yep. But that's not why we moved here."

"So, why did you move here?"

"To live in a better place for my children. Where we moved from was fine, but we wanted to live somewhere that our kids could have the benefits of associating with more members of the Church. Plus, the high school that our kids would've gone to isn't the best. It's not real safe. We just wanted to find a better environment to raise our family."

That conversation got me thinking. What *does* make a community a good place to raise a Latter-day Saint family? I had been raised in Southern California during my childhood years and in the Philadelphia area during my adolescent years. I had lived in Utah since going to school at Brigham Young University. My parents were from small towns in Southeastern Idaho. And my wife was born and raised in Logan, Utah. All of us seemed to turn out okay, despite the variety and the diversity of the communities in which we had been raised.

About five years after that conversation, my wife and I took our five children and we moved across the country to Northern Illinois because of new employment. We moved near a community that hadn't fared well in national ranking systems. But we figured that home and community are what you make of them. So off we went, with our five children—the oldest being 15.

Now, nearly 10 years later, our oldest children are grown and gone. For the most part, they all consider Illinois their home. Yes, they grew up in a non-LDS community, attended early-morning seminary, had to drive 20 minutes to get to church meetings, the whole thing. And somehow they have all survived and are active in the Church today.

So, why this book?

First, a bit about what this book is *not*. It is *not* a book recommending that all LDS families relocate to the top-rated communities. It is *not* a book advocating one community above another. It is *not* a book that argues one particular metropolitan area is more livable, more desirable, more blessed, or better than any other particular area. And it *certainly is not* a book that judges lifestyles or decisions that individuals, neighborhoods, cultures, or communities have adopted over the decades and, in some cases, over the centuries.

Next, what this book *is*. It *is* a book of data based on LDS values and lifestyles. It *is* a reference book to help families and future families make more informed decisions about their futures. It *is* a book that adds another perspective—another factor or sets of factors—to the mortal decisions we all need to make from time to time. It *is* a book of data that will help you as you plan where to go to school, where to raise a family, whether to accept a job offer, what challenges you may face, and what opportunities you may have as you move to other parts of the United States.

This book was researched and written to simply help you make better decisions for your future.

Now for the *hows*.

First, how did I go about gathering the data? All of the data found in this book and used in the rating and ranking process is publicly available data, mostly from state and federal government sources. But that does not mean that it is easy to find, categorize, properly weight (more about that later) or compare. It took much time just to identify the data that is most pertinent to LDS families. For instance, you'll find that climate is not even addressed in this book. But climate is a huge factor for many people, and for a variety of reasons. But, you'll see that "number of negative establishments" in a given metropolitan area is included. You likely won't find, for instance, the number of off-track wagering facilities considered in other lists, books, or city rating and ranking systems. Nor will you find the number of liquor licenses, the number and proximity of LDS temples, or the rate of stay-at-home moms. Yet as I've worked on and researched this book, these data were identified as data of interest to Latter-day Saint families.

Second, how did I select the cities to be rated? Few people would argue that the best data is that which is at the lowest possible geographic or other level. For example, when looking at geographic divisions, we could say that, on average, about 86 percent of American adults have graduated from high school. However, this figure does not hold true when comparing states. Some states have higher graduation rates, and others have lower rates. The national figure is even less relevant when considering rural versus urban areas within states. And then it becomes even less accurate when looking at metropolitan areas. Even within metropolitan areas, there are a number of unique cities and towns, each with their own unique history, tradition, values, employment, schools, housing, etc. And then to look at individual cities or towns, the national data is completely irrelevant. Finally, if one were to research various neighborhoods, or census tracks, within cities, data would finally become both extremely relevant and extremely accurate. It would also become extremely expensive.

So the trick is to find the lowest geographic subdivision with the greatest number of affordable, accurate, and relevant data.

Next, when comparing community to community, you need to have comparable data. To look at graduation rates, for example, the researcher needs to consider how the graduation rates were calculated, and then compare like data across communities.

Unfortunately, current high school graduation rates are one of those data that are not measured or reported in consistent methods across communities. So we used our own method of calculating "graduation rates." We took the total number of freshmen entering high school in 2005 and subtracted the total number of seniors graduating four years later. In cases where schools or school districts had combined or separated in the intervening years (for instance, when the "graduating" class was much larger or much smaller than the corresponding freshman class), the data was obviously skewed and was disregarded.

And so, the question remains: What level of community should we select? The answer came in the federal government's Metropolitan Statistical Area designations. We used 361 of these areas because the data is most plentiful, most accurate, and most affordable at that level. Many of the MSAs have smaller *divisions;* there are also *Micropolitan Statistical Areas.* However, we chose to utilize MSAs for the reasons cited above.

Because these areas are sometimes quite large—some have millions of residents—and can be relatively small—fewer than 100,000 residents—you will need to sort through the data and even seek out your own primary and secondary research as you consider the data presented in this volume.

Third, how did I organize the data? It's organized into seven broad categories: LDS Culture, Education, Crime, Economic Environment, Health, Households, and Housing. More details about these categories are in Chapter 2.

Fourth, how did I weight the variables? This is the most subjective element of this entire effort. For example, what is more important in making a decision about whether to move to a particular community?

Which is more important to you?		
Proximity to a temple	OR	Teen smoking rates?
Teen smoking rates	OR	Property tax rates?
Property tax rates	OR	Ratio of stay-at-home moms?
Stay-at-home moms	OR	Unemployment rate?
Unemployment rate	OR	Median cost of a large home?
Median home cost	OR	Median age of home?

You get the idea. It's impossible for one person or group of researchers to adequately and fairly weight such diverse elements of a community, especially when the weighting needs to factor in LDS values and lifestyles.

Another example: One family may find it most desirable to live near an LDS temple and surrounded by other members of the Church. Another family may believe it is more important to live where fewer members of the Church live in order to have more missionary opportunities.

Which family is right? Is either family right? Is either family wrong? The answer is obvious. Neither family is right, and neither family is wrong.

So, given the propensity for diverse LDS families to have diverse needs and desires, how did I weight the factors? I used my best judgment, looking at the totality of data available to me.

There are two weightings that were used. First, weighting within a category. For this, I used what I consider to be middle-of-the-road subjectivity. For example, when looking at crime, I weighted violent crime—that is, murder, assault, etc.—more heavily than nonviolent crimes such as burglary or theft. I weighted proximity to temples more heavily than proximity to significant Church historical sites, and both of those more heavily than commute times (which determine time away from family). In the Health category, I weighted teen unhealthy behavior slightly heavier than adult unhealthy behavior—that is, teen smoking is considered more of a detriment than adult smoking. In the Economic Environment category, most of the data received equal weight. However, trends in unemployment were weighted more heavily than some other factors. And in the Education category, the ratio of adults with four-year college degrees or higher was rated more heavily than public school data, such as student-teacher ratios. These are just some examples of intra-category weightings.

When it comes to inter-category ratings, the questions—and therefore, the subjectivity—become even more difficult to handle. Is it more important to live where wages are high and expenses are low versus where education is highly valued or versus proximity to other Church members? Inter-category ratings are even more subject to personal lifestyle choices, family preferences, and your own upbringing. And so the weighting used in the inter-category considerations is only slight.

In some cases, data for particular metropolitan areas was not available. In those instances, we had three options: substitute national or regional averages, substitute statewide data, or do nothing. As you go through this book, you will see the cases where data is simply not included for a particular metropolitan area. <u>A blank cell, or a cell with the notation "0," indicates the data is not available</u>. For example, the current (May 2010) median list price of four-bedroom homes is not available for all metropolitan areas; it would not be reliable nor would it be accurate to substitute regional or statewide data for this category. The same argument applies to certain crime data: the vast majority of communities utilize the FBI's standard crime definitions and reporting systems, but a handful of communities do not. However, for crime rating purposes, we at times used average crime data to get a more realistic picture of crime in the community than we would have without using the data at all.

Finally, once all the data within categories were weighted, and all the communities scored, the final scores for each of the seven categories were converted to a 0 to 100 index. A score of 100 represents the best in a category; 0 represents the worst. You will discover that in some categories, such as Crime, the lowest score may be 0 or close to it. In other categories, such as housing, the lowest score may be significantly higher than 0. The indexing system tells you how different the communities are in the particular categories. You will innately sense that a community with a crime index of 88, compared to a community with a crime index of 15, is a much safer place to live. On the other hand, a community with an Education score of 88, compared to a community with an Education index of 72, may not be all that more favorable.

All data used in this book is the latest data available. In most cases, that means 2009 or later. In some cases, data was not available for all communities for the same year; this seems to be more likely the case in the Health category. In these cases, the most recent data available for each community was used.

Back to the *hows*. The fifth *how* would be, **How does one use this book?** You can use this book in a number of ways. Perhaps the easiest and quickest way is to look at Chapter 3 to see the list of final rankings for each of the seven categories. These tables are listed both in alphabetical order (by primary city in a metropolitan area), as well as by ranking. You can also look at the more detailed data in Chapter 3 to see tables of key data for each of the seven categories. Much, but not all, of the data used in calculations for each category can be found in this section.

Finally, you can read through Chapter 4 to see how each of the communities was ranked and rated.

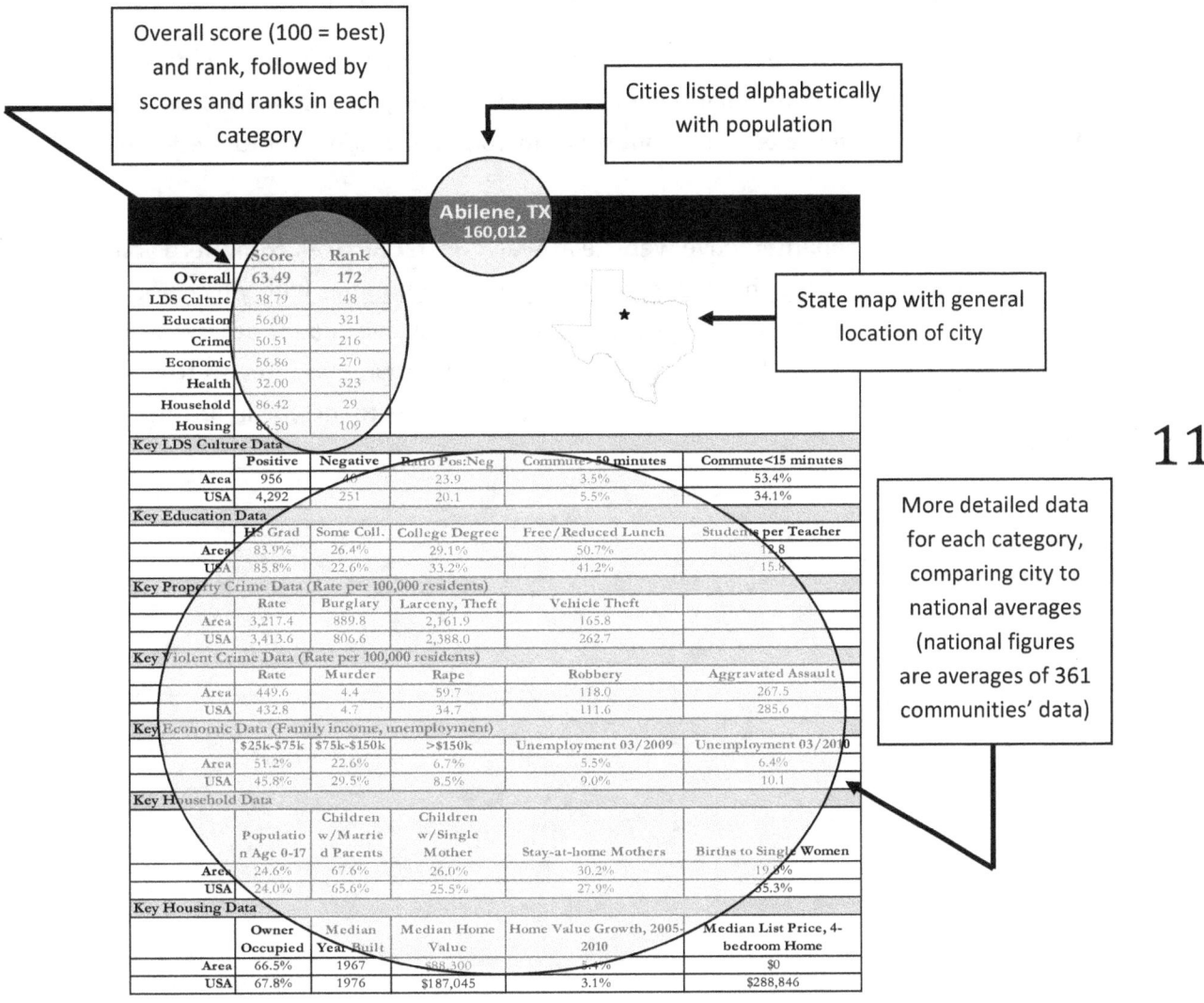

The sixth *how* is this: **How can a person find more data on the communities?** Most communities have websites, chambers of commerce, travel and tourism bureaus, and other local sources for valuable data and information. There are also other rankings and ratings of communities in various periodicals and books. And the U.S. Census

Bureau, Bureau of Labor Statistics, Centers for Disease Control and Prevention, and other federal government sources likewise have data available, either online or in print form.

Finally, **how can a person give more input? Will there be future editions of this book? Can a community move up or down in future editions?**

We recognize that data is just that: data. And our weighting system may not accurately reflect your own weighting system. So we want your input—not just about the communities themselves, but about other factors to consider in future editions of this book.

We've set up an interactive website at **www.BestLDSPlaces.com.** Here you can leave your own comments and your own ratings for communities with which you are familiar—whether you've lived there, are living there, have visited, or otherwise know about the pros and cons of the various communities. **We invite you to visit the website and leave your own feedback** for others to view, and for us to include in future editions of this book.

Table 1: Metropolitan Statistical Areas and 2009 Population (MSAs in bold)

Area	Population	Area	Population
Abilene, TX	**160,070**	**Anderson, IN**	**131,417**
Callahan County, TX	13,426	Madison County, IN	131,417
Jones County, TX	18,961	**Anderson, SC**	**184,901**
Taylor County, TX	127,683	Anderson County, SC	184,901
Akron, OH	**699,935**	**Ann Arbor, MI**	**347,563**
Portage County, OH	157,530	Washtenaw County, MI	347,563
Summit County, OH	542,405	**Anniston-Oxford, AL**	**114,081**
Albany, GA	**165,440**	Calhoun County, AL	114,081
Baker County, GA	3,637	**Appleton, WI**	**221,894**
Dougherty County, GA	95,859	Calumet County, WI	44,739
Lee County, GA	34,410	Outagamie County, WI	177,155
Terrell County, GA	10,320	**Asheville, NC**	**412,672**
Worth County, GA	21,214	Buncombe County, NC	231,452
Albany-Schenectady-Troy, NY	**857,592**	Haywood County, NC	57,109
Albany County, NY	298,284	Henderson County, NC	103,669
Rensselaer County, NY	155,541	Madison County, NC	20,442
Saratoga County, NY	220,069	**Athens-Clarke County, GA**	**192,222**
Schenectady County, NY	152,169	Clarke County, GA	116,342
Schoharie County, NY	31,529	Madison County, GA	28,232
Albuquerque, NM	**857,903**	Oconee County, GA	33,320
Bernalillo County, NM	642,527	Oglethorpe County, GA	14,328
Sandoval County, NM	125,988	**Atlanta-Sandy Springs-Marietta, GA**	**5,475,213**
Torrance County, NM	16,475	Barrow County, GA	72,158
Valencia County, NM	72,913	Bartow County, GA	96,217
Alexandria, LA	**154,101**	Butts County, GA	24,392
Grant Parish, LA	20,164	Carroll County, GA	114,778
Rapides Parish, LA	133,937	Cherokee County, GA	215,084
Allentown-Bthlhm-Easton, PA-NJ	**816,012**	Clayton County, GA	275,772
Warren County, NJ	109,638	Cobb County, GA	714,692
Carbon County, PA	63,865	Coweta County, GA	127,111
Lehigh County, PA	343,519	Dawson County, GA	22,555
Northampton County, PA	298,990	DeKalb County, GA	747,274
Altoona, PA	**126,122**	Douglas County, GA	129,703
Blair County, PA	126,122	Fayette County, GA	106,788
Amarillo, TX	**246,474**	Forsyth County, GA	174,520
Armstrong County, TX	2,065	Fulton County, GA	1,033,756
Carson County, TX	6,110	Gwinnett County, GA	808,167
Potter County, TX	121,816	Haralson County, GA	28,890
Randall County, TX	116,483	Heard County, GA	11,528
Ames, IA	**87,214**	Henry County, GA	195,370
Story County, IA	87,214	Jasper County, GA	13,953
Anchorage, AK	**374,553**	Lamar County, GA	17,550
Anchorage Municipality, AK	286,174	Meriwether County, GA	22,783
Matanuska-Susitna Borough, AK	88,379	Newton County, GA	99,944

Metropolitan Statistical Areas and 2009 Population, Continued (MSAs in bold)

Paulding County, GA 136,655	St. Helena Parish, LA 10,551
Pickens County, GA 31,264	West Baton Rouge Parish, LA 22,638
Pike County, GA 17,721	West Feliciana Parish, LA 15,055
Rockdale County, GA 84,569	**Battle Creek, MI 135,616**
Spalding County, GA 64,708	Calhoun County, MI 135,616
Walton County, GA 87,311	**Bay City, MI 107,434**
Atlantic City-Hammonton, NJ 271,712	Bay County, MI 107,434
Atlantic County, NJ 271,712	**Beaumont-Port Arthur, TX 378,477**
Auburn-Opelika, AL 135,883	Hardin County, TX 53,424
Lee County, AL 135,883	Jefferson County, TX 243,237
Augusta-Richmond County, GA-SC 539,154	Orange County, TX 81,816
Burke County, GA 22,797	**Bellingham, WA 200,434**
Columbia County, GA 112,958	Whatcom County, WA 200,434
McDuffie County, GA 21,862	**Bend, OR 158,629**
Richmond County, GA 199,768	Deschutes County, OR 158,629
Aiken County, SC 156,017	**Billings, MT 154,553**
Edgefield County, SC 25,752	Carbon County, MT 9,756
Austin-Round Rock, TX 1,705,075	Yellowstone County, MT 144,797
Bastrop County, TX 74,876	**Binghamton, NY 244,694**
Caldwell County, TX 37,810	Broome County, NY 194,630
Hays County, TX 155,545	Tioga County, NY 50,064
Travis County, TX 1,026,158	**Birmingham-Hoover, AL 1,131,070**
Williamson County, TX 410,686	Bibb County, AL 21,587
Bakersfield, CA 807,407	Blount County, AL 58,345
Kern County, CA 807,407	Chilton County, AL 42,971
Baltimore-Towson, MD 2,690,886	Jefferson County, AL 665,027
Anne Arundel County, MD 521,209	St. Clair County, AL 81,895
Baltimore County, MD 789,814	Shelby County, AL 192,503
Carroll County, MD 170,089	Walker County, AL 68,742
Harford County, MD 242,514	**Bismarck, ND 106,286**
Howard County, MD 281,884	Burleigh County, ND 79,822
Queen Anne's County, MD 47,958	Morton County, ND 26,464
Baltimore city, MD 637,418	**Blacksburg-Christiansburg-Radford, VA 159,587**
Bangor, ME 149,419	Giles County, VA 17,358
Penobscot County, ME 149,419	Montgomery County, VA 91,023
Barnstable Town, MA 221,151	Pulaski County, VA 35,022
Barnstable County, MA 221,151	Radford city, VA 16,184
Baton Rouge, LA 786,947	**Bloomington, IN 185,598**
Ascension Parish, LA 104,822	Greene County, IN 32,463
East Baton Rouge Parish, LA 434,633	Monroe County, IN 130,738
East Feliciana Parish, LA 20,970	Owen County, IN 22,397
Iberville Parish, LA 32,505	**Bloomington-Normal, IL 167,699**
Livingston Parish, LA 123,326	McLean County, IL 167,699
Pointe Coupee Parish, LA 22,447	

Metropolitan Statistical Areas and 2009 Population, Continued (MSAs in bold)

Area	Population	Area	Population
Boise City-Nampa, ID	**606,376**	**Cape Coral-Fort Myers, FL**	**586,908**
Ada County, ID	384,656	Lee County, FL	586,908
Boise County, ID	7,445	**Casper, WY**	**74,508**
Canyon County, ID	186,615	Natrona County, WY	74,508
Gem County, ID	16,437	**Cedar Rapids, IA**	**256,324**
Owyhee County, ID	11,223	Benton County, IA	26,734
Boston-Cambridge-Quincy, MA-NH	**4,588,680**	Jones County, IA	20,364
Norfolk County, MA	666,303	Linn County, IA	209,226
Plymouth County, MA	498,344	**Champaign-Urbana, IL**	**226,132**
Suffolk County, MA	753,580	Champaign County, IL	195,671
Middlesex County, MA	1,505,006	Ford County, IL	13,911
Essex County, MA	742,582	Piatt County, IL	16,550
Rockingham County, NH	299,276	**Charleston, WV**	**304,214**
Strafford County, NH	123,589	Boone County, WV	24,709
Boulder, CO	**303,482**	Clay County, WV	10,022
Boulder County, CO	303,482	Kanawha County, WV	191,663
Bowling Green, KY	**120,595**	Lincoln County, WV	22,147
Edmonson County, KY	11,926	Putnam County, WV	55,673
Warren County, KY	108,669	**Charleston-North Charleston-Summerville, SC**	**659,191**
Bradenton-Sarasota-Venice, FL	**688,126**	Berkeley County, SC	173,498
Manatee County, FL	318,361	Charleston County, SC	355,276
Sarasota County, FL	369,765	Dorchester County, SC	130,417
Bremerton-Silverdale, WA	**240,862**	**Charlotte-Gastonia-Concord, NC-SC**	**1,745,524**
Kitsap County, WA	240,862	Anson County, NC	25,056
Bridgeport-Stamford-Norwalk, CT	**901,208**	Cabarrus County, NC	172,223
Fairfield County, CT	901,208	Gaston County, NC	208,958
Brownsville-Harlingen, TX	**396,371**	Mecklenburg County, NC	913,639
Cameron County, TX	396,371	Union County, NC	198,645
Brunswick, GA	**103,841**	York County, SC	227,003
Brantley County, GA	15,643	**Charlottesville, VA**	**196,766**
Glynn County, GA	76,820	Albemarle County, VA	94,908
McIntosh County, GA	11,378	Fluvanna County, VA	25,732
Buffalo-Niagara Falls, NY	**1,123,804**	Greene County, VA	18,421
Erie County, NY	909,247	Nelson County, VA	15,487
Niagara County, NY	214,557	Charlottesville city, VA	42,218
Burlington, NC	**150,358**	**Chattanooga, TN-GA**	**524,303**
Alamance County, NC	150,358	Catoosa County, GA	64,035
Burlington-South Burlington, VT	**208,055**	Dade County, GA	16,127
Chittenden County, VT	152,313	Walker County, GA	64,983
Franklin County, VT	48,182	Hamilton County, TN	337,175
Grand Isle County, VT	7,560	Marion County, TN	28,068
Canton-Massillon, OH	**408,005**	Sequatchie County, TN	13,915
Carroll County, OH	28,539	**Cheyenne, WY**	**88,854**
Stark County, OH	379,466	Laramie County, WY	88,854

Metropolitan Statistical Areas and 2009 Population, Continued (MSAs in bold)

Chicago-Naperville-Joliet, IL-IN-WI 9,580,567	Lake County, OH 236,775
Cook County, IL 5,287,037	Lorain County, OH 305,707
DeKalb County, IL 107,333	Medina County, OH 174,035
DuPage County, IL 932,541	**Coeur d'Alene, ID 139,390**
Grundy County, IL 48,421	Kootenai County, ID 139,390
Kane County, IL 511,892	**College Station-Bryan, TX 212,268**
Kendall County, IL 104,821	Brazos County, TX 179,992
McHenry County, IL 320,961	Burleson County, TX 16,570
Will County, IL 685,251	Robertson County, TX 15,706
Jasper County, IN 32,816	**Colorado Springs, CO 626,227**
Lake County, IN 494,211	El Paso County, CO 604,542
Newton County, IN 13,736	Teller County, CO 21,685
Porter County, IN 163,598	**Columbia, MO 166,234**
Lake County, IL 712,567	Boone County, MO 156,377
Kenosha County, WI 165,382	Howard County, MO 9,857
Chico, CA 220,577	**Columbia, SC 744,730**
Butte County, CA 220,577	Calhoun County, SC 14,621
Cincinnati-Middletown, OH-KY-IN 2,171,896	Fairfield County, SC 23,343
Dearborn County, IN 50,502	Kershaw County, SC 60,042
Franklin County, IN 23,148	Lexington County, SC 255,607
Ohio County, IN 5,909	Richland County, SC 372,023
Boone County, KY 118,576	Saluda County, SC 19,094
Bracken County, KY 8,653	**Columbus, GA-AL 292,795**
Campbell County, KY 88,423	Russell County, AL 50,846
Gallatin County, KY 8,202	Chattahoochee County, GA 14,402
Grant County, KY 25,542	Harris County, GA 30,138
Kenton County, KY 158,729	Marion County, GA 6,995
Pendleton County, KY 14,887	Muscogee County, GA 190,414
Brown County, OH 44,003	**Columbus, IN 76,063**
Butler County, OH 363,184	Bartholomew County, IN 76,063
Clermont County, OH 196,364	**Columbus, OH 1,801,848**
Hamilton County, OH 855,062	Delaware County, OH 168,708
Warren County, OH 210,712	Fairfield County, OH 143,712
Clarksville, TN-KY 268,546	Franklin County, OH 1,150,122
Christian County, KY 80,938	Licking County, OH 158,488
Trigg County, KY 13,290	Madison County, OH 42,539
Montgomery County, TN 160,978	Morrow County, OH 34,642
Stewart County, TN 13,340	Pickaway County, OH 54,734
Cleveland, TN 113,358	Union County, OH 48,903
Bradley County, TN 97,710	**Corpus Christi, TX 416,095**
Polk County, TN 15,648	Aransas County, TX 24,826
Cleveland-Elyria-Mentor, OH 2,091,286	Nueces County, TX 323,046
Cuyahoga County, OH 1,275,709	San Patricio County, TX 68,223
Geauga County, OH 99,060	

Metropolitan Statistical Areas and 2009 Population, Continued (MSAs in bold)

Corvallis, OR	**82,605**
Benton County, OR	82,605
Cumberland, MD-WV	**99,736**
Allegany County, MD	72,532
Mineral County, WV	27,204
Dallas-Fort Worth-Arlington, TX	**6,447,615**
Collin County, TX	791,631
Dallas County, TX	2,451,730
Delta County, TX	5,410
Denton County, TX	658,616
Ellis County, TX	151,737
Hunt County, TX	82,831
Kaufman County, TX	103,038
Rockwall County, TX	81,391
Johnson County, TX	156,997
Parker County, TX	114,919
Tarrant County, TX	1,789,900
Wise County, TX	59,415
Dalton, GA	**134,319**
Murray County, GA	40,621
Whitfield County, GA	93,698
Danville, IL	**80,067**
Vermilion County, IL	80,067
Danville, VA	**105,814**
Pittsylvania County, VA	61,414
Danville city, VA	44,400
Davenport-Moline-Rock Island, IA-IL	**379,066**
Henry County, IL	49,314
Mercer County, IL	16,276
Rock Island County, IL	146,826
Scott County, IA	166,650
Dayton, OH	**835,063**
Greene County, OH	159,823
Miami County, OH	101,256
Montgomery County, OH	532,562
Preble County, OH	41,422
Decatur, AL	**151,399**
Lawrence County, AL	34,106
Morgan County, AL	117,293
Decatur, IL	**108,204**
Macon County, IL	108,204
Deltona-Daytona Beach-Ormond Beach, FL	**495,890**
Volusia County, FL	495,890
Denver-Aurora-Broomfield, CO	**2,552,195**
Adams County, CO	440,994
Arapahoe County, CO	565,360
Broomfield County, CO	55,990
Clear Creek County, CO	8,706
Denver County, CO	610,345
Douglas County, CO	288,225
Elbert County, CO	23,287
Gilpin County, CO	5,604
Jefferson County, CO	536,922
Park County, CO	16,762
Des Moines-West Des Moines, IA	**562,906**
Dallas County, IA	61,950
Guthrie County, IA	10,833
Madison County, IA	15,409
Polk County, IA	429,439
Warren County, IA	45,275
Detroit-Warren-Livonia, MI	**4,403,437**
Wayne County, MI	1,925,848
Lapeer County, MI	89,974
Livingston County, MI	183,118
Macomb County, MI	831,427
Oakland County, MI	1,205,508
St. Clair County, MI	167,562
Dothan, AL	**142,693**
Geneva County, AL	25,961
Henry County, AL	16,647
Houston County, AL	100,085
Dover, DE	**157,741**
Kent County, DE	157,741
Dubuque, IA	**93,072**
Dubuque County, IA	93,072
Duluth, MN-WI	**276,368**
Carlton County, MN	34,327
St. Louis County, MN	197,767
Douglas County, WI	44,274
Durham-Chapel Hill, NC	**501,228**
Chatham County, NC	64,772
Durham County, NC	269,706
Orange County, NC	129,083
Person County, NC	37,667
Eau Claire, WI	**160,018**
Chippewa County, WI	60,609
Eau Claire County, WI	99,409

Metropolitan Statistical Areas and 2009 Population, Continued (MSAs in bold)

El Centro, CA	**166,874**
Imperial County, CA	166,874
Elizabethtown, KY	**113,433**
Hardin County, KY	99,770
Larue County, KY	13,663
Elkhart-Goshen, IN	**200,502**
Elkhart County, IN	200,502
Elmira, NY	**88,331**
Chemung County, NY	88,331
El Paso, TX	**751,296**
El Paso County, TX	751,296
Erie, PA	**280,291**
Erie County, PA	280,291
Eugene-Springfield, OR	**351,109**
Lane County, OR	351,109
Evansville, IN-KY	**351,911**
Gibson County, IN	32,750
Posey County, IN	26,004
Vanderburgh County, IN	175,434
Warrick County, IN	58,521
Henderson County, KY	45,496
Webster County, KY	13,706
Fairbanks, AK	**98,660**
Fairbanks North Star Borough, AK	98,660
Fargo, ND-MN	**200,102**
Clay County, MN	56,763
Cass County, ND	143,339
Farmington, NM	**124,131**
San Juan County, NM	124,131
Fayetteville, NC	**360,355**
Cumberland County, NC	315,207
Hoke County, NC	45,148
Fayetteville-Springdale-Rogers, AR-MO	**464,623**
Benton County, AR	225,504
Madison County, AR	15,875
Washington County, AR	200,181
McDonald County, MO	23,063
Flagstaff, AZ	**129,849**
Coconino County, AZ	129,849
Flint, MI	**424,043**
Genesee County, MI	424,043
Florence, SC	**200,653**
Darlington County, SC	66,445
Florence County, SC	134,208
Florence-Muscle Shoals, AL	**144,238**
Colbert County, AL	54,639
Lauderdale County, AL	89,599
Fond du Lac, WI	**100,070**
Fond du Lac County, WI	100,070
Fort Collins-Loveland, CO	**298,382**
Larimer County, CO	298,382
Fort Smith, AR-OK	**293,063**
Crawford County, AR	60,102
Franklin County, AR	18,016
Sebastian County, AR	123,597
Le Flore County, OK	49,915
Sequoyah County, OK	41,433
Fort Walton Beach-Crestview-Destin, FL	**178,473**
Okaloosa County, FL	178,473
Fort Wayne, IN	**414,315**
Allen County, IN	353,888
Wells County, IN	27,566
Whitley County, IN	32,861
Fresno, CA	**915,267**
Fresno County, CA	915,267
Gadsden, AL	**103,645**
Etowah County, AL	103,645
Gainesville, FL	**260,690**
Alachua County, FL	243,574
Gilchrist County, FL	17,116
Gainesville, GA	**187,743**
Hall County, GA	187,743
Glens Falls, NY	**128,774**
Warren County, NY	66,021
Washington County, NY	62,753
Goldsboro, NC	**113,811**
Wayne County, NC	113,811
Grand Forks, ND-MN	**97,190**
Polk County, MN	30,776
Grand Forks County, ND	66,414
Grand Junction, CO	**146,093**
Mesa County, CO	146,093
Grand Rapids-Wyoming, MI	**778,009**
Barry County, MI	58,434
Ionia County, MI	62,574
Kent County, MI	608,315
Newaygo County, MI	48,686

Metropolitan Statistical Areas and 2009 Population, Continued (MSAs in bold)

Area	Population	Area	Population
Great Falls, MT	**82,178**	**Hickory-Lenoir-Morganton, NC**	**365,364**
Cascade County, MT	82,178	Alexander County, NC	36,777
Greeley, CO	**254,759**	Burke County, NC	89,548
Weld County, CO /1	254,759	Caldwell County, NC	79,914
Green Bay, WI	**304,783**	Catawba County, NC	159,125
Brown County, WI	247,319	**Hinesville-Fort Stewart, GA**	**74,420**
Kewaunee County, WI	20,315	Liberty County, GA	62,186
Oconto County, WI	37,149	Long County, GA	12,234
Greensboro-High Point, NC	**714,765**	**Holland-Grand Haven, MI**	**261,957**
Guilford County, NC	480,362	Ottawa County, MI	261,957
Randolph County, NC	142,151	**Honolulu, HI**	**907,574**
Rockingham County, NC	92,252	Honolulu County, HI	907,574
Greenville, NC	**179,715**	**Hot Springs, AR**	**98,479**
Greene County, NC	20,658	Garland County, AR	98,479
Pitt County, NC	159,057	**Houma-Bayou Cane-Thibodaux, LA**	**202,973**
Greenville-Mauldin-Easley, SC	**639,617**	Lafourche Parish, LA	93,682
Greenville County, SC	451,428	Terrebonne Parish, LA	109,291
Laurens County, SC	70,045	**Houston-Sugar Land-Baytown, TX**	**5,867,489**
Pickens County, SC	118,144	Austin County, TX	27,248
Gulfport-Biloxi, MS	**238,772**	Brazoria County, TX	309,208
Hancock County, MS	40,962	Chambers County, TX	31,431
Harrison County, MS	181,191	Fort Bend County, TX	556,870
Stone County, MS	16,619	Galveston County, TX	286,814
Hagerstown-Martinsburg, MD-WV	**266,149**	Harris County, TX	4,070,989
Washington County, MD	145,910	Liberty County, TX	75,779
Berkeley County, WV	103,854	Montgomery County, TX	447,718
Morgan County, WV	16,385	San Jacinto County, TX	24,902
Hanford-Corcoran, CA	**148,764**	Waller County, TX	36,530
Kings County, CA	148,764	**Huntington-Ashland, WV-KY-OH**	**285,624**
Harrisburg-Carlisle, PA	**536,919**	Boyd County, KY	48,527
Cumberland County, PA	232,483	Greenup County, KY	38,020
Dauphin County, PA	258,934	Lawrence County, OH	62,744
Perry County, PA	45,502	Cabell County, WV	95,214
Harrisonburg, VA	**120,271**	Wayne County, WV	41,119
Rockingham County, VA	75,134	**Huntsville, AL**	**406,316**
Harrisonburg city, VA	45,137	Limestone County, AL	78,572
Hartford-West Hartford-East Hartford, CT	**1,195,998**	Madison County, AL	327,744
Hartford County, CT	879,835	**Idaho Falls, ID**	**126,131**
Middlesex County, CT	165,702	Bonneville County, ID	101,329
Tolland County, CT	150,461	Jefferson County, ID	24,802
Hattiesburg, MS	**143,093**		
Forrest County, MS	81,078		
Lamar County, MS	49,980		
Perry County, MS	12,035		

Metropolitan Statistical Areas and 2009 Population, Continued (MSAs in bold)

Indianapolis-Carmel, IN 1,743,658	**Johnstown, PA 143,998**
Boone County, IN 56,287	Cambria County, PA 143,998
Brown County, IN 14,548	**Jonesboro, AR 120,139**
Hamilton County, IN 279,287	Craighead County, AR 95,457
Hancock County, IN 68,334	Poinsett County, AR 24,682
Hendricks County, IN 140,606	**Joplin, MO 174,300**
Johnson County, IN 141,501	Jasper County, MO 118,179
Marion County, IN 890,879	Newton County, MO 56,121
Morgan County, IN 70,876	**Kalamazoo-Portage, MI 326,634**
Putnam County, IN 36,837	Kalamazoo County, MI 248,407
Shelby County, IN 44,503	Van Buren County, MI 78,227
Iowa City, IA 152,263	**Kankakee-Bradley, IL 113,215**
Johnson County, IA 131,005	Kankakee County, IL 113,215
Washington County, IA 21,258	**Kansas City, MO-KS 2,067,585**
Ithaca, NY 101,779	Franklin County, KS 26,441
Tompkins County, NY 101,779	Johnson County, KS 542,737
Jackson, MI 159,828	Leavenworth County, KS 75,227
Jackson County, MI 159,828	Linn County, KS 9,335
Jackson, MS 540,866	Miami County, KS 30,969
Copiah County, MS 29,094	Wyandotte County, KS 155,085
Hinds County, MS 247,631	Bates County, MO 16,761
Madison County, MS 93,097	Caldwell County, MO 9,160
Rankin County, MS 143,124	Cass County, MO 100,184
Simpson County, MS 27,920	Clay County, MO 228,358
Jackson, TN 113,629	Clinton County, MO 21,002
Chester County, TN 16,312	Jackson County, MO 705,708
Madison County, TN 97,317	Lafayette County, MO 32,572
Jacksonville, FL 1,328,144	Platte County, MO 90,688
Baker County, FL 26,336	Ray County, MO 23,358
Clay County, FL 186,756	**Kennewick-Pasco-Richland, WA 245,649**
Duval County, FL 857,040	Benton County, WA 168,294
Nassau County, FL 70,576	Franklin County, WA 77,355
St. Johns County, FL 187,436	**Killeen-Temple-Fort Hood, TX 379,231**
Jacksonville, NC 173,064	Bell County, TX 285,787
Onslow County, NC 173,064	Coryell County, TX 72,529
Janesville, WI 160,155	Lampasas County, TX 20,915
Rock County, WI 160,155	**Kingsport-Bristol-Bristol, TN-VA 305,629**
Jefferson City, MO 147,438	Hawkins County, TN 57,784
Callaway County, MO 43,727	Sullivan County, TN 154,552
Cole County, MO 75,018	Scott County, VA 22,585
Moniteau County, MO 15,132	Washington County, VA 53,018
Osage County, MO 13,561	Bristol city, VA 17,690
Johnson City, TN 197,381	**Kingston, NY 181,440**
Carter County, TN 59,043	Ulster County, NY 181,440
Unicoi County, TN 17,740	
Washington County, TN 120,598	

Metropolitan Statistical Areas and 2009 Population, Continued (MSAs in bold)

Knoxville, TN 699,247	**Lexington-Fayette, KY 470,849**
Anderson County, TN 74,849	Bourbon County, KY 19,729
Blount County, TN 122,784	Clark County, KY 36,159
Knox County, TN 435,725	Fayette County, KY 296,545
Loudon County, TN 46,725	Jessamine County, KY 47,589
Union County, TN 19,164	Scott County, KY 45,841
Kokomo, IN 98,787	Woodford County, KY 24,986
Howard County, IN 82,895	**Lima, OH 104,357**
Tipton County, IN 15,892	Allen County, OH 104,357
La Crosse, WI-MN 132,923	**Lincoln, NE 298,012**
Houston County, MN 19,244	Lancaster County, NE 281,531
La Crosse County, WI 113,679	Seward County, NE 16,481
Lafayette, IN 196,329	**Little Rock-North Little Rock-Conway, AR 685,488**
Benton County, IN 8,613	Faulkner County, AR 109,386
Carroll County, IN 19,752	Grant County, AR 17,760
Tippecanoe County, IN 167,964	Lonoke County, AR 66,677
Lafayette, LA 263,171	Perry County, AR 10,312
Lafayette Parish, LA 210,954	Pulaski County, AR 381,904
St. Martin Parish, LA 52,217	Saline County, AR 99,449
Lake Charles, LA 194,138	**Logan, UT-ID 127,945**
Calcasieu Parish, LA 187,554	Franklin County, ID 12,676
Cameron Parish, LA 6,584	Cache County, UT 115,269
Lake Havasu City-Kingman, AZ 194,825	**Longview, TX 206,874**
Mohave County, AZ 194,825	Gregg County, TX 119,637
Lakeland-Winter Haven, FL 583,403	Rusk County, TX 49,180
Polk County, FL 583,403	Upshur County, TX 38,057
Lancaster, PA 507,766	**Longview, WA 101,966**
Lancaster County, PA 507,766	Cowlitz County, WA 101,966
Lansing-East Lansing, MI 453,603	**Los Angeles-Long Beach-Santa Ana, CA 12,874,797**
Clinton County, MI 69,893	Los Angeles County, CA 9,848,011
Eaton County, MI 106,077	Orange County, CA 3,026,786
Ingham County, MI 277,633	**Louisville/Jefferson County, KY-IN 1,258,577**
Laredo, TX 241,438	Clark County, IN 108,634
Webb County, TX 241,438	Floyd County, IN 74,426
Las Cruces, NM 206,419	Harrison County, IN 37,562
Doña Ana County, NM 206,419	Washington County, IN 27,729
Las Vegas, NV 1,902,834	Bullitt County, KY 75,653
Clark County, NV 1,902,834	Henry County, KY 16,060
Lawrence, KS 116,383	Jefferson County, KY 721,594
Douglas County, KS 116,383	Meade County, KY 26,501
Lawton, OK 113,228	Nelson County, KY 43,550
Comanche County, OK 113,228	Oldham County, KY 58,095
Lebanon, PA 130,506	Shelby County, KY 42,078
Lebanon County, PA 130,506	Spencer County, KY 17,737
Lewiston-Auburn, ME 106,539	Trimble County, KY 8,958
Androscoggin County, ME 106,539	

Metropolitan Statistical Areas and 2009 Population, Continued (MSAs in bold)

Area	Population	Area	Population
Lubbock, TX	**276,659**	LaPorte County, IN	111,063
Crosby County, TX	6,109	**Midland, TX**	**132,316**
Lubbock County, TX	270,550	Midland County, TX	132,316
		Milwaukee-Waukesha-West Allis, WI	**1,559,667**
Lynchburg, VA	**247,447**		
Amherst County, VA	32,482	Milwaukee County, WI	959,521
Appomattox County, VA	14,552	Ozaukee County, WI	86,311
Bedford County, VA	67,154	Washington County, WI	130,681
Campbell County, VA	52,976	Waukesha County, WI	383,154
		Minneapolis-St. Paul-Bloomington, MN-WI	**3,269,814**
Bedford city, VA	6,350		
Lynchburg city, VA	73,933	Anoka County, MN	331,582
Macon, GA	**231,576**	Carver County, MN	92,107
Bibb County, GA	156,060	Chisago County, MN	50,625
Crawford County, GA	12,240	Dakota County, MN	396,500
Jones County, GA	27,740	Hennepin County, MN	1,156,212
Monroe County, GA	25,425	Isanti County, MN	39,442
Twiggs County, GA	10,111	Ramsey County, MN	506,278
Madera-Chowchilla, CA	**148,632**	Scott County, MN	131,939
Madera County, CA	148,632	Sherburne County, MN	87,832
Madison, WI	**570,025**	Washington County, MN	231,958
Columbia County, WI	55,170	Wright County, MN	121,907
Dane County, WI	491,357	Pierce County, WI	40,081
Iowa County, WI	23,498	St. Croix County, WI	83,351
Manchester-Nashua, NH	**405,906**	**Missoula, MT**	**108,623**
Hillsborough County, NH	405,906	Missoula County, MT	108,623
Mansfield, OH	**124,490**	**Mobile, AL**	**411,721**
Richland County, OH	124,490	Mobile County, AL	411,721
McAllen-Edinburg-Mission, TX	**741,152**	**Modesto, CA**	**510,385**
Hidalgo County, TX	741,152	Stanislaus County, CA	510,385
Medford, OR	**201,286**	**Monroe, LA**	**174,086**
Jackson County, OR	201,286	Ouachita Parish, LA	151,502
Memphis, TN-MS-AR	**1,304,926**	Union Parish, LA	22,584
Crittenden County, AR	53,022	**Monroe, MI**	**152,721**
DeSoto County, MS	158,719	Monroe County, MI	152,721
Marshall County, MS	36,900	**Montgomery, AL**	**366,401**
Tate County, MS	27,337	Autauga County, AL	50,756
Tunica County, MS	10,436	Elmore County, AL	79,233
Fayette County, TN	38,785	Lowndes County, AL	12,293
Shelby County, TN	920,232	Montgomery County, AL	224,119
Tipton County, TN	59,495	**Morgantown, WV**	**120,327**
Merced, CA	**245,321**	Monongalia County, WV	90,080
Merced County, CA	245,321	Preston County, WV	30,247
Miami-Fort Lauderdale-Pompano Beach, FL	**5,547,051**		
		Morristown, TN	**137,612**
Broward County, FL	1,766,476	Grainger County, TN	22,857
Miami-Dade County, FL	2,500,625	Hamblen County, TN	63,033
Palm Beach County, FL	1,279,950	Jefferson County, TN	51,722
Michigan City-La Porte, IN	111,063		

Metropolitan Statistical Areas and 2009 Population, Continued (MSAs in bold)

Mount Vernon-Anacortes, WA 119,534	Sussex County, NJ 151,118
Skagit County, WA 119,534	Union County, NJ 526,426
Muncie, IN 115,192	Pike County, PA 60,529
Delaware County, IN 115,192	Bergen County, NJ 895,250
Muskegon-Norton Shores, MI 173,951	Hudson County, NJ 597,924
Muskegon County, MI 173,951	Passaic County, NJ 491,778
Myrtle Beach-North Myrtle Beach-Conway, SC 263,868	Bronx County, NY 1,397,287
Horry County, SC 263,868	Kings County, NY 2,567,098
Napa, CA 134,650	New York County, NY 1,629,054
Napa County, CA 134,650	Putnam County, NY 99,265
Naples-Marco Island, FL 318,537	Queens County, NY 2,306,712
Collier County, FL 318,537	Richmond County, NY 491,730
Nashville-Franklin, TN 1,582,264	Rockland County, NY 300,173
Cannon County, TN 13,860	Westchester County, NY 955,962
Cheatham County, TN 39,876	**Niles-Benton Harbor, MI 160,472**
Davidson County, TN 635,710	Berrien County, MI 160,472
Dickson County, TN 48,230	**Norwich-New London, CT 266,830**
Hickman County, TN 23,805	New London County, CT 266,830
Macon County, TN 22,057	**Ocala, FL 328,547**
Robertson County, TN 66,581	Marion County, FL 328,547
Rutherford County, TN 257,048	**Ocean City, NJ 96,091**
Smith County, TN 19,201	Cape May County, NJ 96,091
Sumner County, TN 158,759	**Odessa, TX 134,625**
Trousdale County, TN 7,922	Ector County, TX 134,625
Williamson County, TN 176,838	**Ogden-Clearfield, UT 541,569**
Wilson County, TN 112,377	Davis County, UT 300,827
New Haven-Milford, CT 848,006	Morgan County, UT 8,908
New Haven County, CT 848,006	Weber County, UT 231,834
New Orleans-Metairie-Kenner, LA 1,189,981	Oklahoma City, OK 1,227,278
Jefferson Parish, LA 443,342	**Canadian County, OK 109,668**
Orleans Parish, LA 354,850	Cleveland County, OK 244,589
Plaquemines Parish, LA 20,942	Grady County, OK 51,649
St. Bernard Parish, LA 40,655	Lincoln County, OK 32,199
St. Charles Parish, LA 51,611	Logan County, OK 39,301
St. John the Baptist Parish, LA 47,086	McClain County, OK 33,168
St. Tammany Parish, LA 231,495	Oklahoma County, OK 716,704
New York-No.Jersey-Long Island 19,069,796	**Olympia, WA 250,979**
Middlesex County, NJ 790,738	Thurston County, WA 250,979
Monmouth County, NJ 644,105	**Omaha-Council Bluffs, NE-IA 849,517**
Ocean County, NJ 573,678	Harrison County, IA 15,328
Somerset County, NJ 326,869	Mills County, IA 15,002
Nassau County, NY 1,357,429	Pottawattamie County, IA 90,224
Suffolk County, NY 1,518,475	Cass County, NE 25,485
Essex County, NJ 769,644	Douglas County, NE 510,199
Hunterdon County, NJ 130,034	Sarpy County, NE 153,504
Morris County, NJ 488,518	Saunders County, NE 20,057

Metropolitan Statistical Areas and 2009 Population, Continued (MSAs in bold)

Washington County, NE 19,718	New Castle County, DE 534,634
Orlando-Kissimmee, FL 2,082,421	Cecil County, MD 100,796
Lake County, FL 312,119	Salem County, NJ 66,342
Orange County, FL 1,086,480	**Phoenix-Mesa-Scottsdale, AZ 4,364,094**
Osceola County, FL 270,618	Maricopa County, AZ 4,023,132
Seminole County, FL 413,204	Pinal County, AZ 340,962
Oshkosh-Neenah, WI 163,370	**Pine Bluff, AR 100,694**
Winnebago County, WI 163,370	Cleveland County, AR 8,436
Owensboro, KY 113,636	Jefferson County, AR 78,705
Daviess County, KY 95,394	Lincoln County, AR 13,553
Hancock County, KY 8,635	**Pittsburgh, PA 2,354,957**
McLean County, KY 9,607	Allegheny County, PA 1,218,494
Oxnard-Thousand Oaks-Ventura, CA 802,983	Armstrong County, PA 67,851
Ventura County, CA 802,983	Beaver County, PA 171,673
Palm Bay-Melbourne-Titusville, FL 536,357	Butler County, PA 184,694
Brevard County, FL 536,357	Fayette County, PA 142,605
Palm Coast, FL 91,622	Washington County, PA 207,389
Flagler County, FL 91,622	Westmoreland County, PA 362,251
Panama City-Lynn Haven-FL 164,767	**Pittsfield, MA 129,288**
Bay County, FL 164,767	Berkshire County, MA 129,288
Parkersburg-Marietta-Vienna, WV-OH 160,905	**Pocatello, ID 90,273**
Washington County, OH 61,048	Bannock County, ID 82,539
Pleasants County, WV 7,364	Power County, ID 7,734
Wirt County, WV 5,605	**Portland-South Portland-Biddeford, ME 516,826**
Wood County, WV 86,888	Cumberland County, ME 278,559
Pascagoula, MS 155,603	Sagadahoc County, ME 36,391
George County, MS 22,681	York County, ME 201,876
Jackson County, MS 132,922	**Portland-Vancouver-Beaverton, OR-WA 2,241,841**
Pensacola-Ferry Pass-Brent, FL 455,102	Clackamas County, OR 386,143
Escambia County, FL 303,343	Columbia County, OR 49,592
Santa Rosa County, FL 151,759	Multnomah County, OR 726,855
Peoria, IL 375,865	Washington County, OR 537,318
Marshall County, IL 12,702	Yamhill County, OR 99,037
Peoria County, IL 185,816	Clark County, WA 432,002
Stark County, IL 6,019	Skamania County, WA 10,894
Tazewell County, IL 132,466	**Port St. Lucie, FL 406,296**
Woodford County, IL 38,862	Martin County, FL 139,794
Philadelphia-Camden-Wlmngtn, PA 5,968,252	St. Lucie County, FL 266,502
Burlington County, NJ 446,108	**Poughkeepsie-Newburgh-Middletown, NY 677,094**
Camden County, NJ 517,879	Dutchess County, NY 293,562
Gloucester County, NJ 289,920	Orange County, NY 383,532
Bucks County, PA 626,015	**Prescott, AZ 215,686**
Chester County, PA 498,894	Yavapai County, AZ 215,686
Delaware County, PA 558,028	
Montgomery County, PA 782,339	
Philadelphia County, PA 1,547,297	

Metropolitan Statistical Areas and 2009 Population, Continued (MSAs in bold)

Providence-New Bedford-Fall River, RI-MA 1,600,642	Prince George County, VA 37,116
Bristol County, MA 547,433	Sussex County, VA 12,116
Bristol County, RI 49,542	Colonial Heights city, VA 17,823
Kent County, RI 168,752	Hopewell city, VA 23,123
Newport County, RI 80,300	Petersburg city, VA 32,986
Providence County, RI 627,690	Richmond city, VA 204,451
Washington County, RI 126,925	**Riverside-San Bernardino-Ontario, CA 4,143,113**
Provo-Orem, UT 555,551	Riverside County, CA 2,125,440
Juab County, UT 10,244	San Bernardino County, CA 2,017,673
Utah County, UT 545,307	**Roanoke, VA 300,399**
Pueblo, CO 157,224	Botetourt County, VA 32,551
Pueblo County, CO 157,224	Craig County, VA 4,969
Punta Gorda, FL 156,952	Franklin County, VA 51,924
Charlotte County, FL 156,952	Roanoke County, VA 91,011
Racine, WI 200,601	Roanoke city, VA 94,482
Racine County, WI 200,601	Salem city, VA 25,462
Raleigh-Cary, NC 1,125,827	**Rochester, MN 185,618**
Franklin County, NC 60,088	Dodge County, MN 19,772
Johnston County, NC 168,525	Olmsted County, MN 143,962
Wake County, NC 897,214	Wabasha County, MN 21,884
Rapid City, SD 124,766	**Rochester, NY 1,035,566**
Meade County, SD 23,916	Livingston County, NY 62,871
Pennington County, SD 100,850	Monroe County, NY 733,703
Reading, PA 407,125	Ontario County, NY 105,650
Berks County, PA 407,125	Orleans County, NY 42,051
Redding, CA 181,099	Wayne County, NY 91,291
Shasta County, CA 181,099	**Rockford, IL 353,722**
Reno-Sparks, NV 419,261	Boone County, IL 54,020
Storey County, NV 4,441	Winnebago County, IL 299,702
Washoe County, NV 414,820	**Rocky Mount, NC 146,596**
Richmond, VA 1,238,187	Edgecombe County, NC 51,853
Amelia County, VA 12,886	Nash County, NC 94,743
Caroline County, VA 27,870	**Rome, GA 96,250**
Charles City County, VA 7,217	Floyd County, GA 96,250
	Sacramento--Arden-Arcade--Roseville, CA 2,127,355
Chesterfield County, VA 306,670	El Dorado County, CA 178,447
Cumberland County, VA 9,757	Placer County, CA 348,552
Dinwiddie County, VA 26,338	Sacramento County, CA 1,400,949
Goochland County, VA 21,311	Yolo County, CA 199,407
Hanover County, VA 99,933	**Saginaw-Saginaw Township North, MI 200,050**
Henrico County, VA 296,415	Saginaw County, MI 200,050
King and Queen County, VA 6,796	**St. Cloud, MN 189,148**
King William County, VA 16,225	Benton County, MN 40,193
Louisa County, VA 33,078	Stearns County, MN 148,955
New Kent County, VA 18,112	
Powhatan County, VA 27,964	

Metropolitan Statistical Areas and 2009 Population, Continued (MSAs in bold)

St. George, UT 137,473	Kendall County, TX 34,053
Washington County, UT 137,473	Medina County, TX 44,728
St. Joseph, MO-KS 126,644	Wilson County, TX 40,749
Doniphan County, KS 7,624	**San Diego-Carlsbad-SanMrcos, CA 3,053,793**
Andrew County, MO 17,052	San Diego County, CA 3,053,793
Buchanan County, MO 89,856	**Sandusky, OH 76,963**
DeKalb County, MO 12,112	Erie County, OH 76,963
St. Louis, MO-IL 2,828,990	**San Francisco-Oakland-Fremont, CA 4,317,853**
Bond County, IL 18,103	Alameda County, CA 1,491,482
Calhoun County, IL 5,019	Contra Costa County, CA 1,041,274
Clinton County, IL 36,368	Marin County, CA 250,750
Jersey County, IL 22,549	San Francisco County, CA 815,358
Macoupin County, IL 47,774	San Mateo County, CA 718,989
Madison County, IL 268,457	**San Jose-Sunnyvale-Santa Clara, CA 1,839,700**
Monroe County, IL 33,236	San Benito County, CA 55,058
St. Clair County, IL 263,617	Santa Clara County, CA 1,784,642
Franklin County, MO 101,263	**San Luis Obispo-Paso Robles, CA 266,971**
Jefferson County, MO 219,046	San Luis Obispo County, CA 266,971
Lincoln County, MO 53,311	**Santa Barbara-Santa Maria-Goleta, CA 407,057**
St. Charles County, MO 355,367	Santa Barbara County, CA 407,057
St. Louis County, MO 992,408	**Santa Cruz-Watsonville, CA 256,218**
Warren County, MO 31,485	Santa Cruz County, CA 256,218
Washington County, MO 24,400	**Santa Fe, NM 147,532**
St. Louis city, MO 356,587	Santa Fe County, NM 147,532
Salem, OR 396,103	**Santa Rosa-Petaluma, CA 472,102**
Marion County, OR 317,981	Sonoma County, CA 472,102
Polk County, OR 78,122	**Savannah, GA 343,092**
Salinas, CA 410,370	Bryan County, GA 32,559
Monterey County, CA 410,370	Chatham County, GA 256,992
Salisbury, MD 120,181	Effingham County, GA 53,541
Somerset County, MD 25,959	**Scranton--Wilkes-Barre, PA 549,454**
Wicomico County, MD 94,222	Lackawanna County, PA 208,801
Salt Lake City, UT 1,130,293	Luzerne County, PA 312,845
Salt Lake County, UT 1,034,989	Wyoming County, PA 27,808
Summit County, UT 36,969	**Seattle-Tacoma-Bellevue, WA 3,407,848**
Tooele County, UT 58,335	King County, WA 1,916,441
San Angelo, TX 110,119	Snohomish County, WA 694,571
Irion County, TX 1,741	Pierce County, WA 796,836
Tom Green County, TX 108,378	**Sebastian-Vero Beach, FL 135,167**
San Antonio, TX 2,072,128	Indian River County, FL 135,167
Atascosa County, TX 44,633	**Sheboygan, WI 114,560**
Bandera County, TX 20,560	Sheboygan County, WI 114,560
Bexar County, TX 1,651,448	**Sherman-Denison, TX 120,030**
Comal County, TX 114,525	Grayson County, TX 120,030

Metropolitan Statistical Areas and 2009 Population, Continued (MSAs in bold)

Shreveport-Bossier City, LA 391,516	Oswego County, NY 121,377
Bossier Parish, LA 111,492	**Tallahassee, FL 360,013**
Caddo Parish, LA 253,623	Gadsden County, FL 47,474
De Soto Parish, LA 26,401	Jefferson County, FL 14,010
Sioux City, IA-NE-SD 144,360	Leon County, FL 265,714
Woodbury County, IA 102,831	Wakulla County, FL 32,815
Dakota County, NE 20,651	**Tampa-St. Petersburg-Clearwater, FL 2,747,272**
Dixon County, NE 6,289	Hernando County, FL 171,233
Union County, SD 14,589	Hillsborough County, FL 1,195,317
Sioux Falls, SD 238,122	Pasco County, FL 471,709
Lincoln County, SD 41,218	Pinellas County, FL 909,013
McCook County, SD 5,619	**Terre Haute, IN 169,825**
Minnehaha County, SD 183,048	Clay County, IN 26,533
Turner County, SD 8,237	Sullivan County, IN 21,153
South Bend-Mishawaka, IN-MI 317,538	Vermillion County, IN 16,172
St. Joseph County, IN 267,613	Vigo County, IN 105,967
Cass County, MI 49,925	**Texarkana, TX-Texarkana, AR 137,486**
Spartanburg, SC 286,822	Miller County, AR 43,522
Spartanburg County, SC 286,822	Bowie County, TX 93,964
Spokane, WA 468,684	**Toledo, OH 672,220**
Spokane County, WA 468,684	Fulton County, OH 42,402
Springfield, IL 208,182	Lucas County, OH 463,493
Menard County, IL 12,466	Ottawa County, OH 40,945
Sangamon County, IL 195,716	Wood County, OH 125,380
Springfield, MA 698,903	**Topeka, KS 230,824**
Franklin County, MA 71,778	Jackson County, KS 13,412
Hampden County, MA 471,081	Jefferson County, KS 18,207
Hampshire County, MA 156,044	Osage County, KS 16,104
Springfield, MO 430,900	Shawnee County, KS 176,255
Christian County, MO 77,455	Wabaunsee County, KS 6,846
Dallas County, MO 16,637	**Trenton-Ewing, NJ 366,222**
Greene County, MO 269,630	Mercer County, NJ 366,222
Polk County, MO 30,626	**Tucson, AZ 1,020,200**
Webster County, MO 36,552	Pima County, AZ 1,020,200
Springfield, OH 139,671	**Tulsa, OK 929,015**
Clark County, OH 139,671	Creek County, OK 70,244
State College, PA 146,212	Okmulgee County, OK 39,292
Centre County, PA 146,212	Osage County, OK 45,051
Stockton, CA 674,860	Pawnee County, OK 16,419
San Joaquin County, CA 674,860	Rogers County, OK 85,654
Sumter, SC 104,495	Tulsa County, OK 601,961
Sumter County, SC 104,495	Wagoner County, OK 70,394
Syracuse, NY 646,084	
Madison County, NY 69,954	
Onondaga County, NY 454,753	

Metropolitan Statistical Areas and 2009 Population, Continued (MSAs in bold)

Area	Population	Area	Population
Tuscaloosa, AL	**210,839**	**Washington, DC- Alexandria, VA**	**5,476,241**
Greene County, AL	8,829	Frederick County, MD	227,980
Hale County, AL	17,975	Montgomery County, MD	971,600
Tuscaloosa County, AL	184,035	District of Columbia, DC	599,657
Tyler, TX	**204,665**	Calvert County, MD	89,212
Smith County, TX	204,665	Charles County, MD	142,226
Utica-Rome, NY	**293,280**	Prince George's County, MD	834,560
Herkimer County, NY	62,236	Arlington County, VA	217,483
Oneida County, NY	231,044	Clarke County, VA	14,588
Valdosta, GA	**135,804**	Fairfax County, VA	1,037,605
Brooks County, GA	16,354	Fauquier County, VA	68,010
Echols County, GA	4,213	Loudoun County, VA	301,171
Lanier County, GA	8,423	Prince William County, VA	379,166
Lowndes County, GA	106,814	Spotsylvania County, VA	120,977
Vallejo-Fairfield, CA	**407,234**	Stafford County, VA	124,166
Solano County, CA	407,234	Warren County, VA	36,713
Victoria, TX	**115,396**	Alexandria city, VA	150,006
Calhoun County, TX	20,573	Fairfax city, VA	24,665
Goliad County, TX	7,033	Falls Church city, VA	11,957
Victoria County, TX	87,790	Fredericksburg city, VA	23,193
Vineland-Millville-Bridgeton, NJ	**157,745**	Manassas city, VA	36,514
Cumberland County, NJ	157,745	Manassas Park city, VA	12,042
Virginia Beach-Norfolk-Newport News, VA-NC	**1,674,498**	Jefferson County, WV	52,750
Currituck County, NC	24,216	**Waterloo-Cedar Falls, IA**	**164,913**
Gloucester County, VA	39,184	Black Hawk County, IA	129,276
Isle of Wight County, VA	35,877	Bremer County, IA	23,460
James City County, VA	63,735	Grundy County, IA	12,177
Mathews County, VA	8,984	**Wausau, WI**	**131,612**
Surry County, VA	7,088	Marathon County, WI	131,612
York County, VA	61,140	**Weirton-Steubenville, WV-OH**	**120,929**
Chesapeake city, VA	222,455	Jefferson County, OH	67,691
Hampton city, VA	144,236	Brooke County, WV	23,509
Newport News city, VA	193,172	Hancock County, WV	29,729
Norfolk city, VA	233,333	**Wenatchee-East Wenatchee, WA**	**109,937**
Poquoson city, VA	11,794	Chelan County, WA	72,372
Portsmouth city, VA	99,321	Douglas County, WA	37,565
Suffolk city, VA	83,659	**Wheeling, WV-OH**	**144,637**
Virginia Beach city, VA	433,575	Belmont County, OH	68,066
Williamsburg city, VA	12,729	Marshall County, WV	32,556
Visalia-Porterville, CA	**429,668**	Ohio County, WV	44,015
Tulare County, CA	429,668	**Wichita, KS**	**612,683**
Waco, TX	**233,378**	Butler County, KS	64,084
McLennan County, TX	233,378	Harvey County, KS	34,247
Warner Robins, GA	**135,715**	Sedgwick County, KS	490,864
Houston County, GA	135,715	Sumner County, KS	23,488

Metropolitan Statistical Areas and 2009 Population, Continued (MSAs in bold)

Wichita Falls, TX	**147,421**
Archer County, TX	8,912
Clay County, TX	10,893
Wichita County, TX	127,616
Williamsport, PA	**116,840**
Lycoming County, PA	116,840
Wilmington, NC	**354,525**
Brunswick County, NC	107,062
New Hanover County, NC	195,085
Pender County, NC	52,378
Winchester, VA-WV	**123,989**
Frederick County, VA	74,972
Winchester city, VA	26,322
Hampshire County, WV	22,695
Winston-Salem, NC	**484,921**
Davie County, NC	41,420
Forsyth County, NC	359,638
Stokes County, NC	46,150
Yadkin County, NC	37,713
Worcester, MA	**803,701**
Worcester County, MA	803,701
Yakima, WA	**239,054**
Yakima County, WA	239,054
York-Hanover, PA	**428,937**
York County, PA	428,937
Youngstown-Warren-Boardman, OH-PA	**562,963**
Mahoning County, OH	236,735
Trumbull County, OH	210,157
Mercer County, PA	116,071
Yuba City, CA	**165,539**
Sutter County, CA	92,614
Yuba County, CA	72,925
Yuma, AZ	**196,972**
Yuma County, AZ	196,972

Chapter 2: The Categories

As mentioned in Chapter 1, we use seven categories to consider the status of the 361 communities ranked and rated in this book. Each category has multiple data sets. Some have as many as nine or ten data sets; others have as few as four or five.

The first category, **LDS Culture,** looks at data such as proximity to LDS temples, proximity to LDS historic sites, stay-at-home mothers, commuting times, and the number and ratio of "negative establishments" versus "positive establishments." "Negative" establishments include such organizations and institutions as gambling halls, liquor stores, bars, strip clubs, casinos, smoke shops, etc. "Positive" establishments include churches, educational institutions, family amusement parks, youth camps, recreation facilities, etc. Sources for data in this category include the Bureau of Labor Statistics, the Census Bureau, and LDS.org.

The second category is **Education.** Here we considered educational attainment, student-teacher ratios in public schools, graduation rates, and school environment issues, such as the number of students qualifying for free and reduced lunch. Sources include the U.S. Department of Education and the Census Bureau.

Third is **Crime.** This includes violent crime (murder, rape, robbery and aggravated assault) and property crime (burglary, larceny, theft, and motor vehicle theft). Sources include the Federal Bureau of Investigation and State of the Cities Data System.

Fourth: **Economic Environment.** Here we considered family income, poverty levels, state income tax rates, complexity and favorability of state income tax system, state sales tax rates, state sales tax exemptions (such as for food or religious items), state income and sales tax revenues, unemployment rates, consumer prices indexes, home costs, home values, and other data. Sources include the U.S. Census Bureau, the Bureau of Labor Statistics, Tax Foundation, National Association of Realtors, and private databases.

The fifth category is **Health.** We examined health from an LDS perspective, including youth and adult drug, tobacco, and alcohol use, teen sexual activity, teen and adult sexually transmitted disease rates, general health, exercise, obesity, etc. Sources include the Centers for Disease Control and Prevention.

Sixth is **Household Characteristics,** including population, percent of population between the ages of 0 and 17, percent of children living with biological parents, percent of children living with married biological parents, percent of children living with single mothers or single fathers, percent of children living with two unmarried adults, percent of children living with same-sex partners, working parents, stay-at-home mothers, rate of new mothers who are working, and rate of births to unwed mothers. All data came from the U.S. Census Bureau.

The final category is **Housing.** Here we looked again at housing costs, housing affordability, age of home, cost of larger home (four-bedroom), owner-occupied versus rented homes, and home value appreciation. Sources for these data include the U.S. Census Bureau, the National Association of Realtors, Freddie Mac, and private databases.

Chapter 3: Community Data

Here you'll find, in Table 2.1, all 361 communities listed in order of highest rank to the lowest rank. Remember, a score of 100 is best and 0 is worst, in all of the categories.

In Table 2.2, you'll see the same ranking, only this time the communities are listed alphabetically.

You will then find tables listing the rankings of the best and worst in each of the seven categories used in our evaluation.

The rest of the tables are various data sets from the seven categories.

Table 2.1: Communities in Order of Ranking

Community	Final Index	Final Ranking
Provo-Orem, UT	100.00	1
St. George, UT	92.52	2
Logan, UT-ID	89.84	3
Ogden-Clearfield, UT	88.48	4
State College, PA	81.04	5
Idaho Falls, ID	80.57	6
Corvallis, OR	79.09	7
Salt Lake City, UT	78.94	8
Bend, OR	78.88	9
Ames, IA	77.08	10
Ithaca, NY	77.01	11
Iowa City, IA	76.91	12
Boise City-Nampa, ID	76.65	13
Lynchburg, VA	76.63	14
Harrisonburg, VA	75.65	15
Appleton, WI	75.54	16
Bismarck, ND	75.06	17
Charlottesville, VA	74.89	18
Holland-Grand Haven, MI	74.70	19
Blacksburg-Christiansburg-Radford, VA	74.34	20
Oshkosh-Neenah, WI	74.30	21
Sheboygan, WI	74.11	22
Lancaster, PA	74.02	23
Boulder, CO	74.01	24
Fort Collins-Loveland, CO	73.19	25
Olympia, WA	73.15	26
Eau Claire, WI	73.06	27
San Luis Obispo-Paso Robles, CA	72.33	28
Jefferson City, MO	72.27	29
Madison, WI	72.15	30
Fayetteville-Springdale-Rogers, AR-MO	72.00	31
Coeur d'Alene, ID	71.90	32
Raleigh-Cary, NC	71.81	33
Elmira, NY	71.69	34
Fond du Lac, WI	71.56	35
Pocatello, ID	71.43	36
St. Cloud, MN	71.23	37
Lincoln, NE	71.14	38
Rochester, MN	71.03	39
Poughkeepsie-Newburgh-Middletown, NY	71.03	40
Lewiston-Auburn, ME	70.92	41
Waterloo-Cedar Falls, IA	70.89	42
Salem, OR	70.80	43
Kennewick-Pasco-Richland, WA	70.69	44
Bangor, ME	70.55	45
Richmond, VA	70.34	46
Columbia, MO	70.20	47
Cedar Rapids, IA	70.15	48
Burlington-South Burlington, VT	70.14	49
Colorado Springs, CO	70.08	50

Communities in Order of Ranking

Community	Final Index	Final Ranking	Community	Final Index	Final Ranking
Mount Vernon-Anacortes, WA	69.91	51	Denver-Aurora-Broomfield, CO	68.24	76
Des Moines-West Des Moines, IA	69.76	52	Medford, OR	68.23	77
Lebanon, PA	69.74	53	Fairbanks, AK	68.18	78
Huntingotn-Ashland, WV-KY	69.73	54	Dubuque, IA	68.16	79
Portland-South Portland-Biddeford, ME	69.60	55	Knoxville, TN	68.12	80
Wausau, WI	69.42	56	Anchorage, AK	68.08	81
Palm Coast, FL	69.37	57	Pittsburgh, PA	68.07	82
Bridgeport-Stamford-Norwalk, CT	69.33	58	Kingsport-Bristol-Bristol, TN-VA	68.05	83
Punta Gorda, FL	69.25	59	Elkhart-Goshen, IN	67.98	84
San Jose-Sunnyvale-Santa Clara, CA	69.22	60	Minneapolis-St. Paul-Bloomington, MN-WI	67.95	85
Harrisburg-Carlisle, PA	69.18	61	York-Hanover, PA	67.90	86
Sioux Falls, SD	69.13	62	La Crosse, WI-MN	67.89	87
Fort Walton Beach-Crestview-Destin, FL	69.13	63	Kingston, NY	67.81	88
Oxnard-Thousand Oaks-Ventura, CA	69.07	64	Honolulu, HI	67.80	89
Rochester, NY	69.07	65	Auburn-Opelika, AL	67.79	90
Omaha-Concl Bluffs, NE-IA	69.03	66	Port St. Lucie, FL	67.76	91
Fargo, ND-MN	68.95	67	Grand Forks, ND-MN	67.74	92
Glens Falls, NY	68.88	68	Grand Junction, CO	67.68	93
Green Bay, WI	68.86	69	Bloomington-Normal, IL	67.48	94
Bellingham, WA	68.77	70	Hickory-Morganton, NC	67.46	95
Greeley, CO	68.75	71	Johnson City, TN	67.43	96
Lafayette, IN	68.69	72	Missoula, MT	67.36	97
Wenatchee-East Wenatchee, WA	68.55	73	Altoona, PA	67.25	98
Syracuse, NY	68.41	74	Warner Robins, GA	67.22	99
Columbus, IN	68.34	75	Norwich-New London, CT	67.21	100

Communities in Order of Ranking

Community	Final Index	Final Ranking	Community	Final Index	Final Ranking
Roanoke, VA	67.10	101	Dalton, GA	66.01	126
Seattle-Tacoma-Bellevue, WA	67.01	102	Decatur, AL	65.92	127
Albany-Schenectady-Troy, NY	67.01	103	Springfield, MO	65.87	128
Ann Arbor, MI	66.99	104	Jacksonville, NC	65.86	129
Sherman-Denison, TX	66.98	105	Ocean City, NJ	65.81	130
Naples-Marco Island, FL	66.98	106	Kansas City, MO-KS	65.57	131
Evansville, IN-KY	66.68	107	Gadsden, AL	65.49	132
Gainesville, GA	66.66	108	Austin-Round Rock, TX	65.49	133
Portland-Vancouver-Beaverton, OR-WA	66.63	109	Great Falls, MT	65.37	134
Trenton-Ewing, NJ	66.61	110	Rapid City, SD	65.35	135
Reading, PA	66.56	111	Barnstable Town, MA	65.30	136
Casper, WY	66.49	112	Grand Rapids-Wyoming, MI	65.03	137
Asheville, NC	66.44	113	Greensboro-High Point, NC	64.98	138
Bloomington, IN	66.33	114	Tyler, TX	64.95	139
Bremerton-Silverdale, WA	66.30	115	Huntsville, AL	64.83	140
Mansfield, OH	66.25	116	Cleveland, TN	64.82	141
Billings, MT	66.25	117	Morgantown, WV	64.70	142
Utica-Rome, NY	66.23	118	Pascagoula, MS	64.69	143
Santa Barbara-Santa Maria-Goleta, CA	66.23	119	Lawrence, KS	64.65	144
Cheyenne, WY	66.21	120	Eugene-Springfield, OR	64.64	145
Williamsport, PA	66.20	121	Duluth, MN-WI	64.61	146
Elizabethtown, KY	66.18	122	Atlanta-Sandy Springs-Marietta, GA	64.56	147
Midland, TX	66.14	123	Parkersburg-Marietta-Vienna, WV-OH	64.52	148
Allentown-Bethlehem-Easton, PA-NJ	66.11	124	Dallas-Fort Worth-Arlington, TX	64.51	149
Binghamton, NY	66.02	125	Chattanooga, TN-GA	64.44	150

Communities in Order of Ranking

Community	Final Index	Final Ranking	Community	Final Index	Final Ranking
Lansing-East Lansing, MI	64.41	151	Boston Metro Area, MA-NH	63.30	176
Janesville, WI	64.40	152	Racine, WI	63.30	177
Champaign-Urbana, IL	64.39	153	Killeen-Fort Hood, TX	63.27	178
Winston-Salem, NC	64.34	154	Goldsboro, NC	63.21	179
Owensboro, KY	64.33	155	Kokomo, IN	63.17	180
Fort Smith, AR-OK	64.30	156	Jonesboro, AR	63.03	181
Sandusky, OH	64.27	157	Scranton--Wilkes-Barre, PA	62.99	182
Erie, PA	64.25	158	Phoenix-Mesa, AZ	62.96	183
Cape Coral-Fort Myers, FL	64.20	159	San Diego-Carlsbad-San Marcos, CA	62.96	184
Weirton-Steubnvlle, WV-OH	64.10	160	Santa Rosa-Petaluma, CA	62.80	185
Hartford-West Hartford-East Hartford, CT	63.91	161	Worcester, MA	62.65	186
Sebastian-Vero Beach, FL	63.85	162	Hagerstown-Martinsburg, MD-WV	62.41	187
Nashville-Davidson--Murfreesboro--Franklin, TN	63.84	163	Monroe, MI	62.26	188
Sioux City, IA-NE-SD	63.82	164	Hanford-Corcoran, CA	62.26	189
Manchester-Nashua, NH	63.82	165	Charlotte-Gastonia-Concord, NC-SC	62.12	190
St. Joseph, MO-KS	63.77	166	Hattiesburg, MS	62.10	191
Kalamazoo-Portage, MI	63.69	167	Washington DC Metro Area	62.10	192
Johnstown, PA	63.66	168	Peoria, IL	62.09	193
Fort Wayne, IN	63.62	169	New York City Area	61.99	194
Florence-Muscle Shoals, AL	63.55	170	El Centro, CA	61.98	195
Salinas, CA	63.50	171	Akron, OH	61.96	196
Abilene, TX	63.49	172	Jackson, MI	61.94	197
Prescott, AZ	63.39	173	Buffalo-Niagara Falls, NY	61.94	198
Napa, CA	63.31	174	Spokane, WA	61.88	199
Santa Cruz-Watsonville, CA	63.31	175	Fayetteville, NC	61.85	200

Communities in Order of Ranking

Community	Final Index	Final Ranking	Community	Final Index	Final Ranking
Athens-Clarke County, GA	61.84	201	Virginia Beach-Norfolk-Newport News, VA-NC	60.73	226
Cincinnati-Middletown, OH-KY-IN	61.80	202	Wichita Falls, TX	60.71	227
Redding, CA	61.76	203	Longview, WA	60.65	228
Sacramento--Arden-Arcade--Roseville, CA	61.74	204	Tuscaloosa, AL	60.58	229
Valdosta, GA	61.72	205	Lakeland-Winter Haven, FL	60.57	230
Oklahoma City, OK	61.67	206	Morristown, TN	60.48	231
Farmington, NM	61.63	207	Springfield, OH	60.47	232
Springfield, IL	61.58	208	Bay City, MI	60.41	233
Durham-Chapel Hill, NC	61.58	209	Gainesville, FL	60.38	234
Riverside-San Bernardino-Ontario, CA	61.56	210	Dover, DE	60.35	235
Birmingham-Hoover, AL	61.44	211	South Bend-Mishawaka, IN-MI	60.33	236
Davenport-Moline-Rock Island, IA-IL	61.36	212	Canton-Massillon, OH	60.28	237
Wilmington, NC	61.32	213	Lake Havasu City-Kingman, AZ	60.24	238
Danville, VA	61.29	214	Indianapolis-Carmel, IN	60.22	239
College Station-Bryan, TX	61.26	215	Lubbock, TX	60.18	240
Cumberland, MD-WV	61.22	216	Monroe, LA	60.10	241
Clarksville, TN-KY	61.15	217	Greenville-Mauldin, SC	60.08	242
McAllen-Edinburg, TX	61.14	218	San Angelo, TX	60.06	243
Wheeling, WV-OH	61.03	219	Modesto, CA	59.99	244
Bowling Green, KY	60.94	220	Muncie, IN	59.99	245
Winchester, VA-WV	60.91	221	Lexington-Fayette, KY	59.98	246
Lake Charles, LA	60.87	222	Bradenton-Sarasota-Venice, FL	59.95	247
Montgomery, AL	60.86	223	Charleston, WV	59.93	248
Topeka, KS	60.84	224	Tulsa, OK	59.90	249
Columbus, OH	60.79	225	St. Louis, MO-IL	59.87	250

Communities in Order of Ranking

Community	Final Index	Final Ranking	Community	Final Index	Final Ranking
Orlando-Kissimmee, FL	59.81	251	Madera-Chowchilla, CA	58.53	276
Pittsfield, MA	59.64	252	Amarillo, TX	58.52	277
Louisville/Jefferson County, KY-IN	59.60	253	Savannah, GA	58.47	278
Pensacola-Ferry Pass-Brent, FL	59.56	254	Chicago-Naperville-Joliet, IL-IN-WI	58.47	279
Rocky Mount, NC	59.54	255	Los Angeles-Long Beach-Santa Ana, CA	58.45	280
Yuma, AZ	59.53	256	Lawton, OK	58.45	281
Michigan City-La Porte, IN	59.50	257	Jacksonville, FL	58.43	282
San Francisco-Oakland-Fremont, CA	59.42	258	Anniston-Oxford, AL	58.35	283
Houston-Sugar Land-Baytown, TX	59.42	259	Springfield, MA	58.29	284
Yakima, WA	59.34	260	Columbia, SC	58.19	285
Tucson, AZ	59.28	261	Joplin, MO	58.09	286
Baton Rouge, LA	59.17	262	Philadelphia-Camden-Wilmington, PA-NJ-DE-MD	57.89	287
Longview, TX	59.11	263	Brownsville-Harlingen, TX	57.86	288
Santa Fe, NM	59.07	264	Merced, CA	57.82	289
Terre Haute, IN	59.01	265	Dothan, AL	57.79	290
Anderson, IN	59.00	266	Little Rock-North Little Rock-Conway, AR	57.76	291
Hinesville-Fort Stewart, GA	58.98	267	Tampa-St. Petersburg-Clearwater, FL	57.75	292
El Paso, TX	58.97	268	Burlington, NC	57.73	293
Flagstaff, AZ	58.93	269	Las Vegas-Paradise, NV	57.67	294
Dayton, OH	58.89	270	Detroit-Warren-Livonia, MI	57.57	295
Palm Bay-Melbourne-Titusville, FL	58.73	271	Panama City-Lynn Haven-Panama City Beach, FL	57.39	296
Wichita, KS	58.68	272	Chico, CA	57.36	297
Reno-Sparks, NV	58.60	273	Albuquerque, NM	57.29	298
Las Cruces, NM	58.60	274	Yuba City, CA	57.29	299
Greenville, NC	58.55	275	Augusta-Richmond County, GA-SC	57.16	300

Communities in Order of Ranking

Community	Final Index	Final Ranking	Community	Final Index	Final Ranking
Alexandria, LA	57.14	301	Columbus, GA-AL	54.81	332
Youngstown, OH	57.14	302	Tallahassee, FL	54.76	333
Deltona-Daytona Beach, FL	57.10	303	Stockton, CA	54.72	334
Bakersfield, CA	57.05	304	Lima, OH	54.72	335
Vallejo-Fairfield, CA	56.99	305	Providence- RI-MA	54.44	336
Cleveland-Elyria-Mentor, OH	56.89	306	Atlantic City-Hammonton, NJ	54.43	337
Texarkana, TX-Texarkana, AR	56.88	307	Battle Creek, MI	54.27	338
Muskegon-Norton Shores, MI	56.86	308	Milwaukee, WI	54.25	339
San Antonio, TX	56.78	309	Waco, TX	54.18	340
New Haven-Milford, CT	56.67	310	Fresno, CA	54.18	341
Rome, GA	56.60	311	Victoria, TX	53.90	342
Niles-Benton Harbor, MI	56.36	312	Gulfport-Biloxi, MS	53.84	343
Flint, MI	56.35	313	Mobile, AL	53.84	344
Jackson, TN	56.33	314	Salisbury, MD	53.48	345
Anderson, SC	56.32	315	Myrtle Beach, SC	53.41	346
Jackson, MS	56.29	316	Vineland-Millville, NJ	53.27	347
Visalia-Porterville, CA	56.26	317	Rockford, IL	53.25	348
Kankakee-Bradley, IL	56.11	318	Lafayette, LA	53.17	349
Brunswick, GA	56.10	319	Corpus Christi, TX	52.81	350
Beaumont-Port Arthur, TX	56.07	320	Toledo, OH	52.67	351
Pueblo, CO	55.86	321	Sumter, SC	52.67	352
Ocala, FL	55.83	322	Hot Springs, AR	52.39	353
Baltimore-Towson, MD	55.82	323	Pine Bluff, AR	52.33	354
Decatur, IL	55.71	324	Albany, GA	52.22	355
Miami-Fort Lauderdale, FL	55.71	325	Memphis, TN-MS-AR	52.14	356
Danville, IL	55.54	326	Odessa, TX	51.78	357
Houma-Bayou Cane, LA	55.44	327	Saginaw, MI	51.64	358
New Orleans, LA	55.06	328	Macon, GA	51.53	359
Laredo, TX	55.00	329	Shreveport-Bossier City, LA	51.39	360
Charleston-N.Charleston, SC	54.97	330	Florence, SC	49.18	361
Spartanburg, SC	54.89	331			

Table 2.2: Communities in Alphabetical Order

Community	Final Index	Final Ranking	Community	Final Index	Final Ranking
Abilene, TX	63.49	172	Bangor, ME	70.55	45
Akron, OH	61.96	196	Barnstable Town, MA	65.30	136
Albany, GA	52.22	355	Baton Rouge, LA	59.17	262
Albany-Schenectady-Troy, NY	67.01	103	Battle Creek, MI	54.27	338
Albuquerque, NM	57.29	298	Bay City, MI	60.41	233
Alexandria, LA	57.14	301	Beaumont-Port Arthur, TX	56.07	320
Allentown-Bethlehem-Easton, PA-NJ	66.11	124	Bellingham, WA	68.77	70
Altoona, PA	67.25	98	Bend, OR	78.88	9
Amarillo, TX	58.52	277	Billings, MT	66.25	117
Ames, IA	77.08	10	Binghamton, NY	66.02	125
Anchorage, AK	68.08	81	Birmingham-Hoover, AL	61.44	211
Anderson, IN	59.00	266	Bismarck, ND	75.06	17
Anderson, SC	56.32	315	Blacksburg-Christiansburg-Radford, VA	74.34	20
Ann Arbor, MI	66.99	104	Bloomington, IN	66.33	114
Anniston-Oxford, AL	58.35	283	Bloomington-Normal, IL	67.48	94
Appleton, WI	75.54	16	Boise City-Nampa, ID	76.65	13
Asheville, NC	66.44	113	Boston-Cambridge-Quincy, MA-NH	63.30	176
Athens-Clarke County, GA	61.84	201	Boulder, CO	74.01	24
Atlanta-Sandy Springs-Marietta, GA	64.56	147	Bowling Green, KY	60.94	220
Atlantic City-Hammonton, NJ	54.43	337	Bradenton-Sarasota-Venice, FL	59.95	247
Auburn-Opelika, AL	67.79	90	Bremerton-Silverdale, WA	66.30	115
Augusta-Richmond County, GA-SC	57.16	300	Bridgeport-Stamford-Norwalk, CT	69.33	58
Austin-Round Rock, TX	65.49	133	Brownsville-Harlingen, TX	57.86	288
Bakersfield, CA	57.05	304	Brunswick, GA	56.10	319
Baltimore-Towson, MD	55.82	323	Buffalo-Niagara Falls, NY	61.94	198

Communities in Alphabetical Order

Community	Final Index	Final Ranking	Community	Final Index	Final Ranking
Burlington, NC	57.73	293	Columbus, IN	68.34	75
Burlington-South Burlington, VT	70.14	49	Columbus, OH	60.79	225
Canton-Massillon, OH	60.28	237	Corpus Christi, TX	52.81	350
Cape Coral-Fort Myers, FL	64.20	159	Corvallis, OR	79.09	7
Casper, WY	66.49	112	Cumberland, MD-WV	61.22	216
Cedar Rapids, IA	70.15	48	Dallas-Fort Worth-Arlington, TX	64.51	149
Champaign-Urbana, IL	64.39	153	Dalton, GA	66.01	126
Charleston, WV	59.93	248	Danville, IL	55.54	326
Charleston-North Charleston-Summerville, SC	54.97	330	Danville, VA	61.29	214
Charlotte-Gastonia-Concord, NC-SC	62.12	190	Davenport-Moline-Rock Island, IA-IL	61.36	212
Charlottesville, VA	74.89	18	Dayton, OH	58.89	270
Chattanooga, TN-GA	64.44	150	Decatur, AL	65.92	127
Cheyenne, WY	66.21	120	Decatur, IL	55.71	324
Chicago-Naperville-Joliet, IL-IN-WI	58.47	279	Deltona-Daytona Beach-Ormond Beach, FL	57.10	303
Chico, CA	57.36	297	Denver-Aurora-Broomfield, CO	68.24	76
Cincinnati-Middletown, OH-KY-IN	61.80	202	Des Moines-West Des Moines, IA	69.76	52
Clarksville, TN-KY	61.15	217	Detroit-Warren-Livonia, MI	57.57	295
Cleveland, TN	64.82	141	Dothan, AL	57.79	290
Cleveland-Elyria-Mentor, OH	56.89	306	Dover, DE	60.35	235
Coeur d'Alene, ID	71.90	32	Dubuque, IA	68.16	79
College Station-Bryan, TX	61.26	215	Duluth, MN-WI	64.61	146
Colorado Springs, CO	70.08	50	Durham-Chapel Hill, NC	61.58	209
Columbia, MO	70.20	47	Eau Claire, WI	73.06	27
Columbia, SC	58.19	285	El Centro, CA	61.98	195
Columbus, GA-AL	54.81	332	El Paso, TX	58.97	268

Communities in Alphabetical Order

Community	Final Index	Final Ranking	Community	Final Index	Final Ranking
Elizabethtown, KY	66.18	122	Goldsboro, NC	63.21	179
Elkhart-Goshen, IN	67.98	84	Grand Forks, ND-MN	67.74	92
Elmira, NY	71.69	34	Grand Junction, CO	67.68	93
Erie, PA	64.25	158	Grand Rapids-Wyoming, MI	65.03	137
Eugene-Springfield, OR	64.64	145	Great Falls, MT	65.37	134
Evansville, IN-KY	66.68	107	Greeley, CO	68.75	71
Fairbanks, AK	68.18	78	Green Bay, WI	68.86	69
Fargo, ND-MN	68.95	67	Greensboro-High Point, NC	64.98	138
Farmington, NM	61.63	207	Greenville, NC	58.55	275
Fayetteville, NC	61.85	200	Greenville-Mauldin-Easley, SC	60.08	242
Fayetteville-Springdale-Rogers, AR-MO	72.00	31	Gulfport-Biloxi, MS	53.84	343
Flagstaff, AZ	58.93	269	Hagerstown-Martinsburg, MD-WV	62.41	187
Flint, MI	56.35	313	Hanford-Corcoran, CA	62.26	189
Florence, SC	49.18	361	Harrisburg-Carlisle, PA	69.18	61
Florence-Muscle Shoals, AL	63.55	170	Harrisonburg, VA	75.65	15
Fond du Lac, WI	71.56	35	Hartford-West Hartford-East Hartford, CT	63.91	161
Fort Collins-Loveland, CO	73.19	25	Hattiesburg, MS	62.10	191
Fort Smith, AR-OK	64.30	156	Hickory-Lenoir-Morganton, NC	67.46	95
Fort Walton Beach-Crestview-Destin, FL	69.13	63	Hinesville-Fort Stewart, GA	58.98	267
Fort Wayne, IN	63.62	169	Holland-Grand Haven, MI	74.70	19
Fresno, CA	54.18	341	Honolulu, HI	67.80	89
Gadsden, AL	65.49	132	Hot Springs, AR	52.39	353
Gainesville, FL	60.38	234	Houma-Bayou Cane-Thibodaux, LA	55.44	327
Gainesville, GA	66.66	108	Houston-Sugar Land-Baytown, TX	59.42	259
Glens Falls, NY	68.88	68	Huntington-Ashland, WV-KY-OH	69.73	54

Communities in Alphabetical Order

Community	Final Index	Final Ranking	Community	Final Index	Final Ranking
Huntsville, AL	64.83	140	La Crosse, WI-MN	67.89	87
Idaho Falls, ID	80.57	6	Lafayette, IN	68.69	72
Indianapolis-Carmel, IN	60.22	239	Lafayette, LA	53.17	349
Iowa City, IA	76.91	12	Lake Charles, LA	60.87	222
Ithaca, NY	77.01	11	Lake Havasu City-Kingman, AZ	60.24	238
Jackson, MI	61.94	197	Lakeland-Winter Haven, FL	60.57	230
Jackson, MS	56.29	316	Lancaster, PA	74.02	23
Jackson, TN	56.33	314	Lansing-East Lansing, MI	64.41	151
Jacksonville, FL	58.43	282	Laredo, TX	55.00	329
Jacksonville, NC	65.86	129	Las Cruces, NM	58.60	274
Janesville, WI	64.40	152	Las Vegas-Paradise, NV	57.67	294
Jefferson City, MO	72.27	29	Lawrence, KS	64.65	144
Johnson City, TN	67.43	96	Lawton, OK	58.45	281
Johnstown, PA	63.66	168	Lebanon, PA	69.74	53
Jonesboro, AR	63.03	181	Lewiston-Auburn, ME	70.92	41
Joplin, MO	58.09	286	Lexington-Fayette, KY	59.98	246
Kalamazoo-Portage, MI	63.69	167	Lima, OH	54.72	335
Kankakee-Bradley, IL	56.11	318	Lincoln, NE	71.14	38
Kansas City, MO-KS	65.57	131	Little Rock-North Little Rock-Conway, AR	57.76	291
Kennewick-Pasco-Richland, WA	70.69	44	Logan, UT-ID	89.84	3
Killeen-Temple-Fort Hood, TX	63.27	178	Longview, TX	59.11	263
Kingsport-Bristol-Bristol, TN-VA	68.05	83	Longview, WA	60.65	228
Kingston, NY	67.81	88	Los Angeles-Long Beach-Santa Ana, CA	58.45	280
Knoxville, TN	68.12	80	Louisville/Jefferson County, KY-IN	59.60	253
Kokomo, IN	63.17	180	Lubbock, TX	60.18	240

Communities in Alphabetical Order

Community	Final Index	Final Ranking	Community	Final Index	Final Ranking
Lynchburg, VA	76.63	14	Muskegon-Norton Shores, MI	56.86	308
Macon, GA	51.53	359	Myrtle Beach-North Myrtle Beach-Conway, SC	53.41	346
Madera-Chowchilla, CA	58.53	276	Napa, CA	63.31	174
Madison, WI	72.15	30	Naples-Marco Island, FL	66.98	106
Manchester-Nashua, NH	63.82	165	Nashville-Davidson--Murfreesboro--Franklin, TN	63.84	163
Mansfield, OH	66.25	116	New Haven-Milford, CT	56.67	310
McAllen-Edinburg-Mission, TX	61.14	218	New Orleans-Metairie-Kenner, LA	55.06	328
Medford, OR	68.23	77	New York-Northern New Jersey-Long Island, NY-NJ-PA	61.99	194
Memphis, TN-MS-AR	52.14	356	Niles-Benton Harbor, MI	56.36	312
Merced, CA	57.82	289	Norwich-New London, CT	67.21	100
Miami-Fort Lauderdale-Pompano Beach, FL	55.71	325	Ocala, FL	55.83	322
Michigan City-La Porte, IN	59.50	257	Ocean City, NJ	65.81	130
Midland, TX	66.14	123	Odessa, TX	51.78	357
Milwaukee-Waukesha-West Allis, WI	54.25	339	Ogden-Clearfield, UT	88.48	4
Minneapolis-St. Paul-Bloomington, MN-WI	67.95	85	Oklahoma City, OK	61.67	206
Missoula, MT	67.36	97	Olympia, WA	73.15	26
Mobile, AL	53.84	344	Omaha-Council Bluffs, NE-IA	69.03	66
Modesto, CA	59.99	244	Orlando-Kissimmee, FL	59.81	251
Monroe, LA	60.10	241	Oshkosh-Neenah, WI	74.30	21
Monroe, MI	62.26	188	Owensboro, KY	64.33	155
Montgomery, AL	60.86	223	Oxnard-Thousand Oaks-Ventura, CA	69.07	64
Morgantown, WV	64.70	142	Palm Bay-Melbourne-Titusville, FL	58.73	271
Morristown, TN	60.48	231	Palm Coast, FL	69.37	57
Mount Vernon-Anacortes, WA	69.91	51	Panama City-Lynn Haven-Panama City Beach, FL	57.39	296
Muncie, IN	59.99	245	Parkersburg-Marietta-Vienna, WV-OH	64.52	148

Communities in Alphabetical Order

Community	Final Index	Final Ranking	Community	Final Index	Final Ranking
Pascagoula, MS	64.69	143	Riverside-San Bernardino-Ontario, CA	61.56	210
Pensacola-Ferry Pass-Brent, FL	59.56	254	Roanoke, VA	67.10	101
Peoria, IL	62.09	193	Rochester, MN	71.03	39
Philadelphia-Camden-Wilmington, PA-NJ-DE-MD	57.89	287	Rochester, NY	69.07	65
Phoenix-Mesa-Scottsdale, AZ	62.96	183	Rockford, IL	53.25	348
Pine Bluff, AR	52.33	354	Rocky Mount, NC	59.54	255
Pittsburgh, PA	68.07	82	Rome, GA	56.60	311
Pittsfield, MA	59.64	252	Sacramento--Arden-Arcade--Roseville, CA	61.74	204
Pocatello, ID	71.43	36	Saginaw-Saginaw Township North, MI	51.64	358
Port St. Lucie, FL	67.76	91	Salem, OR	70.80	43
Portland-South Portland-Biddeford, ME	69.60	55	Salinas, CA	63.50	171
Portland-Vancouver-Beaverton, OR-WA	66.63	109	Salisbury, MD	53.48	345
Poughkeepsie-Newburgh-Middletown, NY	71.03	40	Salt Lake City, UT	78.94	8
Prescott, AZ	63.39	173	San Angelo, TX	60.06	243
Providence-New Bedford-Fall River, RI-MA	54.44	336	San Antonio, TX	56.78	309
Provo-Orem, UT	100.00	1	San Diego-Carlsbad-San Marcos, CA	62.96	184
Pueblo, CO	55.86	321	San Francisco-Oakland-Fremont, CA	59.42	258
Punta Gorda, FL	69.25	59	San Jose-Sunnyvale-Santa Clara, CA	69.22	60
Racine, WI	63.30	177	San Luis Obispo-Paso Robles, CA	72.33	28
Raleigh-Cary, NC	71.81	33	Sandusky, OH	64.27	157
Rapid City, SD	65.35	135	Santa Barbara-Santa Maria-Goleta, CA	66.23	119
Reading, PA	66.56	111	Santa Cruz-Watsonville, CA	63.31	175
Redding, CA	61.76	203	Santa Fe, NM	59.07	264
Reno-Sparks, NV	58.60	273	Santa Rosa-Petaluma, CA	62.80	185
Richmond, VA	70.34	46	Savannah, GA	58.47	278

Communities in Alphabetical Order

Community	Final Index	Final Ranking	Community	Final Index	Final Ranking
Scranton--Wilkes-Barre, PA	62.99	182	Tulsa, OK	59.90	249
Seattle-Tacoma-Bellevue, WA	67.01	102	Tuscaloosa, AL	60.58	229
Sebastian-Vero Beach, FL	63.85	162	Tyler, TX	64.95	139
Sheboygan, WI	74.11	22	Utica-Rome, NY	66.23	118
Sherman-Denison, TX	66.98	105	Valdosta, GA	61.72	205
Shreveport-Bossier City, LA	51.39	360	Vallejo-Fairfield, CA	56.99	305
Sioux City, IA-NE-SD	63.82	164	Victoria, TX	53.90	342
Sioux Falls, SD	69.13	62	Vineland-Millville, NJ	53.27	347
South Bend, IN	60.33	236	Virginia Beach-Norfolk, VA	60.73	226
Spartanburg, SC	54.89	331	Visalia-Porterville, CA	56.26	317
Spokane, WA	61.88	199	Waco, TX	54.18	340
Springfield, IL	61.58	208	Warner Robins, GA	67.22	99
Springfield, MA	58.29	284	Washington DC Metro Area	62.10	192
Springfield, MO	65.87	128	Waterloo-Cedar Falls, IA	70.89	42
Springfield, OH	60.47	232	Wausau, WI	69.42	56
St. Cloud, MN	71.23	37	Weirton-Steubenville, WV	64.10	160
St. George, UT	92.52	2	Wenatchee, WA	68.55	73
St. Joseph, MO-KS	63.77	166	Wheeling, WV-OH	61.03	219
St. Louis, MO-IL	59.87	250	Wichita Falls, TX	60.71	227
State College, PA	81.04	5	Wichita, KS	58.68	272
Stockton, CA	54.72	334	Williamsport, PA	66.20	121
Sumter, SC	52.67	352	Wilmington, NC	61.32	213
Syracuse, NY	68.41	74	Winchester, VA-WV	60.91	221
Tallahassee, FL	54.76	333	Winston-Salem, NC	64.34	154
Tampa-St. Petersburg, FL	57.75	292	Worcester, MA	62.65	186
Terre Haute, IN	59.01	265	Yakima, WA	59.34	260
Texarkana, TX-Texarkana, AR	56.88	307	York-Hanover, PA	67.90	86
Toledo, OH	52.67	351	Youngstown-Warren, OH	57.14	302
Topeka, KS	60.84	224	Yuba City, CA	57.29	299
Trenton-Ewing, NJ	66.61	110	Yuma, AZ	59.53	256
Tucson, AZ	59.28	261			

Tables 3.1 and 3.2: Best and Worst Communities for LDS Culture

Best for LDS Culture	Index	Rank	Worst for LDS Culture	Index	Rank
St. George, UT	100.00	1	Hagerstown-Martinsburg, MD-WV	14.91	337
Provo-Orem, UT	92.25	2	Stockton, CA	14.85	338
Lynchburg, VA	81.87	3	Topeka, KS	14.64	339
Logan, UT-ID	76.55	4	Monroe, MI	14.52	340
Blacksburg-Christiansburg-Radford, VA	72.98	5	Morgantown, WV	14.30	341
Danville, VA	62.36	6	Austin-Round Rock, TX	14.27	342
Charlottesville, VA	59.92	7	Portland-Vancouver-Beaverton, OR-WA	14.26	343
Roanoke, VA	59.82	8	Trenton-Ewing, NJ	14.17	344
Harrisonburg, VA	58.15	9	Bremerton-Silverdale, WA	13.96	345
Hickory-Lenoir-Morganton, NC	57.45	10	Palm Coast, FL	13.59	346
Anniston-Oxford, AL	56.11	11	Houston-Sugar Land-Baytown, TX	13.40	347
Idaho Falls, ID	54.12	12	Santa Cruz-Watsonville, CA	13.33	348
Lubbock, TX	50.81	13	Santa Rosa-Petaluma, CA	12.54	349
Rocky Mount, NC	50.66	14	Minneapolis-St. Paul-Bloomington, MN-WI	12.32	350
Goldsboro, NC	50.10	15	Yuba City, CA	12.02	351
San Antonio, TX	48.50	16	Greeley, CO	11.93	352
Tyler, TX	48.31	17	Atlantic City-Hammonton, NJ	11.28	353
Ogden-Clearfield, UT	48.02	18	Pueblo, CO	11.18	354
Salt Lake City, UT	47.70	19	Pascagoula, MS	10.79	355
Columbia, MO	47.24	20	Visalia-Porterville, CA	10.48	356
Virginia Beach-Norfolk-Newport News, VA-NC	46.90	21	Baltimore-Towson, MD	8.87	357
Lewiston-Auburn, ME	46.56	22	Gulfport-Biloxi, MS	8.02	358
Punta Gorda, FL	46.52	23	Houma-Bayou Cane-Thibodaux, LA	7.71	359
Kingsport-Bristol-Bristol, TN-VA	46.47	24	Deltona-Daytona Beach-Ormond Beach, FL	5.04	360
Gadsden, AL	45.51	25	Vallejo-Fairfield, CA	2.65	361

Tables 4.1 and 4.2: Best and Worst Communities for Education

Best Communities for Education	Index	Rank
St. George, UT	100.00	1
Iowa City, IA	99.57	2
Springfield, IL	99.40	3
Provo-Orem, UT	99.31	4
Salem, OR	97.42	5
Ames, IA	97.04	6
Minneapolis-St. Paul-Bloomington, MN-WI	96.75	7
Lincoln, NE	95.72	8
Columbia, MO	95.26	9
State College, PA	94.70	10
Madison, WI	94.63	11
La Crosse, WI-MN	92.73	12
Salt Lake City, UT	92.38	13
Lawrence, KS	92.29	14
Waterloo-Cedar Falls, IA	92.14	15
Boulder, CO	91.61	16
Ogden-Clearfield, UT	90.55	17
Bremerton-Silverdale, WA	90.19	18
Palm Coast, FL	89.85	19
Colorado Springs, CO	89.34	20
Eau Claire, WI	88.94	21
St. Cloud, MN	88.68	22
Cedar Rapids, IA	88.47	23
Fargo, ND-MN	88.41	24
Logan, UT-ID	88.37	25

Worst Communities for Education	Index	Rank
Spartanburg, SC	52.80	337
Burlington, NC	52.55	338
Elizabethtown, KY	52.44	339
Decatur, IL	52.03	340
Anderson, SC	51.74	341
Rocky Mount, NC	51.36	342
Victoria, TX	51.28	343
Monroe, LA	51.24	344
Reno-Sparks, NV	50.96	345
Houma-Bayou Cane-Thibodaux, LA	50.87	346
Ocala, FL	50.75	347
Danville, VA	50.54	348
Yakima, WA	49.74	349
Hinesville-Fort Stewart, GA	49.69	350
Brownsville-Harlingen, TX	49.46	351
Odessa, TX	49.16	352
New Orleans-Metairie-Kenner, LA	49.06	353
McAllen-Edinburg-Mission, TX	49.01	354
Mobile, AL	48.16	355
Dalton, GA	47.10	356
Sumter, SC	45.85	357
Florence, SC	45.40	358
Gainesville, GA	45.38	359
Macon, GA	42.60	360
Albany, GA	42.56	361

Tables 5.1 and 5.2: Best and Worst Communities for Crime

Best Communities Regarding Crime	Index	Rank	Worst Communities Regarding Crime	Index	Rank
Logan, UT-ID	100.00	1	Miami-Fort Lauderdale-Pompano Beach, FL	29.19	337
State College, PA	96.74	2	Anchorage, AK	28.78	338
Harrisonburg, VA	94.18	3	Little Rock-North Little Rock-Conway, AR	28.44	339
Eau Claire, WI	92.33	4	Orlando-Kissimmee, FL	28.16	340
Provo-Orem, UT	91.57	5	Texarkana, TX-Texarkana, AR	28.10	341
Glens Falls, NY	89.24	6	Lawton, OK	27.81	342
Holland-Grand Haven, MI	88.43	7	Brunswick, GA	27.67	343
Williamsport, PA	88.31	8	Tallahassee, FL	27.56	344
Ithaca, NY	87.94	9	Albuquerque, NM	27.07	345
Appleton, WI	87.52	10	Jacksonville, FL	26.69	346
Corvallis, OR	87.22	11	Salisbury, MD	26.46	347
Portland-South Portland-Biddeford, ME	86.69	12	Hot Springs, AR	25.24	348
Sheboygan, WI	86.42	13	Fayetteville, NC	24.85	349
Lewiston-Auburn, ME	86.37	14	Jackson, TN	24.75	350
Weirton-Steubenville, WV-OH	86.01	15	Rockford, IL	24.56	351
Johnstown, PA	85.34	16	Lubbock, TX	24.43	352
Fond du Lac, WI	84.63	17	Alexandria, LA	23.24	353
Lancaster, PA	84.54	18	Stockton, CA	22.46	354
Bangor, ME	84.18	19	Shreveport-Bossier City, LA	20.36	355
Lebanon, PA	83.45	20	Springfield, IL	19.42	356
St. George, UT	83.32	21	Saginaw-Saginaw Township North, MI	17.15	357
Wheeling, WV-OH	83.17	22	Pine Bluff, AR	16.33	358
Columbus, IN	83.10	23	Florence, SC	15.97	359
Parkersburg-Marietta-Vienna, WV-OH	82.47	24	Myrtle Beach-North Myrtle Beach-Conway, SC	11.29	360
Kingston, NY	82.06	25	Memphis, TN-MS-AR	5.35	361

Tables 6.1 and 6.2: Best and Worst Communities for Economic Environment

Best Communities for Economic Environment	Index	Rank
Fairbanks, AK	100.00	1
Anchorage, AK	99.44	2
Bend, OR	91.11	3
Eugene-Springfield, OR	90.66	4
Elmira, NY	90.22	5
Boulder, CO	90.05	6
Corvallis, OR	87.22	7
Fort Collins-Loveland, CO	86.16	8
State College, PA	83.60	9
Sheboygan, WI	82.55	10
Fond du Lac, WI	82.05	11
Port St. Lucie, FL	81.55	12
Lincoln, NE	80.71	13
Denver-Aurora-Broomfield, CO	80.32	14
Oshkosh-Neenah, WI	79.71	15
Minneapolis-St. Paul-Bloomington, MN-WI	79.60	16
Norwich-New London, CT	79.43	17
Rochester, MN	79.04	18
Colorado Springs, CO	78.93	19
Madison, WI	78.71	20
Ocean City, NJ	78.04	21
Janesville, WI	77.77	22
Barnstable Town, MA	77.65	23
Manchester-Nashua, NH	77.49	24
Appleton, WI	77.38	25

Worst Communities for Economic Environment	Index	Rank
Canton-Massillon, OH	48.47	337
Mobile, AL	48.47	338
San Antonio, TX	48.25	339
Redding, CA	48.14	340
Charleston, WV	47.92	341
Joplin, MO	47.92	342
El Centro, CA	47.36	343
Stockton, CA	47.36	344
Wheeling, WV-OH	46.86	345
Yuba City, CA	46.75	346
Brownsville-Harlingen, TX	46.47	347
Pine Bluff, AR	46.25	348
Chico, CA	45.91	349
Las Cruces, NM	45.80	350
McAllen-Edinburg-Mission, TX	45.80	351
Farmington, NM	45.41	352
Hanford-Corcoran, CA	44.86	353
Madera-Chowchilla, CA	44.02	354
Visalia-Porterville, CA	42.91	355
Hattiesburg, MS	42.52	356
Fresno, CA	41.41	357
Merced, CA	40.13	358
Bakersfield, CA	39.69	359
Texarkana, TX-Texarkana, AR	39.13	360
Yuma, AZ	36.13	361

Tables 7.1 and 7.2: Best and Worst Communities for Health

Best Communities for Health	Index	Rank	Worst Communities for Health	Index	Rank
Provo-Orem, UT	100.00	1	Bridgeport-Stamford-Norwalk, CT	31.88	337
Ogden-Clearfield, UT	85.84	2	Providence-New Bedford-Fall River, RI-MA	31.73	338
Salt Lake City, UT	78.30	3	San Antonio, TX	31.71	339
Logan, UT-ID	63.80	4	Boston-Cambridge-Quincy, MA-NH	31.62	340
St. George, UT	63.80	5	Indianapolis-Carmel, IN	31.17	341
Idaho Falls, ID	63.54	6	Amarillo, TX	31.11	342
Monroe, LA	58.02	7	Lubbock, TX	31.11	343
Lake Charles, LA	57.92	8	Dothan, AL	30.81	344
Alexandria, LA	56.89	9	Houston-Sugar Land-Baytown, TX	29.71	345
Bangor, ME	55.64	10	Virginia Beach-Norfolk-Newport News, VA-NC	29.63	346
Orlando-Kissimmee, FL	54.63	11	Cheyenne, WY	29.61	347
Ames, IA	54.48	12	Brownsville-Harlingen, TX	29.28	348
Dubuque, IA	54.48	13	St. Louis, MO-IL	29.21	349
Iowa City, IA	54.48	14	New Haven-Milford, CT	29.03	350
Waterloo-Cedar Falls, IA	54.48	15	Milwaukee-Waukesha-West Allis, WI	28.48	351
Miami-Fort Lauderdale-Pompano Beach, FL	54.20	16	Manchester-Nashua, NH	27.89	352
Tallahassee, FL	53.83	17	Morgantown, WV	27.63	353
Huntington-Ashland, WV-KY-OH	53.20	18	Laredo, TX	26.70	354
Lewiston-Auburn, ME	53.14	19	Bowling Green, KY	26.56	355
Honolulu, HI	52.83	20	Elizabethtown, KY	26.56	356
Lakeland-Winter Haven, FL	52.75	21	Lexington-Fayette, KY	26.56	357
Bradenton-Sarasota-Venice, FL	52.72	22	Owensboro, KY	26.56	358
Fort Walton Beach-Crestview-Destin, FL	52.72	23	Austin-Round Rock, TX	25.14	359
Pensacola-Ferry Pass-Brent, FL	52.72	24	Casper, WY	22.82	360
Punta Gorda, FL	52.72	25	Wichita Falls, TX	22.23	361

Tables 8.1 and 8.2: Best and Worst Communities for Household Characteristics

Best Communities for Household Characteristics	Index	Rank	Worst Communities for Household Characteristics	Index	Rank
Provo-Orem, UT	100.00	1	Altoona, PA	69.14	337
St. George, UT	98.15	2	Battle Creek, MI	45.06	338
Idaho Falls, ID	96.91	3	Saginaw-Saginaw Township North, MI	45.06	339
Logan, UT-ID	93.21	4	Springfield, IL	45.06	340
Pascagoula, MS	93.21	5	Waco, TX	45.06	341
Boulder, CO	92.59	6	Wheeling, WV-OH	45.06	342
Ogden-Clearfield, UT	92.59	7	Michigan City-La Porte, IN	43.83	343
Bridgeport-Stamford-Norwalk, CT	91.98	8	Shreveport-Bossier City, LA	43.83	344
Elizabethtown, KY	91.98	9	Vineland-Millville-Bridgeton, NJ	43.83	345
Corvallis, OR	91.36	10	Atlantic City-Hammonton, NJ	43.21	346
Jacksonville, NC	91.36	11	Bowling Green, KY	43.21	347
Pocatello, ID	91.36	12	Ocala, FL	43.21	348
Salt Lake City, UT	90.74	13	Santa Fe, NM	43.21	349
Coeur d'Alene, ID	90.12	14	Salisbury, MD	42.59	350
Fayetteville-Springdale-Rogers, AR-MO	90.12	15	Johnstown, PA	41.98	351
McAllen-Edinburg-Mission, TX	90.12	16	Toledo, OH	41.98	352
Santa Cruz-Watsonville, CA	90.12	17	Utica-Rome, NY	41.98	353
Trenton-Ewing, NJ	90.12	18	Youngstown-Warren-Boardman, OH-PA	41.98	354
Harrisonburg, VA	88.27	19	Danville, IL	41.36	355
Lancaster, PA	88.27	20	Binghamton, NY	40.74	356
Mount Vernon-Anacortes, WA	88.27	21	Kankakee-Bradley, IL	40.74	357
Santa Barbara-Santa Maria-Goleta, CA	88.27	22	Pittsfield, MA	40.74	358
Ithaca, NY	87.65	23	Tallahassee, FL	40.74	359
Raleigh-Cary, NC	87.65	24	Lima, OH	39.51	360
San Jose-Sunnyvale-Santa Clara, CA	87.65	25	Anderson, IN	37.65	361

Tables 9.1 and 9.2: Best and Worst Communities for Housing

Best Communities for Housing	Index	Rank	Worst Communities for Housing	Index	Rank
Boise City-Nampa, ID	100.00	1	Milwaukee-Waukesha, WI	66.91	337
Augusta-Richmond Cnty, GA-SC	98.35	2	Philadelphia-Camden-Wilmington, PA-NJ-DE-MD	66.02	338
Lakeland-Winter Haven, FL	97.87	3	Portland-South Portland-Biddeford, ME	65.82	339
Fayetteville, NC	97.73	4	Poughkeepsie-Newburgh-Middletown, NY	65.77	340
Huntsville, AL	97.51	5	Honolulu, HI	65.45	341
Ocala, FL	97.18	6	Scranton--Wilkes-Barre, PA	65.37	342
Austin-Round Rock, TX	97.14	7	Chicago, IL-IN-WI	64.72	343
McAllen-Edinburg-Mission, TX	96.72	8	Pittsfield, MA	63.89	344
Houston-Sugar Land-Baytown, TX	96.22	9	Bridgeport-Stamfrd-Norwlk, CT	63.08	345
Clarksville, TN-KY	96.17	10	Salinas, CA	63.07	346
Fayetteville-Springdale-Rogers, AR-MO	95.47	11	Hartford-West Hartford-East Hartford, CT	62.99	347
Montgomery, AL	94.96	12	Trenton-Ewing, NJ	62.68	348
Dallas-Fort Worth, TX	94.88	13	Chico, CA	62.67	349
Kingsport-Bristol-Bristol, TN-VA	94.68	14	Sandusky, OH	60.90	350
Pascagoula, MS	94.32	15	Santa Rosa-Petaluma, CA	60.85	351
Hinesville-Fort Stewart, GA	94.14	16	Napa, CA	60.80	352
Myrtle Beach-North Myrtle Beach-Conway, SC	94.09	17	San Francisco-Oakland, CA	60.73	353
Columbia, SC	94.00	18	Santa Barbara-Santa Maria-Goleta, CA	60.25	354
Sumter, SC	93.73	19	Worcester, MA	58.42	355
Charlotte-Gastonia, NC-SC	93.69	20	New Haven-Milford, CT	58.22	356
Pensacola-Ferry Pass-Brent, FL	93.62	21	Providence-New Bedford-Fall River, RI-MA	56.05	357
Fort Smith, AR-OK	93.50	22	Boston-Cambridge, MA-NH	54.32	358
Auburn-Opelika, AL	93.15	23	Santa Cruz-Watsonville, CA	53.32	359
Waco, TX	93.13	24	Los Angeles-Long Beach, CA	53.10	360
Coeur d'Alene, ID	93.01	25	New York-No.Jersey, NY-NJ-PA	53.07	361

Table 10: One-way Commute Times

Table 10: One-way Commute Times	< 15 mins	15-29 mins	>29 mins	Table 10: One-way Commute Times	< 15 mins	15-29 mins	>29 mins
Abilene, TX	53%	33%	13%	Bay City, MI	32%	44%	24%
Akron, OH	30%	40%	30%	Beaumont-Port Arthur, TX	34%	41%	25%
Albany, GA	36%	48%	17%	Bellingham, WA	39%	39%	22%
Albany-Schenectady-Troy, NY	29%	42%	29%	Bend, OR	46%	35%	19%
Albuquerque, NM	25%	42%	32%	Billings, MT	40%	46%	14%
Alexandria, LA	34%	41%	26%	Binghamton, NY	39%	40%	21%
Allentown-Bethlehem, PA	29%	36%	36%	Birmingham-Hoover, AL	22%	39%	39%
Altoona, PA	44%	34%	21%	Bismarck, ND	55%	32%	13%
Amarillo, TX	44%	43%	13%	Blacksburg-Christiansburg, VA	43%	37%	21%
Ames, IA	54%	29%	17%	Bloomington, IN	38%	38%	24%
Anchorage, AK	36%	42%	22%	Bloomington-Normal, IL	52%	34%	14%
Anderson, IN	35%	31%	35%	Boise City-Nampa, ID	32%	43%	25%
Anderson, SC	30%	43%	26%	Boston-Cambridge-Quincy, MA	23%	32%	45%
Ann Arbor, MI	29%	40%	31%	Boulder, CO	37%	36%	27%
Anniston-Oxford, AL	30%	43%	27%	Bowling Green, KY	35%	46%	19%
Appleton, WI	36%	42%	22%	Bradenton-Sarasota-Venice, FL	31%	43%	26%
Asheville, NC	31%	42%	27%	Bremerton-Silverdale, WA	27%	34%	39%
Athens-Clarke County, GA	39%	38%	22%	Bridgeport-Stamford, CT	28%	35%	37%
Atlanta-Sandy Springs, GA	19%	33%	48%	Brownsville-Harlingen, TX	37%	41%	22%
Atlantic City-Hammonton, NJ	28%	42%	29%	Brunswick, GA	34%	40%	26%
Auburn-Opelika, AL	37%	40%	23%	Buffalo-Niagara Falls, NY	31%	44%	25%
Augusta-Richmond County, GA	26%	44%	30%	Burlington, NC	33%	38%	29%
Austin-Round Rock, TX	24%	39%	37%	Burlington-South Burlington, VT	32%	39%	29%
Bakersfield, CA	35%	39%	27%	Canton-Massillon, OH	32%	39%	28%
Baltimore-Towson, MD	20%	35%	45%	Cape Coral-Fort Myers, FL	23%	39%	38%
Bangor, ME	36%	38%	26%	Casper, WY	48%	44%	8%
Barnstable Town, MA	36%	36%	28%	Cedar Rapids, IA	39%	38%	22%
Baton Rouge, LA	25%	39%	36%	Champaign-Urbana, IL	41%	41%	17%
Battle Creek, MI	42%	38%	21%	Charleston, WV	33%	36%	31%

Table 10: One-way Commute Times	< 15 mins	15-29 mins	>29 mins	Table 10: One-way Commute Times	< 15 mins	15-29 mins	>29 mins
Charleston-N.Charleston, SC	25%	40%	36%	Decatur, IL	44%	41%	15%
Charlotte-Gastonia, NC-SC	23%	41%	36%	Deltona-Daytona -Ormond, FL	28%	39%	33%
Charlottesville, VA	30%	39%	31%	Denver-Aurora-Broomfield, CO	21%	38%	41%
Chattanooga, TN-GA	26%	43%	31%	Des Moines-W. Des Moines, IA	33%	47%	20%
Cheyenne, WY	53%	38%	9%	Detroit-Warren-Livonia, MI	23%	37%	39%
Chicago-Naperville-Joliet, IL-IN	20%	29%	51%	Dothan, AL	32%	38%	30%
Chico, CA	46%	30%	23%	Dover, DE	32%	36%	32%
Cincinnati-Middletown, OH-KY	26%	41%	34%	Dubuque, IA	48%	40%	12%
Clarksville, TN-KY	31%	41%	27%	Duluth, MN-WI	41%	40%	19%
Cleveland, TN	36%	37%	26%	Durham-Chapel Hill, NC	28%	42%	30%
Cleveland-Elyria-Mentor, OH	26%	40%	34%	Eau Claire, WI	44%	37%	19%
Coeur d'Alene, ID	39%	36%	25%	El Centro, CA	47%	31%	22%
College Station-Bryan, TX	43%	42%	15%	El Paso, TX	34%	40%	27%
Colorado Springs, CO	30%	43%	27%	Elizabethtown, KY	39%	41%	21%
Columbia, MO	39%	43%	18%	Elkhart-Goshen, IN	44%	39%	17%
Columbia, SC	26%	43%	32%	Elmira, NY	23%	47%	31%
Columbus, GA-AL	29%	48%	23%	Erie, PA	39%	43%	18%
Columbus, IN	40%	40%	19%	Eugene-Springfield, OR	38%	42%	20%
Columbus, OH	27%	44%	29%	Evansville, IN-KY	36%	42%	23%
Corpus Christi, TX	39%	42%	19%	Fairbanks, AK	39%	44%	17%
Corvallis, OR	49%	32%	19%	Fargo, ND-MN	51%	39%	10%
Cumberland, MD-WV	37%	37%	27%	Farmington, NM	32%	30%	37%
Dallas-Fort Worth-Arlington, TX	22%	36%	42%	Fayetteville, NC	28%	46%	26%
Dalton, GA	28%	49%	23%	Fayetteville-Springdale, AR-MO	32%	41%	27%
Danville, IL	43%	35%	22%	Flagstaff, AZ	54%	28%	17%
Danville, VA	29%	46%	25%	Flint, MI	30%	38%	32%
Davenport-Moline, IA-IL	37%	45%	18%	Florence, SC	33%	40%	27%
Dayton, OH	33%	44%	24%	Florence-Muscle Shoals, AL	37%	34%	29%
Decatur, AL	30%	36%	34%	Fond du Lac, WI	44%	34%	23%

Table 10: One-way Commute Times	< 15 mins	15-29 mins	>29 mins	Table 10: One-way Commute Times	< 15 mins	15-29 mins	>29 mins
Fort Collins-Loveland, CO	35%	40%	25%	Honolulu, HI	21%	35%	45%
Fort Smith, AR-OK	40%	36%	25%	Hot Springs, AR	32%	41%	26%
Fort Walton Bch-Crestview, FL	36%	32%	33%	Houma-Bayou Cane, LA	36%	30%	34%
Fort Wayne, IN	28%	51%	21%	Houston-Baytown, TX	20%	35%	45%
Fresno, CA	29%	47%	24%	Huntington-Ashland, WV-KY-OH	35%	43%	22%
Gadsden, AL	36%	35%	29%	Huntsville, AL	28%	44%	28%
Gainesville, FL	32%	44%	24%	Idaho Falls, ID	42%	35%	24%
Gainesville, GA	21%	40%	38%	Indianapolis-Carmel, IN	25%	41%	34%
Glens Falls, NY	36%	32%	32%	Iowa City, IA	41%	41%	18%
Goldsboro, NC	39%	38%	23%	Ithaca, NY	40%	42%	17%
Grand Forks, ND-MN	62%	27%	11%	Jackson, MI	31%	39%	30%
Grand Junction, CO	42%	41%	17%	Jackson, MS	24%	45%	31%
Grand Rapids-Wyoming, MI	29%	46%	25%	Jackson, TN	35%	45%	20%
Great Falls, MT	54%	34%	12%	Jacksonville, FL	23%	40%	37%
Greeley, CO	29%	35%	37%	Jacksonville, NC	37%	37%	27%
Green Bay, WI	39%	41%	20%	Janesville, WI	39%	35%	26%
Greensboro-High Point, NC	31%	44%	26%	Jefferson City, MO	42%	34%	24%
Greenville, NC	36%	42%	22%	Johnson City, TN	37%	38%	25%
Greenville-Mauldin-Easley, SC	27%	46%	26%	Johnstown, PA	35%	38%	27%
Gulfport-Biloxi, MS	28%	41%	31%	Jonesboro, AR	40%	41%	18%
Hagerstown-Martinsburg, MD	28%	32%	40%	Joplin, MO	40%	41%	19%
Hanford-Corcoran, CA	35%	38%	27%	Kalamazoo-Portage, MI	34%	42%	24%
Harrisburg-Carlisle, PA	33%	42%	25%	Kankakee-Bradley, IL	40%	31%	29%
Harrisonburg, VA	37%	40%	23%	Kansas City, MO-KS	27%	42%	31%
Hartford-W/E Hartford, CT	28%	42%	30%	Kennewick-Pasco-Richland, WA	36%	44%	20%
Hattiesburg, MS	32%	39%	29%	Killeen-Temple-Fort Hood, TX	38%	40%	22%
Hickory-Lenoir-Morganton, NC	32%	43%	25%	Kingsport-Bristol-Bristol, TN-VA	32%	41%	27%
Hinesville-Fort Stewart, GA	36%	31%	33%	Kingston, NY	31%	31%	37%
Holland-Grand Haven, MI	36%	44%	20%	Knoxville, TN	29%	45%	26%

Table 10: One-way Commute Times	< 15 mins	15-29 mins	>29 mins	Table 10: One-way Commute Times	< 15 mins	15-29 mins	>29 mins
Kokomo, IN	45%	35%	20%	McAllen-Edinburg, TX	30%	46%	24%
La Crosse, WI-MN	41%	41%	18%	Medford, OR	41%	45%	14%
Lafayette, IN	42%	42%	16%	Memphis, TN-MS-AR	24%	43%	33%
Lafayette, LA	31%	45%	25%	Merced, CA	37%	30%	33%
Lake Charles, LA	39%	40%	20%	Miami-Fort Lauderdale, FL	20%	35%	45%
Lake Havasu City, AZ	39%	44%	17%	Michigan City-La Porte, IN	37%	37%	26%
Lakeland-Winter Haven, FL	25%	40%	35%	Midland, TX	40%	43%	17%
Lancaster, PA	35%	38%	27%	Milwaukee-Waukesha, WI	28%	42%	30%
Lansing-E.Lansing, MI	33%	45%	22%	Minneapolis-St. Paul	25%	40%	34%
Laredo, TX	31%	42%	27%	Missoula, MT	45%	39%	15%
Las Cruces, NM	38%	43%	19%	Mobile, AL	23%	43%	34%
Las Vegas-Paradise, NV	20%	45%	35%	Modesto, CA	33%	36%	31%
Lawrence, KS	46%	30%	25%	Monroe, LA	35%	43%	22%
Lawton, OK	45%	43%	12%	Monroe, MI	29%	38%	33%
Lebanon, PA	32%	34%	34%	Montgomery, AL	26%	47%	27%
Lewiston-Auburn, ME	37%	35%	28%	Morgantown, WV	30%	40%	31%
Lexington-Fayette, KY	32%	43%	25%	Morristown, TN	29%	40%	31%
Lima, OH	40%	41%	19%	Mount Vernon, WA	34%	34%	31%
Lincoln, NE	38%	48%	14%	Muncie, IN	40%	41%	19%
Little Rock-N.Little Rock, AR	32%	39%	29%	Muskegon-N. Shores, MI	35%	41%	24%
Logan, UT-ID	51%	36%	13%	Myrtle Beach, SC	32%	41%	27%
Longview, TX	35%	37%	28%	Napa, CA	42%	31%	27%
Longview, WA	38%	35%	27%	Naples-Marco Island, FL	27%	43%	29%
Los Angeles Metro Area, CA	21%	35%	44%	Nashville Metro Area, TN	23%	37%	39%
Louisville Metro Area, KY-IN	25%	44%	30%	New Haven-Milford, CT	29%	38%	32%
Lubbock, TX	48%	41%	12%	New Orleans-Metairie, LA	26%	37%	37%
Lynchburg, VA	34%	40%	26%	New York City Metro Area	18%	27%	55%
Macon, GA	29%	43%	28%	Niles-Benton Harbor, MI	38%	43%	18%
Madera-Chowchilla, CA	37%	31%	32%	Norwich-New London, CT	33%	38%	29%
Madison, WI	32%	42%	26%	Ocala, FL	25%	45%	31%
Manchester-Nashua, NH	28%	35%	37%	Ocean City, NJ	37%	35%	28%
Mansfield, OH	41%	41%	18%	Odessa, TX	38%	43%	18%

Table 10: One-way Commute Times	< 15 mins	15-29 mins	>29 mins	Table 10: One-way Commute Times	< 15 mins	15-29 mins	>29 mins
Ogden-Clearfield, UT	32%	40%	29%	Racine, WI	34%	36%	30%
Oklahoma City, OK	30%	44%	26%	Raleigh-Cary, NC	23%	43%	34%
Olympia, WA	28%	45%	28%	Rapid City, SD	42%	43%	15%
Omaha-Council Bluffs, NE-IA	34%	46%	20%	Reading, PA	31%	40%	29%
Orlando-Kissimmee, FL	21%	38%	41%	Redding, CA	41%	44%	15%
Oshkosh-Neenah, WI	42%	40%	17%	Reno-Sparks, NV	33%	43%	24%
Owensboro, KY	41%	40%	19%	Richmond, VA	23%	43%	34%
Oxnard-Thousand Oaks, CA	30%	35%	36%	Riverside-Ontario, CA	25%	33%	42%
Palm Bay-Melbourne, FL	25%	43%	32%	Roanoke, VA	33%	43%	25%
Palm Coast, FL	29%	33%	38%	Rochester, MN	42%	42%	16%
Panama City Metro Area, FL	36%	44%	20%	Rochester, NY	32%	44%	24%
Parkersburg-Marietta, WV-OH	36%	42%	22%	Rockford, IL	32%	42%	26%
Pascagoula, MS	23%	39%	38%	Rocky Mount, NC	36%	43%	21%
Pensacola-Ferry Pass-Brent, FL	30%	40%	30%	Rome, GA	31%	44%	25%
Peoria, IL	34%	44%	22%	Sacramento, CA	26%	38%	36%
Philadelphia Metro, PA-NJ-DE	23%	34%	43%	Saginaw, MI	36%	39%	25%
Phoenix-Mesa-Scottsdale, AZ	23%	36%	41%	Salem, OR	39%	38%	23%
Pine Bluff, AR	31%	42%	27%	Salinas, CA	48%	35%	17%
Pittsburgh, PA	28%	35%	37%	Salisbury, MD	45%	35%	19%
Pittsfield, MA	42%	36%	21%	Salt Lake City, UT	25%	39%	37%
Pocatello, ID	60%	27%	13%	San Angelo, TX	31%	40%	30%
Port St. Lucie, FL	32%	35%	33%	San Antonio, TX	33%	40%	27%
Portland-South Portland, ME	26%	39%	36%	San Diego-Carlsbad, CA	35%	39%	25%
Portland-Vancouver, OR-WA	23%	38%	38%	San Francisco-Oakland, CA	28%	43%	29%
Poughkeepsie-Newburgh, NY	29%	29%	42%	San Jose-Santa Clara, CA	51%	37%	12%
Prescott, AZ	36%	37%	27%	San Luis Obispo, CA	24%	39%	37%
Providence-New Bedford, RI-MA	31%	37%	32%	Sandusky, OH	26%	42%	32%
Provo-Orem, UT	43%	33%	24%	Santa Barbara, CA	48%	31%	21%
Pueblo, CO	40%	37%	23%	Santa Cruz-Watsonville, CA	21%	33%	45%
Punta Gorda, FL	33%	35%	32%	Santa Fe, NM	22%	43%	34%

Table 10: One-way Commute Times	< 15 mins	15-29 mins	>29 mins	Table 10: One-way Commute Times	< 15 mins	15-29 mins	>29 mins
Santa Rosa, CA	41%	36%	23%	Tucson, AZ	25%	39%	36%
Savannah, GA	44%	34%	22%	Tulsa, OK	31%	45%	25%
Scranton, PA	28%	34%	38%	Tuscaloosa, AL	33%	41%	26%
Seattle-Tacoma, WA	32%	39%	29%	Tyler, TX	31%	43%	26%
Sebastian, FL	33%	33%	34%	Utica-Rome, NY	41%	37%	21%
Sheboygan, WI	24%	47%	29%	Valdosta, GA	38%	45%	17%
Sherman-Denison, TX	38%	40%	23%	Vallejo-Fairfield, CA	26%	30%	44%
Shrevepor, LA	22%	36%	42%	Victoria, TX	42%	32%	26%
Sioux City, IA-NE-SD	34%	46%	20%	Vineland-Millville, NJ	40%	30%	30%
Sioux Falls, SD	50%	33%	17%	Virginia Beach-Norfolk, VA-NC	26%	42%	33%
South Bend-Mishawaka, IN-MI	38%	38%	24%	Visalia-Porterville, CA	42%	35%	24%
Spartanburg, SC	30%	47%	23%	Waco, TX	40%	44%	16%
Spokane, WA	44%	43%	13%	Warner Robins, GA	33%	49%	18%
Springfield, IL	41%	47%	12%	Washington DC Metro Area	16%	30%	54%
Springfield, MA	34%	43%	23%	Waterloo-Cedar Falls, IA	51%	37%	12%
Springfield, MO	27%	48%	25%	Wausau, WI	39%	44%	17%
Springfield, OH	29%	46%	25%	Weirton-Steubenville, WV-OH	36%	34%	30%
St. Cloud, MN	33%	47%	19%	Wenatchee-E.Wenatchee, WA	47%	35%	18%
St. George, UT	33%	40%	28%	Wheeling, WV-OH	33%	42%	26%
St. Joseph, MO-KS	31%	43%	26%	Wichita Falls, TX	36%	46%	18%
St. Louis, MO-IL	36%	38%	26%	Wichita, KS	49%	38%	13%
State College, PA	39%	39%	21%	Williamsport, PA	40%	41%	19%
Stockton, CA	31%	35%	33%	Wilmington, NC	33%	42%	25%
Sumter, SC	35%	42%	22%	Winchester, VA-WV	26%	37%	36%
Syracuse, NY	33%	44%	23%	Winston-Salem, NC	32%	44%	24%
Tallahassee, FL	28%	44%	29%	Worcester, MA	28%	33%	39%
Tampa, FL	25%	38%	38%	Yakima, WA	40%	41%	19%
Terre Haute, IN	39%	39%	22%	York-Hanover, PA	27%	37%	36%
Texarkana, TX	41%	40%	20%	Youngstown-Warren, OH-PA	37%	40%	23%
Toledo, OH	36%	45%	20%	Yuba City, CA	29%	29%	43%
Topeka, KS	36%	42%	22%	Yuma, AZ	38%	41%	21%
Trenton-Ewing, NJ	32%	37%	32%				

61

Table 11.1: Top 25 Shortest Commute Times					
	<10 minutes	10-19 minutes	20-29 minutes	30-44 minutes	>44 minutes
Grand Forks, ND-MN	35.75%	43.85%	9.78%	6.41%	4.20%
Logan, UT-ID	30.42%	42.32%	14.38%	6.16%	6.71%
Pocatello, ID	30.20%	47.53%	9.13%	6.03%	7.11%
Abilene, TX	29.87%	42.76%	14.19%	6.66%	6.52%
Wenatchee-East Wenatchee, WA	28.25%	38.37%	15.35%	8.99%	9.04%
El Centro, CA	27.48%	32.81%	17.64%	14.71%	7.35%
Great Falls, MT	27.16%	46.06%	14.69%	7.51%	4.59%
Ames, IA	27.01%	41.03%	15.44%	10.16%	6.37%
Flagstaff, AZ	26.87%	44.90%	10.79%	8.46%	8.98%
Waterloo-Cedar Falls, IA	26.33%	44.31%	17.58%	7.33%	4.45%
San Angelo, TX	26.15%	48.44%	13.00%	5.76%	6.64%
Sheboygan, WI	25.64%	42.97%	14.02%	10.02%	7.35%
Cheyenne, WY	25.61%	52.38%	12.77%	5.67%	3.57%
Bismarck, ND	24.90%	48.45%	13.45%	7.13%	6.08%
Vineland-Millville-Bridgeton, NJ	24.26%	27.26%	18.43%	13.67%	16.38%
Bloomington-Normal, IL	24.03%	47.82%	13.74%	8.42%	5.99%
Fond du Lac, WI	23.58%	37.22%	16.66%	13.68%	8.86%
Jacksonville, NC	23.24%	29.66%	20.23%	16.03%	10.85%
Pittsfield, MA	23.22%	37.98%	17.58%	11.15%	10.07%
Chico, CA	23.15%	38.71%	15.12%	12.54%	10.49%
Battle Creek, MI	22.89%	37.44%	19.02%	12.61%	8.04%
Duluth, MN-WI	22.87%	35.00%	22.92%	11.67%	7.54%
Lawrence, KS	22.86%	37.60%	14.74%	12.95%	11.84%
Fargo, ND-MN	22.79%	51.12%	15.69%	5.96%	4.44%
Victoria, TX	22.78%	36.64%	14.48%	12.22%	13.87%

Table 11.2: Bottom 25: Longest Commute Times	<10 minutes	10-19 minutes	20-29 minutes	30-44 minutes	>44 minutes
Gainesville, GA	10.14%	28.74%	22.75%	19.52%	18.86%
Merced, CA	18.46%	33.87%	15.15%	13.51%	19.01%
Worcester, MA	13.91%	27.60%	19.93%	19.38%	19.17%
Allentown-Bethlehem-Easton, PA-NJ	14.34%	28.52%	21.53%	16.41%	19.19%
Santa Cruz-Watsonville, CA	11.77%	31.79%	18.47%	18.30%	19.68%
Los Angeles-Long Beach-Santa Ana, CA	8.94%	26.61%	20.28%	24.32%	19.85%
Philadelphia-Camden-Wilmington, PA-NJ-DE-MD	10.93%	25.77%	20.36%	22.77%	20.17%
Hinesville-Fort Stewart, GA	14.10%	39.82%	13.36%	12.47%	20.25%
Houston-Sugar Land-Baytown, TX	8.69%	25.03%	20.82%	25.02%	20.44%
Stockton, CA	15.07%	32.78%	19.02%	12.37%	20.77%
Bremerton-Silverdale, WA	12.99%	28.75%	19.46%	17.94%	20.86%
Boston-Cambridge-Quincy, MA-NH	10.98%	24.25%	19.51%	24.04%	21.22%
Baltimore-Towson, MD	8.51%	24.43%	21.64%	24.19%	21.24%
Hagerstown-Martinsburg, MD-WV	12.37%	28.92%	18.78%	18.59%	21.34%
Bridgeport-Stamford-Norwalk, CT	12.12%	30.94%	19.78%	15.71%	21.45%
San Francisco-Oakland-Fremont, CA	8.57%	26.76%	19.24%	23.49%	21.94%
Winchester, VA-WV	12.71%	28.84%	22.21%	13.62%	22.62%
Atlanta-Sandy Springs-Marietta, GA	8.57%	23.60%	20.18%	24.26%	23.38%
Riverside-San Bernardino-Ontario, CA	11.74%	27.44%	18.40%	19.03%	23.39%
Yuba City, CA	14.61%	30.78%	12.06%	17.99%	24.55%
Poughkeepsie-Newburgh-Middletown, NY	15.41%	26.42%	16.24%	16.10%	25.83%
Vallejo-Fairfield, CA	11.97%	28.99%	15.00%	18.20%	25.84%
Chicago-Naperville-Joliet, IL-IN-WI	9.15%	22.39%	17.67%	24.70%	26.09%
Washington-Arlington-Alexandria, DC-VA-MD-WV	6.89%	20.08%	18.59%	25.77%	28.67%
New York-Northern New Jersey-Long Island, NY-NJ-PA	8.29%	20.79%	16.21%	22.77%	31.95%

Table 12.1: Most College-Educated Communities: Top 25	Some College	College Degree	Total	Rank
Boulder, CO	17.0%	63.5%	80.5%	1
Ann Arbor, MI	20.2%	57.7%	77.9%	2
Corvallis, OR	24.8%	53.1%	77.9%	3
Iowa City, IA	19.6%	56.1%	75.7%	4
Provo-Orem, UT	30.0%	45.6%	75.6%	5
Lawrence, KS	20.5%	54.5%	74.9%	6
Ames, IA	20.1%	53.8%	74.0%	7
Ithaca, NY	15.3%	57.6%	72.9%	8
Fort Collins-Loveland, CO	21.7%	50.9%	72.6%	9
Scranton--Wilkes-Barre, PA	22.3%	48.6%	70.8%	10
Barnstable Town, MA	20.2%	50.5%	70.7%	11
Lincoln, NE	25.0%	45.4%	70.3%	12
Washington-Arlington-Alexandria, DC-VA-MD-WV	17.8%	52.4%	70.2%	13
Shreveport-Bossier City, LA	24.6%	45.3%	70.0%	14
Madison, WI	21.2%	48.7%	69.9%	15
Logan, UT-ID	25.2%	44.6%	69.8%	16
Colorado Springs, CO	25.5%	44.3%	69.8%	17
Fargo, ND-MN	23.3%	46.1%	69.5%	18
Santa Cruz-Watsonville, CA	19.0%	50.4%	69.4%	19
Olympia, WA	26.6%	42.6%	69.2%	20
Gainesville, FL	16.3%	52.9%	69.2%	21
Raleigh-Cary, NC	19.9%	49.3%	69.1%	22
Rochester, MN	21.4%	47.6%	69.0%	23
Santa Fe, NM	18.1%	50.8%	68.8%	24
Bremerton-Silverdale, WA	30.8%	37.9%	68.8%	25

Table 12.2: Least College-Educated Communities: Bottom 25	Some College	College Degree	Total	Rank
Winchester, VA-WV	16.5%	27.8%	44.3%	337
Hagerstown-Martinsburg, MD-WV	20.8%	23.3%	44.2%	338
Mansfield, OH	21.4%	22.5%	43.9%	339
Lima, OH	21.3%	22.5%	43.8%	340
Yakima, WA	22.5%	21.3%	43.8%	341
Pine Bluff, AR	22.7%	21.0%	43.8%	342
Anderson, IN	19.3%	24.4%	43.6%	343
Youngstown-Warren-Boardman, OH-PA	18.6%	24.8%	43.4%	344
Lancaster, PA	14.4%	28.8%	43.2%	345
Visalia-Porterville, CA	23.0%	20.1%	43.1%	346
Merced, CA	23.0%	19.5%	42.6%	347
Rocky Mount, NC	18.8%	23.5%	42.3%	348
El Centro, CA	24.5%	17.5%	42.0%	349
Altoona, PA	16.7%	24.6%	41.3%	350
Hanford-Corcoran, CA	24.3%	16.9%	41.2%	351
Lebanon, PA	15.9%	24.9%	40.8%	352
Morristown, TN	20.8%	19.9%	40.7%	353
Elizabethtown, KY	17.4%	23.2%	40.6%	354
Brownsville-Harlingen, TX	18.5%	22.0%	40.5%	355
Cumberland, MD-WV	18.4%	20.9%	39.3%	356
Johnstown, PA	14.8%	23.9%	38.8%	357
Vineland-Millville-Bridgeton, NJ	17.2%	19.4%	36.6%	358
Dalton, GA	19.1%	17.4%	36.5%	359
Houma-Bayou Cane-Thibodaux, LA	16.9%	17.9%	34.8%	360
McAllen-Edinburg-Mission, TX	15.5%	18.5%	34.0%	361

Table 13.1: Top 25 Communities with Lowest Property Crime*	Property crime	Burglary	Larceny, Theft	Vehicle theft	Rank
Harrisonburg, VA	1544.8	319.4	1129.8	95.5	1
Logan, UT-ID	1641	319.4	1279.2	42.4	2
Kingston, NY	1760.8	446.5	1260.5	53.8	3
Lebanon, PA	1760.9	307.5	1381.3	72.2	4
Glens Falls, NY	1767.9	271.2	1465	31.7	5
State College, PA	1794.5	339.7	1406.8	48	6
Elizabethtown, KY	1809.1	385.2	1351.7	72.2	7
Wausau, WI	1814.5	385	1359.7	69.8	8
Holland-Grand Haven, MI	1837.8	363.6	1417.2	57	9
New York-City Area	1863.1	300.6	1391.1	171.3	10
Fond du Lac, WI	1868.4	235.7	1560.2	72.5	11
Santa Rosa-Petaluma, CA	1880.3	445.3	1258.8	176.2	12
Naples-Marco Island, FL	1928.9	424.3	1404.5	100.1	13
Johnstown, PA	1955.6	388.1	1491.8	75.7	14
Sioux Falls, SD	1968.2	349.3	1489.1	129.8	15
Wheeling, WV-OH	2001.9	445.3	1422.4	134.2	16
Oxnard-Thousand Oaks-Ventura, CA	2012.8	410	1432.7	170.2	17
Weirton-Steubenville, WV-OH	2015.9	432	1475.3	108.6	18
Poughkeepsie-Newburgh-Middletown, NY	2048.6	340.1	1628.7	79.8	19
Williamsport, PA	2063.3	460.6	1527.9	74.8	20
Bridgeport-Stamford-Norwalk, CT	2082.3	355.8	1488.7	237.9	21
Worcester, MA	2093.9	552.4	1369.4	172	22
Iowa City, IA	2095.6	494.3	1507.6	93.8	23
Lancaster, PA	2102.4	377.1	1619.8	105.4	24
Rochester, MN	2110.3	397.1	1572.6	140.6	25

Rate per 100,000 residents

*Note: Does not include the following communities, whose data is not complete: Anderson, SC; Anniston-Oxford, AL; Atlantic City-Hammonton, NJ; Baton Rouge, LA; Boulder, CO; Canton-Massillon, OH; Chicago-Naperville-Joliet, IL-IN-WI; Detroit-Warren-Livonia, MI; Fargo, ND-MN; Gulfport-Biloxi, MS; Huntington-Ashland, WV-KY-OH; Kansas City, MO-KS; Lake Charles, LA; Manchester-Nashua, NH; New Haven-Milford, CT; Owensboro, KY; Peoria, IL; Rockford, IL; Springfield, IL; Terre Haute, IN; Tucson, AZ.

Table 13.2: Bottom 25 Communities with the Highest Property Crime*	Property crime	Burglary	Larceny, Theft	Vehicle theft	Rank
Ocean City, NJ	4845.2	1010.4	3726.7	108.1	315
Winston-Salem, NC	4850.4	1426	3102.5	321.9	316
Brownsville-Harlingen, TX	4864.2	1035.6	3634.7	193.9	317
Mobile, AL	4887.4	1269.4	3179.2	438.9	318
Albuquerque, NM	4905.8	1132.5	3085.4	687.9	319
Stockton, CA	4923.4	1123.5	3148.6	651.2	320
Greenville, NC	5028.6	1624.9	3141	262.7	321
Lubbock, TX	5078.9	1334.6	3490.5	253.9	322
Monroe, LA	5133.1	1416.4	3518.5	198.2	323
Pueblo, CO	5,148.5	1,152.4	3,582.2	413.9	324
Yakima, WA	5210.2	1300	3138.7	771.5	325
Jackson, TN	5244	1312.1	3462.1	469.7	326
Wichita Falls, TX	5287.4	1233.3	3667.6	386.5	327
Little Rock-North Little Rock, AR	5362.5	1468.5	3524.7	369.2	328
Macon, GA	5382.2	1326	3517.3	538.9	329
Florence, SC	5384	1314.5	3641.1	428.4	330
Corpus Christi, TX	5427	1173.9	4046.1	207.1	331
Memphis, TN-MS-AR	5748.5	1652	3570	526.5	332
Pine Bluff, AR	5805.5	2049	3226.4	530.1	333
San Antonio, TX	5923.7	1197.8	4271.5	454.4	334
Columbus, GA-AL	5979.9	1398.5	3915.3	666.1	335
Fayetteville, NC	6022.1	1786.4	3846.8	388.9	336
Laredo, TX	6184.7	938.4	4505.4	740.9	337
Hot Springs, AR	6599.8	1940.1	4278.7	381	338
Myrtle Beach-North Myrtle Beach-Conway, SC	6,896.8	1,457.8	4,830.7	608.3	339

Rate per 100,000 residents

*Note: Does not include the following communities, whose data is not complete: Anderson, SC; Anniston-Oxford, AL; Atlantic City-Hammonton, NJ; Baton Rouge, LA; Boulder, CO; Canton-Massillon, OH; Chicago-Naperville-Joliet, IL-IN-WI; Detroit-Warren-Livonia, MI; Fargo, ND-MN; Gulfport-Biloxi, MS; Huntington-Ashland, WV-KY-OH; Kansas City, MO-KS; Lake Charles, LA; Manchester-Nashua, NH; New Haven-Milford, CT; Owensboro, KY; Peoria, IL; Rockford, IL; Springfield, IL; Terre Haute, IN; Tucson, AZ.

Table 14.1: Top 25 Communities with the Lowest Violent Crime*	Violent crime	Murder	Rape	Robbery	Aggr. Assault	Rank
Logan, UT-ID	72.8	1.6	28.8	1.6	40.8	1
Bangor, ME	76	1.3	9.4	25.6	39.7	2
Provo-Orem, UT	91.4	0.6	25.4	13.2	52.3	3
State College, PA	92	0	13.7	17.8	60.4	4
Columbus, IN	94.6	2.7	6.7	18.6	66.6	5
Eau Claire, WI	100.7	1.3	18.9	14.5	66.1	6
Sheboygan, WI	102.9	0	14	25.3	63.7	7
Appleton, WI	115.5	0.9	18.6	10.9	85	8
Corvallis, OR	134.4	1.2	24.4	24.4	84.3	9
Portland-South Portland-Biddeford, ME	134.7	2.1	33.1	39.3	60.1	10
Ithaca, NY	134.9	2	13.8	34.5	84.7	11
Harrisonburg, VA	145.4	1.7	17.7	23.7	102.3	12
Lewiston-Auburn, ME	149.9	1.9	33.7	45	69.3	13
Williamsport, PA	154.7	1.7	14.6	51.6	86.8	14
Elkhart-Goshen, IN	157.2	4	34.6	102.2	16.5	15
Ogden-Clearfield, UT	158.3	1.7	29.9	45	81.7	16
Glens Falls, NY	175.4	1.5	30.9	10	132.9	17
Parkersburg-Marietta-Vienna, WV-OH	176.7	2.5	27.4	20.5	126.3	18
Holland-Grand Haven, MI	176.8	1.5	50.1	22.3	102.9	19
Bend, OR	181.2	0	33.2	30.1	117.9	20
Anderson, IN	181.4	3.1	24.6	67.6	86.1	21
Weirton-Steubenville, WV-OH	184.3	2.5	14	42	125.9	22
St. George, UT	189.2	1.4	22.5	22.5	142.8	23
Wenatchee-E. Wenatchee, WA	190.2	4.6	46.2	20.3	119.1	24
Morgantown, WV	191.0	2.6	35.6	41.7	111.2	25

Rate per 100,000 residents

*Note: Does not include the following communities, whose data is not complete: Anniston-Oxford, AL; Augusta-Richmond County, GA-SC; Boulder, CO; Canton-Massillon, OH; Chattanooga, TN-GA; Chicago-Naperville-Joliet, IL-IN-WI; Davenport-Moline-Rock Island, IA-IL; Duluth, MN-WI; Fargo, ND-MN; Farmington, NM; Grand Forks, ND-MN; Gulfport-Biloxi, MS; Huntington-Ashland, WV-KY-OH; Kansas City, MO-KS; La Crosse, WI-MN; Lake Charles, LA; Manchester-Nashua, NH; Minneapolis-St.Paul-Bloomington, MN-WI; New Haven-Milford, CT; Owensboro, KY; Peoria, IL; Raleigh-Cary, NC; Rochester, MN; Rockford, IL; Springfield, IL; Springfield, MO; St. Cloud, MN; Terre Haute, IN.

Table 14.2: Bottom 25 Communities with the Highest Violent Crime*	Violent crime	Murder	Rape	Robbery	Aggr. Assault	Rank
Baltimore-Towson, MD	761	11.3	20.1	268.4	461.2	309
Miami-Fort Lauderdale-Pompano Beach, FL	765.4	7.6	29.5	276.9	451.5	310
Fairbanks, AK	775.3	8	120.3	82.9	564.1	311
Nashville-Davidson--Murfreesboro--Franklin, TN	781.2	6.5	35.6	186.5	552.6	312
Albuquerque, NM	798.7	7.6	61.5	188.3	541.4	313
Gainesville, FL	798.7	2.3	52.1	140.1	604.2	314
Jackson, TN	815.9	8.8	37.1	228.7	541.3	315
Orlando-Kissimmee, FL	820.6	7.9	38.8	239.4	534.5	316
Jacksonville, FL	820.9	9.7	28.9	251	531.3	317
Brunswick, GA	822.1	19.7	26.6	164.2	611.7	318
Las Vegas-Paradise, NV	840.4	7.3	47.1	307.6	478.4	319
Lubbock, TX	841	3.3	40.1	115.8	681.8	320
Texarkana, TX-Texarkana, AR	873.3	3.7	37.1	120.9	711.6	321
Lawton, OK	890.9	5.3	70.3	178.4	637	322
Tallahassee, FL	894.5	4.3	51.7	226.1	612.4	323
Stockton, CA	902.9	5.1	25.1	296.9	575.8	324
Salisbury, MD	919.4	6.7	32.5	192.4	687.9	325
Anchorage, AK	922.9	3.3	88	183.1	648.5	326
Alexandria, LA	933.8	6.7	29.3	133.8	764.0	327
Myrtle Beach-North Myrtle Beach-Conway, SC	948.1	4.9	56.6	194.2	692.5	328
Pine Bluff, AR	949.1	20.8	85.4	260.1	582.7	329
Florence, SC	1002.5	11	44.9	169.2	777.3	330
Shreveport-Bossier City, LA	1048.3	9.5	37.8	157.9	843.1	331
Saginaw-Saginaw Township North, MI	1192.6	12	54.6	197.3	928.6	332
Memphis, TN-MS-AR	1207.3	12.6	40.4	408.5	745.8	333

Rate per 100,000 residents

*Note: Does not include the following communities, whose data is not complete: Anniston-Oxford, AL; Augusta-Richmond County, GA-SC; Boulder, CO; Canton-Massillon, OH; Chattanooga, TN-GA; Chicago-Naperville-Joliet, IL-IN-WI; Davenport-Moline-Rock Island, IA-IL; Duluth, MN-WI; Fargo, ND-MN; Farmington, NM; Grand Forks, ND-MN; Gulfport-Biloxi, MS; Huntington-Ashland, WV-KY-OH; Kansas City, MO-KS; La Crosse, WI-MN; Lake Charles, LA; Manchester-Nashua, NH; Minneapolis-St.Paul-Bloomington, MN-WI; New Haven-Milford, CT; Owensboro, KY; Peoria, IL; Raleigh-Cary, NC; Rochester, MN; Rockford, IL; Springfield, IL; Springfield, MO; St. Cloud, MN; Terre Haute, IN.

Table 15.1: Top 25 Communities with Most Families Earning Most Income	<$25k	$25k to $75k	$75k to $150k	>$150K	Rank
Bridgeport-Stamford-Norwalk, CT	8.7%	25.8%	33.1%	32.5%	1
Santa Fe, NM	7.9%	27.8%	34.0%	30.4%	2
Washington DC Metro Area	7.4%	27.7%	36.3%	28.6%	3
Trenton-Ewing, NJ	10.1%	30.4%	32.9%	26.6%	4
Santa Cruz-Watsonville, CA	10.6%	29.1%	34.5%	25.9%	5
Boulder, CO	7.9%	32.0%	35.1%	25.0%	6
Boston-Cambridge-Quincy, MA-NH	10.3%	30.8%	36.7%	22.1%	7
New York-Northern New Jersey-Long Island, NY-NJ-PA	14.3%	34.0%	31.6%	20.0%	8
Oxnard-Thousand Oaks-Ventura, CA	8.7%	33.5%	37.8%	19.9%	9
Scranton--Wilkes-Barre, PA	12.8%	32.7%	34.7%	19.9%	10
Napa, CA	10.3%	38.7%	33.3%	17.7%	11
Baltimore-Towson, MD	10.4%	35.3%	36.6%	17.7%	12
Naples-Marco Island, FL	11.8%	39.4%	31.1%	17.6%	13
Hartford-W. Hartford-E. Hartford, CT	10.0%	34.1%	38.6%	17.3%	14
Sandusky, OH	13.6%	36.7%	32.8%	17.0%	15
Shreveport-Bossier City, LA	9.4%	36.2%	37.6%	16.9%	16
Charlottesville, VA	10.0%	39.6%	33.6%	16.8%	17
Raleigh-Cary, NC	10.5%	38.0%	34.9%	16.6%	18
Sebastian-Vero Beach, FL	10.5%	37.4%	35.6%	16.5%	19
Ann Arbor, MI	12.5%	32.1%	38.9%	16.5%	20
Philadelphia-Camden-Wilmington, PA-NJ-DE-MD	12.6%	35.6%	35.5%	16.3%	21
Poughkeepsie-Newburgh-Middletown, NY	9.0%	33.6%	41.1%	16.2%	22
Los Angeles-Long Beach-Santa Ana, CA	16.6%	38.1%	29.2%	16.1%	23
Minneapolis-St. Paul-Bloomington, MN-WI	8.3%	36.0%	39.6%	16.1%	24
Anchorage, AK	7.1%	33.8%	43.3%	15.9%	25

Table 15.2: Bottom 25 Communities with Most Families Earning Least Income	<$25k	$25k to $75k	$75k to $150k	>$150K	Rank
Bakersfield, CA	23.8%	44.3%	24.2%	7.7%	337
Jonesboro, AR	23.8%	44.3%	26.3%	5.5%	338
Fresno, CA	23.9%	43.6%	24.7%	7.9%	339
Fort Smith, AR-OK	23.9%	51.2%	20.7%	4.1%	340
Rocky Mount, NC	24.0%	43.5%	26.0%	6.4%	341
Florence, SC	24.1%	50.0%	20.9%	5.0%	342
Texarkana, TX-Texarkana, AR	24.2%	45.7%	24.7%	5.3%	343
Huntington-Ashland, WV-KY-OH	24.2%	51.2%	19.7%	4.9%	344
Anniston-Oxford, AL	24.3%	47.5%	25.4%	2.8%	345
Alexandria, LA	24.3%	44.6%	26.1%	4.9%	346
Monroe, LA	24.5%	43.6%	24.9%	7.1%	347
Danville, VA	25.1%	52.1%	19.2%	3.7%	348
Visalia-Porterville, CA	25.5%	45.7%	23.4%	5.4%	349
Joplin, MO	26.1%	50.2%	19.8%	3.9%	350
Pine Bluff, AR	26.5%	48.4%	22.5%	2.6%	351
Yuma, AZ	26.8%	52.2%	17.8%	3.2%	352
Merced, CA	27.0%	44.1%	23.4%	5.6%	353
Albany, GA	27.5%	41.4%	23.4%	7.7%	354
Macon, GA	28.3%	40.9%	24.0%	6.8%	355
Laredo, TX	29.2%	46.7%	19.7%	4.5%	356
Las Cruces, NM	30.3%	42.2%	23.4%	4.1%	357
El Centro, CA	31.3%	45.3%	18.9%	4.5%	358
Elmira, NY	31.4%	45.0%	18.9%	4.7%	359
Brownsville-Harlingen, TX	37.4%	44.7%	14.6%	3.3%	360
McAllen-Edinburg-Mission, TX	39.2%	41.6%	15.4%	3.8%	361

Table 16.1: Top 25 Communities with the Lowest Unemployment Rate*	Unemployment 3/2009	Unemployment 3/2010	Change	Rank
Houma-Bayou Cane-Thibodaux, LA	3.9%	4.6%	0.7%	1
Fargo, ND-MN	5.2%	4.9%	-0.3%	2
Lincoln, NE	4.6%	4.9%	0.3%	3
Bismarck, ND	4.9%	5.0%	0.1%	4
Lafayette, LA	4.4%	5.0%	0.6%	5
Iowa City, IA	3.8%	5.1%	1.3%	6
Grand Forks, ND-MN	5.8%	5.3%	-0.5%	7
Ames, IA	4.0%	5.4%	1.4%	8
Lawton, OK	5.0%	5.4%	0.4%	9
Sioux Falls, SD	5.3%	5.4%	0.1%	10
Ithaca, NY	5.6%	5.5%	-0.1%	11
Logan, UT-ID	5.5%	5.5%	0.0%	12
Amarillo, TX	4.8%	5.6%	0.8%	13
Honolulu, HI	5.5%	5.6%	0.1%	14
Lawrence, KS	5.9%	5.6%	-0.3%	15
Rapid City, SD	5.4%	5.6%	0.2%	16
Midland, TX	4.8%	5.7%	0.9%	17
Alexandria, LA	6.1%	5.8%	-0.3%	18
Lake Charles, LA	5.5%	5.8%	0.3%	19
Shreveport-Bossier City, LA	6.7%	5.8%	-0.9%	20
College Station-Bryan, TX	5.0%	5.9%	0.9%	21
Lubbock, TX	4.8%	5.9%	1.1%	22
Omaha-Council Bluffs, NE-IA	5.2%	5.9%	0.7%	23
Baton Rouge, LA	5.6%	6.0%	0.4%	24
Burlington-South Burlington, VT	6.9%	6.0%	-0.9%	25

*As of March 2010

Does not include the following communities, whose complete data was not available: Bradenton-Sarasota-Venice, FL; Davenport-Moline-Rock Island, IA-IL; Fort Walton Beach-Crestview-Destin, FL.

Table 16.2: Bottom 25 Communities with the Highest Unemployment Rate*	Unemployment 3/2009	Unemployment 3/2010	Change	Rank
Elkhart-Goshen, IN	20.1%	15.2%	-4.9%	334
Jackson, MI	12.7%	15.2%	2.5%	335
Kankakee-Bradley, IL	12.0%	15.2%	3.2%	336
Santa Cruz-Watsonville, CA	12.6%	15.3%	2.7%	337
Detroit-Warren-Livonia, MI	14.3%	15.5%	1.2%	338
Bend, OR	16.7%	15.8%	-0.9%	339
Monroe, MI	13.8%	16.0%	2.2%	340
Flint, MI	14.8%	16.3%	1.5%	341
Ocean City, NJ	15.2%	16.3%	1.1%	342
Muskegon-Norton Shores, MI	14.6%	16.5%	1.9%	343
Palm Coast, FL	13.7%	16.6%	2.9%	344
Salinas, CA	14.8%	16.8%	2.0%	345
Madera-Chowchilla, CA	14.8%	17.5%	2.7%	346
Redding, CA	15.8%	17.7%	1.9%	347
Rockford, IL	14.1%	17.9%	3.8%	348
Bakersfield, CA	15.2%	18.3%	3.1%	349
Stockton, CA	15.6%	18.4%	2.8%	350
Hanford-Corcoran, CA	15.5%	18.6%	3.1%	351
Fresno, CA	15.9%	18.7%	2.8%	352
Modesto, CA	16.5%	19.2%	2.7%	353
Visalia-Porterville, CA	16.6%	19.4%	2.8%	354
Yuma, AZ	15.8%	19.9%	4.1%	355
Yuba City, CA	18.3%	21.7%	3.4%	356
Merced, CA	19.0%	22.1%	3.1%	357
El Centro, CA	24.8%	27.0%	2.2%	358

*As of March 2010

Does not include the following communities, whose complete data was not available: Bradenton-Sarasota-Venice, FL; Davenport-Moline-Rock Island, IA-IL; Fort Walton Beach-Crestview-Destin, FL.

Table 17.1: Top 25 Communities with Children Living with Married Parents	Children living with married parents	Children living with single father	Children living with single mother	Rank
Salinas, CA	84.1%	4.9%	10.2%	1
Provo-Orem, UT	83.4%	4.2%	12.1%	2
Fond du Lac, WI	82.1%	6.1%	11.8%	3
Logan, UT-ID	81.5%	6.3%	11.5%	4
Holland-Grand Haven, MI	80.1%	5.3%	13.9%	5
Ogden-Clearfield, UT	79.0%	5.1%	15.0%	6
Idaho Falls, ID	78.0%	4.7%	15.6%	7
Boulder, CO	77.4%	7.3%	14.8%	8
Pocatello, ID	77.2%	5.2%	16.2%	9
Appleton, WI	76.9%	7.0%	15.1%	10
Cleveland, TN	76.9%	2.9%	16.6%	11
Sioux Falls, SD	76.4%	2.9%	18.3%	12
Fort Collins-Loveland, CO	76.3%	6.4%	15.8%	13
Corvallis, OR	76.1%	5.2%	18.7%	14
Rochester, MN	75.9%	8.0%	15.5%	15
Bismarck, ND	75.7%	4.1%	20.0%	16
Santa Fe, NM	75.7%	7.9%	16.0%	17
Bridgeport-Stamford-Norwalk, CT	75.6%	5.0%	18.9%	18
State College, PA	75.5%	5.8%	17.7%	19
Bend, OR	75.2%	9.2%	15.7%	20
San Francisco-Oakland-Fremont, CA	74.9%	7.4%	17.0%	21
Harrisonburg, VA	74.8%	8.7%	15.4%	22
Poughkeepsie-Newburgh-Middletown, NY	74.5%	7.3%	17.4%	23
Ames, IA	74.4%	5.7%	19.1%	24
Grand Junction, CO	74.4%	7.9%	16.7%	25

Table 17.2: Bottom 25 Communities with Children Living with Married Parents	Children living with married parents	Children living with single father	Children living with single mother	Rank
Las Cruces, NM	57.0%	8.8%	33.7%	337
Flagstaff, AZ	56.8%	10.3%	31.2%	338
Monroe, LA	56.5%	4.9%	38.1%	339
Burlington, NC	56.3%	4.9%	37.2%	340
Danville, IL	56.2%	9.2%	29.2%	341
Dothan, AL	56.2%	7.5%	35.3%	342
Pittsfield, MA	56.0%	12.2%	29.2%	343
Jackson, MS	55.8%	5.6%	37.8%	344
Punta Gorda, FL	55.7%	17.0%	25.9%	345
Saginaw-Saginaw Township North, MI	55.3%	7.8%	36.5%	346
Kankakee-Bradley, IL	55.2%	5.8%	38.7%	347
Anderson, IN	55.1%	9.7%	33.2%	348
Florence, SC	54.8%	7.7%	36.8%	349
Macon, GA	54.7%	7.2%	37.3%	350
Rocky Mount, NC	54.7%	7.2%	37.4%	351
Greenville, NC	54.6%	7.2%	37.5%	352
Memphis, TN-MS-AR	53.6%	7.5%	38.0%	353
Longview, WA	53.3%	16.7%	25.5%	354
Vineland-Millville-Bridgeton, NJ	52.5%	15.6%	31.1%	355
Sumter, SC	52.0%	5.9%	40.0%	356
Columbus, GA-AL	50.9%	5.7%	42.3%	357
Albany, GA	50.1%	6.0%	43.7%	358
Fayetteville, NC	50.0%	7.7%	41.4%	359
Spartanburg, SC	49.3%	9.7%	39.7%	360
Pine Bluff, AR	46.4%	10.6%	42.9%	361

Table 18.1: Top 25 Communities with Stay-at-Home Mothers	Stay-at-home mothers	Rank
Salinas, CA	49.9%	1
Provo-Orem, UT	48.3%	2
Hinesville-Fort Stewart, GA	46.4%	3
McAllen-Edinburg-Mission, TX	45.7%	4
Brownsville-Harlingen, TX	43.7%	5
Farmington, NM	43.4%	6
Logan, UT-ID	42.7%	7
Laredo, TX	41.5%	8
Longview, TX	41.3%	9
Hanford-Corcoran, CA	41.1%	10
Elmira, NY	40.8%	11
Killeen-Temple-Fort Hood, TX	40.4%	12
Visalia-Porterville, CA	40.4%	13
Clarksville, TN-KY	40.3%	14
Cleveland, TN	40.3%	15
Pascagoula, MS	40.0%	16
Houston-Sugar Land-Baytown, TX	39.8%	17
Fairbanks, AK	39.6%	18
Kennewick-Pasco-Richland, WA	39.5%	19
Odessa, TX	38.8%	20
Mount Vernon-Anacortes, WA	38.8%	21
Bridgeport-Stamford-Norwalk, CT	38.6%	22
Madera-Chowchilla, CA	38.5%	23
Bakersfield, CA	38.3%	24
Merced, CA	38.2%	25

Table 18.2: Bottom 25 Communities with Stay-at-Home Mothers	Stay-at-home mothers	Rank
San Diego-Carlsbad-San Marcos, CA	17.9%	337
Cheyenne, WY	17.9%	338
Madison, WI	17.8%	339
Duluth, MN-WI	17.8%	340
Grand Forks, ND-MN	17.6%	341
Muncie, IN	17.4%	342
Columbia, MO	17.3%	343
Fond du Lac, WI	17.1%	344
Atlantic City-Hammonton, NJ	16.8%	345
Janesville, WI	15.9%	346
Sioux Falls, SD	15.7%	347
Eau Claire, WI	15.6%	348
Rochester, MN	15.3%	349
Bismarck, ND	15.2%	350
Salem, OR	14.1%	351
Glens Falls, NY	14.1%	352
Jefferson City, MO	13.8%	353
St. Cloud, MN	13.3%	354
La Crosse, WI-MN	13.2%	355
Oshkosh-Neenah, WI	13.1%	356
Lincoln, NE	12.9%	357
Dubuque, IA	12.2%	358
Fargo, ND-MN	11.9%	359
Danville, IL	11.4%	360
Springfield, IL	10.2%	361

Table 19.1 and 19.2: Best and Worst Communities for Positive Establishments

Table 19.1: Top 25 Communities for Positive Establishments	Positive Establishments	Negative Establishments	Ratio Positive:Negative	Rank
St. George, UT	529	6	88.2	1
Provo-Orem, UT	3811	48	79.4	2
Lynchburg, VA	1320	17	77.6	3
Danville, VA	1836	28	65.6	4
Charlottesville, VA	2010	32	62.8	5
Blacksburg, VA	2361	41	57.6	6
Harrisonburg, VA	1451	26	55.8	7
Hickory, NC	2861	52	55.0	8
Anniston, AL	1712	32	53.5	9
Roanoke, VA	2424	46	52.7	10
Goldsboro, NC	1551	30	51.7	11
Logan, UT-ID	886	19	46.6	12
Gadsden, AL	1767	38	46.5	13
Tyler, TX	1787	40	44.7	14
Richmond, VA	5761	131	44.0	15
Virginia Beach, VA	7237	168	43.1	16
Lewiston, ME	2049	48	42.7	17
Rocky Mount, NC	1651	39	42.3	18
Bangor, ME	1074	26	41.3	19
Farmington, NM	453	11	41.2	20
Las Cruces, NM	822	20	41.1	21
Gainesville, GA	4544	112	40.6	22
Ogden, UT	2085	53	39.3	23
Salt Lake City, UT	6314	162	39.0	24
Kingsport, TN-VA	2631	70	37.6	25

Table 19.2: Bottom 25 Communities for Positive Establishments	Positive Establishments	Negative Establishments	Ratio Positive:Negative	Rank
Gulfport-Biloxi, MS	1507	166	9.1	337
Houma, LA	1100	126	8.7	338
Reno-Sparks, NV	1668	195	8.6	339
Sioux Falls, SD	1152	136	8.5	340
Milwaukee, WI	7137	859	8.3	341
Myrtle Beach, SC	1453	179	8.1	342
Vallejo-Fairfield, CA	11012	1376	8.0	343
Dubuque, IA	803	102	7.9	344
Billings, MT	813	104	7.8	345
Rapid City, SD	782	102	7.7	346
Pueblo, CO	842	110	7.7	347
St. Cloud, MN	1033	135	7.7	348
Eau Claire, WI	1044	139	7.5	349
Fond du Lac, WI	1650	223	7.4	350
Oshkosh-Neenah, WI	2126	292	7.3	351
Duluth, MN-WI	970	143	6.8	352
Appleton, WI	2680	396	6.8	353
Green Bay, WI	2161	330	6.5	354
La Crosse, WI-MN	1038	161	6.4	355
Great Falls, MT	434	70	6.2	356
Wausau, WI	814	132	6.2	357
Las Vegas, NV	5637	987	5.7	358
Deltona, FL	2885	506	5.7	359
Sheboygan, WI	1040	190	5.5	360
Visalia, CA	225	121	1.9	361

Chapter 4: Community Data

In Chapter 4, we present detailed data about each of the 361 communities we have ranked. They are presented in alphabetical order, by largest city in the metropolitan area.

Remember that the scores for each of the seven categories, as well as the overall scores, are based on an indexing system where 100 is best and 0 Is worst. This way you will be able to determine the relative differences between two or more communities.

Blank cells indicate that the data for that community is not available.

The data presented here is not all of the data considered in the ranking and evaluation process, but it is key data that most LDS families would find of value.

Abilene, TX
160,012

	Score	Rank
Overall	**63.49**	**172**
LDS Culture	38.79	48
Education	56.00	321
Crime	50.51	216
Economic	56.86	270
Health	32.00	323
Household	86.42	29
Housing	86.50	109

Key LDS Culture Data
	Positive	Negative	Ratio Pos:Neg	Commute>59 minutes	Commute<15 minutes
Area	956	40	23.9	3.5%	53.4%
USA	4,292	251	20.1	5.5%	34.1%

Key Education Data
	HS Grad	Some Coll.	College Degree	Free/Reduced Lunch	Students per Teacher
Area	83.9%	26.4%	29.1%	50.7%	12.8
USA	85.8%	22.6%	33.2%	41.2%	15.8

Key Property Crime Data (Rate per 100,000 residents)
	Rate	Burglary	Larceny, Theft	Vehicle Theft
Area	3,217.4	889.8	2,161.9	165.8
USA	3,413.6	806.6	2,388.0	262.7

Key Violent Crime Data (Rate per 100,000 residents)
	Rate	Murder	Rape	Robbery	Aggravated Assault
Area	449.6	4.4	59.7	118.0	267.5
USA	432.8	4.7	34.7	111.6	285.6

Key Economic Data (Family income, unemployment)
	$25k-$75k	$75k-$150k	>$150k	Unemployment 03/2009	Unemployment 03/2010
Area	51.2%	22.6%	6.7%	5.5%	6.4%
USA	45.8%	29.5%	8.5%	9.0%	10.1

Key Household Data
	Population Age 0-17	Children w/Married Parents	Children w/Single Mother	Stay-at-home Mothers	Births to Single Women
Area	24.6%	67.6%	26.0%	30.2%	19.8%
USA	24.0%	65.6%	25.5%	27.9%	35.3%

Key Housing Data
	Owner Occupied	Median Year Built	Median Home Value	Home Value Growth, 2005-2010	Median List Price, 4-bedroom Home
Area	66.5%	1967	$88,300	5.4%	
USA	67.8%	1976	$187,045	3.1%	$288,846

Akron, OH
698,553

	Score	Rank
Overall	61.96	196
LDS Culture	30.67	133
Education	75.16	124
Crime	58.50	153
Economic	53.70	309
Health	39.69	218
Household	63.58	189
Housing	76.05	271

Key LDS Culture Data

	Positive	Negative	Ratio Pos:Neg	Commute>59 minutes	Commute<15 minutes
Area	8,635	587	14.7	4.7%	30.4%
USA	4,292	251	20.1	5.5%	34.1%

Key Education Data

	HS Grad	Some Coll.	College Degree	Free/Reduced Lunch	Students per Teacher
Area	90.1%	20.0%	37.2%		16.5
USA	85.8%	22.6%	33.2%	41.2%	15.8

Key Property Crime Data (Rate per 100,000 residents)

	Rate	Burglary	Larceny, Theft	Vehicle Theft	
Area	3,312.3	882.7	2,213.0	216.6	
USA	3,413.6	806.6	2,388.0	262.7	

Key Violent Crime Data (Rate per 100,000 residents)

	Rate	Murder	Rape	Robbery	Aggravated Assault
Area	347.2	3.4	40.3	141.0	162.4
USA	432.8	4.7	34.7	111.6	285.6

Key Economic Data (Family income, unemployment)

	$25k-$75k	$75k-$150k	>$150k	Unemployment 03/2009	Unemployment 03/2010
Area	44.5%	30.7%	10.3%	9.6%	11.6%
USA	45.8%	29.5%	8.5%	9.0%	10.1

Key Household Data

	Population Age 0-17	Children w/Married Parents	Children w/Single Mother	Stay-at-home Mothers	Births to Single Women
Area	22.9%	65.2%	28.3%	28.4%	35.9%
USA	24.0%	65.6%	25.5%	27.9%	35.3%

Key Housing Data

	Owner Occupied	Median Year Built	Median Home Value	Home Value Growth, 2005-2010	Median List Price, 4-bedroom Home
Area	68.6%	1964	$148,300	0.3%	$229,500
USA	67.8%	1976	$187,045	3.1%	$288,846

Albany, GA
163,074

	Score	Rank
Overall	52.22	355
LDS Culture	33.58	97
Education	42.56	361
Crime	42.75	268
Economic	49.97	330
Health	40.98	197
Household	45.06	336
Housing	79.94	209

Key LDS Culture Data

	Positive	Negative	Ratio Pos:Neg	Commute>59 minutes	Commute<15 minutes
Area	966	42	23.0	2.5%	35.6%
USA	4,292	251	20.1	5.5%	34.1%

Key Education Data

	HS Grad	Some Coll.	College Degree	Free/Reduced Lunch	Students per Teacher
Area	79.7%	23.0%	22.9%	66.1%	15.0
USA	85.8%	22.6%	33.2%	41.2%	15.8

Key Property Crime Data (Rate per 100,000 residents)

	Rate	Burglary	Larceny, Theft	Vehicle Theft	
Area	4,593.2	1,273.5	3,006.4	313.4	
USA	3,413.6	806.6	2,388.0	262.7	

Key Violent Crime Data (Rate per 100,000 residents)

	Rate	Murder	Rape	Robbery	Aggravated Assault
Area	472.2	9.1	23.6	138.8	300.6
USA	432.8	4.7	34.7	111.6	285.6

Key Economic Data (Family income, unemployment)

	$25k-$75k	$75k-$150k	>$150k	Unemployment 03/2009	Unemployment 03/2010
Area	41.4%	23.4%	7.7%	7.9%	10.9%
USA	45.8%	29.5%	8.5%	9.0%	10.1

Key Household Data

	Population Age 0-17	Children w/Married Parents	Children w/Single Mother	Stay-at-home Mothers	Births to Single Women
Area	26.0%	50.1%	43.7%	25.2%	63.5%
USA	24.0%	65.6%	25.5%	27.9%	35.3%

Key Housing Data

	Owner Occupied	Median Year Built	Median Home Value	Home Value Growth, 2005-2010	Median List Price, 4-bedroom Home
Area	59.9%	1980	$101,400	3.3%	$310,000
USA	67.8%	1976	$187,045	3.1%	$288,846

Albany-Schenectady-Troy, NY
853,919

	Score	Rank
Overall	**67.01**	**103**
LDS Culture	24.63	225
Education	86.25	35
Crime	67.31	102
Economic	74.65	47
Health	49.20	45
Household	56.79	248
Housing	70.87	324

Key LDS Culture Data
	Positive	Negative	Ratio Pos:Neg	Commute>59 minutes	Commute<15 minutes
Area	4,237	329	12.9	4.2%	29.3%
USA	4,292	251	20.1	5.5%	34.1%

Key Education Data
	HS Grad	Some Coll.	College Degree	Free/Reduced Lunch	Students per Teacher
Area	90.7%	17.7%	44.0%	26.1%	13.2
USA	85.8%	22.6%	33.2%	41.2%	15.8

Key Property Crime Data (Rate per 100,000 residents)
	Rate	Burglary	Larceny, Theft	Vehicle Theft	
Area	2,573.3	510.7	1,960.1	102.5	
USA	3,413.6	806.6	2,388.0	262.7	

Key Violent Crime Data (Rate per 100,000 residents)
	Rate	Murder	Rape	Robbery	Aggravated Assault
Area	327.8	2.7	21.0	111.6	192.5
USA	432.8	4.7	34.7	111.6	285.6

Key Economic Data (Family income, unemployment)
	$25k-$75k	$75k-$150k	>$150k	Unemployment 03/2009	Unemployment 03/2010
Area	39.1%	38.7%	11.1%	7.1%	7.2%
USA	45.8%	29.5%	8.5%	9.0%	10.1

Key Household Data
	Population Age 0-17	Children w/Married Parents	Children w/Single Mother	Stay-at-home Mothers	Births to Single Women
Area	21.2%	65.6%	24.7%	26.1%	40.5%
USA	24.0%	65.6%	25.5%	27.9%	35.3%

Key Housing Data
	Owner Occupied	Median Year Built	Median Home Value	Home Value Growth, 2005-2010	Median List Price, 4-bedroom Home
Area	67.1%	1965	$197,400	6.0%	
USA	67.8%	1976	$187,045	3.1%	$288,846

Albuquerque, NM
841,408

	Score	Rank
Overall	57.29	298
LDS Culture	34.06	91
Education	59.17	304
Crime	27.07	345
Economic	58.20	255
Health	44.38	156
Household	55.56	268
Housing	88.94	64

Key LDS Culture Data

	Positive	Negative	Ratio Pos:Neg	Commute>59 minutes	Commute<15 minutes
Area	3,454	121	28.5	5.8%	25.2%
USA	4,292	251	20.1	5.5%	34.1%

Key Education Data

	HS Grad	Some Coll.	College Degree	Free/Reduced Lunch	Students per Teacher
Area	86.5%	24.7%	36.4%	52.8%	14.7
USA	85.8%	22.6%	33.2%	41.2%	15.8

Key Property Crime Data (Rate per 100,000 residents)

	Rate	Burglary	Larceny, Theft	Vehicle Theft
Area	4,905.8	1,132.5	3,085.4	687.9
USA	3,413.6	806.6	2,388.0	262.7

Key Violent Crime Data (Rate per 100,000 residents)

	Rate	Murder	Rape	Robbery	Aggravated Assault
Area	798.7	7.6	61.5	188.3	541.4
USA	432.8	4.7	34.7	111.6	285.6

Key Economic Data (Family income, unemployment)

	$25k-$75k	$75k-$150k	>$150k	Unemployment 03/2009	Unemployment 03/2010
Area	43.6%	29.6%	9.2%	6.7%	9.2%
USA	45.8%	29.5%	8.5%	9.0%	10.1

Key Household Data

	Population Age 0-17	Children w/Married Parents	Children w/Single Mother	Stay-at-home Mothers	Births to Single Women
Area	24.8%	63.3%	28.3%	31.6%	45.1%
USA	24.0%	65.6%	25.5%	27.9%	35.3%

Key Housing Data

	Owner Occupied	Median Year Built	Median Home Value	Home Value Growth, 2005-2010	Median List Price, 4-bedroom Home
Area	67.8%	1983	$192,500	5.7%	$284,900
USA	67.8%	1976	$187,045	3.1%	$288,846

Alexandria, LA
151,428

	Score	Rank
Overall	57.14	301
LDS Culture	32.62	115
Education	58.00	309
Crime	23.24	353
Economic	54.75	296
Health	56.89	9
Household	52.47	283
Housing	88.42	73

Key LDS Culture Data

	Positive	Negative	Ratio Pos:Neg	Commute>59 minutes	Commute<15 minutes
Area	1,117	35	31.9	5.1%	33.5%
USA	4,292	251	20.1	5.5%	34.1%

Key Education Data

	HS Grad	Some Coll.	College Degree	Free/Reduced Lunch	Students per Teacher
Area	82.4%	22.7%	23.2%	65.5%	14.2
USA	85.8%	22.6%	33.2%	41.2%	15.8

Key Property Crime Data (Rate per 100,000 residents)

	Rate	Burglary	Larceny, Theft	Vehicle Theft
Area	4,467.1	1,158.0	3,020.2	288.8
USA	3,413.6	806.6	2,388.0	262.7

Key Violent Crime Data (Rate per 100,000 residents)

	Rate	Murder	Rape	Robbery	Aggravated Assault
Area	933.8	6.7	29.3	133.8	764.0
USA	432.8	4.7	34.7	111.6	285.6

Key Economic Data (Family income, unemployment)

	$25k-$75k	$75k-$150k	>$150k	Unemployment 03/2009	Unemployment 03/2010
Area	44.6%	26.1%	4.9%	6.1%	5.8%
USA	45.8%	29.5%	8.5%	9.0%	10.1

Key Household Data

	Population Age 0-17	Children w/Married Parents	Children w/Single Mother	Stay-at-home Mothers	Births to Single Women
Area	25.3%	60.1%	32.6%	33.7%	51.2%
USA	24.0%	65.6%	25.5%	27.9%	35.3%

Key Housing Data

	Owner Occupied	Median Year Built	Median Home Value	Home Value Growth, 2005-2010	Median List Price, 4-bedroom Home
Area	69.7%	1978	$105,200	4.7%	
USA	67.8%	1976	$187,045	3.1%	$288,846

Allentown-Bethlehem-Easton, PA-NJ
808,210

	Score	Rank
Overall	66.11	124
LDS Culture	18.17	309
Education	79.43	74
Crime	74.51	55
Economic	64.37	160
Health	46.01	131
Household	69.14	151
Housing	72.32	314

Key LDS Culture Data

	Positive	Negative	Ratio Pos:Neg	Commute>59 minutes	Commute<15 minutes
Area	7,688	494	15.6	12.1%	28.5%
USA	4,292	251	20.1	5.5%	34.1%

Key Education Data

	HS Grad	Some Coll.	College Degree	Free/Reduced Lunch	Students per Teacher
Area	86.8%	17.0%	34.4%	29.3%	15.1
USA	85.8%	22.6%	33.2%	41.2%	15.8

Key Property Crime Data (Rate per 100,000 residents)

	Rate	Burglary	Larceny, Theft	Vehicle Theft
Area	2,596.8	459.0	1,992.6	145.2
USA	3,413.6	806.6	2,388.0	262.7

Key Violent Crime Data (Rate per 100,000 residents)

	Rate	Murder	Rape	Robbery	Aggravated Assault
Area	247.9	2.8	15.5	103.3	126.2
USA	432.8	4.7	34.7	111.6	285.6

Key Economic Data (Family income, unemployment)

	$25k-$75k	$75k-$150k	>$150k	Unemployment 03/2009	Unemployment 03/2010
Area	42.9%	34.9%	10.8%	8.6%	10.2%
USA	45.8%	29.5%	8.5%	9.0%	10.1

Key Household Data

	Population Age 0-17	Children w/Married Parents	Children w/Single Mother	Stay-at-home Mothers	Births to Single Women
Area	22.6%	67.9%	23.3%	26.7%	32.3%
USA	24.0%	65.6%	25.5%	27.9%	35.3%

Key Housing Data

	Owner Occupied	Median Year Built	Median Home Value	Home Value Growth, 2005-2010	Median List Price, 4-bedroom Home
Area	73.7%	1967	$226,200	4.7%	$315,500
USA	67.8%	1976	$187,045	3.1%	$288,846

Altoona, PA
125,174

	Score	Rank
Overall	67.25	98
LDS Culture	37.77	59
Education	69.41	192
Crime	74.53	54
Economic	57.70	262
Health	47.33	92
Household	69.14	337
Housing	75.33	279

Key LDS Culture Data

	Positive	Negative	Ratio Pos:Neg	Commute>59 minutes	Commute<15 minutes
Area	1,516	119	12.7	2.6%	44.5%
USA	4,292	251	20.1	5.5%	34.1%

Key Education Data

	HS Grad	Some Coll.	College Degree	Free/Reduced Lunch	Students per Teacher
Area	88.3%	16.7%	24.6%	40.9%	13.6
USA	85.8%	22.6%	33.2%	41.2%	15.8

Key Property Crime Data (Rate per 100,000 residents)

	Rate	Burglary	Larceny, Theft	Vehicle Theft
Area	2,124.2	518.3	1,517.2	88.8
USA	3,413.6	806.6	2,388.0	262.7

Key Violent Crime Data (Rate per 100,000 residents)

	Rate	Murder	Rape	Robbery	Aggravated Assault
Area	296.7	3.2	24.0	72.8	196.7
USA	432.8	4.7	34.7	111.6	285.6

Key Economic Data (Family income, unemployment)

	$25k-$75k	$75k-$150k	>$150k	Unemployment 03/2009	Unemployment 03/2010
Area	51.8%	24.0%	3.9%	7.4%	8.6%
USA	45.8%	29.5%	8.5%	9.0%	10.1

Key Household Data

	Population Age 0-17	Children w/Married Parents	Children w/Single Mother	Stay-at-home Mothers	Births to Single Women
Area	21.2%	57.5%	29.9%	27.0%	59.3%
USA	24.0%	65.6%	25.5%	27.9%	35.3%

Key Housing Data

	Owner Occupied	Median Year Built	Median Home Value	Home Value Growth, 2005-2010	Median List Price, 4-bedroom Home
Area	71.9%	1956	$96,800	3.8%	
USA	67.8%	1976	$187,045	3.1%	$288,846

Amarillo, TX
242,640

	Score	Rank
Overall	58.52	277
LDS Culture	34.58	82
Education	66.23	230
Crime	35.71	316
Economic	63.04	183
Health	31.11	342
Household	56.17	257
Housing	88.40	74

Key LDS Culture Data

	Positive	Negative	Ratio Pos:Neg	Commute>59 minutes	Commute<15 minutes
Area	1,230	87	14.1	1.9%	44.3%
USA	4,292	251	20.1	5.5%	34.1%

Key Education Data

	HS Grad	Some Coll.	College Degree	Free/Reduced Lunch	Students per Teacher
Area	83.9%	29.6%	27.7%	52.5%	14.1
USA	85.8%	22.6%	33.2%	41.2%	15.8

Key Property Crime Data (Rate per 100,000 residents)

	Rate	Burglary	Larceny, Theft	Vehicle Theft	
Area	4,555.5	1,075.3	3,150.6	329.6	
USA	3,413.6	806.6	2,388.0	262.7	

Key Violent Crime Data (Rate per 100,000 residents)

	Rate	Murder	Rape	Robbery	Aggravated Assault
Area	638.0	6.1	54.9	134.7	442.2
USA	432.8	4.7	34.7	111.6	285.6

Key Economic Data (Family income, unemployment)

	$25k-$75k	$75k-$150k	>$150k	Unemployment 03/2009	Unemployment 03/2010
Area	46.8%	27.0%	9.0%	4.8%	5.6%
USA	45.8%	29.5%	8.5%	9.0%	10.1

Key Household Data

	Population Age 0-17	Children w/Married Parents	Children w/Single Mother	Stay-at-home Mothers	Births to Single Women
Area	26.4%	61.7%	28.7%	27.3%	37.9%
USA	24.0%	65.6%	25.5%	27.9%	35.3%

Key Housing Data

	Owner Occupied	Median Year Built	Median Home Value	Home Value Growth, 2005-2010	Median List Price, 4-bedroom Home
Area	64.8%	1970	$110,000	3.5%	$234,000
USA	67.8%	1976	$187,045	3.1%	$288,846

Ames, IA
86,754

	Score	Rank
Overall	77.08	10
LDS Culture	43.25	29
Education	97.04	6
Crime	70.06	75
Economic	68.26	105
Health	54.48	12
Household	83.95	38
Housing	77.23	257

Key LDS Culture Data

	Positive	Negative	Ratio Pos:Neg	Commute>59 minutes	Commute<15 minutes
Area	1,911	137	13.9	2.2%	54.2%
USA	4,292	251	20.1	5.5%	34.1%

Key Education Data

	HS Grad	Some Coll.	College Degree	Free/Reduced Lunch	Students per Teacher
Area	93.7%	20.1%	53.8%	17.8%	14.6
USA	85.8%	22.6%	33.2%	41.2%	15.8

Key Property Crime Data (Rate per 100,000 residents)

	Rate	Burglary	Larceny, Theft	Vehicle Theft
Area	2,686.0	583.5	1,984.4	118.1
USA	3,413.6	806.6	2,388.0	262.7

Key Violent Crime Data (Rate per 100,000 residents)

	Rate	Murder	Rape	Robbery	Aggravated Assault
Area	286.5	5.8	44.4	11.7	224.5
USA	432.8	4.7	34.7	111.6	285.6

Key Economic Data (Family income, unemployment)

	$25k-$75k	$75k-$150k	>$150k	Unemployment 03/2009	Unemployment 03/2010
Area	36.3%	42.0%	9.4%	4.0%	5.4%
USA	45.8%	29.5%	8.5%	9.0%	10.1

Key Household Data

	Population Age 0-17	Children w/Married Parents	Children w/Single Mother	Stay-at-home Mothers	Births to Single Women
Area	17.7%	74.4%	19.1%	23.1%	17.8%
USA	24.0%	65.6%	25.5%	27.9%	35.3%

Key Housing Data

	Owner Occupied	Median Year Built	Median Home Value	Home Value Growth, 2005-2010	Median List Price, 4-bedroom Home
Area	55.3%	1972	$154,600	1.6%	
USA	67.8%	1976	$187,045	3.1%	$288,846

Anchorage, AK
364,701

	Score	Rank
Overall	**68.08**	**81**
LDS Culture	29.22	154
Education	83.43	46
Crime	28.78	338
Economic	99.44	2
Health	44.76	153
Household	72.22	130
Housing	78.72	234

Key LDS Culture Data

	Positive	Negative	Ratio Pos:Neg	Commute>59 minutes	Commute<15 minutes
Area	1,608	89	18.1	6.3%	36.1%
USA	4,292	251	20.1	5.5%	34.1%

Key Education Data

	HS Grad	Some Coll.	College Degree	Free/Reduced Lunch	Students per Teacher
Area	92.9%	28.8%	39.2%	30.4%	17.8
USA	85.8%	22.6%	33.2%	41.2%	15.8

Key Property Crime Data (Rate per 100,000 residents)

	Rate	Burglary	Larceny, Theft	Vehicle Theft
Area	3,379.3	423.9	2,687.0	268.4
USA	3,413.6	806.6	2,388.0	262.7

Key Violent Crime Data (Rate per 100,000 residents)

	Rate	Murder	Rape	Robbery	Aggravated Assault
Area	922.9	3.3	88.0	183.1	648.5
USA	432.8	4.7	34.7	111.6	285.6

Key Economic Data (Family income, unemployment)

	$25k-$75k	$75k-$150k	>$150k	Unemployment 03/2009	Unemployment 03/2010
Area	33.8%	43.3%	15.9%	7.3%	8.6%
USA	45.8%	29.5%	8.5%	9.0%	10.1

Key Household Data

	Population Age 0-17	Children w/Married Parents	Children w/Single Mother	Stay-at-home Mothers	Births to Single Women
Area	26.0%	67.0%	20.5%	29.2%	25.7%
USA	24.0%	65.6%	25.5%	27.9%	35.3%

Key Housing Data

	Owner Occupied	Median Year Built	Median Home Value	Home Value Growth, 2005-2010	Median List Price, 4-bedroom Home
Area	66.1%	1983	$260,500	5.0%	$345,000
USA	67.8%	1976	$187,045	3.1%	$288,846

Anderson, IN
131,501

	Score	Rank
Overall	59.00	266
LDS Culture	21.05	270
Education	66.56	228
Crime	74.76	51
Economic	65.81	141
Health	34.59	290
Household	37.65	361
Housing	77.93	246

Key LDS Culture Data

	Positive	Negative	Ratio Pos:Neg	Commute>59 minutes	Commute<15 minutes
Area	5,365	285	18.8	10.3%	34.5%
USA	4,292	251	20.1	5.5%	34.1%

Key Education Data

	HS Grad	Some Coll.	College Degree	Free/Reduced Lunch	Students per Teacher
Area	86.4%	19.3%	24.4%	45.9%	17.7
USA	85.8%	22.6%	33.2%	41.2%	15.8

Key Property Crime Data (Rate per 100,000 residents)

	Rate	Burglary	Larceny, Theft	Vehicle Theft	
Area	3,211.5	738.5	2,257.1	215.9	
USA	3,413.6	806.6	2,388.0	262.7	

Key Violent Crime Data (Rate per 100,000 residents)

	Rate	Murder	Rape	Robbery	Aggravated Assault
Area	181.4	3.1	24.6	67.6	86.1
USA	432.8	4.7	34.7	111.6	285.6

Key Economic Data (Family income, unemployment)

	$25k-$75k	$75k-$150k	>$150k	Unemployment 03/2009	Unemployment 03/2010
Area	51.3%	27.3%	3.5%	11.4%	11.9%
USA	45.8%	29.5%	8.5%	9.0%	10.1

Key Household Data

	Population Age 0-17	Children w/Married Parents	Children w/Single Mother	Stay-at-home Mothers	Births to Single Women
Area	22.7%	55.1%	33.2%	21.2%	49.4%
USA	24.0%	65.6%	25.5%	27.9%	35.3%

Key Housing Data

	Owner Occupied	Median Year Built	Median Home Value	Home Value Growth, 2005-2010	Median List Price, 4-bedroom Home
Area	77.0%	1963	$95,100	0.0%	
USA	67.8%	1976	$187,045	3.1%	$288,846

Anderson, SC
182,825

	Score	Rank
Overall	56.32	315
LDS Culture	30.06	145
Education	51.74	341
Crime	37.66	304
Economic	60.20	227
Health	37.46	250
Household	56.17	258
Housing	87.83	87

Key LDS Culture Data

	Positive	Negative	Ratio Pos:Neg	Commute>59 minutes	Commute<15 minutes
Area	2,434	128	19.0	2.5%	30.5%
USA	4,292	251	20.1	5.5%	34.1%

Key Education Data

	HS Grad	Some Coll.	College Degree	Free/Reduced Lunch	Students per Teacher
Area	81.5%	20.6%	27.4%	45.2%	15.0
USA	85.8%	22.6%	33.2%	41.2%	15.8

Key Property Crime Data (Rate per 100,000 residents)

	Rate	Burglary	Larceny, Theft	Vehicle Theft	
Area			3,182.4	544.5	
USA	3,413.6	806.6	2,388.0	262.7	

Key Violent Crime Data (Rate per 100,000 residents)

	Rate	Murder	Rape	Robbery	Aggravated Assault
Area	656.2	9.9	30.1	111.7	504.5
USA	432.8	4.7	34.7	111.6	285.6

Key Economic Data (Family income, unemployment)

	$25k-$75k	$75k-$150k	>$150k	Unemployment 03/2009	Unemployment 03/2010
Area	49.1%	25.7%	5.3%	11.7%	12.5%
USA	45.8%	29.5%	8.5%	9.0%	10.1

Key Household Data

	Population Age 0-17	Children w/Married Parents	Children w/Single Mother	Stay-at-home Mothers	Births to Single Women
Area	23.8%	66.0%	28.5%	23.9%	47.9%
USA	24.0%	65.6%	25.5%	27.9%	35.3%

Key Housing Data

	Owner Occupied	Median Year Built	Median Home Value	Home Value Growth, 2005-2010	Median List Price, 4-bedroom Home
Area	76.6%	1983	$122,600	3.2%	
USA	67.8%	1976	$187,045	3.1%	$288,846

Ann Arbor, MI
347,376

	Score	Rank
Overall	**66.99**	**104**
LDS Culture	17.29	317
Education	86.99	32
Crime	61.35	143
Economic	69.71	90
Health	36.88	262
Household	81.48	57
Housing	75.85	275

Key LDS Culture Data

	Positive	Negative	Ratio Pos:Neg	Commute>59 minutes	Commute<15 minutes
Area	11,069	760	14.6	5.4%	29.2%
USA	4,292	251	20.1	5.5%	34.1%

Key Education Data

	HS Grad	Some Coll.	College Degree	Free/Reduced Lunch	Students per Teacher
Area	93.7%	20.2%	57.7%	21.8%	17.4
USA	85.8%	22.6%	33.2%	41.2%	15.8

Key Property Crime Data (Rate per 100,000 residents)

	Rate	Burglary	Larceny, Theft	Vehicle Theft
Area	2,719.1	656.7	1,886.9	175.5
USA	3,413.6	806.6	2,388.0	262.7

Key Violent Crime Data (Rate per 100,000 residents)

	Rate	Murder	Rape	Robbery	Aggravated Assault
Area	376.7	3.1	36.5	84.5	252.6
USA	432.8	4.7	34.7	111.6	285.6

Key Economic Data (Family income, unemployment)

	$25k-$75k	$75k-$150k	>$150k	Unemployment 03/2009	Unemployment 03/2010
Area	32.1%	38.9%	16.5%	7.8%	9.6%
USA	45.8%	29.5%	8.5%	9.0%	10.1

Key Household Data

	Population Age 0-17	Children w/Married Parents	Children w/Single Mother	Stay-at-home Mothers	Births to Single Women
Area	21.4%	72.4%	20.2%	28.7%	30.3%
USA	24.0%	65.6%	25.5%	27.9%	35.3%

Key Housing Data

	Owner Occupied	Median Year Built	Median Home Value	Home Value Growth, 2005-2010	Median List Price, 4-bedroom Home
Area	62.5%	1977	$223,500	-3.2%	$275,000
USA	67.8%	1976	$187,045	3.1%	$288,846

93

Anniston-Oxford, AL
113,419

	Score	Rank
Overall	58.35	283
LDS Culture	56.11	11
Education	57.42	312
Crime	38.55	299
Economic	56.48	277
Health	33.58	305
Household	46.30	323
Housing	85.70	126

Key LDS Culture Data

	Positive	Negative	Ratio Pos:Neg	Commute>59 minutes	Commute<15 minutes
Area	1,712	32	53.5	4.6%	30.4%
USA	4,292	251	20.1	5.5%	34.1%

Key Education Data

	HS Grad	Some Coll.	College Degree	Free/Reduced Lunch	Students per Teacher
Area	80.4%	24.8%	21.5%	53.5%	15.5
USA	85.8%	22.6%	33.2%	41.2%	15.8

Key Property Crime Data (Rate per 100,000 residents)

	Rate	Burglary	Larceny, Theft	Vehicle Theft
Area		1,554.7	3,474.2	404.8
USA	3,413.6	806.6	2,388.0	262.7

Key Violent Crime Data (Rate per 100,000 residents)

	Rate	Murder	Rape	Robbery	Aggravated Assault
Area		11.0	40.6	244.9	445.3
USA	432.8	4.7	34.7	111.6	285.6

Key Economic Data (Family income, unemployment)

	$25k-$75k	$75k-$150k	>$150k	Unemployment 03/2009	Unemployment 03/2010
Area	47.5%	25.4%	2.8%	9.4%	11.0%
USA	45.8%	29.5%	8.5%	9.0%	10.1

Key Household Data

	Population Age 0-17	Children w/Married Parents	Children w/Single Mother	Stay-at-home Mothers	Births to Single Women
Area	23.1%	60.1%	28.6%	27.7%	40.7%
USA	24.0%	65.6%	25.5%	27.9%	35.3%

Key Housing Data

	Owner Occupied	Median Year Built	Median Home Value	Home Value Growth, 2005-2010	Median List Price, 4-bedroom Home
Area	74.8%	1977	$99,800	4.0%	
USA	67.8%	1976	$187,045	3.1%	$288,846

Appleton, WI
219,720

	Score	Rank
Overall	75.54	16
LDS Culture	19.24	296
Education	87.01	31
Crime	87.52	10
Economic	77.38	25
Health	39.16	224
Household	87.04	26
Housing	87.04	97

Key LDS Culture Data
	Positive	Negative	Ratio Pos:Neg	Commute>59 minutes	Commute<15 minutes
Area	2,680	396	6.8	3.4%	36.5%
USA	4,292	251	20.1	5.5%	34.1%

Key Education Data
	HS Grad	Some Coll.	College Degree	Free/Reduced Lunch	Students per Teacher
Area	92.1%	20.0%	36.5%	21.7%	15.5
USA	85.8%	22.6%	33.2%	41.2%	15.8

Key Property Crime Data (Rate per 100,000 residents)
	Rate	Burglary	Larceny, Theft	Vehicle Theft	
Area	2,524.2	301.9	2,150.0	72.3	
USA	3,413.6	806.6	2,388.0	262.7	

Key Violent Crime Data (Rate per 100,000 residents)
	Rate	Murder	Rape	Robbery	Aggravated Assault
Area	115.5	0.9	18.6	10.9	85.0
USA	432.8	4.7	34.7	111.6	285.6

Key Economic Data (Family income, unemployment)
	$25k-$75k	$75k-$150k	>$150k	Unemployment 03/2009	Unemployment 03/2010
Area	47.4%	35.6%	8.4%	9.2%	9.2%
USA	45.8%	29.5%	8.5%	9.0%	10.1

Key Household Data
	Population Age 0-17	Children w/Married Parents	Children w/Single Mother	Stay-at-home Mothers	Births to Single Women
Area	25.3%	76.9%	15.1%	19.9%	17.9%
USA	24.0%	65.6%	25.5%	27.9%	35.3%

Key Housing Data
	Owner Occupied	Median Year Built	Median Home Value	Home Value Growth, 2005-2010	Median List Price, 4-bedroom Home
Area	75.2%	1975	$157,800	1.9%	$199,900
USA	67.8%	1976	$187,045	3.1%	$288,846

Asheville, NC
409,092

	Score	Rank
Overall	66.44	113
LDS Culture	34.39	86
Education	65.72	236
Crime	68.53	86
Economic	63.70	172
Health	41.11	193
Household	77.78	76
Housing	74.81	284

Key LDS Culture Data

	Positive	Negative	Ratio Pos:Neg	Commute>59 minutes	Commute<15 minutes
Area	2,892	100	28.9	4.2%	31.2%
USA	4,292	251	20.1	5.5%	34.1%

Key Education Data

	HS Grad	Some Coll.	College Degree	Free/Reduced Lunch	Students per Teacher
Area	86.1%	22.7%	36.9%	39.6%	14.5
USA	85.8%	22.6%	33.2%	41.2%	15.8

Key Property Crime Data (Rate per 100,000 residents)

	Rate	Burglary	Larceny, Theft	Vehicle Theft
Area	2,868.3	821.5	1,815.7	231.1
USA	3,413.6	806.6	2,388.0	262.7

Key Violent Crime Data (Rate per 100,000 residents)

	Rate	Murder	Rape	Robbery	Aggravated Assault
Area	284.0	2.2	23.2	87.8	170.8
USA	432.8	4.7	34.7	111.6	285.6

Key Economic Data (Family income, unemployment)

	$25k-$75k	$75k-$150k	>$150k	Unemployment 03/2009	Unemployment 03/2010
Area	51.6%	23.4%	6.8%	9.2%	9.4%
USA	45.8%	29.5%	8.5%	9.0%	10.1

Key Household Data

	Population Age 0-17	Children w/Married Parents	Children w/Single Mother	Stay-at-home Mothers	Births to Single Women
Area	21.1%	65.6%	24.3%	33.7%	22.3%
USA	24.0%	65.6%	25.5%	27.9%	35.3%

Key Housing Data

	Owner Occupied	Median Year Built	Median Home Value	Home Value Growth, 2005-2010	Median List Price, 4-bedroom Home
Area	69.8%	1981	$191,500	6.3%	$422,500
USA	67.8%	1976	$187,045	3.1%	$288,846

Athens-Clarke County, GA

194,988

	Score	Rank
Overall	**61.84**	**201**
LDS Culture	24.36	231
Education	77.11	104
Crime	46.04	245
Economic	63.87	170
Health	40.98	198
Household	58.64	234
Housing	85.57	131

Key LDS Culture Data

	Positive	Negative	Ratio Pos:Neg	Commute>59 minutes	Commute<15 minutes
Area	2,302	102	22.6	6.3%	39.3%
USA	4,292	251	20.1	5.5%	34.1%

Key Education Data

	HS Grad	Some Coll.	College Degree	Free/Reduced Lunch	Students per Teacher
Area	82.0%	18.2%	38.2%	51.7%	13.1
USA	85.8%	22.6%	33.2%	41.2%	15.8

Key Property Crime Data (Rate per 100,000 residents)

	Rate	Burglary	Larceny, Theft	Vehicle Theft
Area	4,740.4	1,210.2	3,234.8	295.4
USA	3,413.6	806.6	2,388.0	262.7

Key Violent Crime Data (Rate per 100,000 residents)

	Rate	Murder	Rape	Robbery	Aggravated Assault
Area	409.6	2.6	33.8	132.6	240.5
USA	432.8	4.7	34.7	111.6	285.6

Key Economic Data (Family income, unemployment)

	$25k-$75k	$75k-$150k	>$150k	Unemployment 03/2009	Unemployment 03/2010
Area	44.1%	25.4%	10.3%	6.9%	7.9%
USA	45.8%	29.5%	8.5%	9.0%	10.1

Key Household Data

	Population Age 0-17	Children w/Married Parents	Children w/Single Mother	Stay-at-home Mothers	Births to Single Women
Area	22.4%	58.7%	35.3%	35.2%	46.4%
USA	24.0%	65.6%	25.5%	27.9%	35.3%

Key Housing Data

	Owner Occupied	Median Year Built	Median Home Value	Home Value Growth, 2005-2010	Median List Price, 4-bedroom Home
Area	59.1%	1984	$168,900	3.1%	
USA	67.8%	1976	$187,045	3.1%	$288,846

Atlanta-Sandy Springs-Marietta, GA
5,368,070

	Score	Rank
Overall	64.56	147
LDS Culture	22.49	250
Education	73.56	141
Crime	44.29	260
Economic	67.82	114
Health	43.48	164
Household	72.22	131
Housing	90.10	53

Key LDS Culture Data

	Positive	Negative	Ratio Pos:Neg	Commute>59 minutes	Commute<15 minutes
Area	20,106	790	25.5	12.2%	19.1%
USA	4,292	251	20.1	5.5%	34.1%

Key Education Data

	HS Grad	Some Coll.	College Degree	Free/Reduced Lunch	Students per Teacher
Area	87.3%	20.4%	41.2%	45.6%	14.2
USA	85.8%	22.6%	33.2%	41.2%	15.8

Key Property Crime Data (Rate per 100,000 residents)

	Rate	Burglary	Larceny, Theft	Vehicle Theft	
Area	3,995.0	1,077.2	2,418.0	499.8	
USA	3,413.6	806.6	2,388.0	262.7	

Key Violent Crime Data (Rate per 100,000 residents)

	Rate	Murder	Rape	Robbery	Aggravated Assault
Area	500.9	7.4	19.8	218.4	255.4
USA	432.8	4.7	34.7	111.6	285.6

Key Economic Data (Family income, unemployment)

	$25k-$75k	$75k-$150k	>$150k	Unemployment 03/2009	Unemployment 03/2010
Area	40.1%	32.7%	14.2%	8.8%	10.4%
USA	45.8%	29.5%	8.5%	9.0%	10.1

Key Household Data

	Population Age 0-17	Children w/Married Parents	Children w/Single Mother	Stay-at-home Mothers	Births to Single Women
Area	26.8%	65.7%	26.8%	30.0%	35.6%
USA	24.0%	65.6%	25.5%	27.9%	35.3%

Key Housing Data

	Owner Occupied	Median Year Built	Median Home Value	Home Value Growth, 2005-2010	Median List Price, 4-bedroom Home
Area	68.6%	1990	$199,300	1.5%	$214,600
USA	67.8%	1976	$187,045	3.1%	$288,846

Atlantic City-Hammonton, NJ

270,681

	Score	Rank
Overall	54.43	337
LDS Culture	11.28	353
Education	72.79	154
Crime	47.31	238
Economic	60.20	228
Health	45.09	145
Household	43.21	346
Housing	69.13	330

Key LDS Culture Data

	Positive	Negative	Ratio Pos:Neg	Commute>59 minutes	Commute<15 minutes
Area	2,412	189	12.8	5.9%	28.1%
USA	4,292	251	20.1	5.5%	34.1%

Key Education Data

	HS Grad	Some Coll.	College Degree	Free/Reduced Lunch	Students per Teacher
Area	83.0%	18.7%	31.5%	39.3%	14.1
USA	85.8%	22.6%	33.2%	41.2%	15.8

Key Property Crime Data (Rate per 100,000 residents)

	Rate	Burglary	Larceny, Theft	Vehicle Theft
Area			2,596.1	167.0
USA	3,413.6	806.6	2,388.0	262.7

Key Violent Crime Data (Rate per 100,000 residents)

	Rate	Murder	Rape	Robbery	Aggravated Assault
Area	486.0	7.7	24.7	193.9	259.8
USA	432.8	4.7	34.7	111.6	285.6

Key Economic Data (Family income, unemployment)

	$25k-$75k	$75k-$150k	>$150k	Unemployment 03/2009	Unemployment 03/2010
Area	41.0%	34.6%	8.6%	11.9%	13.6%
USA	45.8%	29.5%	8.5%	9.0%	10.1

Key Household Data

	Population Age 0-17	Children w/Married Parents	Children w/Single Mother	Stay-at-home Mothers	Births to Single Women
Area	23.8%	60.0%	32.3%	16.8%	44.1%
USA	24.0%	65.6%	25.5%	27.9%	35.3%

Key Housing Data

	Owner Occupied	Median Year Built	Median Home Value	Home Value Growth, 2005-2010	Median List Price, 4-bedroom Home
Area	72.3%	1977	$273,000	4.5%	$369,900
USA	67.8%	1976	$187,045	3.1%	$288,846

Auburn-Opelika, AL
133,010

	Score	Rank
Overall	67.79	90
LDS Culture	40.52	44
Education	73.72	139
Crime	41.95	273
Economic	66.59	130
Health	33.58	306
Household	85.19	31
Housing	93.15	23

Key LDS Culture Data
	Positive	Negative	Ratio Pos:Neg	Commute>59 minutes	Commute<15 minutes
Area	1,450	47	30.9	2.4%	36.6%
USA	4,292	251	20.1	5.5%	34.1%

Key Education Data
	HS Grad	Some Coll.	College Degree	Free/Reduced Lunch	Students per Teacher
Area	85.6%	20.7%	37.5%	41.4%	14.2
USA	85.8%	22.6%	33.2%	41.2%	15.8

Key Property Crime Data (Rate per 100,000 residents)
	Rate	Burglary	Larceny, Theft	Vehicle Theft
Area	4,835.9	1,618.2	3,060.3	157.4
USA	3,413.6	806.6	2,388.0	262.7

Key Violent Crime Data (Rate per 100,000 residents)
	Rate	Murder	Rape	Robbery	Aggravated Assault
Area	464.6	4.5	48.9	137.8	273.3
USA	432.8	4.7	34.7	111.6	285.6

Key Economic Data (Family income, unemployment)
	$25k-$75k	$75k-$150k	>$150k	Unemployment 03/2009	Unemployment 03/2010
Area	47.1%	26.0%	8.4%	7.8%	9.3%
USA	45.8%	29.5%	8.5%	9.0%	10.1

Key Household Data
	Population Age 0-17	Children w/Married Parents	Children w/Single Mother	Stay-at-home Mothers	Births to Single Women
Area	22.2%	70.7%	23.9%	28.3%	28.7%
USA	24.0%	65.6%	25.5%	27.9%	35.3%

Key Housing Data
	Owner Occupied	Median Year Built	Median Home Value	Home Value Growth, 2005-2010	Median List Price, 4-bedroom Home
Area	65.7%	1991	$145,700	4.8%	
USA	67.8%	1976	$187,045	3.1%	$288,846

Augusta-Richmond County, GA-SC
537,309

	Score	Rank
Overall	57.16	300
LDS Culture	22.01	259
Education	54.29	330
Crime	41.17	277
Economic	55.42	288
Health	45.94	132
Household	49.38	301
Housing	98.35	2

Key LDS Culture Data

	Positive	Negative	Ratio Pos:Neg	Commute>59 minutes	Commute<15 minutes
Area	2,867	144	19.9	4.3%	25.8%
USA	4,292	251	20.1	5.5%	34.1%

Key Education Data

	HS Grad	Some Coll.	College Degree	Free/Reduced Lunch	Students per Teacher
Area	82.0%	20.9%	29.4%	54.7%	14.8
USA	85.8%	22.6%	33.2%	41.2%	15.8

Key Property Crime Data (Rate per 100,000 residents)

	Rate	Burglary	Larceny, Theft	Vehicle Theft
Area	4,836.8	1,177.0	3,177.4	482.5
USA	3,413.6	806.6	2,388.0	262.7

Key Violent Crime Data (Rate per 100,000 residents)

	Rate	Murder	Rape	Robbery	Aggravated Assault
Area		7.7	47.6	191.0	
USA	432.8	4.7	34.7	111.6	285.6

Key Economic Data (Family income, unemployment)

	$25k-$75k	$75k-$150k	>$150k	Unemployment 03/2009	Unemployment 03/2010
Area	45.8%	24.7%	8.1%	8.7%	9.2%
USA	45.8%	29.5%	8.5%	9.0%	10.1

Key Household Data

	Population Age 0-17	Children w/Married Parents	Children w/Single Mother	Stay-at-home Mothers	Births to Single Women
Area	25.5%	57.0%	35.7%	32.4%	59.4%
USA	24.0%	65.6%	25.5%	27.9%	35.3%

Key Housing Data

	Owner Occupied	Median Year Built	Median Home Value	Home Value Growth, 2005-2010	Median List Price, 4-bedroom Home
Area	70.1%	1982	$120,700	5.3%	$207,000
USA	67.8%	1976	$187,045	3.1%	$288,846

Austin-Round Rock, TX
1,650,887

	Score	Rank
Overall	**65.49**	**133**
LDS Culture	14.27	342
Education	77.86	96
Crime	55.89	165
Economic	68.15	107
Health	25.14	359
Household	81.48	58
Housing	97.14	7

Key LDS Culture Data

	Positive	Negative	Ratio Pos:Neg	Commute>59 minutes	Commute<15 minutes
Area	6,894	427	16.1	6.4%	24.4%
USA	4,292	251	20.1	5.5%	34.1%

Key Education Data

	HS Grad	Some Coll.	College Degree	Free/Reduced Lunch	Students per Teacher
Area	86.5%	21.7%	45.0%	43.1%	14.4
USA	85.8%	22.6%	33.2%	41.2%	15.8

Key Property Crime Data (Rate per 100,000 residents)

	Rate	Burglary	Larceny, Theft	Vehicle Theft	
Area	3,904.4	788.7	2,904.5	211.1	
USA	3,413.6	806.6	2,388.0	262.7	

Key Violent Crime Data (Rate per 100,000 residents)

	Rate	Murder	Rape	Robbery	Aggravated Assault
Area	345.5	2.0	28.8	93.9	220.8
USA	432.8	4.7	34.7	111.6	285.6

Key Economic Data (Family income, unemployment)

	$25k-$75k	$75k-$150k	>$150k	Unemployment 03/2009	Unemployment 03/2010
Area	38.2%	34.3%	14.8%	6.6%	7.1%
USA	45.8%	29.5%	8.5%	9.0%	10.1

Key Household Data

	Population Age 0-17	Children w/Married Parents	Children w/Single Mother	Stay-at-home Mothers	Births to Single Women
Area	26.0%	69.3%	22.6%	32.4%	28.3%
USA	24.0%	65.6%	25.5%	27.9%	35.3%

Key Housing Data

	Owner Occupied	Median Year Built	Median Home Value	Home Value Growth, 2005-2010	Median List Price, 4-bedroom Home
Area	60.6%	1991	$188,500	5.7%	$274,000
USA	67.8%	1976	$187,045	3.1%	$288,846

Bakersfield, CA
800,458

	Score	Rank
Overall	57.05	304
LDS Culture	19.49	289
Education	70.98	173
Crime	41.16	278
Economic	39.69	359
Health	48.59	59
Household	66.67	167
Housing	79.25	222

Key LDS Culture Data

	Positive	Negative	Ratio Pos:Neg	Commute>59 minutes	Commute<15 minutes
Area	2,132	125	17.1	6.8%	34.5%
USA	4,292	251	20.1	5.5%	34.1%

Key Education Data

	HS Grad	Some Coll.	College Degree	Free/Reduced Lunch	Students per Teacher
Area	70.2%	23.8%	22.0%	59.6%	18.3
USA	85.8%	22.6%	33.2%	41.2%	15.8

Key Property Crime Data (Rate per 100,000 residents)

	Rate	Burglary	Larceny, Theft	Vehicle Theft	
Area	3,967.1	1,150.3	2,166.1	650.6	
USA	3,413.6	806.6	2,388.0	262.7	

Key Violent Crime Data (Rate per 100,000 residents)

	Rate	Murder	Rape	Robbery	Aggravated Assault
Area	575.8	7.1	29.0	160.3	379.5
USA	432.8	4.7	34.7	111.6	285.6

Key Economic Data (Family income, unemployment)

	$25k-$75k	$75k-$150k	>$150k	Unemployment 03/2009	Unemployment 03/2010
Area	44.3%	24.2%	7.7%	15.2%	18.3%
USA	45.8%	29.5%	8.5%	9.0%	10.1

Key Household Data

	Population Age 0-17	Children w/Married Parents	Children w/Single Mother	Stay-at-home Mothers	Births to Single Women
Area	29.8%	62.3%	24.7%	38.3%	38.3%
USA	24.0%	65.6%	25.5%	27.9%	35.3%

Key Housing Data

	Owner Occupied	Median Year Built	Median Home Value	Home Value Growth, 2005-2010	Median List Price, 4-bedroom Home
Area	59.6%	1983	$222,400	1.0%	$219,900
USA	67.8%	1976	$187,045	3.1%	$288,846

Baltimore-Towson, MD
2,667,117

	Score	Rank
Overall	55.82	323
LDS Culture	8.87	357
Education	74.69	131
Crime	34.94	321
Economic	68.32	103
Health	44.47	155
Household	56.79	249
Housing	69.88	326

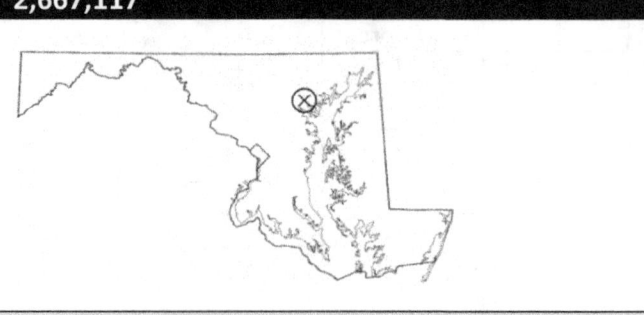

Key LDS Culture Data

	Positive	Negative	Ratio Pos:Neg	Commute>59 minutes	Commute<15 minutes
Area	15,695	1044	15.0	11.2%	19.8%
USA	4,292	251	20.1	5.5%	34.1%

Key Education Data

	HS Grad	Some Coll.	College Degree	Free/Reduced Lunch	Students per Teacher
Area	87.7%	20.3%	40.3%	33.9%	14.3
USA	85.8%	22.6%	33.2%	41.2%	15.8

Key Property Crime Data (Rate per 100,000 residents)

	Rate	Burglary	Larceny, Theft	Vehicle Theft
Area	3,572.3	717.1	2,435.6	419.6
USA	3,413.6	806.6	2,388.0	262.7

Key Violent Crime Data (Rate per 100,000 residents)

	Rate	Murder	Rape	Robbery	Aggravated Assault
Area	761.0	11.3	20.1	268.4	461.2
USA	432.8	4.7	34.7	111.6	285.6

Key Economic Data (Family income, unemployment)

	$25k-$75k	$75k-$150k	>$150k	Unemployment 03/2009	Unemployment 03/2010
Area	35.3%	36.6%	17.7%	7.1%	8.0%
USA	45.8%	29.5%	8.5%	9.0%	10.1

Key Household Data

	Population Age 0-17	Children w/Married Parents	Children w/Single Mother	Stay-at-home Mothers	Births to Single Women
Area	23.6%	64.4%	28.1%	24.4%	37.1%
USA	24.0%	65.6%	25.5%	27.9%	35.3%

Key Housing Data

	Owner Occupied	Median Year Built	Median Home Value	Home Value Growth, 2005-2010	Median List Price, 4-bedroom Home
Area	67.9%	1973	$310,600	5.2%	$399,900
USA	67.8%	1976	$187,045	3.1%	$288,846

Bangor, ME
148,651

	Score	Rank
Overall	70.55	45
LDS Culture	45.34	26
Education	70.95	174
Crime	84.18	19
Economic	64.65	156
Health	55.64	10
Household	56.17	259
Housing	75.44	278

Key LDS Culture Data

	Positive	Negative	Ratio Pos:Neg	Commute>59 minutes	Commute<15 minutes
Area	1,074	26	41.3	7.2%	36.4%
USA	4,292	251	20.1	5.5%	34.1%

Key Education Data

	HS Grad	Some Coll.	College Degree	Free/Reduced Lunch	Students per Teacher
Area	89.1%	22.3%	30.9%	37.9%	8.6
USA	85.8%	22.6%	33.2%	41.2%	15.8

Key Property Crime Data (Rate per 100,000 residents)

	Rate	Burglary	Larceny, Theft	Vehicle Theft
Area	3,250.1	550.4	2,595.4	104.3
USA	3,413.6	806.6	2,388.0	262.7

Key Violent Crime Data (Rate per 100,000 residents)

	Rate	Murder	Rape	Robbery	Aggravated Assault
Area	76.0	1.3	9.4	25.6	39.7
USA	432.8	4.7	34.7	111.6	285.6

Key Economic Data (Family income, unemployment)

	$25k-$75k	$75k-$150k	>$150k	Unemployment 03/2009	Unemployment 03/2010
Area	51.2%	25.5%	4.9%	8.1%	8.2%
USA	45.8%	29.5%	8.5%	9.0%	10.1

Key Household Data

	Population Age 0-17	Children w/Married Parents	Children w/Single Mother	Stay-at-home Mothers	Births to Single Women
Area	20.2%	64.8%	23.7%	22.3%	32.4%
USA	24.0%	65.6%	25.5%	27.9%	35.3%

Key Housing Data

	Owner Occupied	Median Year Built	Median Home Value	Home Value Growth, 2005-2010	Median List Price, 4-bedroom Home
Area	67.6%	1974	$136,200	4.0%	
USA	67.8%	1976	$187,045	3.1%	$288,846

Barnstable Town, MA
221,049

	Score	Rank
Overall	65.30	136
LDS Culture	15.89	331
Education	87.23	29
Crime	53.46	185
Economic	77.65	23
Health	34.63	289
Household	76.54	84
Housing	73.31	304

Key LDS Culture Data

	Positive	Negative	Ratio Pos:Neg	Commute>59 minutes	Commute<15 minutes
Area	2,323	179	13.0	10.6%	36.2%
USA	4,292	251	20.1	5.5%	34.1%

Key Education Data

	HS Grad	Some Coll.	College Degree	Free/Reduced Lunch	Students per Teacher
Area	96.1%	20.2%	50.5%	18.2%	12.4
USA	85.8%	22.6%	33.2%	41.2%	15.8

Key Property Crime Data (Rate per 100,000 residents)

	Rate	Burglary	Larceny, Theft	Vehicle Theft	
Area	2,978.5	974.9	1,901.9	101.7	
USA	3,413.6	806.6	2,388.0	262.7	

Key Violent Crime Data (Rate per 100,000 residents)

	Rate	Murder	Rape	Robbery	Aggravated Assault
Area	434.8	0.9	35.8	42.5	355.6
USA	432.8	4.7	34.7	111.6	285.6

Key Economic Data (Family income, unemployment)

	$25k-$75k	$75k-$150k	>$150k	Unemployment 03/2009	Unemployment 03/2010
Area	41.3%	34.6%	14.9%	10.3%	11.5%
USA	45.8%	29.5%	8.5%	9.0%	10.1

Key Household Data

	Population Age 0-17	Children w/Married Parents	Children w/Single Mother	Stay-at-home Mothers	Births to Single Women
Area	17.7%	72.7%	21.6%	22.6%	30.7%
USA	24.0%	65.6%	25.5%	27.9%	35.3%

Key Housing Data

	Owner Occupied	Median Year Built	Median Home Value	Home Value Growth, 2005-2010	Median List Price, 4-bedroom Home
Area	81.2%	1978	$393,300	0.0%	
USA	67.8%	1976	$187,045	3.1%	$288,846

Baton Rouge, LA
777,650

	Score	Rank
Overall	**59.17**	**262**
LDS Culture	27.16	179
Education	63.04	269
Crime	40.27	285
Economic	59.70	232
Health	52.48	29
Household	46.30	324
Housing	90.46	49

Key LDS Culture Data

	Positive	Negative	Ratio Pos:Neg	Commute>59 minutes	Commute<15 minutes
Area	3,733	180	20.7	8.5%	24.7%
USA	4,292	251	20.1	5.5%	34.1%

Key Education Data

	HS Grad	Some Coll.	College Degree	Free/Reduced Lunch	Students per Teacher
Area	84.1%	22.3%	29.5%	61.0%	14.7
USA	85.8%	22.6%	33.2%	41.2%	15.8

Key Property Crime Data (Rate per 100,000 residents)

	Rate	Burglary	Larceny, Theft	Vehicle Theft
Area		1,099.3	2,679.5	
USA	3,413.6	806.6	2,388.0	262.7

Key Violent Crime Data (Rate per 100,000 residents)

	Rate	Murder	Rape	Robbery	Aggravated Assault
Area	622.5	13.4	20.8	182.2	406.1
USA	432.8	4.7	34.7	111.6	285.6

Key Economic Data (Family income, unemployment)

	$25k-$75k	$75k-$150k	>$150k	Unemployment 03/2009	Unemployment 03/2010
Area	41.2%	31.6%	8.9%	5.6%	6.0%
USA	45.8%	29.5%	8.5%	9.0%	10.1

Key Household Data

	Population Age 0-17	Children w/Married Parents	Children w/Single Mother	Stay-at-home Mothers	Births to Single Women
Area	25.5%	59.7%	30.7%	27.0%	59.2%
USA	24.0%	65.6%	25.5%	27.9%	35.3%

Key Housing Data

	Owner Occupied	Median Year Built	Median Home Value	Home Value Growth, 2005-2010	Median List Price, 4-bedroom Home
Area	68.3%	1981	$153,000	6.0%	$255,000
USA	67.8%	1976	$187,045	3.1%	$288,846

Battle Creek, MI
135,861

	Score	Rank
Overall	54.27	338
LDS Culture	35.22	79
Education	64.69	246
Crime	33.19	329
Economic	61.20	208
Health	36.88	263
Household	45.06	338
Housing	71.73	320

Key LDS Culture Data

	Positive	Negative	Ratio Pos:Neg	Commute>59 minutes	Commute<15 minutes
Area	2,700	136	19.9	3.5%	41.7%
USA	4,292	251	20.1	5.5%	34.1%

Key Education Data

	HS Grad	Some Coll.	College Degree	Free/Reduced Lunch	Students per Teacher
Area	88.1%	25.9%	26.5%	45.6%	15.5
USA	85.8%	22.6%	33.2%	41.2%	15.8

Key Property Crime Data (Rate per 100,000 residents)

	Rate	Burglary	Larceny, Theft	Vehicle Theft
Area	4,240.2	1,140.4	2,938.7	161.1
USA	3,413.6	806.6	2,388.0	262.7

Key Violent Crime Data (Rate per 100,000 residents)

	Rate	Murder	Rape	Robbery	Aggravated Assault
Area	729.5	3.7	78.3	117.5	529.9
USA	432.8	4.7	34.7	111.6	285.6

Key Economic Data (Family income, unemployment)

	$25k-$75k	$75k-$150k	>$150k	Unemployment 03/2009	Unemployment 03/2010
Area	51.5%	24.6%	5.7%	11.3%	13.2%
USA	45.8%	29.5%	8.5%	9.0%	10.1

Key Household Data

	Population Age 0-17	Children w/Married Parents	Children w/Single Mother	Stay-at-home Mothers	Births to Single Women
Area	23.9%	59.7%	28.3%	27.0%	45.7%
USA	24.0%	65.6%	25.5%	27.9%	35.3%

Key Housing Data

	Owner Occupied	Median Year Built	Median Home Value	Home Value Growth, 2005-2010	Median List Price, 4-bedroom Home
Area	69.7%	1957	$113,200	-0.6%	
USA	67.8%	1976	$187,045	3.1%	$288,846

Bay City, MI
107,495

	Score	Rank
Overall	60.41	233
LDS Culture	25.93	197
Education	63.70	260
Crime	67.45	97
Economic	63.59	174
Health	36.88	264
Household	56.79	250
Housing	73.06	308

Key LDS Culture Data

	Positive	Negative	Ratio Pos:Neg	Commute>59 minutes	Commute<15 minutes
Area	2,323	162	14.3	4.7%	31.6%
USA	4,292	251	20.1	5.5%	34.1%

Key Education Data

	HS Grad	Some Coll.	College Degree	Free/Reduced Lunch	Students per Teacher
Area	88.3%	23.4%	31.0%	40.5%	18.6
USA	85.8%	22.6%	33.2%	41.2%	15.8

Key Property Crime Data (Rate per 100,000 residents)

	Rate	Burglary	Larceny, Theft	Vehicle Theft
Area	2,617.0	591.7	1,894.6	130.8
USA	3,413.6	806.6	2,388.0	262.7

Key Violent Crime Data (Rate per 100,000 residents)

	Rate	Murder	Rape	Robbery	Aggravated Assault
Area	321.7	2.8	63.0	52.7	203.2
USA	432.8	4.7	34.7	111.6	285.6

Key Economic Data (Family income, unemployment)

	$25k-$75k	$75k-$150k	>$150k	Unemployment 03/2009	Unemployment 03/2010
Area	50.8%	30.3%	5.1%	11.8%	14.6%
USA	45.8%	29.5%	8.5%	9.0%	10.1

Key Household Data

	Population Age 0-17	Children w/Married Parents	Children w/Single Mother	Stay-at-home Mothers	Births to Single Women
Area	22.1%	68.3%	23.6%	22.6%	45.3%
USA	24.0%	65.6%	25.5%	27.9%	35.3%

Key Housing Data

	Owner Occupied	Median Year Built	Median Home Value	Home Value Growth, 2005-2010	Median List Price, 4-bedroom Home
Area	77.2%	1961	$116,100	-2.2%	
USA	67.8%	1976	$187,045	3.1%	$288,846

Beaumont-Port Arthur, TX
380,260

	Score	Rank
Overall	56.07	320
LDS Culture	28.69	159
Education	54.16	332
Crime	43.12	267
Economic	55.48	287
Health	32.00	324
Household	61.73	210
Housing	84.34	153

Key LDS Culture Data

	Positive	Negative	Ratio Pos:Neg	Commute>59 minutes	Commute<15 minutes
Area	2,179	97	22.5	4.7%	34.2%
USA	4,292	251	20.1	5.5%	34.1%

Key Education Data

	HS Grad	Some Coll.	College Degree	Free/Reduced Lunch	Students per Teacher
Area	83.3%	23.9%	24.7%	52.4%	14.2
USA	85.8%	22.6%	33.2%	41.2%	15.8

Key Property Crime Data (Rate per 100,000 residents)

	Rate	Burglary	Larceny, Theft	Vehicle Theft	
Area	3,864.4	1,209.1	2,395.3	260.1	
USA	3,413.6	806.6	2,388.0	262.7	

Key Violent Crime Data (Rate per 100,000 residents)

	Rate	Murder	Rape	Robbery	Aggravated Assault
Area	541.8	4.8	44.8	159.6	332.6
USA	432.8	4.7	34.7	111.6	285.6

Key Economic Data (Family income, unemployment)

	$25k-$75k	$75k-$150k	>$150k	Unemployment 03/2009	Unemployment 03/2010
Area	44.0%	29.1%	7.8%	8.8%	10.8%
USA	45.8%	29.5%	8.5%	9.0%	10.1

Key Household Data

	Population Age 0-17	Children w/Married Parents	Children w/Single Mother	Stay-at-home Mothers	Births to Single Women
Area	24.4%	63.3%	28.5%	36.0%	40.7%
USA	24.0%	65.6%	25.5%	27.9%	35.3%

Key Housing Data

	Owner Occupied	Median Year Built	Median Home Value	Home Value Growth, 2005-2010	Median List Price, 4-bedroom Home
Area	69.7%	1972	$89,000	4.9%	
USA	67.8%	1976	$187,045	3.1%	$288,846

Bellingham, WA
196,529

	Score	Rank
Overall	**68.77**	**70**
LDS Culture	28.25	167
Education	75.90	117
Crime	68.16	89
Economic	63.31	180
Health	47.39	90
Household	77.16	80
Housing	80.77	200

Key LDS Culture Data

	Positive	Negative	Ratio Pos:Neg	Commute>59 minutes	Commute<15 minutes
Area	1,758	80	22.0	5.0%	38.8%
USA	4,292	251	20.1	5.5%	34.1%

Key Education Data

	HS Grad	Some Coll.	College Degree	Free/Reduced Lunch	Students per Teacher
Area	91.2%	26.6%	39.4%	37.9%	19.2
USA	85.8%	22.6%	33.2%	41.2%	15.8

Key Property Crime Data (Rate per 100,000 residents)

	Rate	Burglary	Larceny, Theft	Vehicle Theft	
Area	3,658.4	741.6	2,726.7	190.2	
USA	3,413.6	806.6	2,388.0	262.7	

Key Violent Crime Data (Rate per 100,000 residents)

	Rate	Murder	Rape	Robbery	Aggravated Assault
Area	225.8	1.0	35.6	44.2	145.0
USA	432.8	4.7	34.7	111.6	285.6

Key Economic Data (Family income, unemployment)

	$25k-$75k	$75k-$150k	>$150k	Unemployment 03/2009	Unemployment 03/2010
Area	50.1%	30.9%	6.3%	8.1%	9.5%
USA	45.8%	29.5%	8.5%	9.0%	10.1

Key Household Data

	Population Age 0-17	Children w/Married Parents	Children w/Single Mother	Stay-at-home Mothers	Births to Single Women
Area	21.8%	66.0%	27.5%	27.3%	26.6%
USA	24.0%	65.6%	25.5%	27.9%	35.3%

Key Housing Data

	Owner Occupied	Median Year Built	Median Home Value	Home Value Growth, 2005-2010	Median List Price, 4-bedroom Home
Area	61.4%	1984	$308,000	6.8%	
USA	67.8%	1976	$187,045	3.1%	$288,846

Bend, OR
158,456

	Score	Rank
Overall	78.88	9
LDS Culture	35.22	78
Education	87.50	28
Crime	77.19	42
Economic	91.11	3
Health	46.31	123
Household	82.10	52
Housing	86.41	113

Key LDS Culture Data

	Positive	Negative	Ratio Pos:Neg	Commute>59 minutes	Commute<15 minutes
Area	695	35	19.9	2.7%	45.5%
USA	4,292	251	20.1	5.5%	34.1%

Key Education Data

	HS Grad	Some Coll.	College Degree	Free/Reduced Lunch	Students per Teacher
Area	92.4%	25.4%	39.7%	33.3%	20.8
USA	85.8%	22.6%	33.2%	41.2%	15.8

Key Property Crime Data (Rate per 100,000 residents)

	Rate	Burglary	Larceny, Theft	Vehicle Theft
Area	2,961.1	565.5	2,240.1	155.5
USA	3,413.6	806.6	2,388.0	262.7

Key Violent Crime Data (Rate per 100,000 residents)

	Rate	Murder	Rape	Robbery	Aggravated Assault
Area	181.2	0.0	33.2	30.1	117.9
USA	432.8	4.7	34.7	111.6	285.6

Key Economic Data (Family income, unemployment)

	$25k-$75k	$75k-$150k	>$150k	Unemployment 03/2009	Unemployment 03/2010
Area	50.5%	29.9%	7.8%	16.7%	15.8%
USA	45.8%	29.5%	8.5%	9.0%	10.1

Key Household Data

	Population Age 0-17	Children w/Married Parents	Children w/Single Mother	Stay-at-home Mothers	Births to Single Women
Area	22.3%	75.2%	15.7%	26.9%	25.7%
USA	24.0%	65.6%	25.5%	27.9%	35.3%

Key Housing Data

	Owner Occupied	Median Year Built	Median Home Value	Home Value Growth, 2005-2010	Median List Price, 4-bedroom Home
Area	67.5%	1993	$331,600	4.8%	$363,800
USA	67.8%	1976	$187,045	3.1%	$288,846

Billings, MT
151,975

	Score	Rank
Overall	**66.25**	**117**
LDS Culture	33.42	100
Education	79.31	77
Crime	67.87	92
Economic	69.87	86
Health	41.64	188
Household	53.70	279
Housing	79.00	228

Key LDS Culture Data

	Positive	Negative	Ratio Pos:Neg	Commute>59 minutes	Commute<15 minutes
Area	813	104	7.8	2.4%	40.3%
USA	4,292	251	20.1	5.5%	34.1%

Key Education Data

	HS Grad	Some Coll.	College Degree	Free/Reduced Lunch	Students per Teacher
Area	92.2%	23.4%	35.5%	29.9%	14.4
USA	85.8%	22.6%	33.2%	41.2%	15.8

Key Property Crime Data (Rate per 100,000 residents)

	Rate	Burglary	Larceny, Theft	Vehicle Theft
Area	3,428.6	518.0	2,689.3	221.4
USA	3,413.6	806.6	2,388.0	262.7

Key Violent Crime Data (Rate per 100,000 residents)

	Rate	Murder	Rape	Robbery	Aggravated Assault
Area	240.5	2.0	35.7	36.3	166.5
USA	432.8	4.7	34.7	111.6	285.6

Key Economic Data (Family income, unemployment)

	$25k-$75k	$75k-$150k	>$150k	Unemployment 03/2009	Unemployment 03/2010
Area	47.5%	29.1%	8.1%	4.5%	6.1%
USA	45.8%	29.5%	8.5%	9.0%	10.1

Key Household Data

	Population Age 0-17	Children w/Married Parents	Children w/Single Mother	Stay-at-home Mothers	Births to Single Women
Area	23.7%	63.3%	23.7%	30.2%	38.6%
USA	24.0%	65.6%	25.5%	27.9%	35.3%

Key Housing Data

	Owner Occupied	Median Year Built	Median Home Value	Home Value Growth, 2005-2010	Median List Price, 4-bedroom Home
Area	68.4%	1976	$175,600	5.5%	
USA	67.8%	1976	$187,045	3.1%	$288,846

Binghamton, NY
245,189

	Score	Rank
Overall	66.02	125
LDS Culture	28.42	163
Education	79.97	69
Crime	73.64	60
Economic	65.81	142
Health	49.20	46
Household	40.74	356
Housing	85.56	132

Key LDS Culture Data

	Positive	Negative	Ratio Pos:Neg	Commute>59 minutes	Commute<15 minutes
Area	1,301	107	12.2	3.6%	39.0%
USA	4,292	251	20.1	5.5%	34.1%

Key Education Data

	HS Grad	Some Coll.	College Degree	Free/Reduced Lunch	Students per Teacher
Area	90.0%	17.9%	37.9%	37.9%	11.8
USA	85.8%	22.6%	33.2%	41.2%	15.8

Key Property Crime Data (Rate per 100,000 residents)

	Rate	Burglary	Larceny, Theft	Vehicle Theft	
Area	2,792.5	439.2	2,294.2	59.0	
USA	3,413.6	806.6	2,388.0	262.7	

Key Violent Crime Data (Rate per 100,000 residents)

	Rate	Murder	Rape	Robbery	Aggravated Assault
Area	236.9	0.8	34.6	53.3	148.2
USA	432.8	4.7	34.7	111.6	285.6

Key Economic Data (Family income, unemployment)

	$25k-$75k	$75k-$150k	>$150k	Unemployment 03/2009	Unemployment 03/2010
Area	47.8%	27.1%	8.2%	8.4%	8.9%
USA	45.8%	29.5%	8.5%	9.0%	10.1

Key Household Data

	Population Age 0-17	Children w/Married Parents	Children w/Single Mother	Stay-at-home Mothers	Births to Single Women
Area	20.3%	59.9%	26.7%	22.4%	64.7%
USA	24.0%	65.6%	25.5%	27.9%	35.3%

Key Housing Data

	Owner Occupied	Median Year Built	Median Home Value	Home Value Growth, 2005-2010	Median List Price, 4-bedroom Home
Area	69.0%	1958	$99,300	7.0%	$174,900
USA	67.8%	1976	$187,045	3.1%	$288,846

Birmingham-Hoover, AL
1,117,348

	Score	Rank
Overall	61.44	211
LDS Culture	35.11	80
Education	66.96	222
Crime	36.77	309
Economic	64.48	158
Health	41.57	189
Household	63.58	190
Housing	85.52	133

Key LDS Culture Data

	Positive	Negative	Ratio Pos:Neg	Commute>59 minutes	Commute<15 minutes
Area	5,650	190	29.7	6.6%	22.1%
USA	4,292	251	20.1	5.5%	34.1%

Key Education Data

	HS Grad	Some Coll.	College Degree	Free/Reduced Lunch	Students per Teacher
Area	85.2%	22.5%	33.2%	43.3%	14.8
USA	85.8%	22.6%	33.2%	41.2%	15.8

Key Property Crime Data (Rate per 100,000 residents)

	Rate	Burglary	Larceny, Theft	Vehicle Theft
Area	4,738.2	1,253.6	3,093.8	390.8
USA	3,413.6	806.6	2,388.0	262.7

Key Violent Crime Data (Rate per 100,000 residents)

	Rate	Murder	Rape	Robbery	Aggravated Assault
Area	594.1	10.3	42.0	243.1	298.7
USA	432.8	4.7	34.7	111.6	285.6

Key Economic Data (Family income, unemployment)

	$25k-$75k	$75k-$150k	>$150k	Unemployment 03/2009	Unemployment 03/2010
Area	43.7%	29.6%	10.1%	8.6%	10.3%
USA	45.8%	29.5%	8.5%	9.0%	10.1

Key Household Data

	Population Age 0-17	Children w/Married Parents	Children w/Single Mother	Stay-at-home Mothers	Births to Single Women
Area	24.5%	65.5%	28.8%	30.5%	40.1%
USA	24.0%	65.6%	25.5%	27.9%	35.3%

Key Housing Data

	Owner Occupied	Median Year Built	Median Home Value	Home Value Growth, 2005-2010	Median List Price, 4-bedroom Home
Area	71.9%	1980	$146,400	3.7%	$269,900
USA	67.8%	1976	$187,045	3.1%	$288,846

Bismarck, ND
104,944

	Score	Rank
Overall	75.06	17
LDS Culture	39.15	47
Education	84.68	41
Crime	81.94	26
Economic	66.76	127
Health	48.58	79
Household	76.54	85
Housing	83.63	165

Key LDS Culture Data

	Positive	Negative	Ratio Pos:Neg	Commute>59 minutes	Commute<15 minutes
Area	572	40	14.3	4.4%	54.6%
USA	4,292	251	20.1	5.5%	34.1%

Key Education Data

	HS Grad	Some Coll.	College Degree	Free/Reduced Lunch	Students per Teacher
Area	90.6%	20.4%	44.8%	24.3%	14.1
USA	85.8%	22.6%	33.2%	41.2%	15.8

Key Property Crime Data (Rate per 100,000 residents)

	Rate	Burglary	Larceny, Theft	Vehicle Theft
Area	2,169.9	304.9	1,731.2	133.8
USA	3,413.6	806.6	2,388.0	262.7

Key Violent Crime Data (Rate per 100,000 residents)

	Rate	Murder	Rape	Robbery	Aggravated Assault
Area	212.2	1.9	44.0	13.4	152.9
USA	432.8	4.7	34.7	111.6	285.6

Key Economic Data (Family income, unemployment)

	$25k-$75k	$75k-$150k	>$150k	Unemployment 03/2009	Unemployment 03/2010
Area	41.7%	40.2%	4.4%	4.9%	5.0%
USA	45.8%	29.5%	8.5%	9.0%	10.1

Key Household Data

	Population Age 0-17	Children w/Married Parents	Children w/Single Mother	Stay-at-home Mothers	Births to Single Women
Area	22.3%	75.7%	20.0%	15.2%	23.2%
USA	24.0%	65.6%	25.5%	27.9%	35.3%

Key Housing Data

	Owner Occupied	Median Year Built	Median Home Value	Home Value Growth, 2005-2010	Median List Price, 4-bedroom Home
Area	73.1%	1978	$148,100	5.6%	
USA	67.8%	1976	$187,045	3.1%	$288,846

Blacksburg-Christiansburg-Radford, VA
158,922

	Score	Rank
Overall	74.34	20
LDS Culture	72.98	5
Education	69.70	191
Crime	75.17	49
Economic	61.15	209
Health	36.28	277
Household	82.72	49
Housing	78.69	235

Key LDS Culture Data

	Positive	Negative	Ratio Pos:Neg	Commute>59 minutes	Commute<15 minutes
Area	2,361	41	57.6	2.3%	42.7%
USA	4,292	251	20.1	5.5%	34.1%

Key Education Data

	HS Grad	Some Coll.	College Degree	Free/Reduced Lunch	Students per Teacher
Area	83.9%	19.9%	35.5%	37.8%	15.1
USA	85.8%	22.6%	33.2%	41.2%	15.8

Key Property Crime Data (Rate per 100,000 residents)

	Rate	Burglary	Larceny, Theft	Vehicle Theft
Area	2,724.1	588.0	2,013.2	122.9
USA	3,413.6	806.6	2,388.0	262.7

Key Violent Crime Data (Rate per 100,000 residents)

	Rate	Murder	Rape	Robbery	Aggravated Assault
Area	227.5	3.8	36.8	26.6	160.3
USA	432.8	4.7	34.7	111.6	285.6

Key Economic Data (Family income, unemployment)

	$25k-$75k	$75k-$150k	>$150k	Unemployment 03/2009	Unemployment 03/2010
Area	45.9%	28.2%	7.1%	9.0%	9.5%
USA	45.8%	29.5%	8.5%	9.0%	10.1

Key Household Data

	Population Age 0-17	Children w/Married Parents	Children w/Single Mother	Stay-at-home Mothers	Births to Single Women
Area	16.4%	69.5%	23.4%	26.6%	5.3%
USA	24.0%	65.6%	25.5%	27.9%	35.3%

Key Housing Data

	Owner Occupied	Median Year Built	Median Home Value	Home Value Growth, 2005-2010	Median List Price, 4-bedroom Home
Area	62.4%	1976	$155,100	4.8%	
USA	67.8%	1976	$187,045	3.1%	$288,846

Bloomington, IN
183,623

	Score	Rank
Overall	66.33	114
LDS Culture	30.38	140
Education	78.85	83
Crime	78.26	38
Economic	64.70	155
Health	34.59	291
Household	56.17	260
Housing	82.37	182

Key LDS Culture Data

	Positive	Negative	Ratio Pos:Neg	Commute>59 minutes	Commute<15 minutes
Area	1,414	58	24.4	6.5%	38.4%
USA	4,292	251	20.1	5.5%	34.1%

Key Education Data

	HS Grad	Some Coll.	College Degree	Free/Reduced Lunch	Students per Teacher
Area	88.3%	22.1%	39.4%	31.2%	17.0
USA	85.8%	22.6%	33.2%	41.2%	15.8

Key Property Crime Data (Rate per 100,000 residents)

	Rate	Burglary	Larceny, Theft	Vehicle Theft	
Area	2,618.0	618.5	1,848.9	150.6	
USA	3,413.6	806.6	2,388.0	262.7	

Key Violent Crime Data (Rate per 100,000 residents)

	Rate	Murder	Rape	Robbery	Aggravated Assault
Area	205.3	2.2	25.5	35.7	141.9
USA	432.8	4.7	34.7	111.6	285.6

Key Economic Data (Family income, unemployment)

	$25k-$75k	$75k-$150k	>$150k	Unemployment 03/2009	Unemployment 03/2010
Area	48.2%	24.8%	8.1%	7.2%	7.8%
USA	45.8%	29.5%	8.5%	9.0%	10.1

Key Household Data

	Population Age 0-17	Children w/Married Parents	Children w/Single Mother	Stay-at-home Mothers	Births to Single Women
Area	19.1%	62.0%	31.8%	19.8%	21.9%
USA	24.0%	65.6%	25.5%	27.9%	35.3%

Key Housing Data

	Owner Occupied	Median Year Built	Median Home Value	Home Value Growth, 2005-2010	Median List Price, 4-bedroom Home
Area	62.1%	1979	$122,300	3.2%	
USA	67.8%	1976	$187,045	3.1%	$288,846

Bloomington-Normal, IL
165,298

	Score	Rank
Overall	67.48	94
LDS Culture	42.31	30
Education	78.36	90
Crime	50.59	213
Economic	71.48	67
Health	47.30	101
Household	65.43	174
Housing	77.24	256

Key LDS Culture Data

	Positive	Negative	Ratio Pos:Neg	Commute>59 minutes	Commute<15 minutes
Area	1,301	101	12.9	2.7%	52.0%
USA	4,292	251	20.1	5.5%	34.1%

Key Education Data

	HS Grad	Some Coll.	College Degree	Free/Reduced Lunch	Students per Teacher
Area	94.2%	19.4%	46.3%	23.5%	18.1
USA	85.8%	22.6%	33.2%	41.2%	15.8

Key Property Crime Data (Rate per 100,000 residents)

	Rate	Burglary	Larceny, Theft	Vehicle Theft	
Area	2,812.6				
USA	3,413.6	806.6	2,388.0	262.7	

Key Violent Crime Data (Rate per 100,000 residents)

	Rate	Murder	Rape	Robbery	Aggravated Assault
Area	497.4				
USA	432.8	4.7	34.7	111.6	285.6

Key Economic Data (Family income, unemployment)

	$25k-$75k	$75k-$150k	>$150k	Unemployment 03/2009	Unemployment 03/2010
Area	38.8%	41.8%	11.6%	6.6%	8.6%
USA	45.8%	29.5%	8.5%	9.0%	10.1

Key Household Data

	Population Age 0-17	Children w/Married Parents	Children w/Single Mother	Stay-at-home Mothers	Births to Single Women
Area	22.7%	72.1%	23.1%	21.1%	43.0%
USA	24.0%	65.6%	25.5%	27.9%	35.3%

Key Housing Data

	Owner Occupied	Median Year Built	Median Home Value	Home Value Growth, 2005-2010	Median List Price, 4-bedroom Home
Area	68.1%	1977	$157,200	1.9%	
USA	67.8%	1976	$187,045	3.1%	$288,846

Boise City-Nampa, ID
596,289

	Score	Rank
Overall	**76.65**	**13**
LDS Culture	37.50	62
Education	79.11	80
Crime	78.68	35
Economic	61.87	199
Health	47.34	91
Household	87.04	27
Housing	100.00	1

Key LDS Culture Data

	Positive	Negative	Ratio Pos:Neg	Commute>59 minutes	Commute<15 minutes
Area	2,737	122	22.4	3.7%	31.6%
USA	4,292	251	20.1	5.5%	34.1%

Key Education Data

	HS Grad	Some Coll.	College Degree	Free/Reduced Lunch	Students per Teacher
Area	88.6%	27.8%	35.7%	33.1%	18.9
USA	85.8%	22.6%	33.2%	41.2%	15.8

Key Property Crime Data (Rate per 100,000 residents)

	Rate	Burglary	Larceny, Theft	Vehicle Theft	
Area	2,259.8	487.7	1,658.9	113.2	
USA	3,413.6	806.6	2,388.0	262.7	

Key Violent Crime Data (Rate per 100,000 residents)

	Rate	Murder	Rape	Robbery	Aggravated Assault
Area	237.9	0.8	38.5	21.2	177.4
USA	432.8	4.7	34.7	111.6	285.6

Key Economic Data (Family income, unemployment)

	$25k-$75k	$75k-$150k	>$150k	Unemployment 03/2009	Unemployment 03/2010
Area	49.7%	29.1%	7.3%	8.5%	9.9%
USA	45.8%	29.5%	8.5%	9.0%	10.1

Key Household Data

	Population Age 0-17	Children w/Married Parents	Children w/Single Mother	Stay-at-home Mothers	Births to Single Women
Area	27.7%	70.7%	18.5%	34.2%	23.6%
USA	24.0%	65.6%	25.5%	27.9%	35.3%

Key Housing Data

	Owner Occupied	Median Year Built	Median Home Value	Home Value Growth, 2005-2010	Median List Price, 4-bedroom Home
Area	70.6%	1991	$203,900	5.6%	$189,000
USA	67.8%	1976	$187,045	3.1%	$288,846

Boston-Cambridge-Quincy, MA-NH
4,522,858

	Score	Rank
Overall	63.30	176
LDS Culture	24.75	219
Education	82.85	50
Crime	64.11	113
Economic	73.54	53
Health	31.62	340
Household	74.69	104
Housing	54.32	358

Key LDS Culture Data

	Positive	Negative	Ratio Pos:Neg	Commute>59 minutes	Commute<15 minutes
Area	21,689	1204	18.0	10.5%	22.7%
USA	4,292	251	20.1	5.5%	34.1%

Key Education Data

	HS Grad	Some Coll.	College Degree	Free/Reduced Lunch	Students per Teacher
Area	89.9%	15.9%	49.0%	26.6%	13.6
USA	85.8%	22.6%	33.2%	41.2%	15.8

Key Property Crime Data (Rate per 100,000 residents)

	Rate	Burglary	Larceny, Theft	Vehicle Theft
Area	2,260.1	453.7	1,618.9	187.5
USA	3,413.6	806.6	2,388.0	262.7

Key Violent Crime Data (Rate per 100,000 residents)

	Rate	Murder	Rape	Robbery	Aggravated Assault
Area	394.7	2.6	22.7	110.1	259.3
USA	432.8	4.7	34.7	111.6	285.6

Key Economic Data (Family income, unemployment)

	$25k-$75k	$75k-$150k	>$150k	Unemployment 03/2009	Unemployment 03/2010
Area	30.8%	36.7%	22.1%	7.3%	8.3%
USA	45.8%	29.5%	8.5%	9.0%	10.1

Key Household Data

	Population Age 0-17	Children w/Married Parents	Children w/Single Mother	Stay-at-home Mothers	Births to Single Women
Area	22.1%	70.4%	22.9%	26.2%	28.0%
USA	24.0%	65.6%	25.5%	27.9%	35.3%

Key Housing Data

	Owner Occupied	Median Year Built	Median Home Value	Home Value Growth, 2005-2010	Median List Price, 4-bedroom Home
Area	63.7%	1959	$385,100	-0.4%	$499,900
USA	67.8%	1976	$187,045	3.1%	$288,846

Boulder, CO
293,161

	Score	Rank
Overall	74.01	24
LDS Culture	19.27	294
Education	91.61	16
Crime	64.10	114
Economic	90.05	6
Health	42.83	171
Household	92.59	6
Housing	74.12	295

Key LDS Culture Data

	Positive	Negative	Ratio Pos:Neg	Commute>59 minutes	Commute<15 minutes
Area	6,023	510	11.8	4.5%	37.2%
USA	4,292	251	20.1	5.5%	34.1%

Key Education Data

	HS Grad	Some Coll.	College Degree	Free/Reduced Lunch	Students per Teacher
Area	92.7%	17.0%	63.5%	22.7%	17.5
USA	85.8%	22.6%	33.2%	41.2%	15.8

Key Property Crime Data (Rate per 100,000 residents)

	Rate	Burglary	Larceny, Theft	Vehicle Theft	
Area		444.1	1,881.1	136.9	
USA	3,413.6	806.6	2,388.0	262.7	

Key Violent Crime Data (Rate per 100,000 residents)

	Rate	Murder	Rape	Robbery	Aggravated Assault
Area		1.4	30.3	25.3	160.0
USA	432.8	4.7	34.7	111.6	285.6

Key Economic Data (Family income, unemployment)

	$25k-$75k	$75k-$150k	>$150k	Unemployment 03/2009	Unemployment 03/2010
Area	32.0%	35.1%	25.0%	6.8%	6.4%
USA	45.8%	29.5%	8.5%	9.0%	10.1

Key Household Data

	Population Age 0-17	Children w/Married Parents	Children w/Single Mother	Stay-at-home Mothers	Births to Single Women
Area	21.1%	77.4%	14.8%	36.3%	15.8%
USA	24.0%	65.6%	25.5%	27.9%	35.3%

Key Housing Data

	Owner Occupied	Median Year Built	Median Home Value	Home Value Growth, 2005-2010	Median List Price, 4-bedroom Home
Area	65.1%	1983	$358,600	2.3%	$495,000
USA	67.8%	1976	$187,045	3.1%	$288,846

Bowling Green, KY
117,219

	Score	Rank
Overall	60.94	220
LDS Culture	32.37	116
Education	70.45	178
Crime	62.92	128
Economic	66.93	123
Health	26.56	355
Household	43.21	347
Housing	88.32	76

Key LDS Culture Data

	Positive	Negative	Ratio Pos:Neg	Commute>59 minutes	Commute<15 minutes
Area	1,168	54	21.6	3.2%	35.4%
USA	4,292	251	20.1	5.5%	34.1%

Key Education Data

	HS Grad	Some Coll.	College Degree	Free/Reduced Lunch	Students per Teacher
Area	83.0%	22.0%	30.8%	46.6%	16.6
USA	85.8%	22.6%	33.2%	41.2%	15.8

Key Property Crime Data (Rate per 100,000 residents)

	Rate	Burglary	Larceny, Theft	Vehicle Theft
Area	3,203.7	648.9	2,422.1	132.7
USA	3,413.6	806.6	2,388.0	262.7

Key Violent Crime Data (Rate per 100,000 residents)

	Rate	Murder	Rape	Robbery	Aggravated Assault
Area	309.6	0.0	45.1	80.8	183.7
USA	432.8	4.7	34.7	111.6	285.6

Key Economic Data (Family income, unemployment)

	$25k-$75k	$75k-$150k	>$150k	Unemployment 03/2009	Unemployment 03/2010
Area	45.2%	26.6%	5.3%	10.2%	9.8%
USA	45.8%	29.5%	8.5%	9.0%	10.1

Key Household Data

	Population Age 0-17	Children w/Married Parents	Children w/Single Mother	Stay-at-home Mothers	Births to Single Women
Area	23.0%	57.7%	28.1%	18.4%	46.5%
USA	24.0%	65.6%	25.5%	27.9%	35.3%

Key Housing Data

	Owner Occupied	Median Year Built	Median Home Value	Home Value Growth, 2005-2010	Median List Price, 4-bedroom Home
Area	61.5%	1984	$131,300	2.3%	
USA	67.8%	1976	$187,045	3.1%	$288,846

Bradenton-Sarasota-Venice, FL
687,823

	Score	Rank
Overall	59.95	247
LDS Culture	16.35	326
Education	72.20	159
Crime	37.18	305
Economic	69.09	94
Health	52.72	22
Household	56.17	261
Housing	80.69	202

Key LDS Culture Data
	Positive	Negative	Ratio Pos:Neg	Commute>59 minutes	Commute<15 minutes
Area	4,793	355	13.5	5.1%	31.3%
USA	4,292	251	20.1	5.5%	34.1%

Key Education Data
	HS Grad	Some Coll.	College Degree	Free/Reduced Lunch	Students per Teacher
Area	88.5%	22.0%	34.8%	39.8%	15.3
USA	85.8%	22.6%	33.2%	41.2%	15.8

Key Property Crime Data (Rate per 100,000 residents)
	Rate	Burglary	Larceny, Theft	Vehicle Theft
Area	4,256.5	1,055.4	2,982.4	218.7
USA	3,413.6	806.6	2,388.0	262.7

Key Violent Crime Data (Rate per 100,000 residents)
	Rate	Murder	Rape	Robbery	Aggravated Assault
Area	636.3	4.0	27.8	166.9	437.5
USA	432.8	4.7	34.7	111.6	285.6

Key Economic Data (Family income, unemployment)
	$25k-$75k	$75k-$150k	>$150k	Unemployment 03/2009	Unemployment 03/2010
Area	48.0%	28.3%	9.3%		
USA	45.8%	29.5%	8.5%	9.0%	10.1

Key Household Data
	Population Age 0-17	Children w/Married Parents	Children w/Single Mother	Stay-at-home Mothers	Births to Single Women
Area	18.4%	63.1%	29.0%	27.7%	41.6%
USA	24.0%	65.6%	25.5%	27.9%	35.3%

Key Housing Data
	Owner Occupied	Median Year Built	Median Home Value	Home Value Growth, 2005-2010	Median List Price, 4-bedroom Home
Area	74.2%	1984	$237,300	0.1%	
USA	67.8%	1976	$187,045	3.1%	$288,846

Bremerton-Silverdale, WA
239,769

	Score	Rank
Overall	66.30	115
LDS Culture	13.96	345
Education	90.19	18
Crime	54.89	174
Economic	72.37	61
Health	47.12	114
Household	74.07	110
Housing	72.57	312

Key LDS Culture Data
	Positive	Negative	Ratio Pos:Neg	Commute>59 minutes	Commute<15 minutes
Area	15,494	745	20.8	15.6%	26.9%
USA	4,292	251	20.1	5.5%	34.1%

Key Education Data
	HS Grad	Some Coll.	College Degree	Free/Reduced Lunch	Students per Teacher
Area	92.6%	30.8%	37.9%	27.4%	19.4
USA	85.8%	22.6%	33.2%	41.2%	15.8

Key Property Crime Data (Rate per 100,000 residents)
	Rate	Burglary	Larceny, Theft	Vehicle Theft
Area	2,696.5	705.6	1,859.2	131.8
USA	3,413.6	806.6	2,388.0	262.7

Key Violent Crime Data (Rate per 100,000 residents)
	Rate	Murder	Rape	Robbery	Aggravated Assault
Area	464.4	2.1	82.1	47.2	333.0
USA	432.8	4.7	34.7	111.6	285.6

Key Economic Data (Family income, unemployment)
	$25k-$75k	$75k-$150k	>$150k	Unemployment 03/2009	Unemployment 03/2010
Area	38.8%	38.5%	10.3%	7.8%	8.5%
USA	45.8%	29.5%	8.5%	9.0%	10.1

Key Household Data
	Population Age 0-17	Children w/Married Parents	Children w/Single Mother	Stay-at-home Mothers	Births to Single Women
Area	23.1%	66.7%	24.5%	33.8%	35.6%
USA	24.0%	65.6%	25.5%	27.9%	35.3%

Key Housing Data
	Owner Occupied	Median Year Built	Median Home Value	Home Value Growth, 2005-2010	Median List Price, 4-bedroom Home
Area	69.2%	1984	$304,100	6.1%	$397,500
USA	67.8%	1976	$187,045	3.1%	$288,846

Bridgeport-Stamford-Norwalk, CT
895,030

	Score	Rank
Overall	69.33	58
LDS Culture	33.15	104
Education	80.97	63
Crime	72.11	67
Economic	71.43	71
Health	31.88	337
Household	91.98	8
Housing	63.08	345

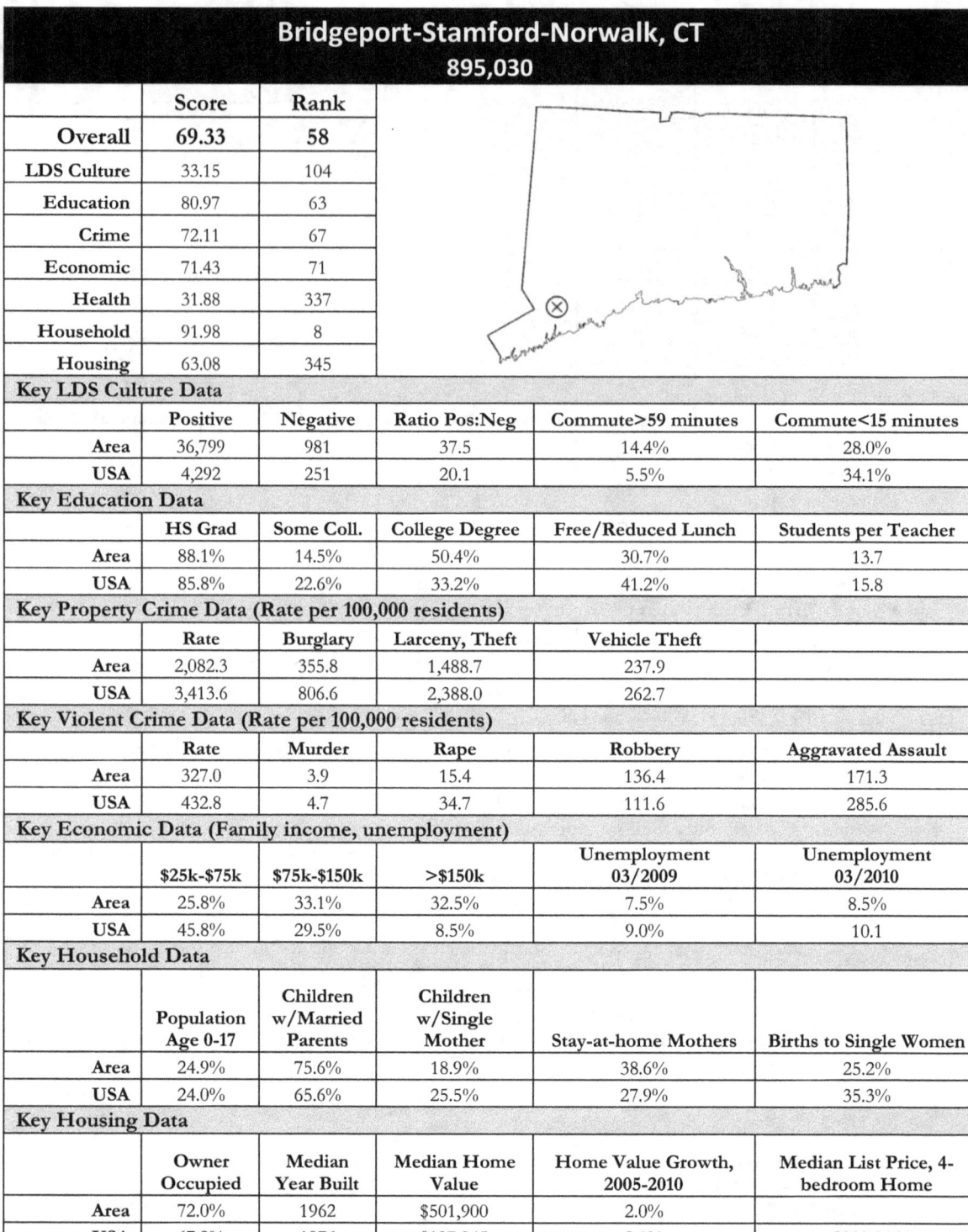

Key LDS Culture Data
	Positive	Negative	Ratio Pos:Neg	Commute>59 minutes	Commute<15 minutes
Area	36,799	981	37.5	14.4%	28.0%
USA	4,292	251	20.1	5.5%	34.1%

Key Education Data
	HS Grad	Some Coll.	College Degree	Free/Reduced Lunch	Students per Teacher
Area	88.1%	14.5%	50.4%	30.7%	13.7
USA	85.8%	22.6%	33.2%	41.2%	15.8

Key Property Crime Data (Rate per 100,000 residents)
	Rate	Burglary	Larceny, Theft	Vehicle Theft	
Area	2,082.3	355.8	1,488.7	237.9	
USA	3,413.6	806.6	2,388.0	262.7	

Key Violent Crime Data (Rate per 100,000 residents)
	Rate	Murder	Rape	Robbery	Aggravated Assault
Area	327.0	3.9	15.4	136.4	171.3
USA	432.8	4.7	34.7	111.6	285.6

Key Economic Data (Family income, unemployment)
	$25k-$75k	$75k-$150k	>$150k	Unemployment 03/2009	Unemployment 03/2010
Area	25.8%	33.1%	32.5%	7.5%	8.5%
USA	45.8%	29.5%	8.5%	9.0%	10.1

Key Household Data
	Population Age 0-17	Children w/Married Parents	Children w/Single Mother	Stay-at-home Mothers	Births to Single Women
Area	24.9%	75.6%	18.9%	38.6%	25.2%
USA	24.0%	65.6%	25.5%	27.9%	35.3%

Key Housing Data
	Owner Occupied	Median Year Built	Median Home Value	Home Value Growth, 2005-2010	Median List Price, 4-bedroom Home
Area	72.0%	1962	$501,900	2.0%	
USA	67.8%	1976	$187,045	3.1%	$288,846

Brownsville-Harlingen, TX
392,736

	Score	Rank
Overall	57.86	288
LDS Culture	33.79	95
Education	49.46	351
Crime	44.22	262
Economic	46.47	347
Health	29.28	348
Household	77.78	77
Housing	89.98	54

Key LDS Culture Data

	Positive	Negative	Ratio Pos:Neg	Commute>59 minutes	Commute<15 minutes
Area	1,557	67	23.2	2.7%	36.7%
USA	4,292	251	20.1	5.5%	34.1%

Key Education Data

	HS Grad	Some Coll.	College Degree	Free/Reduced Lunch	Students per Teacher
Area	63.2%	18.5%	22.0%	19.4%	15.2
USA	85.8%	22.6%	33.2%	41.2%	15.8

Key Property Crime Data (Rate per 100,000 residents)

	Rate	Burglary	Larceny, Theft	Vehicle Theft	
Area	4,864.2	1,035.6	3,634.7	193.9	
USA	3,413.6	806.6	2,388.0	262.7	

Key Violent Crime Data (Rate per 100,000 residents)

	Rate	Murder	Rape	Robbery	Aggravated Assault
Area	422.8	3.3	33.8	81.5	304.3
USA	432.8	4.7	34.7	111.6	285.6

Key Economic Data (Family income, unemployment)

	$25k-$75k	$75k-$150k	>$150k	Unemployment 03/2009	Unemployment 03/2010
Area	44.7%	14.6%	3.3%	9.4%	11.0%
USA	45.8%	29.5%	8.5%	9.0%	10.1

Key Household Data

	Population Age 0-17	Children w/Married Parents	Children w/Single Mother	Stay-at-home Mothers	Births to Single Women
Area	34.0%	65.4%	27.6%	43.7%	32.4%
USA	24.0%	65.6%	25.5%	27.9%	35.3%

Key Housing Data

	Owner Occupied	Median Year Built	Median Home Value	Home Value Growth, 2005-2010	Median List Price, 4-bedroom Home
Area	67.4%	1984	$76,500	3.3%	
USA	67.8%	1976	$187,045	3.1%	$288,846

Brunswick, GA
99,793

	Score	Rank
Overall	56.10	319
LDS Culture	27.47	176
Education	54.20	331
Crime	27.67	343
Economic	58.87	242
Health	40.98	199
Household	64.20	186
Housing	86.36	114

Key LDS Culture Data

	Positive	Negative	Ratio Pos:Neg	Commute>59 minutes	Commute<15 minutes
Area	738	35	21.1	3.1%	34.5%
USA	4,292	251	20.1	5.5%	34.1%

Key Education Data

	HS Grad	Some Coll.	College Degree	Free/Reduced Lunch	Students per Teacher
Area	85.6%	20.6%	30.9%	51.5%	14.4
USA	85.8%	22.6%	33.2%	41.2%	15.8

Key Property Crime Data (Rate per 100,000 residents)

	Rate	Burglary	Larceny, Theft	Vehicle Theft	
Area	4,560.1	1,073.9	3,190.2	296.0	
USA	3,413.6	806.6	2,388.0	262.7	

Key Violent Crime Data (Rate per 100,000 residents)

	Rate	Murder	Rape	Robbery	Aggravated Assault
Area	822.1	19.7	26.6	164.2	611.7
USA	432.8	4.7	34.7	111.6	285.6

Key Economic Data (Family income, unemployment)

	$25k-$75k	$75k-$150k	>$150k	Unemployment 03/2009	Unemployment 03/2010
Area	44.4%	27.5%	7.7%	8.1%	10.0%
USA	45.8%	29.5%	8.5%	9.0%	10.1

Key Household Data

	Population Age 0-17	Children w/Married Parents	Children w/Single Mother	Stay-at-home Mothers	Births to Single Women
Area	24.9%	63.2%	26.7%	34.8%	37.9%
USA	24.0%	65.6%	25.5%	27.9%	35.3%

Key Housing Data

	Owner Occupied	Median Year Built	Median Home Value	Home Value Growth, 2005-2010	Median List Price, 4-bedroom Home
Area	69.5%	1984	$158,500	5.9%	
USA	67.8%	1976	$187,045	3.1%	$288,846

Buffalo-Niagara Falls, NY
1,124,309

	Score	Rank
Overall	61.94	198
LDS Culture	28.32	164
Education	78.68	87
Crime	49.82	220
Economic	68.59	100
Health	41.10	194
Household	51.85	287
Housing	78.85	232

Key LDS Culture Data

	Positive	Negative	Ratio Pos:Neg	Commute>59 minutes	Commute<15 minutes
Area	5,769	479	12.0	3.2%	31.4%
USA	4,292	251	20.1	5.5%	34.1%

Key Education Data

	HS Grad	Some Coll.	College Degree	Free/Reduced Lunch	Students per Teacher
Area	88.7%	18.9%	38.5%	38.5%	12.9
USA	85.8%	22.6%	33.2%	41.2%	15.8

Key Property Crime Data (Rate per 100,000 residents)

	Rate	Burglary	Larceny, Theft	Vehicle Theft
Area	3,110.3	699.8	2,173.5	237.0
USA	3,413.6	806.6	2,388.0	262.7

Key Violent Crime Data (Rate per 100,000 residents)

	Rate	Murder	Rape	Robbery	Aggravated Assault
Area	489.2	3.9	25.5	178.2	281.6
USA	432.8	4.7	34.7	111.6	285.6

Key Economic Data (Family income, unemployment)

	$25k-$75k	$75k-$150k	>$150k	Unemployment 03/2009	Unemployment 03/2010
Area	44.0%	32.3%	7.6%	8.8%	8.6%
USA	45.8%	29.5%	8.5%	9.0%	10.1

Key Household Data

	Population Age 0-17	Children w/Married Parents	Children w/Single Mother	Stay-at-home Mothers	Births to Single Women
Area	21.5%	62.8%	29.6%	24.2%	45.2%
USA	24.0%	65.6%	25.5%	27.9%	35.3%

Key Housing Data

	Owner Occupied	Median Year Built	Median Home Value	Home Value Growth, 2005-2010	Median List Price, 4-bedroom Home
Area	66.7%	1957	$115,900	3.7%	$195,000
USA	67.8%	1976	$187,045	3.1%	$288,846

Burlington, NC
148,053

	Score	Rank
Overall	57.73	293
LDS Culture	36.94	68
Education	52.55	338
Crime	45.33	250
Economic	55.42	289
Health	37.16	256
Household	52.47	284
Housing	90.29	51

Key LDS Culture Data

	Positive	Negative	Ratio Pos:Neg	Commute>59 minutes	Commute<15 minutes
Area	5,884	185	31.8	3.7%	33.0%
USA	4,292	251	20.1	5.5%	34.1%

Key Education Data

	HS Grad	Some Coll.	College Degree	Free/Reduced Lunch	Students per Teacher
Area	79.3%	22.9%	27.8%	40.7%	15.1
USA	85.8%	22.6%	33.2%	41.2%	15.8

Key Property Crime Data (Rate per 100,000 residents)

	Rate	Burglary	Larceny, Theft	Vehicle Theft
Area	4,039.2	1,202.7	2,652.1	184.3
USA	3,413.6	806.6	2,388.0	262.7

Key Violent Crime Data (Rate per 100,000 residents)

	Rate	Murder	Rape	Robbery	Aggravated Assault
Area	472.3	2.7	22.4	114.5	332.7
USA	432.8	4.7	34.7	111.6	285.6

Key Economic Data (Family income, unemployment)

	$25k-$75k	$75k-$150k	>$150k	Unemployment 03/2009	Unemployment 03/2010
Area	46.6%	27.2%	4.7%	11.5%	12.1%
USA	45.8%	29.5%	8.5%	9.0%	10.1

Key Household Data

	Population Age 0-17	Children w/Married Parents	Children w/Single Mother	Stay-at-home Mothers	Births to Single Women
Area	23.9%	56.3%	37.2%	28.1%	46.7%
USA	24.0%	65.6%	25.5%	27.9%	35.3%

Key Housing Data

	Owner Occupied	Median Year Built	Median Home Value	Home Value Growth, 2005-2010	Median List Price, 4-bedroom Home
Area	66.0%	1984	$130,800	1.9%	$229,900
USA	67.8%	1976	$187,045	3.1%	$288,846

Burlington-South Burlington, VT
209,005

	Score	Rank
Overall	70.14	49
LDS Culture	38.16	54
Education	83.47	45
Crime	71.64	69
Economic	75.10	46
Health	43.70	158
Household	64.81	179
Housing	72.88	309

Key LDS Culture Data

	Positive	Negative	Ratio Pos:Neg	Commute>59 minutes	Commute<15 minutes
Area	1,832	79	23.2	3.5%	32.0%
USA	4,292	251	20.1	5.5%	34.1%

Key Education Data

	HS Grad	Some Coll.	College Degree	Free/Reduced Lunch	Students per Teacher
Area	91.8%	16.9%	44.5%	23.1%	11.8
USA	85.8%	22.6%	33.2%	41.2%	15.8

Key Property Crime Data (Rate per 100,000 residents)

	Rate	Burglary	Larceny, Theft	Vehicle Theft	
Area	3,596.4	694.7	2,781.0	120.7	
USA	3,413.6	806.6	2,388.0	262.7	

Key Violent Crime Data (Rate per 100,000 residents)

	Rate	Murder	Rape	Robbery	Aggravated Assault
Area	191.5	0.5	27.9	27.4	135.7
USA	432.8	4.7	34.7	111.6	285.6

Key Economic Data (Family income, unemployment)

	$25k-$75k	$75k-$150k	>$150k	Unemployment 03/2009	Unemployment 03/2010
Area	42.6%	36.8%	10.1%	6.9%	6.0%
USA	45.8%	29.5%	8.5%	9.0%	10.1

Key Household Data

	Population Age 0-17	Children w/Married Parents	Children w/Single Mother	Stay-at-home Mothers	Births to Single Women
Area	22.2%	66.6%	25.3%	21.0%	31.3%
USA	24.0%	65.6%	25.5%	27.9%	35.3%

Key Housing Data

	Owner Occupied	Median Year Built	Median Home Value	Home Value Growth, 2005-2010	Median List Price, 4-bedroom Home
Area	70.5%	1976	$250,900	4.3%	$344,000
USA	67.8%	1976	$187,045	3.1%	$288,846

Canton-Massillon, OH
408,245

	Score	Rank
Overall	60.28	237
LDS Culture	27.75	173
Education	75.41	123
Crime	48.70	229
Economic	48.47	337
Health	47.55	89
Household	60.49	220
Housing	78.18	243

Key LDS Culture Data

	Positive	Negative	Ratio Pos:Neg	Commute>59 minutes	Commute<15 minutes
Area	7,268	443	16.4	5.7%	32.4%
USA	4,292	251	20.1	5.5%	34.1%

Key Education Data

	HS Grad	Some Coll.	College Degree	Free/Reduced Lunch	Students per Teacher
Area	87.7%	21.0%	25.1%		18.6
USA	85.8%	22.6%	33.2%	41.2%	15.8

Key Property Crime Data (Rate per 100,000 residents)

	Rate	Burglary	Larceny, Theft	Vehicle Theft	
Area		903.4	2,531.2	216.9	
USA	3,413.6	806.6	2,388.0	262.7	

Key Violent Crime Data (Rate per 100,000 residents)

	Rate	Murder	Rape	Robbery	Aggravated Assault
Area		3.3	34.4	143.3	
USA	432.8	4.7	34.7	111.6	285.6

Key Economic Data (Family income, unemployment)

	$25k-$75k	$75k-$150k	>$150k	Unemployment 03/2009	Unemployment 03/2010
Area	50.7%	26.0%	6.9%	10.8%	13.5%
USA	45.8%	29.5%	8.5%	9.0%	10.1

Key Household Data

	Population Age 0-17	Children w/Married Parents	Children w/Single Mother	Stay-at-home Mothers	Births to Single Women
Area	22.6%	64.6%	26.6%	19.4%	24.6%
USA	24.0%	65.6%	25.5%	27.9%	35.3%

Key Housing Data

	Owner Occupied	Median Year Built	Median Home Value	Home Value Growth, 2005-2010	Median List Price, 4-bedroom Home
Area	69.8%	1964	$128,200	-0.1%	$174,900
USA	67.8%	1976	$187,045	3.1%	$288,846

Cape Coral-Fort Myers, FL
593,136

	Score	Rank
Overall	**64.20**	**159**
LDS Culture	19.90	285
Education	74.26	135
Crime	47.95	235
Economic	65.43	146
Health	46.83	118
Household	74.07	111
Housing	83.20	173

Key LDS Culture Data

	Positive	Negative	Ratio Pos:Neg	Commute>59 minutes	Commute<15 minutes
Area	4,212	187	22.5	5.1%	23.0%
USA	4,292	251	20.1	5.5%	34.1%

Key Education Data

	HS Grad	Some Coll.	College Degree	Free/Reduced Lunch	Students per Teacher
Area	87.9%	23.2%	32.6%	46.2%	16.0
USA	85.8%	22.6%	33.2%	41.2%	15.8

Key Property Crime Data (Rate per 100,000 residents)

	Rate	Burglary	Larceny, Theft	Vehicle Theft
Area	3,509.1	1,025.5	2,236.6	247.0
USA	3,413.6	806.6	2,388.0	262.7

Key Violent Crime Data (Rate per 100,000 residents)

	Rate	Murder	Rape	Robbery	Aggravated Assault
Area	468.8	7.6	26.0	128.2	307.0
USA	432.8	4.7	34.7	111.6	285.6

Key Economic Data (Family income, unemployment)

	$25k-$75k	$75k-$150k	>$150k	Unemployment 03/2009	Unemployment 03/2010
Area	47.9%	28.5%	9.1%	11.3%	13.5%
USA	45.8%	29.5%	8.5%	9.0%	10.1

Key Household Data

	Population Age 0-17	Children w/Married Parents	Children w/Single Mother	Stay-at-home Mothers	Births to Single Women
Area	20.8%	67.4%	23.0%	28.4%	22.2%
USA	24.0%	65.6%	25.5%	27.9%	35.3%

Key Housing Data

	Owner Occupied	Median Year Built	Median Home Value	Home Value Growth, 2005-2010	Median List Price, 4-bedroom Home
Area	75.0%	1989	$211,700	-1.0%	
USA	67.8%	1976	$187,045	3.1%	$288,846

Casper, WY
73,129

	Score	Rank
Overall	66.49	112
LDS Culture	26.54	189
Education	78.88	82
Crime	63.93	117
Economic	76.10	37
Health	22.82	360
Household	75.93	90
Housing	82.15	184

Key LDS Culture Data

	Positive	Negative	Ratio Pos:Neg	Commute>59 minutes	Commute<15 minutes
Area	421	28	15.0	3.6%	48.2%
USA	4,292	251	20.1	5.5%	34.1%

Key Education Data

	HS Grad	Some Coll.	College Degree	Free/Reduced Lunch	Students per Teacher
Area	93.2%	30.0%	32.5%	33.7%	14.4
USA	85.8%	22.6%	33.2%	41.2%	15.8

Key Property Crime Data (Rate per 100,000 residents)

	Rate	Burglary	Larceny, Theft	Vehicle Theft	
Area	3,785.7	682.6	2,895.6	207.5	
USA	3,413.6	806.6	2,388.0	262.7	

Key Violent Crime Data (Rate per 100,000 residents)

	Rate	Murder	Rape	Robbery	Aggravated Assault
Area	264.9	1.4	49.1	28.7	185.7
USA	432.8	4.7	34.7	111.6	285.6

Key Economic Data (Family income, unemployment)

	$25k-$75k	$75k-$150k	>$150k	Unemployment 03/2009	Unemployment 03/2010
Area	45.1%	31.9%	11.2%	5.7%	7.8%
USA	45.8%	29.5%	8.5%	9.0%	10.1

Key Household Data

	Population Age 0-17	Children w/Married Parents	Children w/Single Mother	Stay-at-home Mothers	Births to Single Women
Area	24.5%	73.3%	20.5%	30.1%	45.1%
USA	24.0%	65.6%	25.5%	27.9%	35.3%

Key Housing Data

	Owner Occupied	Median Year Built	Median Home Value	Home Value Growth, 2005-2010	Median List Price, 4-bedroom Home
Area	70.2%	1973	$191,200	7.2%	
USA	67.8%	1976	$187,045	3.1%	$288,846

Cedar Rapids, IA
255,452

	Score	Rank
Overall	70.15	48
LDS Culture	29.30	153
Education	88.47	23
Crime	74.73	52
Economic	60.70	220
Health	45.73	138
Household	67.90	161
Housing	82.98	176

Key LDS Culture Data

	Positive	Negative	Ratio Pos:Neg	Commute>59 minutes	Commute<15 minutes
Area	1,790	136	13.2	3.3%	39.3%
USA	4,292	251	20.1	5.5%	34.1%

Key Education Data

	HS Grad	Some Coll.	College Degree	Free/Reduced Lunch	Students per Teacher
Area	92.4%	24.7%	37.5%	27.3%	14.1
USA	85.8%	22.6%	33.2%	41.2%	15.8

Key Property Crime Data (Rate per 100,000 residents)

	Rate	Burglary	Larceny, Theft	Vehicle Theft
Area	2,965.0	659.8	2,129.6	175.5
USA	3,413.6	806.6	2,388.0	262.7

Key Violent Crime Data (Rate per 100,000 residents)

	Rate	Murder	Rape	Robbery	Aggravated Assault
Area	207.3	2.0	19.2	55.6	130.5
USA	432.8	4.7	34.7	111.6	285.6

Key Economic Data (Family income, unemployment)

	$25k-$75k	$75k-$150k	>$150k	Unemployment 03/2009	Unemployment 03/2010
Area	42.4%	35.0%	9.6%	5.6%	7.4%
USA	45.8%	29.5%	8.5%	9.0%	10.1

Key Household Data

	Population Age 0-17	Children w/Married Parents	Children w/Single Mother	Stay-at-home Mothers	Births to Single Women
Area	24.4%	68.3%	24.2%	18.8%	26.7%
USA	24.0%	65.6%	25.5%	27.9%	35.3%

Key Housing Data

	Owner Occupied	Median Year Built	Median Home Value	Home Value Growth, 2005-2010	Median List Price, 4-bedroom Home
Area	74.3%	1970	$135,800	1.8%	$219,500
USA	67.8%	1976	$187,045	3.1%	$288,846

Champaign-Urbana, IL
222,716

	Score	Rank
Overall	64.39	153
LDS Culture	40.76	42
Education	80.70	67
Crime	46.43	244
Economic	60.92	213
Health	47.30	102
Household	52.47	285
Housing	84.30	154

Key LDS Culture Data

	Positive	Negative	Ratio Pos:Neg	Commute>59 minutes	Commute<15 minutes
Area	1,355	84	16.1	2.3%	41.4%
USA	4,292	251	20.1	5.5%	34.1%

Key Education Data

	HS Grad	Some Coll.	College Degree	Free/Reduced Lunch	Students per Teacher
Area	92.1%	20.5%	47.5%	35.8%	15.8
USA	85.8%	22.6%	33.2%	41.2%	15.8

Key Property Crime Data (Rate per 100,000 residents)

	Rate	Burglary	Larceny, Theft	Vehicle Theft	
Area	2,997.0	608.0	2,177.0	212.0	
USA	3,413.6	806.6	2,388.0	262.7	

Key Violent Crime Data (Rate per 100,000 residents)

	Rate	Murder	Rape	Robbery	Aggravated Assault
Area	592.0	3.0	21.0	125.0	443.0
USA	432.8	4.7	34.7	111.6	285.6

Key Economic Data (Family income, unemployment)

	$25k-$75k	$75k-$150k	>$150k	Unemployment 03/2009	Unemployment 03/2010
Area	45.2%	31.7%	8.5%	7.4%	9.5%
USA	45.8%	29.5%	8.5%	9.0%	10.1

Key Household Data

	Population Age 0-17	Children w/Married Parents	Children w/Single Mother	Stay-at-home Mothers	Births to Single Women
Area	20.2%	64.4%	22.9%	21.3%	39.7%
USA	24.0%	65.6%	25.5%	27.9%	35.3%

Key Housing Data

	Owner Occupied	Median Year Built	Median Home Value	Home Value Growth, 2005-2010	Median List Price, 4-bedroom Home
Area	57.9%	1970	$140,500	2.6%	$225,000
USA	67.8%	1976	$187,045	3.1%	$288,846

Charleston, WV
300,975

	Score	Rank
Overall	**59.93**	**248**
LDS Culture	25.57	205
Education	63.72	259
Crime	51.46	202
Economic	47.92	341
Health	39.60	221
Household	68.52	156
Housing	87.52	91

Key LDS Culture Data

	Positive	Negative	Ratio Pos:Neg	Commute>59 minutes	Commute<15 minutes
Area	1,799	95	18.9	6.3%	33.3%
USA	4,292	251	20.1	5.5%	34.1%

Key Education Data

	HS Grad	Some Coll.	College Degree	Free/Reduced Lunch	Students per Teacher
Area	84.2%	19.5%	26.5%	49.5%	14.2
USA	85.8%	22.6%	33.2%	41.2%	15.8

Key Property Crime Data (Rate per 100,000 residents)

	Rate	Burglary	Larceny, Theft	Vehicle Theft	
Area	3,360.7	740.8	2,348.1	271.9	
USA	3,413.6	806.6	2,388.0	262.7	

Key Violent Crime Data (Rate per 100,000 residents)

	Rate	Murder	Rape	Robbery	Aggravated Assault
Area	420.5	4.6	26.0	74.1	315.7
USA	432.8	4.7	34.7	111.6	285.6

Key Economic Data (Family income, unemployment)

	$25k-$75k	$75k-$150k	>$150k	Unemployment 03/2009	Unemployment 03/2010
Area	49.6%	25.4%	6.0%	6.4%	8.8%
USA	45.8%	29.5%	8.5%	9.0%	10.1

Key Household Data

	Population Age 0-17	Children w/Married Parents	Children w/Single Mother	Stay-at-home Mothers	Births to Single Women
Area	21.7%	65.7%	26.8%	33.1%	36.0%
USA	24.0%	65.6%	25.5%	27.9%	35.3%

Key Housing Data

	Owner Occupied	Median Year Built	Median Home Value	Home Value Growth, 2005-2010	Median List Price, 4-bedroom Home
Area	72.6%	1971	$101,400	2.9%	$234,900
USA	67.8%	1976	$187,045	3.1%	$288,846

Charleston-North Charleston-Summerville, SC
644,506

	Score	Rank
Overall	**54.97**	**330**
LDS Culture	20.30	277
Education	59.34	302
Crime	34.67	323
Economic	65.37	148
Health	38.89	237
Household	48.77	305
Housing	85.18	139

Key LDS Culture Data

	Positive	Negative	Ratio Pos:Neg	Commute>59 minutes	Commute<15 minutes
Area	3,306	184	18.0	4.9%	24.6%
USA	4,292	251	20.1	5.5%	34.1%

Key Education Data

	HS Grad	Some Coll.	College Degree	Free/Reduced Lunch	Students per Teacher
Area	87.5%	21.1%	37.5%	46.2%	14.7
USA	85.8%	22.6%	33.2%	41.2%	15.8

Key Property Crime Data (Rate per 100,000 residents)

	Rate	Burglary	Larceny, Theft	Vehicle Theft	
Area	4,004.0	847.5	2,731.1	425.3	
USA	3,413.6	806.6	2,388.0	262.7	

Key Violent Crime Data (Rate per 100,000 residents)

	Rate	Murder	Rape	Robbery	Aggravated Assault
Area	720.9	7.5	40.5	208.8	464.1
USA	432.8	4.7	34.7	111.6	285.6

Key Economic Data (Family income, unemployment)

	$25k-$75k	$75k-$150k	>$150k	Unemployment 03/2009	Unemployment 03/2010
Area	41.6%	30.7%	10.0%	9.0%	9.8%
USA	45.8%	29.5%	8.5%	9.0%	10.1

Key Household Data

	Population Age 0-17	Children w/Married Parents	Children w/Single Mother	Stay-at-home Mothers	Births to Single Women
Area	24.5%	60.8%	31.4%	25.8%	46.9%
USA	24.0%	65.6%	25.5%	27.9%	35.3%

Key Housing Data

	Owner Occupied	Median Year Built	Median Home Value	Home Value Growth, 2005-2010	Median List Price, 4-bedroom Home
Area	68.8%	1985	$208,000	6.0%	$299,900
USA	67.8%	1976	$187,045	3.1%	$288,846

Charlotte-Gastonia-Concord, NC-SC
1,701,600

	Score	Rank
Overall	62.12	190
LDS Culture	24.07	236
Education	66.77	223
Crime	34.21	325
Economic	67.09	121
Health	39.64	219
Household	72.84	127
Housing	93.69	20

Key LDS Culture Data

	Positive	Negative	Ratio Pos:Neg	Commute>59 minutes	Commute<15 minutes
Area	8,609	316	27.2	5.5%	23.2%
USA	4,292	251	20.1	5.5%	34.1%

Key Education Data

	HS Grad	Some Coll.	College Degree	Free/Reduced Lunch	Students per Teacher
Area	86.4%	22.3%	39.9%	30.5%	14.9
USA	85.8%	22.6%	33.2%	41.2%	15.8

Key Property Crime Data (Rate per 100,000 residents)

	Rate	Burglary	Larceny, Theft	Vehicle Theft	
Area	4,661.4	1,193.9	3,020.4	447.1	
USA	3,413.6	806.6	2,388.0	262.7	

Key Violent Crime Data (Rate per 100,000 residents)

	Rate	Murder	Rape	Robbery	Aggravated Assault
Area	661.0	8.1	30.6	227.6	394.8
USA	432.8	4.7	34.7	111.6	285.6

Key Economic Data (Family income, unemployment)

	$25k-$75k	$75k-$150k	>$150k	Unemployment 03/2009	Unemployment 03/2010
Area	42.5%	30.9%	12.6%	11.1%	11.9%
USA	45.8%	29.5%	8.5%	9.0%	10.1

Key Household Data

	Population Age 0-17	Children w/Married Parents	Children w/Single Mother	Stay-at-home Mothers	Births to Single Women
Area	26.2%	66.5%	24.7%	27.6%	33.1%
USA	24.0%	65.6%	25.5%	27.9%	35.3%

Key Housing Data

	Owner Occupied	Median Year Built	Median Home Value	Home Value Growth, 2005-2010	Median List Price, 4-bedroom Home
Area	68.2%	1990	$179,500	4.4%	$254,900
USA	67.8%	1976	$187,045	3.1%	$288,846

Charlottesville, VA
193,684

	Score	Rank
Overall	74.89	18
LDS Culture	59.92	7
Education	78.16	94
Crime	78.21	39
Economic	75.82	42
Health	36.28	278
Household	70.37	143
Housing	81.49	191

Key LDS Culture Data
	Positive	Negative	Ratio Pos:Neg	Commute>59 minutes	Commute<15 minutes
Area	2,010	32	62.8	5.1%	29.8%
USA	4,292	251	20.1	5.5%	34.1%

Key Education Data
	HS Grad	Some Coll.	College Degree	Free/Reduced Lunch	Students per Teacher
Area	86.7%	16.7%	47.3%	29.3%	16.1
USA	85.8%	22.6%	33.2%	41.2%	15.8

Key Property Crime Data (Rate per 100,000 residents)
	Rate	Burglary	Larceny, Theft	Vehicle Theft	
Area	2,550.9	348.6	2,042.9	159.4	
USA	3,413.6	806.6	2,388.0	262.7	

Key Violent Crime Data (Rate per 100,000 residents)
	Rate	Murder	Rape	Robbery	Aggravated Assault
Area	212.9	4.6	30.3	63.8	114.1
USA	432.8	4.7	34.7	111.6	285.6

Key Economic Data (Family income, unemployment)
	$25k-$75k	$75k-$150k	>$150k	Unemployment 03/2009	Unemployment 03/2010
Area	39.6%	33.6%	16.8%	5.4%	6.4%
USA	45.8%	29.5%	8.5%	9.0%	10.1

Key Household Data
	Population Age 0-17	Children w/Married Parents	Children w/Single Mother	Stay-at-home Mothers	Births to Single Women
Area	21.0%	72.9%	19.8%	23.5%	35.6%
USA	24.0%	65.6%	25.5%	27.9%	35.3%

Key Housing Data
	Owner Occupied	Median Year Built	Median Home Value	Home Value Growth, 2005-2010	Median List Price, 4-bedroom Home
Area	65.6%	1985	$288,800	5.6%	
USA	67.8%	1976	$187,045	3.1%	$288,846

Chattanooga, TN-GA
518,515

	Score	Rank
Overall	64.44	150
LDS Culture	32.73	112
Education	61.89	280
Crime	45.33	251
Economic	67.98	111
Health	44.79	151
Household	71.60	136
Housing	88.88	65

Key LDS Culture Data

	Positive	Negative	Ratio Pos:Neg	Commute>59 minutes	Commute<15 minutes
Area	3,813	141	27.0	4.1%	25.9%
USA	4,292	251	20.1	5.5%	34.1%

Key Education Data

	HS Grad	Some Coll.	College Degree	Free/Reduced Lunch	Students per Teacher
Area	83.7%	24.1%	30.2%	50.6%	14.8
USA	85.8%	22.6%	33.2%	41.2%	15.8

Key Property Crime Data (Rate per 100,000 residents)

	Rate	Burglary	Larceny, Theft	Vehicle Theft	
Area	4,404.6	1,022.4	3,029.6	352.5	
USA	3,413.6	806.6	2,388.0	262.7	

Key Violent Crime Data (Rate per 100,000 residents)

	Rate	Murder	Rape	Robbery	Aggravated Assault
Area		5.6	25.1	119.0	
USA	432.8	4.7	34.7	111.6	285.6

Key Economic Data (Family income, unemployment)

	$25k-$75k	$75k-$150k	>$150k	Unemployment 03/2009	Unemployment 03/2010
Area	49.2%	27.4%	7.0%	9.7%	9.5%
USA	45.8%	29.5%	8.5%	9.0%	10.1

Key Household Data

	Population Age 0-17	Children w/Married Parents	Children w/Single Mother	Stay-at-home Mothers	Births to Single Women
Area	22.8%	67.6%	25.9%	30.5%	38.8%
USA	24.0%	65.6%	25.5%	27.9%	35.3%

Key Housing Data

	Owner Occupied	Median Year Built	Median Home Value	Home Value Growth, 2005-2010	Median List Price, 4-bedroom Home
Area	70.7%	1977	$142,900	3.4%	$249,900
USA	67.8%	1976	$187,045	3.1%	$288,846

Cheyenne, WY
87,542

	Score	Rank
Overall	66.21	120
LDS Culture	41.62	37
Education	78.60	89
Crime	69.98	76
Economic	77.27	27
Health	29.61	347
Household	51.23	293
Housing	76.25	266

Key LDS Culture Data

	Positive	Negative	Ratio Pos:Neg	Commute>59 minutes	Commute<15 minutes
Area	496	29	17.1	1.5%	53.0%
USA	4,292	251	20.1	5.5%	34.1%

Key Education Data

	HS Grad	Some Coll.	College Degree	Free/Reduced Lunch	Students per Teacher
Area	91.0%	28.3%	33.9%	32.4%	12.9
USA	85.8%	22.6%	33.2%	41.2%	15.8

Key Property Crime Data (Rate per 100,000 residents)

	Rate	Burglary	Larceny, Theft	Vehicle Theft
Area	3,574.4	468.5	2,942.1	163.8
USA	3,413.6	806.6	2,388.0	262.7

Key Violent Crime Data (Rate per 100,000 residents)

	Rate	Murder	Rape	Robbery	Aggravated Assault
Area	210.4	3.4	33.0	34.1	139.9
USA	432.8	4.7	34.7	111.6	285.6

Key Economic Data (Family income, unemployment)

	$25k-$75k	$75k-$150k	>$150k	Unemployment 03/2009	Unemployment 03/2010
Area	41.6%	36.4%	9.0%	6.2%	8.1%
USA	45.8%	29.5%	8.5%	9.0%	10.1

Key Household Data

	Population Age 0-17	Children w/Married Parents	Children w/Single Mother	Stay-at-home Mothers	Births to Single Women
Area	25.4%	62.0%	25.0%	17.9%	48.3%
USA	24.0%	65.6%	25.5%	27.9%	35.3%

Key Housing Data

	Owner Occupied	Median Year Built	Median Home Value	Home Value Growth, 2005-2010	Median List Price, 4-bedroom Home
Area	71.6%	1974	$175,000	3.7%	
USA	67.8%	1976	$187,045	3.1%	$288,846

Chicago-Naperville-Joliet, IL-IN-WI
9,568,532

	Score	Rank
Overall	**58.47**	**279**
LDS Culture	22.28	253
Education	72.95	150
Crime	34.59	324
Economic	61.15	210
Health	38.99	236
Household	80.25	63
Housing	64.72	343

Key LDS Culture Data

	Positive	Negative	Ratio Pos:Neg	Commute>59 minutes	Commute<15 minutes
Area	33,798	2221	15.2	14.4%	19.9%
USA	4,292	251	20.1	5.5%	34.1%

Key Education Data

	HS Grad	Some Coll.	College Degree	Free/Reduced Lunch	Students per Teacher
Area	85.5%	20.5%	39.6%	38.8%	19.1
USA	85.8%	22.6%	33.2%	41.2%	15.8

Key Property Crime Data (Rate per 100,000 residents)

	Rate	Burglary	Larceny, Theft	Vehicle Theft
Area		803.9	2,739.1	569.1
USA	3,413.6	806.6	2,388.0	262.7

Key Violent Crime Data (Rate per 100,000 residents)

	Rate	Murder	Rape	Robbery	Aggravated Assault
Area		13.8		467.4	549.2
USA	432.8	4.7	34.7	111.6	285.6

Key Economic Data (Family income, unemployment)

	$25k-$75k	$75k-$150k	>$150k	Unemployment 03/2009	Unemployment 03/2010
Area	37.3%	34.1%	15.4%	9.6%	11.3%
USA	45.8%	29.5%	8.5%	9.0%	10.1

Key Household Data

	Population Age 0-17	Children w/Married Parents	Children w/Single Mother	Stay-at-home Mothers	Births to Single Women
Area	25.6%	68.0%	24.5%	32.7%	31.2%
USA	24.0%	65.6%	25.5%	27.9%	35.3%

Key Housing Data

	Owner Occupied	Median Year Built	Median Home Value	Home Value Growth, 2005-2010	Median List Price, 4-bedroom Home
Area	68.2%	1969	$269,900	2.2%	$347,900
USA	67.8%	1976	$187,045	3.1%	$288,846

Chico, CA
220,337

	Score	Rank
Overall	57.36	297
LDS Culture	25.12	210
Education	78.32	92
Crime	51.65	200
Economic	45.91	349
Health	48.59	60
Household	55.56	269
Housing	62.67	349

Key LDS Culture Data

	Positive	Negative	Ratio Pos:Neg	Commute>59 minutes	Commute<15 minutes
Area	1,419	77	18.4	6.6%	46.5%
USA	4,292	251	20.1	5.5%	34.1%

Key Education Data

	HS Grad	Some Coll.	College Degree	Free/Reduced Lunch	Students per Teacher
Area	84.4%	30.8%	32.1%	49.5%	17.1
USA	85.8%	22.6%	33.2%	41.2%	15.8

Key Property Crime Data (Rate per 100,000 residents)

	Rate	Burglary	Larceny, Theft	Vehicle Theft	
Area	3,086.2	851.9	1,829.2	405.1	
USA	3,413.6	806.6	2,388.0	262.7	

Key Violent Crime Data (Rate per 100,000 residents)

	Rate	Murder	Rape	Robbery	Aggravated Assault
Area	452.3	4.2	58.8	81.5	307.9
USA	432.8	4.7	34.7	111.6	285.6

Key Economic Data (Family income, unemployment)

	$25k-$75k	$75k-$150k	>$150k	Unemployment 03/2009	Unemployment 03/2010
Area	47.4%	25.7%	5.5%	12.6%	15.1%
USA	45.8%	29.5%	8.5%	9.0%	10.1

Key Household Data

	Population Age 0-17	Children w/Married Parents	Children w/Single Mother	Stay-at-home Mothers	Births to Single Women
Area	20.8%	60.5%	28.7%	34.2%	55.5%
USA	24.0%	65.6%	25.5%	27.9%	35.3%

Key Housing Data

	Owner Occupied	Median Year Built	Median Home Value	Home Value Growth, 2005-2010	Median List Price, 4-bedroom Home
Area	57.7%	1977	$276,900	1.7%	$370,000
USA	67.8%	1976	$187,045	3.1%	$288,846

Cincinnati-Middletown, OH-KY-IN
2,155,435

	Score	Rank
Overall	61.80	202
LDS Culture	27.14	181
Education	76.60	108
Crime	56.24	161
Economic	56.81	272
Health	37.59	249
Household	62.35	205
Housing	79.57	216

Key LDS Culture Data

	Positive	Negative	Ratio Pos:Neg	Commute>59 minutes	Commute<15 minutes
Area	9,414	599	15.7	4.6%	25.7%
USA	4,292	251	20.1	5.5%	34.1%

Key Education Data

	HS Grad	Some Coll.	College Degree	Free/Reduced Lunch	Students per Teacher
Area	87.4%	19.7%	36.0%	8.6%	18.0
USA	85.8%	22.6%	33.2%	41.2%	15.8

Key Property Crime Data (Rate per 100,000 residents)

	Rate	Burglary	Larceny, Theft	Vehicle Theft
Area	3,247.1	763.8	2,303.0	180.3
USA	3,413.6	806.6	2,388.0	262.7

Key Violent Crime Data (Rate per 100,000 residents)

	Rate	Murder	Rape	Robbery	Aggravated Assault
Area	376.9	5.0	38.7	176.7	156.6
USA	432.8	4.7	34.7	111.6	285.6

Key Economic Data (Family income, unemployment)

	$25k-$75k	$75k-$150k	>$150k	Unemployment 03/2009	Unemployment 03/2010
Area	41.6%	34.0%	10.9%	9.0%	10.6%
USA	45.8%	29.5%	8.5%	9.0%	10.1

Key Household Data

	Population Age 0-17	Children w/Married Parents	Children w/Single Mother	Stay-at-home Mothers	Births to Single Women
Area	25.0%	66.2%	25.0%	26.2%	36.6%
USA	24.0%	65.6%	25.5%	27.9%	35.3%

Key Housing Data

	Owner Occupied	Median Year Built	Median Home Value	Home Value Growth, 2005-2010	Median List Price, 4-bedroom Home
Area	69.7%	1974	$161,200	1.2%	$234,900
USA	67.8%	1976	$187,045	3.1%	$288,846

Clarksville, TN-KY
261,068

	Score	Rank
Overall	61.15	217
LDS Culture	22.39	251
Education	64.36	253
Crime	46.56	241
Economic	58.25	253
Health	37.08	261
Household	67.28	163
Housing	96.17	10

Key LDS Culture Data

	Positive	Negative	Ratio Pos:Neg	Commute>59 minutes	Commute<15 minutes
Area	1,424	70	20.3	7.4%	31.5%
USA	4,292	251	20.1	5.5%	34.1%

Key Education Data

	HS Grad	Some Coll.	College Degree	Free/Reduced Lunch	Students per Teacher
Area	87.3%	28.5%	26.1%	46.3%	16.2
USA	85.8%	22.6%	33.2%	41.2%	15.8

Key Property Crime Data (Rate per 100,000 residents)

	Rate	Burglary	Larceny, Theft	Vehicle Theft
Area	3,227.1	968.8	2,060.3	198.0
USA	3,413.6	806.6	2,388.0	262.7

Key Violent Crime Data (Rate per 100,000 residents)

	Rate	Murder	Rape	Robbery	Aggravated Assault
Area	538.2	2.6	36.9	114.4	384.3
USA	432.8	4.7	34.7	111.6	285.6

Key Economic Data (Family income, unemployment)

	$25k-$75k	$75k-$150k	>$150k	Unemployment 03/2009	Unemployment 03/2010
Area	50.1%	24.3%	4.6%	10.2%	10.5%
USA	45.8%	29.5%	8.5%	9.0%	10.1

Key Household Data

	Population Age 0-17	Children w/Married Parents	Children w/Single Mother	Stay-at-home Mothers	Births to Single Women
Area	28.6%	58.6%	30.9%	40.3%	33.0%
USA	24.0%	65.6%	25.5%	27.9%	35.3%

Key Housing Data

	Owner Occupied	Median Year Built	Median Home Value	Home Value Growth, 2005-2010	Median List Price, 4-bedroom Home
Area	66.9%	1988	$122,300	4.4%	$198,000
USA	67.8%	1976	$187,045	3.1%	$288,846

Cleveland, TN
113,081

	Score	Rank
Overall	64.82	141
LDS Culture	37.39	63
Education	62.84	270
Crime	38.60	298
Economic	70.93	76
Health	38.85	238
Household	82.10	53
Housing	84.95	142

Key LDS Culture Data

	Positive	Negative	Ratio Pos:Neg	Commute>59 minutes	Commute<15 minutes
Area	3,688	135	27.3	4.1%	36.1%
USA	4,292	251	20.1	5.5%	34.1%

Key Education Data

	HS Grad	Some Coll.	College Degree	Free/Reduced Lunch	Students per Teacher
Area	77.9%	25.0%	22.0%	49.4%	16.0
USA	85.8%	22.6%	33.2%	41.2%	15.8

Key Property Crime Data (Rate per 100,000 residents)

	Rate	Burglary	Larceny, Theft	Vehicle Theft
Area	3,319.2	766.4	2,367.0	185.8
USA	3,413.6	806.6	2,388.0	262.7

Key Violent Crime Data (Rate per 100,000 residents)

	Rate	Murder	Rape	Robbery	Aggravated Assault
Area	703.8	2.7	32.2	48.2	620.8
USA	432.8	4.7	34.7	111.6	285.6

Key Economic Data (Family income, unemployment)

	$25k-$75k	$75k-$150k	>$150k	Unemployment 03/2009	Unemployment 03/2010
Area	50.9%	21.8%	4.2%	10.6%	10.1%
USA	45.8%	29.5%	8.5%	9.0%	10.1

Key Household Data

	Population Age 0-17	Children w/Married Parents	Children w/Single Mother	Stay-at-home Mothers	Births to Single Women
Area	22.9%	76.9%	16.6%	40.3%	36.2%
USA	24.0%	65.6%	25.5%	27.9%	35.3%

Key Housing Data

	Owner Occupied	Median Year Built	Median Home Value	Home Value Growth, 2005-2010	Median List Price, 4-bedroom Home
Area	68.4%	1980	$131,200	3.7%	
USA	67.8%	1976	$187,045	3.1%	$288,846

Cleveland-Elyria-Mentor, OH
2,088,291

	Score	Rank
Overall	56.89	306
LDS Culture	24.72	220
Education	70.47	177
Crime	53.14	188
Economic	57.53	264
Health	35.87	284
Household	51.85	288
Housing	71.23	322

Key LDS Culture Data

	Positive	Negative	Ratio Pos:Neg	Commute>59 minutes	Commute<15 minutes
Area	11,971	923	13.0	4.4%	26.1%
USA	4,292	251	20.1	5.5%	34.1%

Key Education Data

	HS Grad	Some Coll.	College Degree	Free/Reduced Lunch	Students per Teacher
Area	88.0%	22.5%	34.3%		17.1
USA	85.8%	22.6%	33.2%	41.2%	15.8

Key Property Crime Data (Rate per 100,000 residents)

	Rate	Burglary	Larceny, Theft	Vehicle Theft	
Area	3,003.4	814.4	1,740.5	448.6	
USA	3,413.6	806.6	2,388.0	262.7	

Key Violent Crime Data (Rate per 100,000 residents)

	Rate	Murder	Rape	Robbery	Aggravated Assault
Area	436.5	6.1	35.4	243.9	151.0
USA	432.8	4.7	34.7	111.6	285.6

Key Economic Data (Family income, unemployment)

	$25k-$75k	$75k-$150k	>$150k	Unemployment 03/2009	Unemployment 03/2010
Area	42.9%	31.2%	10.1%	9.1%	9.8%
USA	45.8%	29.5%	8.5%	9.0%	10.1

Key Household Data

	Population Age 0-17	Children w/Married Parents	Children w/Single Mother	Stay-at-home Mothers	Births to Single Women
Area	23.5%	62.7%	29.7%	26.3%	40.8%
USA	24.0%	65.6%	25.5%	27.9%	35.3%

Key Housing Data

	Owner Occupied	Median Year Built	Median Home Value	Home Value Growth, 2005-2010	Median List Price, 4-bedroom Home
Area	68.0%	1960	$153,300	-0.2%	$214,900
USA	67.8%	1976	$187,045	3.1%	$288,846

Coeur d'Alene, ID
137,475

	Score	Rank
Overall	71.90	32
LDS Culture	25.66	203
Education	76.18	115
Crime	67.75	93
Economic	63.15	181
Health	45.18	143
Household	90.12	14
Housing	93.01	25

Key LDS Culture Data

	Positive	Negative	Ratio Pos:Neg	Commute>59 minutes	Commute<15 minutes
Area	2,627	138	19.0	4.6%	39.1%
USA	4,292	251	20.1	5.5%	34.1%

Key Education Data

	HS Grad	Some Coll.	College Degree	Free/Reduced Lunch	Students per Teacher
Area	92.1%	29.8%	34.6%	34.7%	19.2
USA	85.8%	22.6%	33.2%	41.2%	15.8

Key Property Crime Data (Rate per 100,000 residents)

	Rate	Burglary	Larceny, Theft	Vehicle Theft	
Area	2,373.5	505.2	1,717.1	151.2	
USA	3,413.6	806.6	2,388.0	262.7	

Key Violent Crime Data (Rate per 100,000 residents)

	Rate	Murder	Rape	Robbery	Aggravated Assault
Area	343.7	0.7	53.1	21.4	268.5
USA	432.8	4.7	34.7	111.6	285.6

Key Economic Data (Family income, unemployment)

	$25k-$75k	$75k-$150k	>$150k	Unemployment 03/2009	Unemployment 03/2010
Area	54.8%	27.6%	5.1%	9.2%	11.9%
USA	45.8%	29.5%	8.5%	9.0%	10.1

Key Household Data

	Population Age 0-17	Children w/Married Parents	Children w/Single Mother	Stay-at-home Mothers	Births to Single Women
Area	24.6%	70.7%	21.0%	28.4%	19.1%
USA	24.0%	65.6%	25.5%	27.9%	35.3%

Key Housing Data

	Owner Occupied	Median Year Built	Median Home Value	Home Value Growth, 2005-2010	Median List Price, 4-bedroom Home
Area	72.1%	1991	$234,400	7.4%	
USA	67.8%	1976	$187,045	3.1%	$288,846

College Station-Bryan, TX
211,761

	Score	Rank
Overall	61.26	215
LDS Culture	28.79	157
Education	74.77	130
Crime	44.56	258
Economic	53.81	308
Health	32.00	325
Household	72.22	132
Housing	86.66	106

Key LDS Culture Data

	Positive	Negative	Ratio Pos:Neg	Commute>59 minutes	Commute<15 minutes
Area	1,125	64	17.6	3.6%	42.5%
USA	4,292	251	20.1	5.5%	34.1%

Key Education Data

	HS Grad	Some Coll.	College Degree	Free/Reduced Lunch	Students per Teacher
Area	80.8%	15.7%	39.5%	50.4%	13.8
USA	85.8%	22.6%	33.2%	41.2%	15.8

Key Property Crime Data (Rate per 100,000 residents)

	Rate	Burglary	Larceny, Theft	Vehicle Theft	
Area	3,995.0	1,001.7	2,808.2	185.2	
USA	3,413.6	806.6	2,388.0	262.7	

Key Violent Crime Data (Rate per 100,000 residents)

	Rate	Murder	Rape	Robbery	Aggravated Assault
Area	494.8	4.9	54.9	83.1	351.9
USA	432.8	4.7	34.7	111.6	285.6

Key Economic Data (Family income, unemployment)

	$25k-$75k	$75k-$150k	>$150k	Unemployment 03/2009	Unemployment 03/2010
Area	43.6%	25.2%	9.5%	5.0%	5.9%
USA	45.8%	29.5%	8.5%	9.0%	10.1

Key Household Data

	Population Age 0-17	Children w/Married Parents	Children w/Single Mother	Stay-at-home Mothers	Births to Single Women
Area	23.0%	61.6%	31.3%	33.7%	28.7%
USA	24.0%	65.6%	25.5%	27.9%	35.3%

Key Housing Data

	Owner Occupied	Median Year Built	Median Home Value	Home Value Growth, 2005-2010	Median List Price, 4-bedroom Home
Area	51.0%	1986	$137,200	4.4%	
USA	67.8%	1976	$187,045	3.1%	$288,846

Colorado Springs, CO
617,321

	Score	Rank
Overall	70.08	50
LDS Culture	15.19	333
Education	89.34	20
Crime	50.89	209
Economic	78.93	19
Health	44.77	152
Household	83.33	39
Housing	86.94	101

Key LDS Culture Data

	Positive	Negative	Ratio Pos:Neg	Commute>59 minutes	Commute<15 minutes
Area	3,181	261	12.2	4.9%	29.9%
USA	4,292	251	20.1	5.5%	34.1%

Key Education Data

	HS Grad	Some Coll.	College Degree	Free/Reduced Lunch	Students per Teacher
Area	92.3%	25.5%	44.3%	29.1%	16.0
USA	85.8%	22.6%	33.2%	41.2%	15.8

Key Property Crime Data (Rate per 100,000 residents)

	Rate	Burglary	Larceny, Theft	Vehicle Theft	
Area	3,083.6	693.4	2,166.6	223.7	
USA	3,413.6	806.6	2,388.0	262.7	

Key Violent Crime Data (Rate per 100,000 residents)

	Rate	Murder	Rape	Robbery	Aggravated Assault
Area	470.5	5.0	67.1	88.7	309.7
USA	432.8	4.7	34.7	111.6	285.6

Key Economic Data (Family income, unemployment)

	$25k-$75k	$75k-$150k	>$150k	Unemployment 03/2009	Unemployment 03/2010
Area	42.5%	34.0%	11.2%	9.0%	9.0%
USA	45.8%	29.5%	8.5%	9.0%	10.1

Key Household Data

	Population Age 0-17	Children w/Married Parents	Children w/Single Mother	Stay-at-home Mothers	Births to Single Women
Area	25.5%	68.8%	22.9%	36.5%	28.4%
USA	24.0%	65.6%	25.5%	27.9%	35.3%

Key Housing Data

	Owner Occupied	Median Year Built	Median Home Value	Home Value Growth, 2005-2010	Median List Price, 4-bedroom Home
Area	68.0%	1986	$228,000	2.0%	$259,000
USA	67.8%	1976	$187,045	3.1%	$288,846

Columbia, MO
164,929

	Score	Rank
Overall	70.20	47
LDS Culture	47.24	20
Education	95.26	9
Crime	60.41	146
Economic	61.37	205
Health	33.49	311
Household	66.67	168
Housing	85.71	125

Key LDS Culture Data

	Positive	Negative	Ratio Pos:Neg	Commute>59 minutes	Commute<15 minutes
Area	1,793	63	28.5	2.6%	38.8%
USA	4,292	251	20.1	5.5%	34.1%

Key Education Data

	HS Grad	Some Coll.	College Degree	Free/Reduced Lunch	Students per Teacher
Area	91.6%	18.3%	47.7%	30.6%	13.2
USA	85.8%	22.6%	33.2%	41.2%	15.8

Key Property Crime Data (Rate per 100,000 residents)

	Rate	Burglary	Larceny, Theft	Vehicle Theft
Area	3,266.2	700.3	2,438.7	127.3
USA	3,413.6	806.6	2,388.0	262.7

Key Violent Crime Data (Rate per 100,000 residents)

	Rate	Murder	Rape	Robbery	Aggravated Assault
Area	330.0	4.3	16.4	92.6	216.8
USA	432.8	4.7	34.7	111.6	285.6

Key Economic Data (Family income, unemployment)

	$25k-$75k	$75k-$150k	>$150k	Unemployment 03/2009	Unemployment 03/2010
Area	42.9%	31.9%	7.4%	6.4%	6.9%
USA	45.8%	29.5%	8.5%	9.0%	10.1

Key Household Data

	Population Age 0-17	Children w/Married Parents	Children w/Single Mother	Stay-at-home Mothers	Births to Single Women
Area	22.0%	65.9%	23.5%	17.3%	21.6%
USA	24.0%	65.6%	25.5%	27.9%	35.3%

Key Housing Data

	Owner Occupied	Median Year Built	Median Home Value	Home Value Growth, 2005-2010	Median List Price, 4-bedroom Home
Area	56.8%	1986	$148,900	2.9%	
USA	67.8%	1976	$187,045	3.1%	$288,846

Columbia, SC
721,109

	Score	Rank
Overall	**58.19**	**285**
LDS Culture	22.65	246
Education	64.10	255
Crime	33.56	328
Economic	65.26	149
Health	44.81	150
Household	48.77	306
Housing	94.00	18

Key LDS Culture Data

	Positive	Negative	Ratio Pos:Neg	Commute>59 minutes	Commute<15 minutes
Area	3,611	175	20.6	4.1%	25.7%
USA	4,292	251	20.1	5.5%	34.1%

Key Education Data

	HS Grad	Some Coll.	College Degree	Free/Reduced Lunch	Students per Teacher
Area	88.2%	22.3%	39.1%	46.4%	13.8
USA	85.8%	22.6%	33.2%	41.2%	15.8

Key Property Crime Data (Rate per 100,000 residents)

	Rate	Burglary	Larceny, Theft	Vehicle Theft
Area	3,994.3	874.7	2,694.3	425.2
USA	3,413.6	806.6	2,388.0	262.7

Key Violent Crime Data (Rate per 100,000 residents)

	Rate	Murder	Rape	Robbery	Aggravated Assault
Area	747.5	5.5	33.5	160.0	548.5
USA	432.8	4.7	34.7	111.6	285.6

Key Economic Data (Family income, unemployment)

	$25k-$75k	$75k-$150k	>$150k	Unemployment 03/2009	Unemployment 03/2010
Area	43.9%	31.9%	8.6%	8.8%	9.6%
USA	45.8%	29.5%	8.5%	9.0%	10.1

Key Household Data

	Population Age 0-17	Children w/Married Parents	Children w/Single Mother	Stay-at-home Mothers	Births to Single Women
Area	24.2%	60.5%	31.3%	23.7%	47.2%
USA	24.0%	65.6%	25.5%	27.9%	35.3%

Key Housing Data

	Owner Occupied	Median Year Built	Median Home Value	Home Value Growth, 2005-2010	Median List Price, 4-bedroom Home
Area	69.1%	1984	$140,500	4.0%	$205,000
USA	67.8%	1976	$187,045	3.1%	$288,846

Columbus, GA-AL
291,305

	Score	Rank
Overall	54.81	332
LDS Culture	24.60	226
Education	64.17	254
Crime	32.81	331
Economic	56.36	279
Health	33.58	307
Household	49.38	302
Housing	90.56	47

Key LDS Culture Data

	Positive	Negative	Ratio Pos:Neg	Commute>59 minutes	Commute<15 minutes
Area	2,078	91	22.8	3.2%	28.8%
USA	4,292	251	20.1	5.5%	34.1%

Key Education Data

	HS Grad	Some Coll.	College Degree	Free/Reduced Lunch	Students per Teacher
Area	83.4%	25.8%	28.0%	59.9%	14.6
USA	85.8%	22.6%	33.2%	41.2%	15.8

Key Property Crime Data (Rate per 100,000 residents)

	Rate	Burglary	Larceny, Theft	Vehicle Theft
Area	5,979.9	1,398.5	3,915.3	666.1
USA	3,413.6	806.6	2,388.0	262.7

Key Violent Crime Data (Rate per 100,000 residents)

	Rate	Murder	Rape	Robbery	Aggravated Assault
Area	552.0	12.4	31.9	250.2	257.6
USA	432.8	4.7	34.7	111.6	285.6

Key Economic Data (Family income, unemployment)

	$25k-$75k	$75k-$150k	>$150k	Unemployment 03/2009	Unemployment 03/2010
Area	49.4%	22.9%	5.3%	8.4%	9.9%
USA	45.8%	29.5%	8.5%	9.0%	10.1

Key Household Data

	Population Age 0-17	Children w/Married Parents	Children w/Single Mother	Stay-at-home Mothers	Births to Single Women
Area	26.2%	50.9%	42.3%	29.7%	43.8%
USA	24.0%	65.6%	25.5%	27.9%	35.3%

Key Housing Data

	Owner Occupied	Median Year Built	Median Home Value	Home Value Growth, 2005-2010	Median List Price, 4-bedroom Home
Area	61.2%	1978	$132,500	4.4%	$209,000
USA	67.8%	1976	$187,045	3.1%	$288,846

Columbus, IN
75,360

	Score	Rank
Overall	68.34	75
LDS Culture	26.64	186
Education	72.89	151
Crime	83.10	23
Economic	71.48	68
Health	34.59	292
Household	68.52	157
Housing	81.01	197

Key LDS Culture Data

	Positive	Negative	Ratio Pos:Neg	Commute>59 minutes	Commute<15 minutes
Area	1,401	138	10.2	5.0%	40.4%
USA	4,292	251	20.1	5.5%	34.1%

Key Education Data

	HS Grad	Some Coll.	College Degree	Free/Reduced Lunch	Students per Teacher
Area	88.8%	21.4%	36.0%	34.0%	21.1
USA	85.8%	22.6%	33.2%	41.2%	15.8

Key Property Crime Data (Rate per 100,000 residents)

	Rate	Burglary	Larceny, Theft	Vehicle Theft	
Area	3,182.8	291.6	2,719.4	171.8	
USA	3,413.6	806.6	2,388.0	262.7	

Key Violent Crime Data (Rate per 100,000 residents)

	Rate	Murder	Rape	Robbery	Aggravated Assault
Area	94.6	2.7	6.7	18.6	66.6
USA	432.8	4.7	34.7	111.6	285.6

Key Economic Data (Family income, unemployment)

	$25k-$75k	$75k-$150k	>$150k	Unemployment 03/2009	Unemployment 03/2010
Area	47.8%	33.5%	8.2%	9.8%	10.2%
USA	45.8%	29.5%	8.5%	9.0%	10.1

Key Household Data

	Population Age 0-17	Children w/Married Parents	Children w/Single Mother	Stay-at-home Mothers	Births to Single Women
Area	25.5%	67.5%	17.2%	23.0%	25.0%
USA	24.0%	65.6%	25.5%	27.9%	35.3%

Key Housing Data

	Owner Occupied	Median Year Built	Median Home Value	Home Value Growth, 2005-2010	Median List Price, 4-bedroom Home
Area	76.2%	1973	$139,500	2.4%	
USA	67.8%	1976	$187,045	3.1%	$288,846

Columbus, OH
1,773,120

	Score	Rank
Overall	**60.79**	**225**
LDS Culture	35.98	72
Education	70.76	176
Crime	48.15	232
Economic	55.36	290
Health	39.58	222
Household	56.17	262
Housing	83.80	161

Key LDS Culture Data

	Positive	Negative	Ratio Pos:Neg	Commute>59 minutes	Commute<15 minutes
Area	8,799	560	15.7	3.7%	26.9%
USA	4,292	251	20.1	5.5%	34.1%

Key Education Data

	HS Grad	Some Coll.	College Degree	Free/Reduced Lunch	Students per Teacher
Area	89.5%	20.8%	39.4%		18.4
USA	85.8%	22.6%	33.2%	41.2%	15.8

Key Property Crime Data (Rate per 100,000 residents)

	Rate	Burglary	Larceny, Theft	Vehicle Theft
Area	4,324.1	1,176.5	2,780.3	367.3
USA	3,413.6	806.6	2,388.0	262.7

Key Violent Crime Data (Rate per 100,000 residents)

	Rate	Murder	Rape	Robbery	Aggravated Assault
Area	407.7	6.9	51.2	235.9	113.7
USA	432.8	4.7	34.7	111.6	285.6

Key Economic Data (Family income, unemployment)

	$25k-$75k	$75k-$150k	>$150k	Unemployment 03/2009	Unemployment 03/2010
Area	42.3%	32.7%	11.4%	8.0%	9.8%
USA	45.8%	29.5%	8.5%	9.0%	10.1

Key Household Data

	Population Age 0-17	Children w/Married Parents	Children w/Single Mother	Stay-at-home Mothers	Births to Single Women
Area	25.4%	65.3%	25.8%	24.5%	36.3%
USA	24.0%	65.6%	25.5%	27.9%	35.3%

Key Housing Data

	Owner Occupied	Median Year Built	Median Home Value	Home Value Growth, 2005-2010	Median List Price, 4-bedroom Home
Area	64.8%	1977	$166,500	1.2%	$234,900
USA	67.8%	1976	$187,045	3.1%	$288,846

Corpus Christi, TX
415,527

	Score	Rank
Overall	52.81	350
LDS Culture	21.70	266
Education	53.24	336
Crime	31.90	333
Economic	56.36	280
Health	32.00	326
Household	54.94	272
Housing	88.46	72

Key LDS Culture Data

	Positive	Negative	Ratio Pos:Neg	Commute>59 minutes	Commute<15 minutes
Area	2,009	138	14.6	3.4%	38.9%
USA	4,292	251	20.1	5.5%	34.1%

Key Education Data

	HS Grad	Some Coll.	College Degree	Free/Reduced Lunch	Students per Teacher
Area	78.8%	26.1%	25.5%	57.7%	15.0
USA	85.8%	22.6%	33.2%	41.2%	15.8

Key Property Crime Data (Rate per 100,000 residents)

	Rate	Burglary	Larceny, Theft	Vehicle Theft
Area	5,427.0	1,173.9	4,046.1	207.1
USA	3,413.6	806.6	2,388.0	262.7

Key Violent Crime Data (Rate per 100,000 residents)

	Rate	Murder	Rape	Robbery	Aggravated Assault
Area	632.0	5.1	58.4	129.6	438.9
USA	432.8	4.7	34.7	111.6	285.6

Key Economic Data (Family income, unemployment)

	$25k-$75k	$75k-$150k	>$150k	Unemployment 03/2009	Unemployment 03/2010
Area	45.9%	25.2%	7.0%	6.4%	7.9%
USA	45.8%	29.5%	8.5%	9.0%	10.1

Key Household Data

	Population Age 0-17	Children w/Married Parents	Children w/Single Mother	Stay-at-home Mothers	Births to Single Women
Area	26.8%	59.6%	29.6%	32.2%	40.6%
USA	24.0%	65.6%	25.5%	27.9%	35.3%

Key Housing Data

	Owner Occupied	Median Year Built	Median Home Value	Home Value Growth, 2005-2010	Median List Price, 4-bedroom Home
Area	63.2%	1974	$105,500	4.4%	
USA	67.8%	1976	$187,045	3.1%	$288,846

157

Corvallis, OR
81,859

	Score	Rank
Overall	79.09	7
LDS Culture	34.49	83
Education	81.69	60
Crime	87.22	11
Economic	87.22	7
Health	46.31	124
Household	91.36	10
Housing	78.88	229

Key LDS Culture Data

	Positive	Negative	Ratio Pos:Neg	Commute>59 minutes	Commute<15 minutes
Area	2,112	111	19.0	3.0%	49.1%
USA	4,292	251	20.1	5.5%	34.1%

Key Education Data

	HS Grad	Some Coll.	College Degree	Free/Reduced Lunch	Students per Teacher
Area	93.5%	24.8%	53.1%	29.1%	20.3
USA	85.8%	22.6%	33.2%	41.2%	15.8

Key Property Crime Data (Rate per 100,000 residents)

	Rate	Burglary	Larceny, Theft	Vehicle Theft	
Area	2,372.8	402.0	1,840.1	130.7	
USA	3,413.6	806.6	2,388.0	262.7	

Key Violent Crime Data (Rate per 100,000 residents)

	Rate	Murder	Rape	Robbery	Aggravated Assault
Area	134.4	1.2	24.4	24.4	84.3
USA	432.8	4.7	34.7	111.6	285.6

Key Economic Data (Family income, unemployment)

	$25k-$75k	$75k-$150k	>$150k	Unemployment 03/2009	Unemployment 03/2010
Area	39.7%	33.4%	14.8%	8.3%	8.1%
USA	45.8%	29.5%	8.5%	9.0%	10.1

Key Household Data

	Population Age 0-17	Children w/Married Parents	Children w/Single Mother	Stay-at-home Mothers	Births to Single Women
Area	17.7%	76.1%	18.7%	34.3%	
USA	24.0%	65.6%	25.5%	27.9%	35.3%

Key Housing Data

	Owner Occupied	Median Year Built	Median Home Value	Home Value Growth, 2005-2010	Median List Price, 4-bedroom Home
Area	58.0%	1977	$282,300	6.5%	
USA	67.8%	1976	$187,045	3.1%	$288,846

Cumberland, MD-WV
99,033

	Score	Rank
Overall	61.22	216
LDS Culture	19.68	288
Education	73.60	140
Crime	55.11	173
Economic	60.20	229
Health	45.68	139
Household	62.35	206
Housing	75.96	273

Key LDS Culture Data

	Positive	Negative	Ratio Pos:Neg	Commute>59 minutes	Commute<15 minutes
Area	898	52	17.3	11.1%	36.6%
USA	4,292	251	20.1	5.5%	34.1%

Key Education Data

	HS Grad	Some Coll.	College Degree	Free/Reduced Lunch	Students per Teacher
Area	87.7%	18.4%	20.9%	44.2%	13.9
USA	85.8%	22.6%	33.2%	41.2%	15.8

Key Property Crime Data (Rate per 100,000 residents)

	Rate	Burglary	Larceny, Theft	Vehicle Theft	
Area	2,716.7	654.8	1,986.7	75.1	
USA	3,413.6	806.6	2,388.0	262.7	

Key Violent Crime Data (Rate per 100,000 residents)

	Rate	Murder	Rape	Robbery	Aggravated Assault
Area	454.8	5.1	25.4	41.6	382.7
USA	432.8	4.7	34.7	111.6	285.6

Key Economic Data (Family income, unemployment)

	$25k-$75k	$75k-$150k	>$150k	Unemployment 03/2009	Unemployment 03/2010
Area	57.8%	23.6%	4.6%	8.5%	9.9%
USA	45.8%	29.5%	8.5%	9.0%	10.1

Key Household Data

	Population Age 0-17	Children w/Married Parents	Children w/Single Mother	Stay-at-home Mothers	Births to Single Women
Area	19.5%	66.3%	26.7%	21.0%	38.4%
USA	24.0%	65.6%	25.5%	27.9%	35.3%

Key Housing Data

	Owner Occupied	Median Year Built	Median Home Value	Home Value Growth, 2005-2010	Median List Price, 4-bedroom Home
Area	74.2%	1958	$120,000	7.7%	
USA	67.8%	1976	$187,045	3.1%	$288,846

Dallas-Fort Worth-Arlington, TX
6,303,407

	Score	Rank
Overall	64.51	149
LDS Culture	27.27	178
Education	67.83	210
Crime	45.86	248
Economic	62.98	185
Health	33.37	315
Household	81.48	59
Housing	94.88	13

Key LDS Culture Data

	Positive	Negative	Ratio Pos:Neg	Commute>59 minutes	Commute<15 minutes
Area	23,276	1116	20.9	7.9%	22.4%
USA	4,292	251	20.1	5.5%	34.1%

Key Education Data

	HS Grad	Some Coll.	College Degree	Free/Reduced Lunch	Students per Teacher
Area	81.2%	22.5%	35.8%	46.7%	14.8
USA	85.8%	22.6%	33.2%	41.2%	15.8

Key Property Crime Data (Rate per 100,000 residents)

	Rate	Burglary	Larceny, Theft	Vehicle Theft
Area	4,064.1	998.2	2,645.4	420.5
USA	3,413.6	806.6	2,388.0	262.7

Key Violent Crime Data (Rate per 100,000 residents)

	Rate	Murder	Rape	Robbery	Aggravated Assault
Area	457.5	5.5	31.0	185.6	235.3
USA	432.8	4.7	34.7	111.6	285.6

Key Economic Data (Family income, unemployment)

	$25k-$75k	$75k-$150k	>$150k	Unemployment 03/2009	Unemployment 03/2010
Area	40.2%	31.7%	13.4%	7.3%	8.3%
USA	45.8%	29.5%	8.5%	9.0%	10.1

Key Household Data

	Population Age 0-17	Children w/Married Parents	Children w/Single Mother	Stay-at-home Mothers	Births to Single Women
Area	27.9%	69.0%	23.4%	35.6%	30.1%
USA	24.0%	65.6%	25.5%	27.9%	35.3%

Key Housing Data

	Owner Occupied	Median Year Built	Median Home Value	Home Value Growth, 2005-2010	Median List Price, 4-bedroom Home
Area	63.1%	1985	$148,600	2.9%	$244,000
USA	67.8%	1976	$187,045	3.1%	$288,846

Dalton, GA
134,139

	Score	Rank
Overall	66.01	126
LDS Culture	29.13	155
Education	47.10	356
Crime	63.35	125
Economic	72.15	64
Health	43.59	163
Household	84.57	34
Housing	83.36	168

Key LDS Culture Data

	Positive	Negative	Ratio Pos:Neg	Commute>59 minutes	Commute<15 minutes
Area	3,831	137	28.0	3.5%	27.8%
USA	4,292	251	20.1	5.5%	34.1%

Key Education Data

	HS Grad	Some Coll.	College Degree	Free/Reduced Lunch	Students per Teacher
Area	69.2%	19.1%	17.4%	62.5%	14.6
USA	85.8%	22.6%	33.2%	41.2%	15.8

Key Property Crime Data (Rate per 100,000 residents)

	Rate	Burglary	Larceny, Theft	Vehicle Theft
Area	2,911.4	599.5	2,158.0	153.9
USA	3,413.6	806.6	2,388.0	262.7

Key Violent Crime Data (Rate per 100,000 residents)

	Rate	Murder	Rape	Robbery	Aggravated Assault
Area	335.3	0.7	19.2	40.0	275.3
USA	432.8	4.7	34.7	111.6	285.6

Key Economic Data (Family income, unemployment)

	$25k-$75k	$75k-$150k	>$150k	Unemployment 03/2009	Unemployment 03/2010
Area	56.0%	19.3%	4.9%	13.4%	12.6%
USA	45.8%	29.5%	8.5%	9.0%	10.1

Key Household Data

	Population Age 0-17	Children w/Married Parents	Children w/Single Mother	Stay-at-home Mothers	Births to Single Women
Area	29.3%	74.3%	19.0%	34.6%	31.9%
USA	24.0%	65.6%	25.5%	27.9%	35.3%

Key Housing Data

	Owner Occupied	Median Year Built	Median Home Value	Home Value Growth, 2005-2010	Median List Price, 4-bedroom Home
Area	69.7%	1983	$118,700	1.8%	
USA	67.8%	1976	$187,045	3.1%	$288,846

Danville, IL
80,680

	Score	Rank
Overall	55.54	326
LDS Culture	32.88	108
Education	58.53	307
Crime	45.65	249
Economic	56.31	282
Health	47.30	103
Household	41.36	355
Housing	74.15	294

Key LDS Culture Data

	Positive	Negative	Ratio Pos:Neg	Commute>59 minutes	Commute<15 minutes
Area	940	77	12.2	3.2%	43.2%
USA	4,292	251	20.1	5.5%	34.1%

Key Education Data

	HS Grad	Some Coll.	College Degree	Free/Reduced Lunch	Students per Teacher
Area	86.1%	23.4%	22.2%	51.1%	18.9
USA	85.8%	22.6%	33.2%	41.2%	15.8

Key Property Crime Data (Rate per 100,000 residents)

	Rate	Burglary	Larceny, Theft	Vehicle Theft
Area	3,811.0			
USA	3,413.6	806.6	2,388.0	262.7

Key Violent Crime Data (Rate per 100,000 residents)

	Rate	Murder	Rape	Robbery	Aggravated Assault
Area	581.0				
USA	432.8	4.7	34.7	111.6	285.6

Key Economic Data (Family income, unemployment)

	$25k-$75k	$75k-$150k	>$150k	Unemployment 03/2009	Unemployment 03/2010
Area	58.1%	20.7%	5.1%	11.1%	13.7%
USA	45.8%	29.5%	8.5%	9.0%	10.1

Key Household Data

	Population Age 0-17	Children w/Married Parents	Children w/Single Mother	Stay-at-home Mothers	Births to Single Women
Area	24.0%	56.2%	29.2%	11.4%	48.3%
USA	24.0%	65.6%	25.5%	27.9%	35.3%

Key Housing Data

	Owner Occupied	Median Year Built	Median Home Value	Home Value Growth, 2005-2010	Median List Price, 4-bedroom Home
Area	73.3%	1956	$73,200	2.5%	
USA	67.8%	1976	$187,045	3.1%	$288,846

Danville, VA
104,806

	Score	Rank
Overall	61.29	214
LDS Culture	62.36	6
Education	50.54	348
Crime	61.89	134
Economic	54.31	303
Health	36.28	279
Household	48.77	307
Housing	78.86	230

Key LDS Culture Data

	Positive	Negative	Ratio Pos:Neg	Commute>59 minutes	Commute<15 minutes
Area	1,836	28	65.6	5.1%	29.4%
USA	4,292	251	20.1	5.5%	34.1%

Key Education Data

	HS Grad	Some Coll.	College Degree	Free/Reduced Lunch	Students per Teacher
Area	74.7%	22.4%	22.3%	51.7%	15.0
USA	85.8%	22.6%	33.2%	41.2%	15.8

Key Property Crime Data (Rate per 100,000 residents)

	Rate	Burglary	Larceny, Theft	Vehicle Theft
Area	3,196.4	716.1	2,339.1	141.1
USA	3,413.6	806.6	2,388.0	262.7

Key Violent Crime Data (Rate per 100,000 residents)

	Rate	Murder	Rape	Robbery	Aggravated Assault
Area	321.4	12.4	18.1	122.1	168.8
USA	432.8	4.7	34.7	111.6	285.6

Key Economic Data (Family income, unemployment)

	$25k-$75k	$75k-$150k	>$150k	Unemployment 03/2009	Unemployment 03/2010
Area	52.1%	19.2%	3.7%	11.3%	12.5%
USA	45.8%	29.5%	8.5%	9.0%	10.1

Key Household Data

	Population Age 0-17	Children w/Married Parents	Children w/Single Mother	Stay-at-home Mothers	Births to Single Women
Area	20.1%	61.7%	29.2%	27.6%	50.4%
USA	24.0%	65.6%	25.5%	27.9%	35.3%

Key Housing Data

	Owner Occupied	Median Year Built	Median Home Value	Home Value Growth, 2005-2010	Median List Price, 4-bedroom Home
Area	69.9%	1973	$101,700	3.6%	
USA	67.8%	1976	$187,045	3.1%	$288,846

Davenport-Moline-Rock Island, IA-IL
378,879

	Score	Rank
Overall	61.36	212
LDS Culture	28.29	166
Education	72.73	155
Crime	44.32	259
Economic	65.76	143
Health	47.30	104
Household	53.70	280
Housing	81.34	193

Key LDS Culture Data

	Positive	Negative	Ratio Pos:Neg	Commute>59 minutes	Commute<15 minutes
Area	2,366	197	12.0	3.3%	37.3%
USA	4,292	251	20.1	5.5%	34.1%

Key Education Data

	HS Grad	Some Coll.	College Degree	Free/Reduced Lunch	Students per Teacher
Area	88.7%	24.7%	33.6%	38.3%	16.7
USA	85.8%	22.6%	33.2%	41.2%	15.8

Key Property Crime Data (Rate per 100,000 residents)

	Rate	Burglary	Larceny, Theft	Vehicle Theft
Area		912.3	3,584.5	200.6
USA	3,413.6	806.6	2,388.0	262.7

Key Violent Crime Data (Rate per 100,000 residents)

	Rate	Murder	Rape	Robbery	Aggravated Assault
Area		1.9	31.5	142.1	380.1
USA	432.8	4.7	34.7	111.6	285.6

Key Economic Data (Family income, unemployment)

	$25k-$75k	$75k-$150k	>$150k	Unemployment 03/2009	Unemployment 03/2010
Area	46.4%	31.8%	7.7%		
USA	45.8%	29.5%	8.5%	9.0%	10.1

Key Household Data

	Population Age 0-17	Children w/Married Parents	Children w/Single Mother	Stay-at-home Mothers	Births to Single Women
Area	23.7%	63.5%	24.7%	23.4%	42.9%
USA	24.0%	65.6%	25.5%	27.9%	35.3%

Key Housing Data

	Owner Occupied	Median Year Built	Median Home Value	Home Value Growth, 2005-2010	Median List Price, 4-bedroom Home
Area	71.8%	1961	$117,800	2.5%	$192,900
USA	67.8%	1976	$187,045	3.1%	$288,846

Dayton, OH
836,544

	Score	Rank
Overall	58.89	270
LDS Culture	32.68	113
Education	65.37	240
Crime	56.46	160
Economic	54.31	302
Health	39.15	235
Household	50.00	299
Housing	79.68	215

Key LDS Culture Data

	Positive	Negative	Ratio Pos:Neg	Commute>59 minutes	Commute<15 minutes
Area	6,149	362	17.0	3.4%	32.6%
USA	4,292	251	20.1	5.5%	34.1%

Key Education Data

	HS Grad	Some Coll.	College Degree	Free/Reduced Lunch	Students per Teacher
Area	88.8%	24.3%	33.2%		18.2
USA	85.8%	22.6%	33.2%	41.2%	15.8

Key Property Crime Data (Rate per 100,000 residents)

	Rate	Burglary	Larceny, Theft	Vehicle Theft
Area	3,512.7	878.2	2,355.2	279.3
USA	3,413.6	806.6	2,388.0	262.7

Key Violent Crime Data (Rate per 100,000 residents)

	Rate	Murder	Rape	Robbery	Aggravated Assault
Area	359.0	5.2	40.2	159.7	154.0
USA	432.8	4.7	34.7	111.6	285.6

Key Economic Data (Family income, unemployment)

	$25k-$75k	$75k-$150k	>$150k	Unemployment 03/2009	Unemployment 03/2010
Area	48.0%	28.9%	7.9%	10.9%	12.3%
USA	45.8%	29.5%	8.5%	9.0%	10.1

Key Household Data

	Population Age 0-17	Children w/Married Parents	Children w/Single Mother	Stay-at-home Mothers	Births to Single Women
Area	23.1%	60.8%	29.2%	29.2%	37.1%
USA	24.0%	65.6%	25.5%	27.9%	35.3%

Key Housing Data

	Owner Occupied	Median Year Built	Median Home Value	Home Value Growth, 2005-2010	Median List Price, 4-bedroom Home
Area	66.7%	1966	$132,000	0.6%	$184,900
USA	67.8%	1976	$187,045	3.1%	$288,846

Decatur, AL
150,125

	Score	Rank
Overall	65.92	127
LDS Culture	35.38	76
Education	63.05	268
Crime	64.23	112
Economic	57.59	263
Health	35.44	285
Household	80.86	61
Housing	86.16	117

Key LDS Culture Data

	Positive	Negative	Ratio Pos:Neg	Commute>59 minutes	Commute<15 minutes
Area	2,978	85	35.0	3.3%	29.7%
USA	4,292	251	20.1	5.5%	34.1%

Key Education Data

	HS Grad	Some Coll.	College Degree	Free/Reduced Lunch	Students per Teacher
Area	84.1%	26.0%	23.7%	44.4%	14.7
USA	85.8%	22.6%	33.2%	41.2%	15.8

Key Property Crime Data (Rate per 100,000 residents)

	Rate	Burglary	Larceny, Theft	Vehicle Theft
Area	3,793.2	1,024.6	2,645.2	123.3
USA	3,413.6	806.6	2,388.0	262.7

Key Violent Crime Data (Rate per 100,000 residents)

	Rate	Murder	Rape	Robbery	Aggravated Assault
Area	261.3	4.0	26.7	89.3	141.3
USA	432.8	4.7	34.7	111.6	285.6

Key Economic Data (Family income, unemployment)

	$25k-$75k	$75k-$150k	>$150k	Unemployment 03/2009	Unemployment 03/2010
Area	45.8%	28.9%	5.9%	9.4%	11.5%
USA	45.8%	29.5%	8.5%	9.0%	10.1

Key Household Data

	Population Age 0-17	Children w/Married Parents	Children w/Single Mother	Stay-at-home Mothers	Births to Single Women
Area	23.6%	73.6%	17.8%	25.9%	24.1%
USA	24.0%	65.6%	25.5%	27.9%	35.3%

Key Housing Data

	Owner Occupied	Median Year Built	Median Home Value	Home Value Growth, 2005-2010	Median List Price, 4-bedroom Home
Area	71.5%	1981	$119,800	3.4%	
USA	67.8%	1976	$187,045	3.1%	$288,846

Decatur, IL
108,328

	Score	Rank
Overall	55.71	324
LDS Culture	33.22	101
Education	52.03	340
Crime	41.88	274
Economic	50.42	327
Health	47.30	105
Household	56.17	263
Housing	76.21	267

Key LDS Culture Data

	Positive	Negative	Ratio Pos:Neg	Commute>59 minutes	Commute<15 minutes
Area	1,058	84	12.6	3.8%	44.0%
USA	4,292	251	20.1	5.5%	34.1%

Key Education Data

	HS Grad	Some Coll.	College Degree	Free/Reduced Lunch	Students per Teacher
Area	87.4%	25.9%	28.0%	46.2%	19.1
USA	85.8%	22.6%	33.2%	41.2%	15.8

Key Property Crime Data (Rate per 100,000 residents)

	Rate	Burglary	Larceny, Theft	Vehicle Theft	
Area	4,316.1				
USA	3,413.6	806.6	2,388.0	262.7	

Key Violent Crime Data (Rate per 100,000 residents)

	Rate	Murder	Rape	Robbery	Aggravated Assault
Area	700.1				
USA	432.8	4.7	34.7	111.6	285.6

Key Economic Data (Family income, unemployment)

	$25k-$75k	$75k-$150k	>$150k	Unemployment 03/2009	Unemployment 03/2010
Area	48.8%	28.6%	7.6%	9.9%	13.8%
USA	45.8%	29.5%	8.5%	9.0%	10.1

Key Household Data

	Population Age 0-17	Children w/Married Parents	Children w/Single Mother	Stay-at-home Mothers	Births to Single Women
Area	22.7%	64.4%	24.4%	29.1%	52.3%
USA	24.0%	65.6%	25.5%	27.9%	35.3%

Key Housing Data

	Owner Occupied	Median Year Built	Median Home Value	Home Value Growth, 2005-2010	Median List Price, 4-bedroom Home
Area	70.6%	1959	$92,600	2.2%	
USA	67.8%	1976	$187,045	3.1%	$288,846

Deltona-Daytona Beach-Ormond Beach, FL
498,036

	Score	Rank
Overall	57.10	303
LDS Culture	5.04	360
Education	60.37	291
Crime	41.01	281
Economic	56.92	268
Health	50.06	38
Household	69.14	152
Housing	83.59	166

Key LDS Culture Data

	Positive	Negative	Ratio Pos:Neg	Commute>59 minutes	Commute<15 minutes
Area	2,885	506	5.7	8.2%	28.0%
USA	4,292	251	20.1	5.5%	34.1%

Key Education Data

	HS Grad	Some Coll.	College Degree	Free/Reduced Lunch	Students per Teacher
Area	88.4%	25.3%	31.1%	42.5%	14.5
USA	85.8%	22.6%	33.2%	41.2%	15.8

Key Property Crime Data (Rate per 100,000 residents)

	Rate	Burglary	Larceny, Theft	Vehicle Theft
Area	3,843.2	1,016.1	2,539.1	287.9
USA	3,413.6	806.6	2,388.0	262.7

Key Violent Crime Data (Rate per 100,000 residents)

	Rate	Murder	Rape	Robbery	Aggravated Assault
Area	592.4	3.0	32.3	145.2	412.0
USA	432.8	4.7	34.7	111.6	285.6

Key Economic Data (Family income, unemployment)

	$25k-$75k	$75k-$150k	>$150k	Unemployment 03/2009	Unemployment 03/2010
Area	50.8%	27.2%	5.2%	10.0%	12.7%
USA	45.8%	29.5%	8.5%	9.0%	10.1

Key Household Data

	Population Age 0-17	Children w/Married Parents	Children w/Single Mother	Stay-at-home Mothers	Births to Single Women
Area	19.4%	65.8%	24.5%	29.3%	32.2%
USA	24.0%	65.6%	25.5%	27.9%	35.3%

Key Housing Data

	Owner Occupied	Median Year Built	Median Home Value	Home Value Growth, 2005-2010	Median List Price, 4-bedroom Home
Area	76.5%	1985	$198,700	2.5%	
USA	67.8%	1976	$187,045	3.1%	$288,846

Denver-Aurora-Broomfield, CO
2,502,881

	Score	Rank
Overall	68.24	76
LDS Culture	19.32	292
Education	74.84	127
Crime	61.50	140
Economic	80.32	14
Health	46.30	125
Household	83.33	40
Housing	71.95	318

Key LDS Culture Data
	Positive	Negative	Ratio Pos:Neg	Commute>59 minutes	Commute<15 minutes
Area	13,677	1153	11.9	6.4%	20.8%
USA	4,292	251	20.1	5.5%	34.1%

Key Education Data
	HS Grad	Some Coll.	College Degree	Free/Reduced Lunch	Students per Teacher
Area	88.6%	21.9%	44.5%	34.4%	17.9
USA	85.8%	22.6%	33.2%	41.2%	15.8

Key Property Crime Data (Rate per 100,000 residents)
	Rate	Burglary	Larceny, Theft	Vehicle Theft
Area	2,878.1	579.3	1,934.6	364.2
USA	3,413.6	806.6	2,388.0	262.7

Key Violent Crime Data (Rate per 100,000 residents)
	Rate	Murder	Rape	Robbery	Aggravated Assault
Area	358.6	3.2	42.7	89.9	222.8
USA	432.8	4.7	34.7	111.6	285.6

Key Economic Data (Family income, unemployment)
	$25k-$75k	$75k-$150k	>$150k	Unemployment 03/2009	Unemployment 03/2010
Area	37.3%	34.8%	15.4%	8.5%	8.5%
USA	45.8%	29.5%	8.5%	9.0%	10.1

Key Household Data
	Population Age 0-17	Children w/Married Parents	Children w/Single Mother	Stay-at-home Mothers	Births to Single Women
Area	25.4%	70.0%	21.6%	30.0%	25.0%
USA	24.0%	65.6%	25.5%	27.9%	35.3%

Key Housing Data
	Owner Occupied	Median Year Built	Median Home Value	Home Value Growth, 2005-2010	Median List Price, 4-bedroom Home
Area	67.3%	1980	$251,500	0.8%	$300,000
USA	67.8%	1976	$187,045	3.1%	$288,846

Des Moines-West Des Moines, IA
554,247

	Score	Rank
Overall	69.76	52
LDS Culture	33.81	94
Education	86.23	36
Crime	62.69	130
Economic	64.31	161
Health	47.77	86
Household	74.07	112
Housing	78.41	239

Key LDS Culture Data

	Positive	Negative	Ratio Pos:Neg	Commute>59 minutes	Commute<15 minutes
Area	2,639	199	13.3	2.4%	33.4%
USA	4,292	251	20.1	5.5%	34.1%

Key Education Data

	HS Grad	Some Coll.	College Degree	Free/Reduced Lunch	Students per Teacher
Area	91.9%	22.3%	42.7%	31.8%	14.4
USA	85.8%	22.6%	33.2%	41.2%	15.8

Key Property Crime Data (Rate per 100,000 residents)

	Rate	Burglary	Larceny, Theft	Vehicle Theft	
Area	3,001.4	578.2	2,235.5	187.6	
USA	3,413.6	806.6	2,388.0	262.7	

Key Violent Crime Data (Rate per 100,000 residents)

	Rate	Murder	Rape	Robbery	Aggravated Assault
Area	333.0	2.9	44.9	68.3	216.9
USA	432.8	4.7	34.7	111.6	285.6

Key Economic Data (Family income, unemployment)

	$25k-$75k	$75k-$150k	>$150k	Unemployment 03/2009	Unemployment 03/2010
Area	38.8%	38.5%	11.5%	5.5%	7.1%
USA	45.8%	29.5%	8.5%	9.0%	10.1

Key Household Data

	Population Age 0-17	Children w/Married Parents	Children w/Single Mother	Stay-at-home Mothers	Births to Single Women
Area	26.3%	71.8%	19.1%	18.2%	21.6%
USA	24.0%	65.6%	25.5%	27.9%	35.3%

Key Housing Data

	Owner Occupied	Median Year Built	Median Home Value	Home Value Growth, 2005-2010	Median List Price, 4-bedroom Home
Area	72.7%	1974	$157,600	1.9%	$239,900
USA	67.8%	1976	$187,045	3.1%	$288,846

Detroit-Warren-Livonia, MI
4,425,110

	Score	Rank
Overall	57.57	295
LDS Culture	23.97	237
Education	66.61	225
Crime	39.69	290
Economic	69.87	87
Health	32.01	322
Household	59.26	230
Housing	77.75	249

Key LDS Culture Data

	Positive	Negative	Ratio Pos:Neg	Commute>59 minutes	Commute<15 minutes
Area	19,984	1648	12.1	6.8%	23.1%
USA	4,292	251	20.1	5.5%	34.1%

Key Education Data

	HS Grad	Some Coll.	College Degree	Free/Reduced Lunch	Students per Teacher
Area	87.1%	24.0%	34.1%	36.9%	18.2
USA	85.8%	22.6%	33.2%	41.2%	15.8

Key Property Crime Data (Rate per 100,000 residents)

	Rate	Burglary	Larceny, Theft	Vehicle Theft
Area		811.3	1,852.3	
USA	3,413.6	806.6	2,388.0	262.7

Key Violent Crime Data (Rate per 100,000 residents)

	Rate	Murder	Rape	Robbery	Aggravated Assault
Area	709.7	10.9	31.4	208.8	458.5
USA	432.8	4.7	34.7	111.6	285.6

Key Economic Data (Family income, unemployment)

	$25k-$75k	$75k-$150k	>$150k	Unemployment 03/2009	Unemployment 03/2010
Area	40.3%	33.0%	11.5%	14.3%	15.5%
USA	45.8%	29.5%	8.5%	9.0%	10.1

Key Household Data

	Population Age 0-17	Children w/Married Parents	Children w/Single Mother	Stay-at-home Mothers	Births to Single Women
Area	24.6%	63.9%	28.7%	29.9%	37.7%
USA	24.0%	65.6%	25.5%	27.9%	35.3%

Key Housing Data

	Owner Occupied	Median Year Built	Median Home Value	Home Value Growth, 2005-2010	Median List Price, 4-bedroom Home
Area	73.1%	1966	$164,900	-6.1%	$219,900
USA	67.8%	1976	$187,045	3.1%	$288,846

Dothan, AL
140,961

	Score	Rank
Overall	57.79	290
LDS Culture	28.65	160
Education	56.23	320
Crime	51.73	199
Economic	58.64	246
Health	30.81	344
Household	56.79	251
Housing	87.72	88

Key LDS Culture Data

	Positive	Negative	Ratio Pos:Neg	Commute>59 minutes	Commute<15 minutes
Area	1,323	59	22.4	3.5%	31.9%
USA	4,292	251	20.1	5.5%	34.1%

Key Education Data

	HS Grad	Some Coll.	College Degree	Free/Reduced Lunch	Students per Teacher
Area	79.1%	20.6%	25.1%	55.0%	15.3
USA	85.8%	22.6%	33.2%	41.2%	15.8

Key Property Crime Data (Rate per 100,000 residents)

	Rate	Burglary	Larceny, Theft	Vehicle Theft	
Area	3,662.2	914.1	2,545.1	203.0	
USA	3,413.6	806.6	2,388.0	262.7	

Key Violent Crime Data (Rate per 100,000 residents)

	Rate	Murder	Rape	Robbery	Aggravated Assault
Area	402.4	2.8	38.3	154.0	207.2
USA	432.8	4.7	34.7	111.6	285.6

Key Economic Data (Family income, unemployment)

	$25k-$75k	$75k-$150k	>$150k	Unemployment 03/2009	Unemployment 03/2010
Area	50.2%	23.4%	5.3%	8.3%	9.9%
USA	45.8%	29.5%	8.5%	9.0%	10.1

Key Household Data

	Population Age 0-17	Children w/Married Parents	Children w/Single Mother	Stay-at-home Mothers	Births to Single Women
Area	24.1%	56.2%	35.3%	23.0%	38.2%
USA	24.0%	65.6%	25.5%	27.9%	35.3%

Key Housing Data

	Owner Occupied	Median Year Built	Median Home Value	Home Value Growth, 2005-2010	Median List Price, 4-bedroom Home
Area	72.4%	1980	$107,400	4.9%	
USA	67.8%	1976	$187,045	3.1%	$288,846

Dover, DE
155,415

	Score	Rank
Overall	**60.35**	**235**
LDS Culture	17.16	318
Education	60.92	287
Crime	39.47	291
Economic	74.43	49
Health	41.81	186
Household	67.28	164
Housing	85.90	124

Key LDS Culture Data

	Positive	Negative	Ratio Pos:Neg	Commute>59 minutes	Commute<15 minutes
Area	2,047	142	14.4	10.1%	31.8%
USA	4,292	251	20.1	5.5%	34.1%

Key Education Data

	HS Grad	Some Coll.	College Degree	Free/Reduced Lunch	Students per Teacher
Area	85.9%	25.0%	26.0%	34.6%	14.8
USA	85.8%	22.6%	33.2%	41.2%	15.8

Key Property Crime Data (Rate per 100,000 residents)

	Rate	Burglary	Larceny, Theft	Vehicle Theft
Area	3,460.1	737.7	2,495.8	226.6
USA	3,413.6	806.6	2,388.0	262.7

Key Violent Crime Data (Rate per 100,000 residents)

	Rate	Murder	Rape	Robbery	Aggravated Assault
Area	668.8	5.1	63.1	124.9	475.7
USA	432.8	4.7	34.7	111.6	285.6

Key Economic Data (Family income, unemployment)

	$25k-$75k	$75k-$150k	>$150k	Unemployment 03/2009	Unemployment 03/2010
Area	48.6%	34.5%	5.4%	8.1%	9.0%
USA	45.8%	29.5%	8.5%	9.0%	10.1

Key Household Data

	Population Age 0-17	Children w/Married Parents	Children w/Single Mother	Stay-at-home Mothers	Births to Single Women
Area	25.3%	66.6%	25.4%	19.5%	21.9%
USA	24.0%	65.6%	25.5%	27.9%	35.3%

Key Housing Data

	Owner Occupied	Median Year Built	Median Home Value	Home Value Growth, 2005-2010	Median List Price, 4-bedroom Home
Area	73.7%	1989	$215,000	5.1%	
USA	67.8%	1976	$187,045	3.1%	$288,846

Dubuque, IA
92,724

	Score	Rank
Overall	68.16	79
LDS Culture	33.47	98
Education	85.33	38
Crime	58.64	150
Economic	63.31	179
Health	54.48	13
Household	69.75	147
Housing	72.11	316

Key LDS Culture Data

	Positive	Negative	Ratio Pos:Neg	Commute>59 minutes	Commute<15 minutes
Area	803	102	7.9	2.8%	47.8%
USA	4,292	251	20.1	5.5%	34.1%

Key Education Data

	HS Grad	Some Coll.	College Degree	Free/Reduced Lunch	Students per Teacher
Area	90.1%	20.1%	32.3%	32.3%	12.6
USA	85.8%	22.6%	33.2%	41.2%	15.8

Key Property Crime Data (Rate per 100,000 residents)

	Rate	Burglary	Larceny, Theft	Vehicle Theft	
Area	2,378.0	619.8	1,654.9	103.3	
USA	3,413.6	806.6	2,388.0	262.7	

Key Violent Crime Data (Rate per 100,000 residents)

	Rate	Murder	Rape	Robbery	Aggravated Assault
Area	448.7	0.0	28.0	26.9	393.8
USA	432.8	4.7	34.7	111.6	285.6

Key Economic Data (Family income, unemployment)

	$25k-$75k	$75k-$150k	>$150k	Unemployment 03/2009	Unemployment 03/2010
Area	50.8%	31.2%	5.9%	6.7%	7.8%
USA	45.8%	29.5%	8.5%	9.0%	10.1

Key Household Data

	Population Age 0-17	Children w/Married Parents	Children w/Single Mother	Stay-at-home Mothers	Births to Single Women
Area	24.1%	68.9%	23.4%	12.2%	24.6%
USA	24.0%	65.6%	25.5%	27.9%	35.3%

Key Housing Data

	Owner Occupied	Median Year Built	Median Home Value	Home Value Growth, 2005-2010	Median List Price, 4-bedroom Home
Area	75.1%	1964	$137,400	2.8%	
USA	67.8%	1976	$187,045	3.1%	$288,846

Duluth, MN-WI
275,336

	Score	Rank
Overall	64.61	146
LDS Culture	19.25	295
Education	83.30	47
Crime	59.03	149
Economic	75.26	45
Health	40.69	209
Household	62.35	207
Housing	74.40	291

Key LDS Culture Data

	Positive	Negative	Ratio Pos:Neg	Commute>59 minutes	Commute<15 minutes
Area	970	143	6.8	4.2%	40.5%
USA	4,292	251	20.1	5.5%	34.1%

Key Education Data

	HS Grad	Some Coll.	College Degree	Free/Reduced Lunch	Students per Teacher
Area	91.6%	25.6%	36.2%	35.5%	16.7
USA	85.8%	22.6%	33.2%	41.2%	15.8

Key Property Crime Data (Rate per 100,000 residents)

	Rate	Burglary	Larceny, Theft	Vehicle Theft
Area	3,471.0	556.1	2,747.8	167.1
USA	3,413.6	806.6	2,388.0	262.7

Key Violent Crime Data (Rate per 100,000 residents)

	Rate	Murder	Rape	Robbery	Aggravated Assault
Area		1.5		62.9	134.9
USA	432.8	4.7	34.7	111.6	285.6

Key Economic Data (Family income, unemployment)

	$25k-$75k	$75k-$150k	>$150k	Unemployment 03/2009	Unemployment 03/2010
Area	47.9%	31.2%	5.9%	10.0%	9.2%
USA	45.8%	29.5%	8.5%	9.0%	10.1

Key Household Data

	Population Age 0-17	Children w/Married Parents	Children w/Single Mother	Stay-at-home Mothers	Births to Single Women
Area	20.2%	66.6%	25.2%	17.8%	30.4%
USA	24.0%	65.6%	25.5%	27.9%	35.3%

Key Housing Data

	Owner Occupied	Median Year Built	Median Home Value	Home Value Growth, 2005-2010	Median List Price, 4-bedroom Home
Area	71.7%	1960	$148,600	3.4%	$224,900
USA	67.8%	1976	$187,045	3.1%	$288,846

Durham-Chapel Hill, NC
489,762

	Score	Rank
Overall	61.58	209
LDS Culture	31.07	122
Education	72.58	156
Crime	42.52	271
Economic	67.32	118
Health	37.16	257
Household	56.17	264
Housing	88.05	83

Key LDS Culture Data

	Positive	Negative	Ratio Pos:Neg	Commute>59 minutes	Commute<15 minutes
Area	8,016	228	35.2	5.3%	27.9%
USA	4,292	251	20.1	5.5%	34.1%

Key Education Data

	HS Grad	Some Coll.	College Degree	Free/Reduced Lunch	Students per Teacher
Area	86.9%	16.3%	49.9%	40.1%	14.0
USA	85.8%	22.6%	33.2%	41.2%	15.8

Key Property Crime Data (Rate per 100,000 residents)

	Rate	Burglary	Larceny, Theft	Vehicle Theft	
Area	4,252.7	1,244.9	2,730.0	277.8	
USA	3,413.6	806.6	2,388.0	262.7	

Key Violent Crime Data (Rate per 100,000 residents)

	Rate	Murder	Rape	Robbery	Aggravated Assault
Area	514.0	7.8	22.9	231.5	251.8
USA	432.8	4.7	34.7	111.6	285.6

Key Economic Data (Family income, unemployment)

	$25k-$75k	$75k-$150k	>$150k	Unemployment 03/2009	Unemployment 03/2010
Area	38.6%	32.3%	13.8%	7.5%	7.8%
USA	45.8%	29.5%	8.5%	9.0%	10.1

Key Household Data

	Population Age 0-17	Children w/Married Parents	Children w/Single Mother	Stay-at-home Mothers	Births to Single Women
Area	22.7%	63.2%	28.7%	28.7%	39.3%
USA	24.0%	65.6%	25.5%	27.9%	35.3%

Key Housing Data

	Owner Occupied	Median Year Built	Median Home Value	Home Value Growth, 2005-2010	Median List Price, 4-bedroom Home
Area	60.6%	1986	$191,100	4.0%	$329,900
USA	67.8%	1976	$187,045	3.1%	$288,846

Eau Claire, WI
158,742

	Score	Rank
Overall	73.06	27
LDS Culture	24.31	232
Education	88.94	21
Crime	92.33	4
Economic	76.76	32
Health	39.16	225
Household	69.75	148
Housing	77.22	258

Key LDS Culture Data

	Positive	Negative	Ratio Pos:Neg	Commute>59 minutes	Commute<15 minutes
Area	1,044	139	7.5	4.2%	44.1%
USA	4,292	251	20.1	5.5%	34.1%

Key Education Data

	HS Grad	Some Coll.	College Degree	Free/Reduced Lunch	Students per Teacher
Area	90.8%	20.1%	37.9%	32.4%	15.5
USA	85.8%	22.6%	33.2%	41.2%	15.8

Key Property Crime Data (Rate per 100,000 residents)

	Rate	Burglary	Larceny, Theft	Vehicle Theft	
Area	2,166.8	416.0	1,681.6	69.2	
USA	3,413.6	806.6	2,388.0	262.7	

Key Violent Crime Data (Rate per 100,000 residents)

	Rate	Murder	Rape	Robbery	Aggravated Assault
Area	100.7	1.3	18.9	14.5	66.1
USA	432.8	4.7	34.7	111.6	285.6

Key Economic Data (Family income, unemployment)

	$25k-$75k	$75k-$150k	>$150k	Unemployment 03/2009	Unemployment 03/2010
Area	47.7%	32.5%	6.9%	8.9%	8.5%
USA	45.8%	29.5%	8.5%	9.0%	10.1

Key Household Data

	Population Age 0-17	Children w/Married Parents	Children w/Single Mother	Stay-at-home Mothers	Births to Single Women
Area	21.6%	72.9%	20.3%	15.6%	22.6%
USA	24.0%	65.6%	25.5%	27.9%	35.3%

Key Housing Data

	Owner Occupied	Median Year Built	Median Home Value	Home Value Growth, 2005-2010	Median List Price, 4-bedroom Home
Area	70.0%	1972	$151,900	2.3%	
USA	67.8%	1976	$187,045	3.1%	$288,846

	Score	Rank	El Centro, CA		
			163,972		
Overall	61.98	195			
LDS Culture	38.27	53			
Education	56.60	316			
Crime	61.55	138			
Economic	47.36	343			
Health	48.59	61			
Household	59.88	227			
Housing	85.22	138			

Key LDS Culture Data

	Positive	Negative	Ratio Pos:Neg	Commute>59 minutes	Commute<15 minutes
Area	533	16	33.3	5.1%	47.3%
USA	4,292	251	20.1	5.5%	34.1%

Key Education Data

	HS Grad	Some Coll.	College Degree	Free/Reduced Lunch	Students per Teacher
Area	64.2%	24.5%	17.5%	69.1%	18.6
USA	85.8%	22.6%	33.2%	41.2%	15.8

Key Property Crime Data (Rate per 100,000 residents)

	Rate	Burglary	Larceny, Theft	Vehicle Theft	
Area	3,805.1	1,190.2	1,950.8	664.1	
USA	3,413.6	806.6	2,388.0	262.7	

Key Violent Crime Data (Rate per 100,000 residents)

	Rate	Murder	Rape	Robbery	Aggravated Assault
Area	289.6	4.9	13.4	77.6	193.7
USA	432.8	4.7	34.7	111.6	285.6

Key Economic Data (Family income, unemployment)

	$25k-$75k	$75k-$150k	>$150k	Unemployment 03/2009	Unemployment 03/2010
Area	45.3%	18.9%	4.5%	24.8%	27.0%
USA	45.8%	29.5%	8.5%	9.0%	10.1

Key Household Data

	Population Age 0-17	Children w/Married Parents	Children w/Single Mother	Stay-at-home Mothers	Births to Single Women
Area	29.3%	57.9%	34.4%	33.8%	42.3%
USA	24.0%	65.6%	25.5%	27.9%	35.3%

Key Housing Data

	Owner Occupied	Median Year Built	Median Home Value	Home Value Growth, 2005-2010	Median List Price, 4-bedroom Home
Area	55.0%	1983	$214,100	-0.6%	$144,900
USA	67.8%	1976	$187,045	3.1%	$288,846

El Paso, TX
112,431

	Score	Rank
Overall	58.97	268
LDS Culture	20.55	273
Education	62.34	273
Crime	52.09	196
Economic	57.75	261
Health	32.00	327
Household	62.96	198
Housing	90.46	48

Key LDS Culture Data

	Positive	Negative	Ratio Pos:Neg	Commute>59 minutes	Commute<15 minutes
Area	1,337	84	15.9	4.9%	33.8%
USA	4,292	251	20.1	5.5%	34.1%

Key Education Data

	HS Grad	Some Coll.	College Degree	Free/Reduced Lunch	Students per Teacher
Area	87.4%	28.4%	25.7%	46.1%	16.0
USA	85.8%	22.6%	33.2%	41.2%	15.8

Key Property Crime Data (Rate per 100,000 residents)

	Rate	Burglary	Larceny, Theft	Vehicle Theft
Area	3,109.8	368.6	2,322.5	418.7
USA	3,413.6	806.6	2,388.0	262.7

Key Violent Crime Data (Rate per 100,000 residents)

	Rate	Murder	Rape	Robbery	Aggravated Assault
Area	437.1	2.6	28.6	69.7	336.3
USA	432.8	4.7	34.7	111.6	285.6

Key Economic Data (Family income, unemployment)

	$25k-$75k	$75k-$150k	>$150k	Unemployment 03/2009	Unemployment 03/2010
Area	49.7%	32.1%	3.2%	8.5%	9.4%
USA	45.8%	29.5%	8.5%	9.0%	10.1

Key Household Data

	Population Age 0-17	Children w/Married Parents	Children w/Single Mother	Stay-at-home Mothers	Births to Single Women
Area	25.8%	74.2%	17.9%	37.9%	18.5%
USA	24.0%	65.6%	25.5%	27.9%	35.3%

Key Housing Data

	Owner Occupied	Median Year Built	Median Home Value	Home Value Growth, 2005-2010	Median List Price, 4-bedroom Home
Area	66.6%	1984	$139,400	3.0%	
USA	67.8%	1976	$187,045	3.1%	$288,846

Elizabethtown, KY
199,137

	Score	Rank
Overall	66.18	122
LDS Culture	27.32	177
Education	52.44	339
Crime	74.65	53
Economic	65.20	151
Health	26.56	356
Household	91.98	9
Housing	86.24	115

Key LDS Culture Data

	Positive	Negative	Ratio Pos:Neg	Commute>59 minutes	Commute<15 minutes
Area	3,331	195	17.1	2.1%	38.6%
USA	4,292	251	20.1	5.5%	34.1%

Key Education Data

	HS Grad	Some Coll.	College Degree	Free/Reduced Lunch	Students per Teacher
Area	77.4%	17.4%	23.2%	44.4%	17.7
USA	85.8%	22.6%	33.2%	41.2%	15.8

Key Property Crime Data (Rate per 100,000 residents)

	Rate	Burglary	Larceny, Theft	Vehicle Theft	
Area	1,809.1	385.2	1,351.7	72.2	
USA	3,413.6	806.6	2,388.0	262.7	

Key Violent Crime Data (Rate per 100,000 residents)

	Rate	Murder	Rape	Robbery	Aggravated Assault
Area	328.1	0.9	37.4	41.9	247.9
USA	432.8	4.7	34.7	111.6	285.6

Key Economic Data (Family income, unemployment)

	$25k-$75k	$75k-$150k	>$150k	Unemployment 03/2009	Unemployment 03/2010
Area	50.0%	29.3%	5.9%	11.3%	10.2%
USA	45.8%	29.5%	8.5%	9.0%	10.1

Key Household Data

	Population Age 0-17	Children w/Married Parents	Children w/Single Mother	Stay-at-home Mothers	Births to Single Women
Area	28.2%	67.9%	19.7%	35.8%	39.6%
USA	24.0%	65.6%	25.5%	27.9%	35.3%

Key Housing Data

	Owner Occupied	Median Year Built	Median Home Value	Home Value Growth, 2005-2010	Median List Price, 4-bedroom Home
Area	72.9%	1975	$136,600	1.7%	
USA	67.8%	1976	$187,045	3.1%	$288,846

Elkhart-Goshen, IN
87,813

	Score	Rank
Overall	67.98	84
LDS Culture	32.77	111
Education	73.44	143
Crime	74.88	50
Economic	71.21	73
Health	34.59	293
Household	71.60	137
Housing	77.44	255

Key LDS Culture Data

	Positive	Negative	Ratio Pos:Neg	Commute>59 minutes	Commute<15 minutes
Area	1,258	104	12.1	3.8%	44.1%
USA	4,292	251	20.1	5.5%	34.1%

Key Education Data

	HS Grad	Some Coll.	College Degree	Free/Reduced Lunch	Students per Teacher
Area	87.2%	18.9%	30.1%	41.7%	11.1
USA	85.8%	22.6%	33.2%	41.2%	15.8

Key Property Crime Data (Rate per 100,000 residents)

	Rate	Burglary	Larceny, Theft	Vehicle Theft
Area	3,583.9	885.3	2,462.2	236.4
USA	3,413.6	806.6	2,388.0	262.7

Key Violent Crime Data (Rate per 100,000 residents)

	Rate	Murder	Rape	Robbery	Aggravated Assault
Area	157.2	4.0	34.6	102.2	16.5
USA	432.8	4.7	34.7	111.6	285.6

Key Economic Data (Family income, unemployment)

	$25k-$75k	$75k-$150k	>$150k	Unemployment 03/2009	Unemployment 03/2010
Area	48.7%	28.8%	3.7%	20.1%	15.2%
USA	45.8%	29.5%	8.5%	9.0%	10.1

Key Household Data

	Population Age 0-17	Children w/Married Parents	Children w/Single Mother	Stay-at-home Mothers	Births to Single Women
Area	21.9%	68.9%	26.5%	21.0%	35.7%
USA	24.0%	65.6%	25.5%	27.9%	35.3%

Key Housing Data

	Owner Occupied	Median Year Built	Median Home Value	Home Value Growth, 2005-2010	Median List Price, 4-bedroom Home
Area	69.2%	1954	$85,200	4.5%	
USA	67.8%	1976	$187,045	3.1%	$288,846

Elmira, NY
742,062

	Score	Rank
Overall	71.69	34
LDS Culture	32.78	110
Education	66.69	224
Crime	77.49	40
Economic	90.22	5
Health	49.20	47
Household	68.52	158
Housing	74.79	285

Key LDS Culture Data

	Positive	Negative	Ratio Pos:Neg	Commute>59 minutes	Commute<15 minutes
Area	2,280	172	13.3	2.7%	22.8%
USA	4,292	251	20.1	5.5%	34.1%

Key Education Data

	HS Grad	Some Coll.	College Degree	Free/Reduced Lunch	Students per Teacher
Area	71.7%	21.6%	25.8%	68.7%	15.1
USA	85.8%	22.6%	33.2%	41.2%	15.8

Key Property Crime Data (Rate per 100,000 residents)

	Rate	Burglary	Larceny, Theft	Vehicle Theft	
Area	2,433.3	503.3	1,885.4	44.5	
USA	3,413.6	806.6	2,388.0	262.7	

Key Violent Crime Data (Rate per 100,000 residents)

	Rate	Murder	Rape	Robbery	Aggravated Assault
Area	232.8	4.6	20.5	42.2	165.5
USA	432.8	4.7	34.7	111.6	285.6

Key Economic Data (Family income, unemployment)

	$25k-$75k	$75k-$150k	>$150k	Unemployment 03/2009	Unemployment 03/2010
Area	45.0%	18.9%	4.7%	9.5%	8.7%
USA	45.8%	29.5%	8.5%	9.0%	10.1

Key Household Data

	Population Age 0-17	Children w/Married Parents	Children w/Single Mother	Stay-at-home Mothers	Births to Single Women
Area	31.0%	62.1%	30.9%	40.8%	40.4%
USA	24.0%	65.6%	25.5%	27.9%	35.3%

Key Housing Data

	Owner Occupied	Median Year Built	Median Home Value	Home Value Growth, 2005-2010	Median List Price, 4-bedroom Home
Area	65.9%	1980	$107,900	7.0%	
USA	67.8%	1976	$187,045	3.1%	$288,846

Erie, PA
279,175

	Score	Rank
Overall	64.25	158
LDS Culture	30.45	138
Education	71.81	164
Crime	70.37	74
Economic	62.03	196
Health	47.33	93
Household	48.77	308
Housing	81.22	194

Key LDS Culture Data

	Positive	Negative	Ratio Pos:Neg	Commute>59 minutes	Commute<15 minutes
Area	1,617	171	9.5	2.4%	38.5%
USA	4,292	251	20.1	5.5%	34.1%

Key Education Data

	HS Grad	Some Coll.	College Degree	Free/Reduced Lunch	Students per Teacher
Area	89.3%	17.0%	30.1%	44.8%	15.5
USA	85.8%	22.6%	33.2%	41.2%	15.8

Key Property Crime Data (Rate per 100,000 residents)

	Rate	Burglary	Larceny, Theft	Vehicle Theft
Area	2,469.5	624.9	1,747.7	96.9
USA	3,413.6	806.6	2,388.0	262.7

Key Violent Crime Data (Rate per 100,000 residents)

	Rate	Murder	Rape	Robbery	Aggravated Assault
Area	305.6	3.2	45.2	129.1	128.1
USA	432.8	4.7	34.7	111.6	285.6

Key Economic Data (Family income, unemployment)

	$25k-$75k	$75k-$150k	>$150k	Unemployment 03/2009	Unemployment 03/2010
Area	51.0%	27.5%	5.4%	8.6%	10.6%
USA	45.8%	29.5%	8.5%	9.0%	10.1

Key Household Data

	Population Age 0-17	Children w/Married Parents	Children w/Single Mother	Stay-at-home Mothers	Births to Single Women
Area	22.7%	58.1%	32.0%	23.4%	44.4%
USA	24.0%	65.6%	25.5%	27.9%	35.3%

Key Housing Data

	Owner Occupied	Median Year Built	Median Home Value	Home Value Growth, 2005-2010	Median List Price, 4-bedroom Home
Area	69.3%	1961	$112,500	2.7%	$176,900
USA	67.8%	1976	$187,045	3.1%	$288,846

Eugene-Springfield, OR
346,560

	Score	Rank
Overall	**64.64**	**145**
LDS Culture	25.82	200
Education	77.36	101
Crime	53.56	182
Economic	90.66	4
Health	47.57	88
Household	45.68	331
Housing	73.84	300

Key LDS Culture Data

	Positive	Negative	Ratio Pos:Neg	Commute>59 minutes	Commute<15 minutes
Area	1,787	93	19.2	4.0%	37.9%
USA	4,292	251	20.1	5.5%	34.1%

Key Education Data

	HS Grad	Some Coll.	College Degree	Free/Reduced Lunch	Students per Teacher
Area	89.8%	28.2%	35.9%	40.1%	20.4
USA	85.8%	22.6%	33.2%	41.2%	15.8

Key Property Crime Data (Rate per 100,000 residents)

	Rate	Burglary	Larceny, Theft	Vehicle Theft	
Area	4,767.3	880.4	3,271.6	615.3	
USA	3,413.6	806.6	2,388.0	262.7	

Key Violent Crime Data (Rate per 100,000 residents)

	Rate	Murder	Rape	Robbery	Aggravated Assault
Area	327.3	2.3	31.8	87.2	206.0
USA	432.8	4.7	34.7	111.6	285.6

Key Economic Data (Family income, unemployment)

	$25k-$75k	$75k-$150k	>$150k	Unemployment 03/2009	Unemployment 03/2010
Area	50.0%	26.9%	5.7%	13.5%	11.8%
USA	45.8%	29.5%	8.5%	9.0%	10.1

Key Household Data

	Population Age 0-17	Children w/Married Parents	Children w/Single Mother	Stay-at-home Mothers	Births to Single Women
Area	20.0%	60.8%	23.0%	26.1%	44.1%
USA	24.0%	65.6%	25.5%	27.9%	35.3%

Key Housing Data

	Owner Occupied	Median Year Built	Median Home Value	Home Value Growth, 2005-2010	Median List Price, 4-bedroom Home
Area	61.0%	1974	$246,400	6.4%	$324,900
USA	67.8%	1976	$187,045	3.1%	$288,846

Evansville, IN-KY
351,765

	Score	Rank
Overall	**66.68**	**107**
LDS Culture	28.18	168
Education	69.74	189
Crime	71.42	70
Economic	66.09	136
Health	34.59	294
Household	68.52	159
Housing	89.04	63

Key LDS Culture Data

	Positive	Negative	Ratio Pos:Neg	Commute>59 minutes	Commute<15 minutes
Area	2,314	137	16.9	3.2%	35.6%
USA	4,292	251	20.1	5.5%	34.1%

Key Education Data

	HS Grad	Some Coll.	College Degree	Free/Reduced Lunch	Students per Teacher
Area	86.2%	21.7%	28.5%	40.5%	16.4
USA	85.8%	22.6%	33.2%	41.2%	15.8

Key Property Crime Data (Rate per 100,000 residents)

	Rate	Burglary	Larceny, Theft	Vehicle Theft
Area	2,905.5	553.3	2,217.5	134.7
USA	3,413.6	806.6	2,388.0	262.7

Key Violent Crime Data (Rate per 100,000 residents)

	Rate	Murder	Rape	Robbery	Aggravated Assault
Area	249.1	2.9	28.5	54.5	163.2
USA	432.8	4.7	34.7	111.6	285.6

Key Economic Data (Family income, unemployment)

	$25k-$75k	$75k-$150k	>$150k	Unemployment 03/2009	Unemployment 03/2010
Area	45.6%	30.2%	4.9%	9.1%	9.0%
USA	45.8%	29.5%	8.5%	9.0%	10.1

Key Household Data

	Population Age 0-17	Children w/Married Parents	Children w/Single Mother	Stay-at-home Mothers	Births to Single Women
Area	23.3%	64.4%	27.4%	25.9%	31.6%
USA	24.0%	65.6%	25.5%	27.9%	35.3%

Key Housing Data

	Owner Occupied	Median Year Built	Median Home Value	Home Value Growth, 2005-2010	Median List Price, 4-bedroom Home
Area	70.3%	1970	$111,200	1.4%	$191,000
USA	67.8%	1976	$187,045	3.1%	$288,846

Fairbanks, AK
97,970

	Score	Rank
Overall	68.18	78
LDS Culture	24.57	227
Education	70.07	183
Crime	33.06	330
Economic	100.00	1
Health	43.07	167
Household	82.72	50
Housing	83.70	163

Key LDS Culture Data

	Positive	Negative	Ratio Pos:Neg	Commute>59 minutes	Commute<15 minutes
Area	512	40	12.8	2.6%	38.6%
USA	4,292	251	20.1	5.5%	34.1%

Key Education Data

	HS Grad	Some Coll.	College Degree	Free/Reduced Lunch	Students per Teacher
Area	92.1%	31.7%	36.0%	25.1%	18.1
USA	85.8%	22.6%	33.2%	41.2%	15.8

Key Property Crime Data (Rate per 100,000 residents)

	Rate	Burglary	Larceny, Theft	Vehicle Theft	
Area	3,841.5	435.7	3,018.2	387.6	
USA	3,413.6	806.6	2,388.0	262.7	

Key Violent Crime Data (Rate per 100,000 residents)

	Rate	Murder	Rape	Robbery	Aggravated Assault
Area	775.3	8.0	120.3	82.9	564.1
USA	432.8	4.7	34.7	111.6	285.6

Key Economic Data (Family income, unemployment)

	$25k-$75k	$75k-$150k	>$150k	Unemployment 03/2009	Unemployment 03/2010
Area	36.2%	45.1%	11.2%	7.5%	8.7%
USA	45.8%	29.5%	8.5%	9.0%	10.1

Key Household Data

	Population Age 0-17	Children w/Married Parents	Children w/Single Mother	Stay-at-home Mothers	Births to Single Women
Area	28.3%	69.7%	18.4%	39.6%	29.0%
USA	24.0%	65.6%	25.5%	27.9%	35.3%

Key Housing Data

	Owner Occupied	Median Year Built	Median Home Value	Home Value Growth, 2005-2010	Median List Price, 4-bedroom Home
Area	62.1%	1982	$218,100	4.0%	
USA	67.8%	1976	$187,045	3.1%	$288,846

Fargo, ND-MN
194,839

	Score	Rank
Overall	68.95	67
LDS Culture	30.44	139
Education	88.41	24
Crime	63.60	122
Economic	71.48	70
Health	41.26	192
Household	66.05	172
Housing	80.90	199

Key LDS Culture Data

	Positive	Negative	Ratio Pos:Neg	Commute>59 minutes	Commute<15 minutes
Area	860	91	9.5	2.6%	50.5%
USA	4,292	251	20.1	5.5%	34.1%

Key Education Data

	HS Grad	Some Coll.	College Degree	Free/Reduced Lunch	Students per Teacher
Area	93.7%	23.3%	46.1%	24.1%	14.6
USA	85.8%	22.6%	33.2%	41.2%	15.8

Key Property Crime Data (Rate per 100,000 residents)

	Rate	Burglary	Larceny, Theft	Vehicle Theft	
Area			1,902.1	163.6	
USA	3,413.6	806.6	2,388.0	262.7	

Key Violent Crime Data (Rate per 100,000 residents)

	Rate	Murder	Rape	Robbery	Aggravated Assault
Area				18.5	132.3
USA	432.8	4.7	34.7	111.6	285.6

Key Economic Data (Family income, unemployment)

	$25k-$75k	$75k-$150k	>$150k	Unemployment 03/2009	Unemployment 03/2010
Area	47.9%	32.0%	8.9%	5.2%	4.9%
USA	45.8%	29.5%	8.5%	9.0%	10.1%

Key Household Data

	Population Age 0-17	Children w/Married Parents	Children w/Single Mother	Stay-at-home Mothers	Births to Single Women
Area	22.7%	70.1%	21.7%	11.9%	32.3%
USA	24.0%	65.6%	25.5%	27.9%	35.3%

Key Housing Data

	Owner Occupied	Median Year Built	Median Home Value	Home Value Growth, 2005-2010	Median List Price, 4-bedroom Home
Area	58.7%	1978	$150,000	3.7%	
USA	67.8%	1976	$187,045	3.1%	$288,846

Farmington, NM
122,500

	Score	Rank
Overall	61.63	207
LDS Culture	40.81	41
Education	55.36	324
Crime	58.57	151
Economic	45.41	352
Health	52.72	27
Household	54.94	273
Housing	87.38	94

Key LDS Culture Data

	Positive	Negative	Ratio Pos:Neg	Commute>59 minutes	Commute<15 minutes
Area	453	11	41.2	8.1%	32.5%
USA	4,292	251	20.1	5.5%	34.1%

Key Education Data

	HS Grad	Some Coll.	College Degree	Free/Reduced Lunch	Students per Teacher
Area	82.1%	26.7%	23.9%	56.0%	14.7
USA	85.8%	22.6%	33.2%	41.2%	15.8

Key Property Crime Data (Rate per 100,000 residents)

	Rate	Burglary	Larceny, Theft	Vehicle Theft	
Area	2,410.0	941.1	1,254.5	214.4	
USA	3,413.6	806.6	2,388.0	262.7	

Key Violent Crime Data (Rate per 100,000 residents)

	Rate	Murder	Rape	Robbery	Aggravated Assault
Area		6.5	121.8	39.8	
USA	432.8	4.7	34.7	111.6	285.6

Key Economic Data (Family income, unemployment)

	$25k-$75k	$75k-$150k	>$150k	Unemployment 03/2009	Unemployment 03/2010
Area	46.4%	32.6%	4.9%	5.7%	10.7%
USA	45.8%	29.5%	8.5%	9.0%	10.1

Key Household Data

	Population Age 0-17	Children w/Married Parents	Children w/Single Mother	Stay-at-home Mothers	Births to Single Women
Area	27.7%	63.2%	25.3%	43.4%	49.6%
USA	24.0%	65.6%	25.5%	27.9%	35.3%

Key Housing Data

	Owner Occupied	Median Year Built	Median Home Value	Home Value Growth, 2005-2010	Median List Price, 4-bedroom Home
Area	74.1%	1983	$158,500	6.2%	
USA	67.8%	1976	$187,045	3.1%	$288,846

Fayetteville, NC
356,105

	Score	Rank
Overall	61.85	200
LDS Culture	28.64	161
Education	70.43	179
Crime	24.85	349
Economic	59.70	233
Health	44.88	149
Household	70.37	144
Housing	97.73	4

Key LDS Culture Data

	Positive	Negative	Ratio Pos:Neg	Commute>59 minutes	Commute<15 minutes
Area	2,933	107	27.4	3.4%	27.8%
USA	4,292	251	20.1	5.5%	34.1%

Key Education Data

	HS Grad	Some Coll.	College Degree	Free/Reduced Lunch	Students per Teacher
Area	88.4%	29.2%	32.3%	7.7%	14.6
USA	85.8%	22.6%	33.2%	41.2%	15.8

Key Property Crime Data (Rate per 100,000 residents)

	Rate	Burglary	Larceny, Theft	Vehicle Theft
Area	6,022.1	1,786.4	3,846.8	388.9
USA	3,413.6	806.6	2,388.0	262.7

Key Violent Crime Data (Rate per 100,000 residents)

	Rate	Murder	Rape	Robbery	Aggravated Assault
Area	730.2	11.4	31.6	256.0	431.2
USA	432.8	4.7	34.7	111.6	285.6

Key Economic Data (Family income, unemployment)

	$25k-$75k	$75k-$150k	>$150k	Unemployment 03/2009	Unemployment 03/2010
Area	48.1%	26.0%	4.7%	8.8%	9.1%
USA	45.8%	29.5%	8.5%	9.0%	10.1

Key Household Data

	Population Age 0-17	Children w/Married Parents	Children w/Single Mother	Stay-at-home Mothers	Births to Single Women
Area	28.1%	50.0%	41.4%	29.1%	27.3%
USA	24.0%	65.6%	25.5%	27.9%	35.3%

Key Housing Data

	Owner Occupied	Median Year Built	Median Home Value	Home Value Growth, 2005-2010	Median List Price, 4-bedroom Home
Area	61.5%	1984	$122,400	4.8%	$212,500
USA	67.8%	1976	$187,045	3.1%	$288,846

Fayetteville-Springdale-Rogers, AR-MO
442,582

	Score	Rank
Overall	72.00	31
LDS Culture	36.52	71
Education	73.05	147
Crime	69.86	78
Economic	54.64	299
Health	42.02	185
Household	90.12	15
Housing	95.47	11

Key LDS Culture Data

	Positive	Negative	Ratio Pos:Neg	Commute>59 minutes	Commute<15 minutes
Area	1,877	88	21.3	4.0%	32.1%
USA	4,292	251	20.1	5.5%	34.1%

Key Education Data

	HS Grad	Some Coll.	College Degree	Free/Reduced Lunch	Students per Teacher
Area	81.6%	20.0%	29.7%	46.0%	14.1
USA	85.8%	22.6%	33.2%	41.2%	15.8

Key Property Crime Data (Rate per 100,000 residents)

	Rate	Burglary	Larceny, Theft	Vehicle Theft	
Area	2,458.6	602.6	1,734.5	121.5	
USA	3,413.6	806.6	2,388.0	262.7	

Key Violent Crime Data (Rate per 100,000 residents)

	Rate	Murder	Rape	Robbery	Aggravated Assault
Area	312.2	1.8	54.9	21.7	233.8
USA	432.8	4.7	34.7	111.6	285.6

Key Economic Data (Family income, unemployment)

	$25k-$75k	$75k-$150k	>$150k	Unemployment 03/2009	Unemployment 03/2010
Area	49.8%	25.3%	7.7%	5.9%	6.6%
USA	45.8%	29.5%	8.5%	9.0%	10.1

Key Household Data

	Population Age 0-17	Children w/Married Parents	Children w/Single Mother	Stay-at-home Mothers	Births to Single Women
Area	27.0%	70.1%	21.2%	30.0%	17.4%
USA	24.0%	65.6%	25.5%	27.9%	35.3%

Key Housing Data

	Owner Occupied	Median Year Built	Median Home Value	Home Value Growth, 2005-2010	Median List Price, 4-bedroom Home
Area	64.1%	1989	$154,900	2.6%	$240,000
USA	67.8%	1976	$187,045	3.1%	$288,846

Flagstaff, AZ
128,558

	Score	Rank
Overall	58.93	269
LDS Culture	35.40	75
Education	59.75	297
Crime	53.70	179
Economic	57.98	259
Health	43.61	160
Household	48.77	309
Housing	78.66	237

Key LDS Culture Data

	Positive	Negative	Ratio Pos:Neg	Commute>59 minutes	Commute<15 minutes
Area	752	30	25.1	5.7%	54.2%
USA	4,292	251	20.1	5.5%	34.1%

Key Education Data

	HS Grad	Some Coll.	College Degree	Free/Reduced Lunch	Students per Teacher
Area	88.4%	27.4%	40.7%	40.5%	17.4
USA	85.8%	22.6%	33.2%	41.2%	15.8

Key Property Crime Data (Rate per 100,000 residents)

	Rate	Burglary	Larceny, Theft	Vehicle Theft	
Area	3,836.9	558.3	3,170.9	107.8	
USA	3,413.6	806.6	2,388.0	262.7	

Key Violent Crime Data (Rate per 100,000 residents)

	Rate	Murder	Rape	Robbery	Aggravated Assault
Area	372.4	2.3	62.5	56.2	251.4
USA	432.8	4.7	34.7	111.6	285.6

Key Economic Data (Family income, unemployment)

	$25k-$75k	$75k-$150k	>$150k	Unemployment 03/2009	Unemployment 03/2010
Area	45.5%	30.7%	6.9%	7.3%	8.3%
USA	45.8%	29.5%	8.5%	9.0%	10.1

Key Household Data

	Population Age 0-17	Children w/Married Parents	Children w/Single Mother	Stay-at-home Mothers	Births to Single Women
Area	25.4%	56.8%	31.2%	29.3%	51.2%
USA	24.0%	65.6%	25.5%	27.9%	35.3%

Key Housing Data

	Owner Occupied	Median Year Built	Median Home Value	Home Value Growth, 2005-2010	Median List Price, 4-bedroom Home
Area	62.0%	1986	$287,900	6.6%	$449,000
USA	67.8%	1976	$187,045	3.1%	$288,846

Flint, MI
428,790

	Score	Rank
Overall	56.35	313
LDS Culture	21.77	263
Education	57.88	310
Crime	35.07	320
Economic	66.04	138
Health	38.57	242
Household	56.79	252
Housing	85.22	137

Key LDS Culture Data

	Positive	Negative	Ratio Pos:Neg	Commute>59 minutes	Commute<15 minutes
Area	4,273	292	14.6	9.7%	30.4%
USA	4,292	251	20.1	5.5%	34.1%

Key Education Data

	HS Grad	Some Coll.	College Degree	Free/Reduced Lunch	Students per Teacher
Area	88.4%	26.7%	27.3%	40.6%	18.4
USA	85.8%	22.6%	33.2%	41.2%	15.8

Key Property Crime Data (Rate per 100,000 residents)

	Rate	Burglary	Larceny, Theft	Vehicle Theft
Area	3,696.9	1,301.7	2,008.5	386.7
USA	3,413.6	806.6	2,388.0	262.7

Key Violent Crime Data (Rate per 100,000 residents)

	Rate	Murder	Rape	Robbery	Aggravated Assault
Area	744.6	8.6	55.5	217.0	463.5
USA	432.8	4.7	34.7	111.6	285.6

Key Economic Data (Family income, unemployment)

	$25k-$75k	$75k-$150k	>$150k	Unemployment 03/2009	Unemployment 03/2010
Area	47.8%	27.3%	6.2%	14.8%	16.3%
USA	45.8%	29.5%	8.5%	9.0%	10.1

Key Household Data

	Population Age 0-17	Children w/Married Parents	Children w/Single Mother	Stay-at-home Mothers	Births to Single Women
Area	25.3%	58.1%	32.7%	28.9%	42.7%
USA	24.0%	65.6%	25.5%	27.9%	35.3%

Key Housing Data

	Owner Occupied	Median Year Built	Median Home Value	Home Value Growth, 2005-2010	Median List Price, 4-bedroom Home
Area	69.9%	1968	$126,800	-4.5%	$139,900
USA	67.8%	1976	$187,045	3.1%	$288,846

Florence, SC
199,831

	Score	Rank
Overall	49.18	361
LDS Culture	25.90	198
Education	45.40	358
Crime	15.97	359
Economic	54.36	301
Health	37.46	251
Household	45.68	332
Housing	90.59	45

Key LDS Culture Data

	Positive	Negative	Ratio Pos:Neg	Commute>59 minutes	Commute<15 minutes
Area	1,564	81	19.3	4.1%	33.3%
USA	4,292	251	20.1	5.5%	34.1%

Key Education Data

	HS Grad	Some Coll.	College Degree	Free/Reduced Lunch	Students per Teacher
Area	80.8%	17.2%	27.8%	63.6%	14.9
USA	85.8%	22.6%	33.2%	41.2%	15.8

Key Property Crime Data (Rate per 100,000 residents)

	Rate	Burglary	Larceny, Theft	Vehicle Theft	
Area	5,384.0	1,314.5	3,641.1	428.4	
USA	3,413.6	806.6	2,388.0	262.7	

Key Violent Crime Data (Rate per 100,000 residents)

	Rate	Murder	Rape	Robbery	Aggravated Assault
Area	1,002.5	11.0	44.9	169.2	777.3
USA	432.8	4.7	34.7	111.6	285.6

Key Economic Data (Family income, unemployment)

	$25k-$75k	$75k-$150k	>$150k	Unemployment 03/2009	Unemployment 03/2010
Area	50.0%	20.9%	5.0%	11.8%	12.3%
USA	45.8%	29.5%	8.5%	9.0%	10.1

Key Household Data

	Population Age 0-17	Children w/Married Parents	Children w/Single Mother	Stay-at-home Mothers	Births to Single Women
Area	24.6%	54.8%	36.8%	24.6%	75.6%
USA	24.0%	65.6%	25.5%	27.9%	35.3%

Key Housing Data

	Owner Occupied	Median Year Built	Median Home Value	Home Value Growth, 2005-2010	Median List Price, 4-bedroom Home
Area	70.8%	1982	$96,000	3.3%	
USA	67.8%	1976	$187,045	3.1%	$288,846

Florence-Muscle Shoals, AL
143,791

	Score	Rank
Overall	63.55	170
LDS Culture	30.30	141
Education	65.95	235
Crime	52.15	195
Economic	62.98	188
Health	33.58	308
Household	76.54	86
Housing	86.00	121

Key LDS Culture Data

	Positive	Negative	Ratio Pos:Neg	Commute>59 minutes	Commute<15 minutes
Area	996	34	29.3	7.2%	36.7%
USA	4,292	251	20.1	5.5%	34.1%

Key Education Data

	HS Grad	Some Coll.	College Degree	Free/Reduced Lunch	Students per Teacher
Area	82.7%	21.8%	28.4%	45.8%	15.0
USA	85.8%	22.6%	33.2%	41.2%	15.8

Key Property Crime Data (Rate per 100,000 residents)

	Rate	Burglary	Larceny, Theft	Vehicle Theft	
Area	3,646.9	958.4	2,553.3	135.2	
USA	3,413.6	806.6	2,388.0	262.7	

Key Violent Crime Data (Rate per 100,000 residents)

	Rate	Murder	Rape	Robbery	Aggravated Assault
Area	398.7	4.2	33.5	88.5	272.5
USA	432.8	4.7	34.7	111.6	285.6

Key Economic Data (Family income, unemployment)

	$25k-$75k	$75k-$150k	>$150k	Unemployment 03/2009	Unemployment 03/2010
Area	49.5%	27.1%	5.2%	9.5%	10.4%
USA	45.8%	29.5%	8.5%	9.0%	10.1

Key Household Data

	Population Age 0-17	Children w/Married Parents	Children w/Single Mother	Stay-at-home Mothers	Births to Single Women
Area	21.1%	71.8%	22.0%	28.1%	32.7%
USA	24.0%	65.6%	25.5%	27.9%	35.3%

Key Housing Data

	Owner Occupied	Median Year Built	Median Home Value	Home Value Growth, 2005-2010	Median List Price, 4-bedroom Home
Area	74.2%	1978	$107,100	4.5%	
USA	67.8%	1976	$187,045	3.1%	$288,846

Fond du Lac, WI
99,453

	Score	Rank
Overall	71.56	35
LDS Culture	19.79	286
Education	83.75	43
Crime	84.63	17
Economic	82.05	11
Health	39.16	226
Household	72.84	128
Housing	76.65	262

Key LDS Culture Data

	Positive	Negative	Ratio Pos:Neg	Commute>59 minutes	Commute<15 minutes
Area	1,650	223	7.4	5.3%	43.6%
USA	4,292	251	20.1	5.5%	34.1%

Key Education Data

	HS Grad	Some Coll.	College Degree	Free/Reduced Lunch	Students per Teacher
Area	88.4%	21.7%	28.3%	28.5%	15.6
USA	85.8%	22.6%	33.2%	41.2%	15.8

Key Property Crime Data (Rate per 100,000 residents)

	Rate	Burglary	Larceny, Theft	Vehicle Theft	
Area	1,868.4	235.7	1,560.2	72.5	
USA	3,413.6	806.6	2,388.0	262.7	

Key Violent Crime Data (Rate per 100,000 residents)

	Rate	Murder	Rape	Robbery	Aggravated Assault
Area	214.5	1.0	38.3	10.1	165.2
USA	432.8	4.7	34.7	111.6	285.6

Key Economic Data (Family income, unemployment)

	$25k-$75k	$75k-$150k	>$150k	Unemployment 03/2009	Unemployment 03/2010
Area	49.4%	34.3%	6.4%	10.2%	9.9%
USA	45.8%	29.5%	8.5%	9.0%	10.1

Key Household Data

	Population Age 0-17	Children w/Married Parents	Children w/Single Mother	Stay-at-home Mothers	Births to Single Women
Area	22.1%	82.1%	11.8%	17.1%	28.9%
USA	24.0%	65.6%	25.5%	27.9%	35.3%

Key Housing Data

	Owner Occupied	Median Year Built	Median Home Value	Home Value Growth, 2005-2010	Median List Price, 4-bedroom Home
Area	75.1%	1962	$142,600	2.1%	
USA	67.8%	1976	$187,045	3.1%	$288,846

Fort Collins-Loveland, CO
292,825

	Score	Rank
Overall	73.19	25
LDS Culture	16.99	320
Education	87.58	27
Crime	70.60	73
Economic	86.16	8
Health	37.28	255
Household	85.80	30
Housing	84.89	145

Key LDS Culture Data

	Positive	Negative	Ratio Pos:Neg	Commute>59 minutes	Commute<15 minutes
Area	2,775	195	14.2	6.2%	35.2%
USA	4,292	251	20.1	5.5%	34.1%

Key Education Data

	HS Grad	Some Coll.	College Degree	Free/Reduced Lunch	Students per Teacher
Area	92.7%	21.7%	50.9%	24.0%	17.6
USA	85.8%	22.6%	33.2%	41.2%	15.8

Key Property Crime Data (Rate per 100,000 residents)

	Rate	Burglary	Larceny, Theft	Vehicle Theft	
Area	2,783.4	488.4	2,155.4	139.5	
USA	3,413.6	806.6	2,388.0	262.7	

Key Violent Crime Data (Rate per 100,000 residents)

	Rate	Murder	Rape	Robbery	Aggravated Assault
Area	270.5	1.7	44.5	23.3	201.1
USA	432.8	4.7	34.7	111.6	285.6

Key Economic Data (Family income, unemployment)

	$25k-$75k	$75k-$150k	>$150k	Unemployment 03/2009	Unemployment 03/2010
Area	41.3%	34.1%	13.8%	7.2%	7.1%
USA	45.8%	29.5%	8.5%	9.0%	10.1

Key Household Data

	Population Age 0-17	Children w/Married Parents	Children w/Single Mother	Stay-at-home Mothers	Births to Single Women
Area	21.4%	76.3%	15.8%	30.7%	12.5%
USA	24.0%	65.6%	25.5%	27.9%	35.3%

Key Housing Data

	Owner Occupied	Median Year Built	Median Home Value	Home Value Growth, 2005-2010	Median List Price, 4-bedroom Home
Area	67.4%	1988	$246,500	0.8%	$319,000
USA	67.8%	1976	$187,045	3.1%	$288,846

Fort Smith, AR-OK
286,786

	Score	Rank
Overall	64.30	156
LDS Culture	28.86	156
Education	71.30	168
Crime	54.12	177
Economic	51.08	320
Health	49.87	41
Household	63.58	191
Housing	93.50	22

Key LDS Culture Data

	Positive	Negative	Ratio Pos:Neg	Commute>59 minutes	Commute<15 minutes
Area	1,269	56	22.7	3.7%	39.5%
USA	4,292	251	20.1	5.5%	34.1%

Key Education Data

	HS Grad	Some Coll.	College Degree	Free/Reduced Lunch	Students per Teacher
Area	81.6%	24.0%	22.1%	58.3%	14.0
USA	85.8%	22.6%	33.2%	41.2%	15.8

Key Property Crime Data (Rate per 100,000 residents)

	Rate	Burglary	Larceny, Theft	Vehicle Theft	
Area	2,834.0	746.6	1,906.0	181.3	
USA	3,413.6	806.6	2,388.0	262.7	

Key Violent Crime Data (Rate per 100,000 residents)

	Rate	Murder	Rape	Robbery	Aggravated Assault
Area	451.5	2.4	54.8	47.3	346.9
USA	432.8	4.7	34.7	111.6	285.6

Key Economic Data (Family income, unemployment)

	$25k-$75k	$75k-$150k	>$150k	Unemployment 03/2009	Unemployment 03/2010
Area	51.2%	20.7%	4.1%	7.7%	8.3%
USA	45.8%	29.5%	8.5%	9.0%	10.1

Key Household Data

	Population Age 0-17	Children w/Married Parents	Children w/Single Mother	Stay-at-home Mothers	Births to Single Women
Area	26.3%	65.5%	27.2%	31.3%	45.3%
USA	24.0%	65.6%	25.5%	27.9%	35.3%

Key Housing Data

	Owner Occupied	Median Year Built	Median Home Value	Home Value Growth, 2005-2010	Median List Price, 4-bedroom Home
Area	67.8%	1979	$93,700	3.7%	$197,500
USA	67.8%	1976	$187,045	3.1%	$288,846

Fort Walton Beach-Crestview-Destin, FL
179,693

	Score	Rank
Overall	69.13	63
LDS Culture	21.21	268
Education	76.77	107
Crime	57.55	157
Economic	70.21	82
Health	52.72	23
Household	80.86	62
Housing	83.94	159

Key LDS Culture Data

	Positive	Negative	Ratio Pos:Neg	Commute>59 minutes	Commute<15 minutes
Area	1,596	84	19.0	5.5%	35.6%
USA	4,292	251	20.1	5.5%	34.1%

Key Education Data

	HS Grad	Some Coll.	College Degree	Free/Reduced Lunch	Students per Teacher
Area	91.5%	27.4%	37.5%	29.5%	14.3
USA	85.8%	22.6%	33.2%	41.2%	15.8

Key Property Crime Data (Rate per 100,000 residents)

	Rate	Burglary	Larceny, Theft	Vehicle Theft	
Area	3,067.0	579.7	2,324.5	162.8	
USA	3,413.6	806.6	2,388.0	262.7	

Key Violent Crime Data (Rate per 100,000 residents)

	Rate	Murder	Rape	Robbery	Aggravated Assault
Area	381.5	1.7	31.0	77.0	271.9
USA	432.8	4.7	34.7	111.6	285.6

Key Economic Data (Family income, unemployment)

	$25k-$75k	$75k-$150k	>$150k	Unemployment 03/2009	Unemployment 03/2010
Area	49.1%	30.5%	7.9%		
USA	45.8%	29.5%	8.5%	9.0%	10.1

Key Household Data

	Population Age 0-17	Children w/Married Parents	Children w/Single Mother	Stay-at-home Mothers	Births to Single Women
Area	23.7%	66.0%	25.2%	31.9%	23.7%
USA	24.0%	65.6%	25.5%	27.9%	35.3%

Key Housing Data

	Owner Occupied	Median Year Built	Median Home Value	Home Value Growth, 2005-2010	Median List Price, 4-bedroom Home
Area	66.3%	1986	$214,500	4.5%	
USA	67.8%	1976	$187,045	3.1%	$288,846

Fort Wayne, IN
410,247

	Score	Rank
Overall	63.62	169
LDS Culture	21.88	262
Education	67.55	212
Crime	71.93	68
Economic	76.65	33
Health	34.59	295
Household	47.53	316
Housing	87.83	86

Key LDS Culture Data

	Positive	Negative	Ratio Pos:Neg	Commute>59 minutes	Commute<15 minutes
Area	2,612	177	14.8	3.4%	28.5%
USA	4,292	251	20.1	5.5%	34.1%

Key Education Data

	HS Grad	Some Coll.	College Degree	Free/Reduced Lunch	Students per Teacher
Area	88.3%	22.8%	34.2%	40.6%	17.7
USA	85.8%	22.6%	33.2%	41.2%	15.8

Key Property Crime Data (Rate per 100,000 residents)

	Rate	Burglary	Larceny, Theft	Vehicle Theft
Area	3,097.8	708.5	2,186.5	202.8
USA	3,413.6	806.6	2,388.0	262.7

Key Violent Crime Data (Rate per 100,000 residents)

	Rate	Murder	Rape	Robbery	Aggravated Assault
Area	223.6	6.1	30.6	122.0	65.0
USA	432.8	4.7	34.7	111.6	285.6

Key Economic Data (Family income, unemployment)

	$25k-$75k	$75k-$150k	>$150k	Unemployment 03/2009	Unemployment 03/2010
Area	49.3%	29.9%	6.8%	11.3%	11.1%
USA	45.8%	29.5%	8.5%	9.0%	10.1

Key Household Data

	Population Age 0-17	Children w/Married Parents	Children w/Single Mother	Stay-at-home Mothers	Births to Single Women
Area	26.5%	60.4%	28.6%	28.5%	40.1%
USA	24.0%	65.6%	25.5%	27.9%	35.3%

Key Housing Data

	Owner Occupied	Median Year Built	Median Home Value	Home Value Growth, 2005-2010	Median List Price, 4-bedroom Home
Area	73.4%	1973	$113,800	1.0%	$164,900
USA	67.8%	1976	$187,045	3.1%	$288,846

Fresno, CA
909,153

	Score	Rank
Overall	54.18	341
LDS Culture	21.98	260
Education	59.81	296
Crime	45.04	254
Economic	41.41	357
Health	48.59	62
Household	62.96	199
Housing	67.61	336

Key LDS Culture Data

	Positive	Negative	Ratio Pos:Neg	Commute>59 minutes	Commute<15 minutes
Area	4,002	269	14.9	5.0%	29.3%
USA	4,292	251	20.1	5.5%	34.1%

Key Education Data

	HS Grad	Some Coll.	College Degree	Free/Reduced Lunch	Students per Teacher
Area	73.2%	23.7%	27.1%	64.9%	17.8
USA	85.8%	22.6%	33.2%	41.2%	15.8

Key Property Crime Data (Rate per 100,000 residents)

	Rate	Burglary	Larceny, Theft	Vehicle Theft	
Area	4,103.1	846.9	2,592.6	663.7	
USA	3,413.6	806.6	2,388.0	262.7	

Key Violent Crime Data (Rate per 100,000 residents)

	Rate	Murder	Rape	Robbery	Aggravated Assault
Area	472.2	7.2	18.9	141.4	304.7
USA	432.8	4.7	34.7	111.6	285.6

Key Economic Data (Family income, unemployment)

	$25k-$75k	$75k-$150k	>$150k	Unemployment 03/2009	Unemployment 03/2010
Area	43.6%	24.7%	7.9%	15.9%	18.7%
USA	45.8%	29.5%	8.5%	9.0%	10.1

Key Household Data

	Population Age 0-17	Children w/Married Parents	Children w/Single Mother	Stay-at-home Mothers	Births to Single Women
Area	29.7%	60.7%	28.4%	35.2%	38.8%
USA	24.0%	65.6%	25.5%	27.9%	35.3%

Key Housing Data

	Owner Occupied	Median Year Built	Median Home Value	Home Value Growth, 2005-2010	Median List Price, 4-bedroom Home
Area	53.7%	1980	$261,900	-0.4%	$250,500
USA	67.8%	1976	$187,045	3.1%	$288,846

Gadsden, AL
103,303

	Score	Rank
Overall	**65.49**	**132**
LDS Culture	45.51	25
Education	62.09	276
Crime	53.08	190
Economic	59.03	239
Health	33.58	309
Household	83.33	41
Housing	83.32	169

Key LDS Culture Data

	Positive	Negative	Ratio Pos:Neg	Commute>59 minutes	Commute<15 minutes
Area	1,767	38	46.5	9.2%	35.8%
USA	4,292	251	20.1	5.5%	34.1%

Key Education Data

	HS Grad	Some Coll.	College Degree	Free/Reduced Lunch	Students per Teacher
Area	80.9%	24.3%	26.9%	52.1%	15.7
USA	85.8%	22.6%	33.2%	41.2%	15.8

Key Property Crime Data (Rate per 100,000 residents)

	Rate	Burglary	Larceny, Theft	Vehicle Theft
Area	3,665.7	788.1	2,662.0	215.6
USA	3,413.6	806.6	2,388.0	262.7

Key Violent Crime Data (Rate per 100,000 residents)

	Rate	Murder	Rape	Robbery	Aggravated Assault
Area	387.7	4.8	46.4	151.8	184.7
USA	432.8	4.7	34.7	111.6	285.6

Key Economic Data (Family income, unemployment)

	$25k-$75k	$75k-$150k	>$150k	Unemployment 03/2009	Unemployment 03/2010
Area	49.6%	26.1%	5.0%	10.0%	11.1%
USA	45.8%	29.5%	8.5%	9.0%	10.1

Key Household Data

	Population Age 0-17	Children w/Married Parents	Children w/Single Mother	Stay-at-home Mothers	Births to Single Women
Area	23.0%	66.9%	23.3%	37.1%	9.3%
USA	24.0%	65.6%	25.5%	27.9%	35.3%

Key Housing Data

	Owner Occupied	Median Year Built	Median Home Value	Home Value Growth, 2005-2010	Median List Price, 4-bedroom Home
Area	69.8%	1974	$113,200	3.7%	
USA	67.8%	1976	$187,045	3.1%	$288,846

Gainesville, FL
255,393

	Score	Rank
Overall	60.38	234
LDS Culture	30.72	130
Education	71.70	166
Crime	30.18	335
Economic	50.47	325
Health	51.46	35
Household	64.81	180
Housing	87.86	85

Key LDS Culture Data

	Positive	Negative	Ratio Pos:Neg	Commute>59 minutes	Commute<15 minutes
Area	1,981	80	24.8	4.6%	31.9%
USA	4,292	251	20.1	5.5%	34.1%

Key Education Data

	HS Grad	Some Coll.	College Degree	Free/Reduced Lunch	Students per Teacher
Area	89.8%	16.3%	52.9%	43.7%	16.0
USA	85.8%	22.6%	33.2%	41.2%	15.8

Key Property Crime Data (Rate per 100,000 residents)

	Rate	Burglary	Larceny, Theft	Vehicle Theft	
Area	4,240.2	1,115.0	2,861.8	263.4	
USA	3,413.6	806.6	2,388.0	262.7	

Key Violent Crime Data (Rate per 100,000 residents)

	Rate	Murder	Rape	Robbery	Aggravated Assault
Area	798.7	2.3	52.1	140.1	604.2
USA	432.8	4.7	34.7	111.6	285.6

Key Economic Data (Family income, unemployment)

	$25k-$75k	$75k-$150k	>$150k	Unemployment 03/2009	Unemployment 03/2010
Area	40.8%	32.0%	10.7%	6.2%	8.5%
USA	45.8%	29.5%	8.5%	9.0%	10.1

Key Household Data

	Population Age 0-17	Children w/Married Parents	Children w/Single Mother	Stay-at-home Mothers	Births to Single Women
Area	19.3%	58.4%	34.1%	31.7%	34.0%
USA	24.0%	65.6%	25.5%	27.9%	35.3%

Key Housing Data

	Owner Occupied	Median Year Built	Median Home Value	Home Value Growth, 2005-2010	Median List Price, 4-bedroom Home
Area	57.3%	1985	$205,500	5.2%	$250,000
USA	67.8%	1976	$187,045	3.1%	$288,846

Gainesville, GA
184,814

	Score	Rank
Overall	66.66	108
LDS Culture	31.43	119
Education	45.38	359
Crime	74.46	56
Economic	65.26	150
Health	40.98	200
Household	83.33	42
Housing	86.62	107

Key LDS Culture Data

	Positive	Negative	Ratio Pos:Neg	Commute>59 minutes	Commute<15 minutes
Area	4,544	112	40.6	10.2%	21.3%
USA	4,292	251	20.1	5.5%	34.1%

Key Education Data

	HS Grad	Some Coll.	College Degree	Free/Reduced Lunch	Students per Teacher
Area	74.9%	19.7%	26.1%	54.9%	14.2
USA	85.8%	22.6%	33.2%	41.2%	15.8

Key Property Crime Data (Rate per 100,000 residents)

	Rate	Burglary	Larceny, Theft	Vehicle Theft
Area	2,743.2	573.4	1,857.0	312.8
USA	3,413.6	806.6	2,388.0	262.7

Key Violent Crime Data (Rate per 100,000 residents)

	Rate	Murder	Rape	Robbery	Aggravated Assault
Area	233.2	2.2	20.7	58.3	151.9
USA	432.8	4.7	34.7	111.6	285.6

Key Economic Data (Family income, unemployment)

	$25k-$75k	$75k-$150k	>$150k	Unemployment 03/2009	Unemployment 03/2010
Area	44.7%	28.7%	10.9%	8.8%	9.6%
USA	45.8%	29.5%	8.5%	9.0%	10.1

Key Household Data

	Population Age 0-17	Children w/Married Parents	Children w/Single Mother	Stay-at-home Mothers	Births to Single Women
Area	28.7%	73.1%	15.8%	33.8%	22.3%
USA	24.0%	65.6%	25.5%	27.9%	35.3%

Key Housing Data

	Owner Occupied	Median Year Built	Median Home Value	Home Value Growth, 2005-2010	Median List Price, 4-bedroom Home
Area	68.9%	1994	$184,300	2.0%	$259,900
USA	67.8%	1976	$187,045	3.1%	$288,846

Glens Falls, NY
128,775

	Score	Rank
Overall	68.88	68
LDS Culture	23.66	238
Education	78.72	86
Crime	89.24	6
Economic	73.99	51
Health	49.20	48
Household	51.23	294
Housing	75.67	276

Key LDS Culture Data

	Positive	Negative	Ratio Pos:Neg	Commute>59 minutes	Commute<15 minutes
Area	1,260	107	11.8	6.0%	36.3%
USA	4,292	251	20.1	5.5%	34.1%

Key Education Data

	HS Grad	Some Coll.	College Degree	Free/Reduced Lunch	Students per Teacher
Area	87.5%	18.6%	33.3%	29.5%	10.4
USA	85.8%	22.6%	33.2%	41.2%	15.8

Key Property Crime Data (Rate per 100,000 residents)

	Rate	Burglary	Larceny, Theft	Vehicle Theft
Area	1,767.9	271.2	1,465.0	31.7
USA	3,413.6	806.6	2,388.0	262.7

Key Violent Crime Data (Rate per 100,000 residents)

	Rate	Murder	Rape	Robbery	Aggravated Assault
Area	175.4	1.5	30.9	10.0	132.9
USA	432.8	4.7	34.7	111.6	285.6

Key Economic Data (Family income, unemployment)

	$25k-$75k	$75k-$150k	>$150k	Unemployment 03/2009	Unemployment 03/2010
Area	52.0%	28.0%	5.6%	9.1%	9.1%
USA	45.8%	29.5%	8.5%	9.0%	10.1

Key Household Data

	Population Age 0-17	Children w/Married Parents	Children w/Single Mother	Stay-at-home Mothers	Births to Single Women
Area	19.7%	66.7%	21.5%	14.1%	41.9%
USA	24.0%	65.6%	25.5%	27.9%	35.3%

Key Housing Data

	Owner Occupied	Median Year Built	Median Home Value	Home Value Growth, 2005-2010	Median List Price, 4-bedroom Home
Area	67.5%	1968	$166,800	6.2%	$269,900
USA	67.8%	1976	$187,045	3.1%	$288,846

Goldsboro, NC
113,671

	Score	Rank
Overall	63.21	179
LDS Culture	50.10	15
Education	55.95	322
Crime	41.08	280
Economic	54.20	306
Health	49.20	49
Household	63.58	192
Housing	91.19	38

Key LDS Culture Data

	Positive	Negative	Ratio Pos:Neg	Commute>59 minutes	Commute<15 minutes
Area	1,551	30	51.7	6.0%	38.6%
USA	4,292	251	20.1	5.5%	34.1%

Key Education Data

	HS Grad	Some Coll.	College Degree	Free/Reduced Lunch	Students per Teacher
Area	81.5%	26.1%	24.7%	52.3%	14.4
USA	85.8%	22.6%	33.2%	41.2%	15.8

Key Property Crime Data (Rate per 100,000 residents)

	Rate	Burglary	Larceny, Theft	Vehicle Theft
Area	4,819.9	1,486.1	2,951.1	382.7
USA	3,413.6	806.6	2,388.0	262.7

Key Violent Crime Data (Rate per 100,000 residents)

	Rate	Murder	Rape	Robbery	Aggravated Assault
Area	486.3	9.7	5.3	139.6	331.8
USA	432.8	4.7	34.7	111.6	285.6

Key Economic Data (Family income, unemployment)

	$25k-$75k	$75k-$150k	>$150k	Unemployment 03/2009	Unemployment 03/2010
Area	51.8%	21.5%	3.6%	8.9%	9.2%
USA	45.8%	29.5%	8.5%	9.0%	10.1

Key Household Data

	Population Age 0-17	Children w/Married Parents	Children w/Single Mother	Stay-at-home Mothers	Births to Single Women
Area	25.6%	59.0%	33.1%	34.5%	39.0%
USA	24.0%	65.6%	25.5%	27.9%	35.3%

Key Housing Data

	Owner Occupied	Median Year Built	Median Home Value	Home Value Growth, 2005-2010	Median List Price, 4-bedroom Home
Area	63.1%	1983	$112,500	3.5%	
USA	67.8%	1976	$187,045	3.1%	$288,846

Grand Forks, ND-MN
95,796

	Score	Rank
Overall	67.74	92
LDS Culture	30.93	126
Education	78.63	88
Crime	68.08	91
Economic	62.70	191
Health	52.49	28
Household	61.73	211
Housing	79.81	212

Key LDS Culture Data

	Positive	Negative	Ratio Pos:Neg	Commute>59 minutes	Commute<15 minutes
Area	440	44	10.0	2.5%	62.1%
USA	4,292	251	20.1	5.5%	34.1%

Key Education Data

	HS Grad	Some Coll.	College Degree	Free/Reduced Lunch	Students per Teacher
Area	91.3%	22.3%	42.4%	34.7%	12.5
USA	85.8%	22.6%	33.2%	41.2%	15.8

Key Property Crime Data (Rate per 100,000 residents)

	Rate	Burglary	Larceny, Theft	Vehicle Theft	
Area	2,566.8	413.0	2,004.6	149.2	
USA	3,413.6	806.6	2,388.0	262.7	

Key Violent Crime Data (Rate per 100,000 residents)

	Rate	Murder	Rape	Robbery	Aggravated Assault
Area		1.0		16.4	155.4
USA	432.8	4.7	34.7	111.6	285.6

Key Economic Data (Family income, unemployment)

	$25k-$75k	$75k-$150k	>$150k	Unemployment 03/2009	Unemployment 03/2010
Area	43.8%	34.1%	7.4%	5.8%	5.3%
USA	45.8%	29.5%	8.5%	9.0%	10.1

Key Household Data

	Population Age 0-17	Children w/Married Parents	Children w/Single Mother	Stay-at-home Mothers	Births to Single Women
Area	21.7%	71.0%	21.2%	17.6%	47.2%
USA	24.0%	65.6%	25.5%	27.9%	35.3%

Key Housing Data

	Owner Occupied	Median Year Built	Median Home Value	Home Value Growth, 2005-2010	Median List Price, 4-bedroom Home
Area	61.9%	1966	$131,000	4.9%	
USA	67.8%	1976	$187,045	3.1%	$288,846

Grand Junction, CO
143,171

	Score	Rank
Overall	67.68	93
LDS Culture	19.97	284
Education	73.42	144
Crime	62.39	132
Economic	76.10	38
Health	46.30	126
Household	75.93	91
Housing	79.88	210

Key LDS Culture Data

	Positive	Negative	Ratio Pos:Neg	Commute>59 minutes	Commute<15 minutes
Area	718	57	12.6	7.3%	41.9%
USA	4,292	251	20.1	5.5%	34.1%

Key Education Data

	HS Grad	Some Coll.	College Degree	Free/Reduced Lunch	Students per Teacher
Area	90.3%	26.6%	32.3%	37.7%	17.5
USA	85.8%	22.6%	33.2%	41.2%	15.8

Key Property Crime Data (Rate per 100,000 residents)

	Rate	Burglary	Larceny, Theft	Vehicle Theft
Area	2,994.2	588.9	2,184.5	220.9
USA	3,413.6	806.6	2,388.0	262.7

Key Violent Crime Data (Rate per 100,000 residents)

	Rate	Murder	Rape	Robbery	Aggravated Assault
Area	337.0	4.9	58.4	32.4	241.3
USA	432.8	4.7	34.7	111.6	285.6

Key Economic Data (Family income, unemployment)

	$25k-$75k	$75k-$150k	>$150k	Unemployment 03/2009	Unemployment 03/2010
Area	50.0%	29.9%	7.5%	8.7%	10.3%
USA	45.8%	29.5%	8.5%	9.0%	10.1

Key Household Data

	Population Age 0-17	Children w/Married Parents	Children w/Single Mother	Stay-at-home Mothers	Births to Single Women
Area	22.9%	74.4%	16.7%	25.6%	23.1%
USA	24.0%	65.6%	25.5%	27.9%	35.3%

Key Housing Data

	Owner Occupied	Median Year Built	Median Home Value	Home Value Growth, 2005-2010	Median List Price, 4-bedroom Home
Area	69.6%	1984	$224,900	7.1%	$300,000
USA	67.8%	1976	$187,045	3.1%	$288,846

Grand Rapids-Wyoming, MI
776,833

	Score	Rank
Overall	65.03	137
LDS Culture	25.46	206
Education	77.22	102
Crime	53.56	181
Economic	61.98	197
Health	34.86	287
Household	80.25	64
Housing	83.65	164

Key LDS Culture Data

	Positive	Negative	Ratio Pos:Neg	Commute>59 minutes	Commute<15 minutes
Area	4,590	244	18.8	4.9%	29.3%
USA	4,292	251	20.1	5.5%	34.1%

Key Education Data

	HS Grad	Some Coll.	College Degree	Free/Reduced Lunch	Students per Teacher
Area	87.5%	23.9%	34.2%	38.6%	16.9
USA	85.8%	22.6%	33.2%	41.2%	15.8

Key Property Crime Data (Rate per 100,000 residents)

	Rate	Burglary	Larceny, Theft	Vehicle Theft	
Area	2,942.8	673.3	2,122.2	147.3	
USA	3,413.6	806.6	2,388.0	262.7	

Key Violent Crime Data (Rate per 100,000 residents)

	Rate	Murder	Rape	Robbery	Aggravated Assault
Area	440.3	2.3	45.3	127.9	264.7
USA	432.8	4.7	34.7	111.6	285.6

Key Economic Data (Family income, unemployment)

	$25k-$75k	$75k-$150k	>$150k	Unemployment 03/2009	Unemployment 03/2010
Area	45.6%	30.3%	7.4%	11.1%	12.8%
USA	45.8%	29.5%	8.5%	9.0%	10.1

Key Household Data

	Population Age 0-17	Children w/Married Parents	Children w/Single Mother	Stay-at-home Mothers	Births to Single Women
Area	26.4%	68.4%	24.2%	27.4%	32.1%
USA	24.0%	65.6%	25.5%	27.9%	35.3%

Key Housing Data

	Owner Occupied	Median Year Built	Median Home Value	Home Value Growth, 2005-2010	Median List Price, 4-bedroom Home
Area	74.7%	1972	$147,000	-1.5%	$167,900
USA	67.8%	1976	$187,045	3.1%	$288,846

Great Falls, MT
82,026

	Score	Rank
Overall	65.37	134
LDS Culture	31.99	118
Education	68.77	199
Crime	64.75	111
Economic	67.26	119
Health	46.11	128
Household	65.43	175
Housing	74.87	282

Key LDS Culture Data
	Positive	Negative	Ratio Pos:Neg	Commute>59 minutes	Commute<15 minutes
Area	434	70	6.2	1.9%	53.9%
USA	4,292	251	20.1	5.5%	34.1%

Key Education Data
	HS Grad	Some Coll.	College Degree	Free/Reduced Lunch	Students per Teacher
Area	91.6%	29.2%	32.4%	33.9%	14.0
USA	85.8%	22.6%	33.2%	41.2%	15.8

Key Property Crime Data (Rate per 100,000 residents)
	Rate	Burglary	Larceny, Theft	Vehicle Theft	
Area	3,795.9	400.5	3,207.9	187.5	
USA	3,413.6	806.6	2,388.0	262.7	

Key Violent Crime Data (Rate per 100,000 residents)
	Rate	Murder	Rape	Robbery	Aggravated Assault
Area	255.7	2.4	13.4	37.7	202.1
USA	432.8	4.7	34.7	111.6	285.6

Key Economic Data (Family income, unemployment)
	$25k-$75k	$75k-$150k	>$150k	Unemployment 03/2009	Unemployment 03/2010
Area	54.6%	25.8%	4.1%	5.0%	6.5%
USA	45.8%	29.5%	8.5%	9.0%	10.1

Key Household Data
	Population Age 0-17	Children w/Married Parents	Children w/Single Mother	Stay-at-home Mothers	Births to Single Women
Area	24.6%	69.7%	25.1%	19.5%	33.4%
USA	24.0%	65.6%	25.5%	27.9%	35.3%

Key Housing Data
	Owner Occupied	Median Year Built	Median Home Value	Home Value Growth, 2005-2010	Median List Price, 4-bedroom Home
Area	67.0%	1962	$154,400	5.5%	
USA	67.8%	1976	$187,045	3.1%	$288,846

Greeley, CO
249,775

	Score	Rank
Overall	68.75	71
LDS Culture	11.93	352
Education	67.79	211
Crime	69.08	81
Economic	76.54	34
Health	42.67	172
Household	84.57	35
Housing	88.31	77

Key LDS Culture Data

	Positive	Negative	Ratio Pos:Neg	Commute>59 minutes	Commute<15 minutes
Area	2,227	165	13.5	7.6%	28.9%
USA	4,292	251	20.1	5.5%	34.1%

Key Education Data

	HS Grad	Some Coll.	College Degree	Free/Reduced Lunch	Students per Teacher
Area	83.3%	21.6%	36.9%	41.8%	16.1
USA	85.8%	22.6%	33.2%	41.2%	15.8

Key Property Crime Data (Rate per 100,000 residents)

	Rate	Burglary	Larceny, Theft	Vehicle Theft
Area	2,555.2	584.2	1,798.2	172.9
USA	3,413.6	806.6	2,388.0	262.7

Key Violent Crime Data (Rate per 100,000 residents)

	Rate	Murder	Rape	Robbery	Aggravated Assault
Area	310.5	2.4	29.7	38.0	240.5
USA	432.8	4.7	34.7	111.6	285.6

Key Economic Data (Family income, unemployment)

	$25k-$75k	$75k-$150k	>$150k	Unemployment 03/2009	Unemployment 03/2010
Area	44.4%	33.9%	7.6%	9.1%	9.9%
USA	45.8%	29.5%	8.5%	9.0%	10.1

Key Household Data

	Population Age 0-17	Children w/Married Parents	Children w/Single Mother	Stay-at-home Mothers	Births to Single Women
Area	27.3%	73.2%	18.3%	34.8%	25.1%
USA	24.0%	65.6%	25.5%	27.9%	35.3%

Key Housing Data

	Owner Occupied	Median Year Built	Median Home Value	Home Value Growth, 2005-2010	Median List Price, 4-bedroom Home
Area	69.5%	1994	$199,400	-1.2%	$239,000
USA	67.8%	1976	$187,045	3.1%	$288,846

Green Bay, WI
302,935

	Score	Rank
Overall	68.86	69
LDS Culture	19.04	300
Education	85.18	39
Crime	81.41	30
Economic	76.21	35
Health	39.16	227
Household	54.94	274
Housing	85.63	129

Key LDS Culture Data

	Positive	Negative	Ratio Pos:Neg	Commute>59 minutes	Commute<15 minutes
Area	2,161	330	6.5	3.5%	38.7%
USA	4,292	251	20.1	5.5%	34.1%

Key Education Data

	HS Grad	Some Coll.	College Degree	Free/Reduced Lunch	Students per Teacher
Area	89.8%	20.6%	33.1%	30.0%	14.3
USA	85.8%	22.6%	33.2%	41.2%	15.8

Key Property Crime Data (Rate per 100,000 residents)

	Rate	Burglary	Larceny, Theft	Vehicle Theft	
Area	2,346.6	412.2	1,832.2	102.2	
USA	3,413.6	806.6	2,388.0	262.7	

Key Violent Crime Data (Rate per 100,000 residents)

	Rate	Murder	Rape	Robbery	Aggravated Assault
Area	199.5	0.7	35.0	36.9	127.0
USA	432.8	4.7	34.7	111.6	285.6

Key Economic Data (Family income, unemployment)

	$25k-$75k	$75k-$150k	>$150k	Unemployment 03/2009	Unemployment 03/2010
Area	49.4%	32.5%	7.2%	9.1%	9.1%
USA	45.8%	29.5%	8.5%	9.0%	10.1

Key Household Data

	Population Age 0-17	Children w/Married Parents	Children w/Single Mother	Stay-at-home Mothers	Births to Single Women
Area	24.0%	66.3%	24.1%	20.1%	39.1%
USA	24.0%	65.6%	25.5%	27.9%	35.3%

Key Housing Data

	Owner Occupied	Median Year Built	Median Home Value	Home Value Growth, 2005-2010	Median List Price, 4-bedroom Home
Area	71.8%	1975	$158,400	0.8%	$189,900
USA	67.8%	1976	$187,045	3.1%	$288,846

Greensboro-High Point, NC
705,684

	Score	Rank
Overall	64.98	138
LDS Culture	36.59	70
Education	69.75	188
Crime	40.44	284
Economic	61.70	202
Health	49.89	40
Household	67.90	162
Housing	90.42	50

Key LDS Culture Data

	Positive	Negative	Ratio Pos:Neg	Commute>59 minutes	Commute<15 minutes
Area	6,658	212	31.4	3.5%	30.8%
USA	4,292	251	20.1	5.5%	34.1%

Key Education Data

	HS Grad	Some Coll.	College Degree	Free/Reduced Lunch	Students per Teacher
Area	82.9%	21.8%	32.2%	14.4%	14.8
USA	85.8%	22.6%	33.2%	41.2%	15.8

Key Property Crime Data (Rate per 100,000 residents)

	Rate	Burglary	Larceny, Theft	Vehicle Theft
Area	4,650.5	1,440.9	2,905.0	304.5
USA	3,413.6	806.6	2,388.0	262.7

Key Violent Crime Data (Rate per 100,000 residents)

	Rate	Murder	Rape	Robbery	Aggravated Assault
Area	519.0	6.4	27.7	211.4	273.6
USA	432.8	4.7	34.7	111.6	285.6

Key Economic Data (Family income, unemployment)

	$25k-$75k	$75k-$150k	>$150k	Unemployment 03/2009	Unemployment 03/2010
Area	50.2%	24.3%	8.0%	11.0%	11.5%
USA	45.8%	29.5%	8.5%	9.0%	10.1

Key Household Data

	Population Age 0-17	Children w/Married Parents	Children w/Single Mother	Stay-at-home Mothers	Births to Single Women
Area	23.6%	64.3%	26.1%	25.4%	29.3%
USA	24.0%	65.6%	25.5%	27.9%	35.3%

Key Housing Data

	Owner Occupied	Median Year Built	Median Home Value	Home Value Growth, 2005-2010	Median List Price, 4-bedroom Home
Area	68.3%	1982	$138,600	2.3%	$255,000
USA	67.8%	1976	$187,045	3.1%	$288,846

Greenville, NC
173,136

	Score	Rank
Overall	58.55	275
LDS Culture	41.33	39
Education	62.64	271
Crime	35.53	318
Economic	58.59	247
Health	37.16	258
Household	51.85	289
Housing	88.36	75

Key LDS Culture Data

	Positive	Negative	Ratio Pos:Neg	Commute>59 minutes	Commute<15 minutes
Area	2,537	69	36.8	4.3%	36.0%
USA	4,292	251	20.1	5.5%	34.1%

Key Education Data

	HS Grad	Some Coll.	College Degree	Free/Reduced Lunch	Students per Teacher
Area	84.5%	22.5%	36.5%	37.7%	14.0
USA	85.8%	22.6%	33.2%	41.2%	15.8

Key Property Crime Data (Rate per 100,000 residents)

	Rate	Burglary	Larceny, Theft	Vehicle Theft	
Area	5,028.6	1,624.9	3,141.0	262.7	
USA	3,413.6	806.6	2,388.0	262.7	

Key Violent Crime Data (Rate per 100,000 residents)

	Rate	Murder	Rape	Robbery	Aggravated Assault
Area	591.4	4.6	16.0	176.6	394.3
USA	432.8	4.7	34.7	111.6	285.6

Key Economic Data (Family income, unemployment)

	$25k-$75k	$75k-$150k	>$150k	Unemployment 03/2009	Unemployment 03/2010
Area	44.4%	26.2%	5.9%	10.2%	10.3%
USA	45.8%	29.5%	8.5%	9.0%	10.1

Key Household Data

	Population Age 0-17	Children w/Married Parents	Children w/Single Mother	Stay-at-home Mothers	Births to Single Women
Area	23.6%	54.6%	37.5%	26.0%	44.7%
USA	24.0%	65.6%	25.5%	27.9%	35.3%

Key Housing Data

	Owner Occupied	Median Year Built	Median Home Value	Home Value Growth, 2005-2010	Median List Price, 4-bedroom Home
Area	58.3%	1987	$121,100	2.6%	
USA	67.8%	1976	$187,045	3.1%	$288,846

Hagerstown-Martinsburg, MD-WV
263,613

	Score	Rank
Overall	62.41	187
LDS Culture	14.91	337
Education	69.12	195
Crime	73.87	58
Economic	61.76	201
Health	49.20	44
Household	48.77	310
Housing	82.56	179

Key LDS Culture Data

	Positive	Negative	Ratio Pos:Neg	Commute>59 minutes	Commute<15 minutes
Area	3,273	194	16.9	13.5%	27.6%
USA	4,292	251	20.1	5.5%	34.1%

Key Education Data

	HS Grad	Some Coll.	College Degree	Free/Reduced Lunch	Students per Teacher
Area	82.2%	20.8%	23.3%	38.9%	14.6
USA	85.8%	22.6%	33.2%	41.2%	15.8

Key Property Crime Data (Rate per 100,000 residents)

	Rate	Burglary	Larceny, Theft	Vehicle Theft
Area	2,437.7	546.9	1,721.7	169.1
USA	3,413.6	806.6	2,388.0	262.7

Key Violent Crime Data (Rate per 100,000 residents)

	Rate	Murder	Rape	Robbery	Aggravated Assault
Area	271.2	2.3	12.4	67.4	189.1
USA	432.8	4.7	34.7	111.6	285.6

Key Economic Data (Family income, unemployment)

	$25k-$75k	$75k-$150k	>$150k	Unemployment 03/2009	Unemployment 03/2010
Area	47.6%	31.2%	7.7%	9.7%	10.9%
USA	45.8%	29.5%	8.5%	9.0%	10.1

Key Household Data

	Population Age 0-17	Children w/Married Parents	Children w/Single Mother	Stay-at-home Mothers	Births to Single Women
Area	23.9%	63.0%	24.0%	23.4%	51.8%
USA	24.0%	65.6%	25.5%	27.9%	35.3%

Key Housing Data

	Owner Occupied	Median Year Built	Median Home Value	Home Value Growth, 2005-2010	Median List Price, 4-bedroom Home
Area	69.6%	1983	$218,700	3.2%	$249,900
USA	67.8%	1976	$187,045	3.1%	$288,846

Hanford-Corcoran, CA
149,518

	Score	Rank
Overall	**62.26**	**189**
LDS Culture	26.62	187
Education	61.95	279
Crime	61.46	141
Economic	44.86	353
Health	48.59	63
Household	79.63	66
Housing	76.11	269

Key LDS Culture Data

	Positive	Negative	Ratio Pos:Neg	Commute>59 minutes	Commute<15 minutes
Area	2,420	160	15.1	2.4%	35.4%
USA	4,292	251	20.1	5.5%	34.1%

Key Education Data

	HS Grad	Some Coll.	College Degree	Free/Reduced Lunch	Students per Teacher
Area	69.2%	24.3%	16.9%	54.9%	17.7
USA	85.8%	22.6%	33.2%	41.2%	15.8

Key Property Crime Data (Rate per 100,000 residents)

	Rate	Burglary	Larceny, Theft	Vehicle Theft
Area	2,412.6	579.3	1,503.5	329.8
USA	3,413.6	806.6	2,388.0	262.7

Key Violent Crime Data (Rate per 100,000 residents)

	Rate	Murder	Rape	Robbery	Aggravated Assault
Area	407.4	4.6	17.9	73.0	311.9
USA	432.8	4.7	34.7	111.6	285.6

Key Economic Data (Family income, unemployment)

	$25k-$75k	$75k-$150k	>$150k	Unemployment 03/2009	Unemployment 03/2010
Area	48.5%	29.0%	5.6%	15.5%	18.6%
USA	45.8%	29.5%	8.5%	9.0%	10.1

Key Household Data

	Population Age 0-17	Children w/Married Parents	Children w/Single Mother	Stay-at-home Mothers	Births to Single Women
Area	27.1%	67.6%	17.1%	41.1%	35.6%
USA	24.0%	65.6%	25.5%	27.9%	35.3%

Key Housing Data

	Owner Occupied	Median Year Built	Median Home Value	Home Value Growth, 2005-2010	Median List Price, 4-bedroom Home
Area	55.3%	1984	$226,300	3.4%	
USA	67.8%	1976	$187,045	3.1%	$288,846

Harrisburg-Carlisle, PA
531,108

	Score	Rank
Overall	**69.18**	**61**
LDS Culture	31.04	123
Education	67.41	215
Crime	71.35	71
Economic	67.70	116
Health	47.33	94
Household	79.01	69
Housing	79.78	213

Key LDS Culture Data

	Positive	Negative	Ratio Pos:Neg	Commute>59 minutes	Commute<15 minutes
Area	5,515	274	20.1	4.0%	32.6%
USA	4,292	251	20.1	5.5%	34.1%

Key Education Data

	HS Grad	Some Coll.	College Degree	Free/Reduced Lunch	Students per Teacher
Area	89.0%	16.6%	34.9%	23.7%	13.3
USA	85.8%	22.6%	33.2%	41.2%	15.8

Key Property Crime Data (Rate per 100,000 residents)

	Rate	Burglary	Larceny, Theft	Vehicle Theft
Area	2,222.3	414.8	1,708.4	99.2
USA	3,413.6	806.6	2,388.0	262.7

Key Violent Crime Data (Rate per 100,000 residents)

	Rate	Murder	Rape	Robbery	Aggravated Assault
Area	320.6	3.6	30.7	137.1	149.3
USA	432.8	4.7	34.7	111.6	285.6

Key Economic Data (Family income, unemployment)

	$25k-$75k	$75k-$150k	>$150k	Unemployment 03/2009	Unemployment 03/2010
Area	41.8%	37.9%	9.3%	7.0%	8.4%
USA	45.8%	29.5%	8.5%	9.0%	10.1

Key Household Data

	Population Age 0-17	Children w/Married Parents	Children w/Single Mother	Stay-at-home Mothers	Births to Single Women
Area	21.9%	68.0%	23.3%	24.7%	27.9%
USA	24.0%	65.6%	25.5%	27.9%	35.3%

Key Housing Data

	Owner Occupied	Median Year Built	Median Home Value	Home Value Growth, 2005-2010	Median List Price, 4-bedroom Home
Area	70.3%	1973	$168,700	4.9%	$265,000
USA	67.8%	1976	$187,045	3.1%	$288,846

Harrisonburg, VA
118,409

	Score	Rank
Overall	75.65	15
LDS Culture	58.15	9
Education	66.96	221
Crime	94.18	3
Economic	62.42	194
Health	36.28	280
Household	88.27	19
Housing	78.81	233

Key LDS Culture Data

	Positive	Negative	Ratio Pos:Neg	Commute>59 minutes	Commute<15 minutes
Area	1,451	26	55.8	3.7%	36.6%
USA	4,292	251	20.1	5.5%	34.1%

Key Education Data

	HS Grad	Some Coll.	College Degree	Free/Reduced Lunch	Students per Teacher
Area	79.8%	15.2%	30.2%	38.2%	15.3
USA	85.8%	22.6%	33.2%	41.2%	15.8

Key Property Crime Data (Rate per 100,000 residents)

	Rate	Burglary	Larceny, Theft	Vehicle Theft	
Area	1,544.8	319.4	1,129.8	95.5	
USA	3,413.6	806.6	2,388.0	262.7	

Key Violent Crime Data (Rate per 100,000 residents)

	Rate	Murder	Rape	Robbery	Aggravated Assault
Area	145.4	1.7	17.7	23.7	102.3
USA	432.8	4.7	34.7	111.6	285.6

Key Economic Data (Family income, unemployment)

	$25k-$75k	$75k-$150k	>$150k	Unemployment 03/2009	Unemployment 03/2010
Area	51.7%	27.4%	6.6%	6.1%	7.2%
USA	45.8%	29.5%	8.5%	9.0%	10.1

Key Household Data

	Population Age 0-17	Children w/Married Parents	Children w/Single Mother	Stay-at-home Mothers	Births to Single Women
Area	20.6%	74.8%	15.4%	30.2%	8.4%
USA	24.0%	65.6%	25.5%	27.9%	35.3%

Key Housing Data

	Owner Occupied	Median Year Built	Median Home Value	Home Value Growth, 2005-2010	Median List Price, 4-bedroom Home
Area	64.5%	1979	$202,900	6.7%	
USA	67.8%	1976	$187,045	3.1%	$288,846

Hartford-West Hartford-East Hartford, CT
1,190,512

	Score	Rank
Overall	63.91	161
LDS Culture	24.96	213
Education	80.96	64
Crime	67.29	103
Economic	72.26	63
Health	34.09	302
Household	67.28	165
Housing	62.99	347

Key LDS Culture Data

	Positive	Negative	Ratio Pos:Neg	Commute>59 minutes	Commute<15 minutes
Area	11,275	851	13.2	4.4%	28.1%
USA	4,292	251	20.1	5.5%	34.1%

Key Education Data

	HS Grad	Some Coll.	College Degree	Free/Reduced Lunch	Students per Teacher
Area	88.4%	18.4%	42.3%	28.3%	13.2
USA	85.8%	22.6%	33.2%	41.2%	15.8

Key Property Crime Data (Rate per 100,000 residents)

	Rate	Burglary	Larceny, Theft	Vehicle Theft	
Area	2,866.8	476.7	2,071.4	318.6	
USA	3,413.6	806.6	2,388.0	262.7	

Key Violent Crime Data (Rate per 100,000 residents)

	Rate	Murder	Rape	Robbery	Aggravated Assault
Area	297.5	4.2	20.8	121.8	150.8
USA	432.8	4.7	34.7	111.6	285.6

Key Economic Data (Family income, unemployment)

	$25k-$75k	$75k-$150k	>$150k	Unemployment 03/2009	Unemployment 03/2010
Area	34.1%	38.6%	17.3%	8.0%	9.5%
USA	45.8%	29.5%	8.5%	9.0%	10.1

Key Household Data

	Population Age 0-17	Children w/Married Parents	Children w/Single Mother	Stay-at-home Mothers	Births to Single Women
Area	22.4%	66.7%	26.5%	23.9%	33.9%
USA	24.0%	65.6%	25.5%	27.9%	35.3%

Key Housing Data

	Owner Occupied	Median Year Built	Median Home Value	Home Value Growth, 2005-2010	Median List Price, 4-bedroom Home
Area	68.7%	1965	$266,500	3.1%	$369,900
USA	67.8%	1976	$187,045	3.1%	$288,846

Hattiesburg, MS
138,752

	Score	Rank
Overall	62.10	191
LDS Culture	23.04	244
Education	68.09	206
Crime	68.10	90
Economic	42.52	356
Health	32.82	318
Household	74.07	114
Housing	89.57	59

Key LDS Culture Data

	Positive	Negative	Ratio Pos:Neg	Commute>59 minutes	Commute<15 minutes
Area	1,138	54	21.1	8.0%	32.4%
USA	4,292	251	20.1	5.5%	34.1%

Key Education Data

	HS Grad	Some Coll.	College Degree	Free/Reduced Lunch	Students per Teacher
Area	83.6%	22.1%	35.8%	61.8%	13.9
USA	85.8%	22.6%	33.2%	41.2%	15.8

Key Property Crime Data (Rate per 100,000 residents)

	Rate	Burglary	Larceny, Theft	Vehicle Theft
Area	3,083.0	830.9	2,027.6	224.5
USA	3,413.6	806.6	2,388.0	262.7

Key Violent Crime Data (Rate per 100,000 residents)

	Rate	Murder	Rape	Robbery	Aggravated Assault
Area	266.4	2.9	39.7	118.5	105.2
USA	432.8	4.7	34.7	111.6	285.6

Key Economic Data (Family income, unemployment)

	$25k-$75k	$75k-$150k	>$150k	Unemployment 03/2009	Unemployment 03/2010
Area	45.9%	26.3%	5.9%	6.7%	8.6%
USA	45.8%	29.5%	8.5%	9.0%	10.1

Key Household Data

	Population Age 0-17	Children w/Married Parents	Children w/Single Mother	Stay-at-home Mothers	Births to Single Women
Area	26.7%	66.1%	29.8%	28.3%	32.6%
USA	24.0%	65.6%	25.5%	27.9%	35.3%

Key Housing Data

	Owner Occupied	Median Year Built	Median Home Value	Home Value Growth, 2005-2010	Median List Price, 4-bedroom Home
Area	66.5%	1984	$113,800	4.7%	
USA	67.8%	1976	$187,045	3.1%	$288,846

Hickory-Lenoir-Morganton, NC
363,036

	Score	Rank
Overall	67.46	95
LDS Culture	57.45	10
Education	58.99	306
Crime	64.04	115
Economic	66.20	134
Health	45.10	144
Household	53.09	282
Housing	87.72	89

Key LDS Culture Data

	Positive	Negative	Ratio Pos:Neg	Commute>59 minutes	Commute<15 minutes
Area	2,861	52	55.0	4.7%	31.6%
USA	4,292	251	20.1	5.5%	34.1%

Key Education Data

	HS Grad	Some Coll.	College Degree	Free/Reduced Lunch	Students per Teacher
Area	77.9%	19.7%	25.5%	38.3%	14.6
USA	85.8%	22.6%	33.2%	41.2%	15.8

Key Property Crime Data (Rate per 100,000 residents)

	Rate	Burglary	Larceny, Theft	Vehicle Theft	
Area	3,485.1	987.9	2,271.1	226.0	
USA	3,413.6	806.6	2,388.0	262.7	

Key Violent Crime Data (Rate per 100,000 residents)

	Rate	Murder	Rape	Robbery	Aggravated Assault
Area	278.8	8.0	18.1	73.4	179.3
USA	432.8	4.7	34.7	111.6	285.6

Key Economic Data (Family income, unemployment)

	$25k-$75k	$75k-$150k	>$150k	Unemployment 03/2009	Unemployment 03/2010
Area	51.6%	21.6%	5.7%	14.9%	14.5%
USA	45.8%	29.5%	8.5%	9.0%	10.1

Key Household Data

	Population Age 0-17	Children w/Married Parents	Children w/Single Mother	Stay-at-home Mothers	Births to Single Women
Area	23.0%	65.2%	26.8%	23.2%	50.6%
USA	24.0%	65.6%	25.5%	27.9%	35.3%

Key Housing Data

	Owner Occupied	Median Year Built	Median Home Value	Home Value Growth, 2005-2010	Median List Price, 4-bedroom Home
Area	72.1%	1979	$123,000	3.6%	$285,000
USA	67.8%	1976	$187,045	3.1%	$288,846

Hinesville-Fort Stewart, GA
71,710

	Score	Rank
Overall	58.98	267
LDS Culture	17.48	315
Education	49.69	350
Crime	47.30	239
Economic	58.87	243
Health	40.98	201
Household	69.75	149
Housing	94.14	16

Key LDS Culture Data

	Positive	Negative	Ratio Pos:Neg	Commute>59 minutes	Commute<15 minutes
Area	989	50	19.8	12.0%	36.0%
USA	4,292	251	20.1	5.5%	34.1%

Key Education Data

	HS Grad	Some Coll.	College Degree	Free/Reduced Lunch	Students per Teacher
Area	82.7%	27.6%	21.2%	59.4%	15.9
USA	85.8%	22.6%	33.2%	41.2%	15.8

Key Property Crime Data (Rate per 100,000 residents)

	Rate	Burglary	Larceny, Theft	Vehicle Theft
Area	3,899.5	1,288.6	2,448.5	162.3
USA	3,413.6	806.6	2,388.0	262.7

Key Violent Crime Data (Rate per 100,000 residents)

	Rate	Murder	Rape	Robbery	Aggravated Assault
Area	442.1	7.0	28.0	100.7	306.4
USA	432.8	4.7	34.7	111.6	285.6

Key Economic Data (Family income, unemployment)

	$25k-$75k	$75k-$150k	>$150k	Unemployment 03/2009	Unemployment 03/2010
Area	54.6%	18.3%	4.1%	7.1%	8.5%
USA	45.8%	29.5%	8.5%	9.0%	10.1

Key Household Data

	Population Age 0-17	Children w/Married Parents	Children w/Single Mother	Stay-at-home Mothers	Births to Single Women
Area	33.3%	57.5%	34.7%	46.4%	31.9%
USA	24.0%	65.6%	25.5%	27.9%	35.3%

Key Housing Data

	Owner Occupied	Median Year Built	Median Home Value	Home Value Growth, 2005-2010	Median List Price, 4-bedroom Home
Area	46.9%	1994	$128,900	5.7%	
USA	67.8%	1976	$187,045	3.1%	$288,846

Holland-Grand Haven, MI
260,364

	Score	Rank
Overall	74.70	19
LDS Culture	38.02	55
Education	78.72	85
Crime	88.43	7
Economic	75.88	41
Health	36.88	265
Household	71.60	138
Housing	89.47	61

Key LDS Culture Data

	Positive	Negative	Ratio Pos:Neg	Commute>59 minutes	Commute<15 minutes
Area	4,289	238	18.0	1.7%	35.8%
USA	4,292	251	20.1	5.5%	34.1%

Key Education Data

	HS Grad	Some Coll.	College Degree	Free/Reduced Lunch	Students per Teacher
Area	90.5%	21.8%	36.8%	26.9%	17.7
USA	85.8%	22.6%	33.2%	41.2%	15.8

Key Property Crime Data (Rate per 100,000 residents)

	Rate	Burglary	Larceny, Theft	Vehicle Theft	
Area	1,837.8	363.6	1,417.2	57.0	
USA	3,413.6	806.6	2,388.0	262.7	

Key Violent Crime Data (Rate per 100,000 residents)

	Rate	Murder	Rape	Robbery	Aggravated Assault
Area	176.8	1.5	50.1	22.3	102.9
USA	432.8	4.7	34.7	111.6	285.6

Key Economic Data (Family income, unemployment)

	$25k-$75k	$75k-$150k	>$150k	Unemployment 03/2009	Unemployment 03/2010
Area	49.5%	33.0%	7.7%	12.5%	14.0%
USA	45.8%	29.5%	8.5%	9.0%	10.1

Key Household Data

	Population Age 0-17	Children w/Married Parents	Children w/Single Mother	Stay-at-home Mothers	Births to Single Women
Area	25.7%	80.1%	13.9%	25.1%	35.7%
USA	24.0%	65.6%	25.5%	27.9%	35.3%

Key Housing Data

	Owner Occupied	Median Year Built	Median Home Value	Home Value Growth, 2005-2010	Median List Price, 4-bedroom Home
Area	81.4%	1981	$165,100	-0.1%	$199,900
USA	67.8%	1976	$187,045	3.1%	$288,846

Honolulu, HI
905,034

	Score	Rank
Overall	67.80	89
LDS Culture	38.38	52
Education	67.12	219
Crime	63.45	124
Economic	65.43	147
Health	52.83	20
Household	82.10	54
Housing	65.45	341

Key LDS Culture Data

	Positive	Negative	Ratio Pos:Neg	Commute>59 minutes	Commute<15 minutes
Area	4,218	180	23.4	9.0%	20.5%
USA	4,292	251	20.1	5.5%	34.1%

Key Education Data

	HS Grad	Some Coll.	College Degree	Free/Reduced Lunch	Students per Teacher
Area	90.5%	22.2%	40.3%	37.7%	15.9
USA	85.8%	22.6%	33.2%	41.2%	15.8

Key Property Crime Data (Rate per 100,000 residents)

	Rate	Burglary	Larceny, Theft	Vehicle Theft	
Area	3,506.5	702.8	2,369.2	434.5	
USA	3,413.6	806.6	2,388.0	262.7	

Key Violent Crime Data (Rate per 100,000 residents)

	Rate	Murder	Rape	Robbery	Aggravated Assault
Area	284.1	2.0	22.4	102.4	157.3
USA	432.8	4.7	34.7	111.6	285.6

Key Economic Data (Family income, unemployment)

	$25k-$75k	$75k-$150k	>$150k	Unemployment 03/2009	Unemployment 03/2010
Area	36.0%	39.4%	15.4%	5.5%	5.6%
USA	45.8%	29.5%	8.5%	9.0%	10.1

Key Household Data

	Population Age 0-17	Children w/Married Parents	Children w/Single Mother	Stay-at-home Mothers	Births to Single Women
Area	22.0%	71.8%	19.3%	26.7%	25.5%
USA	24.0%	65.6%	25.5%	27.9%	35.3%

Key Housing Data

	Owner Occupied	Median Year Built	Median Home Value	Home Value Growth, 2005-2010	Median List Price, 4-bedroom Home
Area	58.2%	1974	$574,100	7.0%	$669,000
USA	67.8%	1976	$187,045	3.1%	$288,846

Hot Springs, AR
97,465

	Score	Rank
Overall	52.39	353
LDS Culture	21.74	264
Education	60.53	289
Crime	25.24	348
Economic	48.75	336
Health	40.43	212
Household	48.15	313
Housing	91.13	41

Key LDS Culture Data

	Positive	Negative	Ratio Pos:Neg	Commute>59 minutes	Commute<15 minutes
Area	1,137	58	19.6	8.9%	32.4%
USA	4,292	251	20.1	5.5%	34.1%

Key Education Data

	HS Grad	Some Coll.	College Degree	Free/Reduced Lunch	Students per Teacher
Area	83.9%	26.7%	23.8%	53.6%	13.2
USA	85.8%	22.6%	33.2%	41.2%	15.8

Key Property Crime Data (Rate per 100,000 residents)

	Rate	Burglary	Larceny, Theft	Vehicle Theft
Area	6,599.8	1,940.1	4,278.7	381.0
USA	3,413.6	806.6	2,388.0	262.7

Key Violent Crime Data (Rate per 100,000 residents)

	Rate	Murder	Rape	Robbery	Aggravated Assault
Area	659.4	4.1	45.2	121.2	488.9
USA	432.8	4.7	34.7	111.6	285.6

Key Economic Data (Family income, unemployment)

	$25k-$75k	$75k-$150k	>$150k	Unemployment 03/2009	Unemployment 03/2010
Area	52.6%	20.2%	5.0%	6.9%	8.3%
USA	45.8%	29.5%	8.5%	9.0%	10.1

Key Household Data

	Population Age 0-17	Children w/Married Parents	Children w/Single Mother	Stay-at-home Mothers	Births to Single Women
Area	21.7%	59.8%	31.6%	34.4%	46.6%
USA	24.0%	65.6%	25.5%	27.9%	35.3%

Key Housing Data

	Owner Occupied	Median Year Built	Median Home Value	Home Value Growth, 2005-2010	Median List Price, 4-bedroom Home
Area	71.4%	1984	$127,100	6.3%	
USA	67.8%	1976	$187,045	3.1%	$288,846

Houma-Bayou Cane-Thibodaux, LA
201,148

	Score	Rank
Overall	**55.44**	**327**
LDS Culture	7.71	359
Education	50.87	346
Crime	50.73	211
Economic	54.64	300
Health	42.25	176
Household	64.20	187
Housing	85.06	140

Key LDS Culture Data

	Positive	Negative	Ratio Pos:Neg	Commute>59 minutes	Commute<15 minutes
Area	1,100	126	8.7	11.5%	36.1%
USA	4,292	251	20.1	5.5%	34.1%

Key Education Data

	HS Grad	Some Coll.	College Degree	Free/Reduced Lunch	Students per Teacher
Area	74.2%	16.9%	17.9%	59.4%	13.8
USA	85.8%	22.6%	33.2%	41.2%	15.8

Key Property Crime Data (Rate per 100,000 residents)

	Rate	Burglary	Larceny, Theft	Vehicle Theft
Area	3,174.6	523.3	2,438.7	212.7
USA	3,413.6	806.6	2,388.0	262.7

Key Violent Crime Data (Rate per 100,000 residents)

	Rate	Murder	Rape	Robbery	Aggravated Assault
Area	453.9	5.4	25.6	85.2	337.7
USA	432.8	4.7	34.7	111.6	285.6

Key Economic Data (Family income, unemployment)

	$25k-$75k	$75k-$150k	>$150k	Unemployment 03/2009	Unemployment 03/2010
Area	42.4%	28.3%	8.7%	3.9%	4.6%
USA	45.8%	29.5%	8.5%	9.0%	10.1

Key Household Data

	Population Age 0-17	Children w/Married Parents	Children w/Single Mother	Stay-at-home Mothers	Births to Single Women
Area	25.7%	66.2%	25.1%	36.1%	52.9%
USA	24.0%	65.6%	25.5%	27.9%	35.3%

Key Housing Data

	Owner Occupied	Median Year Built	Median Home Value	Home Value Growth, 2005-2010	Median List Price, 4-bedroom Home
Area	76.2%	1977	$122,000	6.3%	
USA	67.8%	1976	$187,045	3.1%	$288,846

Houston-Sugar Land-Baytown, TX
5,722,952

	Score	Rank
Overall	59.42	259
LDS Culture	13.40	347
Education	63.50	264
Crime	36.99	307
Economic	58.48	250
Health	29.71	345
Household	82.72	51
Housing	96.22	9

Key LDS Culture Data

	Positive	Negative	Ratio Pos:Neg	Commute>59 minutes	Commute<15 minutes
Area	21,803	1438	15.2	10.3%	19.6%
USA	4,292	251	20.1	5.5%	34.1%

Key Education Data

	HS Grad	Some Coll.	College Degree	Free/Reduced Lunch	Students per Teacher
Area	80.1%	22.0%	34.2%	49.5%	15.4
USA	85.8%	22.6%	33.2%	41.2%	15.8

Key Property Crime Data (Rate per 100,000 residents)

	Rate	Burglary	Larceny, Theft	Vehicle Theft	
Area	3,810.5	953.6	2,413.5	443.5	
USA	3,413.6	806.6	2,388.0	262.7	

Key Violent Crime Data (Rate per 100,000 residents)

	Rate	Murder	Rape	Robbery	Aggravated Assault
Area	688.3	7.8	30.8	255.4	394.4
USA	432.8	4.7	34.7	111.6	285.6

Key Economic Data (Family income, unemployment)

	$25k-$75k	$75k-$150k	>$150k	Unemployment 03/2009	Unemployment 03/2010
Area	40.1%	29.4%	14.4%	6.8%	8.5%
USA	45.8%	29.5%	8.5%	9.0%	10.1

Key Household Data

	Population Age 0-17	Children w/Married Parents	Children w/Single Mother	Stay-at-home Mothers	Births to Single Women
Area	28.2%	67.6%	23.9%	39.8%	32.4%
USA	24.0%	65.6%	25.5%	27.9%	35.3%

Key Housing Data

	Owner Occupied	Median Year Built	Median Home Value	Home Value Growth, 2005-2010	Median List Price, 4-bedroom Home
Area	63.4%	1984	$142,400	4.9%	$228,000
USA	67.8%	1976	$187,045	3.1%	$288,846

Huntington-Ashland, WV-KY-OH
284,234

	Score	Rank
Overall	69.73	54
LDS Culture	38.50	51
Education	61.40	284
Crime	81.63	29
Economic	49.03	334
Health	53.20	18
Household	74.69	105
Housing	88.71	68

Key LDS Culture Data

	Positive	Negative	Ratio Pos:Neg	Commute>59 minutes	Commute<15 minutes
Area	1,815	77	23.6	3.3%	35.0%
USA	4,292	251	20.1	5.5%	34.1%

Key Education Data

	HS Grad	Some Coll.	College Degree	Free/Reduced Lunch	Students per Teacher
Area	83.1%	20.1%	25.2%	37.8%	15.1
USA	85.8%	22.6%	33.2%	41.2%	15.8

Key Property Crime Data (Rate per 100,000 residents)

	Rate	Burglary	Larceny, Theft	Vehicle Theft	
Area		829.3	1,891.5	231.8	
USA	3,413.6	806.6	2,388.0	262.7	

Key Violent Crime Data (Rate per 100,000 residents)

	Rate	Murder	Rape	Robbery	Aggravated Assault
Area		2.5	25.5	82.9	110.9
USA	432.8	4.7	34.7	111.6	285.6

Key Economic Data (Family income, unemployment)

	$25k-$75k	$75k-$150k	>$150k	Unemployment 03/2009	Unemployment 03/2010
Area	51.2%	19.7%	4.9%	7.8%	9.0%
USA	45.8%	29.5%	8.5%	9.0%	10.1

Key Household Data

	Population Age 0-17	Children w/Married Parents	Children w/Single Mother	Stay-at-home Mothers	Births to Single Women
Area	21.4%	64.0%	24.9%	31.2%	23.8%
USA	24.0%	65.6%	25.5%	27.9%	35.3%

Key Housing Data

	Owner Occupied	Median Year Built	Median Home Value	Home Value Growth, 2005-2010	Median List Price, 4-bedroom Home
Area	70.1%	1970	$93,000	4.0%	$190,000
USA	67.8%	1976	$187,045	3.1%	$288,846

Huntsville, AL
395,645

	Score	Rank
Overall	64.83	140
LDS Culture	33.09	106
Education	72.97	149
Crime	48.42	230
Economic	66.54	131
Health	33.58	310
Household	63.58	193
Housing	97.51	5

Key LDS Culture Data

	Positive	Negative	Ratio Pos:Neg	Commute>59 minutes	Commute<15 minutes
Area	2,745	100	27.5	2.6%	28.0%
USA	4,292	251	20.1	5.5%	34.1%

Key Education Data

	HS Grad	Some Coll.	College Degree	Free/Reduced Lunch	Students per Teacher
Area	86.8%	21.5%	40.5%	31.5%	14.8
USA	85.8%	22.6%	33.2%	41.2%	15.8

Key Property Crime Data (Rate per 100,000 residents)

	Rate	Burglary	Larceny, Theft	Vehicle Theft
Area	3,993.4	952.3	2,675.2	366.0
USA	3,413.6	806.6	2,388.0	262.7

Key Violent Crime Data (Rate per 100,000 residents)

	Rate	Murder	Rape	Robbery	Aggravated Assault
Area	421.4	4.8	33.3	131.2	252.1
USA	432.8	4.7	34.7	111.6	285.6

Key Economic Data (Family income, unemployment)

	$25k-$75k	$75k-$150k	>$150k	Unemployment 03/2009	Unemployment 03/2010
Area	42.6%	33.8%	11.5%	7.1%	8.4%
USA	45.8%	29.5%	8.5%	9.0%	10.1

Key Household Data

	Population Age 0-17	Children w/Married Parents	Children w/Single Mother	Stay-at-home Mothers	Births to Single Women
Area	24.1%	67.8%	25.7%	30.9%	53.8%
USA	24.0%	65.6%	25.5%	27.9%	35.3%

Key Housing Data

	Owner Occupied	Median Year Built	Median Home Value	Home Value Growth, 2005-2010	Median List Price, 4-bedroom Home
Area	72.7%	1987	$154,200	5.5%	$256,900
USA	67.8%	1976	$187,045	3.1%	$288,846

Idaho Falls, ID
123,995

	Score	Rank
Overall	80.57	6
LDS Culture	54.12	12
Education	79.33	75
Crime	73.83	59
Economic	63.98	167
Health	63.54	6
Household	96.91	3
Housing	84.95	143

Key LDS Culture Data

	Positive	Negative	Ratio Pos:Neg	Commute>59 minutes	Commute<15 minutes
Area	840	32	26.3	10.0%	41.7%
USA	4,292	251	20.1	5.5%	34.1%

Key Education Data

	HS Grad	Some Coll.	College Degree	Free/Reduced Lunch	Students per Teacher
Area	90.1%	27.3%	36.2%	35.1%	19.8
USA	85.8%	22.6%	33.2%	41.2%	15.8

Key Property Crime Data (Rate per 100,000 residents)

	Rate	Burglary	Larceny, Theft	Vehicle Theft
Area	2,326.7	479.2	1,724.1	123.5
USA	3,413.6	806.6	2,388.0	262.7

Key Violent Crime Data (Rate per 100,000 residents)

	Rate	Murder	Rape	Robbery	Aggravated Assault
Area	283.2	1.6	42.0	12.3	227.2
USA	432.8	4.7	34.7	111.6	285.6

Key Economic Data (Family income, unemployment)

	$25k-$75k	$75k-$150k	>$150k	Unemployment 03/2009	Unemployment 03/2010
Area	52.4%	28.0%	5.6%	6.1%	7.6%
USA	45.8%	29.5%	8.5%	9.0%	10.1

Key Household Data

	Population Age 0-17	Children w/Married Parents	Children w/Single Mother	Stay-at-home Mothers	Births to Single Women
Area	30.8%	78.0%	15.6%	34.7%	6.2%
USA	24.0%	65.6%	25.5%	27.9%	35.3%

Key Housing Data

	Owner Occupied	Median Year Built	Median Home Value	Home Value Growth, 2005-2010	Median List Price, 4-bedroom Home
Area	73.3%	1979	$164,900	5.5%	
USA	67.8%	1976	$187,045	3.1%	$288,846

Indianapolis-Carmel, IN
1,715,128

	Score	Rank
Overall	60.22	239
LDS Culture	19.98	283
Education	71.94	162
Crime	38.13	300
Economic	71.21	72
Health	31.17	341
Household	67.28	166
Housing	86.42	112

Key LDS Culture Data

	Positive	Negative	Ratio Pos:Neg	Commute>59 minutes	Commute<15 minutes
Area	8,190	465	17.6	4.8%	24.9%
USA	4,292	251	20.1	5.5%	34.1%

Key Education Data

	HS Grad	Some Coll.	College Degree	Free/Reduced Lunch	Students per Teacher
Area	88.7%	20.5%	38.9%	37.9%	17.6
USA	85.8%	22.6%	33.2%	41.2%	15.8

Key Property Crime Data (Rate per 100,000 residents)

	Rate	Burglary	Larceny, Theft	Vehicle Theft	
Area	4,033.2	1,015.4	2,574.5	443.4	
USA	3,413.6	806.6	2,388.0	262.7	

Key Violent Crime Data (Rate per 100,000 residents)

	Rate	Murder	Rape	Robbery	Aggravated Assault
Area	638.3	7.4	34.9	250.0	346.0
USA	432.8	4.7	34.7	111.6	285.6

Key Economic Data (Family income, unemployment)

	$25k-$75k	$75k-$150k	>$150k	Unemployment 03/2009	Unemployment 03/2010
Area	41.2%	34.0%	11.1%	8.9%	9.5%
USA	45.8%	29.5%	8.5%	9.0%	10.1

Key Household Data

	Population Age 0-17	Children w/Married Parents	Children w/Single Mother	Stay-at-home Mothers	Births to Single Women
Area	26.6%	65.9%	26.0%	26.5%	35.8%
USA	24.0%	65.6%	25.5%	27.9%	35.3%

Key Housing Data

	Owner Occupied	Median Year Built	Median Home Value	Home Value Growth, 2005-2010	Median List Price, 4-bedroom Home
Area	69.4%	1980	$147,200	1.2%	$204,300
USA	67.8%	1976	$187,045	3.1%	$288,846

Iowa City, IA
149,437

	Score	Rank
Overall	76.91	12
LDS Culture	38.68	50
Education	99.57	2
Crime	75.55	48
Economic	66.93	124
Health	54.48	14
Household	79.63	67
Housing	78.34	242

Key LDS Culture Data

	Positive	Negative	Ratio Pos:Neg	Commute>59 minutes	Commute<15 minutes
Area	1,956	142	13.8	2.8%	40.6%
USA	4,292	251	20.1	5.5%	34.1%

Key Education Data

	HS Grad	Some Coll.	College Degree	Free/Reduced Lunch	Students per Teacher
Area	95.5%	19.6%	56.1%	24.8%	14.9
USA	85.8%	22.6%	33.2%	41.2%	15.8

Key Property Crime Data (Rate per 100,000 residents)

	Rate	Burglary	Larceny, Theft	Vehicle Theft
Area	2,095.6	494.3	1,507.6	93.8
USA	3,413.6	806.6	2,388.0	262.7

Key Violent Crime Data (Rate per 100,000 residents)

	Rate	Murder	Rape	Robbery	Aggravated Assault
Area	288.7	5.4	35.5	50.9	196.9
USA	432.8	4.7	34.7	111.6	285.6

Key Economic Data (Family income, unemployment)

	$25k-$75k	$75k-$150k	>$150k	Unemployment 03/2009	Unemployment 03/2010
Area	39.2%	37.0%	12.8%	3.8%	5.1%
USA	45.8%	29.5%	8.5%	9.0%	10.1

Key Household Data

	Population Age 0-17	Children w/Married Parents	Children w/Single Mother	Stay-at-home Mothers	Births to Single Women
Area	21.6%	72.7%	20.8%	20.4%	13.1%
USA	24.0%	65.6%	25.5%	27.9%	35.3%

Key Housing Data

	Owner Occupied	Median Year Built	Median Home Value	Home Value Growth, 2005-2010	Median List Price, 4-bedroom Home
Area	64.3%	1980	$171,100	2.5%	
USA	67.8%	1976	$187,045	3.1%	$288,846

Ithaca, NY
101,136

	Score	Rank
Overall	77.01	11
LDS Culture	38.76	49
Education	85.12	40
Crime	87.94	9
Economic	70.82	77
Health	49.20	50
Household	87.65	23
Housing	74.32	292

Key LDS Culture Data

	Positive	Negative	Ratio Pos:Neg	Commute>59 minutes	Commute<15 minutes
Area	1,289	93	13.9	2.6%	40.1%
USA	4,292	251	20.1	5.5%	34.1%

Key Education Data

	HS Grad	Some Coll.	College Degree	Free/Reduced Lunch	Students per Teacher
Area	95.2%	15.3%	57.6%	31.9%	11.0
USA	85.8%	22.6%	33.2%	41.2%	15.8

Key Property Crime Data (Rate per 100,000 residents)

	Rate	Burglary	Larceny, Theft	Vehicle Theft	
Area	2,292.5	417.4	1,821.0	54.1	
USA	3,413.6	806.6	2,388.0	262.7	

Key Violent Crime Data (Rate per 100,000 residents)

	Rate	Murder	Rape	Robbery	Aggravated Assault
Area	134.9	2.0	13.8	34.5	84.7
USA	432.8	4.7	34.7	111.6	285.6

Key Economic Data (Family income, unemployment)

	$25k-$75k	$75k-$150k	>$150k	Unemployment 03/2009	Unemployment 03/2010
Area	39.7%	35.1%	10.5%	5.6%	5.5%
USA	45.8%	29.5%	8.5%	9.0%	10.1

Key Household Data

	Population Age 0-17	Children w/Married Parents	Children w/Single Mother	Stay-at-home Mothers	Births to Single Women
Area	15.4%	70.4%	21.2%	24.1%	14.4%
USA	24.0%	65.6%	25.5%	27.9%	35.3%

Key Housing Data

	Owner Occupied	Median Year Built	Median Home Value	Home Value Growth, 2005-2010	Median List Price, 4-bedroom Home
Area	55.2%	1972	$168,100	5.7%	
USA	67.8%	1976	$187,045	3.1%	$288,846

Jackson, MI
160,180

	Score	Rank
Overall	61.94	197
LDS Culture	25.12	211
Education	66.21	232
Crime	60.12	147
Economic	60.98	212
Health	36.88	266
Household	73.46	119
Housing	74.45	290

Key LDS Culture Data

	Positive	Negative	Ratio Pos:Neg	Commute>59 minutes	Commute<15 minutes
Area	1,953	106	18.4	6.2%	30.7%
USA	4,292	251	20.1	5.5%	34.1%

Key Education Data

	HS Grad	Some Coll.	College Degree	Free/Reduced Lunch	Students per Teacher
Area	89.0%	25.4%	25.9%	38.1%	16.8
USA	85.8%	22.6%	33.2%	41.2%	15.8

Key Property Crime Data (Rate per 100,000 residents)

	Rate	Burglary	Larceny, Theft	Vehicle Theft	
Area	2,757.4	622.8	1,982.9	151.7	
USA	3,413.6	806.6	2,388.0	262.7	

Key Violent Crime Data (Rate per 100,000 residents)

	Rate	Murder	Rape	Robbery	Aggravated Assault
Area	386.0	2.5	73.4	53.0	257.1
USA	432.8	4.7	34.7	111.6	285.6

Key Economic Data (Family income, unemployment)

	$25k-$75k	$75k-$150k	>$150k	Unemployment 03/2009	Unemployment 03/2010
Area	51.9%	29.0%	5.0%	12.7%	15.2%
USA	45.8%	29.5%	8.5%	9.0%	10.1

Key Household Data

	Population Age 0-17	Children w/Married Parents	Children w/Single Mother	Stay-at-home Mothers	Births to Single Women
Area	23.6%	71.8%	21.6%	25.9%	35.9%
USA	24.0%	65.6%	25.5%	27.9%	35.3%

Key Housing Data

	Owner Occupied	Median Year Built	Median Home Value	Home Value Growth, 2005-2010	Median List Price, 4-bedroom Home
Area	76.9%	1968	$135,000	-2.6%	
USA	67.8%	1976	$187,045	3.1%	$288,846

Jackson, MS
534,767

	Score	Rank
Overall	56.29	316
LDS Culture	23.14	240
Education	63.09	267
Crime	50.57	214
Economic	50.25	328
Health	35.26	286
Household	46.30	325
Housing	92.37	29

Key LDS Culture Data

	Positive	Negative	Ratio Pos:Neg	Commute>59 minutes	Commute<15 minutes
Area	2,839	134	21.2	3.9%	24.1%
USA	4,292	251	20.1	5.5%	34.1%

Key Education Data

	HS Grad	Some Coll.	College Degree	Free/Reduced Lunch	Students per Teacher
Area	85.9%	22.7%	37.8%	62.9%	15.6
USA	85.8%	22.6%	33.2%	41.2%	15.8

Key Property Crime Data (Rate per 100,000 residents)

	Rate	Burglary	Larceny, Theft	Vehicle Theft
Area	3,797.0	1,159.5	2,225.5	412.0
USA	3,413.6	806.6	2,388.0	262.7

Key Violent Crime Data (Rate per 100,000 residents)

	Rate	Murder	Rape	Robbery	Aggravated Assault
Area	408.1	14.1	40.3	197.8	155.9
USA	432.8	4.7	34.7	111.6	285.6

Key Economic Data (Family income, unemployment)

	$25k-$75k	$75k-$150k	>$150k	Unemployment 03/2009	Unemployment 03/2010
Area	42.6%	27.5%	8.6%	7.0%	8.7%
USA	45.8%	29.5%	8.5%	9.0%	10.1

Key Household Data

	Population Age 0-17	Children w/Married Parents	Children w/Single Mother	Stay-at-home Mothers	Births to Single Women
Area	26.2%	55.8%	37.8%	21.9%	48.2%
USA	24.0%	65.6%	25.5%	27.9%	35.3%

Key Housing Data

	Owner Occupied	Median Year Built	Median Home Value	Home Value Growth, 2005-2010	Median List Price, 4-bedroom Home
Area	66.9%	1981	$132,900	3.3%	$249,900
USA	67.8%	1976	$187,045	3.1%	$288,846

Jackson, TN
110,285

	Score	Rank
Overall	56.33	314
LDS Culture	33.62	96
Education	59.59	301
Crime	24.75	350
Economic	62.76	190
Health	38.85	239
Household	56.17	265
Housing	85.50	134

Key LDS Culture Data

	Positive	Negative	Ratio Pos:Neg	Commute>59 minutes	Commute<15 minutes
Area	1,383	60	23.1	3.7%	34.7%
USA	4,292	251	20.1	5.5%	34.1%

Key Education Data

	HS Grad	Some Coll.	College Degree	Free/Reduced Lunch	Students per Teacher
Area	86.2%	24.5%	29.4%	62.9%	15.7
USA	85.8%	22.6%	33.2%	41.2%	15.8

Key Property Crime Data (Rate per 100,000 residents)

	Rate	Burglary	Larceny, Theft	Vehicle Theft	
Area	5,244.0	1,312.1	3,462.1	469.7	
USA	3,413.6	806.6	2,388.0	262.7	

Key Violent Crime Data (Rate per 100,000 residents)

	Rate	Murder	Rape	Robbery	Aggravated Assault
Area	815.9	8.8	37.1	228.7	541.3
USA	432.8	4.7	34.7	111.6	285.6

Key Economic Data (Family income, unemployment)

	$25k-$75k	$75k-$150k	>$150k	Unemployment 03/2009	Unemployment 03/2010
Area	51.0%	26.2%	6.6%	10.5%	11.2%
USA	45.8%	29.5%	8.5%	9.0%	10.1

Key Household Data

	Population Age 0-17	Children w/Married Parents	Children w/Single Mother	Stay-at-home Mothers	Births to Single Women
Area	24.6%	65.2%	26.2%	20.1%	54.3%
USA	24.0%	65.6%	25.5%	27.9%	35.3%

Key Housing Data

	Owner Occupied	Median Year Built	Median Home Value	Home Value Growth, 2005-2010	Median List Price, 4-bedroom Home
Area	67.7%	1984	$116,600	2.0%	
USA	67.8%	1976	$187,045	3.1%	$288,846

Jacksonville, FL
1,315,218

	Score	Rank
Overall	58.43	282
LDS Culture	19.07	298
Education	60.04	295
Crime	26.69	346
Economic	58.25	254
Health	52.43	30
Household	66.67	169
Housing	91.56	35

Key LDS Culture Data

	Positive	Negative	Ratio Pos:Neg	Commute>59 minutes	Commute<15 minutes
Area	5,071	235	21.6	5.3%	23.1%
USA	4,292	251	20.1	5.5%	34.1%

Key Education Data

	HS Grad	Some Coll.	College Degree	Free/Reduced Lunch	Students per Teacher
Area	87.6%	24.8%	33.0%	33.9%	16.0
USA	85.8%	22.6%	33.2%	41.2%	15.8

Key Property Crime Data (Rate per 100,000 residents)

	Rate	Burglary	Larceny, Theft	Vehicle Theft	
Area	4,781.3	1,192.4	3,213.4	375.5	
USA	3,413.6	806.6	2,388.0	262.7	

Key Violent Crime Data (Rate per 100,000 residents)

	Rate	Murder	Rape	Robbery	Aggravated Assault
Area	820.9	9.7	28.9	251.0	531.3
USA	432.8	4.7	34.7	111.6	285.6

Key Economic Data (Family income, unemployment)

	$25k-$75k	$75k-$150k	>$150k	Unemployment 03/2009	Unemployment 03/2010
Area	44.3%	32.6%	10.3%	9.0%	11.9%
USA	45.8%	29.5%	8.5%	9.0%	10.1

Key Household Data

	Population Age 0-17	Children w/Married Parents	Children w/Single Mother	Stay-at-home Mothers	Births to Single Women
Area	24.7%	65.1%	27.6%	26.7%	28.9%
USA	24.0%	65.6%	25.5%	27.9%	35.3%

Key Housing Data

	Owner Occupied	Median Year Built	Median Home Value	Home Value Growth, 2005-2010	Median List Price, 4-bedroom Home
Area	68.1%	1988	$204,900	4.1%	$240,000
USA	67.8%	1976	$187,045	3.1%	$288,846

Jacksonville, NC
165,938

	Score	Rank
Overall	65.86	129
LDS Culture	18.97	301
Education	62.18	274
Crime	55.62	168
Economic	66.04	137
Health	37.16	259
Household	91.36	11
Housing	90.98	44

Key LDS Culture Data

	Positive	Negative	Ratio Pos:Neg	Commute>59 minutes	Commute<15 minutes
Area	1,120	68	16.5	5.4%	36.6%
USA	4,292	251	20.1	5.5%	34.1%

Key Education Data

	HS Grad	Some Coll.	College Degree	Free/Reduced Lunch	Students per Teacher
Area	88.3%	32.4%	27.7%	39.3%	15.7
USA	85.8%	22.6%	33.2%	41.2%	15.8

Key Property Crime Data (Rate per 100,000 residents)

	Rate	Burglary	Larceny, Theft	Vehicle Theft
Area	3,590.4	1,022.0	2,359.6	208.8
USA	3,413.6	806.6	2,388.0	262.7

Key Violent Crime Data (Rate per 100,000 residents)

	Rate	Murder	Rape	Robbery	Aggravated Assault
Area	364.1	6.7	36.4	86.8	234.3
USA	432.8	4.7	34.7	111.6	285.6

Key Economic Data (Family income, unemployment)

	$25k-$75k	$75k-$150k	>$150k	Unemployment 03/2009	Unemployment 03/2010
Area	50.9%	27.5%	4.8%	8.2%	8.0%
USA	45.8%	29.5%	8.5%	9.0%	10.1

Key Household Data

	Population Age 0-17	Children w/Married Parents	Children w/Single Mother	Stay-at-home Mothers	Births to Single Women
Area	27.7%	69.2%	24.9%	35.6%	18.4%
USA	24.0%	65.6%	25.5%	27.9%	35.3%

Key Housing Data

	Owner Occupied	Median Year Built	Median Home Value	Home Value Growth, 2005-2010	Median List Price, 4-bedroom Home
Area	62.3%	1988	$141,100	6.6%	
USA	67.8%	1976	$187,045	3.1%	$288,846

Janesville, WI
160,213

	Score	Rank
Overall	64.40	152
LDS Culture	26.15	193
Education	74.85	126
Crime	67.35	100
Economic	77.77	22
Health	39.16	228
Household	54.94	275
Housing	72.75	311

Key LDS Culture Data
	Positive	Negative	Ratio Pos:Neg	Commute>59 minutes	Commute<15 minutes
Area	2,734	285	9.6	4.5%	38.6%
USA	4,292	251	20.1	5.5%	34.1%

Key Education Data
	HS Grad	Some Coll.	College Degree	Free/Reduced Lunch	Students per Teacher
Area	87.9%	21.7%	29.1%	34.8%	14.7
USA	85.8%	22.6%	33.2%	41.2%	15.8

Key Property Crime Data (Rate per 100,000 residents)
	Rate	Burglary	Larceny, Theft	Vehicle Theft	
Area	3,401.3	615.8	2,615.3	170.2	
USA	3,413.6	806.6	2,388.0	262.7	

Key Violent Crime Data (Rate per 100,000 residents)
	Rate	Murder	Rape	Robbery	Aggravated Assault
Area	247.4	2.5	34.9	71.1	139.0
USA	432.8	4.7	34.7	111.6	285.6

Key Economic Data (Family income, unemployment)
	$25k-$75k	$75k-$150k	>$150k	Unemployment 03/2009	Unemployment 03/2010
Area	47.0%	34.4%	4.4%	13.7%	12.8%
USA	45.8%	29.5%	8.5%	9.0%	10.1

Key Household Data
	Population Age 0-17	Children w/Married Parents	Children w/Single Mother	Stay-at-home Mothers	Births to Single Women
Area	24.6%	64.0%	25.8%	15.9%	28.3%
USA	24.0%	65.6%	25.5%	27.9%	35.3%

Key Housing Data
	Owner Occupied	Median Year Built	Median Home Value	Home Value Growth, 2005-2010	Median List Price, 4-bedroom Home
Area	73.6%	1967	$145,900	1.6%	
USA	67.8%	1976	$187,045	3.1%	$288,846

Jefferson City, MO
145,387

	Score	Rank
Overall	72.27	29
LDS Culture	42.08	34
Education	84.14	42
Crime	67.02	104
Economic	76.15	36
Health	33.49	312
Household	81.48	60
Housing	79.08	225

Key LDS Culture Data

	Positive	Negative	Ratio Pos:Neg	Commute>59 minutes	Commute<15 minutes
Area	1,493	66	22.6	3.4%	42.0%
USA	4,292	251	20.1	5.5%	34.1%

Key Education Data

	HS Grad	Some Coll.	College Degree	Free/Reduced Lunch	Students per Teacher
Area	88.4%	21.5%	34.6%	39.1%	11.9
USA	85.8%	22.6%	33.2%	41.2%	15.8

Key Property Crime Data (Rate per 100,000 residents)

	Rate	Burglary	Larceny, Theft	Vehicle Theft	
Area	2,643.5	502.2	2,006.7	134.6	
USA	3,413.6	806.6	2,388.0	262.7	

Key Violent Crime Data (Rate per 100,000 residents)

	Rate	Murder	Rape	Robbery	Aggravated Assault
Area	323.6	2.1	28.2	30.2	263.1
USA	432.8	4.7	34.7	111.6	285.6

Key Economic Data (Family income, unemployment)

	$25k-$75k	$75k-$150k	>$150k	Unemployment 03/2009	Unemployment 03/2010
Area	50.8%	35.1%	5.5%	7.8%	7.9%
USA	45.8%	29.5%	8.5%	9.0%	10.1

Key Household Data

	Population Age 0-17	Children w/Married Parents	Children w/Single Mother	Stay-at-home Mothers	Births to Single Women
Area	23.3%	71.7%	19.0%	13.8%	25.3%
USA	24.0%	65.6%	25.5%	27.9%	35.3%

Key Housing Data

	Owner Occupied	Median Year Built	Median Home Value	Home Value Growth, 2005-2010	Median List Price, 4-bedroom Home
Area	74.3%	1978	$136,700	2.5%	
USA	67.8%	1976	$187,045	3.1%	$288,846

Johnson City, TN
195,849

	Score	Rank
Overall	67.43	96
LDS Culture	42.04	35
Education	69.22	193
Crime	60.98	144
Economic	60.81	215
Health	38.85	240
Household	75.93	92
Housing	84.57	148

Key LDS Culture Data

	Positive	Negative	Ratio Pos:Neg	Commute>59 minutes	Commute<15 minutes
Area	2,630	70	37.6	4.7%	37.5%
USA	4,292	251	20.1	5.5%	34.1%

Key Education Data

	HS Grad	Some Coll.	College Degree	Free/Reduced Lunch	Students per Teacher
Area	82.0%	21.6%	28.2%	47.8%	15.1
USA	85.8%	22.6%	33.2%	41.2%	15.8

Key Property Crime Data (Rate per 100,000 residents)

	Rate	Burglary	Larceny, Theft	Vehicle Theft	
Area	2,863.7	660.1	2,061.5	142.1	
USA	3,413.6	806.6	2,388.0	262.7	

Key Violent Crime Data (Rate per 100,000 residents)

	Rate	Murder	Rape	Robbery	Aggravated Assault
Area	365.7	1.5	22.6	38.0	303.7
USA	432.8	4.7	34.7	111.6	285.6

Key Economic Data (Family income, unemployment)

	$25k-$75k	$75k-$150k	>$150k	Unemployment 03/2009	Unemployment 03/2010
Area	54.5%	19.4%	6.0%	9.6%	10.0%
USA	45.8%	29.5%	8.5%	9.0%	10.1

Key Household Data

	Population Age 0-17	Children w/Married Parents	Children w/Single Mother	Stay-at-home Mothers	Births to Single Women
Area	20.5%	71.1%	19.5%	33.2%	32.0%
USA	24.0%	65.6%	25.5%	27.9%	35.3%

Key Housing Data

	Owner Occupied	Median Year Built	Median Home Value	Home Value Growth, 2005-2010	Median List Price, 4-bedroom Home
Area	71.2%	1979	$123,900	4.6%	
USA	67.8%	1976	$187,045	3.1%	$288,846

Johnstown, PA
144,319

	Score	Rank
Overall	63.66	168
LDS Culture	24.39	230
Education	75.55	121
Crime	85.34	16
Economic	58.42	251
Health	47.33	95
Household	41.98	351
Housing	75.23	280

Key LDS Culture Data

	Positive	Negative	Ratio Pos:Neg	Commute>59 minutes	Commute<15 minutes
Area	2,584	205	12.6	3.5%	35.5%
USA	4,292	251	20.1	5.5%	34.1%

Key Education Data

	HS Grad	Some Coll.	College Degree	Free/Reduced Lunch	Students per Teacher
Area	88.3%	14.8%	23.9%	41.1%	14.0
USA	85.8%	22.6%	33.2%	41.2%	15.8

Key Property Crime Data (Rate per 100,000 residents)

	Rate	Burglary	Larceny, Theft	Vehicle Theft
Area	1,955.6	388.1	1,491.8	75.7
USA	3,413.6	806.6	2,388.0	262.7

Key Violent Crime Data (Rate per 100,000 residents)

	Rate	Murder	Rape	Robbery	Aggravated Assault
Area	197.8	4.2	14.6	40.3	138.8
USA	432.8	4.7	34.7	111.6	285.6

Key Economic Data (Family income, unemployment)

	$25k-$75k	$75k-$150k	>$150k	Unemployment 03/2009	Unemployment 03/2010
Area	52.6%	24.3%	2.6%	8.5%	10.3%
USA	45.8%	29.5%	8.5%	9.0%	10.1

Key Household Data

	Population Age 0-17	Children w/Married Parents	Children w/Single Mother	Stay-at-home Mothers	Births to Single Women
Area	19.5%	62.0%	29.8%	22.0%	60.7%
USA	24.0%	65.6%	25.5%	27.9%	35.3%

Key Housing Data

	Owner Occupied	Median Year Built	Median Home Value	Home Value Growth, 2005-2010	Median List Price, 4-bedroom Home
Area	73.0%	1950	$84,600	3.5%	
USA	67.8%	1976	$187,045	3.1%	$288,846

Jonesboro, AR
120,336

	Score	Rank
Overall	63.03	181
LDS Culture	29.32	152
Education	70.02	185
Crime	51.32	205
Economic	51.36	318
Health	40.43	213
Household	74.07	115
Housing	87.65	90

Key LDS Culture Data

	Positive	Negative	Ratio Pos:Neg	Commute>59 minutes	Commute<15 minutes
Area	927	40	23.2	6.1%	40.4%
USA	4,292	251	20.1	5.5%	34.1%

Key Education Data

	HS Grad	Some Coll.	College Degree	Free/Reduced Lunch	Students per Teacher
Area	83.1%	20.9%	24.7%	55.0%	11.6
USA	85.8%	22.6%	33.2%	41.2%	15.8

Key Property Crime Data (Rate per 100,000 residents)

	Rate	Burglary	Larceny, Theft	Vehicle Theft
Area	4,012.5	1,566.0	2,307.7	138.8
USA	3,413.6	806.6	2,388.0	262.7

Key Violent Crime Data (Rate per 100,000 residents)

	Rate	Murder	Rape	Robbery	Aggravated Assault
Area	389.2	6.0	47.7	82.6	252.9
USA	432.8	4.7	34.7	111.6	285.6

Key Economic Data (Family income, unemployment)

	$25k-$75k	$75k-$150k	>$150k	Unemployment 03/2009	Unemployment 03/2010
Area	44.3%	26.3%	5.5%	6.8%	7.6%
USA	45.8%	29.5%	8.5%	9.0%	10.1

Key Household Data

	Population Age 0-17	Children w/Married Parents	Children w/Single Mother	Stay-at-home Mothers	Births to Single Women
Area	25.0%	64.6%	28.8%	30.1%	35.2%
USA	24.0%	65.6%	25.5%	27.9%	35.3%

Key Housing Data

	Owner Occupied	Median Year Built	Median Home Value	Home Value Growth, 2005-2010	Median List Price, 4-bedroom Home
Area	65.1%	1984	$96,500	1.9%	
USA	67.8%	1976	$187,045	3.1%	$288,846

Joplin, MO
172,933

	Score	Rank
Overall	58.09	286
LDS Culture	39.45	46
Education	66.05	233
Crime	49.32	225
Economic	47.92	342
Health	33.49	313
Household	51.85	290
Housing	84.41	150

Key LDS Culture Data

	Positive	Negative	Ratio Pos:Neg	Commute>59 minutes	Commute<15 minutes
Area	1,454	74	19.6	2.5%	39.8%
USA	4,292	251	20.1	5.5%	34.1%

Key Education Data

	HS Grad	Some Coll.	College Degree	Free/Reduced Lunch	Students per Teacher
Area	81.4%	22.9%	24.7%	48.1%	14.5
USA	85.8%	22.6%	33.2%	41.2%	15.8

Key Property Crime Data (Rate per 100,000 residents)

	Rate	Burglary	Larceny, Theft	Vehicle Theft
Area	4,423.6	838.6	3,287.4	297.5
USA	3,413.6	806.6	2,388.0	262.7

Key Violent Crime Data (Rate per 100,000 residents)

	Rate	Murder	Rape	Robbery	Aggravated Assault
Area	390.1	4.1	43.4	41.1	301.5
USA	432.8	4.7	34.7	111.6	285.6

Key Economic Data (Family income, unemployment)

	$25k-$75k	$75k-$150k	>$150k	Unemployment 03/2009	Unemployment 03/2010
Area	50.2%	19.8%	3.9%	8.0%	9.1%
USA	45.8%	29.5%	8.5%	9.0%	10.1

Key Household Data

	Population Age 0-17	Children w/Married Parents	Children w/Single Mother	Stay-at-home Mothers	Births to Single Women
Area	25.8%	60.5%	31.5%	26.9%	39.1%
USA	24.0%	65.6%	25.5%	27.9%	35.3%

Key Housing Data

	Owner Occupied	Median Year Built	Median Home Value	Home Value Growth, 2005-2010	Median List Price, 4-bedroom Home
Area	67.4%	1977	$96,200	3.2%	
USA	67.8%	1976	$187,045	3.1%	$288,846

Kalamazoo-Portage, MI
323,713

	Score	Rank
Overall	63.69	167
LDS Culture	30.29	142
Education	77.57	100
Crime	48.14	233
Economic	60.70	219
Health	36.88	267
Household	70.37	145
Housing	84.44	149

Key LDS Culture Data

	Positive	Negative	Ratio Pos:Neg	Commute>59 minutes	Commute<15 minutes
Area	2,699	140	19.3	3.9%	33.8%
USA	4,292	251	20.1	5.5%	34.1%

Key Education Data

	HS Grad	Some Coll.	College Degree	Free/Reduced Lunch	Students per Teacher
Area	90.7%	26.1%	37.2%	39.9%	16.4
USA	85.8%	22.6%	33.2%	41.2%	15.8

Key Property Crime Data (Rate per 100,000 residents)

	Rate	Burglary	Larceny, Theft	Vehicle Theft	
Area	3,711.4	918.7	2,586.8	205.9	
USA	3,413.6	806.6	2,388.0	262.7	

Key Violent Crime Data (Rate per 100,000 residents)

	Rate	Murder	Rape	Robbery	Aggravated Assault
Area	442.9	1.9	58.8	105.1	277.1
USA	432.8	4.7	34.7	111.6	285.6

Key Economic Data (Family income, unemployment)

	$25k-$75k	$75k-$150k	>$150k	Unemployment 03/2009	Unemployment 03/2010
Area	48.2%	28.7%	7.4%	10.2%	12.7%
USA	45.8%	29.5%	8.5%	9.0%	10.1

Key Household Data

	Population Age 0-17	Children w/Married Parents	Children w/Single Mother	Stay-at-home Mothers	Births to Single Women
Area	23.4%	65.4%	25.3%	25.2%	24.1%
USA	24.0%	65.6%	25.5%	27.9%	35.3%

Key Housing Data

	Owner Occupied	Median Year Built	Median Home Value	Home Value Growth, 2005-2010	Median List Price, 4-bedroom Home
Area	69.8%	1971	$146,500	0.0%	$193,900
USA	67.8%	1976	$187,045	3.1%	$288,846

Kankakee-Bradley, IL
112,524

	Score	Rank
Overall	56.11	318
LDS Culture	22.01	258
Education	64.44	251
Crime	52.77	192
Economic	53.03	310
Health	47.30	106
Household	40.74	357
Housing	79.51	217

Key LDS Culture Data

	Positive	Negative	Ratio Pos:Neg	Commute>59 minutes	Commute<15 minutes
Area	1,011	102	9.9	10.4%	40.3%
USA	4,292	251	20.1	5.5%	34.1%

Key Education Data

	HS Grad	Some Coll.	College Degree	Free/Reduced Lunch	Students per Teacher
Area	85.3%	24.8%	25.8%	43.3%	19.4
USA	85.8%	22.6%	33.2%	41.2%	15.8

Key Property Crime Data (Rate per 100,000 residents)

	Rate	Burglary	Larceny, Theft	Vehicle Theft	
Area	3,037.7				
USA	3,413.6	806.6	2,388.0	262.7	

Key Violent Crime Data (Rate per 100,000 residents)

	Rate	Murder	Rape	Robbery	Aggravated Assault
Area	392.8				
USA	432.8	4.7	34.7	111.6	285.6

Key Economic Data (Family income, unemployment)

	$25k-$75k	$75k-$150k	>$150k	Unemployment 03/2009	Unemployment 03/2010
Area	46.7%	32.0%	5.6%	12.0%	15.2%
USA	45.8%	29.5%	8.5%	9.0%	10.1

Key Household Data

	Population Age 0-17	Children w/Married Parents	Children w/Single Mother	Stay-at-home Mothers	Births to Single Women
Area	25.1%	55.2%	38.7%	18.9%	49.8%
USA	24.0%	65.6%	25.5%	27.9%	35.3%

Key Housing Data

	Owner Occupied	Median Year Built	Median Home Value	Home Value Growth, 2005-2010	Median List Price, 4-bedroom Home
Area	68.9%	1970	$148,900	3.6%	
USA	67.8%	1976	$187,045	3.1%	$288,846

Kansas City, MO-KS
2,001,074

	Score	Rank
Overall	65.57	131
LDS Culture	36.60	69
Education	82.08	59
Crime	42.10	272
Economic	69.04	96
Health	33.25	317
Household	73.46	120
Housing	83.93	160

Key LDS Culture Data

	Positive	Negative	Ratio Pos:Neg	Commute>59 minutes	Commute<15 minutes
Area	8,898	542	16.4	3.6%	27.3%
USA	4,292	251	20.1	5.5%	34.1%

Key Education Data

	HS Grad	Some Coll.	College Degree	Free/Reduced Lunch	Students per Teacher
Area	90.1%	23.2%	39.2%	33.3%	14.4
USA	85.8%	22.6%	33.2%	41.2%	15.8

Key Property Crime Data (Rate per 100,000 residents)

	Rate	Burglary	Larceny, Theft	Vehicle Theft
Area		866.2	2,785.4	612.2
USA	3,413.6	806.6	2,388.0	262.7

Key Violent Crime Data (Rate per 100,000 residents)

	Rate	Murder	Rape	Robbery	Aggravated Assault
Area		7.2	47.6	178.9	470.3
USA	432.8	4.7	34.7	111.6	285.6

Key Economic Data (Family income, unemployment)

	$25k-$75k	$75k-$150k	>$150k	Unemployment 03/2009	Unemployment 03/2010
Area	42.2%	34.9%	10.7%	8.4%	9.3%
USA	45.8%	29.5%	8.5%	9.0%	10.1

Key Household Data

	Population Age 0-17	Children w/Married Parents	Children w/Single Mother	Stay-at-home Mothers	Births to Single Women
Area	25.7%	66.9%	24.3%	25.7%	27.9%
USA	24.0%	65.6%	25.5%	27.9%	35.3%

Key Housing Data

	Owner Occupied	Median Year Built	Median Home Value	Home Value Growth, 2005-2010	Median List Price, 4-bedroom Home
Area	69.0%	1975	$162,100	1.4%	$243,000
USA	67.8%	1976	$187,045	3.1%	$288,846

Kennewick-Pasco-Richland, WA
235,841

	Score	Rank
Overall	70.69	44
LDS Culture	33.18	102
Education	68.50	202
Crime	73.52	61
Economic	60.76	218
Health	50.08	37
Household	79.01	70
Housing	88.25	79

Key LDS Culture Data

	Positive	Negative	Ratio Pos:Neg	Commute>59 minutes	Commute<15 minutes
Area	1,018	58	17.6	3.1%	36.1%
USA	4,292	251	20.1	5.5%	34.1%

Key Education Data

	HS Grad	Some Coll.	College Degree	Free/Reduced Lunch	Students per Teacher
Area	81.6%	25.0%	31.9%	49.1%	20.0
USA	85.8%	22.6%	33.2%	41.2%	15.8

Key Property Crime Data (Rate per 100,000 residents)

	Rate	Burglary	Larceny, Theft	Vehicle Theft
Area	2,637.7	607.0	1,835.2	195.4
USA	3,413.6	806.6	2,388.0	262.7

Key Violent Crime Data (Rate per 100,000 residents)

	Rate	Murder	Rape	Robbery	Aggravated Assault
Area	254.3	0.9	40.5	45.6	167.2
USA	432.8	4.7	34.7	111.6	285.6

Key Economic Data (Family income, unemployment)

	$25k-$75k	$75k-$150k	>$150k	Unemployment 03/2009	Unemployment 03/2010
Area	43.4%	32.4%	7.7%	8.1%	8.2%
USA	45.8%	29.5%	8.5%	9.0%	10.1

Key Household Data

	Population Age 0-17	Children w/Married Parents	Children w/Single Mother	Stay-at-home Mothers	Births to Single Women
Area	28.6%	68.9%	18.5%	39.5%	31.0%
USA	24.0%	65.6%	25.5%	27.9%	35.3%

Key Housing Data

	Owner Occupied	Median Year Built	Median Home Value	Home Value Growth, 2005-2010	Median List Price, 4-bedroom Home
Area	70.7%	1980	$161,300	3.2%	$240,000
USA	67.8%	1976	$187,045	3.1%	$288,846

Killeen-Temple-Fort Hood, TX
379,159

	Score	Rank
Overall	63.27	178
LDS Culture	28.47	162
Education	67.38	216
Crime	54.50	176
Economic	60.70	221
Health	32.00	328
Household	71.60	139
Housing	91.09	42

Key LDS Culture Data
	Positive	Negative	Ratio Pos:Neg	Commute>59 minutes	Commute<15 minutes
Area	1,444	65	22.2	4.1%	37.9%
USA	4,292	251	20.1	5.5%	34.1%

Key Education Data
	HS Grad	Some Coll.	College Degree	Free/Reduced Lunch	Students per Teacher
Area	89.0%	29.1%	31.4%	46.6%	14.2
USA	85.8%	22.6%	33.2%	41.2%	15.8

Key Property Crime Data (Rate per 100,000 residents)
	Rate	Burglary	Larceny, Theft	Vehicle Theft	
Area	3,171.7	915.4	2,116.8	139.4	
USA	3,413.6	806.6	2,388.0	262.7	

Key Violent Crime Data (Rate per 100,000 residents)
	Rate	Murder	Rape	Robbery	Aggravated Assault
Area	403.5	4.3	39.4	102.1	257.7
USA	432.8	4.7	34.7	111.6	285.6

Key Economic Data (Family income, unemployment)
	$25k-$75k	$75k-$150k	>$150k	Unemployment 03/2009	Unemployment 03/2010
Area	52.6%	24.4%	7.0%	6.4%	7.3%
USA	45.8%	29.5%	8.5%	9.0%	10.1

Key Household Data
	Population Age 0-17	Children w/Married Parents	Children w/Single Mother	Stay-at-home Mothers	Births to Single Women
Area	29.9%	62.3%	28.2%	40.4%	28.5%
USA	24.0%	65.6%	25.5%	27.9%	35.3%

Key Housing Data
	Owner Occupied	Median Year Built	Median Home Value	Home Value Growth, 2005-2010	Median List Price, 4-bedroom Home
Area	59.6%	1988	$116,400	3.8%	
USA	67.8%	1976	$187,045	3.1%	$288,846

Kingsport-Bristol-Bristol, TN-VA
302,975

	Score	Rank
Overall	**68.05**	**83**
LDS Culture	46.47	24
Education	76.99	106
Crime	56.78	159
Economic	54.20	304
Health	43.68	159
Household	63.58	194
Housing	94.68	14

Key LDS Culture Data

	Positive	Negative	Ratio Pos:Neg	Commute>59 minutes	Commute<15 minutes
Area	2,631	70	37.6	3.8%	32.2%
USA	4,292	251	20.1	5.5%	34.1%

Key Education Data

	HS Grad	Some Coll.	College Degree	Free/Reduced Lunch	Students per Teacher
Area	80.2%	21.3%	26.0%	46.6%	14.8
USA	85.8%	22.6%	33.2%	41.2%	15.8

Key Property Crime Data (Rate per 100,000 residents)

	Rate	Burglary	Larceny, Theft	Vehicle Theft
Area	3,439.2	822.6	2,402.4	214.2
USA	3,413.6	806.6	2,388.0	262.7

Key Violent Crime Data (Rate per 100,000 residents)

	Rate	Murder	Rape	Robbery	Aggravated Assault
Area	359.3	5.3	38.8	39.5	275.7
USA	432.8	4.7	34.7	111.6	285.6

Key Economic Data (Family income, unemployment)

	$25k-$75k	$75k-$150k	>$150k	Unemployment 03/2009	Unemployment 03/2010
Area	52.5%	19.7%	4.6%	9.1%	9.8%
USA	45.8%	29.5%	8.5%	9.0%	10.1

Key Household Data

	Population Age 0-17	Children w/Married Parents	Children w/Single Mother	Stay-at-home Mothers	Births to Single Women
Area	20.6%	68.4%	22.4%	29.1%	35.3%
USA	24.0%	65.6%	25.5%	27.9%	35.3%

Key Housing Data

	Owner Occupied	Median Year Built	Median Home Value	Home Value Growth, 2005-2010	Median List Price, 4-bedroom Home
Area	74.4%	1976	$109,300	5.1%	$239,000
USA	67.8%	1976	$187,045	3.1%	$288,846

Kingston, NY
181,670

	Score	Rank
Overall	67.81	88
LDS Culture	22.56	248
Education	78.31	93
Crime	82.06	25
Economic	74.10	50
Health	49.20	51
Household	60.49	221
Housing	68.12	333

Key LDS Culture Data
	Positive	Negative	Ratio Pos:Neg	Commute>59 minutes	Commute<15 minutes
Area	2,470	159	15.5	10.3%	31.4%
USA	4,292	251	20.1	5.5%	34.1%

Key Education Data
	HS Grad	Some Coll.	College Degree	Free/Reduced Lunch	Students per Teacher
Area	88.7%	21.2%	37.1%	28.0%	13.0
USA	85.8%	22.6%	33.2%	41.2%	15.8

Key Property Crime Data (Rate per 100,000 residents)
	Rate	Burglary	Larceny, Theft	Vehicle Theft	
Area	1,760.8	446.5	1,260.5	53.8	
USA	3,413.6	806.6	2,388.0	262.7	

Key Violent Crime Data (Rate per 100,000 residents)
	Rate	Murder	Rape	Robbery	Aggravated Assault
Area	253.4	3.3	28.0	38.9	183.2
USA	432.8	4.7	34.7	111.6	285.6

Key Economic Data (Family income, unemployment)
	$25k-$75k	$75k-$150k	>$150k	Unemployment 03/2009	Unemployment 03/2010
Area	41.5%	36.1%	9.8%	7.7%	8.0%
USA	45.8%	29.5%	8.5%	9.0%	10.1

Key Household Data
	Population Age 0-17	Children w/Married Parents	Children w/Single Mother	Stay-at-home Mothers	Births to Single Women
Area	20.5%	63.7%	27.4%	24.2%	30.3%
USA	24.0%	65.6%	25.5%	27.9%	35.3%

Key Housing Data
	Owner Occupied	Median Year Built	Median Home Value	Home Value Growth, 2005-2010	Median List Price, 4-bedroom Home
Area	65.6%	1961	$243,300	3.1%	
USA	67.8%	1976	$187,045	3.1%	$288,846

Knoxville, TN
689,179

	Score	Rank
Overall	68.12	80
LDS Culture	24.94	214
Education	79.58	72
Crime	45.29	252
Economic	66.15	135
Health	51.79	33
Household	82.10	55
Housing	87.00	98

Key LDS Culture Data

	Positive	Negative	Ratio Pos:Neg	Commute>59 minutes	Commute<15 minutes
Area	4,320	186	23.2	3.4%	29.1%
USA	4,292	251	20.1	5.5%	34.1%

Key Education Data

	HS Grad	Some Coll.	College Degree	Free/Reduced Lunch	Students per Teacher
Area	87.0%	21.2%	35.8%	40.2%	15.6
USA	85.8%	22.6%	33.2%	41.2%	15.8

Key Property Crime Data (Rate per 100,000 residents)

	Rate	Burglary	Larceny, Theft	Vehicle Theft
Area	3,722.1	977.4	2,440.1	304.6
USA	3,413.6	806.6	2,388.0	262.7

Key Violent Crime Data (Rate per 100,000 residents)

	Rate	Murder	Rape	Robbery	Aggravated Assault
Area	507.2	5.8	33.9	129.8	337.7
USA	432.8	4.7	34.7	111.6	285.6

Key Economic Data (Family income, unemployment)

	$25k-$75k	$75k-$150k	>$150k	Unemployment 03/2009	Unemployment 03/2010
Area	46.7%	28.3%	9.2%	8.8%	8.9%
USA	45.8%	29.5%	8.5%	9.0%	10.1

Key Household Data

	Population Age 0-17	Children w/Married Parents	Children w/Single Mother	Stay-at-home Mothers	Births to Single Women
Area	22.0%	68.1%	24.2%	30.8%	28.9%
USA	24.0%	65.6%	25.5%	27.9%	35.3%

Key Housing Data

	Owner Occupied	Median Year Built	Median Home Value	Home Value Growth, 2005-2010	Median List Price, 4-bedroom Home
Area	69.9%	1982	$155,600	4.7%	$279,900
USA	67.8%	1976	$187,045	3.1%	$288,846

Kokomo, IN
100,211

	Score	Rank
Overall	63.17	180
LDS Culture	30.64	135
Education	71.23	170
Crime	63.10	127
Economic	76.82	31
Health	34.59	296
Household	56.79	253
Housing	71.89	319

Key LDS Culture Data
	Positive	Negative	Ratio Pos:Neg	Commute>59 minutes	Commute<15 minutes
Area	1,776	121	14.7	4.8%	44.8%
USA	4,292	251	20.1	5.5%	34.1%

Key Education Data
	HS Grad	Some Coll.	College Degree	Free/Reduced Lunch	Students per Teacher
Area	86.7%	24.3%	24.6%	35.2%	16.0
USA	85.8%	22.6%	33.2%	41.2%	15.8

Key Property Crime Data (Rate per 100,000 residents)
	Rate	Burglary	Larceny, Theft	Vehicle Theft	
Area	3,660.6	860.7	2,673.4	126.5	
USA	3,413.6	806.6	2,388.0	262.7	

Key Violent Crime Data (Rate per 100,000 residents)
	Rate	Murder	Rape	Robbery	Aggravated Assault
Area	280.2	3.0	24.1	68.3	184.8
USA	432.8	4.7	34.7	111.6	285.6

Key Economic Data (Family income, unemployment)
	$25k-$75k	$75k-$150k	>$150k	Unemployment 03/2009	Unemployment 03/2010
Area	49.2%	27.5%	6.3%	13.8%	13.5%
USA	45.8%	29.5%	8.5%	9.0%	10.1

Key Household Data
	Population Age 0-17	Children w/Married Parents	Children w/Single Mother	Stay-at-home Mothers	Births to Single Women
Area	24.1%	67.2%	19.1%	26.6%	44.7%
USA	24.0%	65.6%	25.5%	27.9%	35.3%

Key Housing Data
	Owner Occupied	Median Year Built	Median Home Value	Home Value Growth, 2005-2010	Median List Price, 4-bedroom Home
Area	69.6%	1968	$116,400	-0.9%	
USA	67.8%	1976	$187,045	3.1%	$288,846

La Crosse, WI-MN
131,872

	Score	Rank
Overall	**67.89**	**87**
LDS Culture	27.79	172
Education	92.73	12
Crime	66.81	105
Economic	69.43	91
Health	39.16	229
Household	62.96	200
Housing	76.47	264

Key LDS Culture Data

	Positive	Negative	Ratio Pos:Neg	Commute>59 minutes	Commute<15 minutes
Area	1,038	161	6.4	2.3%	40.9%
USA	4,292	251	20.1	5.5%	34.1%

Key Education Data

	HS Grad	Some Coll.	College Degree	Free/Reduced Lunch	Students per Teacher
Area	93.2%	22.2%	43.2%	28.2%	14.0
USA	85.8%	22.6%	33.2%	41.2%	15.8

Key Property Crime Data (Rate per 100,000 residents)

	Rate	Burglary	Larceny, Theft	Vehicle Theft	
Area	2,616.8	407.5	2,104.3	105.1	
USA	3,413.6	806.6	2,388.0	262.7	

Key Violent Crime Data (Rate per 100,000 residents)

	Rate	Murder	Rape	Robbery	Aggravated Assault
Area		0.8		29.7	159.2
USA	432.8	4.7	34.7	111.6	285.6

Key Economic Data (Family income, unemployment)

	$25k-$75k	$75k-$150k	>$150k	Unemployment 03/2009	Unemployment 03/2010
Area	47.5%	32.1%	6.4%	7.7%	7.8%
USA	45.8%	29.5%	8.5%	9.0%	10.1

Key Household Data

	Population Age 0-17	Children w/Married Parents	Children w/Single Mother	Stay-at-home Mothers	Births to Single Women
Area	21.7%	68.4%	20.9%	13.2%	25.5%
USA	24.0%	65.6%	25.5%	27.9%	35.3%

Key Housing Data

	Owner Occupied	Median Year Built	Median Home Value	Home Value Growth, 2005-2010	Median List Price, 4-bedroom Home
Area	70.2%	1971	$150,200	2.8%	
USA	67.8%	1976	$187,045	3.1%	$288,846

Lafayette, IN
190,721

	Score	Rank
Overall	68.69	72
LDS Culture	30.62	136
Education	82.17	58
Crime	73.33	62
Economic	65.59	144
Health	34.59	297
Household	74.69	106
Housing	79.47	218

Key LDS Culture Data

	Positive	Negative	Ratio Pos:Neg	Commute>59 minutes	Commute<15 minutes
Area	1,407	96	14.7	4.0%	42.4%
USA	4,292	251	20.1	5.5%	34.1%

Key Education Data

	HS Grad	Some Coll.	College Degree	Free/Reduced Lunch	Students per Teacher
Area	90.2%	18.7%	39.8%	35.6%	17.1
USA	85.8%	22.6%	33.2%	41.2%	15.8

Key Property Crime Data (Rate per 100,000 residents)

	Rate	Burglary	Larceny, Theft	Vehicle Theft	
Area	2,825.0	602.7	2,057.3	165.1	
USA	3,413.6	806.6	2,388.0	262.7	

Key Violent Crime Data (Rate per 100,000 residents)

	Rate	Murder	Rape	Robbery	Aggravated Assault
Area	236.8	2.1	21.2	35.1	178.5
USA	432.8	4.7	34.7	111.6	285.6

Key Economic Data (Family income, unemployment)

	$25k-$75k	$75k-$150k	>$150k	Unemployment 03/2009	Unemployment 03/2010
Area	47.0%	30.6%	6.9%	8.8%	9.4%
USA	45.8%	29.5%	8.5%	9.0%	10.1

Key Household Data

	Population Age 0-17	Children w/Married Parents	Children w/Single Mother	Stay-at-home Mothers	Births to Single Women
Area	21.9%	69.1%	25.5%	24.3%	20.9%
USA	24.0%	65.6%	25.5%	27.9%	35.3%

Key Housing Data

	Owner Occupied	Median Year Built	Median Home Value	Home Value Growth, 2005-2010	Median List Price, 4-bedroom Home
Area	60.0%	1975	$124,800	1.8%	
USA	67.8%	1976	$187,045	3.1%	$288,846

Lafayette, LA
259,073

	Score	Rank
Overall	53.17	349
LDS Culture	16.45	324
Education	53.67	335
Crime	33.68	327
Economic	50.92	322
Health	51.33	36
Household	46.30	326
Housing	88.64	71

Key LDS Culture Data

	Positive	Negative	Ratio Pos:Neg	Commute>59 minutes	Commute<15 minutes
Area	2,601	191	13.6	6.0%	30.6%
USA	4,292	251	20.1	5.5%	34.1%

Key Education Data

	HS Grad	Some Coll.	College Degree	Free/Reduced Lunch	Students per Teacher
Area	80.9%	22.2%	26.9%	59.3%	14.8
USA	85.8%	22.6%	33.2%	41.2%	15.8

Key Property Crime Data (Rate per 100,000 residents)

	Rate	Burglary	Larceny, Theft	Vehicle Theft	
Area	3,965.2	875.4	2,798.2	291.7	
USA	3,413.6	806.6	2,388.0	262.7	

Key Violent Crime Data (Rate per 100,000 residents)

	Rate	Murder	Rape	Robbery	Aggravated Assault
Area	747.8	5.8	45.0	161.4	535.7
USA	432.8	4.7	34.7	111.6	285.6

Key Economic Data (Family income, unemployment)

	$25k-$75k	$75k-$150k	>$150k	Unemployment 03/2009	Unemployment 03/2010
Area	40.1%	27.7%	10.3%	4.4%	5.0%
USA	45.8%	29.5%	8.5%	9.0%	10.1

Key Household Data

	Population Age 0-17	Children w/Married Parents	Children w/Single Mother	Stay-at-home Mothers	Births to Single Women
Area	25.7%	59.8%	32.8%	26.9%	51.5%
USA	24.0%	65.6%	25.5%	27.9%	35.3%

Key Housing Data

	Owner Occupied	Median Year Built	Median Home Value	Home Value Growth, 2005-2010	Median List Price, 4-bedroom Home
Area	68.3%	1981	$132,700	5.4%	
USA	67.8%	1976	$187,045	3.1%	$288,846

Lake Charles, LA
191,454

	Score	Rank
Overall	60.87	222
LDS Culture	22.10	257
Education	60.14	293
Crime	56.93	158
Economic	57.31	267
Health	57.92	8
Household	46.30	327
Housing	89.62	57

Key LDS Culture Data

	Positive	Negative	Ratio Pos:Neg	Commute>59 minutes	Commute<15 minutes
Area	1,261	84	15.0	3.4%	39.5%
USA	4,292	251	20.1	5.5%	34.1%

Key Education Data

	HS Grad	Some Coll.	College Degree	Free/Reduced Lunch	Students per Teacher
Area	81.2%	19.7%	26.1%	54.8%	14.0
USA	85.8%	22.6%	33.2%	41.2%	15.8

Key Property Crime Data (Rate per 100,000 residents)

	Rate	Burglary	Larceny, Theft	Vehicle Theft	
Area		1,548.6	2,775.7	393.0	
USA	3,413.6	806.6	2,388.0	262.7	

Key Violent Crime Data (Rate per 100,000 residents)

	Rate	Murder	Rape	Robbery	Aggravated Assault
Area		19.3	79.9	159.2	394.4
USA	432.8	4.7	34.7	111.6	285.6

Key Economic Data (Family income, unemployment)

	$25k-$75k	$75k-$150k	>$150k	Unemployment 03/2009	Unemployment 03/2010
Area	45.9%	26.4%	7.2%	5.5%	5.8%
USA	45.8%	29.5%	8.5%	9.0%	10.1

Key Household Data

	Population Age 0-17	Children w/Married Parents	Children w/Single Mother	Stay-at-home Mothers	Births to Single Women
Area	25.4%	60.6%	29.4%	37.0%	44.4%
USA	24.0%	65.6%	25.5%	27.9%	35.3%

Key Housing Data

	Owner Occupied	Median Year Built	Median Home Value	Home Value Growth, 2005-2010	Median List Price, 4-bedroom Home
Area	72.4%	1978	$112,300	5.6%	
USA	67.8%	1976	$187,045	3.1%	$288,846

Lake Havasu City-Kingman, AZ
196,281

	Score	Rank
Overall	60.24	238
LDS Culture	22.24	256
Education	58.35	308
Crime	68.61	85
Economic	60.37	226
Health	43.61	161
Household	48.77	311
Housing	84.35	152

Key LDS Culture Data

	Positive	Negative	Ratio Pos:Neg	Commute>59 minutes	Commute<15 minutes
Area	349	23	15.2	4.3%	39.2%
USA	4,292	251	20.1	5.5%	34.1%

Key Education Data

	HS Grad	Some Coll.	College Degree	Free/Reduced Lunch	Students per Teacher
Area	81.9%	29.0%	18.5%	47.8%	21.3
USA	85.8%	22.6%	33.2%	41.2%	15.8

Key Property Crime Data (Rate per 100,000 residents)

	Rate	Burglary	Larceny, Theft	Vehicle Theft	
Area	3,560.6	950.8	2,346.8	263.0	
USA	3,413.6	806.6	2,388.0	262.7	

Key Violent Crime Data (Rate per 100,000 residents)

	Rate	Murder	Rape	Robbery	Aggravated Assault
Area	225.9	4.0	25.6	32.6	163.6
USA	432.8	4.7	34.7	111.6	285.6

Key Economic Data (Family income, unemployment)

	$25k-$75k	$75k-$150k	>$150k	Unemployment 03/2009	Unemployment 03/2010
Area	56.9%	19.3%	3.5%	10.8%	10.7%
USA	45.8%	29.5%	8.5%	9.0%	10.1

Key Household Data

	Population Age 0-17	Children w/Married Parents	Children w/Single Mother	Stay-at-home Mothers	Births to Single Women
Area	22.0%	61.5%	24.3%	24.2%	51.4%
USA	24.0%	65.6%	25.5%	27.9%	35.3%

Key Housing Data

	Owner Occupied	Median Year Built	Median Home Value	Home Value Growth, 2005-2010	Median List Price, 4-bedroom Home
Area	68.2%	1992	$177,700	1.0%	
USA	67.8%	1976	$187,045	3.1%	$288,846

Lakeland-Winter Haven, FL
580,594

	Score	Rank
Overall	60.57	230
LDS Culture	19.34	291
Education	61.08	286
Crime	44.28	261
Economic	49.47	331
Health	52.75	21
Household	63.58	195
Housing	97.87	3

Key LDS Culture Data

	Positive	Negative	Ratio Pos:Neg	Commute>59 minutes	Commute<15 minutes
Area	4,991	228	21.9	6.8%	25.1%
USA	4,292	251	20.1	5.5%	34.1%

Key Education Data

	HS Grad	Some Coll.	College Degree	Free/Reduced Lunch	Students per Teacher
Area	82.1%	19.8%	25.9%	50.4%	14.3
USA	85.8%	22.6%	33.2%	41.2%	15.8

Key Property Crime Data (Rate per 100,000 residents)

	Rate	Burglary	Larceny, Theft	Vehicle Theft
Area	4,083.7	1,149.9	2,649.9	283.9
USA	3,413.6	806.6	2,388.0	262.7

Key Violent Crime Data (Rate per 100,000 residents)

	Rate	Murder	Rape	Robbery	Aggravated Assault
Area	491.6	7.6	28.5	122.1	333.4
USA	432.8	4.7	34.7	111.6	285.6

Key Economic Data (Family income, unemployment)

	$25k-$75k	$75k-$150k	>$150k	Unemployment 03/2009	Unemployment 03/2010
Area	50.5%	25.5%	4.6%	10.0%	13.0%
USA	45.8%	29.5%	8.5%	9.0%	10.1

Key Household Data

	Population Age 0-17	Children w/Married Parents	Children w/Single Mother	Stay-at-home Mothers	Births to Single Women
Area	24.0%	63.4%	28.0%	31.3%	40.5%
USA	24.0%	65.6%	25.5%	27.9%	35.3%

Key Housing Data

	Owner Occupied	Median Year Built	Median Home Value	Home Value Growth, 2005-2010	Median List Price, 4-bedroom Home
Area	69.7%	1985	$155,200	5.0%	$170,900
USA	67.8%	1976	$187,045	3.1%	$288,846

Lancaster, PA
502,370

	Score	Rank
Overall	74.02	23
LDS Culture	27.07	182
Education	73.75	138
Crime	84.54	18
Economic	71.48	69
Health	49.51	43
Household	88.27	20
Housing	80.03	208

Key LDS Culture Data

	Positive	Negative	Ratio Pos:Neg	Commute>59 minutes	Commute<15 minutes
Area	6,563	318	20.6	5.3%	34.6%
USA	4,292	251	20.1	5.5%	34.1%

Key Education Data

	HS Grad	Some Coll.	College Degree	Free/Reduced Lunch	Students per Teacher
Area	82.0%	14.4%	28.8%	27.5%	14.7
USA	85.8%	22.6%	33.2%	41.2%	15.8

Key Property Crime Data (Rate per 100,000 residents)

	Rate	Burglary	Larceny, Theft	Vehicle Theft	
Area	2,102.4	377.1	1,619.8	105.4	
USA	3,413.6	806.6	2,388.0	262.7	

Key Violent Crime Data (Rate per 100,000 residents)

	Rate	Murder	Rape	Robbery	Aggravated Assault
Area	191.2	1.4	23.9	70.8	95.1
USA	432.8	4.7	34.7	111.6	285.6

Key Economic Data (Family income, unemployment)

	$25k-$75k	$75k-$150k	>$150k	Unemployment 03/2009	Unemployment 03/2010
Area	49.2%	32.0%	8.9%	7.2%	8.4%
USA	45.8%	29.5%	8.5%	9.0%	10.1

Key Household Data

	Population Age 0-17	Children w/Married Parents	Children w/Single Mother	Stay-at-home Mothers	Births to Single Women
Area	24.9%	74.3%	18.4%	37.1%	21.3%
USA	24.0%	65.6%	25.5%	27.9%	35.3%

Key Housing Data

	Owner Occupied	Median Year Built	Median Home Value	Home Value Growth, 2005-2010	Median List Price, 4-bedroom Home
Area	70.6%	1974	$191,500	5.4%	$229,900
USA	67.8%	1976	$187,045	3.1%	$288,846

Lansing-East Lansing, MI
454,035

	Score	Rank
Overall	64.41	151
LDS Culture	35.30	77
Education	79.21	78
Crime	55.79	166
Economic	68.98	97
Health	34.37	301
Household	57.41	243
Housing	81.97	186

Key LDS Culture Data

	Positive	Negative	Ratio Pos:Neg	Commute>59 minutes	Commute<15 minutes
Area	2,944	118	24.9	4.7%	33.2%
USA	4,292	251	20.1	5.5%	34.1%

Key Education Data

	HS Grad	Some Coll.	College Degree	Free/Reduced Lunch	Students per Teacher
Area	92.6%	25.7%	40.2%	32.3%	17.2
USA	85.8%	22.6%	33.2%	41.2%	15.8

Key Property Crime Data (Rate per 100,000 residents)

	Rate	Burglary	Larceny, Theft	Vehicle Theft
Area	2,731.7	684.5	1,901.1	146.2
USA	3,413.6	806.6	2,388.0	262.7

Key Violent Crime Data (Rate per 100,000 residents)

	Rate	Murder	Rape	Robbery	Aggravated Assault
Area	435.8	2.9	50.9	83.8	298.3
USA	432.8	4.7	34.7	111.6	285.6

Key Economic Data (Family income, unemployment)

	$25k-$75k	$75k-$150k	>$150k	Unemployment 03/2009	Unemployment 03/2010
Area	44.1%	33.2%	7.6%	10.5%	11.8%
USA	45.8%	29.5%	8.5%	9.0%	10.1

Key Household Data

	Population Age 0-17	Children w/Married Parents	Children w/Single Mother	Stay-at-home Mothers	Births to Single Women
Area	22.4%	64.5%	27.3%	25.7%	38.4%
USA	24.0%	65.6%	25.5%	27.9%	35.3%

Key Housing Data

	Owner Occupied	Median Year Built	Median Home Value	Home Value Growth, 2005-2010	Median List Price, 4-bedroom Home
Area	69.9%	1971	$153,500	-2.4%	$179,900
USA	67.8%	1976	$187,045	3.1%	$288,846

Laredo, TX
236,941

	Score	Rank
Overall	55.00	329
LDS Culture	24.86	218
Education	53.82	333
Crime	29.67	336
Economic	50.25	329
Health	26.70	354
Household	75.93	93
Housing	91.46	37

Key LDS Culture Data

	Positive	Negative	Ratio Pos:Neg	Commute>59 minutes	Commute<15 minutes
Area	707	39	18.1	3.6%	31.4%
USA	4,292	251	20.1	5.5%	34.1%

Key Education Data

	HS Grad	Some Coll.	College Degree	Free/Reduced Lunch	Students per Teacher
Area	65.1%	20.3%	24.5%	49.4%	16.0
USA	85.8%	22.6%	33.2%	41.2%	15.8

Key Property Crime Data (Rate per 100,000 residents)

	Rate	Burglary	Larceny, Theft	Vehicle Theft
Area	6,184.7	938.4	4,505.4	740.9
USA	3,413.6	806.6	2,388.0	262.7

Key Violent Crime Data (Rate per 100,000 residents)

	Rate	Murder	Rape	Robbery	Aggravated Assault
Area	602.1	4.6	34.4	135.0	428.1
USA	432.8	4.7	34.7	111.6	285.6

Key Economic Data (Family income, unemployment)

	$25k-$75k	$75k-$150k	>$150k	Unemployment 03/2009	Unemployment 03/2010
Area	46.7%	19.7%	4.5%	8.0%	9.2%
USA	45.8%	29.5%	8.5%	9.0%	10.1

Key Household Data

	Population Age 0-17	Children w/Married Parents	Children w/Single Mother	Stay-at-home Mothers	Births to Single Women
Area	37.3%	65.8%	27.5%	41.5%	38.6%
USA	24.0%	65.6%	25.5%	27.9%	35.3%

Key Housing Data

	Owner Occupied	Median Year Built	Median Home Value	Home Value Growth, 2005-2010	Median List Price, 4-bedroom Home
Area	64.9%	1990	$107,600	3.6%	
USA	67.8%	1976	$187,045	3.1%	$288,846

Las Cruces, NM
201,603

	Score	Rank
Overall	58.60	274
LDS Culture	45.15	27
Education	54.47	329
Crime	51.61	201
Economic	45.80	350
Health	37.70	246
Household	50.00	300
Housing	91.03	43

Key LDS Culture Data

	Positive	Negative	Ratio Pos:Neg	Commute>59 minutes	Commute<15 minutes
Area	822	20	41.1	3.1%	37.6%
USA	4,292	251	20.1	5.5%	34.1%

Key Education Data

	HS Grad	Some Coll.	College Degree	Free/Reduced Lunch	Students per Teacher
Area	75.5%	23.9%	30.9%	69.9%	15.3
USA	85.8%	22.6%	33.2%	41.2%	15.8

Key Property Crime Data (Rate per 100,000 residents)

	Rate	Burglary	Larceny, Theft	Vehicle Theft	
Area	3,191.3	701.6	2,265.8	223.9	
USA	3,413.6	806.6	2,388.0	262.7	

Key Violent Crime Data (Rate per 100,000 residents)

	Rate	Murder	Rape	Robbery	Aggravated Assault
Area	432.5	4.5	34.3	46.7	347.1
USA	432.8	4.7	34.7	111.6	285.6

Key Economic Data (Family income, unemployment)

	$25k-$75k	$75k-$150k	>$150k	Unemployment 03/2009	Unemployment 03/2010
Area	42.2%	23.4%	4.1%	6.6%	9.0%
USA	45.8%	29.5%	8.5%	9.0%	10.1

Key Household Data

	Population Age 0-17	Children w/Married Parents	Children w/Single Mother	Stay-at-home Mothers	Births to Single Women
Area	27.5%	57.0%	33.7%	31.6%	37.6%
USA	24.0%	65.6%	25.5%	27.9%	35.3%

Key Housing Data

	Owner Occupied	Median Year Built	Median Home Value	Home Value Growth, 2005-2010	Median List Price, 4-bedroom Home
Area	66.7%	1987	$152,200	5.7%	
USA	67.8%	1976	$187,045	3.1%	$288,846

Las Vegas-Paradise, NV
1,865,746

	Score	Rank
Overall	57.67	294
LDS Culture	18.30	307
Education	56.43	318
Crime	31.03	334
Economic	61.70	204
Health	36.69	274
Household	73.46	121
Housing	92.18	33

Key LDS Culture Data

	Positive	Negative	Ratio Pos:Neg	Commute>59 minutes	Commute<15 minutes
Area	5,637	987	5.7	4.8%	20.2%
USA	4,292	251	20.1	5.5%	34.1%

Key Education Data

	HS Grad	Some Coll.	College Degree	Free/Reduced Lunch	Students per Teacher
Area	83.2%	25.8%	28.6%	42.2%	19.5
USA	85.8%	22.6%	33.2%	41.2%	15.8

Key Property Crime Data (Rate per 100,000 residents)

	Rate	Burglary	Larceny, Theft	Vehicle Theft
Area	3,667.7	1,015.7	1,905.4	746.6
USA	3,413.6	806.6	2,388.0	262.7

Key Violent Crime Data (Rate per 100,000 residents)

	Rate	Murder	Rape	Robbery	Aggravated Assault
Area	840.4	7.3	47.1	307.6	478.4
USA	432.8	4.7	34.7	111.6	285.6

Key Economic Data (Family income, unemployment)

	$25k-$75k	$75k-$150k	>$150k	Unemployment 03/2009	Unemployment 03/2010
Area	46.3%	31.9%	9.6%	10.6%	13.8%
USA	45.8%	29.5%	8.5%	9.0%	10.1

Key Household Data

	Population Age 0-17	Children w/Married Parents	Children w/Single Mother	Stay-at-home Mothers	Births to Single Women
Area	26.4%	63.9%	24.4%	32.6%	29.8%
USA	24.0%	65.6%	25.5%	27.9%	35.3%

Key Housing Data

	Owner Occupied	Median Year Built	Median Home Value	Home Value Growth, 2005-2010	Median List Price, 4-bedroom Home
Area	58.2%	1995	$273,300	-3.9%	$199,900
USA	67.8%	1976	$187,045	3.1%	$288,846

Lawrence, KS
114,748

	Score	Rank
Overall	**64.65**	**144**
LDS Culture	24.64	224
Education	92.29	14
Crime	47.68	236
Economic	73.54	54
Health	38.40	244
Household	64.81	181
Housing	73.21	306

Key LDS Culture Data

	Positive	Negative	Ratio Pos:Neg	Commute>59 minutes	Commute<15 minutes
Area	4,083	317	12.9	3.9%	45.5%
USA	4,292	251	20.1	5.5%	34.1%

Key Education Data

	HS Grad	Some Coll.	College Degree	Free/Reduced Lunch	Students per Teacher
Area	94.7%	20.5%	54.5%	28.4%	14.7
USA	85.8%	22.6%	33.2%	41.2%	15.8

Key Property Crime Data (Rate per 100,000 residents)

	Rate	Burglary	Larceny, Theft	Vehicle Theft
Area	4,649.0	837.0	3,617.2	194.8
USA	3,413.6	806.6	2,388.0	262.7

Key Violent Crime Data (Rate per 100,000 residents)

	Rate	Murder	Rape	Robbery	Aggravated Assault
Area	396.4	3.5	42.4	68.4	282.2
USA	432.8	4.7	34.7	111.6	285.6

Key Economic Data (Family income, unemployment)

	$25k-$75k	$75k-$150k	>$150k	Unemployment 03/2009	Unemployment 03/2010
Area	40.0%	36.7%	11.2%	5.9%	5.6%
USA	45.8%	29.5%	8.5%	9.0%	10.1

Key Household Data

	Population Age 0-17	Children w/Married Parents	Children w/Single Mother	Stay-at-home Mothers	Births to Single Women
Area	18.9%	66.0%	27.2%	29.2%	34.0%
USA	24.0%	65.6%	25.5%	27.9%	35.3%

Key Housing Data

	Owner Occupied	Median Year Built	Median Home Value	Home Value Growth, 2005-2010	Median List Price, 4-bedroom Home
Area	53.8%	1983	$181,400	1.9%	
USA	67.8%	1976	$187,045	3.1%	$288,846

Lawton, OK
111,772

	Score	Rank
Overall	58.45	281
LDS Culture	30.72	129
Education	69.21	194
Crime	27.81	342
Economic	51.03	321
Health	42.91	169
Household	66.67	170
Housing	86.46	110

Key LDS Culture Data

	Positive	Negative	Ratio Pos:Neg	Commute>59 minutes	Commute<15 minutes
Area	886	60	14.8	2.1%	44.8%
USA	4,292	251	20.1	5.5%	34.1%

Key Education Data

	HS Grad	Some Coll.	College Degree	Free/Reduced Lunch	Students per Teacher
Area	89.7%	26.9%	27.1%	52.0%	15.0
USA	85.8%	22.6%	33.2%	41.2%	15.8

Key Property Crime Data (Rate per 100,000 residents)

	Rate	Burglary	Larceny, Theft	Vehicle Theft
Area	3,887.8	1,342.5	2,336.2	209.1
USA	3,413.6	806.6	2,388.0	262.7

Key Violent Crime Data (Rate per 100,000 residents)

	Rate	Murder	Rape	Robbery	Aggravated Assault
Area	890.9	5.3	70.3	178.4	637.0
USA	432.8	4.7	34.7	111.6	285.6

Key Economic Data (Family income, unemployment)

	$25k-$75k	$75k-$150k	>$150k	Unemployment 03/2009	Unemployment 03/2010
Area	50.6%	23.6%	3.7%	5.0%	5.4%
USA	45.8%	29.5%	8.5%	9.0%	10.1

Key Household Data

	Population Age 0-17	Children w/Married Parents	Children w/Single Mother	Stay-at-home Mothers	Births to Single Women
Area	28.0%	58.9%	32.7%	23.7%	21.7%
USA	24.0%	65.6%	25.5%	27.9%	35.3%

Key Housing Data

	Owner Occupied	Median Year Built	Median Home Value	Home Value Growth, 2005-2010	Median List Price, 4-bedroom Home
Area	60.7%	1974	$103,300	4.5%	
USA	67.8%	1976	$187,045	3.1%	$288,846

Lebanon, PA
128,934

	Score	Rank
Overall	69.74	53
LDS Culture	25.87	199
Education	71.02	172
Crime	83.45	20
Economic	70.76	80
Health	47.33	96
Household	70.37	146
Housing	78.40	241

Key LDS Culture Data

	Positive	Negative	Ratio Pos:Neg	Commute>59 minutes	Commute<15 minutes
Area	7,788	404	19.3	6.5%	31.8%
USA	4,292	251	20.1	5.5%	34.1%

Key Education Data

	HS Grad	Some Coll.	College Degree	Free/Reduced Lunch	Students per Teacher
Area	84.6%	15.9%	24.9%	27.4%	14.6
USA	85.8%	22.6%	33.2%	41.2%	15.8

Key Property Crime Data (Rate per 100,000 residents)

	Rate	Burglary	Larceny, Theft	Vehicle Theft	
Area	1,760.9	307.5	1,381.3	72.2	
USA	3,413.6	806.6	2,388.0	262.7	

Key Violent Crime Data (Rate per 100,000 residents)

	Rate	Murder	Rape	Robbery	Aggravated Assault
Area	238.4	1.6	16.3	45.8	174.7
USA	432.8	4.7	34.7	111.6	285.6

Key Economic Data (Family income, unemployment)

	$25k-$75k	$75k-$150k	>$150k	Unemployment 03/2009	Unemployment 03/2010
Area	51.1%	33.6%	5.0%	6.7%	8.0%
USA	45.8%	29.5%	8.5%	9.0%	10.1

Key Household Data

	Population Age 0-17	Children w/Married Parents	Children w/Single Mother	Stay-at-home Mothers	Births to Single Women
Area	22.3%	71.9%	18.4%	22.8%	40.6%
USA	24.0%	65.6%	25.5%	27.9%	35.3%

Key Housing Data

	Owner Occupied	Median Year Built	Median Home Value	Home Value Growth, 2005-2010	Median List Price, 4-bedroom Home
Area	74.3%	1972	$161,100	5.4%	
USA	67.8%	1976	$187,045	3.1%	$288,846

Lewiston-Auburn, ME
106,877

	Score	Rank
Overall	70.92	41
LDS Culture	46.56	22
Education	69.07	196
Crime	86.37	14
Economic	68.04	110
Health	53.14	19
Household	61.11	216
Housing	70.50	325

Key LDS Culture Data

	Positive	Negative	Ratio Pos:Neg	Commute>59 minutes	Commute<15 minutes
Area	2,049	48	42.7	4.5%	36.7%
USA	4,292	251	20.1	5.5%	34.1%

Key Education Data

	HS Grad	Some Coll.	College Degree	Free/Reduced Lunch	Students per Teacher
Area	86.8%	21.4%	26.8%	41.2%	9.1
USA	85.8%	22.6%	33.2%	41.2%	15.8

Key Property Crime Data (Rate per 100,000 residents)

	Rate	Burglary	Larceny, Theft	Vehicle Theft	
Area	2,310.8	461.0	1,754.2	95.6	
USA	3,413.6	806.6	2,388.0	262.7	

Key Violent Crime Data (Rate per 100,000 residents)

	Rate	Murder	Rape	Robbery	Aggravated Assault
Area	149.9	1.9	33.7	45.0	69.3
USA	432.8	4.7	34.7	111.6	285.6

Key Economic Data (Family income, unemployment)

	$25k-$75k	$75k-$150k	>$150k	Unemployment 03/2009	Unemployment 03/2010
Area	48.0%	27.5%	6.7%	9.2%	8.8%
USA	45.8%	29.5%	8.5%	9.0%	10.1

Key Household Data

	Population Age 0-17	Children w/Married Parents	Children w/Single Mother	Stay-at-home Mothers	Births to Single Women
Area	22.6%	64.6%	20.9%	20.6%	25.2%
USA	24.0%	65.6%	25.5%	27.9%	35.3%

Key Housing Data

	Owner Occupied	Median Year Built	Median Home Value	Home Value Growth, 2005-2010	Median List Price, 4-bedroom Home
Area	67.2%	1970	$161,500	3.6%	
USA	67.8%	1976	$187,045	3.1%	$288,846

Lexington-Fayette, KY
452,563

	Score	Rank
Overall	59.98	246
LDS Culture	30.93	125
Education	69.73	190
Crime	48.95	227
Economic	64.26	163
Health	26.56	357
Household	57.41	244
Housing	86.77	103

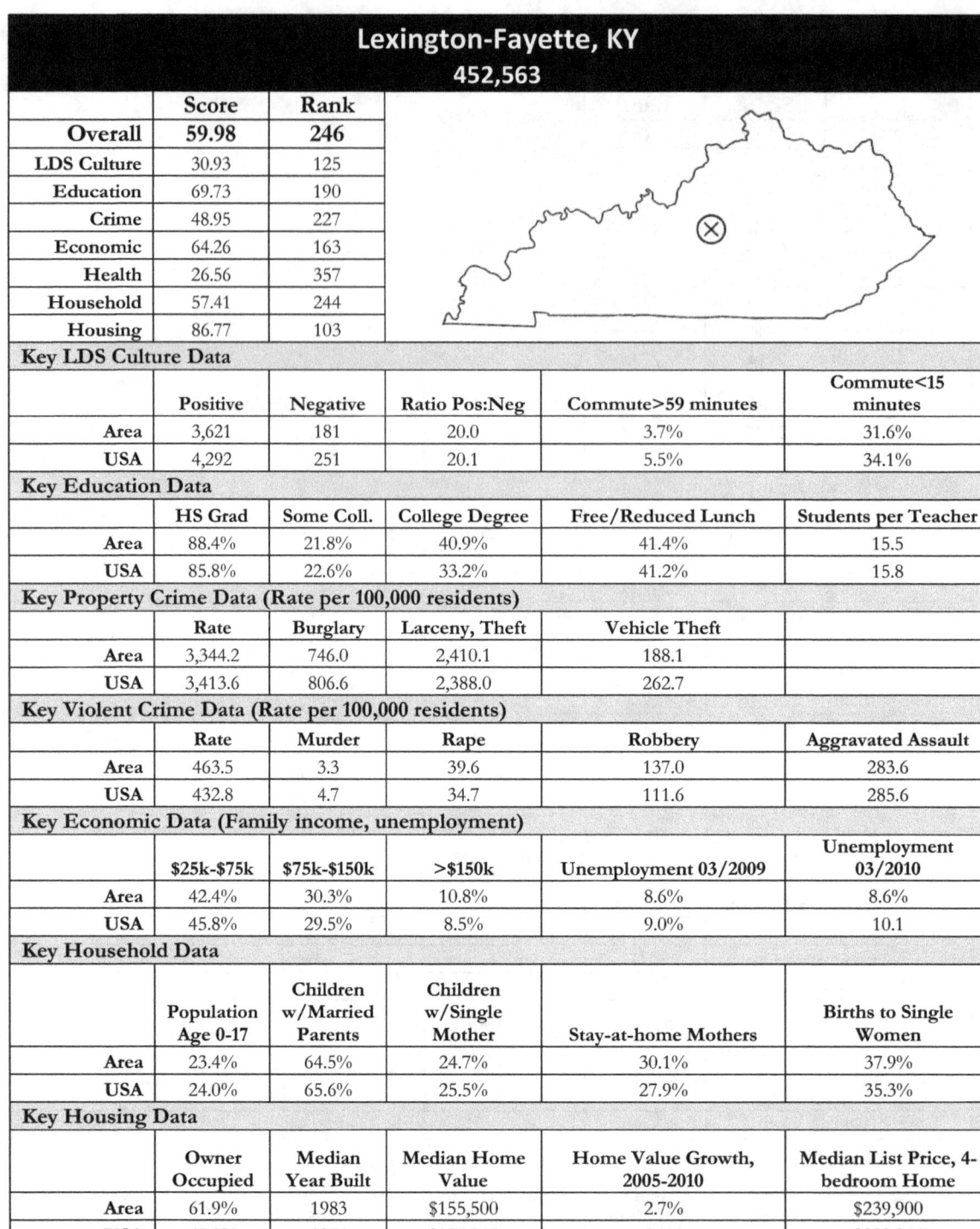

Key LDS Culture Data

	Positive	Negative	Ratio Pos:Neg	Commute>59 minutes	Commute<15 minutes
Area	3,621	181	20.0	3.7%	31.6%
USA	4,292	251	20.1	5.5%	34.1%

Key Education Data

	HS Grad	Some Coll.	College Degree	Free/Reduced Lunch	Students per Teacher
Area	88.4%	21.8%	40.9%	41.4%	15.5
USA	85.8%	22.6%	33.2%	41.2%	15.8

Key Property Crime Data (Rate per 100,000 residents)

	Rate	Burglary	Larceny, Theft	Vehicle Theft	
Area	3,344.2	746.0	2,410.1	188.1	
USA	3,413.6	806.6	2,388.0	262.7	

Key Violent Crime Data (Rate per 100,000 residents)

	Rate	Murder	Rape	Robbery	Aggravated Assault
Area	463.5	3.3	39.6	137.0	283.6
USA	432.8	4.7	34.7	111.6	285.6

Key Economic Data (Family income, unemployment)

	$25k-$75k	$75k-$150k	>$150k	Unemployment 03/2009	Unemployment 03/2010
Area	42.4%	30.3%	10.8%	8.6%	8.6%
USA	45.8%	29.5%	8.5%	9.0%	10.1

Key Household Data

	Population Age 0-17	Children w/Married Parents	Children w/Single Mother	Stay-at-home Mothers	Births to Single Women
Area	23.4%	64.5%	24.7%	30.1%	37.9%
USA	24.0%	65.6%	25.5%	27.9%	35.3%

Key Housing Data

	Owner Occupied	Median Year Built	Median Home Value	Home Value Growth, 2005-2010	Median List Price, 4-bedroom Home
Area	61.9%	1983	$155,500	2.7%	$239,900
USA	67.8%	1976	$187,045	3.1%	$288,846

Lima, OH
105,168

	Score	Rank
Overall	**54.72**	**335**
LDS Culture	33.00	107
Education	62.04	277
Crime	39.15	295
Economic	61.37	207
Health	42.19	177
Household	39.51	360
Housing	73.64	302

Key LDS Culture Data

	Positive	Negative	Ratio Pos:Neg	Commute>59 minutes	Commute<15 minutes
Area	1,787	103	17.3	4.4%	39.6%
USA	4,292	251	20.1	5.5%	34.1%

Key Education Data

	HS Grad	Some Coll.	College Degree	Free/Reduced Lunch	Students per Teacher
Area	88.2%	21.3%	22.5%		16.8
USA	85.8%	22.6%	33.2%	41.2%	15.8

Key Property Crime Data (Rate per 100,000 residents)

	Rate	Burglary	Larceny, Theft	Vehicle Theft
Area	4,618.4	1,294.3	3,083.7	240.4
USA	3,413.6	806.6	2,388.0	262.7

Key Violent Crime Data (Rate per 100,000 residents)

	Rate	Murder	Rape	Robbery	Aggravated Assault
Area	552.3	1.9	80.1	180.3	290.0
USA	432.8	4.7	34.7	111.6	285.6

Key Economic Data (Family income, unemployment)

	$25k-$75k	$75k-$150k	>$150k	Unemployment 03/2009	Unemployment 03/2010
Area	54.6%	23.9%	5.1%	12.0%	12.2%
USA	45.8%	29.5%	8.5%	9.0%	10.1

Key Household Data

	Population Age 0-17	Children w/Married Parents	Children w/Single Mother	Stay-at-home Mothers	Births to Single Women
Area	24.3%	57.7%	30.9%	19.2%	40.1%
USA	24.0%	65.6%	25.5%	27.9%	35.3%

Key Housing Data

	Owner Occupied	Median Year Built	Median Home Value	Home Value Growth, 2005-2010	Median List Price, 4-bedroom Home
Area	69.6%	1963	$104,700	2.1%	
USA	67.8%	1976	$187,045	3.1%	$288,846

Lincoln, NE
295,575

	Score	Rank
Overall	71.14	38
LDS Culture	24.69	222
Education	95.72	8
Crime	47.97	234
Economic	80.71	13
Health	48.14	82
Household	75.93	94
Housing	83.02	175

Key LDS Culture Data

	Positive	Negative	Ratio Pos:Neg	Commute>59 minutes	Commute<15 minutes
Area	1,656	128	12.9	2.7%	38.5%
USA	4,292	251	20.1	5.5%	34.1%

Key Education Data

	HS Grad	Some Coll.	College Degree	Free/Reduced Lunch	Students per Teacher
Area	92.7%	25.0%	45.4%	34.0%	13.8
USA	85.8%	22.6%	33.2%	41.2%	15.8

Key Property Crime Data (Rate per 100,000 residents)

	Rate	Burglary	Larceny, Theft	Vehicle Theft	
Area	3,726.6	581.4	3,021.6	123.5	
USA	3,413.6	806.6	2,388.0	262.7	

Key Violent Crime Data (Rate per 100,000 residents)

	Rate	Murder	Rape	Robbery	Aggravated Assault
Area	445.1	2.0	40.3	73.4	329.3
USA	432.8	4.7	34.7	111.6	285.6

Key Economic Data (Family income, unemployment)

	$25k-$75k	$75k-$150k	>$150k	Unemployment 03/2009	Unemployment 03/2010
Area	46.0%	37.0%	6.8%	4.6%	4.9%
USA	45.8%	29.5%	8.5%	9.0%	10.1

Key Household Data

	Population Age 0-17	Children w/Married Parents	Children w/Single Mother	Stay-at-home Mothers	Births to Single Women
Area	23.6%	74.1%	18.3%	12.9%	16.2%
USA	24.0%	65.6%	25.5%	27.9%	35.3%

Key Housing Data

	Owner Occupied	Median Year Built	Median Home Value	Home Value Growth, 2005-2010	Median List Price, 4-bedroom Home
Area	65.1%	1974	$147,100	1.4%	$195,900
USA	67.8%	1976	$187,045	3.1%	$288,846

Little Rock-North Little Rock-Conway, AR
677,063

	Score	Rank
Overall	57.76	291
LDS Culture	30.65	134
Education	70.21	181
Crime	28.44	339
Economic	51.47	317
Health	40.99	196
Household	57.41	245
Housing	91.18	39

Key LDS Culture Data

	Positive	Negative	Ratio Pos:Neg	Commute>59 minutes	Commute<15 minutes
Area	3,623	184	19.7	3.8%	31.7%
USA	4,292	251	20.1	5.5%	34.1%

Key Education Data

	HS Grad	Some Coll.	College Degree	Free/Reduced Lunch	Students per Teacher
Area	88.1%	23.8%	32.1%	49.6%	13.4
USA	85.8%	22.6%	33.2%	41.2%	15.8

Key Property Crime Data (Rate per 100,000 residents)

	Rate	Burglary	Larceny, Theft	Vehicle Theft
Area	5,362.5	1,468.5	3,524.7	369.2
USA	3,413.6	806.6	2,388.0	262.7

Key Violent Crime Data (Rate per 100,000 residents)

	Rate	Murder	Rape	Robbery	Aggravated Assault
Area	718.4	9.5	53.8	196.5	458.6
USA	432.8	4.7	34.7	111.6	285.6

Key Economic Data (Family income, unemployment)

	$25k-$75k	$75k-$150k	>$150k	Unemployment 03/2009	Unemployment 03/2010
Area	46.7%	27.0%	7.3%	5.8%	7.2%
USA	45.8%	29.5%	8.5%	9.0%	10.1

Key Household Data

	Population Age 0-17	Children w/Married Parents	Children w/Single Mother	Stay-at-home Mothers	Births to Single Women
Area	25.3%	60.3%	29.8%	24.7%	42.9%
USA	24.0%	65.6%	25.5%	27.9%	35.3%

Key Housing Data

	Owner Occupied	Median Year Built	Median Home Value	Home Value Growth, 2005-2010	Median List Price, 4-bedroom Home
Area	65.0%	1983	$134,000	3.6%	$240,000
USA	67.8%	1976	$187,045	3.1%	$288,846

Logan, UT-ID
124,526

	Score	Rank
Overall	89.84	3
LDS Culture	76.55	4
Education	88.37	25
Crime	100.00	1
Economic	73.10	58
Health	63.80	4
Household	93.21	4
Housing	81.10	196

Key LDS Culture Data

	Positive	Negative	Ratio Pos:Neg	Commute>59 minutes	Commute<15 minutes
Area	886	19	46.6	3.7%	50.8%
USA	4,292	251	20.1	5.5%	34.1%

Key Education Data

	HS Grad	Some Coll.	College Degree	Free/Reduced Lunch	Students per Teacher
Area	92.7%	25.2%	44.6%	30.9%	22.6
USA	85.8%	22.6%	33.2%	41.2%	15.8

Key Property Crime Data (Rate per 100,000 residents)

	Rate	Burglary	Larceny, Theft	Vehicle Theft
Area	1,641.0	319.4	1,279.2	42.4
USA	3,413.6	806.6	2,388.0	262.7

Key Violent Crime Data (Rate per 100,000 residents)

	Rate	Murder	Rape	Robbery	Aggravated Assault
Area	72.8	1.6	28.8	1.6	40.8
USA	432.8	4.7	34.7	111.6	285.6

Key Economic Data (Family income, unemployment)

	$25k-$75k	$75k-$150k	>$150k	Unemployment 03/2009	Unemployment 03/2010
Area	56.6%	23.9%	7.1%	5.5%	5.5%
USA	45.8%	29.5%	8.5%	9.0%	10.1

Key Household Data

	Population Age 0-17	Children w/Married Parents	Children w/Single Mother	Stay-at-home Mothers	Births to Single Women
Area	32.1%	81.5%	11.5%	42.7%	23.8%
USA	24.0%	65.6%	25.5%	27.9%	35.3%

Key Housing Data

	Owner Occupied	Median Year Built	Median Home Value	Home Value Growth, 2005-2010	Median List Price, 4-bedroom Home
Area	66.3%	1984	$194,600	4.7%	
USA	67.8%	1976	$187,045	3.1%	$288,846

Longview, TX
210,664

	Score	Rank
Overall	59.11	263
LDS Culture	24.65	223
Education	60.78	288
Crime	35.82	315
Economic	64.31	162
Health	32.00	329
Household	71.60	140
Housing	89.86	55

Key LDS Culture Data

	Positive	Negative	Ratio Pos:Neg	Commute>59 minutes	Commute<15 minutes
Area	1,580	69	22.9	6.2%	35.4%
USA	4,292	251	20.1	5.5%	34.1%

Key Education Data

	HS Grad	Some Coll.	College Degree	Free/Reduced Lunch	Students per Teacher
Area	82.6%	23.4%	25.8%	50.5%	13.4
USA	85.8%	22.6%	33.2%	41.2%	15.8

Key Property Crime Data (Rate per 100,000 residents)

	Rate	Burglary	Larceny, Theft	Vehicle Theft
Area	4,563.3	1,091.5	3,081.3	390.5
USA	3,413.6	806.6	2,388.0	262.7

Key Violent Crime Data (Rate per 100,000 residents)

	Rate	Murder	Rape	Robbery	Aggravated Assault
Area	634.6	7.3	47.4	139.1	440.8
USA	432.8	4.7	34.7	111.6	285.6

Key Economic Data (Family income, unemployment)

	$25k-$75k	$75k-$150k	>$150k	Unemployment 03/2009	Unemployment 03/2010
Area	48.7%	29.0%	6.1%	6.5%	7.6%
USA	45.8%	29.5%	8.5%	9.0%	10.1

Key Household Data

	Population Age 0-17	Children w/Married Parents	Children w/Single Mother	Stay-at-home Mothers	Births to Single Women
Area	25.4%	67.1%	23.3%	41.3%	37.5%
USA	24.0%	65.6%	25.5%	27.9%	35.3%

Key Housing Data

	Owner Occupied	Median Year Built	Median Home Value	Home Value Growth, 2005-2010	Median List Price, 4-bedroom Home
Area	67.1%	1975	$96,700	5.6%	
USA	67.8%	1976	$187,045	3.1%	$288,846

Longview, WA
101,254

	Score	Rank
Overall	60.65	228
LDS Culture	16.99	321
Education	71.26	169
Crime	61.54	139
Economic	69.87	88
Health	48.12	83
Household	46.30	328
Housing	74.83	283

Key LDS Culture Data

	Positive	Negative	Ratio Pos:Neg	Commute>59 minutes	Commute<15 minutes
Area	740	52	14.2	7.9%	37.6%
USA	4,292	251	20.1	5.5%	34.1%

Key Education Data

	HS Grad	Some Coll.	College Degree	Free/Reduced Lunch	Students per Teacher
Area	85.7%	30.3%	26.5%	39.9%	19.5
USA	85.8%	22.6%	33.2%	41.2%	15.8

Key Property Crime Data (Rate per 100,000 residents)

	Rate	Burglary	Larceny, Theft	Vehicle Theft	
Area	3,747.1	723.8	2,696.3	326.9	
USA	3,413.6	806.6	2,388.0	262.7	

Key Violent Crime Data (Rate per 100,000 residents)

	Rate	Murder	Rape	Robbery	Aggravated Assault
Area	292.5	2.0	92.6	61.1	136.9
USA	432.8	4.7	34.7	111.6	285.6

Key Economic Data (Family income, unemployment)

	$25k-$75k	$75k-$150k	>$150k	Unemployment 03/2009	Unemployment 03/2010
Area	49.5%	27.1%	6.1%	13.3%	13.5%
USA	45.8%	29.5%	8.5%	9.0%	10.1

Key Household Data

	Population Age 0-17	Children w/Married Parents	Children w/Single Mother	Stay-at-home Mothers	Births to Single Women
Area	24.1%	53.3%	25.5%	29.3%	54.5%
USA	24.0%	65.6%	25.5%	27.9%	35.3%

Key Housing Data

	Owner Occupied	Median Year Built	Median Home Value	Home Value Growth, 2005-2010	Median List Price, 4-bedroom Home
Area	68.1%	1971	$210,800	5.7%	
USA	67.8%	1976	$187,045	3.1%	$288,846

Los Angeles-Long Beach-Santa Ana, CA
12,872,808

	Score	Rank
Overall	58.45	280
LDS Culture	28.29	165
Education	63.54	261
Crime	54.08	178
Economic	55.09	292
Health	47.27	110
Household	73.46	122
Housing	53.10	360

Key LDS Culture Data

	Positive	Negative	Ratio Pos:Neg	Commute>59 minutes	Commute<15 minutes
Area	35,192	2068	17.0	11.0%	21.0%
USA	4,292	251	20.1	5.5%	34.1%

Key Education Data

	HS Grad	Some Coll.	College Degree	Free/Reduced Lunch	Students per Teacher
Area	76.8%	19.9%	37.0%	53.6%	18.9
USA	85.8%	22.6%	33.2%	41.2%	15.8

Key Property Crime Data (Rate per 100,000 residents)

	Rate	Burglary	Larceny, Theft	Vehicle Theft
Area	2,512.2	513.6	1,501.9	496.7
USA	3,413.6	806.6	2,388.0	262.7

Key Violent Crime Data (Rate per 100,000 residents)

	Rate	Murder	Rape	Robbery	Aggravated Assault
Area	523.8	6.8	20.2	231.2	265.5
USA	432.8	4.7	34.7	111.6	285.6

Key Economic Data (Family income, unemployment)

	$25k-$75k	$75k-$150k	>$150k	Unemployment 03/2009	Unemployment 03/2010
Area	38.1%	29.2%	16.1%	10.3%	11.7%
USA	45.8%	29.5%	8.5%	9.0%	10.1

Key Household Data

	Population Age 0-17	Children w/Married Parents	Children w/Single Mother	Stay-at-home Mothers	Births to Single Women
Area	25.8%	66.5%	23.8%	37.8%	34.5%
USA	24.0%	65.6%	25.5%	27.9%	35.3%

Key Housing Data

	Owner Occupied	Median Year Built	Median Home Value	Home Value Growth, 2005-2010	Median List Price, 4-bedroom Home
Area	51.2%	1964	$553,900	2.4%	$599,000
USA	67.8%	1976	$187,045	3.1%	$288,846

Louisville/Jefferson County, KY-IN
1,244,363

	Score	Rank
Overall	**59.60**	**253**
LDS Culture	30.69	132
Education	65.31	241
Crime	50.02	218
Economic	69.43	92
Health	33.70	304
Household	46.91	319
Housing	86.09	119

Key LDS Culture Data

	Positive	Negative	Ratio Pos:Neg	Commute>59 minutes	Commute<15 minutes
Area	5,921	402	14.7	4.1%	25.3%
USA	4,292	251	20.1	5.5%	34.1%

Key Education Data

	HS Grad	Some Coll.	College Degree	Free/Reduced Lunch	Students per Teacher
Area	87.0%	22.3%	31.1%	46.4%	16.8
USA	85.8%	22.6%	33.2%	41.2%	15.8

Key Property Crime Data (Rate per 100,000 residents)

	Rate	Burglary	Larceny, Theft	Vehicle Theft	
Area	3,584.0	848.0	2,441.0	295.0	
USA	3,413.6	806.6	2,388.0	262.7	

Key Violent Crime Data (Rate per 100,000 residents)

	Rate	Murder	Rape	Robbery	Aggravated Assault
Area	424.7	6.4	25.9	172.2	220.2
USA	432.8	4.7	34.7	111.6	285.6

Key Economic Data (Family income, unemployment)

	$25k-$75k	$75k-$150k	>$150k	Unemployment 03/2009	Unemployment 03/2010
Area	45.1%	30.7%	7.5%	10.5%	10.7%
USA	45.8%	29.5%	8.5%	9.0%	10.1

Key Household Data

	Population Age 0-17	Children w/Married Parents	Children w/Single Mother	Stay-at-home Mothers	Births to Single Women
Area	24.3%	61.8%	29.0%	22.4%	47.6%
USA	24.0%	65.6%	25.5%	27.9%	35.3%

Key Housing Data

	Owner Occupied	Median Year Built	Median Home Value	Home Value Growth, 2005-2010	Median List Price, 4-bedroom Home
Area	70.3%	1975	$147,700	2.3%	$229,900
USA	67.8%	1976	$187,045	3.1%	$288,846

Lubbock, TX
270,120

	Score	Rank
Overall	60.18	240
LDS Culture	50.81	13
Education	70.04	184
Crime	24.43	352
Economic	63.37	177
Health	31.11	343
Household	56.79	254
Housing	89.35	62

Key LDS Culture Data

	Positive	Negative	Ratio Pos:Neg	Commute>59 minutes	Commute<15 minutes
Area	1,705	62	27.5	2.9%	47.6%
USA	4,292	251	20.1	5.5%	34.1%

Key Education Data

	HS Grad	Some Coll.	College Degree	Free/Reduced Lunch	Students per Teacher
Area	83.4%	25.1%	32.8%	52.9%	13.2
USA	85.8%	22.6%	33.2%	41.2%	15.8

Key Property Crime Data (Rate per 100,000 residents)

	Rate	Burglary	Larceny, Theft	Vehicle Theft
Area	5,078.9	1,334.6	3,490.5	253.9
USA	3,413.6	806.6	2,388.0	262.7

Key Violent Crime Data (Rate per 100,000 residents)

	Rate	Murder	Rape	Robbery	Aggravated Assault
Area	841.0	3.3	40.1	115.8	681.8
USA	432.8	4.7	34.7	111.6	285.6

Key Economic Data (Family income, unemployment)

	$25k-$75k	$75k-$150k	>$150k	Unemployment 03/2009	Unemployment 03/2010
Area	46.5%	30.0%	7.5%	4.8%	5.9%
USA	45.8%	29.5%	8.5%	9.0%	10.1

Key Household Data

	Population Age 0-17	Children w/Married Parents	Children w/Single Mother	Stay-at-home Mothers	Births to Single Women
Area	25.2%	63.1%	27.8%	26.2%	42.2%
USA	24.0%	65.6%	25.5%	27.9%	35.3%

Key Housing Data

	Owner Occupied	Median Year Built	Median Home Value	Home Value Growth, 2005-2010	Median List Price, 4-bedroom Home
Area	62.5%	1974	$99,500	3.0%	
USA	67.8%	1976	$187,045	3.1%	$288,846

Lynchburg, VA
246,071

	Score	Rank
Overall	76.63	14
LDS Culture	81.87	3
Education	64.46	250
Crime	80.20	33
Economic	64.15	166
Health	36.28	281
Household	77.78	78
Housing	86.67	105

Key LDS Culture Data

	Positive	Negative	Ratio Pos:Neg	Commute>59 minutes	Commute<15 minutes
Area	1,320	17	77.6	4.1%	34.4%
USA	4,292	251	20.1	5.5%	34.1%

Key Education Data

	HS Grad	Some Coll.	College Degree	Free/Reduced Lunch	Students per Teacher
Area	82.7%	25.0%	27.6%	37.3%	15.8
USA	85.8%	22.6%	33.2%	41.2%	15.8

Key Property Crime Data (Rate per 100,000 residents)

	Rate	Burglary	Larceny, Theft	Vehicle Theft
Area	2,212.3	350.8	1,725.4	136.1
USA	3,413.6	806.6	2,388.0	262.7

Key Violent Crime Data (Rate per 100,000 residents)

	Rate	Murder	Rape	Robbery	Aggravated Assault
Area	226.5	3.3	32.7	52.3	138.2
USA	432.8	4.7	34.7	111.6	285.6

Key Economic Data (Family income, unemployment)

	$25k-$75k	$75k-$150k	>$150k	Unemployment 03/2009	Unemployment 03/2010
Area	51.8%	27.8%	5.4%	7.4%	8.4%
USA	45.8%	29.5%	8.5%	9.0%	10.1

Key Household Data

	Population Age 0-17	Children w/Married Parents	Children w/Single Mother	Stay-at-home Mothers	Births to Single Women
Area	21.5%	68.3%	23.4%	32.2%	35.7%
USA	24.0%	65.6%	25.5%	27.9%	35.3%

Key Housing Data

	Owner Occupied	Median Year Built	Median Home Value	Home Value Growth, 2005-2010	Median List Price, 4-bedroom Home
Area	72.5%	1979	$156,500	6.1%	$265,000
USA	67.8%	1976	$187,045	3.1%	$288,846

Macon, GA
235,132

	Score	Rank
Overall	51.53	359
LDS Culture	22.25	255
Education	42.60	360
Crime	36.00	313
Economic	52.14	313
Health	40.98	202
Household	46.91	320
Housing	89.51	60

Key LDS Culture Data

	Positive	Negative	Ratio Pos:Neg	Commute>59 minutes	Commute<15 minutes
Area	2,381	118	20.2	4.8%	29.1%
USA	4,292	251	20.1	5.5%	34.1%

Key Education Data

	HS Grad	Some Coll.	College Degree	Free/Reduced Lunch	Students per Teacher
Area	79.7%	21.4%	27.6%	65.4%	15.0
USA	85.8%	22.6%	33.2%	41.2%	15.8

Key Property Crime Data (Rate per 100,000 residents)

	Rate	Burglary	Larceny, Theft	Vehicle Theft
Area	5,382.2	1,326.0	3,517.3	538.9
USA	3,413.6	806.6	2,388.0	262.7

Key Violent Crime Data (Rate per 100,000 residents)

	Rate	Murder	Rape	Robbery	Aggravated Assault
Area	542.8	10.0	28.7	201.6	302.5
USA	432.8	4.7	34.7	111.6	285.6

Key Economic Data (Family income, unemployment)

	$25k-$75k	$75k-$150k	>$150k	Unemployment 03/2009	Unemployment 03/2010
Area	40.9%	24.0%	6.8%	8.4%	10.6%
USA	45.8%	29.5%	8.5%	9.0%	10.1

Key Household Data

	Population Age 0-17	Children w/Married Parents	Children w/Single Mother	Stay-at-home Mothers	Births to Single Women
Area	25.3%	54.7%	37.3%	27.9%	60.6%
USA	24.0%	65.6%	25.5%	27.9%	35.3%

Key Housing Data

	Owner Occupied	Median Year Built	Median Home Value	Home Value Growth, 2005-2010	Median List Price, 4-bedroom Home
Area	65.1%	1980	$121,400	2.5%	$195,000
USA	67.8%	1976	$187,045	3.1%	$288,846

Madera-Chowchilla, CA
148,333

	Score	Rank
Overall	**58.53**	**276**
LDS Culture	17.46	316
Education	67.32	217
Crime	58.27	154
Economic	44.02	354
Health	48.59	64
Household	60.49	222
Housing	79.16	224

Key LDS Culture Data

	Positive	Negative	Ratio Pos:Neg	Commute>59 minutes	Commute<15 minutes
Area	3,528	239	14.8	7.7%	36.7%
USA	4,292	251	20.1	5.5%	34.1%

Key Education Data

	HS Grad	Some Coll.	College Degree	Free/Reduced Lunch	Students per Teacher
Area	68.6%	25.8%	19.5%	64.0%	18.0
USA	85.8%	22.6%	33.2%	41.2%	15.8

Key Property Crime Data (Rate per 100,000 residents)

	Rate	Burglary	Larceny, Theft	Vehicle Theft	
Area	2,186.9	700.3	1,145.5	341.1	
USA	3,413.6	806.6	2,388.0	262.7	

Key Violent Crime Data (Rate per 100,000 residents)

	Rate	Murder	Rape	Robbery	Aggravated Assault
Area	499.5	6.7	24.8	124.2	343.8
USA	432.8	4.7	34.7	111.6	285.6

Key Economic Data (Family income, unemployment)

	$25k-$75k	$75k-$150k	>$150k	Unemployment 03/2009	Unemployment 03/2010
Area	47.4%	23.6%	8.0%	14.8%	17.5%
USA	45.8%	29.5%	8.5%	9.0%	10.1

Key Household Data

	Population Age 0-17	Children w/Married Parents	Children w/Single Mother	Stay-at-home Mothers	Births to Single Women
Area	27.6%	67.5%	22.3%	38.5%	40.6%
USA	24.0%	65.6%	25.5%	27.9%	35.3%

Key Housing Data

	Owner Occupied	Median Year Built	Median Home Value	Home Value Growth, 2005-2010	Median List Price, 4-bedroom Home
Area	59.6%	1987	$292,500	-0.1%	$220,000
USA	67.8%	1976	$187,045	3.1%	$288,846

Madison, WI
561,505

	Score	Rank
Overall	72.15	30
LDS Culture	21.65	267
Education	94.63	11
Crime	73.13	63
Economic	78.71	20
Health	39.16	230
Household	75.93	95
Housing	79.45	221

Key LDS Culture Data

	Positive	Negative	Ratio Pos:Neg	Commute>59 minutes	Commute<15 minutes
Area	2,918	307	9.5	3.8%	31.7%
USA	4,292	251	20.1	5.5%	34.1%

Key Education Data

	HS Grad	Some Coll.	College Degree	Free/Reduced Lunch	Students per Teacher
Area	94.0%	21.2%	48.7%	23.1%	13.6
USA	85.8%	22.6%	33.2%	41.2%	15.8

Key Property Crime Data (Rate per 100,000 residents)

	Rate	Burglary	Larceny, Theft	Vehicle Theft	
Area	2,802.1	582.1	2,084.0	136.1	
USA	3,413.6	806.6	2,388.0	262.7	

Key Violent Crime Data (Rate per 100,000 residents)

	Rate	Murder	Rape	Robbery	Aggravated Assault
Area	241.4	2.5	19.9	80.9	138.1
USA	432.8	4.7	34.7	111.6	285.6

Key Economic Data (Family income, unemployment)

	$25k-$75k	$75k-$150k	>$150k	Unemployment 03/2009	Unemployment 03/2010
Area	36.8%	42.1%	11.9%	6.4%	7.0%
USA	45.8%	29.5%	8.5%	9.0%	10.1

Key Household Data

	Population Age 0-17	Children w/Married Parents	Children w/Single Mother	Stay-at-home Mothers	Births to Single Women
Area	22.0%	73.0%	19.2%	17.8%	23.4%
USA	24.0%	65.6%	25.5%	27.9%	35.3%

Key Housing Data

	Owner Occupied	Median Year Built	Median Home Value	Home Value Growth, 2005-2010	Median List Price, 4-bedroom Home
Area	64.6%	1978	$232,600	2.5%	$284,900
USA	67.8%	1976	$187,045	3.1%	$288,846

Manchester-Nashua, NH
402,042

	Score	Rank
Overall	63.82	165
LDS Culture	21.94	261
Education	82.21	57
Crime	56.03	163
Economic	77.49	24
Health	27.89	352
Household	75.93	96
Housing	67.73	335

Key LDS Culture Data

	Positive	Negative	Ratio Pos:Neg	Commute>59 minutes	Commute<15 minutes
Area	6,033	243	24.8	10.0%	28.0%
USA	4,292	251	20.1	5.5%	34.1%

Key Education Data

	HS Grad	Some Coll.	College Degree	Free/Reduced Lunch	Students per Teacher
Area	89.8%	18.1%	44.1%	19.6%	14.1
USA	85.8%	22.6%	33.2%	41.2%	15.8

Key Property Crime Data (Rate per 100,000 residents)

	Rate	Burglary	Larceny, Theft	Vehicle Theft	
Area		494.7	1,570.1	213.7	
USA	3,413.6	806.6	2,388.0	262.7	

Key Violent Crime Data (Rate per 100,000 residents)

	Rate	Murder	Rape	Robbery	Aggravated Assault
Area		2.6	23.0	101.4	282.6
USA	432.8	4.7	34.7	111.6	285.6

Key Economic Data (Family income, unemployment)

	$25k-$75k	$75k-$150k	>$150k	Unemployment 03/2009	Unemployment 03/2010
Area	35.4%	39.3%	15.8%	6.2%	7.3%
USA	45.8%	29.5%	8.5%	9.0%	10.1

Key Household Data

	Population Age 0-17	Children w/Married Parents	Children w/Single Mother	Stay-at-home Mothers	Births to Single Women
Area	24.3%	70.4%	20.1%	24.9%	31.7%
USA	24.0%	65.6%	25.5%	27.9%	35.3%

Key Housing Data

	Owner Occupied	Median Year Built	Median Home Value	Home Value Growth, 2005-2010	Median List Price, 4-bedroom Home
Area	69.0%	1978	$277,800	0.2%	$350,000
USA	67.8%	1976	$187,045	3.1%	$288,846

Mansfield, OH
124,999

	Score	Rank
Overall	66.25	116
LDS Culture	34.48	84
Education	66.61	226
Crime	68.95	82
Economic	64.26	164
Health	42.19	178
Household	74.07	116
Housing	74.25	293

Key LDS Culture Data

	Positive	Negative	Ratio Pos:Neg	Commute>59 minutes	Commute<15 minutes
Area	2,073	109	19.0	7.4%	41.2%
USA	4,292	251	20.1	5.5%	34.1%

Key Education Data

	HS Grad	Some Coll.	College Degree	Free/Reduced Lunch	Students per Teacher
Area	84.6%	21.4%	22.5%		15.8
USA	85.8%	22.6%	33.2%	41.2%	15.8

Key Property Crime Data (Rate per 100,000 residents)

	Rate	Burglary	Larceny, Theft	Vehicle Theft
Area	4,094.4	1,125.9	2,856.0	112.5
USA	3,413.6	806.6	2,388.0	262.7

Key Violent Crime Data (Rate per 100,000 residents)

	Rate	Murder	Rape	Robbery	Aggravated Assault
Area	195.5	2.4	39.1	76.6	77.4
USA	432.8	4.7	34.7	111.6	285.6

Key Economic Data (Family income, unemployment)

	$25k-$75k	$75k-$150k	>$150k	Unemployment 03/2009	Unemployment 03/2010
Area	55.4%	25.0%	5.8%	13.2%	13.4%
USA	45.8%	29.5%	8.5%	9.0%	10.1

Key Household Data

	Population Age 0-17	Children w/Married Parents	Children w/Single Mother	Stay-at-home Mothers	Births to Single Women
Area	22.7%	66.7%	25.6%	28.9%	26.8%
USA	24.0%	65.6%	25.5%	27.9%	35.3%

Key Housing Data

	Owner Occupied	Median Year Built	Median Home Value	Home Value Growth, 2005-2010	Median List Price, 4-bedroom Home
Area	70.5%	1962	$115,500	-1.0%	
USA	67.8%	1976	$187,045	3.1%	$288,846

McAllen-Edinburg-Mission, TX
726,604

	Score	Rank
Overall	61.14	218
LDS Culture	27.15	180
Education	49.01	354
Crime	51.21	206
Economic	45.80	351
Health	32.00	330
Household	90.12	16
Housing	96.72	8

Key LDS Culture Data

	Positive	Negative	Ratio Pos:Neg	Commute>59 minutes	Commute<15 minutes
Area	2,591	125	20.7	4.2%	30.1%
USA	4,292	251	20.1	5.5%	34.1%

Key Education Data

	HS Grad	Some Coll.	College Degree	Free/Reduced Lunch	Students per Teacher
Area	58.3%	15.5%	18.5%	19.8%	15.3
USA	85.8%	22.6%	33.2%	41.2%	15.8

Key Property Crime Data (Rate per 100,000 residents)

	Rate	Burglary	Larceny, Theft	Vehicle Theft	
Area	4,616.2	1,019.0	3,204.6	392.6	
USA	3,413.6	806.6	2,388.0	262.7	

Key Violent Crime Data (Rate per 100,000 residents)

	Rate	Murder	Rape	Robbery	Aggravated Assault
Area	360.1	7.0	24.1	91.5	237.5
USA	432.8	4.7	34.7	111.6	285.6

Key Economic Data (Family income, unemployment)

	$25k-$75k	$75k-$150k	>$150k	Unemployment 03/2009	Unemployment 03/2010
Area	41.6%	15.4%	3.8%	9.8%	11.6%
USA	45.8%	29.5%	8.5%	9.0%	10.1

Key Household Data

	Population Age 0-17	Children w/Married Parents	Children w/Single Mother	Stay-at-home Mothers	Births to Single Women
Area	35.9%	68.1%	28.2%	45.7%	28.9%
USA	24.0%	65.6%	25.5%	27.9%	35.3%

Key Housing Data

	Owner Occupied	Median Year Built	Median Home Value	Home Value Growth, 2005-2010	Median List Price, 4-bedroom Home
Area	69.4%	1991	$72,300	2.9%	
USA	67.8%	1976	$187,045	3.1%	$288,846

Medford, OR
201,138

	Score	Rank
Overall	68.23	77
LDS Culture	30.69	131
Education	76.19	114
Crime	75.74	47
Economic	77.21	28
Health	44.08	157
Household	59.88	228
Housing	73.76	301

Key LDS Culture Data

	Positive	Negative	Ratio Pos:Neg	Commute>59 minutes	Commute<15 minutes
Area	1,480	75	19.7	3.1%	40.8%
USA	4,292	251	20.1	5.5%	34.1%

Key Education Data

	HS Grad	Some Coll.	College Degree	Free/Reduced Lunch	Students per Teacher
Area	89.9%	28.7%	31.6%	40.4%	21.1
USA	85.8%	22.6%	33.2%	41.2%	15.8

Key Property Crime Data (Rate per 100,000 residents)

	Rate	Burglary	Larceny, Theft	Vehicle Theft
Area	2,654.7	354.2	2,183.0	117.6
USA	3,413.6	806.6	2,388.0	262.7

Key Violent Crime Data (Rate per 100,000 residents)

	Rate	Murder	Rape	Robbery	Aggravated Assault
Area	228.7	1.0	36.7	33.7	157.2
USA	432.8	4.7	34.7	111.6	285.6

Key Economic Data (Family income, unemployment)

	$25k-$75k	$75k-$150k	>$150k	Unemployment 03/2009	Unemployment 03/2010
Area	51.0%	22.7%	5.6%	14.3%	13.6%
USA	45.8%	29.5%	8.5%	9.0%	10.1

Key Household Data

	Population Age 0-17	Children w/Married Parents	Children w/Single Mother	Stay-at-home Mothers	Births to Single Women
Area	21.5%	63.0%	26.7%	25.1%	38.8%
USA	24.0%	65.6%	25.5%	27.9%	35.3%

Key Housing Data

	Owner Occupied	Median Year Built	Median Home Value	Home Value Growth, 2005-2010	Median List Price, 4-bedroom Home
Area	61.8%	1983	$285,000	2.8%	$369,000
USA	67.8%	1976	$187,045	3.1%	$288,846

Memphis, TN-MS-AR
1,288,506

	Score	Rank
Overall	52.14	356
LDS Culture	25.93	196
Education	59.60	299
Crime	5.35	361
Economic	56.48	278
Health	47.00	116
Household	49.38	303
Housing	90.58	46

Key LDS Culture Data

	Positive	Negative	Ratio Pos:Neg	Commute>59 minutes	Commute<15 minutes
Area	6,075	314	19.3	4.4%	24.1%
USA	4,292	251	20.1	5.5%	34.1%

Key Education Data

	HS Grad	Some Coll.	College Degree	Free/Reduced Lunch	Students per Teacher
Area	84.1%	24.0%	31.2%	58.7%	16.6
USA	85.8%	22.6%	33.2%	41.2%	15.8

Key Property Crime Data (Rate per 100,000 residents)

	Rate	Burglary	Larceny, Theft	Vehicle Theft
Area	5,748.5	1,652.0	3,570.0	526.5
USA	3,413.6	806.6	2,388.0	262.7

Key Violent Crime Data (Rate per 100,000 residents)

	Rate	Murder	Rape	Robbery	Aggravated Assault
Area	1,207.3	12.6	40.4	408.5	745.8
USA	432.8	4.7	34.7	111.6	285.6

Key Economic Data (Family income, unemployment)

	$25k-$75k	$75k-$150k	>$150k	Unemployment 03/2009	Unemployment 03/2010
Area	42.9%	27.1%	10.0%	9.6%	10.6%
USA	45.8%	29.5%	8.5%	9.0%	10.1

Key Household Data

	Population Age 0-17	Children w/Married Parents	Children w/Single Mother	Stay-at-home Mothers	Births to Single Women
Area	27.1%	53.6%	38.0%	28.4%	50.3%
USA	24.0%	65.6%	25.5%	27.9%	35.3%

Key Housing Data

	Owner Occupied	Median Year Built	Median Home Value	Home Value Growth, 2005-2010	Median List Price, 4-bedroom Home
Area	65.7%	1982	$141,300	2.1%	$219,900
USA	67.8%	1976	$187,045	3.1%	$288,846

Merced, CA
246,117

	Score	Rank
Overall	57.82	289
LDS Culture	28.03	171
Education	67.87	209
Crime	40.87	283
Economic	40.13	358
Health	48.59	65
Household	64.81	182
Housing	80.45	205

Key LDS Culture Data

	Positive	Negative	Ratio Pos:Neg	Commute>59 minutes	Commute<15 minutes
Area	1,260	58	21.7	12.7%	37.1%
USA	4,292	251	20.1	5.5%	34.1%

Key Education Data

	HS Grad	Some Coll.	College Degree	Free/Reduced Lunch	Students per Teacher
Area	66.3%	23.0%	19.5%	69.9%	17.9
USA	85.8%	22.6%	33.2%	41.2%	15.8

Key Property Crime Data (Rate per 100,000 residents)

	Rate	Burglary	Larceny, Theft	Vehicle Theft
Area	3,625.2	910.8	2,273.2	441.1
USA	3,413.6	806.6	2,388.0	262.7

Key Violent Crime Data (Rate per 100,000 residents)

	Rate	Murder	Rape	Robbery	Aggravated Assault
Area	619.1	8.4	28.1	107.3	475.3
USA	432.8	4.7	34.7	111.6	285.6

Key Economic Data (Family income, unemployment)

	$25k-$75k	$75k-$150k	>$150k	Unemployment 03/2009	Unemployment 03/2010
Area	44.1%	23.4%	5.6%	19.0%	22.1%
USA	45.8%	29.5%	8.5%	9.0%	10.1

Key Household Data

	Population Age 0-17	Children w/Married Parents	Children w/Single Mother	Stay-at-home Mothers	Births to Single Women
Area	31.2%	61.6%	27.5%	38.2%	38.1%
USA	24.0%	65.6%	25.5%	27.9%	35.3%

Key Housing Data

	Owner Occupied	Median Year Built	Median Home Value	Home Value Growth, 2005-2010	Median List Price, 4-bedroom Home
Area	53.2%	1982	$239,800	-6.0%	$149,000
USA	67.8%	1976	$187,045	3.1%	$288,846

Miami-Fort Lauderdale-Pompano Beach, FL
5,414,772

	Score	Rank
Overall	**55.71**	**325**
LDS Culture	25.18	209
Education	57.63	311
Crime	29.19	337
Economic	56.59	276
Health	54.20	16
Household	59.26	231
Housing	75.19	281

Key LDS Culture Data

	Positive	Negative	Ratio Pos:Neg	Commute>59 minutes	Commute<15 minutes
Area	20,812	886	23.5	8.5%	19.9%
USA	4,292	251	20.1	5.5%	34.1%

Key Education Data

	HS Grad	Some Coll.	College Degree	Free/Reduced Lunch	Students per Teacher
Area	82.7%	18.1%	37.5%	50.4%	15.5
USA	85.8%	22.6%	33.2%	41.2%	15.8

Key Property Crime Data (Rate per 100,000 residents)

	Rate	Burglary	Larceny, Theft	Vehicle Theft	
Area	4,762.9	1,018.5	3,245.0	499.4	
USA	3,413.6	806.6	2,388.0	262.7	

Key Violent Crime Data (Rate per 100,000 residents)

	Rate	Murder	Rape	Robbery	Aggravated Assault
Area	765.4	7.6	29.5	276.9	451.5
USA	432.8	4.7	34.7	111.6	285.6

Key Economic Data (Family income, unemployment)

	$25k-$75k	$75k-$150k	>$150k	Unemployment 03/2009	Unemployment 03/2010
Area	43.4%	26.6%	11.8%	9.2%	11.5%
USA	45.8%	29.5%	8.5%	9.0%	10.1

Key Household Data

	Population Age 0-17	Children w/Married Parents	Children w/Single Mother	Stay-at-home Mothers	Births to Single Women
Area	22.2%	61.6%	29.3%	27.8%	35.9%
USA	24.0%	65.6%	25.5%	27.9%	35.3%

Key Housing Data

	Owner Occupied	Median Year Built	Median Home Value	Home Value Growth, 2005-2010	Median List Price, 4-bedroom Home
Area	66.9%	1980	$275,500	2.8%	$356,000
USA	67.8%	1976	$187,045	3.1%	$288,846

Michigan City-La Porte, IN
110,888

	Score	Rank
Overall	59.50	257
LDS Culture	19.12	297
Education	71.42	167
Crime	69.21	80
Economic	67.87	113
Health	34.59	298
Household	43.83	343
Housing	75.49	277

Key LDS Culture Data

	Positive	Negative	Ratio Pos:Neg	Commute>59 minutes	Commute<15 minutes
Area	2,886	248	11.6	8.4%	36.6%
USA	4,292	251	20.1	5.5%	34.1%

Key Education Data

	HS Grad	Some Coll.	College Degree	Free/Reduced Lunch	Students per Teacher
Area	86.3%	19.9%	25.2%	43.6%	18.1
USA	85.8%	22.6%	33.2%	41.2%	15.8

Key Property Crime Data (Rate per 100,000 residents)

	Rate	Burglary	Larceny, Theft	Vehicle Theft	
Area	4,045.6	806.9	3,003.4	235.2	
USA	3,413.6	806.6	2,388.0	262.7	

Key Violent Crime Data (Rate per 100,000 residents)

	Rate	Murder	Rape	Robbery	Aggravated Assault
Area	195.1	4.6	25.5	87.5	77.5
USA	432.8	4.7	34.7	111.6	285.6

Key Economic Data (Family income, unemployment)

	$25k-$75k	$75k-$150k	>$150k	Unemployment 03/2009	Unemployment 03/2010
Area	50.5%	29.0%	4.7%	12.3%	13.2%
USA	45.8%	29.5%	8.5%	9.0%	10.1

Key Household Data

	Population Age 0-17	Children w/Married Parents	Children w/Single Mother	Stay-at-home Mothers	Births to Single Women
Area	22.8%	62.9%	23.7%	18.5%	72.4%
USA	24.0%	65.6%	25.5%	27.9%	35.3%

Key Housing Data

	Owner Occupied	Median Year Built	Median Home Value	Home Value Growth, 2005-2010	Median List Price, 4-bedroom Home
Area	75.0%	1965	$120,300	2.4%	
USA	67.8%	1976	$187,045	3.1%	$288,846

Midland, TX
129,494

	Score	Rank
Overall	66.14	123
LDS Culture	31.21	121
Education	59.03	305
Crime	53.55	183
Economic	73.15	57
Health	32.00	331
Household	87.04	28
Housing	88.11	81

Key LDS Culture Data

	Positive	Negative	Ratio Pos:Neg	Commute>59 minutes	Commute<15 minutes
Area	1,210	79	15.3	3.8%	39.8%
USA	4,292	251	20.1	5.5%	34.1%

Key Education Data

	HS Grad	Some Coll.	College Degree	Free/Reduced Lunch	Students per Teacher
Area	82.3%	26.6%	27.4%	46.8%	15.1
USA	85.8%	22.6%	33.2%	41.2%	15.8

Key Property Crime Data (Rate per 100,000 residents)

	Rate	Burglary	Larceny, Theft	Vehicle Theft
Area	3,254.6	833.8	2,276.1	144.7
USA	3,413.6	806.6	2,388.0	262.7

Key Violent Crime Data (Rate per 100,000 residents)

	Rate	Murder	Rape	Robbery	Aggravated Assault
Area	405.2	3.1	55.5	78.2	268.3
USA	432.8	4.7	34.7	111.6	285.6

Key Economic Data (Family income, unemployment)

	$25k-$75k	$75k-$150k	>$150k	Unemployment 03/2009	Unemployment 03/2010
Area	40.2%	32.4%	15.3%	4.8%	5.7%
USA	45.8%	29.5%	8.5%	9.0%	10.1

Key Household Data

	Population Age 0-17	Children w/Married Parents	Children w/Single Mother	Stay-at-home Mothers	Births to Single Women
Area	28.0%	69.7%	24.8%	31.8%	19.6%
USA	24.0%	65.6%	25.5%	27.9%	35.3%

Key Housing Data

	Owner Occupied	Median Year Built	Median Home Value	Home Value Growth, 2005-2010	Median List Price, 4-bedroom Home
Area	70.4%	1976	$136,500	11.5%	
USA	67.8%	1976	$187,045	3.1%	$288,846

Milwaukee-Waukesha-West Allis, WI
1,549,308

	Score	Rank
Overall	54.25	339
LDS Culture	16.18	327
Education	71.98	160
Crime	43.16	266
Economic	69.32	93
Health	28.48	351
Household	51.85	291
Housing	66.91	337

Key LDS Culture Data

	Positive	Negative	Ratio Pos:Neg	Commute>59 minutes	Commute<15 minutes
Area	7,137	859	8.3	3.6%	27.9%
USA	4,292	251	20.1	5.5%	34.1%

Key Education Data

	HS Grad	Some Coll.	College Degree	Free/Reduced Lunch	Students per Teacher
Area	88.9%	22.4%	38.1%	38.5%	16.7
USA	85.8%	22.6%	33.2%	41.2%	15.8

Key Property Crime Data (Rate per 100,000 residents)

	Rate	Burglary	Larceny, Theft	Vehicle Theft
Area	3,829.3	608.0	2,739.7	481.6
USA	3,413.6	806.6	2,388.0	262.7

Key Violent Crime Data (Rate per 100,000 residents)

	Rate	Murder	Rape	Robbery	Aggravated Assault
Area	544.7	4.9	20.3	235.3	284.2
USA	432.8	4.7	34.7	111.6	285.6

Key Economic Data (Family income, unemployment)

	$25k-$75k	$75k-$150k	>$150k	Unemployment 03/2009	Unemployment 03/2010
Area	40.6%	36.0%	10.5%	8.9%	9.8%
USA	45.8%	29.5%	8.5%	9.0%	10.1

Key Household Data

	Population Age 0-17	Children w/Married Parents	Children w/Single Mother	Stay-at-home Mothers	Births to Single Women
Area	25.0%	62.0%	29.9%	23.1%	39.4%
USA	24.0%	65.6%	25.5%	27.9%	35.3%

Key Housing Data

	Owner Occupied	Median Year Built	Median Home Value	Home Value Growth, 2005-2010	Median List Price, 4-bedroom Home
Area	63.8%	1961	$212,200	2.5%	$279,900
USA	67.8%	1976	$187,045	3.1%	$288,846

Minneapolis-St. Paul-Bloomington, MN-WI
3,229,878

	Score	Rank
Overall	67.95	85
LDS Culture	12.32	350
Education	96.75	7
Crime	55.79	167
Economic	79.60	16
Health	36.46	275
Household	75.93	97
Housing	78.86	231

Key LDS Culture Data

	Positive	Negative	Ratio Pos:Neg	Commute>59 minutes	Commute<15 minutes
Area	11,771	844	13.9	5.2%	25.5%
USA	4,292	251	20.1	5.5%	34.1%

Key Education Data

	HS Grad	Some Coll.	College Degree	Free/Reduced Lunch	Students per Teacher
Area	92.7%	22.2%	46.5%	29.1%	17.2
USA	85.8%	22.6%	33.2%	41.2%	15.8

Key Property Crime Data (Rate per 100,000 residents)

	Rate	Burglary	Larceny, Theft	Vehicle Theft	
Area	3,272.6	576.4	2,452.9	243.3	
USA	3,413.6	806.6	2,388.0	262.7	

Key Violent Crime Data (Rate per 100,000 residents)

	Rate	Murder	Rape	Robbery	Aggravated Assault
Area		2.7		116.9	171.2
USA	432.8	4.7	34.7	111.6	285.6

Key Economic Data (Family income, unemployment)

	$25k-$75k	$75k-$150k	>$150k	Unemployment 03/2009	Unemployment 03/2010
Area	36.0%	39.6%	16.1%	8.4%	7.8%
USA	45.8%	29.5%	8.5%	9.0%	10.1

Key Household Data

	Population Age 0-17	Children w/Married Parents	Children w/Single Mother	Stay-at-home Mothers	Births to Single Women
Area	25.1%	72.2%	19.2%	21.7%	27.9%
USA	24.0%	65.6%	25.5%	27.9%	35.3%

Key Housing Data

	Owner Occupied	Median Year Built	Median Home Value	Home Value Growth, 2005-2010	Median List Price, 4-bedroom Home
Area	73.8%	1978	$247,500	-0.1%	$285,000
USA	67.8%	1976	$187,045	3.1%	$288,846

Missoula, MT
107,320

	Score	Rank
Overall	67.36	97
LDS Culture	26.65	185
Education	83.72	44
Crime	68.89	84
Economic	66.87	125
Health	42.61	174
Household	64.20	188
Housing	79.01	226

Key LDS Culture Data
	Positive	Negative	Ratio Pos:Neg	Commute>59 minutes	Commute<15 minutes
Area	701	69	10.2	2.8%	45.5%
USA	4,292	251	20.1	5.5%	34.1%

Key Education Data
	HS Grad	Some Coll.	College Degree	Free/Reduced Lunch	Students per Teacher
Area	93.0%	23.1%	45.1%	33.5%	15.2
USA	85.8%	22.6%	33.2%	41.2%	15.8

Key Property Crime Data (Rate per 100,000 residents)
	Rate	Burglary	Larceny, Theft	Vehicle Theft
Area	2,914.5	337.0	2,428.1	149.4
USA	3,413.6	806.6	2,388.0	262.7

Key Violent Crime Data (Rate per 100,000 residents)
	Rate	Murder	Rape	Robbery	Aggravated Assault
Area	275.4	1.9	28.9	22.4	222.2
USA	432.8	4.7	34.7	111.6	285.6

Key Economic Data (Family income, unemployment)
	$25k-$75k	$75k-$150k	>$150k	Unemployment 03/2009	Unemployment 03/2010
Area	48.4%	28.8%	9.1%	6.1%	7.7%
USA	45.8%	29.5%	8.5%	9.0%	10.1

Key Household Data
	Population Age 0-17	Children w/Married Parents	Children w/Single Mother	Stay-at-home Mothers	Births to Single Women
Area	20.9%	71.7%	20.6%	25.6%	53.7%
USA	24.0%	65.6%	25.5%	27.9%	35.3%

Key Housing Data
	Owner Occupied	Median Year Built	Median Home Value	Home Value Growth, 2005-2010	Median List Price, 4-bedroom Home
Area	62.9%	1979	$248,300	4.7%	
USA	67.8%	1976	$187,045	3.1%	$288,846

Mobile, AL
406,309

	Score	Rank
Overall	53.84	344
LDS Culture	28.72	158
Education	48.16	355
Crime	41.14	279
Economic	48.47	338
Health	32.21	321
Household	54.32	278
Housing	92.22	32

Key LDS Culture Data

	Positive	Negative	Ratio Pos:Neg	Commute>59 minutes	Commute<15 minutes
Area	2,610	116	22.5	5.2%	23.0%
USA	4,292	251	20.1	5.5%	34.1%

Key Education Data

	HS Grad	Some Coll.	College Degree	Free/Reduced Lunch	Students per Teacher
Area	83.4%	21.3%	26.9%	63.0%	15.3
USA	85.8%	22.6%	33.2%	41.2%	15.8

Key Property Crime Data (Rate per 100,000 residents)

	Rate	Burglary	Larceny, Theft	Vehicle Theft
Area	4,887.4	1,269.4	3,179.2	438.9
USA	3,413.6	806.6	2,388.0	262.7

Key Violent Crime Data (Rate per 100,000 residents)

	Rate	Murder	Rape	Robbery	Aggravated Assault
Area	477.6	16.0	16.0	292.8	152.8
USA	432.8	4.7	34.7	111.6	285.6

Key Economic Data (Family income, unemployment)

	$25k-$75k	$75k-$150k	>$150k	Unemployment 03/2009	Unemployment 03/2010
Area	46.5%	25.0%	6.2%	9.2%	11.7%
USA	45.8%	29.5%	8.5%	9.0%	10.1

Key Household Data

	Population Age 0-17	Children w/Married Parents	Children w/Single Mother	Stay-at-home Mothers	Births to Single Women
Area	26.3%	58.5%	34.3%	32.9%	43.6%
USA	24.0%	65.6%	25.5%	27.9%	35.3%

Key Housing Data

	Owner Occupied	Median Year Built	Median Home Value	Home Value Growth, 2005-2010	Median List Price, 4-bedroom Home
Area	68.7%	1977	$125,700	6.3%	$220,000
USA	67.8%	1976	$187,045	3.1%	$288,846

Modesto, CA
510,694

	Score	Rank
Overall	**59.99**	**244**
LDS Culture	15.15	335
Education	68.64	201
Crime	40.00	289
Economic	50.53	324
Health	48.59	66
Household	80.25	65
Housing	81.52	190

Key LDS Culture Data

	Positive	Negative	Ratio Pos:Neg	Commute>59 minutes	Commute<15 minutes
Area	3,189	186	17.1	11.8%	33.4%
USA	4,292	251	20.1	5.5%	34.1%

Key Education Data

	HS Grad	Some Coll.	College Degree	Free/Reduced Lunch	Students per Teacher
Area	75.1%	25.9%	21.7%	54.5%	18.3
USA	85.8%	22.6%	33.2%	41.2%	15.8

Key Property Crime Data (Rate per 100,000 residents)

	Rate	Burglary	Larceny, Theft	Vehicle Theft
Area	4,483.2	1,092.1	2,627.3	763.8
USA	3,413.6	806.6	2,388.0	262.7

Key Violent Crime Data (Rate per 100,000 residents)

	Rate	Murder	Rape	Robbery	Aggravated Assault
Area	547.2	6.0	27.3	156.7	357.3
USA	432.8	4.7	34.7	111.6	285.6

Key Economic Data (Family income, unemployment)

	$25k-$75k	$75k-$150k	>$150k	Unemployment 03/2009	Unemployment 03/2010
Area	45.6%	28.4%	8.3%	16.5%	19.2%
USA	45.8%	29.5%	8.5%	9.0%	10.1

Key Household Data

	Population Age 0-17	Children w/Married Parents	Children w/Single Mother	Stay-at-home Mothers	Births to Single Women
Area	28.4%	70.1%	21.0%	32.0%	35.3%
USA	24.0%	65.6%	25.5%	27.9%	35.3%

Key Housing Data

	Owner Occupied	Median Year Built	Median Home Value	Home Value Growth, 2005-2010	Median List Price, 4-bedroom Home
Area	62.2%	1981	$276,100	-4.3%	$190,000
USA	67.8%	1976	$187,045	3.1%	$288,846

Monroe, LA
171,708

	Score	Rank
Overall	60.10	241
LDS Culture	29.66	146
Education	51.24	344
Crime	39.29	293
Economic	51.58	314
Health	58.02	7
Household	68.52	160
Housing	87.04	96

Key LDS Culture Data

	Positive	Negative	Ratio Pos:Neg	Commute>59 minutes	Commute<15 minutes
Area	1,508	64	23.6	3.9%	34.9%
USA	4,292	251	20.1	5.5%	34.1%

Key Education Data

	HS Grad	Some Coll.	College Degree	Free/Reduced Lunch	Students per Teacher
Area	83.4%	22.3%	27.3%	60.7%	14.5
USA	85.8%	22.6%	33.2%	41.2%	15.8

Key Property Crime Data (Rate per 100,000 residents)

	Rate	Burglary	Larceny, Theft	Vehicle Theft	
Area	5,133.1	1,416.4	3,518.5	198.2	
USA	3,413.6	806.6	2,388.0	262.7	

Key Violent Crime Data (Rate per 100,000 residents)

	Rate	Murder	Rape	Robbery	Aggravated Assault
Area	493.8	6.3	16.7	111.8	359.0
USA	432.8	4.7	34.7	111.6	285.6

Key Economic Data (Family income, unemployment)

	$25k-$75k	$75k-$150k	>$150k	Unemployment 03/2009	Unemployment 03/2010
Area	43.6%	24.9%	7.1%	6.4%	6.6%
USA	45.8%	29.5%	8.5%	9.0%	10.1

Key Household Data

	Population Age 0-17	Children w/Married Parents	Children w/Single Mother	Stay-at-home Mothers	Births to Single Women
Area	25.9%	56.5%	38.1%	25.8%	28.8%
USA	24.0%	65.6%	25.5%	27.9%	35.3%

Key Housing Data

	Owner Occupied	Median Year Built	Median Home Value	Home Value Growth, 2005-2010	Median List Price, 4-bedroom Home
Area	63.7%	1980	$115,100	3.3%	
USA	67.8%	1976	$187,045	3.1%	$288,846

Monroe, MI
152,949

	Score	Rank
Overall	62.26	188
LDS Culture	14.52	340
Education	71.81	163
Crime	75.76	46
Economic	66.81	126
Health	36.88	268
Household	59.88	229
Housing	73.57	303

Key LDS Culture Data

	Positive	Negative	Ratio Pos:Neg	Commute>59 minutes	Commute<15 minutes
Area	5,976	523	11.4	5.8%	28.6%
USA	4,292	251	20.1	5.5%	34.1%

Key Education Data

	HS Grad	Some Coll.	College Degree	Free/Reduced Lunch	Students per Teacher
Area	88.5%	23.0%	25.0%	23.9%	18.0
USA	85.8%	22.6%	33.2%	41.2%	15.8

Key Property Crime Data (Rate per 100,000 residents)

	Rate	Burglary	Larceny, Theft	Vehicle Theft
Area	2,478.4	610.8	1,733.2	134.4
USA	3,413.6	806.6	2,388.0	262.7

Key Violent Crime Data (Rate per 100,000 residents)

	Rate	Murder	Rape	Robbery	Aggravated Assault
Area	246.7	1.3	56.8	40.5	148.1
USA	432.8	4.7	34.7	111.6	285.6

Key Economic Data (Family income, unemployment)

	$25k-$75k	$75k-$150k	>$150k	Unemployment 03/2009	Unemployment 03/2010
Area	43.8%	36.4%	6.8%	13.8%	16.0%
USA	45.8%	29.5%	8.5%	9.0%	10.1

Key Household Data

	Population Age 0-17	Children w/Married Parents	Children w/Single Mother	Stay-at-home Mothers	Births to Single Women
Area	23.6%	66.5%	27.1%	22.1%	42.9%
USA	24.0%	65.6%	25.5%	27.9%	35.3%

Key Housing Data

	Owner Occupied	Median Year Built	Median Home Value	Home Value Growth, 2005-2010	Median List Price, 4-bedroom Home
Area	79.7%	1974	$169,400	-3.6%	
USA	67.8%	1976	$187,045	3.1%	$288,846

Montgomery, AL
369,407

	Score	Rank
Overall	60.86	223
LDS Culture	33.17	103
Education	60.06	294
Crime	52.61	194
Economic	58.09	257
Health	44.48	154
Household	46.91	321
Housing	94.96	12

Key LDS Culture Data

	Positive	Negative	Ratio Pos:Neg	Commute>59 minutes	Commute<15 minutes
Area	2,050	63	32.5	3.8%	26.1%
USA	4,292	251	20.1	5.5%	34.1%

Key Education Data

	HS Grad	Some Coll.	College Degree	Free/Reduced Lunch	Students per Teacher
Area	84.1%	22.5%	32.3%	57.4%	15.4
USA	85.8%	22.6%	33.2%	41.2%	15.8

Key Property Crime Data (Rate per 100,000 residents)

	Rate	Burglary	Larceny, Theft	Vehicle Theft
Area	4,731.8	1,287.1	3,115.4	329.3
USA	3,413.6	806.6	2,388.0	262.7

Key Violent Crime Data (Rate per 100,000 residents)

	Rate	Murder	Rape	Robbery	Aggravated Assault
Area	339.3	7.6	26.8	149.7	155.2
USA	432.8	4.7	34.7	111.6	285.6

Key Economic Data (Family income, unemployment)

	$25k-$75k	$75k-$150k	>$150k	Unemployment 03/2009	Unemployment 03/2010
Area	42.8%	29.6%	7.6%	9.1%	10.3%
USA	45.8%	29.5%	8.5%	9.0%	10.1

Key Household Data

	Population Age 0-17	Children w/Married Parents	Children w/Single Mother	Stay-at-home Mothers	Births to Single Women
Area	25.4%	59.2%	34.2%	21.4%	46.9%
USA	24.0%	65.6%	25.5%	27.9%	35.3%

Key Housing Data

	Owner Occupied	Median Year Built	Median Home Value	Home Value Growth, 2005-2010	Median List Price, 4-bedroom Home
Area	69.4%	1982	$125,800	4.2%	$239,800
USA	67.8%	1976	$187,045	3.1%	$288,846

Morgantown, WV
119,145

	Score	Rank
Overall	64.70	142
LDS Culture	14.30	341
Education	71.96	161
Crime	81.82	27
Economic	55.25	291
Health	27.63	353
Household	79.63	68
Housing	84.27	155

Key LDS Culture Data

	Positive	Negative	Ratio Pos:Neg	Commute>59 minutes	Commute<15 minutes
Area	1,789	160	11.2	5.2%	29.7%
USA	4,292	251	20.1	5.5%	34.1%

Key Education Data

	HS Grad	Some Coll.	College Degree	Free/Reduced Lunch	Students per Teacher
Area	85.2%	13.5%	32.8%	42.2%	14.5
USA	85.8%	22.6%	33.2%	41.2%	15.8

Key Property Crime Data (Rate per 100,000 residents)

	Rate	Burglary	Larceny, Theft	Vehicle Theft
Area	2,386.3	496.7	1,775.0	114.6
USA	3,413.6	806.6	2,388.0	262.7

Key Violent Crime Data (Rate per 100,000 residents)

	Rate	Murder	Rape	Robbery	Aggravated Assault
Area	191.0	2.6	35.6	41.7	111.2
USA	432.8	4.7	34.7	111.6	285.6

Key Economic Data (Family income, unemployment)

	$25k-$75k	$75k-$150k	>$150k	Unemployment 03/2009	Unemployment 03/2010
Area	52.6%	26.1%	5.4%	4.8%	6.6%
USA	45.8%	29.5%	8.5%	9.0%	10.1

Key Household Data

	Population Age 0-17	Children w/Married Parents	Children w/Single Mother	Stay-at-home Mothers	Births to Single Women
Area	19.1%	71.2%	20.3%	33.7%	23.5%
USA	24.0%	65.6%	25.5%	27.9%	35.3%

Key Housing Data

	Owner Occupied	Median Year Built	Median Home Value	Home Value Growth, 2005-2010	Median List Price, 4-bedroom Home
Area	65.7%	1973	$122,300	5.5%	
USA	67.8%	1976	$187,045	3.1%	$288,846

Morristown, TN
137,887

	Score	Rank
Overall	60.48	231
LDS Culture	30.98	124
Education	55.22	326
Crime	53.45	186
Economic	60.09	230
Health	38.85	241
Household	60.49	223
Housing	88.72	67

Key LDS Culture Data

	Positive	Negative	Ratio Pos:Neg	Commute>59 minutes	Commute<15 minutes
Area	1,443	48	30.1	5.7%	28.6%
USA	4,292	251	20.1	5.5%	34.1%

Key Education Data

	HS Grad	Some Coll.	College Degree	Free/Reduced Lunch	Students per Teacher
Area	75.7%	20.8%	19.9%	52.8%	16.3
USA	85.8%	22.6%	33.2%	41.2%	15.8

Key Property Crime Data (Rate per 100,000 residents)

	Rate	Burglary	Larceny, Theft	Vehicle Theft	
Area	3,605.0	808.9	2,537.9	258.1	
USA	3,413.6	806.6	2,388.0	262.7	

Key Violent Crime Data (Rate per 100,000 residents)

	Rate	Murder	Rape	Robbery	Aggravated Assault
Area	386.8	2.2	30.9	56.6	297.1
USA	432.8	4.7	34.7	111.6	285.6

Key Economic Data (Family income, unemployment)

	$25k-$75k	$75k-$150k	>$150k	Unemployment 03/2009	Unemployment 03/2010
Area	52.4%	22.0%	2.6%	13.7%	13.4%
USA	45.8%	29.5%	8.5%	9.0%	10.1

Key Household Data

	Population Age 0-17	Children w/Married Parents	Children w/Single Mother	Stay-at-home Mothers	Births to Single Women
Area	23.5%	64.9%	26.4%	23.9%	32.6%
USA	24.0%	65.6%	25.5%	27.9%	35.3%

Key Housing Data

	Owner Occupied	Median Year Built	Median Home Value	Home Value Growth, 2005-2010	Median List Price, 4-bedroom Home
Area	75.3%	1983	$117,700	4.6%	
USA	67.8%	1976	$187,045	3.1%	$288,846

Mount Vernon-Anacortes, WA
118,000

	Score	Rank
Overall	**69.91**	**51**
LDS Culture	22.27	254
Education	76.38	112
Crime	66.01	109
Economic	65.15	152
Health	48.12	84
Household	88.27	21
Housing	82.09	185

Key LDS Culture Data

	Positive	Negative	Ratio Pos:Neg	Commute>59 minutes	Commute<15 minutes
Area	2,687	133	20.2	10.0%	34.1%
USA	4,292	251	20.1	5.5%	34.1%

Key Education Data

	HS Grad	Some Coll.	College Degree	Free/Reduced Lunch	Students per Teacher
Area	87.8%	27.0%	35.4%	44.6%	20.0
USA	85.8%	22.6%	33.2%	41.2%	15.8

Key Property Crime Data (Rate per 100,000 residents)

	Rate	Burglary	Larceny, Theft	Vehicle Theft
Area	4,524.7	904.1	3,331.3	289.2
USA	3,413.6	806.6	2,388.0	262.7

Key Violent Crime Data (Rate per 100,000 residents)

	Rate	Murder	Rape	Robbery	Aggravated Assault
Area	205.5	7.6	42.3	46.5	109.1
USA	432.8	4.7	34.7	111.6	285.6

Key Economic Data (Family income, unemployment)

	$25k-$75k	$75k-$150k	>$150k	Unemployment 03/2009	Unemployment 03/2010
Area	50.2%	32.5%	7.4%	9.8%	11.5%
USA	45.8%	29.5%	8.5%	9.0%	10.1

Key Household Data

	Population Age 0-17	Children w/Married Parents	Children w/Single Mother	Stay-at-home Mothers	Births to Single Women
Area	23.5%	72.3%	21.9%	38.8%	12.9%
USA	24.0%	65.6%	25.5%	27.9%	35.3%

Key Housing Data

	Owner Occupied	Median Year Built	Median Home Value	Home Value Growth, 2005-2010	Median List Price, 4-bedroom Home
Area	70.9%	1981	$292,200	6.5%	
USA	67.8%	1976	$187,045	3.1%	$288,846

Muncie, IN
114,685

	Score	Rank
Overall	**59.99**	**245**
LDS Culture	26.13	194
Education	74.23	136
Crime	61.73	136
Economic	67.04	122
Health	34.59	299
Household	48.15	314
Housing	72.80	310

Key LDS Culture Data

	Positive	Negative	Ratio Pos:Neg	Commute>59 minutes	Commute<15 minutes
Area	2,331	160	14.6	5.6%	40.1%
USA	4,292	251	20.1	5.5%	34.1%

Key Education Data

	HS Grad	Some Coll.	College Degree	Free/Reduced Lunch	Students per Teacher
Area	83.9%	21.3%	27.3%	41.3%	15.9
USA	85.8%	22.6%	33.2%	41.2%	15.8

Key Property Crime Data (Rate per 100,000 residents)

	Rate	Burglary	Larceny, Theft	Vehicle Theft	
Area	3,049.3	595.1	2,287.2	167.0	
USA	3,413.6	806.6	2,388.0	262.7	

Key Violent Crime Data (Rate per 100,000 residents)

	Rate	Murder	Rape	Robbery	Aggravated Assault
Area	338.4	0.9	33.9	73.9	229.7
USA	432.8	4.7	34.7	111.6	285.6

Key Economic Data (Family income, unemployment)

	$25k-$75k	$75k-$150k	>$150k	Unemployment 03/2009	Unemployment 03/2010
Area	55.6%	24.2%	4.8%	10.8%	11.7%
USA	45.8%	29.5%	8.5%	9.0%	10.1

Key Household Data

	Population Age 0-17	Children w/Married Parents	Children w/Single Mother	Stay-at-home Mothers	Births to Single Women
Area	20.2%	61.0%	25.1%	17.4%	30.6%
USA	24.0%	65.6%	25.5%	27.9%	35.3%

Key Housing Data

	Owner Occupied	Median Year Built	Median Home Value	Home Value Growth, 2005-2010	Median List Price, 4-bedroom Home
Area	69.2%	1962	$92,200	-0.9%	
USA	67.8%	1976	$187,045	3.1%	$288,846

Muskegon-Norton Shores, MI
174,344

	Score	Rank
Overall	**56.86**	**308**
LDS Culture	29.48	149
Education	60.14	292
Crime	44.83	257
Economic	56.92	269
Health	36.88	269
Household	61.73	212
Housing	74.66	287

Key LDS Culture Data

	Positive	Negative	Ratio Pos:Neg	Commute>59 minutes	Commute<15 minutes
Area	2,001	109	18.4	3.8%	35.2%
USA	4,292	251	20.1	5.5%	34.1%

Key Education Data

	HS Grad	Some Coll.	College Degree	Free/Reduced Lunch	Students per Teacher
Area	87.1%	26.0%	25.1%	47.4%	17.7
USA	85.8%	22.6%	33.2%	41.2%	15.8

Key Property Crime Data (Rate per 100,000 residents)

	Rate	Burglary	Larceny, Theft	Vehicle Theft	
Area	4,222.7	759.4	3,259.2	204.1	
USA	3,413.6	806.6	2,388.0	262.7	

Key Violent Crime Data (Rate per 100,000 residents)

	Rate	Murder	Rape	Robbery	Aggravated Assault
Area	464.2	2.3	64.0	100.9	297.0
USA	432.8	4.7	34.7	111.6	285.6

Key Economic Data (Family income, unemployment)

	$25k-$75k	$75k-$150k	>$150k	Unemployment 03/2009	Unemployment 03/2010
Area	51.6%	23.3%	3.9%	14.6%	16.5%
USA	45.8%	29.5%	8.5%	9.0%	10.1

Key Household Data

	Population Age 0-17	Children w/Married Parents	Children w/Single Mother	Stay-at-home Mothers	Births to Single Women
Area	24.7%	66.4%	29.0%	19.1%	42.7%
USA	24.0%	65.6%	25.5%	27.9%	35.3%

Key Housing Data

	Owner Occupied	Median Year Built	Median Home Value	Home Value Growth, 2005-2010	Median List Price, 4-bedroom Home
Area	76.3%	1967	$116,600	-1.1%	
USA	67.8%	1976	$187,045	3.1%	$288,846

Myrtle Beach-North Myrtle Beach-Conway, SC
257,380

	Score	Rank
Overall	53.41	346
LDS Culture	16.01	329
Education	55.28	325
Crime	11.29	360
Economic	64.26	165
Health	41.09	195
Household	60.49	224
Housing	94.09	17

Key LDS Culture Data

	Positive	Negative	Ratio Pos:Neg	Commute>59 minutes	Commute<15 minutes
Area	1,453	179	8.1	3.6%	31.8%
USA	4,292	251	20.1	5.5%	34.1%

Key Education Data

	HS Grad	Some Coll.	College Degree	Free/Reduced Lunch	Students per Teacher
Area	85.7%	21.6%	29.5%	54.5%	15.3
USA	85.8%	22.6%	33.2%	41.2%	15.8

Key Property Crime Data (Rate per 100,000 residents)

	Rate	Burglary	Larceny, Theft	Vehicle Theft	
Area	6,896.8	1,457.8	4,830.7	608.3	
USA	3,413.6	806.6	2,388.0	262.7	

Key Violent Crime Data (Rate per 100,000 residents)

	Rate	Murder	Rape	Robbery	Aggravated Assault
Area	948.1	4.9	56.6	194.2	692.5
USA	432.8	4.7	34.7	111.6	285.6

Key Economic Data (Family income, unemployment)

	$25k-$75k	$75k-$150k	>$150k	Unemployment 03/2009	Unemployment 03/2010
Area	50.0%	25.2%	5.0%	12.8%	13.2%
USA	45.8%	29.5%	8.5%	9.0%	10.1

Key Household Data

	Population Age 0-17	Children w/Married Parents	Children w/Single Mother	Stay-at-home Mothers	Births to Single Women
Area	21.4%	60.5%	29.6%	31.8%	34.4%
USA	24.0%	65.6%	25.5%	27.9%	35.3%

Key Housing Data

	Owner Occupied	Median Year Built	Median Home Value	Home Value Growth, 2005-2010	Median List Price, 4-bedroom Home
Area	70.4%	1993	$179,400	5.7%	$310,000
USA	67.8%	1976	$187,045	3.1%	$288,846

Napa, CA
133,433

	Score	Rank
Overall	**63.31**	**174**
LDS Culture	23.05	243
Education	74.27	134
Crime	50.26	217
Economic	63.81	171
Health	48.59	67
Household	85.19	32
Housing	60.80	352

Key LDS Culture Data

	Positive	Negative	Ratio Pos:Neg	Commute>59 minutes	Commute<15 minutes
Area	10,020	623	16.1	6.6%	42.0%
USA	4,292	251	20.1	5.5%	34.1%

Key Education Data

	HS Grad	Some Coll.	College Degree	Free/Reduced Lunch	Students per Teacher
Area	79.5%	22.2%	37.4%	40.5%	15.9
USA	85.8%	22.6%	33.2%	41.2%	15.8

Key Property Crime Data (Rate per 100,000 residents)

	Rate	Burglary	Larceny, Theft	Vehicle Theft
Area	2,446.9	577.7	1,638.3	230.9
USA	3,413.6	806.6	2,388.0	262.7

Key Violent Crime Data (Rate per 100,000 residents)

	Rate	Murder	Rape	Robbery	Aggravated Assault
Area	625.8	0.8	29.3	52.7	543.1
USA	432.8	4.7	34.7	111.6	285.6

Key Economic Data (Family income, unemployment)

	$25k-$75k	$75k-$150k	>$150k	Unemployment 03/2009	Unemployment 03/2010
Area	38.7%	33.3%	17.7%	8.6%	10.7%
USA	45.8%	29.5%	8.5%	9.0%	10.1

Key Household Data

	Population Age 0-17	Children w/Married Parents	Children w/Single Mother	Stay-at-home Mothers	Births to Single Women
Area	22.5%	73.9%	16.5%	37.6%	23.3%
USA	24.0%	65.6%	25.5%	27.9%	35.3%

Key Housing Data

	Owner Occupied	Median Year Built	Median Home Value	Home Value Growth, 2005-2010	Median List Price, 4-bedroom Home
Area	64.9%	1972	$608,100	-1.0%	$630,000
USA	67.8%	1976	$187,045	3.1%	$288,846

Naples-Marco Island, FL
315,258

	Score	Rank
Overall	66.98	106
LDS Culture	25.63	204
Education	67.95	207
Crime	69.95	77
Economic	63.59	175
Health	45.75	136
Household	79.01	71
Housing	77.61	253

Key LDS Culture Data

	Positive	Negative	Ratio Pos:Neg	Commute>59 minutes	Commute<15 minutes
Area	4,489	187	24.0	3.6%	27.3%
USA	4,292	251	20.1	5.5%	34.1%

Key Education Data

	HS Grad	Some Coll.	College Degree	Free/Reduced Lunch	Students per Teacher
Area	83.3%	19.2%	37.8%	44.3%	14.8
USA	85.8%	22.6%	33.2%	41.2%	15.8

Key Property Crime Data (Rate per 100,000 residents)

	Rate	Burglary	Larceny, Theft	Vehicle Theft	
Area	1,928.9	424.3	1,404.5	100.1	
USA	3,413.6	806.6	2,388.0	262.7	

Key Violent Crime Data (Rate per 100,000 residents)

	Rate	Murder	Rape	Robbery	Aggravated Assault
Area	366.2	2.5	17.5	73.0	273.3
USA	432.8	4.7	34.7	111.6	285.6

Key Economic Data (Family income, unemployment)

	$25k-$75k	$75k-$150k	>$150k	Unemployment 03/2009	Unemployment 03/2010
Area	39.4%	31.1%	17.6%	9.2%	12.3%
USA	45.8%	29.5%	8.5%	9.0%	10.1

Key Household Data

	Population Age 0-17	Children w/Married Parents	Children w/Single Mother	Stay-at-home Mothers	Births to Single Women
Area	20.3%	71.4%	19.7%	37.0%	38.2%
USA	24.0%	65.6%	25.5%	27.9%	35.3%

Key Housing Data

	Owner Occupied	Median Year Built	Median Home Value	Home Value Growth, 2005-2010	Median List Price, 4-bedroom Home
Area	77.1%	1992	$346,300	0.9%	$779,000
USA	67.8%	1976	$187,045	3.1%	$288,846

Nashville-Davidson--Murfreesboro--Franklin, TN
1,552,922

	Score	Rank
Overall	63.84	163
LDS Culture	24.91	217
Education	69.83	187
Crime	33.84	326
Economic	65.98	139
Health	48.67	58
Household	75.93	98
Housing	90.19	52

Key LDS Culture Data

	Positive	Negative	Ratio Pos:Neg	Commute>59 minutes	Commute<15 minutes
Area	7,280	314	23.2	6.1%	23.2%
USA	4,292	251	20.1	5.5%	34.1%

Key Education Data

	HS Grad	Some Coll.	College Degree	Free/Reduced Lunch	Students per Teacher
Area	85.7%	21.4%	35.4%	42.0%	15.7
USA	85.8%	22.6%	33.2%	41.2%	15.8

Key Property Crime Data (Rate per 100,000 residents)

	Rate	Burglary	Larceny, Theft	Vehicle Theft
Area	3,617.9	768.9	2,605.2	243.8
USA	3,413.6	806.6	2,388.0	262.7

Key Violent Crime Data (Rate per 100,000 residents)

	Rate	Murder	Rape	Robbery	Aggravated Assault
Area	781.2	6.5	35.6	186.5	552.6
USA	432.8	4.7	34.7	111.6	285.6

Key Economic Data (Family income, unemployment)

	$25k-$75k	$75k-$150k	>$150k	Unemployment 03/2009	Unemployment 03/2010
Area	44.4%	30.5%	11.0%	9.3%	9.5%
USA	45.8%	29.5%	8.5%	9.0%	10.1

Key Household Data

	Population Age 0-17	Children w/Married Parents	Children w/Single Mother	Stay-at-home Mothers	Births to Single Women
Area	24.8%	68.1%	23.8%	31.0%	31.4%
USA	24.0%	65.6%	25.5%	27.9%	35.3%

Key Housing Data

	Owner Occupied	Median Year Built	Median Home Value	Home Value Growth, 2005-2010	Median List Price, 4-bedroom Home
Area	69.5%	1985	$174,500	4.8%	$299,900
USA	67.8%	1976	$187,045	3.1%	$288,846

New Haven-Milford, CT
846,101

	Score	Rank
Overall	**56.67**	**310**
LDS Culture	22.33	252
Education	77.84	97
Crime	49.75	221
Economic	67.59	117
Health	29.03	350
Household	58.64	235
Housing	58.22	356

Key LDS Culture Data
	Positive	Negative	Ratio Pos:Neg	Commute>59 minutes	Commute<15 minutes
Area	12,661	829	15.3	6.5%	29.5%
USA	4,292	251	20.1	5.5%	34.1%

Key Education Data
	HS Grad	Some Coll.	College Degree	Free/Reduced Lunch	Students per Teacher
Area	88.3%	18.3%	40.6%	35.1%	13.7
USA	85.8%	22.6%	33.2%	41.2%	15.8

Key Property Crime Data (Rate per 100,000 residents)
	Rate	Burglary	Larceny, Theft	Vehicle Theft
Area		560.9	2,449.5	382.7
USA	3,413.6	806.6	2,388.0	262.7

Key Violent Crime Data (Rate per 100,000 residents)
	Rate	Murder	Rape	Robbery	Aggravated Assault
Area		2.9	19.6	186.7	236.5
USA	432.8	4.7	34.7	111.6	285.6

Key Economic Data (Family income, unemployment)
	$25k-$75k	$75k-$150k	>$150k	Unemployment 03/2009	Unemployment 03/2010
Area	34.2%	36.6%	15.8%	8.0%	9.3%
USA	45.8%	29.5%	8.5%	9.0%	10.1

Key Household Data
	Population Age 0-17	Children w/Married Parents	Children w/Single Mother	Stay-at-home Mothers	Births to Single Women
Area	23.1%	63.8%	29.2%	23.3%	33.2%
USA	24.0%	65.6%	25.5%	27.9%	35.3%

Key Housing Data
	Owner Occupied	Median Year Built	Median Home Value	Home Value Growth, 2005-2010	Median List Price, 4-bedroom Home
Area	64.3%	1965	$283,400	2.4%	$399,900
USA	67.8%	1976	$187,045	3.1%	$288,846

New Orleans-Metairie-Kenner, LA
1,134,029

	Score	Rank
Overall	**55.06**	**328**
LDS Culture	17.09	319
Education	49.06	353
Crime	38.98	296
Economic	60.70	222
Health	49.84	42
Household	55.56	270
Housing	81.82	188

Key LDS Culture Data

	Positive	Negative	Ratio Pos:Neg	Commute>59 minutes	Commute<15 minutes
Area	5,043	540	9.3	6.9%	25.8%
USA	4,292	251	20.1	5.5%	34.1%

Key Education Data

	HS Grad	Some Coll.	College Degree	Free/Reduced Lunch	Students per Teacher
Area	83.6%	23.2%	28.8%	65.7%	13.6
USA	85.8%	22.6%	33.2%	41.2%	15.8

Key Property Crime Data (Rate per 100,000 residents)

	Rate	Burglary	Larceny, Theft	Vehicle Theft
Area	4,000.7	1,039.2	2,434.1	527.4
USA	3,413.6	806.6	2,388.0	262.7

Key Violent Crime Data (Rate per 100,000 residents)

	Rate	Murder	Rape	Robbery	Aggravated Assault
Area	622.3	22.4	23.2	185.0	391.6
USA	432.8	4.7	34.7	111.6	285.6

Key Economic Data (Family income, unemployment)

	$25k-$75k	$75k-$150k	>$150k	Unemployment 03/2009	Unemployment 03/2010
Area	43.2%	29.1%	10.5%	5.8%	6.0%
USA	45.8%	29.5%	8.5%	9.0%	10.1

Key Household Data

	Population Age 0-17	Children w/Married Parents	Children w/Single Mother	Stay-at-home Mothers	Births to Single Women
Area	23.5%	60.1%	31.1%	31.5%	51.6%
USA	24.0%	65.6%	25.5%	27.9%	35.3%

Key Housing Data

	Owner Occupied	Median Year Built	Median Home Value	Home Value Growth, 2005-2010	Median List Price, 4-bedroom Home
Area	67.0%	1976	$184,200	4.6%	$249,900
USA	67.8%	1976	$187,045	3.1%	$288,846

New York-Northern New Jersey-Long Island, NY-NJ-PA
19,006,798

	Score	Rank
Overall	61.99	194
LDS Culture	18.94	302
Education	70.00	186
Crime	67.56	94
Economic	66.31	132
Health	45.08	146
Household	76.54	87
Housing	53.07	361

Key LDS Culture Data

	Positive	Negative	Ratio Pos:Neg	Commute>59 minutes	Commute<15 minutes
Area	34,796	2117	16.4	20.1%	18.3%
USA	4,292	251	20.1	5.5%	34.1%

Key Education Data

	HS Grad	Some Coll.	College Degree	Free/Reduced Lunch	Students per Teacher
Area	83.8%	15.8%	41.5%	44.2%	14.1
USA	85.8%	22.6%	33.2%	41.2%	15.8

Key Property Crime Data (Rate per 100,000 residents)

	Rate	Burglary	Larceny, Theft	Vehicle Theft	
Area	1,863.1	300.6	1,391.1	171.3	
USA	3,413.6	806.6	2,388.0	262.7	

Key Violent Crime Data (Rate per 100,000 residents)

	Rate	Murder	Rape	Robbery	Aggravated Assault
Area	398.7	4.5	9.7	182.6	201.9
USA	432.8	4.7	34.7	111.6	285.6

Key Economic Data (Family income, unemployment)

	$25k-$75k	$75k-$150k	>$150k	Unemployment 03/2009	Unemployment 03/2010
Area	34.0%	31.6%	20.0%	8.3%	9.3%
USA	45.8%	29.5%	8.5%	9.0%	10.1

Key Household Data

	Population Age 0-17	Children w/Married Parents	Children w/Single Mother	Stay-at-home Mothers	Births to Single Women
Area	23.3%	66.0%	27.1%	32.9%	29.0%
USA	24.0%	65.6%	25.5%	27.9%	35.3%

Key Housing Data

	Owner Occupied	Median Year Built	Median Home Value	Home Value Growth, 2005-2010	Median List Price, 4-bedroom Home
Area	53.4%	1958	$462,700	4.4%	$499,000
USA	67.8%	1976	$187,045	3.1%	$288,846

Niles-Benton Harbor, MI
159,481

	Score	Rank
Overall	56.36	312
LDS Culture	26.32	191
Education	69.01	197
Crime	55.26	171
Economic	54.70	298
Health	36.88	270
Household	47.53	317
Housing	71.68	321

Key LDS Culture Data

	Positive	Negative	Ratio Pos:Neg	Commute>59 minutes	Commute<15 minutes
Area	3,785	256	14.8	3.0%	38.4%
USA	4,292	251	20.1	5.5%	34.1%

Key Education Data

	HS Grad	Some Coll.	College Degree	Free/Reduced Lunch	Students per Teacher
Area	87.8%	26.8%	30.8%	41.5%	16.3
USA	85.8%	22.6%	33.2%	41.2%	15.8

Key Property Crime Data (Rate per 100,000 residents)

	Rate	Burglary	Larceny, Theft	Vehicle Theft
Area	3,178.8	659.3	2,377.6	141.9
USA	3,413.6	806.6	2,388.0	262.7

Key Violent Crime Data (Rate per 100,000 residents)

	Rate	Murder	Rape	Robbery	Aggravated Assault
Area	394.6	1.3	69.0	66.5	257.8
USA	432.8	4.7	34.7	111.6	285.6

Key Economic Data (Family income, unemployment)

	$25k-$75k	$75k-$150k	>$150k	Unemployment 03/2009	Unemployment 03/2010
Area	47.2%	26.0%	6.5%	12.4%	14.9%
USA	45.8%	29.5%	8.5%	9.0%	10.1

Key Household Data

	Population Age 0-17	Children w/Married Parents	Children w/Single Mother	Stay-at-home Mothers	Births to Single Women
Area	24.1%	60.9%	31.3%	27.7%	41.6%
USA	24.0%	65.6%	25.5%	27.9%	35.3%

Key Housing Data

	Owner Occupied	Median Year Built	Median Home Value	Home Value Growth, 2005-2010	Median List Price, 4-bedroom Home
Area	72.6%	1961	$147,100	2.3%	
USA	67.8%	1976	$187,045	3.1%	$288,846

Norwich-New London, CT
264,519

	Score	Rank
Overall	67.21	100
LDS Culture	34.20	88
Education	82.22	56
Crime	66.55	106
Economic	79.43	17
Health	36.35	276
Household	63.58	196
Housing	68.68	332

Key LDS Culture Data

	Positive	Negative	Ratio Pos:Neg	Commute>59 minutes	Commute<15 minutes
Area	3,973	290	13.7	5.9%	33.5%
USA	4,292	251	20.1	5.5%	34.1%

Key Education Data

	HS Grad	Some Coll.	College Degree	Free/Reduced Lunch	Students per Teacher
Area	92.0%	19.8%	39.5%	22.8%	13.2
USA	85.8%	22.6%	33.2%	41.2%	15.8

Key Property Crime Data (Rate per 100,000 residents)

	Rate	Burglary	Larceny, Theft	Vehicle Theft	
Area	2,469.3	492.3	1,852.5	124.5	
USA	3,413.6	806.6	2,388.0	262.7	

Key Violent Crime Data (Rate per 100,000 residents)

	Rate	Murder	Rape	Robbery	Aggravated Assault
Area	346.7	4.2	39.4	63.3	239.8
USA	432.8	4.7	34.7	111.6	285.6

Key Economic Data (Family income, unemployment)

	$25k-$75k	$75k-$150k	>$150k	Unemployment 03/2009	Unemployment 03/2010
Area	36.4%	39.7%	14.6%	7.9%	8.9%
USA	45.8%	29.5%	8.5%	9.0%	10.1

Key Household Data

	Population Age 0-17	Children w/Married Parents	Children w/Single Mother	Stay-at-home Mothers	Births to Single Women
Area	22.7%	65.0%	27.8%	23.5%	24.2%
USA	24.0%	65.6%	25.5%	27.9%	35.3%

Key Housing Data

	Owner Occupied	Median Year Built	Median Home Value	Home Value Growth, 2005-2010	Median List Price, 4-bedroom Home
Area	68.6%	1969	$277,000	2.3%	
USA	67.8%	1976	$187,045	3.1%	$288,846

Ocala, FL
329,628

	Score	Rank
Overall	**55.83**	**322**
LDS Culture	20.21	279
Education	50.75	347
Crime	49.33	224
Economic	48.92	335
Health	48.44	81
Household	43.21	348
Housing	97.18	6

Key LDS Culture Data

	Positive	Negative	Ratio Pos:Neg	Commute>59 minutes	Commute<15 minutes
Area	3,064	134	22.9	6.3%	24.9%
USA	4,292	251	20.1	5.5%	34.1%

Key Education Data

	HS Grad	Some Coll.	College Degree	Free/Reduced Lunch	Students per Teacher
Area	84.8%	21.8%	25.6%	53.8%	15.5
USA	85.8%	22.6%	33.2%	41.2%	15.8

Key Property Crime Data (Rate per 100,000 residents)

	Rate	Burglary	Larceny, Theft	Vehicle Theft
Area	2,527.7	717.0	1,658.0	152.8
USA	3,413.6	806.6	2,388.0	262.7

Key Violent Crime Data (Rate per 100,000 residents)

	Rate	Murder	Rape	Robbery	Aggravated Assault
Area	629.4	6.7	50.0	94.6	478.1
USA	432.8	4.7	34.7	111.6	285.6

Key Economic Data (Family income, unemployment)

	$25k-$75k	$75k-$150k	>$150k	Unemployment 03/2009	Unemployment 03/2010
Area	54.3%	20.2%	4.1%	12.0%	15.0%
USA	45.8%	29.5%	8.5%	9.0%	10.1

Key Household Data

	Population Age 0-17	Children w/Married Parents	Children w/Single Mother	Stay-at-home Mothers	Births to Single Women
Area	19.9%	60.3%	29.1%	30.4%	70.0%
USA	24.0%	65.6%	25.5%	27.9%	35.3%

Key Housing Data

	Owner Occupied	Median Year Built	Median Home Value	Home Value Growth, 2005-2010	Median List Price, 4-bedroom Home
Area	74.8%	1990	$162,200	4.7%	$200,000
USA	67.8%	1976	$187,045	3.1%	$288,846

Ocean City, NJ
95,838

	Score	Rank
Overall	65.81	130
LDS Culture	15.26	332
Education	80.75	66
Crime	53.38	187
Economic	78.04	21
Health	45.04	147
Household	73.46	123
Housing	76.10	270

Key LDS Culture Data

	Positive	Negative	Ratio Pos:Neg	Commute>59 minutes	Commute<15 minutes
Area	2,797	228	12.3	8.6%	36.5%
USA	4,292	251	20.1	5.5%	34.1%

Key Education Data

	HS Grad	Some Coll.	College Degree	Free/Reduced Lunch	Students per Teacher
Area	91.2%	19.3%	33.4%	30.7%	13.8
USA	85.8%	22.6%	33.2%	41.2%	15.8

Key Property Crime Data (Rate per 100,000 residents)

	Rate	Burglary	Larceny, Theft	Vehicle Theft	
Area	4,845.2	1,010.4	3,726.7	108.1	
USA	3,413.6	806.6	2,388.0	262.7	

Key Violent Crime Data (Rate per 100,000 residents)

	Rate	Murder	Rape	Robbery	Aggravated Assault
Area	325.3	0.0	32.5	78.7	214.0
USA	432.8	4.7	34.7	111.6	285.6

Key Economic Data (Family income, unemployment)

	$25k-$75k	$75k-$150k	>$150k	Unemployment 03/2009	Unemployment 03/2010
Area	44.8%	34.5%	11.5%	15.2%	16.3%
USA	45.8%	29.5%	8.5%	9.0%	10.1

Key Household Data

	Population Age 0-17	Children w/Married Parents	Children w/Single Mother	Stay-at-home Mothers	Births to Single Women
Area	19.9%	72.6%	20.2%	18.0%	22.3%
USA	24.0%	65.6%	25.5%	27.9%	35.3%

Key Housing Data

	Owner Occupied	Median Year Built	Median Home Value	Home Value Growth, 2005-2010	Median List Price, 4-bedroom Home
Area	76.0%	1973	$351,000	4.3%	
USA	67.8%	1976	$187,045	3.1%	$288,846

Odessa, TX
131,941

	Score	Rank
Overall	51.78	357
LDS Culture	18.11	311
Education	49.16	352
Crime	40.21	286
Economic	56.86	271
Health	32.00	332
Household	46.91	322
Housing	88.74	66

Key LDS Culture Data

	Positive	Negative	Ratio Pos:Neg	Commute>59 minutes	Commute<15 minutes
Area	1,209	78	15.5	5.3%	38.5%
USA	4,292	251	20.1	5.5%	34.1%

Key Education Data

	HS Grad	Some Coll.	College Degree	Free/Reduced Lunch	Students per Teacher
Area	75.3%	27.3%	18.2%	48.1%	15.6
USA	85.8%	22.6%	33.2%	41.2%	15.8

Key Property Crime Data (Rate per 100,000 residents)

	Rate	Burglary	Larceny, Theft	Vehicle Theft	
Area	4,003.6	913.3	2,802.7	287.6	
USA	3,413.6	806.6	2,388.0	262.7	

Key Violent Crime Data (Rate per 100,000 residents)

	Rate	Murder	Rape	Robbery	Aggravated Assault
Area	593.6	7.6	3.1	67.3	515.6
USA	432.8	4.7	34.7	111.6	285.6

Key Economic Data (Family income, unemployment)

	$25k-$75k	$75k-$150k	>$150k	Unemployment 03/2009	Unemployment 03/2010
Area	44.2%	28.4%	7.8%	6.7%	8.5%
USA	45.8%	29.5%	8.5%	9.0%	10.1

Key Household Data

	Population Age 0-17	Children w/Married Parents	Children w/Single Mother	Stay-at-home Mothers	Births to Single Women
Area	29.9%	57.1%	32.0%	38.8%	66.5%
USA	24.0%	65.6%	25.5%	27.9%	35.3%

Key Housing Data

	Owner Occupied	Median Year Built	Median Home Value	Home Value Growth, 2005-2010	Median List Price, 4-bedroom Home
Area	67.0%	1965	$77,900	11.0%	
USA	67.8%	1976	$187,045	3.1%	$288,846

Ogden-Clearfield, UT
531,580

	Score	Rank
Overall	88.48	4
LDS Culture	48.02	18
Education	90.55	17
Crime	81.66	28
Economic	75.99	40
Health	85.84	2
Household	92.59	7
Housing	92.72	27

Key LDS Culture Data

	Positive	Negative	Ratio Pos:Neg	Commute>59 minutes	Commute<15 minutes
Area	2,085	53	39.3	6.3%	31.6%
USA	4,292	251	20.1	5.5%	34.1%

Key Education Data

	HS Grad	Some Coll.	College Degree	Free/Reduced Lunch	Students per Teacher
Area	92.3%	29.5%	37.4%	31.2%	24.6
USA	85.8%	22.6%	33.2%	41.2%	15.8

Key Property Crime Data (Rate per 100,000 residents)

	Rate	Burglary	Larceny, Theft	Vehicle Theft
Area	2,718.6	447.0	2,130.9	140.7
USA	3,413.6	806.6	2,388.0	262.7

Key Violent Crime Data (Rate per 100,000 residents)

	Rate	Murder	Rape	Robbery	Aggravated Assault
Area	158.3	1.7	29.9	45.0	81.7
USA	432.8	4.7	34.7	111.6	285.6

Key Economic Data (Family income, unemployment)

	$25k-$75k	$75k-$150k	>$150k	Unemployment 03/2009	Unemployment 03/2010
Area	48.2%	34.8%	7.7%	6.9%	7.3%
USA	45.8%	29.5%	8.5%	9.0%	10.1

Key Household Data

	Population Age 0-17	Children w/Married Parents	Children w/Single Mother	Stay-at-home Mothers	Births to Single Women
Area	31.3%	79.0%	15.0%	37.1%	11.5%
USA	24.0%	65.6%	25.5%	27.9%	35.3%

Key Housing Data

	Owner Occupied	Median Year Built	Median Home Value	Home Value Growth, 2005-2010	Median List Price, 4-bedroom Home
Area	76.8%	1983	$214,100	5.5%	$214,900
USA	67.8%	1976	$187,045	3.1%	$288,846

Oklahoma City, OK
1,202,714

	Score	Rank
Overall	61.67	206
LDS Culture	25.03	212
Education	63.49	265
Crime	39.38	292
Economic	59.20	238
Health	41.56	190
Household	77.16	81
Housing	89.64	56

Key LDS Culture Data

	Positive	Negative	Ratio Pos:Neg	Commute>59 minutes	Commute<15 minutes
Area	5,918	323	18.3	3.6%	30.1%
USA	4,292	251	20.1	5.5%	34.1%

Key Education Data

	HS Grad	Some Coll.	College Degree	Free/Reduced Lunch	Students per Teacher
Area	87.1%	26.7%	32.8%	50.1%	16.3
USA	85.8%	22.6%	33.2%	41.2%	15.8

Key Property Crime Data (Rate per 100,000 residents)

	Rate	Burglary	Larceny, Theft	Vehicle Theft
Area	4,294.8	1,158.6	2,705.7	430.6
USA	3,413.6	806.6	2,388.0	262.7

Key Violent Crime Data (Rate per 100,000 residents)

	Rate	Murder	Rape	Robbery	Aggravated Assault
Area	581.5	6.3	43.3	153.4	378.5
USA	432.8	4.7	34.7	111.6	285.6

Key Economic Data (Family income, unemployment)

	$25k-$75k	$75k-$150k	>$150k	Unemployment 03/2009	Unemployment 03/2010
Area	46.8%	28.2%	8.0%	5.7%	6.1%
USA	45.8%	29.5%	8.5%	9.0%	10.1

Key Household Data

	Population Age 0-17	Children w/Married Parents	Children w/Single Mother	Stay-at-home Mothers	Births to Single Women
Area	25.1%	65.3%	24.6%	31.4%	28.6%
USA	24.0%	65.6%	25.5%	27.9%	35.3%

Key Housing Data

	Owner Occupied	Median Year Built	Median Home Value	Home Value Growth, 2005-2010	Median List Price, 4-bedroom Home
Area	65.8%	1977	$122,300	3.4%	$225,000
USA	67.8%	1976	$187,045	3.1%	$288,846

Olympia, WA
245,181

	Score	Rank
Overall	73.15	26
LDS Culture	35.56	73
Education	86.96	33
Crime	66.23	108
Economic	73.54	52
Health	47.23	111
Household	75.31	99
Housing	84.25	156

Key LDS Culture Data

	Positive	Negative	Ratio Pos:Neg	Commute>59 minutes	Commute<15 minutes
Area	3,987	197	20.2	7.9%	27.5%
USA	4,292	251	20.1	5.5%	34.1%

Key Education Data

	HS Grad	Some Coll.	College Degree	Free/Reduced Lunch	Students per Teacher
Area	93.0%	26.6%	42.6%	28.6%	19.7
USA	85.8%	22.6%	33.2%	41.2%	15.8

Key Property Crime Data (Rate per 100,000 residents)

	Rate	Burglary	Larceny, Theft	Vehicle Theft	
Area	3,404.5	704.5	2,506.2	193.9	
USA	3,413.6	806.6	2,388.0	262.7	

Key Violent Crime Data (Rate per 100,000 residents)

	Rate	Murder	Rape	Robbery	Aggravated Assault
Area	259.4	1.6	36.2	46.1	175.4
USA	432.8	4.7	34.7	111.6	285.6

Key Economic Data (Family income, unemployment)

	$25k-$75k	$75k-$150k	>$150k	Unemployment 03/2009	Unemployment 03/2010
Area	41.6%	38.6%	9.6%	7.9%	8.6%
USA	45.8%	29.5%	8.5%	9.0%	10.1

Key Household Data

	Population Age 0-17	Children w/Married Parents	Children w/Single Mother	Stay-at-home Mothers	Births to Single Women
Area	22.0%	64.4%	25.4%	30.4%	25.0%
USA	24.0%	65.6%	25.5%	27.9%	35.3%

Key Housing Data

	Owner Occupied	Median Year Built	Median Home Value	Home Value Growth, 2005-2010	Median List Price, 4-bedroom Home
Area	67.5%	1986	$269,100	6.8%	$300,000
USA	67.8%	1976	$187,045	3.1%	$288,846

Omaha-Council Bluffs, NE-IA
837,779

	Score	Rank
Overall	**69.03**	**66**
LDS Culture	40.27	45
Education	79.47	73
Crime	51.18	207
Economic	75.38	44
Health	45.88	134
Household	64.81	183
Housing	85.68	127

Key LDS Culture Data

	Positive	Negative	Ratio Pos:Neg	Commute>59 minutes	Commute<15 minutes
Area	3,891	368	10.6	2.4%	34.2%
USA	4,292	251	20.1	5.5%	34.1%

Key Education Data

	HS Grad	Some Coll.	College Degree	Free/Reduced Lunch	Students per Teacher
Area	91.0%	24.5%	39.6%	36.2%	14.6
USA	85.8%	22.6%	33.2%	41.2%	15.8

Key Property Crime Data (Rate per 100,000 residents)

	Rate	Burglary	Larceny, Theft	Vehicle Theft	
Area	3,482.2	620.5	2,435.8	425.8	
USA	3,413.6	806.6	2,388.0	262.7	

Key Violent Crime Data (Rate per 100,000 residents)

	Rate	Murder	Rape	Robbery	Aggravated Assault
Area	417.3	6.0	37.1	124.8	249.4
USA	432.8	4.7	34.7	111.6	285.6

Key Economic Data (Family income, unemployment)

	$25k-$75k	$75k-$150k	>$150k	Unemployment 03/2009	Unemployment 03/2010
Area	44.1%	33.7%	10.4%	5.2%	5.9%
USA	45.8%	29.5%	8.5%	9.0%	10.1

Key Household Data

	Population Age 0-17	Children w/Married Parents	Children w/Single Mother	Stay-at-home Mothers	Births to Single Women
Area	26.8%	69.0%	21.4%	20.9%	32.6%
USA	24.0%	65.6%	25.5%	27.9%	35.3%

Key Housing Data

	Owner Occupied	Median Year Built	Median Home Value	Home Value Growth, 2005-2010	Median List Price, 4-bedroom Home
Area	68.3%	1974	$145,700	1.6%	$234,000
USA	67.8%	1976	$187,045	3.1%	$288,846

Orlando-Kissimmee, FL
2,054,574

	Score	Rank
Overall	59.81	251
LDS Culture	17.63	313
Education	70.21	180
Crime	28.16	340
Economic	58.75	245
Health	54.63	11
Household	62.96	201
Housing	91.17	40

Key LDS Culture Data

	Positive	Negative	Ratio Pos:Neg	Commute>59 minutes	Commute<15 minutes
Area	10,352	519	19.9	6.5%	20.9%
USA	4,292	251	20.1	5.5%	34.1%

Key Education Data

	HS Grad	Some Coll.	College Degree	Free/Reduced Lunch	Students per Teacher
Area	87.5%	21.7%	36.1%	44.2%	15.9
USA	85.8%	22.6%	33.2%	41.2%	15.8

Key Property Crime Data (Rate per 100,000 residents)

	Rate	Burglary	Larceny, Theft	Vehicle Theft	
Area	4,468.4	1,212.5	2,853.6	402.2	
USA	3,413.6	806.6	2,388.0	262.7	

Key Violent Crime Data (Rate per 100,000 residents)

	Rate	Murder	Rape	Robbery	Aggravated Assault
Area	820.6	7.9	38.8	239.4	534.5
USA	432.8	4.7	34.7	111.6	285.6

Key Economic Data (Family income, unemployment)

	$25k-$75k	$75k-$150k	>$150k	Unemployment 03/2009	Unemployment 03/2010
Area	48.2%	26.9%	9.4%	9.5%	12.1%
USA	45.8%	29.5%	8.5%	9.0%	10.1

Key Household Data

	Population Age 0-17	Children w/Married Parents	Children w/Single Mother	Stay-at-home Mothers	Births to Single Women
Area	23.8%	63.4%	27.9%	28.4%	34.1%
USA	24.0%	65.6%	25.5%	27.9%	35.3%

Key Housing Data

	Owner Occupied	Median Year Built	Median Home Value	Home Value Growth, 2005-2010	Median List Price, 4-bedroom Home
Area	67.3%	1988	$232,200	4.5%	$230,000
USA	67.8%	1976	$187,045	3.1%	$288,846

Oshkosh-Neenah, WI
162,111

	Score	Rank
Overall	74.30	21
LDS Culture	37.36	64
Education	87.75	26
Crime	80.88	31
Economic	79.71	15
Health	39.16	231
Household	74.69	107
Housing	76.87	260

Key LDS Culture Data

	Positive	Negative	Ratio Pos:Neg	Commute>59 minutes	Commute<15 minutes
Area	2,126	292	7.3	2.5%	42.5%
USA	4,292	251	20.1	5.5%	34.1%

Key Education Data

	HS Grad	Some Coll.	College Degree	Free/Reduced Lunch	Students per Teacher
Area	88.5%	19.2%	33.3%	28.2%	14.8
USA	85.8%	22.6%	33.2%	41.2%	15.8

Key Property Crime Data (Rate per 100,000 residents)

	Rate	Burglary	Larceny, Theft	Vehicle Theft
Area	2,435.8	501.5	1,845.8	88.5
USA	3,413.6	806.6	2,388.0	262.7

Key Violent Crime Data (Rate per 100,000 residents)

	Rate	Murder	Rape	Robbery	Aggravated Assault
Area	196.1	1.8	17.2	25.8	151.2
USA	432.8	4.7	34.7	111.6	285.6

Key Economic Data (Family income, unemployment)

	$25k-$75k	$75k-$150k	>$150k	Unemployment 03/2009	Unemployment 03/2010
Area	45.8%	37.3%	7.3%	8.4%	8.4%
USA	45.8%	29.5%	8.5%	9.0%	10.1

Key Household Data

	Population Age 0-17	Children w/Married Parents	Children w/Single Mother	Stay-at-home Mothers	Births to Single Women
Area	21.4%	74.0%	19.9%	13.1%	17.2%
USA	24.0%	65.6%	25.5%	27.9%	35.3%

Key Housing Data

	Owner Occupied	Median Year Built	Median Home Value	Home Value Growth, 2005-2010	Median List Price, 4-bedroom Home
Area	70.3%	1969	$145,900	1.8%	
USA	67.8%	1976	$187,045	3.1%	$288,846

Owensboro, KY
110,553

	Score	Rank
Overall	64.33	155
LDS Culture	42.12	33
Education	72.79	153
Crime	63.68	120
Economic	65.87	140
Health	26.56	358
Household	58.02	239
Housing	83.45	167

Key LDS Culture Data

	Positive	Negative	Ratio Pos:Neg	Commute>59 minutes	Commute<15 minutes
Area	2,350	133	17.7	3.4%	41.3%
USA	4,292	251	20.1	5.5%	34.1%

Key Education Data

	HS Grad	Some Coll.	College Degree	Free/Reduced Lunch	Students per Teacher
Area	84.8%	21.9%	26.1%	43.8%	15.3
USA	85.8%	22.6%	33.2%	41.2%	15.8

Key Property Crime Data (Rate per 100,000 residents)

	Rate	Burglary	Larceny, Theft	Vehicle Theft
Area		538.9	1,880.9	139.2
USA	3,413.6	806.6	2,388.0	262.7

Key Violent Crime Data (Rate per 100,000 residents)

	Rate	Murder	Rape	Robbery	Aggravated Assault
Area		4.6	29.1	60.8	121.5
USA	432.8	4.7	34.7	111.6	285.6

Key Economic Data (Family income, unemployment)

	$25k-$75k	$75k-$150k	>$150k	Unemployment 03/2009	Unemployment 03/2010
Area	54.1%	22.4%	4.6%	9.9%	9.7%
USA	45.8%	29.5%	8.5%	9.0%	10.1

Key Household Data

	Population Age 0-17	Children w/Married Parents	Children w/Single Mother	Stay-at-home Mothers	Births to Single Women
Area	23.6%	66.3%	24.0%	29.8%	44.6%
USA	24.0%	65.6%	25.5%	27.9%	35.3%

Key Housing Data

	Owner Occupied	Median Year Built	Median Home Value	Home Value Growth, 2005-2010	Median List Price, 4-bedroom Home
Area	69.4%	1971	$96,500	1.7%	
USA	67.8%	1976	$187,045	3.1%	$288,846

Oxnard-Thousand Oaks-Ventura, CA
797,740

	Score	Rank
Overall	69.07	64
LDS Culture	17.54	314
Education	81.55	62
Crime	78.34	36
Economic	64.59	157
Health	48.59	68
Household	84.57	36
Housing	67.75	334

Key LDS Culture Data

	Positive	Negative	Ratio Pos:Neg	Commute>59 minutes	Commute<15 minutes
Area	19,925	802	24.8	10.1%	29.6%
USA	4,292	251	20.1	5.5%	34.1%

Key Education Data

	HS Grad	Some Coll.	College Degree	Free/Reduced Lunch	Students per Teacher
Area	82.0%	24.8%	38.1%	39.6%	19.4
USA	85.8%	22.6%	33.2%	41.2%	15.8

Key Property Crime Data (Rate per 100,000 residents)

	Rate	Burglary	Larceny, Theft	Vehicle Theft
Area	2,012.8	410.0	1,432.7	170.2
USA	3,413.6	806.6	2,388.0	262.7

Key Violent Crime Data (Rate per 100,000 residents)

	Rate	Murder	Rape	Robbery	Aggravated Assault
Area	267.2	3.9	15.5	108.4	139.4
USA	432.8	4.7	34.7	111.6	285.6

Key Economic Data (Family income, unemployment)

	$25k-$75k	$75k-$150k	>$150k	Unemployment 03/2009	Unemployment 03/2010
Area	33.5%	37.8%	19.9%	9.2%	11.2%
USA	45.8%	29.5%	8.5%	9.0%	10.1

Key Household Data

	Population Age 0-17	Children w/Married Parents	Children w/Single Mother	Stay-at-home Mothers	Births to Single Women
Area	25.9%	72.4%	18.9%	35.0%	31.9%
USA	24.0%	65.6%	25.5%	27.9%	35.3%

Key Housing Data

	Owner Occupied	Median Year Built	Median Home Value	Home Value Growth, 2005-2010	Median List Price, 4-bedroom Home
Area	66.3%	1976	$566,200	-0.8%	
USA	67.8%	1976	$187,045	3.1%	$288,846

Palm Bay-Melbourne-Titusville, FL
536,521

	Score	Rank
Overall	58.73	271
LDS Culture	15.17	334
Education	68.32	203
Crime	38.64	297
Economic	58.81	244
Health	45.75	137
Household	69.14	153
Housing	80.74	201

Key LDS Culture Data

	Positive	Negative	Ratio Pos:Neg	Commute>59 minutes	Commute<15 minutes
Area	2,782	162	17.2	6.5%	25.1%
USA	4,292	251	20.1	5.5%	34.1%

Key Education Data

	HS Grad	Some Coll.	College Degree	Free/Reduced Lunch	Students per Teacher
Area	90.2%	24.5%	37.0%	30.5%	15.3
USA	85.8%	22.6%	33.2%	41.2%	15.8

Key Property Crime Data (Rate per 100,000 residents)

	Rate	Burglary	Larceny, Theft	Vehicle Theft	
Area	3,471.3	918.6	2,316.6	236.0	
USA	3,413.6	806.6	2,388.0	262.7	

Key Violent Crime Data (Rate per 100,000 residents)

	Rate	Murder	Rape	Robbery	Aggravated Assault
Area	686.9	4.1	33.3	123.4	526.0
USA	432.8	4.7	34.7	111.6	285.6

Key Economic Data (Family income, unemployment)

	$25k-$75k	$75k-$150k	>$150k	Unemployment 03/2009	Unemployment 03/2010
Area	47.3%	29.4%	8.3%	9.6%	12.2%
USA	45.8%	29.5%	8.5%	9.0%	10.1

Key Household Data

	Population Age 0-17	Children w/Married Parents	Children w/Single Mother	Stay-at-home Mothers	Births to Single Women
Area	19.9%	65.1%	23.4%	28.1%	34.3%
USA	24.0%	65.6%	25.5%	27.9%	35.3%

Key Housing Data

	Owner Occupied	Median Year Built	Median Home Value	Home Value Growth, 2005-2010	Median List Price, 4-bedroom Home
Area	75.3%	1985	$193,900	0.5%	
USA	67.8%	1976	$187,045	3.1%	$288,846

Palm Coast, FL
91,247

	Score	Rank
Overall	69.37	57
LDS Culture	13.59	346
Education	89.85	19
Crime	73.03	64
Economic	57.53	265
Health	45.32	142
Household	79.01	72
Housing	86.50	108

Key LDS Culture Data

	Positive	Negative	Ratio Pos:Neg	Commute>59 minutes	Commute<15 minutes
Area	2,338	152	15.4	6.6%	29.0%
USA	4,292	251	20.1	5.5%	34.1%

Key Education Data

	HS Grad	Some Coll.	College Degree	Free/Reduced Lunch	Students per Teacher
Area	90.9%	24.1%	30.6%	35.6%	13.6
USA	85.8%	22.6%	33.2%	41.2%	15.8

Key Property Crime Data (Rate per 100,000 residents)

	Rate	Burglary	Larceny, Theft	Vehicle Theft	
Area	2,329.9	575.5	1,610.2	144.1	
USA	3,413.6	806.6	2,388.0	262.7	

Key Violent Crime Data (Rate per 100,000 residents)

	Rate	Murder	Rape	Robbery	Aggravated Assault
Area	291.5	0.0	14.9	59.8	216.8
USA	432.8	4.7	34.7	111.6	285.6

Key Economic Data (Family income, unemployment)

	$25k-$75k	$75k-$150k	>$150k	Unemployment 03/2009	Unemployment 03/2010
Area	56.9%	22.9%	4.4%	13.7%	16.6%
USA	45.8%	29.5%	8.5%	9.0%	10.1

Key Household Data

	Population Age 0-17	Children w/Married Parents	Children w/Single Mother	Stay-at-home Mothers	Births to Single Women
Area	18.8%	67.3%	18.9%	28.7%	17.4%
USA	24.0%	65.6%	25.5%	27.9%	35.3%

Key Housing Data

	Owner Occupied	Median Year Built	Median Home Value	Home Value Growth, 2005-2010	Median List Price, 4-bedroom Home
Area	76.9%	1997	$221,600	0.4%	
USA	67.8%	1976	$187,045	3.1%	$288,846

Panama City-Lynn Haven-Panama City Beach, FL
163,946

	Score	Rank
Overall	57.39	296
LDS Culture	21.72	265
Education	59.61	298
Crime	37.04	306
Economic	61.81	200
Health	48.82	57
Household	58.02	240
Housing	80.96	198

Key LDS Culture Data

	Positive	Negative	Ratio Pos:Neg	Commute>59 minutes	Commute<15 minutes
Area	1,371	94	14.6	3.1%	36.0%
USA	4,292	251	20.1	5.5%	34.1%

Key Education Data

	HS Grad	Some Coll.	College Degree	Free/Reduced Lunch	Students per Teacher
Area	87.0%	24.4%	29.1%	45.2%	14.8
USA	85.8%	22.6%	33.2%	41.2%	15.8

Key Property Crime Data (Rate per 100,000 residents)

	Rate	Burglary	Larceny, Theft	Vehicle Theft	
Area	4,100.4	984.7	2,894.4	221.3	
USA	3,413.6	806.6	2,388.0	262.7	

Key Violent Crime Data (Rate per 100,000 residents)

	Rate	Murder	Rape	Robbery	Aggravated Assault
Area	656.1	6.7	57.3	104.9	487.2
USA	432.8	4.7	34.7	111.6	285.6

Key Economic Data (Family income, unemployment)

	$25k-$75k	$75k-$150k	>$150k	Unemployment 03/2009	Unemployment 03/2010
Area	54.7%	23.9%	7.1%	8.6%	10.4%
USA	45.8%	29.5%	8.5%	9.0%	10.1

Key Household Data

	Population Age 0-17	Children w/Married Parents	Children w/Single Mother	Stay-at-home Mothers	Births to Single Women
Area	23.0%	66.9%	25.7%	29.1%	36.9%
USA	24.0%	65.6%	25.5%	27.9%	35.3%

Key Housing Data

	Owner Occupied	Median Year Built	Median Home Value	Home Value Growth, 2005-2010	Median List Price, 4-bedroom Home
Area	65.4%	1986	$179,900	4.1%	$314,900
USA	67.8%	1976	$187,045	3.1%	$288,846

Parkersburg-Marietta-Vienna, WV-OH
157,943

	Score	Rank
Overall	64.52	148
LDS Culture	37.94	57
Education	71.06	171
Crime	82.47	24
Economic	50.42	326
Health	42.19	179
Household	51.85	292
Housing	77.80	247

Key LDS Culture Data

	Positive	Negative	Ratio Pos:Neg	Commute>59 minutes	Commute<15 minutes
Area	1,055	46	22.9	4.6%	36.2%
USA	4,292	251	20.1	5.5%	34.1%

Key Education Data

	HS Grad	Some Coll.	College Degree	Free/Reduced Lunch	Students per Teacher
Area	87.8%	23.4%	25.3%	25.1%	15.3
USA	85.8%	22.6%	33.2%	41.2%	15.8

Key Property Crime Data (Rate per 100,000 residents)

	Rate	Burglary	Larceny, Theft	Vehicle Theft	
Area	2,457.0	545.8	1,778.0	133.2	
USA	3,413.6	806.6	2,388.0	262.7	

Key Violent Crime Data (Rate per 100,000 residents)

	Rate	Murder	Rape	Robbery	Aggravated Assault
Area	176.7	2.5	27.4	20.5	126.3
USA	432.8	4.7	34.7	111.6	285.6

Key Economic Data (Family income, unemployment)

	$25k-$75k	$75k-$150k	>$150k	Unemployment 03/2009	Unemployment 03/2010
Area	54.8%	22.3%	4.1%	9.1%	10.9%
USA	45.8%	29.5%	8.5%	9.0%	10.1

Key Household Data

	Population Age 0-17	Children w/Married Parents	Children w/Single Mother	Stay-at-home Mothers	Births to Single Women
Area	21.3%	65.2%	23.7%	25.6%	52.7%
USA	24.0%	65.6%	25.5%	27.9%	35.3%

Key Housing Data

	Owner Occupied	Median Year Built	Median Home Value	Home Value Growth, 2005-2010	Median List Price, 4-bedroom Home
Area	74.3%	1966	$102,700	3.0%	
USA	67.8%	1976	$187,045	3.1%	$288,846

Pascagoula, MS
157,563

	Score	Rank
Overall	64.69	143
LDS Culture	10.79	355
Education	56.90	314
Crime	67.45	96
Economic	59.31	237
Health	32.82	319
Household	93.21	5
Housing	94.32	15

Key LDS Culture Data

	Positive	Negative	Ratio Pos:Neg	Commute>59 minutes	Commute<15 minutes
Area	1,819	149	12.2	7.8%	22.6%
USA	4,292	251	20.1	5.5%	34.1%

Key Education Data

	HS Grad	Some Coll.	College Degree	Free/Reduced Lunch	Students per Teacher
Area	85.4%	25.9%	24.3%	56.3%	14.6
USA	85.8%	22.6%	33.2%	41.2%	15.8

Key Property Crime Data (Rate per 100,000 residents)

	Rate	Burglary	Larceny, Theft	Vehicle Theft	
Area	3,400.5	857.5	2,210.3	332.8	
USA	3,413.6	806.6	2,388.0	262.7	

Key Violent Crime Data (Rate per 100,000 residents)

	Rate	Murder	Rape	Robbery	Aggravated Assault
Area	246.3	3.3	40.0	85.2	117.9
USA	432.8	4.7	34.7	111.6	285.6

Key Economic Data (Family income, unemployment)

	$25k-$75k	$75k-$150k	>$150k	Unemployment 03/2009	Unemployment 03/2010
Area	50.4%	28.6%	4.6%	7.9%	10.3%
USA	45.8%	29.5%	8.5%	9.0%	10.1

Key Household Data

	Population Age 0-17	Children w/Married Parents	Children w/Single Mother	Stay-at-home Mothers	Births to Single Women
Area	26.8%	73.5%	21.3%	40.0%	16.7%
USA	24.0%	65.6%	25.5%	27.9%	35.3%

Key Housing Data

	Owner Occupied	Median Year Built	Median Home Value	Home Value Growth, 2005-2010	Median List Price, 4-bedroom Home
Area	75.0%	1984	$130,200	6.7%	
USA	67.8%	1976	$187,045	3.1%	$288,846

Pensacola-Ferry Pass-Brent, FL
452,992

	Score	Rank
Overall	59.56	254
LDS Culture	18.46	305
Education	64.72	245
Crime	41.42	276
Economic	58.53	249
Health	52.72	24
Household	52.47	286
Housing	93.62	21

Key LDS Culture Data

	Positive	Negative	Ratio Pos:Neg	Commute>59 minutes	Commute<15 minutes
Area	2,559	161	15.9	5.8%	30.3%
USA	4,292	251	20.1	5.5%	34.1%

Key Education Data

	HS Grad	Some Coll.	College Degree	Free/Reduced Lunch	Students per Teacher
Area	87.2%	25.3%	33.1%	48.5%	13.7
USA	85.8%	22.6%	33.2%	41.2%	15.8

Key Property Crime Data (Rate per 100,000 residents)

	Rate	Burglary	Larceny, Theft	Vehicle Theft
Area	3,194.4	774.5	2,208.0	211.8
USA	3,413.6	806.6	2,388.0	262.7

Key Violent Crime Data (Rate per 100,000 residents)

	Rate	Murder	Rape	Robbery	Aggravated Assault
Area	663.4	5.3	39.3	158.4	460.4
USA	432.8	4.7	34.7	111.6	285.6

Key Economic Data (Family income, unemployment)

	$25k-$75k	$75k-$150k	>$150k	Unemployment 03/2009	Unemployment 03/2010
Area	49.3%	27.5%	6.2%	8.9%	11.1%
USA	45.8%	29.5%	8.5%	9.0%	10.1

Key Household Data

	Population Age 0-17	Children w/Married Parents	Children w/Single Mother	Stay-at-home Mothers	Births to Single Women
Area	22.5%	60.4%	31.8%	28.6%	36.1%
USA	24.0%	65.6%	25.5%	27.9%	35.3%

Key Housing Data

	Owner Occupied	Median Year Built	Median Home Value	Home Value Growth, 2005-2010	Median List Price, 4-bedroom Home
Area	72.5%	1984	$157,700	4.6%	$239,000
USA	67.8%	1976	$187,045	3.1%	$288,846

Peoria, IL
373,174

	Score	Rank
Overall	62.09	193
LDS Culture	28.16	169
Education	75.78	119
Crime	34.75	322
Economic	56.36	281
Health	47.30	107
Household	75.31	100
Housing	80.45	206

Key LDS Culture Data

	Positive	Negative	Ratio Pos:Neg	Commute>59 minutes	Commute<15 minutes
Area	2,101	177	11.9	3.6%	34.1%
USA	4,292	251	20.1	5.5%	34.1%

Key Education Data

	HS Grad	Some Coll.	College Degree	Free/Reduced Lunch	Students per Teacher
Area	89.4%	23.9%	35.8%	34.8%	18.2
USA	85.8%	22.6%	33.2%	41.2%	15.8

Key Property Crime Data (Rate per 100,000 residents)

	Rate	Burglary	Larceny, Theft	Vehicle Theft
Area		1,403.5	3,879.4	496.1
USA	3,413.6	806.6	2,388.0	262.7

Key Violent Crime Data (Rate per 100,000 residents)

	Rate	Murder	Rape	Robbery	Aggravated Assault
Area		15.0		340.7	489.0
USA	432.8	4.7	34.7	111.6	285.6

Key Economic Data (Family income, unemployment)

	$25k-$75k	$75k-$150k	>$150k	Unemployment 03/2009	Unemployment 03/2010
Area	43.9%	33.1%	10.2%	9.2%	12.3%
USA	45.8%	29.5%	8.5%	9.0%	10.1

Key Household Data

	Population Age 0-17	Children w/Married Parents	Children w/Single Mother	Stay-at-home Mothers	Births to Single Women
Area	23.6%	66.0%	25.8%	28.8%	33.4%
USA	24.0%	65.6%	25.5%	27.9%	35.3%

Key Housing Data

	Owner Occupied	Median Year Built	Median Home Value	Home Value Growth, 2005-2010	Median List Price, 4-bedroom Home
Area	75.4%	1963	$127,000	3.0%	$219,900
USA	67.8%	1976	$187,045	3.1%	$288,846

Philadelphia-Camden-Wilmington, PA-NJ-DE-MD
5,838,471

	Score	Rank
Overall	57.89	287
LDS Culture	16.07	328
Education	75.81	118
Crime	44.97	255
Economic	68.32	104
Health	43.22	166
Household	56.79	255
Housing	66.02	338

Key LDS Culture Data

	Positive	Negative	Ratio Pos:Neg	Commute>59 minutes	Commute<15 minutes
Area	29,820	1640	18.2	10.0%	23.4%
USA	4,292	251	20.1	5.5%	34.1%

Key Education Data

	HS Grad	Some Coll.	College Degree	Free/Reduced Lunch	Students per Teacher
Area	87.6%	17.9%	38.6%	30.6%	14.4
USA	85.8%	22.6%	33.2%	41.2%	15.8

Key Property Crime Data (Rate per 100,000 residents)

	Rate	Burglary	Larceny, Theft	Vehicle Theft
Area	2,982.6	570.4	2,118.8	293.4
USA	3,413.6	806.6	2,388.0	262.7

Key Violent Crime Data (Rate per 100,000 residents)

	Rate	Murder	Rape	Robbery	Aggravated Assault
Area	628.7	9.1	32.6	255.8	331.3
USA	432.8	4.7	34.7	111.6	285.6

Key Economic Data (Family income, unemployment)

	$25k-$75k	$75k-$150k	>$150k	Unemployment 03/2009	Unemployment 03/2010
Area	35.6%	35.5%	16.3%	7.9%	9.4%
USA	45.8%	29.5%	8.5%	9.0%	10.1

Key Household Data

	Population Age 0-17	Children w/Married Parents	Children w/Single Mother	Stay-at-home Mothers	Births to Single Women
Area	23.9%	64.8%	26.7%	26.2%	39.1%
USA	24.0%	65.6%	25.5%	27.9%	35.3%

Key Housing Data

	Owner Occupied	Median Year Built	Median Home Value	Home Value Growth, 2005-2010	Median List Price, 4-bedroom Home
Area	69.8%	1963	$254,400	4.7%	$356,900
USA	67.8%	1976	$187,045	3.1%	$288,846

Phoenix-Mesa-Scottsdale, AZ
4,281,899

	Score	Rank
Overall	62.96	183
LDS Culture	17.76	312
Education	76.32	113
Crime	45.07	253
Economic	59.81	231
Health	39.87	217
Household	72.22	133
Housing	92.70	28

Key LDS Culture Data

	Positive	Negative	Ratio Pos:Neg	Commute>59 minutes	Commute<15 minutes
Area	13,848	689	20.1	7.0%	23.0%
USA	4,292	251	20.1	5.5%	34.1%

Key Education Data

	HS Grad	Some Coll.	College Degree	Free/Reduced Lunch	Students per Teacher
Area	83.7%	25.2%	34.3%	36.2%	20.8
USA	85.8%	22.6%	33.2%	41.2%	15.8

Key Property Crime Data (Rate per 100,000 residents)

	Rate	Burglary	Larceny, Theft	Vehicle Theft	
Area	4,256.2	927.4	2,699.4	629.4	
USA	3,413.6	806.6	2,388.0	262.7	

Key Violent Crime Data (Rate per 100,000 residents)

	Rate	Murder	Rape	Robbery	Aggravated Assault
Area	455.2	6.6	24.3	175.2	249.0
USA	432.8	4.7	34.7	111.6	285.6

Key Economic Data (Family income, unemployment)

	$25k-$75k	$75k-$150k	>$150k	Unemployment 03/2009	Unemployment 03/2010
Area	44.1%	31.8%	10.6%	8.2%	8.9%
USA	45.8%	29.5%	8.5%	9.0%	10.1

Key Household Data

	Population Age 0-17	Children w/Married Parents	Children w/Single Mother	Stay-at-home Mothers	Births to Single Women
Area	27.3%	66.1%	23.1%	35.4%	32.1%
USA	24.0%	65.6%	25.5%	27.9%	35.3%

Key Housing Data

	Owner Occupied	Median Year Built	Median Home Value	Home Value Growth, 2005-2010	Median List Price, 4-bedroom Home
Area	68.4%	1989	$244,100	4.4%	$200,000
USA	67.8%	1976	$187,045	3.1%	$288,846

Pine Bluff, AR
99,876

	Score	Rank
Overall	52.33	354
LDS Culture	32.87	109
Education	61.61	281
Crime	16.33	358
Economic	46.25	348
Health	40.43	214
Household	53.70	281
Housing	84.36	151

Key LDS Culture Data

	Positive	Negative	Ratio Pos:Neg	Commute>59 minutes	Commute<15 minutes
Area	705	41	17.2	4.5%	31.2%
USA	4,292	251	20.1	5.5%	34.1%

Key Education Data

	HS Grad	Some Coll.	College Degree	Free/Reduced Lunch	Students per Teacher
Area	81.4%	22.7%	21.0%	63.9%	13.1
USA	85.8%	22.6%	33.2%	41.2%	15.8

Key Property Crime Data (Rate per 100,000 residents)

	Rate	Burglary	Larceny, Theft	Vehicle Theft
Area	5,805.5	2,049.0	3,226.4	530.1
USA	3,413.6	806.6	2,388.0	262.7

Key Violent Crime Data (Rate per 100,000 residents)

	Rate	Murder	Rape	Robbery	Aggravated Assault
Area	949.1	20.8	85.4	260.1	582.7
USA	432.8	4.7	34.7	111.6	285.6

Key Economic Data (Family income, unemployment)

	$25k-$75k	$75k-$150k	>$150k	Unemployment 03/2009	Unemployment 03/2010
Area	48.4%	22.5%	2.6%	8.6%	9.9%
USA	45.8%	29.5%	8.5%	9.0%	10.1

Key Household Data

	Population Age 0-17	Children w/Married Parents	Children w/Single Mother	Stay-at-home Mothers	Births to Single Women
Area	23.8%	46.4%	42.9%	24.0%	55.9%
USA	24.0%	65.6%	25.5%	27.9%	35.3%

Key Housing Data

	Owner Occupied	Median Year Built	Median Home Value	Home Value Growth, 2005-2010	Median List Price, 4-bedroom Home
Area	67.6%	1975	$77,900	3.8%	
USA	67.8%	1976	$187,045	3.1%	$288,846

333

Pittsburgh, PA
2,351,192

	Score	Rank
Overall	68.07	82
LDS Culture	41.96	36
Education	82.76	52
Crime	67.31	101
Economic	63.09	182
Health	42.62	173
Household	61.11	217
Housing	77.64	251

Key LDS Culture Data

	Positive	Negative	Ratio Pos:Neg	Commute>59 minutes	Commute<15 minutes
Area	12,084	968	12.5	7.5%	27.7%
USA	4,292	251	20.1	5.5%	34.1%

Key Education Data

	HS Grad	Some Coll.	College Degree	Free/Reduced Lunch	Students per Teacher
Area	90.8%	16.5%	37.9%	27.4%	14.5
USA	85.8%	22.6%	33.2%	41.2%	15.8

Key Property Crime Data (Rate per 100,000 residents)

	Rate	Burglary	Larceny, Theft	Vehicle Theft
Area	2,158.1	440.7	1,572.7	144.7
USA	3,413.6	806.6	2,388.0	262.7

Key Violent Crime Data (Rate per 100,000 residents)

	Rate	Murder	Rape	Robbery	Aggravated Assault
Area	370.8	5.2	20.5	120.7	224.4
USA	432.8	4.7	34.7	111.6	285.6

Key Economic Data (Family income, unemployment)

	$25k-$75k	$75k-$150k	>$150k	Unemployment 03/2009	Unemployment 03/2010
Area	46.4%	29.6%	9.1%	7.3%	8.9%
USA	45.8%	29.5%	8.5%	9.0%	10.1

Key Household Data

	Population Age 0-17	Children w/Married Parents	Children w/Single Mother	Stay-at-home Mothers	Births to Single Women
Area	20.5%	65.9%	26.3%	27.8%	37.5%
USA	24.0%	65.6%	25.5%	27.9%	35.3%

Key Housing Data

	Owner Occupied	Median Year Built	Median Home Value	Home Value Growth, 2005-2010	Median List Price, 4-bedroom Home
Area	71.1%	1957	$119,400	3.0%	$245,700
USA	67.8%	1976	$187,045	3.1%	$288,846

Pittsfield, MA
129,395

	Score	Rank
Overall	59.64	252
LDS Culture	25.74	202
Education	77.84	98
Crime	63.26	126
Economic	69.98	84
Health	40.96	207
Household	40.74	358
Housing	63.89	344

Key LDS Culture Data
	Positive	Negative	Ratio Pos:Neg	Commute>59 minutes	Commute<15 minutes
Area	3,561	252	14.1	5.2%	42.4%
USA	4,292	251	20.1	5.5%	34.1%

Key Education Data
	HS Grad	Some Coll.	College Degree	Free/Reduced Lunch	Students per Teacher
Area	92.0%	20.6%	36.7%	31.0%	12.0
USA	85.8%	22.6%	33.2%	41.2%	15.8

Key Property Crime Data (Rate per 100,000 residents)
	Rate	Burglary	Larceny, Theft	Vehicle Theft
Area	2,294.5	787.4	1,406.3	100.8
USA	3,413.6	806.6	2,388.0	262.7

Key Violent Crime Data (Rate per 100,000 residents)
	Rate	Murder	Rape	Robbery	Aggravated Assault
Area	400.3	1.5	59.3	20.8	318.7
USA	432.8	4.7	34.7	111.6	285.6

Key Economic Data (Family income, unemployment)
	$25k-$75k	$75k-$150k	>$150k	Unemployment 03/2009	Unemployment 03/2010
Area	49.2%	27.6%	9.0%	8.7%	9.8%
USA	45.8%	29.5%	8.5%	9.0%	10.1

Key Household Data
	Population Age 0-17	Children w/Married Parents	Children w/Single Mother	Stay-at-home Mothers	Births to Single Women
Area	19.2%	56.0%	29.2%	19.6%	57.0%
USA	24.0%	65.6%	25.5%	27.9%	35.3%

Key Housing Data
	Owner Occupied	Median Year Built	Median Home Value	Home Value Growth, 2005-2010	Median List Price, 4-bedroom Home
Area	67.1%	1955	$208,900	3.9%	
USA	67.8%	1976	$187,045	3.1%	$288,846

Pocatello, ID
87,692

	Score	Rank
Overall	71.43	36
LDS Culture	37.28	65
Education	74.78	129
Crime	68.90	83
Economic	61.09	211
Health	41.66	187
Household	91.36	12
Housing	82.96	177

Key LDS Culture Data
	Positive	Negative	Ratio Pos:Neg	Commute>59 minutes	Commute<15 minutes
Area	550	32	17.2	4.9%	59.6%
USA	4,292	251	20.1	5.5%	34.1%

Key Education Data
	HS Grad	Some Coll.	College Degree	Free/Reduced Lunch	Students per Teacher
Area	90.1%	30.5%	35.2%	37.6%	18.7
USA	85.8%	22.6%	33.2%	41.2%	15.8

Key Property Crime Data (Rate per 100,000 residents)
	Rate	Burglary	Larceny, Theft	Vehicle Theft
Area	2,828.6	385.4	2,343.1	100.0
USA	3,413.6	806.6	2,388.0	262.7

Key Violent Crime Data (Rate per 100,000 residents)
	Rate	Murder	Rape	Robbery	Aggravated Assault
Area	284.2	1.1	51.2	18.2	213.7
USA	432.8	4.7	34.7	111.6	285.6

Key Economic Data (Family income, unemployment)
	$25k-$75k	$75k-$150k	>$150k	Unemployment 03/2009	Unemployment 03/2010
Area	54.7%	28.4%	2.5%	6.5%	8.7%
USA	45.8%	29.5%	8.5%	9.0%	10.1

Key Household Data
	Population Age 0-17	Children w/Married Parents	Children w/Single Mother	Stay-at-home Mothers	Births to Single Women
Area	28.7%	77.2%	16.2%	33.4%	16.5%
USA	24.0%	65.6%	25.5%	27.9%	35.3%

Key Housing Data
	Owner Occupied	Median Year Built	Median Home Value	Home Value Growth, 2005-2010	Median List Price, 4-bedroom Home
Area	72.1%	1974	$146,500	6.0%	
USA	67.8%	1976	$187,045	3.1%	$288,846

Port St. Lucie, FL
514,065

	Score	Rank
Overall	67.76	91
LDS Culture	19.76	287
Education	73.34	145
Crime	49.66	223
Economic	81.55	12
Health	50.00	39
Household	74.07	117
Housing	86.14	118

Key LDS Culture Data

	Positive	Negative	Ratio Pos:Neg	Commute>59 minutes	Commute<15 minutes
Area	2,481	84	29.5	6.3%	32.1%
USA	4,292	251	20.1	5.5%	34.1%

Key Education Data

	HS Grad	Some Coll.	College Degree	Free/Reduced Lunch	Students per Teacher
Area	92.0%	20.5%	42.0%	25.3%	9.3
USA	85.8%	22.6%	33.2%	41.2%	15.8

Key Property Crime Data (Rate per 100,000 residents)

	Rate	Burglary	Larceny, Theft	Vehicle Theft
Area	3,120.9	847.5	2,133.9	139.5
USA	3,413.6	806.6	2,388.0	262.7

Key Violent Crime Data (Rate per 100,000 residents)

	Rate	Murder	Rape	Robbery	Aggravated Assault
Area	490.4	3.2	28.3	125.9	333.0
USA	432.8	4.7	34.7	111.6	285.6

Key Economic Data (Family income, unemployment)

	$25k-$75k	$75k-$150k	>$150k	Unemployment 03/2009	Unemployment 03/2010
Area	44.4%	33.1%	9.8%	5.8%	6.3%
USA	45.8%	29.5%	8.5%	9.0%	10.1

Key Household Data

	Population Age 0-17	Children w/Married Parents	Children w/Single Mother	Stay-at-home Mothers	Births to Single Women
Area	21.5%	68.7%	22.4%	20.5%	29.6%
USA	24.0%	65.6%	25.5%	27.9%	35.3%

Key Housing Data

	Owner Occupied	Median Year Built	Median Home Value	Home Value Growth, 2005-2010	Median List Price, 4-bedroom Home
Area	70.9%	1977	$245,200	-2.8%	$350,000
USA	67.8%	1976	$187,045	3.1%	$288,846

Portland-South Portland-Biddeford, ME
2,209,114

	Score	Rank
Overall	69.60	55
LDS Culture	34.94	81
Education	73.46	142
Crime	86.69	12
Economic	71.04	74
Health	47.72	87
Household	66.67	171
Housing	65.82	339

Key LDS Culture Data

	Positive	Negative	Ratio Pos:Neg	Commute>59 minutes	Commute<15 minutes
Area	9,986	619	16.1	6.6%	25.5%
USA	4,292	251	20.1	5.5%	34.1%

Key Education Data

	HS Grad	Some Coll.	College Degree	Free/Reduced Lunch	Students per Teacher
Area	90.0%	26.4%	41.4%	36.3%	19.6
USA	85.8%	22.6%	33.2%	41.2%	15.8

Key Property Crime Data (Rate per 100,000 residents)

	Rate	Burglary	Larceny, Theft	Vehicle Theft	
Area	2,424.6	468.8	1,862.7	93.0	
USA	3,413.6	806.6	2,388.0	262.7	

Key Violent Crime Data (Rate per 100,000 residents)

	Rate	Murder	Rape	Robbery	Aggravated Assault
Area	134.7	2.1	33.1	39.3	60.1
USA	432.8	4.7	34.7	111.6	285.6

Key Economic Data (Family income, unemployment)

	$25k-$75k	$75k-$150k	>$150k	Unemployment 03/2009	Unemployment 03/2010
Area	40.2%	35.5%	11.7%	11.4%	14.0%
USA	45.8%	29.5%	8.5%	9.0%	10.1

Key Household Data

	Population Age 0-17	Children w/Married Parents	Children w/Single Mother	Stay-at-home Mothers	Births to Single Women
Area	24.1%	70.8%	21.0%	31.4%	28.9%
USA	24.0%	65.6%	25.5%	27.9%	35.3%

Key Housing Data

	Owner Occupied	Median Year Built	Median Home Value	Home Value Growth, 2005-2010	Median List Price, 4-bedroom Home
Area	65.3%	1978	$307,400	2.4%	$349,900
USA	67.8%	1976	$187,045	3.1%	$288,846

Portland-Vancouver-Beaverton, OR-WA
403,768

	Score	Rank
Overall	66.63	109
LDS Culture	14.26	343
Education	73.95	137
Crime	63.88	118
Economic	60.92	214
Health	47.87	85
Household	84.57	37
Housing	81.82	187

Key LDS Culture Data

	Positive	Negative	Ratio Pos:Neg	Commute>59 minutes	Commute<15 minutes
Area	3,064	137	22.4	9.3%	23.4%
USA	4,292	251	20.1	5.5%	34.1%

Key Education Data

	HS Grad	Some Coll.	College Degree	Free/Reduced Lunch	Students per Teacher
Area	84.1%	22.3%	29.0%	46.2%	16.9
USA	85.8%	22.6%	33.2%	41.2%	15.8

Key Property Crime Data (Rate per 100,000 residents)

	Rate	Burglary	Larceny, Theft	Vehicle Theft
Area	3,262.6	495.9	2,403.9	362.9
USA	3,413.6	806.6	2,388.0	262.7

Key Violent Crime Data (Rate per 100,000 residents)

	Rate	Murder	Rape	Robbery	Aggravated Assault
Area	293.1	2.0	37.0	89.9	164.3
USA	432.8	4.7	34.7	111.6	285.6

Key Economic Data (Family income, unemployment)

	$25k-$75k	$75k-$150k	>$150k	Unemployment 03/2009	Unemployment 03/2010
Area	51.0%	26.4%	8.4%	11.1%	11.4%
USA	45.8%	29.5%	8.5%	9.0%	10.1

Key Household Data

	Population Age 0-17	Children w/Married Parents	Children w/Single Mother	Stay-at-home Mothers	Births to Single Women
Area	21.0%	65.7%	22.3%	31.7%	26.8%
USA	24.0%	65.6%	25.5%	27.9%	35.3%

Key Housing Data

	Owner Occupied	Median Year Built	Median Home Value	Home Value Growth, 2005-2010	Median List Price, 4-bedroom Home
Area	76.1%	1987	$209,500	6.4%	$239,000
USA	67.8%	1976	$187,045	3.1%	$288,846

Poughkeepsie-Newburgh-Middletown, NY
672,525

	Score	Rank
Overall	71.03	40
LDS Culture	24.31	233
Education	79.33	76
Crime	76.19	44
Economic	77.32	26
Health	49.20	52
Household	83.33	43
Housing	65.77	340

Key LDS Culture Data

	Positive	Negative	Ratio Pos:Neg	Commute>59 minutes	Commute<15 minutes
Area	4,709	269	17.5	17.6%	29.1%
USA	4,292	251	20.1	5.5%	34.1%

Key Education Data

	HS Grad	Some Coll.	College Degree	Free/Reduced Lunch	Students per Teacher
Area	87.5%	19.7%	39.6%	26.9%	13.5
USA	85.8%	22.6%	33.2%	41.2%	15.8

Key Property Crime Data (Rate per 100,000 residents)

	Rate	Burglary	Larceny, Theft	Vehicle Theft
Area	2,048.6	340.1	1,628.7	79.8
USA	3,413.6	806.6	2,388.0	262.7

Key Violent Crime Data (Rate per 100,000 residents)

	Rate	Murder	Rape	Robbery	Aggravated Assault
Area	286.7	2.7	16.9	85.4	181.7
USA	432.8	4.7	34.7	111.6	285.6

Key Economic Data (Family income, unemployment)

	$25k-$75k	$75k-$150k	>$150k	Unemployment 03/2009	Unemployment 03/2010
Area	33.6%	41.1%	16.2%	7.7%	7.9%
USA	45.8%	29.5%	8.5%	9.0%	10.1

Key Household Data

	Population Age 0-17	Children w/Married Parents	Children w/Single Mother	Stay-at-home Mothers	Births to Single Women
Area	24.4%	74.5%	17.4%	24.5%	26.3%
USA	24.0%	65.6%	25.5%	27.9%	35.3%

Key Housing Data

	Owner Occupied	Median Year Built	Median Home Value	Home Value Growth, 2005-2010	Median List Price, 4-bedroom Home
Area	70.0%	1971	$323,800	1.8%	$385,000
USA	67.8%	1976	$187,045	3.1%	$288,846

Prescott, AZ
215,503

	Score	Rank
Overall	63.39	173
LDS Culture	20.25	278
Education	59.60	300
Crime	68.23	88
Economic	66.26	133
Health	43.61	162
Household	61.73	213
Housing	86.80	102

Key LDS Culture Data

	Positive	Negative	Ratio Pos:Neg	Commute>59 minutes	Commute<15 minutes
Area	896	50	17.9	6.6%	36.2%
USA	4,292	251	20.1	5.5%	34.1%

Key Education Data

	HS Grad	Some Coll.	College Degree	Free/Reduced Lunch	Students per Teacher
Area	88.7%	29.9%	30.0%	38.9%	20.7
USA	85.8%	22.6%	33.2%	41.2%	15.8

Key Property Crime Data (Rate per 100,000 residents)

	Rate	Burglary	Larceny, Theft	Vehicle Theft	
Area	2,300.9	569.6	1,598.0	133.3	
USA	3,413.6	806.6	2,388.0	262.7	

Key Violent Crime Data (Rate per 100,000 residents)

	Rate	Murder	Rape	Robbery	Aggravated Assault
Area	346.2	1.8	19.3	21.1	303.9
USA	432.8	4.7	34.7	111.6	285.6

Key Economic Data (Family income, unemployment)

	$25k-$75k	$75k-$150k	>$150k	Unemployment 03/2009	Unemployment 03/2010
Area	56.0%	26.0%	4.7%	9.8%	10.0%
USA	45.8%	29.5%	8.5%	9.0%	10.1

Key Household Data

	Population Age 0-17	Children w/Married Parents	Children w/Single Mother	Stay-at-home Mothers	Births to Single Women
Area	20.0%	63.0%	25.1%	36.8%	33.7%
USA	24.0%	65.6%	25.5%	27.9%	35.3%

Key Housing Data

	Owner Occupied	Median Year Built	Median Home Value	Home Value Growth, 2005-2010	Median List Price, 4-bedroom Home
Area	70.7%	1992	$251,300	4.2%	$355,000
USA	67.8%	1976	$187,045	3.1%	$288,846

Providence-New Bedford-Fall River, RI-MA
1,596,611

	Score	Rank
Overall	54.44	336
LDS Culture	20.32	276
Education	72.83	152
Crime	61.40	142
Economic	58.03	258
Health	31.73	338
Household	48.77	312
Housing	56.05	357

Key LDS Culture Data

	Positive	Negative	Ratio Pos:Neg	Commute>59 minutes	Commute<15 minutes
Area	10,576	814	13.0	7.1%	30.6%
USA	4,292	251	20.1	5.5%	34.1%

Key Education Data

	HS Grad	Some Coll.	College Degree	Free/Reduced Lunch	Students per Teacher
Area	82.3%	18.1%	35.8%	35.1%	13.7
USA	85.8%	22.6%	33.2%	41.2%	15.8

Key Property Crime Data (Rate per 100,000 residents)

	Rate	Burglary	Larceny, Theft	Vehicle Theft	
Area	2,783.6	603.8	1,911.9	267.8	
USA	3,413.6	806.6	2,388.0	262.7	

Key Violent Crime Data (Rate per 100,000 residents)

	Rate	Murder	Rape	Robbery	Aggravated Assault
Area	369.5	2.6	28.4	98.3	240.3
USA	432.8	4.7	34.7	111.6	285.6

Key Economic Data (Family income, unemployment)

	$25k-$75k	$75k-$150k	>$150k	Unemployment 03/2009	Unemployment 03/2010
Area	38.8%	35.6%	11.5%	11.0%	13.2%
USA	45.8%	29.5%	8.5%	9.0%	10.1

Key Household Data

	Population Age 0-17	Children w/Married Parents	Children w/Single Mother	Stay-at-home Mothers	Births to Single Women
Area	22.0%	62.0%	29.2%	22.0%	37.9%
USA	24.0%	65.6%	25.5%	27.9%	35.3%

Key Housing Data

	Owner Occupied	Median Year Built	Median Home Value	Home Value Growth, 2005-2010	Median List Price, 4-bedroom Home
Area	63.0%	1963	$296,000	0.1%	$389,900
USA	67.8%	1976	$187,045	3.1%	$288,846

Provo-Orem, UT
540,943

	Score	Rank
Overall	100.00	1
LDS Culture	92.25	2
Education	99.31	4
Crime	91.57	5
Economic	72.82	59
Health	99.99	1
Household	100.00	1
Housing	85.30	135

Key LDS Culture Data

	Positive	Negative	Ratio Pos:Neg	Commute>59 minutes	Commute<15 minutes
Area	3,811	48	79.4	4.5%	42.9%
USA	4,292	251	20.1	5.5%	34.1%

Key Education Data

	HS Grad	Some Coll.	College Degree	Free/Reduced Lunch	Students per Teacher
Area	93.5%	30.0%	45.6%	16.2%	24.8
USA	85.8%	22.6%	33.2%	41.2%	15.8

Key Property Crime Data (Rate per 100,000 residents)

	Rate	Burglary	Larceny, Theft	Vehicle Theft	
Area	2,335.5	349.9	1,882.0	103.6	
USA	3,413.6	806.6	2,388.0	262.7	

Key Violent Crime Data (Rate per 100,000 residents)

	Rate	Murder	Rape	Robbery	Aggravated Assault
Area	91.4	0.6	25.4	13.2	52.3
USA	432.8	4.7	34.7	111.6	285.6

Key Economic Data (Family income, unemployment)

	$25k-$75k	$75k-$150k	>$150k	Unemployment 03/2009	Unemployment 03/2010
Area	46.4%	32.7%	9.0%	6.6%	7.3%
USA	45.8%	29.5%	8.5%	9.0%	10.1

Key Household Data

	Population Age 0-17	Children w/Married Parents	Children w/Single Mother	Stay-at-home Mothers	Births to Single Women
Area	34.9%	83.4%	12.1%	48.3%	13.4%
USA	24.0%	65.6%	25.5%	27.9%	35.3%

Key Housing Data

	Owner Occupied	Median Year Built	Median Home Value	Home Value Growth, 2005-2010	Median List Price, 4-bedroom Home
Area	71.9%	1992	$256,500	5.4%	
USA	67.8%	1976	$187,045	3.1%	$288,846

Pueblo, CO
156,737

	Score	Rank
Overall	55.86	321
LDS Culture	11.18	354
Education	59.19	303
Crime	40.08	288
Economic	72.60	60
Health	46.30	127
Household	46.30	329
Housing	82.54	180

Key LDS Culture Data

	Positive	Negative	Ratio Pos:Neg	Commute>59 minutes	Commute<15 minutes
Area	842	110	7.7	5.6%	39.7%
USA	4,292	251	20.1	5.5%	34.1%

Key Education Data

	HS Grad	Some Coll.	College Degree	Free/Reduced Lunch	Students per Teacher
Area	85.5%	31.1%	26.2%	56.4%	17.7
USA	85.8%	22.6%	33.2%	41.2%	15.8

Key Property Crime Data (Rate per 100,000 residents)

	Rate	Burglary	Larceny, Theft	Vehicle Theft	
Area	5,148.5	1,152.4	3,582.2	413.9	
USA	3,413.6	806.6	2,388.0	262.7	

Key Violent Crime Data (Rate per 100,000 residents)

	Rate	Murder	Rape	Robbery	Aggravated Assault
Area	474.2	4.5	29.5	132.8	307.3
USA	432.8	4.7	34.7	111.6	285.6

Key Economic Data (Family income, unemployment)

	$25k-$75k	$75k-$150k	>$150k	Unemployment 03/2009	Unemployment 03/2010
Area	51.9%	23.2%	3.6%	9.4%	9.5%
USA	45.8%	29.5%	8.5%	9.0%	10.1

Key Household Data

	Population Age 0-17	Children w/Married Parents	Children w/Single Mother	Stay-at-home Mothers	Births to Single Women
Area	23.9%	59.4%	29.1%	30.3%	53.1%
USA	24.0%	65.6%	25.5%	27.9%	35.3%

Key Housing Data

	Owner Occupied	Median Year Built	Median Home Value	Home Value Growth, 2005-2010	Median List Price, 4-bedroom Home
Area	67.3%	1972	$139,400	0.9%	$172,900
USA	67.8%	1976	$187,045	3.1%	$288,846

Punta Gorda, FL
150,060

	Score	Rank
Overall	69.25	59
LDS Culture	46.52	23
Education	79.00	81
Crime	58.53	152
Economic	63.65	173
Health	52.72	25
Household	56.17	266
Housing	87.48	92

Key LDS Culture Data

	Positive	Negative	Ratio Pos:Neg	Commute>59 minutes	Commute<15 minutes
Area	3,494	198	17.6	6.1%	32.9%
USA	4,292	251	20.1	5.5%	34.1%

Key Education Data

	HS Grad	Some Coll.	College Degree	Free/Reduced Lunch	Students per Teacher
Area	87.3%	24.1%	29.1%	46.8%	16.3
USA	85.8%	22.6%	33.2%	41.2%	15.8

Key Property Crime Data (Rate per 100,000 residents)

	Rate	Burglary	Larceny, Theft	Vehicle Theft
Area	3,287.8	836.6	2,302.2	149.1
USA	3,413.6	806.6	2,388.0	262.7

Key Violent Crime Data (Rate per 100,000 residents)

	Rate	Murder	Rape	Robbery	Aggravated Assault
Area	348.0	2.0	9.8	47.3	288.9
USA	432.8	4.7	34.7	111.6	285.6

Key Economic Data (Family income, unemployment)

	$25k-$75k	$75k-$150k	>$150k	Unemployment 03/2009	Unemployment 03/2010
Area	52.6%	21.5%	8.0%	11.1%	13.3%
USA	45.8%	29.5%	8.5%	9.0%	10.1

Key Household Data

	Population Age 0-17	Children w/Married Parents	Children w/Single Mother	Stay-at-home Mothers	Births to Single Women
Area	16.0%	55.7%	25.9%	20.9%	28.4%
USA	24.0%	65.6%	25.5%	27.9%	35.3%

Key Housing Data

	Owner Occupied	Median Year Built	Median Home Value	Home Value Growth, 2005-2010	Median List Price, 4-bedroom Home
Area	77.1%	1988	$192,700	-1.5%	$259,900
USA	67.8%	1976	$187,045	3.1%	$288,846

Racine, WI
199,510

	Score	Rank
Overall	63.30	177
LDS Culture	22.64	247
Education	82.78	51
Crime	61.88	135
Economic	69.04	95
Health	39.16	232
Household	61.11	218
Housing	69.26	329

Key LDS Culture Data

	Positive	Negative	Ratio Pos:Neg	Commute>59 minutes	Commute<15 minutes
Area	7,699	493	15.6	5.5%	34.1%
USA	4,292	251	20.1	5.5%	34.1%

Key Education Data

	HS Grad	Some Coll.	College Degree	Free/Reduced Lunch	Students per Teacher
Area	87.6%	22.5%	28.9%	38.3%	15.7
USA	85.8%	22.6%	33.2%	41.2%	15.8

Key Property Crime Data (Rate per 100,000 residents)

	Rate	Burglary	Larceny, Theft	Vehicle Theft
Area	3,134.0	839.8	2,135.8	158.4
USA	3,413.6	806.6	2,388.0	262.7

Key Violent Crime Data (Rate per 100,000 residents)

	Rate	Murder	Rape	Robbery	Aggravated Assault
Area	328.0	5.1	12.8	169.1	141.0
USA	432.8	4.7	34.7	111.6	285.6

Key Economic Data (Family income, unemployment)

	$25k-$75k	$75k-$150k	>$150k	Unemployment 03/2009	Unemployment 03/2010
Area	43.8%	36.0%	8.5%	10.8%	11.5%
USA	45.8%	29.5%	8.5%	9.0%	10.1

Key Household Data

	Population Age 0-17	Children w/Married Parents	Children w/Single Mother	Stay-at-home Mothers	Births to Single Women
Area	24.8%	67.4%	25.8%	26.6%	43.1%
USA	24.0%	65.6%	25.5%	27.9%	35.3%

Key Housing Data

	Owner Occupied	Median Year Built	Median Home Value	Home Value Growth, 2005-2010	Median List Price, 4-bedroom Home
Area	71.5%	1964	$182,900	2.5%	
USA	67.8%	1976	$187,045	3.1%	$288,846

Raleigh-Cary, NC
1,086,404

	Score	Rank
Overall	71.81	33
LDS Culture	30.83	128
Education	78.32	91
Crime	55.53	170
Economic	75.76	43
Health	40.04	216
Household	87.65	24
Housing	92.36	30

Key LDS Culture Data

	Positive	Negative	Ratio Pos:Neg	Commute>59 minutes	Commute<15 minutes
Area	8,128	233	34.9	5.0%	22.6%
USA	4,292	251	20.1	5.5%	34.1%

Key Education Data

	HS Grad	Some Coll.	College Degree	Free/Reduced Lunch	Students per Teacher
Area	89.8%	19.9%	49.3%	2.8%	15.1
USA	85.8%	22.6%	33.2%	41.2%	15.8

Key Property Crime Data (Rate per 100,000 residents)

	Rate	Burglary	Larceny, Theft	Vehicle Theft
Area	2,748.6	692.3	1,872.3	183.9
USA	3,413.6	806.6	2,388.0	262.7

Key Violent Crime Data (Rate per 100,000 residents)

	Rate	Murder	Rape	Robbery	Aggravated Assault
Area		4.7	20.3	132.5	
USA	432.8	4.7	34.7	111.6	285.6

Key Economic Data (Family income, unemployment)

	$25k-$75k	$75k-$150k	>$150k	Unemployment 03/2009	Unemployment 03/2010
Area	38.0%	34.9%	16.6%	8.5%	8.9%
USA	45.8%	29.5%	8.5%	9.0%	10.1

Key Household Data

	Population Age 0-17	Children w/Married Parents	Children w/Single Mother	Stay-at-home Mothers	Births to Single Women
Area	26.2%	73.5%	20.5%	30.3%	26.8%
USA	24.0%	65.6%	25.5%	27.9%	35.3%

Key Housing Data

	Owner Occupied	Median Year Built	Median Home Value	Home Value Growth, 2005-2010	Median List Price, 4-bedroom Home
Area	68.6%	1993	$208,500	4.3%	$319,900
USA	67.8%	1976	$187,045	3.1%	$288,846

Rapid City, SD
122,522

	Score	Rank
Overall	65.35	135
LDS Culture	24.45	228
Education	70.16	182
Crime	58.13	156
Economic	73.26	55
Health	48.89	56
Household	60.49	225
Housing	83.70	162

Key LDS Culture Data

	Positive	Negative	Ratio Pos:Neg	Commute>59 minutes	Commute<15 minutes
Area	782	102	7.7	2.7%	41.8%
USA	4,292	251	20.1	5.5%	34.1%

Key Education Data

	HS Grad	Some Coll.	College Degree	Free/Reduced Lunch	Students per Teacher
Area	92.4%	26.7%	36.2%	30.3%	14.8
USA	85.8%	22.6%	33.2%	41.2%	15.8

Key Property Crime Data (Rate per 100,000 residents)

	Rate	Burglary	Larceny, Theft	Vehicle Theft	
Area	2,735.2	474.8	2,114.8	145.6	
USA	3,413.6	806.6	2,388.0	262.7	

Key Violent Crime Data (Rate per 100,000 residents)

	Rate	Murder	Rape	Robbery	Aggravated Assault
Area	409.8	3.3	119.3	44.4	242.7
USA	432.8	4.7	34.7	111.6	285.6

Key Economic Data (Family income, unemployment)

	$25k-$75k	$75k-$150k	>$150k	Unemployment 03/2009	Unemployment 03/2010
Area	53.0%	26.5%	6.4%	5.4%	5.6%
USA	45.8%	29.5%	8.5%	9.0%	10.1

Key Household Data

	Population Age 0-17	Children w/Married Parents	Children w/Single Mother	Stay-at-home Mothers	Births to Single Women
Area	25.2%	68.3%	26.1%	23.9%	43.9%
USA	24.0%	65.6%	25.5%	27.9%	35.3%

Key Housing Data

	Owner Occupied	Median Year Built	Median Home Value	Home Value Growth, 2005-2010	Median List Price, 4-bedroom Home
Area	65.8%	1981	$160,700	3.9%	
USA	67.8%	1976	$187,045	3.1%	$288,846

Reading, PA
403,595

	Score	Rank
Overall	66.56	111
LDS Culture	34.19	89
Education	77.13	103
Crime	67.38	99
Economic	64.98	154
Health	47.33	97
Household	57.41	246
Housing	78.41	240

Key LDS Culture Data

	Positive	Negative	Ratio Pos:Neg	Commute>59 minutes	Commute<15 minutes
Area	7,232	387	18.7	7.4%	31.3%
USA	4,292	251	20.1	5.5%	34.1%

Key Education Data

	HS Grad	Some Coll.	College Degree	Free/Reduced Lunch	Students per Teacher
Area	83.3%	17.2%	30.0%	32.1%	13.8
USA	85.8%	22.6%	33.2%	41.2%	15.8

Key Property Crime Data (Rate per 100,000 residents)

	Rate	Burglary	Larceny, Theft	Vehicle Theft
Area	2,539.1	528.5	1,716.9	293.8
USA	3,413.6	806.6	2,388.0	262.7

Key Violent Crime Data (Rate per 100,000 residents)

	Rate	Murder	Rape	Robbery	Aggravated Assault
Area	330.6	3.9	16.0	138.2	172.4
USA	432.8	4.7	34.7	111.6	285.6

Key Economic Data (Family income, unemployment)

	$25k-$75k	$75k-$150k	>$150k	Unemployment 03/2009	Unemployment 03/2010
Area	45.0%	31.8%	8.8%	8.5%	10.2%
USA	45.8%	29.5%	8.5%	9.0%	10.1

Key Household Data

	Population Age 0-17	Children w/Married Parents	Children w/Single Mother	Stay-at-home Mothers	Births to Single Women
Area	23.6%	63.9%	25.3%	21.2%	32.8%
USA	24.0%	65.6%	25.5%	27.9%	35.3%

Key Housing Data

	Owner Occupied	Median Year Built	Median Home Value	Home Value Growth, 2005-2010	Median List Price, 4-bedroom Home
Area	72.9%	1970	$184,500	5.3%	$245,000
USA	67.8%	1976	$187,045	3.1%	$288,846

349

Redding, CA
180,214

	Score	Rank
Overall	61.76	203
LDS Culture	37.91	58
Education	75.94	116
Crime	46.04	246
Economic	48.14	340
Health	48.59	69
Household	62.96	202
Housing	76.47	263

Key LDS Culture Data

	Positive	Negative	Ratio Pos:Neg	Commute>59 minutes	Commute<15 minutes
Area	1,116	40	27.9	4.1%	40.9%
USA	4,292	251	20.1	5.5%	34.1%

Key Education Data

	HS Grad	Some Coll.	College Degree	Free/Reduced Lunch	Students per Teacher
Area	88.2%	34.8%	29.7%	46.1%	16.6
USA	85.8%	22.6%	33.2%	41.2%	15.8

Key Property Crime Data (Rate per 100,000 residents)

	Rate	Burglary	Larceny, Theft	Vehicle Theft
Area	2,775.8	793.5	1,735.3	247.0
USA	3,413.6	806.6	2,388.0	262.7

Key Violent Crime Data (Rate per 100,000 residents)

	Rate	Murder	Rape	Robbery	Aggravated Assault
Area	650.1	2.2	73.6	57.6	516.6
USA	432.8	4.7	34.7	111.6	285.6

Key Economic Data (Family income, unemployment)

	$25k-$75k	$75k-$150k	>$150k	Unemployment 03/2009	Unemployment 03/2010
Area	47.0%	25.8%	4.8%	15.8%	17.7%
USA	45.8%	29.5%	8.5%	9.0%	10.1

Key Household Data

	Population Age 0-17	Children w/Married Parents	Children w/Single Mother	Stay-at-home Mothers	Births to Single Women
Area	22.1%	62.1%	27.7%	30.7%	26.7%
USA	24.0%	65.6%	25.5%	27.9%	35.3%

Key Housing Data

	Owner Occupied	Median Year Built	Median Home Value	Home Value Growth, 2005-2010	Median List Price, 4-bedroom Home
Area	65.1%	1980	$279,400	1.5%	
USA	67.8%	1976	$187,045	3.1%	$288,846

Reno-Sparks, NV
414,156

	Score	Rank
Overall	58.60	273
LDS Culture	16.40	325
Education	50.96	345
Crime	44.08	263
Economic	68.48	101
Health	37.34	254
Household	75.31	101
Housing	83.22	172

Key LDS Culture Data

	Positive	Negative	Ratio Pos:Neg	Commute>59 minutes	Commute<15 minutes
Area	1,668	195	8.6	3.9%	33.3%
USA	4,292	251	20.1	5.5%	34.1%

Key Education Data

	HS Grad	Some Coll.	College Degree	Free/Reduced Lunch	Students per Teacher
Area	85.3%	27.7%	34.8%	33.1%	19.1
USA	85.8%	22.6%	33.2%	41.2%	15.8

Key Property Crime Data (Rate per 100,000 residents)

	Rate	Burglary	Larceny, Theft	Vehicle Theft
Area	3,693.8	849.0	2,491.1	353.7
USA	3,413.6	806.6	2,388.0	262.7

Key Violent Crime Data (Rate per 100,000 residents)

	Rate	Murder	Rape	Robbery	Aggravated Assault
Area	538.0	3.6	34.2	153.6	346.7
USA	432.8	4.7	34.7	111.6	285.6

Key Economic Data (Family income, unemployment)

	$25k-$75k	$75k-$150k	>$150k	Unemployment 03/2009	Unemployment 03/2010
Area	40.4%	36.2%	10.0%	11.2%	13.2%
USA	45.8%	29.5%	8.5%	9.0%	10.1

Key Household Data

	Population Age 0-17	Children w/Married Parents	Children w/Single Mother	Stay-at-home Mothers	Births to Single Women
Area	24.2%	67.9%	21.3%	26.8%	25.6%
USA	24.0%	65.6%	25.5%	27.9%	35.3%

Key Housing Data

	Owner Occupied	Median Year Built	Median Home Value	Home Value Growth, 2005-2010	Median List Price, 4-bedroom Home
Area	60.0%	1989	$310,700	-1.0%	$276,000
USA	67.8%	1976	$187,045	3.1%	$288,846

Richmond, VA
1,230,502

	Score	Rank
Overall	70.34	46
LDS Culture	43.28	28
Education	72.40	157
Crime	62.78	129
Economic	69.76	89
Health	42.87	170
Household	74.07	118
Housing	85.91	122

Key LDS Culture Data

	Positive	Negative	Ratio Pos:Neg	Commute>59 minutes	Commute<15 minutes
Area	5,761	131	44.0	5.4%	23.2%
USA	4,292	251	20.1	5.5%	34.1%

Key Education Data

	HS Grad	Some Coll.	College Degree	Free/Reduced Lunch	Students per Teacher
Area	85.2%	21.5%	36.7%	29.0%	17.9
USA	85.8%	22.6%	33.2%	41.2%	15.8

Key Property Crime Data (Rate per 100,000 residents)

	Rate	Burglary	Larceny, Theft	Vehicle Theft
Area	2,824.2	568.5	2,016.4	239.2
USA	3,413.6	806.6	2,388.0	262.7

Key Violent Crime Data (Rate per 100,000 residents)

	Rate	Murder	Rape	Robbery	Aggravated Assault
Area	350.5	6.2	22.2	153.3	168.8
USA	432.8	4.7	34.7	111.6	285.6

Key Economic Data (Family income, unemployment)

	$25k-$75k	$75k-$150k	>$150k	Unemployment 03/2009	Unemployment 03/2010
Area	40.0%	35.5%	13.1%	7.3%	8.4%
USA	45.8%	29.5%	8.5%	9.0%	10.1

Key Household Data

	Population Age 0-17	Children w/Married Parents	Children w/Single Mother	Stay-at-home Mothers	Births to Single Women
Area	23.3%	64.1%	28.3%	27.3%	26.0%
USA	24.0%	65.6%	25.5%	27.9%	35.3%

Key Housing Data

	Owner Occupied	Median Year Built	Median Home Value	Home Value Growth, 2005-2010	Median List Price, 4-bedroom Home
Area	70.4%	1982	$239,500	5.7%	$270,000
USA	67.8%	1976	$187,045	3.1%	$288,846

Riverside-San Bernardino-Ontario, CA
4,115,871

	Score	Rank
Overall	61.56	210
LDS Culture	20.98	272
Education	63.38	266
Crime	51.95	197
Economic	49.31	332
Health	47.21	112
Household	77.78	79
Housing	84.15	157

Key LDS Culture Data

	Positive	Negative	Ratio Pos:Neg	Commute>59 minutes	Commute<15 minutes
Area	11,548	616	18.7	15.1%	25.0%
USA	4,292	251	20.1	5.5%	34.1%

Key Education Data

	HS Grad	Some Coll.	College Degree	Free/Reduced Lunch	Students per Teacher
Area	78.0%	25.1%	26.7%	53.1%	19.5
USA	85.8%	22.6%	33.2%	41.2%	15.8

Key Property Crime Data (Rate per 100,000 residents)

	Rate	Burglary	Larceny, Theft	Vehicle Theft	
Area	3,069.5	804.0	1,759.3	506.2	
USA	3,413.6	806.6	2,388.0	262.7	

Key Violent Crime Data (Rate per 100,000 residents)

	Rate	Murder	Rape	Robbery	Aggravated Assault
Area	449.2	5.0	23.8	151.1	269.3
USA	432.8	4.7	34.7	111.6	285.6

Key Economic Data (Family income, unemployment)

	$25k-$75k	$75k-$150k	>$150k	Unemployment 03/2009	Unemployment 03/2010
Area	43.2%	31.7%	9.5%	12.3%	15.0%
USA	45.8%	29.5%	8.5%	9.0%	10.1

Key Household Data

	Population Age 0-17	Children w/Married Parents	Children w/Single Mother	Stay-at-home Mothers	Births to Single Women
Area	28.5%	67.8%	22.5%	37.7%	32.2%
USA	24.0%	65.6%	25.5%	27.9%	35.3%

Key Housing Data

	Owner Occupied	Median Year Built	Median Home Value	Home Value Growth, 2005-2010	Median List Price, 4-bedroom Home
Area	65.4%	1985	$330,400	-1.7%	$258,000
USA	67.8%	1976	$187,045	3.1%	$288,846

Roanoke, VA
297,029

	Score	Rank
Overall	67.10	101
LDS Culture	59.82	8
Education	65.57	238
Crime	63.51	123
Economic	60.81	216
Health	36.28	282
Household	58.64	236
Housing	85.64	128

Key LDS Culture Data

	Positive	Negative	Ratio Pos:Neg	Commute>59 minutes	Commute<15 minutes
Area	2,424	46	52.7	4.2%	32.7%
USA	4,292	251	20.1	5.5%	34.1%

Key Education Data

	HS Grad	Some Coll.	College Degree	Free/Reduced Lunch	Students per Teacher
Area	85.1%	21.3%	33.7%	34.8%	16.6
USA	85.8%	22.6%	33.2%	41.2%	15.8

Key Property Crime Data (Rate per 100,000 residents)

	Rate	Burglary	Larceny, Theft	Vehicle Theft	
Area	2,859.2	522.8	2,178.6	157.9	
USA	3,413.6	806.6	2,388.0	262.7	

Key Violent Crime Data (Rate per 100,000 residents)

	Rate	Murder	Rape	Robbery	Aggravated Assault
Area	339.0	6.1	29.0	85.7	218.2
USA	432.8	4.7	34.7	111.6	285.6

Key Economic Data (Family income, unemployment)

	$25k-$75k	$75k-$150k	>$150k	Unemployment 03/2009	Unemployment 03/2010
Area	46.0%	31.4%	6.7%	7.0%	8.2%
USA	45.8%	29.5%	8.5%	9.0%	10.1

Key Household Data

	Population Age 0-17	Children w/Married Parents	Children w/Single Mother	Stay-at-home Mothers	Births to Single Women
Area	21.2%	65.2%	26.7%	22.8%	36.5%
USA	24.0%	65.6%	25.5%	27.9%	35.3%

Key Housing Data

	Owner Occupied	Median Year Built	Median Home Value	Home Value Growth, 2005-2010	Median List Price, 4-bedroom Home
Area	69.6%	1973	$166,400	5.3%	$255,000
USA	67.8%	1976	$187,045	3.1%	$288,846

Rochester, MN
182,924

	Score	Rank
Overall	71.03	39
LDS Culture	37.18	66
Education	82.61	55
Crime	65.36	110
Economic	79.04	18
Health	40.69	210
Household	72.84	129
Housing	77.77	248

Key LDS Culture Data

	Positive	Negative	Ratio Pos:Neg	Commute>59 minutes	Commute<15 minutes
Area	1,076	63	17.1	3.5%	42.3%
USA	4,292	251	20.1	5.5%	34.1%

Key Education Data

	HS Grad	Some Coll.	College Degree	Free/Reduced Lunch	Students per Teacher
Area	93.2%	21.4%	47.6%	24.8%	16.7
USA	85.8%	22.6%	33.2%	41.2%	15.8

Key Property Crime Data (Rate per 100,000 residents)

	Rate	Burglary	Larceny, Theft	Vehicle Theft
Area	2,110.3	397.1	1,572.6	140.6
USA	3,413.6	806.6	2,388.0	262.7

Key Violent Crime Data (Rate per 100,000 residents)

	Rate	Murder	Rape	Robbery	Aggravated Assault
Area		2.7		37.7	
USA	432.8	4.7	34.7	111.6	285.6

Key Economic Data (Family income, unemployment)

	$25k-$75k	$75k-$150k	>$150k	Unemployment 03/2009	Unemployment 03/2010
Area	40.2%	36.9%	13.9%	7.4%	6.8%
USA	45.8%	29.5%	8.5%	9.0%	10.1

Key Household Data

	Population Age 0-17	Children w/Married Parents	Children w/Single Mother	Stay-at-home Mothers	Births to Single Women
Area	25.2%	75.9%	15.5%	15.3%	14.8%
USA	24.0%	65.6%	25.5%	27.9%	35.3%

Key Housing Data

	Owner Occupied	Median Year Built	Median Home Value	Home Value Growth, 2005-2010	Median List Price, 4-bedroom Home
Area	78.6%	1980	$178,000	1.3%	
USA	67.8%	1976	$187,045	3.1%	$288,846

Rochester, NY
1,034,090

	Score	Rank
Overall	**69.07**	**65**
LDS Culture	33.14	105
Education	82.68	53
Crime	66.38	107
Economic	70.21	83
Health	46.05	129
Household	62.96	203
Housing	81.48	192

Key LDS Culture Data

	Positive	Negative	Ratio Pos:Neg	Commute>59 minutes	Commute<15 minutes
Area	4,955	283	17.5	3.2%	32.1%
USA	4,292	251	20.1	5.5%	34.1%

Key Education Data

	HS Grad	Some Coll.	College Degree	Free/Reduced Lunch	Students per Teacher
Area	88.6%	18.2%	43.0%	34.9%	11.9
USA	85.8%	22.6%	33.2%	41.2%	15.8

Key Property Crime Data (Rate per 100,000 residents)

	Rate	Burglary	Larceny, Theft	Vehicle Theft	
Area	2,681.8	533.3	1,969.1	179.4	
USA	3,413.6	806.6	2,388.0	262.7	

Key Violent Crime Data (Rate per 100,000 residents)

	Rate	Murder	Rape	Robbery	Aggravated Assault
Area	326.5	4.8	21.2	130.0	170.5
USA	432.8	4.7	34.7	111.6	285.6

Key Economic Data (Family income, unemployment)

	$25k-$75k	$75k-$150k	>$150k	Unemployment 03/2009	Unemployment 03/2010
Area	44.1%	33.0%	8.6%	8.1%	8.2%
USA	45.8%	29.5%	8.5%	9.0%	10.1

Key Household Data

	Population Age 0-17	Children w/Married Parents	Children w/Single Mother	Stay-at-home Mothers	Births to Single Women
Area	22.2%	63.0%	28.3%	22.6%	35.6%
USA	24.0%	65.6%	25.5%	27.9%	35.3%

Key Housing Data

	Owner Occupied	Median Year Built	Median Home Value	Home Value Growth, 2005-2010	Median List Price, 4-bedroom Home
Area	70.4%	1963	$125,100	2.3%	$198,000
USA	67.8%	1976	$187,045	3.1%	$288,846

Rockford, IL
354,394

	Score	Rank
Overall	**53.25**	**348**
LDS Culture	23.40	239
Education	55.01	327
Crime	24.56	351
Economic	51.53	315
Health	47.30	108
Household	55.56	271
Housing	84.09	158

Key LDS Culture Data

	Positive	Negative	Ratio Pos:Neg	Commute>59 minutes	Commute<15 minutes
Area	2,733	238	11.5	8.0%	31.5%
USA	4,292	251	20.1	5.5%	34.1%

Key Education Data

	HS Grad	Some Coll.	College Degree	Free/Reduced Lunch	Students per Teacher
Area	82.9%	21.7%	26.5%	49.3%	19.8
USA	85.8%	22.6%	33.2%	41.2%	15.8

Key Property Crime Data (Rate per 100,000 residents)

	Rate	Burglary	Larceny, Theft	Vehicle Theft
Area		1,725.0	3,877.0	428.4
USA	3,413.6	806.6	2,388.0	262.7

Key Violent Crime Data (Rate per 100,000 residents)

	Rate	Murder	Rape	Robbery	Aggravated Assault
Area		14.1		407.2	864.4
USA	432.8	4.7	34.7	111.6	285.6

Key Economic Data (Family income, unemployment)

	$25k-$75k	$75k-$150k	>$150k	Unemployment 03/2009	Unemployment 03/2010
Area	48.0%	30.8%	6.2%	14.1%	17.9%
USA	45.8%	29.5%	8.5%	9.0%	10.1

Key Household Data

	Population Age 0-17	Children w/Married Parents	Children w/Single Mother	Stay-at-home Mothers	Births to Single Women
Area	25.2%	64.1%	27.2%	28.7%	45.8%
USA	24.0%	65.6%	25.5%	27.9%	35.3%

Key Housing Data

	Owner Occupied	Median Year Built	Median Home Value	Home Value Growth, 2005-2010	Median List Price, 4-bedroom Home
Area	72.0%	1972	$139,800	2.4%	$189,900
USA	67.8%	1976	$187,045	3.1%	$288,846

Rocky Mount, NC
146,356

	Score	Rank
Overall	59.54	255
LDS Culture	50.66	14
Education	51.36	342
Crime	36.75	310
Economic	62.53	193
Health	37.16	260
Household	58.02	241
Housing	85.27	136

Key LDS Culture Data

	Positive	Negative	Ratio Pos:Neg	Commute>59 minutes	Commute<15 minutes
Area	1,651	39	42.3	5.9%	35.6%
USA	4,292	251	20.1	5.5%	34.1%

Key Education Data

	HS Grad	Some Coll.	College Degree	Free/Reduced Lunch	Students per Teacher
Area	78.8%	18.8%	23.5%	58.1%	15.9
USA	85.8%	22.6%	33.2%	41.2%	15.8

Key Property Crime Data (Rate per 100,000 residents)

	Rate	Burglary	Larceny, Theft	Vehicle Theft	
Area	4,693.2	1,445.4	2,977.2	270.6	
USA	3,413.6	806.6	2,388.0	262.7	

Key Violent Crime Data (Rate per 100,000 residents)

	Rate	Murder	Rape	Robbery	Aggravated Assault
Area	599.2	14.2	22.9	223.4	338.7
USA	432.8	4.7	34.7	111.6	285.6

Key Economic Data (Family income, unemployment)

	$25k-$75k	$75k-$150k	>$150k	Unemployment 03/2009	Unemployment 03/2010
Area	43.5%	26.0%	6.4%	13.5%	13.5%
USA	45.8%	29.5%	8.5%	9.0%	10.1

Key Household Data

	Population Age 0-17	Children w/Married Parents	Children w/Single Mother	Stay-at-home Mothers	Births to Single Women
Area	24.5%	54.7%	37.4%	25.4%	36.1%
USA	24.0%	65.6%	25.5%	27.9%	35.3%

Key Housing Data

	Owner Occupied	Median Year Built	Median Home Value	Home Value Growth, 2005-2010	Median List Price, 4-bedroom Home
Area	64.0%	1983	$109,100	2.5%	
USA	67.8%	1976	$187,045	3.1%	$288,846

Rome, GA
95,980

	Score	Rank
Overall	56.60	311
LDS Culture	30.28	143
Education	53.82	334
Crime	47.05	240
Economic	65.54	145
Health	40.98	203
Household	46.30	330
Housing	79.00	227

Key LDS Culture Data

	Positive	Negative	Ratio Pos:Neg	Commute>59 minutes	Commute<15 minutes
Area	1,551	53	29.3	5.3%	31.4%
USA	4,292	251	20.1	5.5%	34.1%

Key Education Data

	HS Grad	Some Coll.	College Degree	Free/Reduced Lunch	Students per Teacher
Area	79.7%	22.1%	23.8%	53.9%	13.3
USA	85.8%	22.6%	33.2%	41.2%	15.8

Key Property Crime Data (Rate per 100,000 residents)

	Rate	Burglary	Larceny, Theft	Vehicle Theft	
Area	3,982.9	831.6	2,876.2	275.1	
USA	3,413.6	806.6	2,388.0	262.7	

Key Violent Crime Data (Rate per 100,000 residents)

	Rate	Murder	Rape	Robbery	Aggravated Assault
Area	438.7	4.2	24.0	78.2	332.4
USA	432.8	4.7	34.7	111.6	285.6

Key Economic Data (Family income, unemployment)

	$25k-$75k	$75k-$150k	>$150k	Unemployment 03/2009	Unemployment 03/2010
Area	44.0%	25.3%	7.6%	9.9%	10.9%
USA	45.8%	29.5%	8.5%	9.0%	10.1

Key Household Data

	Population Age 0-17	Children w/Married Parents	Children w/Single Mother	Stay-at-home Mothers	Births to Single Women
Area	25.1%	59.9%	32.6%	28.3%	54.9%
USA	24.0%	65.6%	25.5%	27.9%	35.3%

Key Housing Data

	Owner Occupied	Median Year Built	Median Home Value	Home Value Growth, 2005-2010	Median List Price, 4-bedroom Home
Area	65.6%	1974	$125,900	1.5%	
USA	67.8%	1976	$187,045	3.1%	$288,846

Sacramento--Arden-Arcade--Roseville, CA
2,109,832

	Score	Rank
Overall	**61.74**	**204**
LDS Culture	16.76	322
Education	76.45	111
Crime	46.46	243
Economic	54.20	305
Health	48.56	80
Household	79.01	73
Housing	74.47	289

Key LDS Culture Data

	Positive	Negative	Ratio Pos:Neg	Commute>59 minutes	Commute<15 minutes
Area	8,363	441	19.0	7.0%	26.2%
USA	4,292	251	20.1	5.5%	34.1%

Key Education Data

	HS Grad	Some Coll.	College Degree	Free/Reduced Lunch	Students per Teacher
Area	87.1%	26.4%	39.2%	40.9%	17.8
USA	85.8%	22.6%	33.2%	41.2%	15.8

Key Property Crime Data (Rate per 100,000 residents)

	Rate	Burglary	Larceny, Theft	Vehicle Theft	
Area	3,333.2	767.2	2,044.3	521.7	
USA	3,413.6	806.6	2,388.0	262.7	

Key Violent Crime Data (Rate per 100,000 residents)

	Rate	Murder	Rape	Robbery	Aggravated Assault
Area	521.8	5.3	27.8	177.9	310.9
USA	432.8	4.7	34.7	111.6	285.6

Key Economic Data (Family income, unemployment)

	$25k-$75k	$75k-$150k	>$150k	Unemployment 03/2009	Unemployment 03/2010
Area	40.3%	34.4%	13.1%	10.7%	13.1%
USA	45.8%	29.5%	8.5%	9.0%	10.1

Key Household Data

	Population Age 0-17	Children w/Married Parents	Children w/Single Mother	Stay-at-home Mothers	Births to Single Women
Area	24.7%	67.6%	22.7%	29.6%	28.7%
USA	24.0%	65.6%	25.5%	27.9%	35.3%

Key Housing Data

	Owner Occupied	Median Year Built	Median Home Value	Home Value Growth, 2005-2010	Median List Price, 4-bedroom Home
Area	62.1%	1982	$348,900	-1.6%	$339,000
USA	67.8%	1976	$187,045	3.1%	$288,846

Saginaw-Saginaw Township North, MI
200,745

	Score	Rank
Overall	51.64	358
LDS Culture	26.83	184
Education	62.51	272
Crime	17.15	357
Economic	56.70	274
Health	36.88	271
Household	45.06	339
Housing	86.01	120

Key LDS Culture Data

	Positive	Negative	Ratio Pos:Neg	Commute>59 minutes	Commute<15 minutes
Area	3,195	208	15.4	4.7%	36.3%
USA	4,292	251	20.1	5.5%	34.1%

Key Education Data

	HS Grad	Some Coll.	College Degree	Free/Reduced Lunch	Students per Teacher
Area	87.5%	24.0%	28.2%	46.4%	16.7
USA	85.8%	22.6%	33.2%	41.2%	15.8

Key Property Crime Data (Rate per 100,000 residents)

	Rate	Burglary	Larceny, Theft	Vehicle Theft
Area	3,355.9	1,265.2	1,887.8	202.9
USA	3,413.6	806.6	2,388.0	262.7

Key Violent Crime Data (Rate per 100,000 residents)

	Rate	Murder	Rape	Robbery	Aggravated Assault
Area	1,192.6	12.0	54.6	197.3	928.6
USA	432.8	4.7	34.7	111.6	285.6

Key Economic Data (Family income, unemployment)

	$25k-$75k	$75k-$150k	>$150k	Unemployment 03/2009	Unemployment 03/2010
Area	47.2%	24.3%	6.4%	12.4%	14.2%
USA	45.8%	29.5%	8.5%	9.0%	10.1

Key Household Data

	Population Age 0-17	Children w/Married Parents	Children w/Single Mother	Stay-at-home Mothers	Births to Single Women
Area	24.0%	55.3%	36.5%	26.4%	49.1%
USA	24.0%	65.6%	25.5%	27.9%	35.3%

Key Housing Data

	Owner Occupied	Median Year Built	Median Home Value	Home Value Growth, 2005-2010	Median List Price, 4-bedroom Home
Area	73.0%	1965	$113,000	-2.2%	$139,900
USA	67.8%	1976	$187,045	3.1%	$288,846

Salem, OR
186,954

	Score	Rank
Overall	70.80	43
LDS Culture	20.06	280
Education	97.42	5
Crime	67.41	98
Economic	60.59	223
Health	51.61	34
Household	77.16	82
Housing	79.73	214

Key LDS Culture Data

	Positive	Negative	Ratio Pos:Neg	Commute>59 minutes	Commute<15 minutes
Area	1,033	135	7.7	6.5%	39.0%
USA	4,292	251	20.1	5.5%	34.1%

Key Education Data

	HS Grad	Some Coll.	College Degree	Free/Reduced Lunch	Students per Teacher
Area	91.3%	25.2%	33.1%	29.7%	16.9
USA	85.8%	22.6%	33.2%	41.2%	15.8

Key Property Crime Data (Rate per 100,000 residents)

	Rate	Burglary	Larceny, Theft	Vehicle Theft	
Area	3,446.1	605.3	2,530.2	310.6	
USA	3,413.6	806.6	2,388.0	262.7	

Key Violent Crime Data (Rate per 100,000 residents)

	Rate	Murder	Rape	Robbery	Aggravated Assault
Area	244.5	4.1	25.8	54.9	159.8
USA	432.8	4.7	34.7	111.6	285.6

Key Economic Data (Family income, unemployment)

	$25k-$75k	$75k-$150k	>$150k	Unemployment 03/2009	Unemployment 03/2010
Area	47.7%	33.8%	6.5%	5.8%	6.7%
USA	45.8%	29.5%	8.5%	9.0%	10.1

Key Household Data

	Population Age 0-17	Children w/Married Parents	Children w/Single Mother	Stay-at-home Mothers	Births to Single Women
Area	22.6%	73.8%	17.1%	14.1%	17.4%
USA	24.0%	65.6%	25.5%	27.9%	35.3%

Key Housing Data

	Owner Occupied	Median Year Built	Median Home Value	Home Value Growth, 2005-2010	Median List Price, 4-bedroom Home
Area	74.4%	1980	$171,000	0.9%	
USA	67.8%	1976	$187,045	3.1%	$288,846

Salinas, CA
137,589

	Score	Rank
Overall	63.50	171
LDS Culture	34.41	85
Education	73.27	146
Crime	52.68	193
Economic	62.98	186
Health	48.59	70
Household	72.22	134
Housing	63.07	346

Key LDS Culture Data

	Positive	Negative	Ratio Pos:Neg	Commute>59 minutes	Commute<15 minutes
Area	529	6	88.2	4.2%	48.0%
USA	4,292	251	20.1	5.5%	34.1%

Key Education Data

	HS Grad	Some Coll.	College Degree	Free/Reduced Lunch	Students per Teacher
Area	90.9%	29.5%	32.8%	31.5%	22.8
USA	85.8%	22.6%	33.2%	41.2%	15.8

Key Property Crime Data (Rate per 100,000 residents)

	Rate	Burglary	Larceny, Theft	Vehicle Theft
Area	2,828.9	752.3	1,610.3	466.3
USA	3,413.6	806.6	2,388.0	262.7

Key Violent Crime Data (Rate per 100,000 residents)

	Rate	Murder	Rape	Robbery	Aggravated Assault
Area	485.7	8.9	24.4	144.5	308.0
USA	432.8	4.7	34.7	111.6	285.6

Key Economic Data (Family income, unemployment)

	$25k-$75k	$75k-$150k	>$150k	Unemployment 03/2009	Unemployment 03/2010
Area	56.8%	23.3%	6.5%	14.8%	16.8%
USA	45.8%	29.5%	8.5%	9.0%	10.1

Key Household Data

	Population Age 0-17	Children w/Married Parents	Children w/Single Mother	Stay-at-home Mothers	Births to Single Women
Area	29.2%	84.1%	10.2%	49.9%	5.1%
USA	24.0%	65.6%	25.5%	27.9%	35.3%

Key Housing Data

	Owner Occupied	Median Year Built	Median Home Value	Home Value Growth, 2005-2010	Median List Price, 4-bedroom Home
Area	69.6%	1996	$262,400	5.2%	
USA	67.8%	1976	$187,045	3.1%	$288,846

Salisbury, MD
124,754

	Score	Rank
Overall	53.48	345
LDS Culture	26.12	195
Education	63.77	258
Crime	26.46	347
Economic	56.70	275
Health	45.68	140
Household	42.59	350
Housing	81.59	189

Key LDS Culture Data

	Positive	Negative	Ratio Pos:Neg	Commute>59 minutes	Commute<15 minutes
Area	831	49	17.0	6.1%	45.5%
USA	4,292	251	20.1	5.5%	34.1%

Key Education Data

	HS Grad	Some Coll.	College Degree	Free/Reduced Lunch	Students per Teacher
Area	86.0%	22.3%	24.7%	44.4%	13.1
USA	85.8%	22.6%	33.2%	41.2%	15.8

Key Property Crime Data (Rate per 100,000 residents)

	Rate	Burglary	Larceny, Theft	Vehicle Theft
Area	3,910.0	1,013.5	2,686.6	209.9
USA	3,413.6	806.6	2,388.0	262.7

Key Violent Crime Data (Rate per 100,000 residents)

	Rate	Murder	Rape	Robbery	Aggravated Assault
Area	919.4	6.7	32.5	192.4	687.9
USA	432.8	4.7	34.7	111.6	285.6

Key Economic Data (Family income, unemployment)

	$25k-$75k	$75k-$150k	>$150k	Unemployment 03/2009	Unemployment 03/2010
Area	53.6%	27.6%	4.5%	8.9%	9.6%
USA	45.8%	29.5%	8.5%	9.0%	10.1

Key Household Data

	Population Age 0-17	Children w/Married Parents	Children w/Single Mother	Stay-at-home Mothers	Births to Single Women
Area	22.3%	69.5%	20.2%	27.9%	35.5%
USA	24.0%	65.6%	25.5%	27.9%	35.3%

Key Housing Data

	Owner Occupied	Median Year Built	Median Home Value	Home Value Growth, 2005-2010	Median List Price, 4-bedroom Home
Area	69.2%	1965	$112,200	2.2%	
USA	67.8%	1976	$187,045	3.1%	$288,846

Salt Lake City, UT
2,813,373

	Score	Rank
Overall	**78.94**	**8**
LDS Culture	47.70	19
Education	92.38	13
Crime	51.80	198
Economic	60.53	224
Health	78.30	3
Household	90.74	13
Housing	84.76	146

Key LDS Culture Data

	Positive	Negative	Ratio Pos:Neg	Commute>59 minutes	Commute<15 minutes
Area	12,716	782	16.3	5.8%	24.5%
USA	4,292	251	20.1	5.5%	34.1%

Key Education Data

	HS Grad	Some Coll.	College Degree	Free/Reduced Lunch	Students per Teacher
Area	88.4%	23.8%	36.9%	33.6%	15.9
USA	85.8%	22.6%	33.2%	41.2%	15.8

Key Property Crime Data (Rate per 100,000 residents)

	Rate	Burglary	Larceny, Theft	Vehicle Theft	
Area	4,724.9	713.3	3,539.1	472.5	
USA	3,413.6	806.6	2,388.0	262.7	

Key Violent Crime Data (Rate per 100,000 residents)

	Rate	Murder	Rape	Robbery	Aggravated Assault
Area	348.4	1.9	39.7	92.1	214.6
USA	432.8	4.7	34.7	111.6	285.6

Key Economic Data (Family income, unemployment)

	$25k-$75k	$75k-$150k	>$150k	Unemployment 03/2009	Unemployment 03/2010
Area	42.4%	33.9%	10.4%	6.5%	7.1%
USA	45.8%	29.5%	8.5%	9.0%	10.1

Key Household Data

	Population Age 0-17	Children w/Married Parents	Children w/Single Mother	Stay-at-home Mothers	Births to Single Women
Area	24.1%	64.4%	26.7%	24.1%	34.3%
USA	24.0%	65.6%	25.5%	27.9%	35.3%

Key Housing Data

	Owner Occupied	Median Year Built	Median Home Value	Home Value Growth, 2005-2010	Median List Price, 4-bedroom Home
Area	72.5%	1971	$164,500	2.5%	$259,000
USA	67.8%	1976	$187,045	3.1%	$288,846

San Angelo, TX
391,680

	Score	Rank
Overall	60.06	243
LDS Culture	34.39	87
Education	63.53	262
Crime	51.33	204
Economic	52.86	311
Health	32.00	333
Household	64.81	184
Housing	86.21	116

Key LDS Culture Data

	Positive	Negative	Ratio Pos:Neg	Commute>59 minutes	Commute<15 minutes
Area	2,992	169	17.7	6.8%	30.7%
USA	4,292	251	20.1	5.5%	34.1%

Key Education Data

	HS Grad	Some Coll.	College Degree	Free/Reduced Lunch	Students per Teacher
Area	83.8%	26.5%	30.2%	49.6%	19.3
USA	85.8%	22.6%	33.2%	41.2%	15.8

Key Property Crime Data (Rate per 100,000 residents)

	Rate	Burglary	Larceny, Theft	Vehicle Theft
Area	4,448.5	1,041.8	3,177.0	229.8
USA	3,413.6	806.6	2,388.0	262.7

Key Violent Crime Data (Rate per 100,000 residents)

	Rate	Murder	Rape	Robbery	Aggravated Assault
Area	367.3	5.5	63.7	60.9	237.1
USA	432.8	4.7	34.7	111.6	285.6

Key Economic Data (Family income, unemployment)

	$25k-$75k	$75k-$150k	>$150k	Unemployment 03/2009	Unemployment 03/2010
Area	49.4%	28.4%	6.0%	6.0%	6.5%
USA	45.8%	29.5%	8.5%	9.0%	10.1

Key Household Data

	Population Age 0-17	Children w/Married Parents	Children w/Single Mother	Stay-at-home Mothers	Births to Single Women
Area	25.6%	68.0%	23.4%	32.5%	32.3%
USA	24.0%	65.6%	25.5%	27.9%	35.3%

Key Housing Data

	Owner Occupied	Median Year Built	Median Home Value	Home Value Growth, 2005-2010	Median List Price, 4-bedroom Home
Area	63.8%	1977	$224,600	5.7%	$274,500
USA	67.8%	1976	$187,045	3.1%	$288,846

San Antonio, TX
408,238

	Score	Rank
Overall	56.78	309
LDS Culture	48.50	16
Education	54.70	328
Crime	32.27	332
Economic	48.25	339
Health	31.71	339
Household	65.43	177
Housing	83.25	171

Key LDS Culture Data

	Positive	Negative	Ratio Pos:Neg	Commute>59 minutes	Commute<15 minutes
Area	2,368	125	18.9	4.2%	33.5%
USA	4,292	251	20.1	5.5%	34.1%

Key Education Data

	HS Grad	Some Coll.	College Degree	Free/Reduced Lunch	Students per Teacher
Area	70.4%	20.3%	29.1%	60.2%	18.0
USA	85.8%	22.6%	33.2%	41.2%	15.8

Key Property Crime Data (Rate per 100,000 residents)

	Rate	Burglary	Larceny, Theft	Vehicle Theft	
Area	5,923.7	1,197.8	4,271.5	454.4	
USA	3,413.6	806.6	2,388.0	262.7	

Key Violent Crime Data (Rate per 100,000 residents)

	Rate	Murder	Rape	Robbery	Aggravated Assault
Area	570.5	7.7	31.7	152.3	378.7
USA	432.8	4.7	34.7	111.6	285.6

Key Economic Data (Family income, unemployment)

	$25k-$75k	$75k-$150k	>$150k	Unemployment 03/2009	Unemployment 03/2010
Area	43.5%	29.9%	11.6%	6.3%	7.3%
USA	45.8%	29.5%	8.5%	9.0%	10.1

Key Household Data

	Population Age 0-17	Children w/Married Parents	Children w/Single Mother	Stay-at-home Mothers	Births to Single Women
Area	27.3%	63.9%	22.1%	32.1%	27.8%
USA	24.0%	65.6%	25.5%	27.9%	35.3%

Key Housing Data

	Owner Occupied	Median Year Built	Median Home Value	Home Value Growth, 2005-2010	Median List Price, 4-bedroom Home
Area	51.9%	1973	$535,700	-3.1%	$823,900
USA	67.8%	1976	$187,045	3.1%	$288,846

San Diego-Carlsbad-San Marcos, CA
121,675

	Score	Rank
Overall	62.96	184
LDS Culture	15.15	336
Education	77.07	105
Crime	55.14	172
Economic	53.86	307
Health	47.11	115
Household	83.33	44
Housing	72.04	317

Key LDS Culture Data

	Positive	Negative	Ratio Pos:Neg	Commute>59 minutes	Commute<15 minutes
Area	1,643	84	19.6	5.1%	35.3%
USA	4,292	251	20.1	5.5%	34.1%

Key Education Data

	HS Grad	Some Coll.	College Degree	Free/Reduced Lunch	Students per Teacher
Area	84.6%	21.5%	25.1%	47.1%	13.4
USA	85.8%	22.6%	33.2%	41.2%	15.8

Key Property Crime Data (Rate per 100,000 residents)

	Rate	Burglary	Larceny, Theft	Vehicle Theft
Area	2,829.3	568.3	1,590.6	670.4
USA	3,413.6	806.6	2,388.0	262.7

Key Violent Crime Data (Rate per 100,000 residents)

	Rate	Murder	Rape	Robbery	Aggravated Assault
Area	432.1	3.0	28.4	134.9	265.9
USA	432.8	4.7	34.7	111.6	285.6

Key Economic Data (Family income, unemployment)

	$25k-$75k	$75k-$150k	>$150k	Unemployment 03/2009	Unemployment 03/2010
Area	47.5%	30.9%	6.8%	9.0%	11.0%
USA	45.8%	29.5%	8.5%	9.0%	10.1

Key Household Data

	Population Age 0-17	Children w/Married Parents	Children w/Single Mother	Stay-at-home Mothers	Births to Single Women
Area	21.7%	61.3%	28.3%	17.9%	65.8%
USA	24.0%	65.6%	25.5%	27.9%	35.3%

Key Housing Data

	Owner Occupied	Median Year Built	Median Home Value	Home Value Growth, 2005-2010	Median List Price, 4-bedroom Home
Area	64.9%	1980	$201,300	6.3%	
USA	67.8%	1976	$187,045	3.1%	$288,846

San Francisco-Oakland-Fremont, CA
1,112,866

	Score	Rank
Overall	59.42	258
LDS Culture	19.35	290
Education	75.63	120
Crime	40.14	287
Economic	63.37	178
Health	38.49	243
Household	83.33	45
Housing	60.73	353

Key LDS Culture Data

	Positive	Negative	Ratio Pos:Neg	Commute>59 minutes	Commute<15 minutes
Area	6,314	162	39.0	4.0%	28.0%
USA	4,292	251	20.1	5.5%	34.1%

Key Education Data

	HS Grad	Some Coll.	College Degree	Free/Reduced Lunch	Students per Teacher
Area	88.9%	25.3%	38.6%	34.3%	24.0
USA	85.8%	22.6%	33.2%	41.2%	15.8

Key Property Crime Data (Rate per 100,000 residents)

	Rate	Burglary	Larceny, Theft	Vehicle Theft
Area	3,626.0	678.9	2,213.1	734.0
USA	3,413.6	806.6	2,388.0	262.7

Key Violent Crime Data (Rate per 100,000 residents)

	Rate	Murder	Rape	Robbery	Aggravated Assault
Area	635.8	8.1	26.4	309.0	292.3
USA	432.8	4.7	34.7	111.6	285.6

Key Economic Data (Family income, unemployment)

	$25k-$75k	$75k-$150k	>$150k	Unemployment 03/2009	Unemployment 03/2010
Area	44.4%	35.6%	10.5%	8.3%	10.1%
USA	45.8%	29.5%	8.5%	9.0%	10.1

Key Household Data

	Population Age 0-17	Children w/Married Parents	Children w/Single Mother	Stay-at-home Mothers	Births to Single Women
Area	29.6%	74.9%	17.0%	35.8%	20.6%
USA	24.0%	65.6%	25.5%	27.9%	35.3%

Key Housing Data

	Owner Occupied	Median Year Built	Median Home Value	Home Value Growth, 2005-2010	Median List Price, 4-bedroom Home
Area	69.5%	1979	$256,000	6.7%	
USA	67.8%	1976	$187,045	3.1%	$288,846

San Jose-Sunnyvale-Santa Clara, CA
109,787

	Score	Rank
Overall	69.22	60
LDS Culture	19.04	299
Education	80.95	65
Crime	67.46	95
Economic	73.21	56
Health	45.87	135
Household	87.65	25
Housing	69.71	328

Key LDS Culture Data

	Positive	Negative	Ratio Pos:Neg	Commute>59 minutes	Commute<15 minutes
Area	598	25	23.9	5.5%	50.9%
USA	4,292	251	20.1	5.5%	34.1%

Key Education Data

	HS Grad	Some Coll.	College Degree	Free/Reduced Lunch	Students per Teacher
Area	81.0%	23.7%	27.5%	49.4%	14.2
USA	85.8%	22.6%	33.2%	41.2%	15.8

Key Property Crime Data (Rate per 100,000 residents)

	Rate	Burglary	Larceny, Theft	Vehicle Theft
Area	2,558.8	468.2	1,588.1	502.4
USA	3,413.6	806.6	2,388.0	262.7

Key Violent Crime Data (Rate per 100,000 residents)

	Rate	Murder	Rape	Robbery	Aggravated Assault
Area	327.6	2.9	21.5	92.6	210.6
USA	432.8	4.7	34.7	111.6	285.6

Key Economic Data (Family income, unemployment)

	$25k-$75k	$75k-$150k	>$150k	Unemployment 03/2009	Unemployment 03/2010
Area	56.5%	24.2%	2.9%	10.5%	12.3%
USA	45.8%	29.5%	8.5%	9.0%	10.1

Key Household Data

	Population Age 0-17	Children w/Married Parents	Children w/Single Mother	Stay-at-home Mothers	Births to Single Women
Area	25.2%	64.3%	25.7%	26.7%	31.0%
USA	24.0%	65.6%	25.5%	27.9%	35.3%

Key Housing Data

	Owner Occupied	Median Year Built	Median Home Value	Home Value Growth, 2005-2010	Median List Price, 4-bedroom Home
Area	65.4%	1973	$96,800	6.4%	
USA	67.8%	1976	$187,045	3.1%	$288,846

San Luis Obispo-Paso Robles, CA
2,032,024

	Score	Rank
Overall	72.33	28
LDS Culture	37.51	61
Education	80.57	68
Crime	72.40	65
Economic	63.98	168
Health	48.59	71
Household	82.10	56
Housing	78.66	236

Key LDS Culture Data

	Positive	Negative	Ratio Pos:Neg	Commute>59 minutes	Commute<15 minutes
Area	8,261	555	14.9	5.9%	24.0%
USA	4,292	251	20.1	5.5%	34.1%

Key Education Data

	HS Grad	Some Coll.	College Degree	Free/Reduced Lunch	Students per Teacher
Area	81.7%	24.1%	31.5%	46.0%	15.1
USA	85.8%	22.6%	33.2%	41.2%	15.8

Key Property Crime Data (Rate per 100,000 residents)

	Rate	Burglary	Larceny, Theft	Vehicle Theft	
Area	2,345.9	576.8	1,637.9	131.2	
USA	3,413.6	806.6	2,388.0	262.7	

Key Violent Crime Data (Rate per 100,000 residents)

	Rate	Murder	Rape	Robbery	Aggravated Assault
Area	296.6	1.5	40.3	42.6	212.2
USA	432.8	4.7	34.7	111.6	285.6

Key Economic Data (Family income, unemployment)

	$25k-$75k	$75k-$150k	>$150k	Unemployment 03/2009	Unemployment 03/2010
Area	44.2%	29.1%	8.6%	8.4%	10.6%
USA	45.8%	29.5%	8.5%	9.0%	10.1

Key Household Data

	Population Age 0-17	Children w/Married Parents	Children w/Single Mother	Stay-at-home Mothers	Births to Single Women
Area	27.6%	64.6%	26.9%	32.8%	37.7%
USA	24.0%	65.6%	25.5%	27.9%	35.3%

Key Housing Data

	Owner Occupied	Median Year Built	Median Home Value	Home Value Growth, 2005-2010	Median List Price, 4-bedroom Home
Area	65.8%	1984	$126,300	5.6%	$235,000
USA	67.8%	1976	$187,045	3.1%	$288,846

Sandusky, OH
3,001,072

	Score	Rank
Overall	64.27	157
LDS Culture	42.27	31
Education	81.64	61
Crime	60.55	145
Economic	63.48	176
Health	42.19	180
Household	61.11	219
Housing	60.90	350

Key LDS Culture Data

	Positive	Negative	Ratio Pos:Neg	Commute>59 minutes	Commute<15 minutes
Area	12,001	700	17.1	5.9%	25.6%
USA	4,292	251	20.1	5.5%	34.1%

Key Education Data

	HS Grad	Some Coll.	College Degree	Free/Reduced Lunch	Students per Teacher
Area	85.0%	23.7%	42.3%	44.3%	18.1
USA	85.8%	22.6%	33.2%	41.2%	15.8

Key Property Crime Data (Rate per 100,000 residents)

	Rate	Burglary	Larceny, Theft	Vehicle Theft
Area	3,480.5	808.5	2,563.0	109.0
USA	3,413.6	806.6	2,388.0	262.7

Key Violent Crime Data (Rate per 100,000 residents)

	Rate	Murder	Rape	Robbery	Aggravated Assault
Area	316.6	2.6	16.9	76.6	220.6
USA	432.8	4.7	34.7	111.6	285.6

Key Economic Data (Family income, unemployment)

	$25k-$75k	$75k-$150k	>$150k	Unemployment 03/2009	Unemployment 03/2010
Area	36.7%	32.8%	17.0%	9.1%	11.0%
USA	45.8%	29.5%	8.5%	9.0%	10.1

Key Household Data

	Population Age 0-17	Children w/Married Parents	Children w/Single Mother	Stay-at-home Mothers	Births to Single Women
Area	24.8%	68.2%	23.1%	34.7%	27.4%
USA	24.0%	65.6%	25.5%	27.9%	35.3%

Key Housing Data

	Owner Occupied	Median Year Built	Median Home Value	Home Value Growth, 2005-2010	Median List Price, 4-bedroom Home
Area	56.4%	1977	$482,900	-1.9%	$565,000
USA	67.8%	1976	$187,045	3.1%	$288,846

Santa Barbara-Santa Maria-Goleta, CA
77,062

	Score	Rank
Overall	66.23	119
LDS Culture	21.00	271
Education	72.32	158
Crime	61.91	133
Economic	72.32	62
Health	48.59	72
Household	88.27	22
Housing	60.25	354

Key LDS Culture Data

	Positive	Negative	Ratio Pos:Neg	Commute>59 minutes	Commute<15 minutes
Area	1,784	139	12.8	4.3%	48.1%
USA	4,292	251	20.1	5.5%	34.1%

Key Education Data

	HS Grad	Some Coll.	College Degree	Free/Reduced Lunch	Students per Teacher
Area	89.9%	20.3%	28.7%	41.2%	17.2
USA	85.8%	22.6%	33.2%	41.2%	15.8

Key Property Crime Data (Rate per 100,000 residents)

	Rate	Burglary	Larceny, Theft	Vehicle Theft
Area	2,335.9	505.3	1,629.0	201.6
USA	3,413.6	806.6	2,388.0	262.7

Key Violent Crime Data (Rate per 100,000 residents)

	Rate	Murder	Rape	Robbery	Aggravated Assault
Area	410.4	3.5	33.8	72.5	300.7
USA	432.8	4.7	34.7	111.6	285.6

Key Economic Data (Family income, unemployment)

	$25k-$75k	$75k-$150k	>$150k	Unemployment 03/2009	Unemployment 03/2010
Area	46.3%	32.5%	5.0%	12.6%	12.9%
USA	45.8%	29.5%	8.5%	9.0%	10.1

Key Household Data

	Population Age 0-17	Children w/Married Parents	Children w/Single Mother	Stay-at-home Mothers	Births to Single Women
Area	22.3%	70.2%	24.7%	19.6%	64.4%
USA	24.0%	65.6%	25.5%	27.9%	35.3%

Key Housing Data

	Owner Occupied	Median Year Built	Median Home Value	Home Value Growth, 2005-2010	Median List Price, 4-bedroom Home
Area	73.4%	1965	$145,700	-0.4%	
USA	67.8%	1976	$187,045	3.1%	$288,846

Santa Cruz-Watsonville, CA
4,274,531

	Score	Rank
Overall	63.31	175
LDS Culture	13.33	348
Education	86.45	34
Crime	48.99	226
Economic	65.15	153
Health	48.59	73
Household	90.12	17
Housing	53.32	359

Key LDS Culture Data

	Positive	Negative	Ratio Pos:Neg	Commute>59 minutes	Commute<15 minutes
Area	24,795	1467	16.9	11.1%	21.2%
USA	4,292	251	20.1	5.5%	34.1%

Key Education Data

	HS Grad	Some Coll.	College Degree	Free/Reduced Lunch	Students per Teacher
Area	86.9%	19.0%	50.4%	34.1%	16.9
USA	85.8%	22.6%	33.2%	41.2%	15.8

Key Property Crime Data (Rate per 100,000 residents)

	Rate	Burglary	Larceny, Theft	Vehicle Theft	
Area	3,152.8	634.0	2,240.4	278.4	
USA	3,413.6	806.6	2,388.0	262.7	

Key Violent Crime Data (Rate per 100,000 residents)

	Rate	Murder	Rape	Robbery	Aggravated Assault
Area	498.8	3.2	30.8	110.4	354.4
USA	432.8	4.7	34.7	111.6	285.6

Key Economic Data (Family income, unemployment)

	$25k-$75k	$75k-$150k	>$150k	Unemployment 03/2009	Unemployment 03/2010
Area	29.1%	34.5%	25.9%	12.6%	15.3%
USA	45.8%	29.5%	8.5%	9.0%	10.1

Key Household Data

	Population Age 0-17	Children w/Married Parents	Children w/Single Mother	Stay-at-home Mothers	Births to Single Women
Area	21.6%	70.8%	21.5%	30.5%	28.0%
USA	24.0%	65.6%	25.5%	27.9%	35.3%

Key Housing Data

	Owner Occupied	Median Year Built	Median Home Value	Home Value Growth, 2005-2010	Median List Price, 4-bedroom Home
Area	56.9%	1964	$674,800	2.2%	$795,000
USA	67.8%	1976	$187,045	3.1%	$288,846

Santa Fe, NM
1,819,087

	Score	Rank
Overall	59.07	264
LDS Culture	37.60	60
Education	64.40	252
Crime	54.68	175
Economic	63.04	184
Health	43.41	165
Household	43.21	349
Housing	72.46	313

Key LDS Culture Data

	Positive	Negative	Ratio Pos:Neg	Commute>59 minutes	Commute<15 minutes
Area	16,529	767	21.6	6.0%	22.4%
USA	4,292	251	20.1	5.5%	34.1%

Key Education Data

	HS Grad	Some Coll.	College Degree	Free/Reduced Lunch	Students per Teacher
Area	85.3%	18.1%	50.8%	35.3%	18.1
USA	85.8%	22.6%	33.2%	41.2%	15.8

Key Property Crime Data (Rate per 100,000 residents)

	Rate	Burglary	Larceny, Theft	Vehicle Theft
Area	3,200.4	1,670.6	1,375.3	154.6
USA	3,413.6	806.6	2,388.0	262.7

Key Violent Crime Data (Rate per 100,000 residents)

	Rate	Murder	Rape	Robbery	Aggravated Assault
Area	398.6	9.0	39.5	65.9	284.2
USA	432.8	4.7	34.7	111.6	285.6

Key Economic Data (Family income, unemployment)

	$25k-$75k	$75k-$150k	>$150k	Unemployment 03/2009	Unemployment 03/2010
Area	27.8%	34.0%	30.4%	5.7%	7.7%
USA	45.8%	29.5%	8.5%	9.0%	10.1

Key Household Data

	Population Age 0-17	Children w/Married Parents	Children w/Single Mother	Stay-at-home Mothers	Births to Single Women
Area	24.4%	75.7%	16.0%	34.4%	24.0%
USA	24.0%	65.6%	25.5%	27.9%	35.3%

Key Housing Data

	Owner Occupied	Median Year Built	Median Home Value	Home Value Growth, 2005-2010	Median List Price, 4-bedroom Home
Area	60.5%	1971	$724,000	2.1%	$775,000
USA	67.8%	1976	$187,045	3.1%	$288,846

Santa Rosa-Petaluma, CA
265,297

	Score	Rank
Overall	**62.80**	**185**
LDS Culture	12.54	349
Education	76.52	110
Crime	63.86	119
Economic	68.15	108
Health	48.59	74
Household	72.22	135
Housing	60.85	351

Key LDS Culture Data

	Positive	Negative	Ratio Pos:Neg	Commute>59 minutes	Commute<15 minutes
Area	1,972	113	17.5	4.1%	41.3%
USA	4,292	251	20.1	5.5%	34.1%

Key Education Data

	HS Grad	Some Coll.	College Degree	Free/Reduced Lunch	Students per Teacher
Area	88.4%	26.5%	41.1%	34.2%	17.4
USA	85.8%	22.6%	33.2%	41.2%	15.8

Key Property Crime Data (Rate per 100,000 residents)

	Rate	Burglary	Larceny, Theft	Vehicle Theft	
Area	1,880.3	445.3	1,258.8	176.2	
USA	3,413.6	806.6	2,388.0	262.7	

Key Violent Crime Data (Rate per 100,000 residents)

	Rate	Murder	Rape	Robbery	Aggravated Assault
Area	439.0	2.6	31.3	59.2	345.8
USA	432.8	4.7	34.7	111.6	285.6

Key Economic Data (Family income, unemployment)

	$25k-$75k	$75k-$150k	>$150k	Unemployment 03/2009	Unemployment 03/2010
Area	40.5%	34.6%	13.1%	9.5%	11.3%
USA	45.8%	29.5%	8.5%	9.0%	10.1

Key Household Data

	Population Age 0-17	Children w/Married Parents	Children w/Single Mother	Stay-at-home Mothers	Births to Single Women
Area	18.7%	69.9%	21.4%	30.0%	26.2%
USA	24.0%	65.6%	25.5%	27.9%	35.3%

Key Housing Data

	Owner Occupied	Median Year Built	Median Home Value	Home Value Growth, 2005-2010	Median List Price, 4-bedroom Home
Area	63.1%	1983	$532,600	0.2%	$629,000
USA	67.8%	1976	$187,045	3.1%	$288,846

Savannah, GA
405,396

	Score	Rank
Overall	58.47	278
LDS Culture	18.27	308
Education	55.72	323
Crime	42.64	270
Economic	70.54	81
Health	40.98	204
Household	69.14	154
Housing	77.64	252

Key LDS Culture Data

	Positive	Negative	Ratio Pos:Neg	Commute>59 minutes	Commute<15 minutes
Area	1,969	143	13.8	5.3%	43.8%
USA	4,292	251	20.1	5.5%	34.1%

Key Education Data

	HS Grad	Some Coll.	College Degree	Free/Reduced Lunch	Students per Teacher
Area	80.9%	21.6%	41.8%	51.1%	18.3
USA	85.8%	22.6%	33.2%	41.2%	15.8

Key Property Crime Data (Rate per 100,000 residents)

	Rate	Burglary	Larceny, Theft	Vehicle Theft	
Area	4,381.0	1,095.2	2,837.9	447.9	
USA	3,413.6	806.6	2,388.0	262.7	

Key Violent Crime Data (Rate per 100,000 residents)

	Rate	Murder	Rape	Robbery	Aggravated Assault
Area	497.5	8.1	17.4	269.4	202.6
USA	432.8	4.7	34.7	111.6	285.6

Key Economic Data (Family income, unemployment)

	$25k-$75k	$75k-$150k	>$150k	Unemployment 03/2009	Unemployment 03/2010
Area	38.8%	33.0%	15.2%	7.5%	8.8%
USA	45.8%	29.5%	8.5%	9.0%	10.1

Key Household Data

	Population Age 0-17	Children w/Married Parents	Children w/Single Mother	Stay-at-home Mothers	Births to Single Women
Area	23.6%	70.8%	19.8%	34.7%	19.4%
USA	24.0%	65.6%	25.5%	27.9%	35.3%

Key Housing Data

	Owner Occupied	Median Year Built	Median Home Value	Home Value Growth, 2005-2010	Median List Price, 4-bedroom Home
Area	54.0%	1972	$557,400	-1.4%	$835,000
USA	67.8%	1976	$187,045	3.1%	$288,846

Scranton--Wilkes-Barre, PA
253,137

	Score	Rank
Overall	62.99	182
LDS Culture	22.72	245
Education	87.20	30
Crime	75.91	45
Economic	67.82	115
Health	36.76	273
Household	48.15	315
Housing	65.37	342

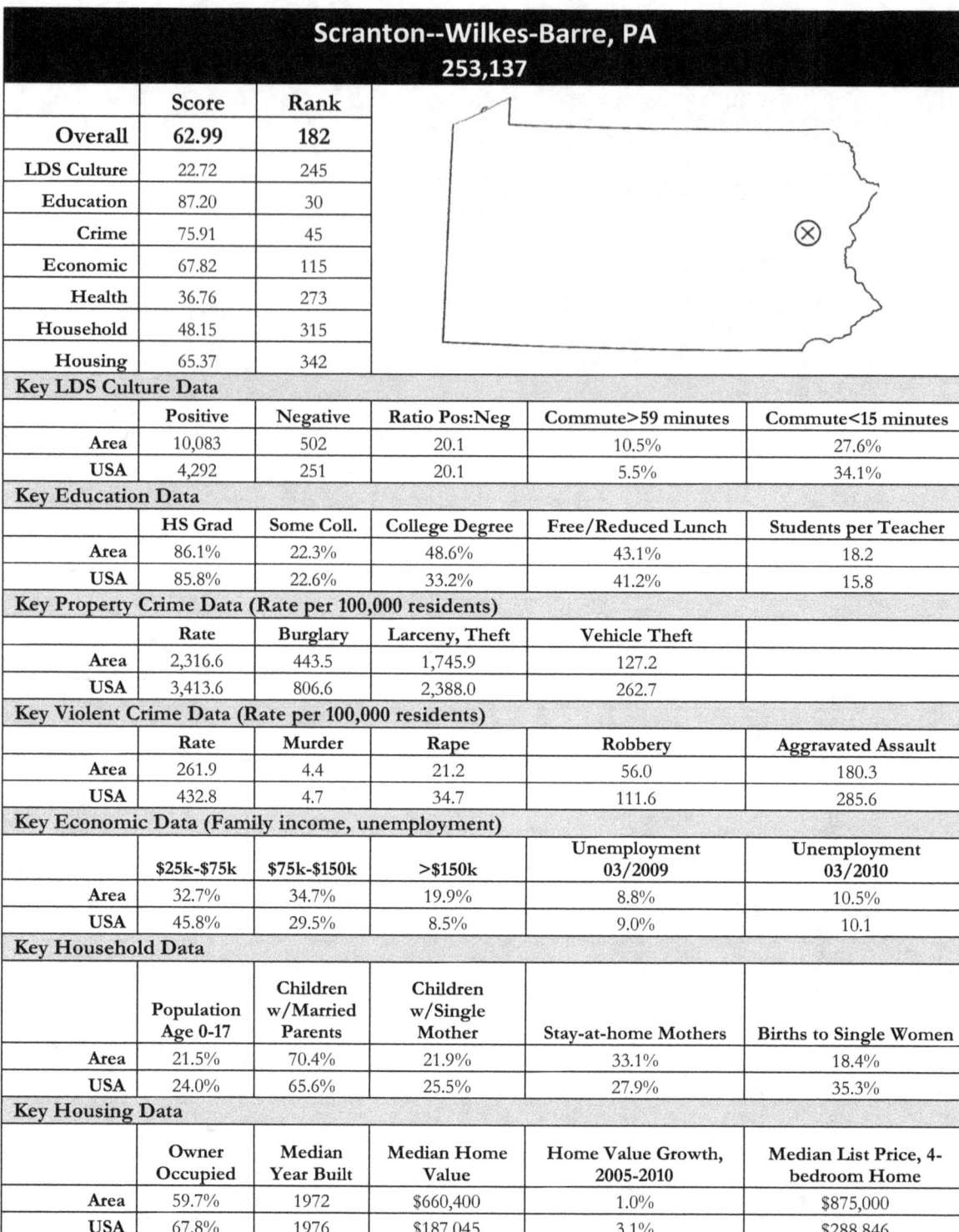

Key LDS Culture Data

	Positive	Negative	Ratio Pos:Neg	Commute>59 minutes	Commute<15 minutes
Area	10,083	502	20.1	10.5%	27.6%
USA	4,292	251	20.1	5.5%	34.1%

Key Education Data

	HS Grad	Some Coll.	College Degree	Free/Reduced Lunch	Students per Teacher
Area	86.1%	22.3%	48.6%	43.1%	18.2
USA	85.8%	22.6%	33.2%	41.2%	15.8

Key Property Crime Data (Rate per 100,000 residents)

	Rate	Burglary	Larceny, Theft	Vehicle Theft
Area	2,316.6	443.5	1,745.9	127.2
USA	3,413.6	806.6	2,388.0	262.7

Key Violent Crime Data (Rate per 100,000 residents)

	Rate	Murder	Rape	Robbery	Aggravated Assault
Area	261.9	4.4	21.2	56.0	180.3
USA	432.8	4.7	34.7	111.6	285.6

Key Economic Data (Family income, unemployment)

	$25k-$75k	$75k-$150k	>$150k	Unemployment 03/2009	Unemployment 03/2010
Area	32.7%	34.7%	19.9%	8.8%	10.5%
USA	45.8%	29.5%	8.5%	9.0%	10.1

Key Household Data

	Population Age 0-17	Children w/Married Parents	Children w/Single Mother	Stay-at-home Mothers	Births to Single Women
Area	21.5%	70.4%	21.9%	33.1%	18.4%
USA	24.0%	65.6%	25.5%	27.9%	35.3%

Key Housing Data

	Owner Occupied	Median Year Built	Median Home Value	Home Value Growth, 2005-2010	Median List Price, 4-bedroom Home
Area	59.7%	1972	$660,400	1.0%	$875,000
USA	67.8%	1976	$187,045	3.1%	$288,846

Seattle-Tacoma-Bellevue, WA
143,937

	Score	Rank
Overall	**67.01**	**102**
LDS Culture	18.80	304
Education	74.79	128
Crime	49.73	222
Economic	77.21	29
Health	46.04	130
Household	83.33	46
Housing	79.82	211

Key LDS Culture Data

	Positive	Negative	Ratio Pos:Neg	Commute>59 minutes	Commute<15 minutes
Area	1,302	40	32.6	4.4%	32.0%
USA	4,292	251	20.1	5.5%	34.1%

Key Education Data

	HS Grad	Some Coll.	College Degree	Free/Reduced Lunch	Students per Teacher
Area	84.5%	19.7%	45.2%	60.5%	15.1
USA	85.8%	22.6%	33.2%	41.2%	15.8

Key Property Crime Data (Rate per 100,000 residents)

	Rate	Burglary	Larceny, Theft	Vehicle Theft
Area	4,436.8	863.2	2,781.1	792.5
USA	3,413.6	806.6	2,388.0	262.7

Key Violent Crime Data (Rate per 100,000 residents)

	Rate	Murder	Rape	Robbery	Aggravated Assault
Area	385.1	3.1	36.4	131.9	213.7
USA	432.8	4.7	34.7	111.6	285.6

Key Economic Data (Family income, unemployment)

	$25k-$75k	$75k-$150k	>$150k	Unemployment 03/2009	Unemployment 03/2010
Area	38.8%	29.8%	14.7%	8.6%	9.0%
USA	45.8%	29.5%	8.5%	9.0%	10.1

Key Household Data

	Population Age 0-17	Children w/Married Parents	Children w/Single Mother	Stay-at-home Mothers	Births to Single Women
Area	20.7%	58.6%	28.1%	26.5%	47.2%
USA	24.0%	65.6%	25.5%	27.9%	35.3%

Key Housing Data

	Owner Occupied	Median Year Built	Median Home Value	Home Value Growth, 2005-2010	Median List Price, 4-bedroom Home
Area	72.4%	1987	$319,700	4.0%	
USA	67.8%	1976	$187,045	3.1%	$288,846

Sebastian-Vero Beach, FL
466,741

	Score	Rank
Overall	63.85	162
LDS Culture	25.29	207
Education	76.58	109
Crime	58.24	155
Economic	54.70	297
Health	52.72	26
Household	66.05	173
Housing	75.86	274

Key LDS Culture Data
	Positive	Negative	Ratio Pos:Neg	Commute>59 minutes	Commute<15 minutes
Area	3,721	405	9.2	9.9%	33.2%
USA	4,292	251	20.1	5.5%	34.1%

Key Education Data
	HS Grad	Some Coll.	College Degree	Free/Reduced Lunch	Students per Teacher
Area	86.6%	26.8%	39.8%	28.0%	16.9
USA	85.8%	22.6%	33.2%	41.2%	15.8

Key Property Crime Data (Rate per 100,000 residents)
	Rate	Burglary	Larceny, Theft	Vehicle Theft	
Area	3,229.5	820.0	2,295.0	114.6	
USA	3,413.6	806.6	2,388.0	262.7	

Key Violent Crime Data (Rate per 100,000 residents)
	Rate	Murder	Rape	Robbery	Aggravated Assault
Area	357.2	3.0	29.4	76.9	248.0
USA	432.8	4.7	34.7	111.6	285.6

Key Economic Data (Family income, unemployment)
	$25k-$75k	$75k-$150k	>$150k	Unemployment 03/2009	Unemployment 03/2010
Area	37.4%	35.6%	16.5%	11.2%	13.9%
USA	45.8%	29.5%	8.5%	9.0%	10.1

Key Household Data
	Population Age 0-17	Children w/Married Parents	Children w/Single Mother	Stay-at-home Mothers	Births to Single Women
Area	22.1%	67.1%	23.5%	32.0%	27.9%
USA	24.0%	65.6%	25.5%	27.9%	35.3%

Key Housing Data
	Owner Occupied	Median Year Built	Median Home Value	Home Value Growth, 2005-2010	Median List Price, 4-bedroom Home
Area	63.5%	1977	$518,700	-1.5%	$575,000
USA	67.8%	1976	$187,045	3.1%	$288,846

Sheboygan, WI
334,353

	Score	Rank
Overall	74.11	22
LDS Culture	31.35	120
Education	82.65	54
Crime	86.42	13
Economic	82.55	10
Health	39.16	233
Household	79.01	74
Housing	74.08	296

Key LDS Culture Data

	Positive	Negative	Ratio Pos:Neg	Commute>59 minutes	Commute<15 minutes
Area	2,352	150	15.7	3.0%	24.0%
USA	4,292	251	20.1	5.5%	34.1%

Key Education Data

	HS Grad	Some Coll.	College Degree	Free/Reduced Lunch	Students per Teacher
Area	87.5%	23.1%	34.5%	49.8%	13.6
USA	85.8%	22.6%	33.2%	41.2%	15.8

Key Property Crime Data (Rate per 100,000 residents)

	Rate	Burglary	Larceny, Theft	Vehicle Theft	
Area	2,757.9	407.3	2,272.9	77.6	
USA	3,413.6	806.6	2,388.0	262.7	

Key Violent Crime Data (Rate per 100,000 residents)

	Rate	Murder	Rape	Robbery	Aggravated Assault
Area	102.9	0.0	14.0	25.3	63.7
USA	432.8	4.7	34.7	111.6	285.6

Key Economic Data (Family income, unemployment)

	$25k-$75k	$75k-$150k	>$150k	Unemployment 03/2009	Unemployment 03/2010
Area	44.9%	29.7%	8.1%	10.1%	10.0%
USA	45.8%	29.5%	8.5%	9.0%	10.1

Key Household Data

	Population Age 0-17	Children w/Married Parents	Children w/Single Mother	Stay-at-home Mothers	Births to Single Women
Area	25.7%	58.0%	35.0%	32.4%	27.4%
USA	24.0%	65.6%	25.5%	27.9%	35.3%

Key Housing Data

	Owner Occupied	Median Year Built	Median Home Value	Home Value Growth, 2005-2010	Median List Price, 4-bedroom Home
Area	60.2%	1985	$183,900	5.1%	$253,900
USA	67.8%	1976	$187,045	3.1%	$288,846

Sherman-Denison, TX
549,621

	Score	Rank
Overall	66.98	105
LDS Culture	27.58	174
Education	68.28	204
Crime	68.50	87
Economic	66.65	129
Health	32.00	334
Household	74.69	108
Housing	91.84	34

Key LDS Culture Data

	Positive	Negative	Ratio Pos:Neg	Commute>59 minutes	Commute<15 minutes
Area	3,139	293	10.7	4.9%	37.8%
USA	4,292	251	20.1	5.5%	34.1%

Key Education Data

	HS Grad	Some Coll.	College Degree	Free/Reduced Lunch	Students per Teacher
Area	87.1%	18.1%	28.9%	35.6%	13.1
USA	85.8%	22.6%	33.2%	41.2%	15.8

Key Property Crime Data (Rate per 100,000 residents)

	Rate	Burglary	Larceny, Theft	Vehicle Theft
Area	2,911.3	750.4	2,033.0	127.8
USA	3,413.6	806.6	2,388.0	262.7

Key Violent Crime Data (Rate per 100,000 residents)

	Rate	Murder	Rape	Robbery	Aggravated Assault
Area	279.9	2.5	12.5	39.3	225.6
USA	432.8	4.7	34.7	111.6	285.6

Key Economic Data (Family income, unemployment)

	$25k-$75k	$75k-$150k	>$150k	Unemployment 03/2009	Unemployment 03/2010
Area	50.1%	26.6%	5.4%	8.0%	8.5%
USA	45.8%	29.5%	8.5%	9.0%	10.1

Key Household Data

	Population Age 0-17	Children w/Married Parents	Children w/Single Mother	Stay-at-home Mothers	Births to Single Women
Area	20.3%	64.2%	26.3%	26.4%	42.1%
USA	24.0%	65.6%	25.5%	27.9%	35.3%

Key Housing Data

	Owner Occupied	Median Year Built	Median Home Value	Home Value Growth, 2005-2010	Median List Price, 4-bedroom Home
Area	67.8%	1951	$126,600	5.8%	$219,900
USA	67.8%	1976	$187,045	3.1%	$288,846

Shreveport-Bossier City, LA
3,344,813

	Score	Rank
Overall	51.39	360
LDS Culture	18.12	310
Education	61.48	283
Crime	20.36	355
Economic	56.14	283
Health	49.04	55
Household	43.83	344
Housing	80.59	203

Key LDS Culture Data

	Positive	Negative	Ratio Pos:Neg	Commute>59 minutes	Commute<15 minutes
Area	16,769	788	21.3	9.1%	21.7%
USA	4,292	251	20.1	5.5%	34.1%

Key Education Data

	HS Grad	Some Coll.	College Degree	Free/Reduced Lunch	Students per Teacher
Area	91.3%	24.6%	45.3%	30.9%	20.4
USA	85.8%	22.6%	33.2%	41.2%	15.8

Key Property Crime Data (Rate per 100,000 residents)

	Rate	Burglary	Larceny, Theft	Vehicle Theft
Area	4,015.8	874.0	2,821.6	320.2
USA	3,413.6	806.6	2,388.0	262.7

Key Violent Crime Data (Rate per 100,000 residents)

	Rate	Murder	Rape	Robbery	Aggravated Assault
Area	1,048.3	9.5	37.8	157.9	843.1
USA	432.8	4.7	34.7	111.6	285.6

Key Economic Data (Family income, unemployment)

	$25k-$75k	$75k-$150k	>$150k	Unemployment 03/2009	Unemployment 03/2010
Area	36.2%	37.6%	16.9%	6.7%	5.8%
USA	45.8%	29.5%	8.5%	9.0%	10.1

Key Household Data

	Population Age 0-17	Children w/Married Parents	Children w/Single Mother	Stay-at-home Mothers	Births to Single Women
Area	23.0%	70.1%	20.3%	31.5%	22.9%
USA	24.0%	65.6%	25.5%	27.9%	35.3%

Key Housing Data

	Owner Occupied	Median Year Built	Median Home Value	Home Value Growth, 2005-2010	Median List Price, 4-bedroom Home
Area	63.5%	1978	$381,300	5.8%	$420,000
USA	67.8%	1976	$187,045	3.1%	$288,846

Sioux City, IA-NE-SD
132,315

	Score	Rank
Overall	63.82	164
LDS Culture	25.76	201
Education	83.17	49
Crime	74.18	57
Economic	60.76	217
Health	46.47	120
Household	45.68	333
Housing	73.26	305

Key LDS Culture Data

	Positive	Negative	Ratio Pos:Neg	Commute>59 minutes	Commute<15 minutes
Area	2,787	118	23.6	5.4%	34.3%
USA	4,292	251	20.1	5.5%	34.1%

Key Education Data

	HS Grad	Some Coll.	College Degree	Free/Reduced Lunch	Students per Teacher
Area	86.9%	22.6%	36.7%	41.0%	17.3
USA	85.8%	22.6%	33.2%	41.2%	15.8

Key Property Crime Data (Rate per 100,000 residents)

	Rate	Burglary	Larceny, Theft	Vehicle Theft
Area	2,350.8	465.0	1,751.6	134.3
USA	3,413.6	806.6	2,388.0	262.7

Key Violent Crime Data (Rate per 100,000 residents)

	Rate	Murder	Rape	Robbery	Aggravated Assault
Area	276.9	4.2	32.2	39.9	200.7
USA	432.8	4.7	34.7	111.6	285.6

Key Economic Data (Family income, unemployment)

	$25k-$75k	$75k-$150k	>$150k	Unemployment 03/2009	Unemployment 03/2010
Area	47.9%	25.2%	12.6%	5.2%	6.8%
USA	45.8%	29.5%	8.5%	9.0%	10.1

Key Household Data

	Population Age 0-17	Children w/Married Parents	Children w/Single Mother	Stay-at-home Mothers	Births to Single Women
Area	19.0%	63.0%	25.8%	35.5%	27.1%
USA	24.0%	65.6%	25.5%	27.9%	35.3%

Key Housing Data

	Owner Occupied	Median Year Built	Median Home Value	Home Value Growth, 2005-2010	Median List Price, 4-bedroom Home
Area	74.5%	1987	$202,800	0.6%	
USA	67.8%	1976	$187,045	3.1%	$288,846

Sioux Falls, SD
114,561

	Score	Rank
Overall	69.13	62
LDS Culture	29.58	148
Education	83.20	48
Crime	80.07	34
Economic	62.59	192
Health	42.05	184
Household	63.58	197
Housing	82.24	183

Key LDS Culture Data

	Positive	Negative	Ratio Pos:Neg	Commute>59 minutes	Commute<15 minutes
Area	1,040	190	5.5	3.9%	50.0%
USA	4,292	251	20.1	5.5%	34.1%

Key Education Data

	HS Grad	Some Coll.	College Degree	Free/Reduced Lunch	Students per Teacher
Area	90.4%	21.2%	31.2%	24.3%	14.4
USA	85.8%	22.6%	33.2%	41.2%	15.8

Key Property Crime Data (Rate per 100,000 residents)

	Rate	Burglary	Larceny, Theft	Vehicle Theft
Area	1,968.2	349.3	1,489.1	129.8
USA	3,413.6	806.6	2,388.0	262.7

Key Violent Crime Data (Rate per 100,000 residents)

	Rate	Murder	Rape	Robbery	Aggravated Assault
Area	253.3	3.0	63.0	20.1	167.1
USA	432.8	4.7	34.7	111.6	285.6

Key Economic Data (Family income, unemployment)

	$25k-$75k	$75k-$150k	>$150k	Unemployment 03/2009	Unemployment 03/2010
Area	50.5%	35.3%	5.2%	5.3%	5.4%
USA	45.8%	29.5%	8.5%	9.0%	10.1

Key Household Data

	Population Age 0-17	Children w/Married Parents	Children w/Single Mother	Stay-at-home Mothers	Births to Single Women
Area	23.3%	76.4%	18.3%	15.7%	5.3%
USA	24.0%	65.6%	25.5%	27.9%	35.3%

Key Housing Data

	Owner Occupied	Median Year Built	Median Home Value	Home Value Growth, 2005-2010	Median List Price, 4-bedroom Home
Area	73.0%	1964	$156,300	2.5%	
USA	67.8%	1976	$187,045	3.1%	$288,846

South Bend-Mishawaka, IN-MI
118,804

	Score	Rank
Overall	60.33	236
LDS Culture	26.15	192
Education	65.71	237
Crime	48.30	231
Economic	62.81	189
Health	36.88	272
Household	70.99	142
Housing	76.01	272

Key LDS Culture Data

	Positive	Negative	Ratio Pos:Neg	Commute>59 minutes	Commute<15 minutes
Area	1,389	53	26.2	8.3%	38.2%
USA	4,292	251	20.1	5.5%	34.1%

Key Education Data

	HS Grad	Some Coll.	College Degree	Free/Reduced Lunch	Students per Teacher
Area	86.1%	28.6%	23.5%	43.5%	13.0
USA	85.8%	22.6%	33.2%	41.2%	15.8

Key Property Crime Data (Rate per 100,000 residents)

	Rate	Burglary	Larceny, Theft	Vehicle Theft
Area	4,432.7	1,199.6	2,937.5	295.6
USA	3,413.6	806.6	2,388.0	262.7

Key Violent Crime Data (Rate per 100,000 residents)

	Rate	Murder	Rape	Robbery	Aggravated Assault
Area	400.6	5.7	43.0	162.7	189.2
USA	432.8	4.7	34.7	111.6	285.6

Key Economic Data (Family income, unemployment)

	$25k-$75k	$75k-$150k	>$150k	Unemployment 03/2009	Unemployment 03/2010
Area	46.8%	29.7%	4.3%	11.9%	12.4%
USA	45.8%	29.5%	8.5%	9.0%	10.1

Key Household Data

	Population Age 0-17	Children w/Married Parents	Children w/Single Mother	Stay-at-home Mothers	Births to Single Women
Area	24.2%	66.0%	25.9%	32.6%	32.8%
USA	24.0%	65.6%	25.5%	27.9%	35.3%

Key Housing Data

	Owner Occupied	Median Year Built	Median Home Value	Home Value Growth, 2005-2010	Median List Price, 4-bedroom Home
Area	72.8%	1976	$96,800	2.8%	
USA	67.8%	1976	$187,045	3.1%	$288,846

Spartanburg, SC
387,764

	Score	Rank
Overall	54.89	331
LDS Culture	18.44	306
Education	52.80	337
Crime	35.62	317
Economic	60.53	225
Health	37.46	252
Household	62.35	209
Housing	84.76	147

Key LDS Culture Data

	Positive	Negative	Ratio Pos:Neg	Commute>59 minutes	Commute<15 minutes
Area	2,528	163	15.5	3.1%	29.6%
USA	4,292	251	20.1	5.5%	34.1%

Key Education Data

	HS Grad	Some Coll.	College Degree	Free/Reduced Lunch	Students per Teacher
Area	85.0%	22.5%	27.2%	57.1%	15.1
USA	85.8%	22.6%	33.2%	41.2%	15.8

Key Property Crime Data (Rate per 100,000 residents)

	Rate	Burglary	Larceny, Theft	Vehicle Theft
Area	4,282.0	1,094.7	2,808.4	378.9
USA	3,413.6	806.6	2,388.0	262.7

Key Violent Crime Data (Rate per 100,000 residents)

	Rate	Murder	Rape	Robbery	Aggravated Assault
Area	669.4	6.8	44.4	152.0	466.2
USA	432.8	4.7	34.7	111.6	285.6

Key Economic Data (Family income, unemployment)

	$25k-$75k	$75k-$150k	>$150k	Unemployment 03/2009	Unemployment 03/2010
Area	48.0%	24.6%	6.2%	11.6%	12.3%
USA	45.8%	29.5%	8.5%	9.0%	10.1

Key Household Data

	Population Age 0-17	Children w/Married Parents	Children w/Single Mother	Stay-at-home Mothers	Births to Single Women
Area	25.8%	49.3%	39.7%	25.1%	49.0%
USA	24.0%	65.6%	25.5%	27.9%	35.3%

Key Housing Data

	Owner Occupied	Median Year Built	Median Home Value	Home Value Growth, 2005-2010	Median List Price, 4-bedroom Home
Area	63.9%	1975	$117,600	4.5%	$265,000
USA	67.8%	1976	$187,045	3.1%	$288,846

Spokane, WA
143,589

	Score	Rank
Overall	61.88	199
LDS Culture	23.06	242
Education	74.45	132
Crime	49.82	219
Economic	56.81	273
Health	45.56	141
Household	69.14	155
Housing	77.95	245

Key LDS Culture Data

	Positive	Negative	Ratio Pos:Neg	Commute>59 minutes	Commute<15 minutes
Area	805	88	9.1	2.5%	44.2%
USA	4,292	251	20.1	5.5%	34.1%

Key Education Data

	HS Grad	Some Coll.	College Degree	Free/Reduced Lunch	Students per Teacher
Area	86.0%	21.0%	30.0%	42.1%	13.6
USA	85.8%	22.6%	33.2%	41.2%	15.8

Key Property Crime Data (Rate per 100,000 residents)

	Rate	Burglary	Larceny, Theft	Vehicle Theft	
Area	3,811.6	791.7	2,536.5	483.4	
USA	3,413.6	806.6	2,388.0	262.7	

Key Violent Crime Data (Rate per 100,000 residents)

	Rate	Murder	Rape	Robbery	Aggravated Assault
Area	415.4	4.1	29.5	121.1	260.7
USA	432.8	4.7	34.7	111.6	285.6

Key Economic Data (Family income, unemployment)

	$25k-$75k	$75k-$150k	>$150k	Unemployment 03/2009	Unemployment 03/2010
Area	50.8%	25.9%	4.9%	9.7%	10.5%
USA	45.8%	29.5%	8.5%	9.0%	10.1

Key Household Data

	Population Age 0-17	Children w/Married Parents	Children w/Single Mother	Stay-at-home Mothers	Births to Single Women
Area	27.6%	62.4%	24.4%	22.6%	49.5%
USA	24.0%	65.6%	25.5%	27.9%	35.3%

Key Housing Data

	Owner Occupied	Median Year Built	Median Home Value	Home Value Growth, 2005-2010	Median List Price, 4-bedroom Home
Area	68.4%	1958	$97,400	2.1%	
USA	67.8%	1976	$187,045	3.1%	$288,846

Springfield, IL
232,647

	Score	Rank
Overall	61.58	208
LDS Culture	30.49	137
Education	99.40	3
Crime	19.42	356
Economic	70.76	79
Health	47.30	109
Household	45.06	340
Housing	82.46	181

Key LDS Culture Data

	Positive	Negative	Ratio Pos:Neg	Commute>59 minutes	Commute<15 minutes
Area	1,152	136	8.5	2.0%	40.9%
USA	4,292	251	20.1	5.5%	34.1%

Key Education Data

	HS Grad	Some Coll.	College Degree	Free/Reduced Lunch	Students per Teacher
Area	92.8%	23.7%	38.7%	8.2%	14.9
USA	85.8%	22.6%	33.2%	41.2%	15.8

Key Property Crime Data (Rate per 100,000 residents)

	Rate	Burglary	Larceny, Theft	Vehicle Theft	
Area		1,679.4	4,620.3	362.0	
USA	3,413.6	806.6	2,388.0	262.7	

Key Violent Crime Data (Rate per 100,000 residents)

	Rate	Murder	Rape	Robbery	Aggravated Assault
Area		5.2		306.1	1,142.8
USA	432.8	4.7	34.7	111.6	285.6

Key Economic Data (Family income, unemployment)

	$25k-$75k	$75k-$150k	>$150k	Unemployment 03/2009	Unemployment 03/2010
Area	47.1%	33.3%	9.9%	7.0%	9.3%
USA	45.8%	29.5%	8.5%	9.0%	10.1

Key Household Data

	Population Age 0-17	Children w/Married Parents	Children w/Single Mother	Stay-at-home Mothers	Births to Single Women
Area	25.7%	70.4%	23.7%	10.2%	38.8%
USA	24.0%	65.6%	25.5%	27.9%	35.3%

Key Housing Data

	Owner Occupied	Median Year Built	Median Home Value	Home Value Growth, 2005-2010	Median List Price, 4-bedroom Home
Area	69.3%	1978	$148,400	3.4%	
USA	67.8%	1976	$187,045	3.1%	$288,846

Springfield, MO
280,738

	Score	Rank
Overall	65.87	128
LDS Culture	40.74	43
Education	67.03	220
Crime	46.49	242
Economic	61.37	206
Health	33.49	314
Household	85.19	33
Housing	88.08	82

Key LDS Culture Data

	Positive	Negative	Ratio Pos:Neg	Commute>59 minutes	Commute<15 minutes
Area	3,363	212	15.9	3.8%	27.2%
USA	4,292	251	20.1	5.5%	34.1%

Key Education Data

	HS Grad	Some Coll.	College Degree	Free/Reduced Lunch	Students per Teacher
Area	78.4%	19.4%	29.9%	48.9%	14.7
USA	85.8%	22.6%	33.2%	41.2%	15.8

Key Property Crime Data (Rate per 100,000 residents)

	Rate	Burglary	Larceny, Theft	Vehicle Theft	
Area	4,548.1	764.1	3,468.9	315.1	
USA	3,413.6	806.6	2,388.0	262.7	

Key Violent Crime Data (Rate per 100,000 residents)

	Rate	Murder	Rape	Robbery	Aggravated Assault
Area		2.6	31.2	76.5	
USA	432.8	4.7	34.7	111.6	285.6

Key Economic Data (Family income, unemployment)

	$25k-$75k	$75k-$150k	>$150k	Unemployment 03/2009	Unemployment 03/2010
Area	49.1%	26.7%	6.3%	8.9%	9.4%
USA	45.8%	29.5%	8.5%	9.0%	10.1

Key Household Data

	Population Age 0-17	Children w/Married Parents	Children w/Single Mother	Stay-at-home Mothers	Births to Single Women
Area	23.9%	67.7%	25.3%	28.3%	54.2%
USA	24.0%	65.6%	25.5%	27.9%	35.3%

Key Housing Data

	Owner Occupied	Median Year Built	Median Home Value	Home Value Growth, 2005-2010	Median List Price, 4-bedroom Home
Area	67.9%	1981	$115,600	2.8%	$209,900
USA	67.8%	1976	$187,045	3.1%	$288,846

Springfield, OH
462,677

	Score	Rank
Overall	60.47	232
LDS Culture	28.06	170
Education	65.06	243
Crime	62.57	131
Economic	58.37	252
Health	42.19	181
Household	51.23	296
Housing	80.26	207

Key LDS Culture Data

	Positive	Negative	Ratio Pos:Neg	Commute>59 minutes	Commute<15 minutes
Area	2,679	127	21.1	3.0%	29.1%
USA	4,292	251	20.1	5.5%	34.1%

Key Education Data

	HS Grad	Some Coll.	College Degree	Free/Reduced Lunch	Students per Teacher
Area	92.4%	28.4%	38.8%	39.6%	19.1
USA	85.8%	22.6%	33.2%	41.2%	15.8

Key Property Crime Data (Rate per 100,000 residents)

	Rate	Burglary	Larceny, Theft	Vehicle Theft	
Area	4,447.5	868.6	3,280.3	298.6	
USA	3,413.6	806.6	2,388.0	262.7	

Key Violent Crime Data (Rate per 100,000 residents)

	Rate	Murder	Rape	Robbery	Aggravated Assault
Area	246.4	7.1	27.1	104.3	107.9
USA	432.8	4.7	34.7	111.6	285.6

Key Economic Data (Family income, unemployment)

	$25k-$75k	$75k-$150k	>$150k	Unemployment 03/2009	Unemployment 03/2010
Area	48.2%	29.8%	7.5%	10.2%	11.7%
USA	45.8%	29.5%	8.5%	9.0%	10.1

Key Household Data

	Population Age 0-17	Children w/Married Parents	Children w/Single Mother	Stay-at-home Mothers	Births to Single Women
Area	23.4%	65.0%	24.1%	32.8%	31.1%
USA	24.0%	65.6%	25.5%	27.9%	35.3%

Key Housing Data

	Owner Occupied	Median Year Built	Median Home Value	Home Value Growth, 2005-2010	Median List Price, 4-bedroom Home
Area	64.5%	1975	$207,300	7.5%	$235,000
USA	67.8%	1976	$187,045	3.1%	$288,846

St. Cloud, MN
207,728

	Score	Rank
Overall	71.23	37
LDS Culture	20.02	282
Education	88.68	22
Crime	69.39	79
Economic	77.04	30
Health	40.69	211
Household	75.31	102
Housing	85.63	130

Key LDS Culture Data

	Positive	Negative	Ratio Pos:Neg	Commute>59 minutes	Commute<15 minutes
Area	1,482	156	9.5	2.9%	33.5%
USA	4,292	251	20.1	5.5%	34.1%

Key Education Data

	HS Grad	Some Coll.	College Degree	Free/Reduced Lunch	Students per Teacher
Area	91.8%	23.8%	37.2%	31.8%	16.6
USA	85.8%	22.6%	33.2%	41.2%	15.8

Key Property Crime Data (Rate per 100,000 residents)

	Rate	Burglary	Larceny, Theft	Vehicle Theft
Area	2,570.1	335.4	2,125.4	109.3
USA	3,413.6	806.6	2,388.0	262.7

Key Violent Crime Data (Rate per 100,000 residents)

	Rate	Murder	Rape	Robbery	Aggravated Assault
Area		0.5		28.1	115.2
USA	432.8	4.7	34.7	111.6	285.6

Key Economic Data (Family income, unemployment)

	$25k-$75k	$75k-$150k	>$150k	Unemployment 03/2009	Unemployment 03/2010
Area	41.2%	36.2%	8.6%	11.9%	11.6%
USA	45.8%	29.5%	8.5%	9.0%	10.1

Key Household Data

	Population Age 0-17	Children w/Married Parents	Children w/Single Mother	Stay-at-home Mothers	Births to Single Women
Area	23.4%	64.8%	26.1%	13.3%	51.9%
USA	24.0%	65.6%	25.5%	27.9%	35.3%

Key Housing Data

	Owner Occupied	Median Year Built	Median Home Value	Home Value Growth, 2005-2010	Median List Price, 4-bedroom Home
Area	75.0%	1972	$115,900	2.3%	$224,900
USA	67.8%	1976	$187,045	3.1%	$288,846

St. George, UT
687,558

	Score	Rank
Overall	92.52	2
LDS Culture	100.00	1
Education	100.00	1
Crime	83.32	21
Economic	59.37	236
Health	63.80	5
Household	98.15	2
Housing	88.65	70

Key LDS Culture Data

	Positive	Negative	Ratio Pos:Neg	Commute>59 minutes	Commute<15 minutes
Area	7,870	591	13.3	4.6%	32.6%
USA	4,292	251	20.1	5.5%	34.1%

Key Education Data

	HS Grad	Some Coll.	College Degree	Free/Reduced Lunch	Students per Teacher
Area	86.7%	18.1%	38.3%	41.9%	12.4
USA	85.8%	22.6%	33.2%	41.2%	15.8

Key Property Crime Data (Rate per 100,000 residents)

	Rate	Burglary	Larceny, Theft	Vehicle Theft
Area	2,249.0	481.2	1,641.9	125.9
USA	3,413.6	806.6	2,388.0	262.7

Key Violent Crime Data (Rate per 100,000 residents)

	Rate	Murder	Rape	Robbery	Aggravated Assault
Area	189.2	1.4	22.5	22.5	142.8
USA	432.8	4.7	34.7	111.6	285.6

Key Economic Data (Family income, unemployment)

	$25k-$75k	$75k-$150k	>$150k	Unemployment 03/2009	Unemployment 03/2010
Area	40.3%	35.0%	7.9%	9.1%	9.7%
USA	45.8%	29.5%	8.5%	9.0%	10.1

Key Household Data

	Population Age 0-17	Children w/Married Parents	Children w/Single Mother	Stay-at-home Mothers	Births to Single Women
Area	21.6%	59.3%	31.2%	19.5%	39.7%
USA	24.0%	65.6%	25.5%	27.9%	35.3%

Key Housing Data

	Owner Occupied	Median Year Built	Median Home Value	Home Value Growth, 2005-2010	Median List Price, 4-bedroom Home
Area	66.0%	1959	$223,400	3.0%	$285,000
USA	67.8%	1976	$187,045	3.1%	$288,846

St. Joseph, MO-KS
425,508

	Score	Rank
Overall	63.77	166
LDS Culture	32.66	114
Education	78.00	95
Crime	56.22	162
Economic	57.98	260
Health	38.40	245
Household	62.35	208
Housing	83.32	170

Key LDS Culture Data

	Positive	Negative	Ratio Pos:Neg	Commute>59 minutes	Commute<15 minutes
Area	2,036	78	26.1	4.0%	30.7%
USA	4,292	251	20.1	5.5%	34.1%

Key Education Data

	HS Grad	Some Coll.	College Degree	Free/Reduced Lunch	Students per Teacher
Area	88.0%	24.8%	31.6%	39.0%	14.5
USA	85.8%	22.6%	33.2%	41.2%	15.8

Key Property Crime Data (Rate per 100,000 residents)

	Rate	Burglary	Larceny, Theft	Vehicle Theft
Area	3,693.7	849.7	2,628.7	215.3
USA	3,413.6	806.6	2,388.0	262.7

Key Violent Crime Data (Rate per 100,000 residents)

	Rate	Murder	Rape	Robbery	Aggravated Assault
Area	352.6	2.4	17.1	75.5	257.5
USA	432.8	4.7	34.7	111.6	285.6

Key Economic Data (Family income, unemployment)

	$25k-$75k	$75k-$150k	>$150k	Unemployment 03/2009	Unemployment 03/2010
Area	50.1%	27.0%	5.5%	8.8%	9.1%
USA	45.8%	29.5%	8.5%	9.0%	10.1

Key Household Data

	Population Age 0-17	Children w/Married Parents	Children w/Single Mother	Stay-at-home Mothers	Births to Single Women
Area	23.6%	71.2%	20.1%	29.6%	17.3%
USA	24.0%	65.6%	25.5%	27.9%	35.3%

Key Housing Data

	Owner Occupied	Median Year Built	Median Home Value	Home Value Growth, 2005-2010	Median List Price, 4-bedroom Home
Area	66.4%	1985	$133,300	2.9%	$199,000
USA	67.8%	1976	$187,045	3.1%	$288,846

St. Louis, MO-IL
139,859

	Score	Rank
Overall	59.87	250
LDS Culture	32.04	117
Education	65.51	239
Crime	45.98	247
Economic	70.98	75
Health	29.21	349
Household	65.43	176
Housing	74.74	286

Key LDS Culture Data

	Positive	Negative	Ratio Pos:Neg	Commute>59 minutes	Commute<15 minutes
Area	4,941	295	16.7	5.2%	36.4%
USA	4,292	251	20.1	5.5%	34.1%

Key Education Data

	HS Grad	Some Coll.	College Degree	Free/Reduced Lunch	Students per Teacher
Area	86.7%	23.7%	24.2%		18.2
USA	85.8%	22.6%	33.2%	41.2%	15.8

Key Property Crime Data (Rate per 100,000 residents)

	Rate	Burglary	Larceny, Theft	Vehicle Theft
Area	3,400.0	684.6	2,336.7	378.7
USA	3,413.6	806.6	2,388.0	262.7

Key Violent Crime Data (Rate per 100,000 residents)

	Rate	Murder	Rape	Robbery	Aggravated Assault
Area	525.8	8.3	20.3	149.7	347.6
USA	432.8	4.7	34.7	111.6	285.6

Key Economic Data (Family income, unemployment)

	$25k-$75k	$75k-$150k	>$150k	Unemployment 03/2009	Unemployment 03/2010
Area	53.3%	25.7%	4.3%	9.8%	10.9%
USA	45.8%	29.5%	8.5%	9.0%	10.1

Key Household Data

	Population Age 0-17	Children w/Married Parents	Children w/Single Mother	Stay-at-home Mothers	Births to Single Women
Area	23.2%	64.3%	23.9%	28.4%	42.7%
USA	24.0%	65.6%	25.5%	27.9%	35.3%

Key Housing Data

	Owner Occupied	Median Year Built	Median Home Value	Home Value Growth, 2005-2010	Median List Price, 4-bedroom Home
Area	71.4%	1962	$110,700	0.2%	
USA	67.8%	1976	$187,045	3.1%	$288,846

State College, PA
144,779

	Score	Rank
Overall	81.04	5
LDS Culture	33.44	99
Education	94.70	10
Crime	96.74	2
Economic	83.60	9
Health	47.33	98
Household	83.33	47
Housing	80.51	204

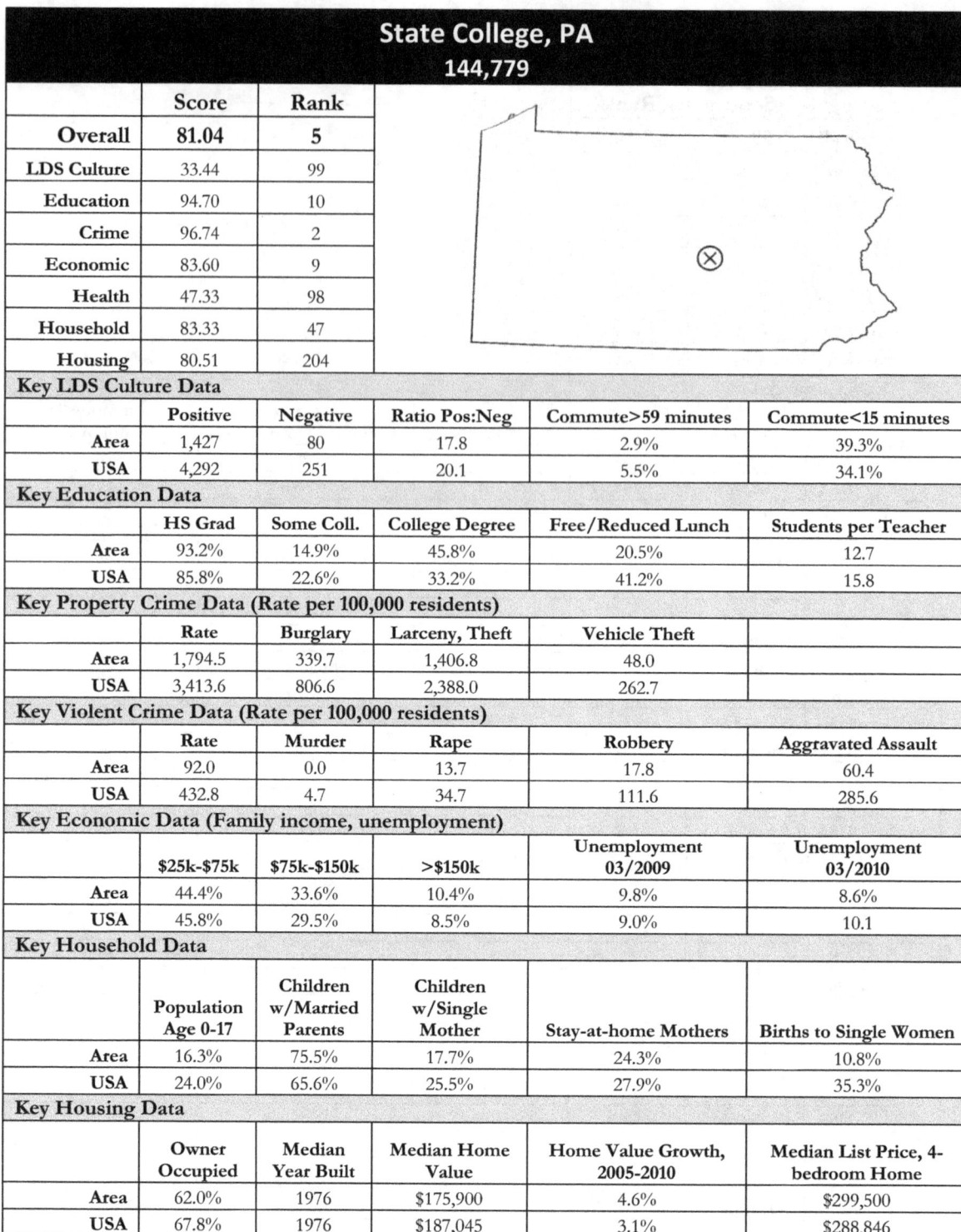

Key LDS Culture Data
	Positive	Negative	Ratio Pos:Neg	Commute>59 minutes	Commute<15 minutes
Area	1,427	80	17.8	2.9%	39.3%
USA	4,292	251	20.1	5.5%	34.1%

Key Education Data
	HS Grad	Some Coll.	College Degree	Free/Reduced Lunch	Students per Teacher
Area	93.2%	14.9%	45.8%	20.5%	12.7
USA	85.8%	22.6%	33.2%	41.2%	15.8

Key Property Crime Data (Rate per 100,000 residents)
	Rate	Burglary	Larceny, Theft	Vehicle Theft	
Area	1,794.5	339.7	1,406.8	48.0	
USA	3,413.6	806.6	2,388.0	262.7	

Key Violent Crime Data (Rate per 100,000 residents)
	Rate	Murder	Rape	Robbery	Aggravated Assault
Area	92.0	0.0	13.7	17.8	60.4
USA	432.8	4.7	34.7	111.6	285.6

Key Economic Data (Family income, unemployment)
	$25k-$75k	$75k-$150k	>$150k	Unemployment 03/2009	Unemployment 03/2010
Area	44.4%	33.6%	10.4%	9.8%	8.6%
USA	45.8%	29.5%	8.5%	9.0%	10.1

Key Household Data
	Population Age 0-17	Children w/Married Parents	Children w/Single Mother	Stay-at-home Mothers	Births to Single Women
Area	16.3%	75.5%	17.7%	24.3%	10.8%
USA	24.0%	65.6%	25.5%	27.9%	35.3%

Key Housing Data
	Owner Occupied	Median Year Built	Median Home Value	Home Value Growth, 2005-2010	Median List Price, 4-bedroom Home
Area	62.0%	1976	$175,900	4.6%	$299,500
USA	67.8%	1976	$187,045	3.1%	$288,846

Stockton, CA
672,388

	Score	Rank
Overall	54.72	334
LDS Culture	14.85	338
Education	64.75	244
Crime	22.46	354
Economic	47.36	344
Health	48.59	75
Household	73.46	124
Housing	79.46	220

Key LDS Culture Data

	Positive	Negative	Ratio Pos:Neg	Commute>59 minutes	Commute<15 minutes
Area	4,486	267	16.8	15.7%	31.5%
USA	4,292	251	20.1	5.5%	34.1%

Key Education Data

	HS Grad	Some Coll.	College Degree	Free/Reduced Lunch	Students per Teacher
Area	75.7%	25.8%	23.8%	51.9%	18.1
USA	85.8%	22.6%	33.2%	41.2%	15.8

Key Property Crime Data (Rate per 100,000 residents)

	Rate	Burglary	Larceny, Theft	Vehicle Theft
Area	4,923.4	1,123.5	3,148.6	651.2
USA	3,413.6	806.6	2,388.0	262.7

Key Violent Crime Data (Rate per 100,000 residents)

	Rate	Murder	Rape	Robbery	Aggravated Assault
Area	902.9	5.1	25.1	296.9	575.8
USA	432.8	4.7	34.7	111.6	285.6

Key Economic Data (Family income, unemployment)

	$25k-$75k	$75k-$150k	>$150k	Unemployment 03/2009	Unemployment 03/2010
Area	39.9%	31.1%	9.9%	15.6%	18.4%
USA	45.8%	29.5%	8.5%	9.0%	10.1

Key Household Data

	Population Age 0-17	Children w/Married Parents	Children w/Single Mother	Stay-at-home Mothers	Births to Single Women
Area	28.9%	62.7%	26.1%	34.1%	27.4%
USA	24.0%	65.6%	25.5%	27.9%	35.3%

Key Housing Data

	Owner Occupied	Median Year Built	Median Home Value	Home Value Growth, 2005-2010	Median List Price, 4-bedroom Home
Area	59.1%	1982	$311,300	-5.0%	$225,000
USA	67.8%	1976	$187,045	3.1%	$288,846

Sumter, SC
104,148

	Score	Rank
Overall	52.67	352
LDS Culture	27.48	175
Education	45.85	357
Crime	35.10	319
Economic	50.58	323
Health	37.46	253
Household	47.53	318
Housing	93.73	19

Key LDS Culture Data

	Positive	Negative	Ratio Pos:Neg	Commute>59 minutes	Commute<15 minutes
Area	1,357	52	26.1	5.6%	35.3%
USA	4,292	251	20.1	5.5%	34.1%

Key Education Data

	HS Grad	Some Coll.	College Degree	Free/Reduced Lunch	Students per Teacher
Area	83.8%	24.1%	29.1%	65.1%	16.5
USA	85.8%	22.6%	33.2%	41.2%	15.8

Key Property Crime Data (Rate per 100,000 residents)

	Rate	Burglary	Larceny, Theft	Vehicle Theft
Area	3,732.1	1,202.2	2,170.4	359.5
USA	3,413.6	806.6	2,388.0	262.7

Key Violent Crime Data (Rate per 100,000 residents)

	Rate	Murder	Rape	Robbery	Aggravated Assault
Area	740.1	12.5	22.0	166.8	538.8
USA	432.8	4.7	34.7	111.6	285.6

Key Economic Data (Family income, unemployment)

	$25k-$75k	$75k-$150k	>$150k	Unemployment 03/2009	Unemployment 03/2010
Area	51.4%	21.6%	5.4%	12.0%	13.0%
USA	45.8%	29.5%	8.5%	9.0%	10.1

Key Household Data

	Population Age 0-17	Children w/Married Parents	Children w/Single Mother	Stay-at-home Mothers	Births to Single Women
Area	26.3%	52.0%	40.0%	30.7%	50.3%
USA	24.0%	65.6%	25.5%	27.9%	35.3%

Key Housing Data

	Owner Occupied	Median Year Built	Median Home Value	Home Value Growth, 2005-2010	Median List Price, 4-bedroom Home
Area	71.4%	1987	$97,500	4.0%	
USA	67.8%	1976	$187,045	3.1%	$288,846

Syracuse, NY
643,794

	Score	Rank
Overall	68.41	74
LDS Culture	30.20	144
Education	79.65	71
Crime	70.80	72
Economic	68.20	106
Health	49.20	53
Household	58.02	242
Housing	82.61	178

Key LDS Culture Data

	Positive	Negative	Ratio Pos:Neg	Commute>59 minutes	Commute<15 minutes
Area	3,488	246	14.2	3.4%	32.6%
USA	4,292	251	20.1	5.5%	34.1%

Key Education Data

	HS Grad	Some Coll.	College Degree	Free/Reduced Lunch	Students per Teacher
Area	88.5%	18.6%	39.6%	34.4%	12.8
USA	85.8%	22.6%	33.2%	41.2%	15.8

Key Property Crime Data (Rate per 100,000 residents)

	Rate	Burglary	Larceny, Theft	Vehicle Theft
Area	2,404.2	572.9	1,710.1	121.2
USA	3,413.6	806.6	2,388.0	262.7

Key Violent Crime Data (Rate per 100,000 residents)

	Rate	Murder	Rape	Robbery	Aggravated Assault
Area	307.7	4.8	25.4	82.9	194.6
USA	432.8	4.7	34.7	111.6	285.6

Key Economic Data (Family income, unemployment)

	$25k-$75k	$75k-$150k	>$150k	Unemployment 03/2009	Unemployment 03/2010
Area	43.5%	33.1%	8.4%	8.3%	8.5%
USA	45.8%	29.5%	8.5%	9.0%	10.1

Key Household Data

	Population Age 0-17	Children w/Married Parents	Children w/Single Mother	Stay-at-home Mothers	Births to Single Women
Area	22.3%	62.8%	26.3%	21.1%	38.3%
USA	24.0%	65.6%	25.5%	27.9%	35.3%

Key Housing Data

	Owner Occupied	Median Year Built	Median Home Value	Home Value Growth, 2005-2010	Median List Price, 4-bedroom Home
Area	68.5%	1962	$116,900	3.9%	$199,900
USA	67.8%	1976	$187,045	3.1%	$288,846

Tallahassee, FL
358,833

	Score	Rank
Overall	54.76	333
LDS Culture	26.61	188
Education	64.67	247
Crime	27.56	344
Economic	52.70	312
Health	53.83	17
Household	40.74	359
Housing	85.04	141

Key LDS Culture Data

	Positive	Negative	Ratio Pos:Neg	Commute>59 minutes	Commute<15 minutes
Area	1,934	77	25.1	3.0%	27.6%
USA	4,292	251	20.1	5.5%	34.1%

Key Education Data

	HS Grad	Some Coll.	College Degree	Free/Reduced Lunch	Students per Teacher
Area	88.8%	23.5%	39.4%	38.8%	14.9
USA	85.8%	22.6%	33.2%	41.2%	15.8

Key Property Crime Data (Rate per 100,000 residents)

	Rate	Burglary	Larceny, Theft	Vehicle Theft
Area	3,907.5	1,331.7	2,363.3	212.5
USA	3,413.6	806.6	2,388.0	262.7

Key Violent Crime Data (Rate per 100,000 residents)

	Rate	Murder	Rape	Robbery	Aggravated Assault
Area	894.5	4.3	51.7	226.1	612.4
USA	432.8	4.7	34.7	111.6	285.6

Key Economic Data (Family income, unemployment)

	$25k-$75k	$75k-$150k	>$150k	Unemployment 03/2009	Unemployment 03/2010
Area	42.3%	30.8%	8.0%	6.6%	8.7%
USA	45.8%	29.5%	8.5%	9.0%	10.1

Key Household Data

	Population Age 0-17	Children w/Married Parents	Children w/Single Mother	Stay-at-home Mothers	Births to Single Women
Area	21.0%	58.8%	32.2%	21.4%	50.8%
USA	24.0%	65.6%	25.5%	27.9%	35.3%

Key Housing Data

	Owner Occupied	Median Year Built	Median Home Value	Home Value Growth, 2005-2010	Median List Price, 4-bedroom Home
Area	61.7%	1986	$179,100	4.5%	$280,000
USA	67.8%	1976	$187,045	3.1%	$288,846

Tampa-St. Petersburg-Clearwater, FL
2,733,761

	Score	Rank
Overall	57.75	292
LDS Culture	15.93	330
Education	61.99	278
Crime	36.77	308
Economic	57.42	266
Health	52.32	32
Household	58.64	237
Housing	87.26	95

Key LDS Culture Data

	Positive	Negative	Ratio Pos:Neg	Commute>59 minutes	Commute<15 minutes
Area	13,505	749	18.0	7.1%	24.7%
USA	4,292	251	20.1	5.5%	34.1%

Key Education Data

	HS Grad	Some Coll.	College Degree	Free/Reduced Lunch	Students per Teacher
Area	86.5%	21.6%	34.3%	44.7%	14.9
USA	85.8%	22.6%	33.2%	41.2%	15.8

Key Property Crime Data (Rate per 100,000 residents)

	Rate	Burglary	Larceny, Theft	Vehicle Theft
Area	4,115.1	1,041.5	2,748.0	325.6
USA	3,413.6	806.6	2,388.0	262.7

Key Violent Crime Data (Rate per 100,000 residents)

	Rate	Murder	Rape	Robbery	Aggravated Assault
Area	660.8	5.6	34.7	176.5	444.0
USA	432.8	4.7	34.7	111.6	285.6

Key Economic Data (Family income, unemployment)

	$25k-$75k	$75k-$150k	>$150k	Unemployment 03/2009	Unemployment 03/2010
Area	47.7%	27.3%	8.7%	10.1%	12.7%
USA	45.8%	29.5%	8.5%	9.0%	10.1

Key Household Data

	Population Age 0-17	Children w/Married Parents	Children w/Single Mother	Stay-at-home Mothers	Births to Single Women
Area	21.7%	60.2%	28.3%	28.2%	35.1%
USA	24.0%	65.6%	25.5%	27.9%	35.3%

Key Housing Data

	Owner Occupied	Median Year Built	Median Home Value	Home Value Growth, 2005-2010	Median List Price, 4-bedroom Home
Area	69.3%	1981	$193,700	2.6%	$249,900
USA	67.8%	1976	$187,045	3.1%	$288,846

Terre Haute, IN
168,982

	Score	Rank
Overall	59.01	265
LDS Culture	20.06	281
Education	67.89	208
Crime	53.63	180
Economic	59.70	234
Health	34.59	300
Household	65.43	178
Housing	77.11	259

Key LDS Culture Data

	Positive	Negative	Ratio Pos:Neg	Commute>59 minutes	Commute<15 minutes
Area	1,270	100	12.7	5.9%	38.9%
USA	4,292	251	20.1	5.5%	34.1%

Key Education Data

	HS Grad	Some Coll.	College Degree	Free/Reduced Lunch	Students per Teacher
Area	85.8%	21.7%	26.6%	46.0%	16.3
USA	85.8%	22.6%	33.2%	41.2%	15.8

Key Property Crime Data (Rate per 100,000 residents)

	Rate	Burglary	Larceny, Theft	Vehicle Theft	
Area		921.6	3,321.3	921.6	
USA	3,413.6	806.6	2,388.0	262.7	

Key Violent Crime Data (Rate per 100,000 residents)

	Rate	Murder	Rape	Robbery	Aggravated Assault
Area		3.6	29.7	76.1	159.2
USA	432.8	4.7	34.7	111.6	285.6

Key Economic Data (Family income, unemployment)

	$25k-$75k	$75k-$150k	>$150k	Unemployment 03/2009	Unemployment 03/2010
Area	49.3%	24.5%	4.8%	10.8%	11.6%
USA	45.8%	29.5%	8.5%	9.0%	10.1

Key Household Data

	Population Age 0-17	Children w/Married Parents	Children w/Single Mother	Stay-at-home Mothers	Births to Single Women
Area	21.4%	65.0%	20.8%	27.0%	34.7%
USA	24.0%	65.6%	25.5%	27.9%	35.3%

Key Housing Data

	Owner Occupied	Median Year Built	Median Home Value	Home Value Growth, 2005-2010	Median List Price, 4-bedroom Home
Area	71.7%	1957	$84,600	0.8%	
USA	67.8%	1976	$187,045	3.1%	$288,846

Texarkana, TX-Texarkana, AR
135,509

	Score	Rank
Overall	56.88	307
LDS Culture	42.19	32
Education	67.45	213
Crime	28.10	341
Economic	39.13	360
Health	40.43	215
Household	59.26	232
Housing	88.17	80

Key LDS Culture Data

	Positive	Negative	Ratio Pos:Neg	Commute>59 minutes	Commute<15 minutes
Area	1,082	39	27.7	2.4%	40.7%
USA	4,292	251	20.1	5.5%	34.1%

Key Education Data

	HS Grad	Some Coll.	College Degree	Free/Reduced Lunch	Students per Teacher
Area	82.0%	27.4%	21.5%	54.6%	12.7
USA	85.8%	22.6%	33.2%	41.2%	15.8

Key Property Crime Data (Rate per 100,000 residents)

	Rate	Burglary	Larceny, Theft	Vehicle Theft
Area	3,989.8	1,139.0	2,589.6	261.2
USA	3,413.6	806.6	2,388.0	262.7

Key Violent Crime Data (Rate per 100,000 residents)

	Rate	Murder	Rape	Robbery	Aggravated Assault
Area	873.3	3.7	37.1	120.9	711.6
USA	432.8	4.7	34.7	111.6	285.6

Key Economic Data (Family income, unemployment)

	$25k-$75k	$75k-$150k	>$150k	Unemployment 03/2009	Unemployment 03/2010
Area	45.7%	24.7%	5.3%	5.6%	7.5%
USA	45.8%	29.5%	8.5%	9.0%	10.1

Key Household Data

	Population Age 0-17	Children w/Married Parents	Children w/Single Mother	Stay-at-home Mothers	Births to Single Women
Area	24.1%	62.4%	35.9%	24.8%	38.6%
USA	24.0%	65.6%	25.5%	27.9%	35.3%

Key Housing Data

	Owner Occupied	Median Year Built	Median Home Value	Home Value Growth, 2005-2010	Median List Price, 4-bedroom Home
Area	63.3%	1980	$88,700	3.4%	
USA	67.8%	1976	$187,045	3.1%	$288,846

Toledo, OH
649,104

	Score	Rank
Overall	52.67	351
LDS Culture	29.44	150
Education	62.12	275
Crime	38.11	301
Economic	55.70	286
Health	34.04	303
Household	41.98	352
Housing	76.37	265

Key LDS Culture Data

	Positive	Negative	Ratio Pos:Neg	Commute>59 minutes	Commute<15 minutes
Area	3,941	296	13.3	3.6%	35.8%
USA	4,292	251	20.1	5.5%	34.1%

Key Education Data

	HS Grad	Some Coll.	College Degree	Free/Reduced Lunch	Students per Teacher
Area	88.4%	22.4%	31.7%		17.4
USA	85.8%	22.6%	33.2%	41.2%	15.8

Key Property Crime Data (Rate per 100,000 residents)

	Rate	Burglary	Larceny, Theft	Vehicle Theft
Area	4,302.5	1,259.5	2,760.0	283.0
USA	3,413.6	806.6	2,388.0	262.7

Key Violent Crime Data (Rate per 100,000 residents)

	Rate	Murder	Rape	Robbery	Aggravated Assault
Area	609.8	3.1	30.3	228.1	348.3
USA	432.8	4.7	34.7	111.6	285.6

Key Economic Data (Family income, unemployment)

	$25k-$75k	$75k-$150k	>$150k	Unemployment 03/2009	Unemployment 03/2010
Area	47.0%	28.3%	7.9%	11.8%	13.0%
USA	45.8%	29.5%	8.5%	9.0%	10.1

Key Household Data

	Population Age 0-17	Children w/Married Parents	Children w/Single Mother	Stay-at-home Mothers	Births to Single Women
Area	23.7%	60.4%	30.1%	19.1%	46.7%
USA	24.0%	65.6%	25.5%	27.9%	35.3%

Key Housing Data

	Owner Occupied	Median Year Built	Median Home Value	Home Value Growth, 2005-2010	Median List Price, 4-bedroom Home
Area	68.1%	1961	$137,400	-1.0%	$187,900
USA	67.8%	1976	$187,045	3.1%	$288,846

Topeka, KS
231,191

	Score	Rank
Overall	60.84	224
LDS Culture	14.64	339
Education	77.75	99
Crime	50.68	212
Economic	69.98	85
Health	46.39	121
Household	51.23	297
Housing	79.47	219

Key LDS Culture Data

	Positive	Negative	Ratio Pos:Neg	Commute>59 minutes	Commute<15 minutes
Area	1,735	150	11.6	6.5%	36.0%
USA	4,292	251	20.1	5.5%	34.1%

Key Education Data

	HS Grad	Some Coll.	College Degree	Free/Reduced Lunch	Students per Teacher
Area	90.8%	24.0%	33.6%	41.7%	13.2
USA	85.8%	22.6%	33.2%	41.2%	15.8

Key Property Crime Data (Rate per 100,000 residents)

	Rate	Burglary	Larceny, Theft	Vehicle Theft	
Area	4,418.7	1,000.3	3,053.6	364.8	
USA	3,413.6	806.6	2,388.0	262.7	

Key Violent Crime Data (Rate per 100,000 residents)

	Rate	Murder	Rape	Robbery	Aggravated Assault
Area	375.7	4.4	24.8	124.1	222.4
USA	432.8	4.7	34.7	111.6	285.6

Key Economic Data (Family income, unemployment)

	$25k-$75k	$75k-$150k	>$150k	Unemployment 03/2009	Unemployment 03/2010
Area	46.6%	32.2%	5.5%	6.9%	6.9%
USA	45.8%	29.5%	8.5%	9.0%	10.1

Key Household Data

	Population Age 0-17	Children w/Married Parents	Children w/Single Mother	Stay-at-home Mothers	Births to Single Women
Area	24.4%	59.9%	30.0%	22.1%	33.0%
USA	24.0%	65.6%	25.5%	27.9%	35.3%

Key Housing Data

	Owner Occupied	Median Year Built	Median Home Value	Home Value Growth, 2005-2010	Median List Price, 4-bedroom Home
Area	69.8%	1972	$116,300	2.5%	
USA	67.8%	1976	$187,045	3.1%	$288,846

Trenton-Ewing, NJ
364,883

	Score	Rank
Overall	66.61	110
LDS Culture	14.17	344
Education	78.81	84
Crime	63.65	121
Economic	71.82	66
Health	45.90	133
Household	90.12	18
Housing	62.68	348

Key LDS Culture Data

	Positive	Negative	Ratio Pos:Neg	Commute>59 minutes	Commute<15 minutes
Area	21,778	1358	16.0	12.5%	31.7%
USA	4,292	251	20.1	5.5%	34.1%

Key Education Data

	HS Grad	Some Coll.	College Degree	Free/Reduced Lunch	Students per Teacher
Area	86.4%	16.6%	45.8%	26.1%	16.4
USA	85.8%	22.6%	33.2%	41.2%	15.8

Key Property Crime Data (Rate per 100,000 residents)

	Rate	Burglary	Larceny, Theft	Vehicle Theft
Area	2,216.6	479.1	1,501.8	235.7
USA	3,413.6	806.6	2,388.0	262.7

Key Violent Crime Data (Rate per 100,000 residents)

	Rate	Murder	Rape	Robbery	Aggravated Assault
Area	404.2	6.6	15.0	199.6	182.9
USA	432.8	4.7	34.7	111.6	285.6

Key Economic Data (Family income, unemployment)

	$25k-$75k	$75k-$150k	>$150k	Unemployment 03/2009	Unemployment 03/2010
Area	30.4%	32.9%	26.6%	7.6%	8.4%
USA	45.8%	29.5%	8.5%	9.0%	10.1

Key Household Data

	Population Age 0-17	Children w/Married Parents	Children w/Single Mother	Stay-at-home Mothers	Births to Single Women
Area	22.9%	72.7%	21.1%	31.3%	12.3%
USA	24.0%	65.6%	25.5%	27.9%	35.3%

Key Housing Data

	Owner Occupied	Median Year Built	Median Home Value	Home Value Growth, 2005-2010	Median List Price, 4-bedroom Home
Area	67.5%	1967	$325,600	3.2%	$400,000
USA	67.8%	1976	$187,045	3.1%	$288,846

Tucson, AZ
1,012,018

	Score	Rank
Overall	59.28	261
LDS Culture	20.34	275
Education	79.12	79
Crime	44.95	256
Economic	59.03	240
Health	39.55	223
Household	51.23	298
Housing	85.90	123

Key LDS Culture Data

	Positive	Negative	Ratio Pos:Neg	Commute>59 minutes	Commute<15 minutes
Area	3,936	171	23.0	5.5%	24.9%
USA	4,292	251	20.1	5.5%	34.1%

Key Education Data

	HS Grad	Some Coll.	College Degree	Free/Reduced Lunch	Students per Teacher
Area	86.9%	26.3%	36.4%	23.6%	18.9
USA	85.8%	22.6%	33.2%	41.2%	15.8

Key Property Crime Data (Rate per 100,000 residents)

	Rate	Burglary	Larceny, Theft	Vehicle Theft
Area		839.0		749.6
USA	3,413.6	806.6	2,388.0	262.7

Key Violent Crime Data (Rate per 100,000 residents)

	Rate	Murder	Rape	Robbery	Aggravated Assault
Area	518.6	9.5	33.4	177.9	297.7
USA	432.8	4.7	34.7	111.6	285.6

Key Economic Data (Family income, unemployment)

	$25k-$75k	$75k-$150k	>$150k	Unemployment 03/2009	Unemployment 03/2010
Area	45.1%	28.6%	8.6%	8.0%	8.6%
USA	45.8%	29.5%	8.5%	9.0%	10.1

Key Household Data

	Population Age 0-17	Children w/Married Parents	Children w/Single Mother	Stay-at-home Mothers	Births to Single Women
Area	23.6%	60.9%	29.1%	31.5%	40.4%
USA	24.0%	65.6%	25.5%	27.9%	35.3%

Key Housing Data

	Owner Occupied	Median Year Built	Median Home Value	Home Value Growth, 2005-2010	Median List Price, 4-bedroom Home
Area	66.0%	1983	$210,200	4.6%	$249,900
USA	67.8%	1976	$187,045	3.1%	$288,846

407

Tulsa, OK
918,154

	Score	Rank
Overall	59.90	249
LDS Culture	24.27	235
Education	66.60	227
Crime	37.80	303
Economic	54.81	295
Health	40.76	208
Household	71.60	141
Housing	88.27	78

Key LDS Culture Data

	Positive	Negative	Ratio Pos:Neg	Commute>59 minutes	Commute<15 minutes
Area	4,437	254	17.5	3.8%	30.8%
USA	4,292	251	20.1	5.5%	34.1%

Key Education Data

	HS Grad	Some Coll.	College Degree	Free/Reduced Lunch	Students per Teacher
Area	87.9%	24.4%	33.3%	52.3%	16.3
USA	85.8%	22.6%	33.2%	41.2%	15.8

Key Property Crime Data (Rate per 100,000 residents)

	Rate	Burglary	Larceny, Theft	Vehicle Theft	
Area	3,657.8	1,056.9	2,257.6	343.3	
USA	3,413.6	806.6	2,388.0	262.7	

Key Violent Crime Data (Rate per 100,000 residents)

	Rate	Murder	Rape	Robbery	Aggravated Assault
Area	686.1	8.0	42.6	135.0	500.4
USA	432.8	4.7	34.7	111.6	285.6

Key Economic Data (Family income, unemployment)

	$25k-$75k	$75k-$150k	>$150k	Unemployment 03/2009	Unemployment 03/2010
Area	46.5%	29.3%	8.2%	6.4%	7.5%
USA	45.8%	29.5%	8.5%	9.0%	10.1

Key Household Data

	Population Age 0-17	Children w/Married Parents	Children w/Single Mother	Stay-at-home Mothers	Births to Single Women
Area	25.8%	67.3%	24.1%	32.9%	37.6%
USA	24.0%	65.6%	25.5%	27.9%	35.3%

Key Housing Data

	Owner Occupied	Median Year Built	Median Home Value	Home Value Growth, 2005-2010	Median List Price, 4-bedroom Home
Area	67.2%	1978	$124,200	3.1%	$225,000
USA	67.8%	1976	$187,045	3.1%	$288,846

Tuscaloosa, AL
208,760

	Score	Rank
Overall	60.58	229
LDS Culture	37.06	67
Education	61.33	285
Crime	40.88	282
Economic	58.87	241
Health	42.38	175
Household	59.26	233
Housing	88.70	69

Key LDS Culture Data

	Positive	Negative	Ratio Pos:Neg	Commute>59 minutes	Commute<15 minutes
Area	1,054	33	31.9	4.5%	33.3%
USA	4,292	251	20.1	5.5%	34.1%

Key Education Data

	HS Grad	Some Coll.	College Degree	Free/Reduced Lunch	Students per Teacher
Area	81.0%	19.1%	29.5%	51.2%	15.7
USA	85.8%	22.6%	33.2%	41.2%	15.8

Key Property Crime Data (Rate per 100,000 residents)

	Rate	Burglary	Larceny, Theft	Vehicle Theft
Area	4,645.8	1,328.7	2,985.1	332.0
USA	3,413.6	806.6	2,388.0	262.7

Key Violent Crime Data (Rate per 100,000 residents)

	Rate	Murder	Rape	Robbery	Aggravated Assault
Area	509.7	8.2	32.3	150.1	319.0
USA	432.8	4.7	34.7	111.6	285.6

Key Economic Data (Family income, unemployment)

	$25k-$75k	$75k-$150k	>$150k	Unemployment 03/2009	Unemployment 03/2010
Area	46.2%	28.3%	6.1%	8.3%	9.6%
USA	45.8%	29.5%	8.5%	9.0%	10.1

Key Household Data

	Population Age 0-17	Children w/Married Parents	Children w/Single Mother	Stay-at-home Mothers	Births to Single Women
Area	23.5%	65.7%	30.2%	31.2%	53.3%
USA	24.0%	65.6%	25.5%	27.9%	35.3%

Key Housing Data

	Owner Occupied	Median Year Built	Median Home Value	Home Value Growth, 2005-2010	Median List Price, 4-bedroom Home
Area	63.8%	1985	$142,800	4.3%	
USA	67.8%	1976	$187,045	3.1%	$288,846

Tyler, TX
201,277

	Score	Rank
Overall	64.95	139
LDS Culture	48.31	17
Education	64.64	248
Crime	47.42	237
Economic	61.98	198
Health	41.34	191
Household	64.81	185
Housing	87.96	84

Key LDS Culture Data

	Positive	Negative	Ratio Pos:Neg	Commute>59 minutes	Commute<15 minutes
Area	1,787	40	44.7	4.1%	31.3%
USA	4,292	251	20.1	5.5%	34.1%

Key Education Data

	HS Grad	Some Coll.	College Degree	Free/Reduced Lunch	Students per Teacher
Area	83.4%	24.4%	33.3%	53.8%	14.4
USA	85.8%	22.6%	33.2%	41.2%	15.8

Key Property Crime Data (Rate per 100,000 residents)

	Rate	Burglary	Larceny, Theft	Vehicle Theft
Area	3,416.0	776.9	2,427.9	211.1
USA	3,413.6	806.6	2,388.0	262.7

Key Violent Crime Data (Rate per 100,000 residents)

	Rate	Murder	Rape	Robbery	Aggravated Assault
Area	491.0	6.4	40.1	78.3	366.2
USA	432.8	4.7	34.7	111.6	285.6

Key Economic Data (Family income, unemployment)

	$25k-$75k	$75k-$150k	>$150k	Unemployment 03/2009	Unemployment 03/2010
Area	47.4%	27.3%	8.0%	7.1%	7.8%
USA	45.8%	29.5%	8.5%	9.0%	10.1

Key Household Data

	Population Age 0-17	Children w/Married Parents	Children w/Single Mother	Stay-at-home Mothers	Births to Single Women
Area	25.3%	67.3%	26.3%	29.9%	49.0%
USA	24.0%	65.6%	25.5%	27.9%	35.3%

Key Housing Data

	Owner Occupied	Median Year Built	Median Home Value	Home Value Growth, 2005-2010	Median List Price, 4-bedroom Home
Area	71.9%	1982	$119,600	6.1%	
USA	67.8%	1976	$187,045	3.1%	$288,846

Utica-Rome, NY
293,790

	Score	Rank
Overall	66.23	118
LDS Culture	34.09	90
Education	75.46	122
Crime	72.29	66
Economic	66.70	128
Health	49.20	54
Household	41.98	353
Housing	84.94	144

Key LDS Culture Data

	Positive	Negative	Ratio Pos:Neg	Commute>59 minutes	Commute<15 minutes
Area	1,562	115	13.6	3.6%	41.4%
USA	4,292	251	20.1	5.5%	34.1%

Key Education Data

	HS Grad	Some Coll.	College Degree	Free/Reduced Lunch	Students per Teacher
Area	86.7%	18.5%	32.8%	41.8%	12.1
USA	85.8%	22.6%	33.2%	41.2%	15.8

Key Property Crime Data (Rate per 100,000 residents)

	Rate	Burglary	Larceny, Theft	Vehicle Theft	
Area	2,384.9	522.1	1,784.3	78.5	
USA	3,413.6	806.6	2,388.0	262.7	

Key Violent Crime Data (Rate per 100,000 residents)

	Rate	Murder	Rape	Robbery	Aggravated Assault
Area	293.7	2.7	20.1	77.5	193.4
USA	432.8	4.7	34.7	111.6	285.6

Key Economic Data (Family income, unemployment)

	$25k-$75k	$75k-$150k	>$150k	Unemployment 03/2009	Unemployment 03/2010
Area	48.9%	28.8%	4.7%	8.2%	8.1%
USA	45.8%	29.5%	8.5%	9.0%	10.1

Key Household Data

	Population Age 0-17	Children w/Married Parents	Children w/Single Mother	Stay-at-home Mothers	Births to Single Women
Area	21.2%	58.3%	29.5%	21.1%	50.3%
USA	24.0%	65.6%	25.5%	27.9%	35.3%

Key Housing Data

	Owner Occupied	Median Year Built	Median Home Value	Home Value Growth, 2005-2010	Median List Price, 4-bedroom Home
Area	67.4%	1956	$99,600	5.5%	$169,000
USA	67.8%	1976	$187,045	3.1%	$288,846

411

Valdosta, GA
133,612

	Score	Rank
Overall	61.72	205
LDS Culture	40.93	40
Education	57.17	313
Crime	50.82	210
Economic	55.81	284
Health	40.98	205
Household	60.49	226
Housing	89.57	58

Key LDS Culture Data

	Positive	Negative	Ratio Pos:Neg	Commute>59 minutes	Commute<15 minutes
Area	895	34	26.3	2.0%	38.0%
USA	4,292	251	20.1	5.5%	34.1%

Key Education Data

	HS Grad	Some Coll.	College Degree	Free/Reduced Lunch	Students per Teacher
Area	83.0%	22.8%	28.2%	57.0%	14.0
USA	85.8%	22.6%	33.2%	41.2%	15.8

Key Property Crime Data (Rate per 100,000 residents)

	Rate	Burglary	Larceny, Theft	Vehicle Theft	
Area	3,565.1	841.8	2,494.9	228.4	
USA	3,413.6	806.6	2,388.0	262.7	

Key Violent Crime Data (Rate per 100,000 residents)

	Rate	Murder	Rape	Robbery	Aggravated Assault
Area	417.1	3.1	32.8	124.5	256.7
USA	432.8	4.7	34.7	111.6	285.6

Key Economic Data (Family income, unemployment)

	$25k-$75k	$75k-$150k	>$150k	Unemployment 03/2009	Unemployment 03/2010
Area	56.4%	19.4%	5.4%	7.4%	8.9%
USA	45.8%	29.5%	8.5%	9.0%	10.1

Key Household Data

	Population Age 0-17	Children w/Married Parents	Children w/Single Mother	Stay-at-home Mothers	Births to Single Women
Area	26.0%	62.8%	29.9%	26.5%	49.1%
USA	24.0%	65.6%	25.5%	27.9%	35.3%

Key Housing Data

	Owner Occupied	Median Year Built	Median Home Value	Home Value Growth, 2005-2010	Median List Price, 4-bedroom Home
Area	65.0%	1986	$128,100	4.8%	
USA	67.8%	1976	$187,045	3.1%	$288,846

Vallejo-Fairfield, CA
407,515

	Score	Rank
Overall	56.99	305
LDS Culture	2.65	361
Education	63.86	257
Crime	42.72	269
Economic	58.20	256
Health	48.59	76
Household	77.16	83
Housing	72.28	315

Key LDS Culture Data

	Positive	Negative	Ratio Pos:Neg	Commute>59 minutes	Commute<15 minutes
Area	11,012	1376	8.0	16.0%	26.2%
USA	4,292	251	20.1	5.5%	34.1%

Key Education Data

	HS Grad	Some Coll.	College Degree	Free/Reduced Lunch	Students per Teacher
Area	85.3%	28.1%	34.2%	38.5%	17.3
USA	85.8%	22.6%	33.2%	41.2%	15.8

Key Property Crime Data (Rate per 100,000 residents)

	Rate	Burglary	Larceny, Theft	Vehicle Theft	
Area	3,622.2	958.4	2,027.9	635.9	
USA	3,413.6	806.6	2,388.0	262.7	

Key Violent Crime Data (Rate per 100,000 residents)

	Rate	Murder	Rape	Robbery	Aggravated Assault
Area	576.9	5.9	30.1	221.8	319.1
USA	432.8	4.7	34.7	111.6	285.6

Key Economic Data (Family income, unemployment)

	$25k-$75k	$75k-$150k	>$150k	Unemployment 03/2009	Unemployment 03/2010
Area	37.2%	38.1%	14.6%	10.3%	13.0%
USA	45.8%	29.5%	8.5%	9.0%	10.1

Key Household Data

	Population Age 0-17	Children w/Married Parents	Children w/Single Mother	Stay-at-home Mothers	Births to Single Women
Area	25.2%	67.6%	22.3%	32.3%	31.3%
USA	24.0%	65.6%	25.5%	27.9%	35.3%

Key Housing Data

	Owner Occupied	Median Year Built	Median Home Value	Home Value Growth, 2005-2010	Median List Price, 4-bedroom Home
Area	63.9%	1980	$388,800	-4.8%	$319,000
USA	67.8%	1976	$187,045	3.1%	$288,846

Victoria, TX
114,153

	Score	Rank
Overall	53.90	342
LDS Culture	26.40	190
Education	51.28	343
Crime	43.84	264
Economic	59.70	235
Health	32.00	335
Household	45.68	335
Housing	86.73	104

Key LDS Culture Data

	Positive	Negative	Ratio Pos:Neg	Commute>59 minutes	Commute<15 minutes
Area	636	32	19.9	6.7%	41.8%
USA	4,292	251	20.1	5.5%	34.1%

Key Education Data

	HS Grad	Some Coll.	College Degree	Free/Reduced Lunch	Students per Teacher
Area	78.7%	24.6%	20.5%	57.7%	14.3
USA	85.8%	22.6%	33.2%	41.2%	15.8

Key Property Crime Data (Rate per 100,000 residents)

	Rate	Burglary	Larceny, Theft	Vehicle Theft
Area	3,947.5	1,056.4	2,732.5	158.7
USA	3,413.6	806.6	2,388.0	262.7

Key Violent Crime Data (Rate per 100,000 residents)

	Rate	Murder	Rape	Robbery	Aggravated Assault
Area	516.3	1.8	53.5	64.0	397.1
USA	432.8	4.7	34.7	111.6	285.6

Key Economic Data (Family income, unemployment)

	$25k-$75k	$75k-$150k	>$150k	Unemployment 03/2009	Unemployment 03/2010
Area	45.7%	27.7%	6.2%	6.6%	8.0%
USA	45.8%	29.5%	8.5%	9.0%	10.1

Key Household Data

	Population Age 0-17	Children w/Married Parents	Children w/Single Mother	Stay-at-home Mothers	Births to Single Women
Area	26.4%	60.2%	25.1%	20.4%	50.4%
USA	24.0%	65.6%	25.5%	27.9%	35.3%

Key Housing Data

	Owner Occupied	Median Year Built	Median Home Value	Home Value Growth, 2005-2010	Median List Price, 4-bedroom Home
Area	69.0%	1975	$100,100	5.5%	
USA	67.8%	1976	$187,045	3.1%	$288,846

Vineland-Millville-Bridgeton, NJ
156,830

	Score	Rank
Overall	53.27	347
LDS Culture	22.56	249
Education	60.51	290
Crime	39.26	294
Economic	55.75	285
Health	46.52	119
Household	43.83	345
Housing	73.15	307

Key LDS Culture Data

	Positive	Negative	Ratio Pos:Neg	Commute>59 minutes	Commute<15 minutes
Area	6,652	324	20.5	7.6%	39.6%
USA	4,292	251	20.1	5.5%	34.1%

Key Education Data

	HS Grad	Some Coll.	College Degree	Free/Reduced Lunch	Students per Teacher
Area	77.9%	17.2%	19.4%	61.8%	13.4
USA	85.8%	22.6%	33.2%	41.2%	15.8

Key Property Crime Data (Rate per 100,000 residents)

	Rate	Burglary	Larceny, Theft	Vehicle Theft
Area	3,744.9	957.9	2,624.3	162.7
USA	3,413.6	806.6	2,388.0	262.7

Key Violent Crime Data (Rate per 100,000 residents)

	Rate	Murder	Rape	Robbery	Aggravated Assault
Area	643.3	9.6	16.0	224.2	393.4
USA	432.8	4.7	34.7	111.6	285.6

Key Economic Data (Family income, unemployment)

	$25k-$75k	$75k-$150k	>$150k	Unemployment 03/2009	Unemployment 03/2010
Area	47.7%	31.9%	4.4%	12.5%	14.4%
USA	45.8%	29.5%	8.5%	9.0%	10.1

Key Household Data

	Population Age 0-17	Children w/Married Parents	Children w/Single Mother	Stay-at-home Mothers	Births to Single Women
Area	24.5%	52.5%	31.1%	24.5%	44.8%
USA	24.0%	65.6%	25.5%	27.9%	35.3%

Key Housing Data

	Owner Occupied	Median Year Built	Median Home Value	Home Value Growth, 2005-2010	Median List Price, 4-bedroom Home
Area	68.5%	1966	$184,500	5.8%	
USA	67.8%	1976	$187,045	3.1%	$288,846

Virginia Beach-Norfolk-Newport News, VA-NC
1,657,534

	Score	Rank
Overall	**60.73**	**226**
LDS Culture	46.90	21
Education	64.58	249
Crime	50.53	215
Economic	63.92	169
Health	29.63	346
Household	56.17	267
Housing	77.69	250

Key LDS Culture Data

	Positive	Negative	Ratio Pos:Neg	Commute>59 minutes	Commute<15 minutes
Area	7,237	168	43.1	4.8%	25.9%
USA	4,292	251	20.1	5.5%	34.1%

Key Education Data

	HS Grad	Some Coll.	College Degree	Free/Reduced Lunch	Students per Teacher
Area	89.0%	26.0%	36.1%	35.0%	17.6
USA	85.8%	22.6%	33.2%	41.2%	15.8

Key Property Crime Data (Rate per 100,000 residents)

	Rate	Burglary	Larceny, Theft	Vehicle Theft	
Area	3,459.8	586.1	2,645.6	228.0	
USA	3,413.6	806.6	2,388.0	262.7	

Key Violent Crime Data (Rate per 100,000 residents)

	Rate	Murder	Rape	Robbery	Aggravated Assault
Area	425.5	6.4	28.7	193.5	196.9
USA	432.8	4.7	34.7	111.6	285.6

Key Economic Data (Family income, unemployment)

	$25k-$75k	$75k-$150k	>$150k	Unemployment 03/2009	Unemployment 03/2010
Area	42.0%	34.8%	9.9%	6.6%	7.8%
USA	45.8%	29.5%	8.5%	9.0%	10.1

Key Household Data

	Population Age 0-17	Children w/Married Parents	Children w/Single Mother	Stay-at-home Mothers	Births to Single Women
Area	24.9%	62.2%	29.9%	27.2%	41.7%
USA	24.0%	65.6%	25.5%	27.9%	35.3%

Key Housing Data

	Owner Occupied	Median Year Built	Median Home Value	Home Value Growth, 2005-2010	Median List Price, 4-bedroom Home
Area	63.6%	1979	$256,400	7.3%	$313,900
USA	67.8%	1976	$187,045	3.1%	$288,846

Visalia-Porterville, CA
426,276

	Score	Rank
Overall	56.26	317
LDS Culture	10.48	356
Education	64.08	256
Crime	43.23	265
Economic	42.91	355
Health	48.59	77
Household	73.46	125
Housing	77.99	244

Key LDS Culture Data

	Positive	Negative	Ratio Pos:Neg	Commute>59 minutes	Commute<15 minutes
Area	225	121	1.9	5.4%	41.5%
USA	4,292	251	20.1	5.5%	34.1%

Key Education Data

	HS Grad	Some Coll.	College Degree	Free/Reduced Lunch	Students per Teacher
Area	67.6%	23.0%	20.1%	70.2%	18.8
USA	85.8%	22.6%	33.2%	41.2%	15.8

Key Property Crime Data (Rate per 100,000 residents)

	Rate	Burglary	Larceny, Theft	Vehicle Theft	
Area	3,959.5	921.3	2,383.9	654.3	
USA	3,413.6	806.6	2,388.0	262.7	

Key Violent Crime Data (Rate per 100,000 residents)

	Rate	Murder	Rape	Robbery	Aggravated Assault
Area	529.1	10.1	24.4	109.9	384.7
USA	432.8	4.7	34.7	111.6	285.6

Key Economic Data (Family income, unemployment)

	$25k-$75k	$75k-$150k	>$150k	Unemployment 03/2009	Unemployment 03/2010
Area	45.7%	23.4%	5.4%	16.6%	19.4%
USA	45.8%	29.5%	8.5%	9.0%	10.1

Key Household Data

	Population Age 0-17	Children w/Married Parents	Children w/Single Mother	Stay-at-home Mothers	Births to Single Women
Area	31.8%	65.9%	23.5%	40.4%	35.3%
USA	24.0%	65.6%	25.5%	27.9%	35.3%

Key Housing Data

	Owner Occupied	Median Year Built	Median Home Value	Home Value Growth, 2005-2010	Median List Price, 4-bedroom Home
Area	58.9%	1981	$223,700	2.4%	$239,000
USA	67.8%	1976	$187,045	3.1%	$288,846

Waco, TX
230,213

	Score	Rank
Overall	54.18	340
LDS Culture	29.65	147
Education	56.51	317
Crime	36.10	312
Economic	54.97	293
Health	32.00	336
Household	45.06	341
Housing	93.13	24

Key LDS Culture Data

	Positive	Negative	Ratio Pos:Neg	Commute>59 minutes	Commute<15 minutes
Area	1,373	74	18.6	3.6%	40.0%
USA	4,292	251	20.1	5.5%	34.1%

Key Education Data

	HS Grad	Some Coll.	College Degree	Free/Reduced Lunch	Students per Teacher
Area	81.3%	23.8%	29.0%	58.0%	14.0
USA	85.8%	22.6%	33.2%	41.2%	15.8

Key Property Crime Data (Rate per 100,000 residents)

	Rate	Burglary	Larceny, Theft	Vehicle Theft
Area	4,682.9	1,214.2	3,231.7	237.0
USA	3,413.6	806.6	2,388.0	262.7

Key Violent Crime Data (Rate per 100,000 residents)

	Rate	Murder	Rape	Robbery	Aggravated Assault
Area	615.4	6.5	66.5	127.9	414.5
USA	432.8	4.7	34.7	111.6	285.6

Key Economic Data (Family income, unemployment)

	$25k-$75k	$75k-$150k	>$150k	Unemployment 03/2009	Unemployment 03/2010
Area	45.7%	26.2%	6.1%	6.3%	7.1%
USA	45.8%	29.5%	8.5%	9.0%	10.1

Key Household Data

	Population Age 0-17	Children w/Married Parents	Children w/Single Mother	Stay-at-home Mothers	Births to Single Women
Area	25.6%	58.0%	31.1%	28.8%	49.4%
USA	24.0%	65.6%	25.5%	27.9%	35.3%

Key Housing Data

	Owner Occupied	Median Year Built	Median Home Value	Home Value Growth, 2005-2010	Median List Price, 4-bedroom Home
Area	58.4%	1975	$108,400	3.5%	$199,900
USA	67.8%	1976	$187,045	3.1%	$288,846

Warner Robins, GA
133,161

	Score	Rank
Overall	**67.22**	**99**
LDS Culture	30.85	127
Education	66.41	229
Crime	53.03	191
Economic	68.98	98
Health	40.98	206
Household	83.33	48
Housing	87.48	93

Key LDS Culture Data

	Positive	Negative	Ratio Pos:Neg	Commute>59 minutes	Commute<15 minutes
Area	2,170	109	19.9	2.9%	33.4%
USA	4,292	251	20.1	5.5%	34.1%

Key Education Data

	HS Grad	Some Coll.	College Degree	Free/Reduced Lunch	Students per Teacher
Area	86.3%	23.4%	33.2%	44.4%	13.8
USA	85.8%	22.6%	33.2%	41.2%	15.8

Key Property Crime Data (Rate per 100,000 residents)

	Rate	Burglary	Larceny, Theft	Vehicle Theft
Area	4,351.1	923.6	3,219.3	208.2
USA	3,413.6	806.6	2,388.0	262.7

Key Violent Crime Data (Rate per 100,000 residents)

	Rate	Murder	Rape	Robbery	Aggravated Assault
Area	353.9	6.0	16.5	81.9	249.5
USA	432.8	4.7	34.7	111.6	285.6

Key Economic Data (Family income, unemployment)

	$25k-$75k	$75k-$150k	>$150k	Unemployment 03/2009	Unemployment 03/2010
Area	42.4%	35.7%	10.2%	6.5%	7.8%
USA	45.8%	29.5%	8.5%	9.0%	10.1

Key Household Data

	Population Age 0-17	Children w/Married Parents	Children w/Single Mother	Stay-at-home Mothers	Births to Single Women
Area	26.8%	68.7%	24.1%	24.1%	28.7%
USA	24.0%	65.6%	25.5%	27.9%	35.3%

Key Housing Data

	Owner Occupied	Median Year Built	Median Home Value	Home Value Growth, 2005-2010	Median List Price, 4-bedroom Home
Area	67.5%	1988	$137,000	2.1%	
USA	67.8%	1976	$187,045	3.1%	$288,846

Washington-Arlington-Alexandria, DC-VA-MD-WV
5,356,474

	Score	Rank
Overall	62.10	192
LDS Culture	24.30	234
Education	61.50	282
Crime	53.11	189
Economic	75.99	39
Health	37.70	247
Household	76.54	88
Housing	69.05	331

Key LDS Culture Data

	Positive	Negative	Ratio Pos:Neg	Commute>59 minutes	Commute<15 minutes
Area	29,415	905	32.5	15.3%	15.7%
USA	4,292	251	20.1	5.5%	34.1%

Key Education Data

	HS Grad	Some Coll.	College Degree	Free/Reduced Lunch	Students per Teacher
Area	89.3%	17.8%	52.4%	28.7%	
USA	85.8%	22.6%	33.2%	41.2%	15.8

Key Property Crime Data (Rate per 100,000 residents)

	Rate	Burglary	Larceny, Theft	Vehicle Theft
Area	3,001.3	421.8	2,153.7	425.7
USA	3,413.6	806.6	2,388.0	262.7

Key Violent Crime Data (Rate per 100,000 residents)

	Rate	Murder	Rape	Robbery	Aggravated Assault
Area	437.8	7.5	18.4	204.6	207.3
USA	432.8	4.7	34.7	111.6	285.6

Key Economic Data (Family income, unemployment)

	$25k-$75k	$75k-$150k	>$150k	Unemployment 03/2009	Unemployment 03/2010
Area	27.7%	36.3%	28.6%	5.7%	6.7%
USA	45.8%	29.5%	8.5%	9.0%	10.1

Key Household Data

	Population Age 0-17	Children w/Married Parents	Children w/Single Mother	Stay-at-home Mothers	Births to Single Women
Area	24.3%	68.5%	24.3%	26.7%	28.4%
USA	24.0%	65.6%	25.5%	27.9%	35.3%

Key Housing Data

	Owner Occupied	Median Year Built	Median Home Value	Home Value Growth, 2005-2010	Median List Price, 4-bedroom Home
Area	67.0%	1979	$430,600	3.5%	$409,000
USA	67.8%	1976	$187,045	3.1%	$288,846

Waterloo-Cedar Falls, IA
162,411

	Score	Rank
Overall	70.89	42
LDS Culture	41.43	38
Education	92.14	15
Crime	55.59	169
Economic	62.98	187
Health	54.48	15
Household	73.46	126
Housing	74.48	288

Key LDS Culture Data

	Positive	Negative	Ratio Pos:Neg	Commute>59 minutes	Commute<15 minutes
Area	1,153	97	11.9	2.8%	51.3%
USA	4,292	251	20.1	5.5%	34.1%

Key Education Data

	HS Grad	Some Coll.	College Degree	Free/Reduced Lunch	Students per Teacher
Area	90.9%	23.7%	33.2%	32.1%	14.4
USA	85.8%	22.6%	33.2%	41.2%	15.8

Key Property Crime Data (Rate per 100,000 residents)

	Rate	Burglary	Larceny, Theft	Vehicle Theft
Area	2,609.3	665.6	1,800.1	143.6
USA	3,413.6	806.6	2,388.0	262.7

Key Violent Crime Data (Rate per 100,000 residents)

	Rate	Murder	Rape	Robbery	Aggravated Assault
Area	467.6	1.8	40.3	75.2	350.2
USA	432.8	4.7	34.7	111.6	285.6

Key Economic Data (Family income, unemployment)

	$25k-$75k	$75k-$150k	>$150k	Unemployment 03/2009	Unemployment 03/2010
Area	53.4%	29.1%	5.3%	10.9%	12.6%
USA	45.8%	29.5%	8.5%	9.0%	10.1

Key Household Data

	Population Age 0-17	Children w/Married Parents	Children w/Single Mother	Stay-at-home Mothers	Births to Single Women
Area	21.8%	66.9%	24.6%	22.7%	24.4%
USA	24.0%	65.6%	25.5%	27.9%	35.3%

Key Housing Data

	Owner Occupied	Median Year Built	Median Home Value	Home Value Growth, 2005-2010	Median List Price, 4-bedroom Home
Area	73.7%	1959	$118,600	3.1%	
USA	67.8%	1976	$187,045	3.1%	$288,846

Wausau, WI
130,962

	Score	Rank
Overall	69.42	56
LDS Culture	23.12	241
Education	86.04	37
Crime	80.43	32
Economic	68.09	109
Health	39.16	234
Household	69.75	150
Housing	78.58	238

Key LDS Culture Data

	Positive	Negative	Ratio Pos:Neg	Commute>59 minutes	Commute<15 minutes
Area	814	132	6.2	3.3%	39.4%
USA	4,292	251	20.1	5.5%	34.1%

Key Education Data

	HS Grad	Some Coll.	College Degree	Free/Reduced Lunch	Students per Teacher
Area	88.1%	18.9%	31.9%	29.1%	14.6
USA	85.8%	22.6%	33.2%	41.2%	15.8

Key Property Crime Data (Rate per 100,000 residents)

	Rate	Burglary	Larceny, Theft	Vehicle Theft	
Area	1,814.5	385.0	1,359.7	69.8	
USA	3,413.6	806.6	2,388.0	262.7	

Key Violent Crime Data (Rate per 100,000 residents)

	Rate	Murder	Rape	Robbery	Aggravated Assault
Area	265.4	2.3	26.8	26.1	210.1
USA	432.8	4.7	34.7	111.6	285.6

Key Economic Data (Family income, unemployment)

	$25k-$75k	$75k-$150k	>$150k	Unemployment 03/2009	Unemployment 03/2010
Area	49.5%	35.5%	5.9%	5.3%	6.9%
USA	45.8%	29.5%	8.5%	9.0%	10.1

Key Household Data

	Population Age 0-17	Children w/Married Parents	Children w/Single Mother	Stay-at-home Mothers	Births to Single Women
Area	23.6%	70.7%	19.3%	21.0%	23.1%
USA	24.0%	65.6%	25.5%	27.9%	35.3%

Key Housing Data

	Owner Occupied	Median Year Built	Median Home Value	Home Value Growth, 2005-2010	Median List Price, 4-bedroom Home
Area	72.2%	1972	$144,800	2.5%	
USA	67.8%	1976	$187,045	3.1%	$288,846

Weirton-Steubenville, WV-OH
122,054

	Score	Rank
Overall	64.10	160
LDS Culture	24.71	221
Education	71.76	165
Crime	86.01	15
Economic	54.92	294
Health	42.19	182
Household	57.41	247
Housing	74.01	298

Key LDS Culture Data

	Positive	Negative	Ratio Pos:Neg	Commute>59 minutes	Commute<15 minutes
Area	5,236	404	13.0	5.0%	35.7%
USA	4,292	251	20.1	5.5%	34.1%

Key Education Data

	HS Grad	Some Coll.	College Degree	Free/Reduced Lunch	Students per Teacher
Area	87.1%	18.6%	26.6%	17.8%	14.9
USA	85.8%	22.6%	33.2%	41.2%	15.8

Key Property Crime Data (Rate per 100,000 residents)

	Rate	Burglary	Larceny, Theft	Vehicle Theft
Area	2,015.9	432.0	1,475.3	108.6
USA	3,413.6	806.6	2,388.0	262.7

Key Violent Crime Data (Rate per 100,000 residents)

	Rate	Murder	Rape	Robbery	Aggravated Assault
Area	184.3	2.5	14.0	42.0	125.9
USA	432.8	4.7	34.7	111.6	285.6

Key Economic Data (Family income, unemployment)

	$25k-$75k	$75k-$150k	>$150k	Unemployment 03/2009	Unemployment 03/2010
Area	54.2%	23.6%	4.2%	9.4%	10.6%
USA	45.8%	29.5%	8.5%	9.0%	10.1

Key Household Data

	Population Age 0-17	Children w/Married Parents	Children w/Single Mother	Stay-at-home Mothers	Births to Single Women
Area	19.6%	65.2%	26.1%	31.1%	38.7%
USA	24.0%	65.6%	25.5%	27.9%	35.3%

Key Housing Data

	Owner Occupied	Median Year Built	Median Home Value	Home Value Growth, 2005-2010	Median List Price, 4-bedroom Home
Area	73.8%	1958	$88,700	1.9%	
USA	67.8%	1976	$187,045	3.1%	$288,846

Wenatchee-East Wenatchee, WA
108,193

	Score	Rank
Overall	**68.55**	**73**
LDS Culture	25.22	208
Education	66.21	231
Crime	77.23	41
Economic	68.65	99
Health	46.37	122
Household	78.40	75
Housing	77.52	254

Key LDS Culture Data

	Positive	Negative	Ratio Pos:Neg	Commute>59 minutes	Commute<15 minutes
Area	519	28	18.5	5.2%	47.2%
USA	4,292	251	20.1	5.5%	34.1%

Key Education Data

	HS Grad	Some Coll.	College Degree	Free/Reduced Lunch	Students per Teacher
Area	83.6%	24.1%	32.1%	53.7%	18.5
USA	85.8%	22.6%	33.2%	41.2%	15.8

Key Property Crime Data (Rate per 100,000 residents)

	Rate	Burglary	Larceny, Theft	Vehicle Theft
Area	2,869.9	478.3	2,234.6	157.0
USA	3,413.6	806.6	2,388.0	262.7

Key Violent Crime Data (Rate per 100,000 residents)

	Rate	Murder	Rape	Robbery	Aggravated Assault
Area	190.2	4.6	46.2	20.3	119.1
USA	432.8	4.7	34.7	111.6	285.6

Key Economic Data (Family income, unemployment)

	$25k-$75k	$75k-$150k	>$150k	Unemployment 03/2009	Unemployment 03/2010
Area	53.0%	25.5%	8.1%	9.3%	9.9%
USA	45.8%	29.5%	8.5%	9.0%	10.1

Key Household Data

	Population Age 0-17	Children w/Married Parents	Children w/Single Mother	Stay-at-home Mothers	Births to Single Women
Area	25.8%	71.1%	22.1%	31.1%	39.3%
USA	24.0%	65.6%	25.5%	27.9%	35.3%

Key Housing Data

	Owner Occupied	Median Year Built	Median Home Value	Home Value Growth, 2005-2010	Median List Price, 4-bedroom Home
Area	69.2%	1980	$258,900	9.4%	
USA	67.8%	1976	$187,045	3.1%	$288,846

Wheeling, WV-OH
144,847

	Score	Rank
Overall	61.03	219
LDS Culture	24.93	215
Education	75.07	125
Crime	83.17	22
Economic	46.86	345
Health	42.19	183
Household	45.06	342
Housing	74.07	297

Key LDS Culture Data

	Positive	Negative	Ratio Pos:Neg	Commute>59 minutes	Commute<15 minutes
Area	2,313	175	13.2	6.0%	32.9%
USA	4,292	251	20.1	5.5%	34.1%

Key Education Data

	HS Grad	Some Coll.	College Degree	Free/Reduced Lunch	Students per Teacher
Area	89.6%	21.7%	23.9%	25.9%	14.8
USA	85.8%	22.6%	33.2%	41.2%	15.8

Key Property Crime Data (Rate per 100,000 residents)

	Rate	Burglary	Larceny, Theft	Vehicle Theft
Area	2,001.9	445.3	1,422.4	134.2
USA	3,413.6	806.6	2,388.0	262.7

Key Violent Crime Data (Rate per 100,000 residents)

	Rate	Murder	Rape	Robbery	Aggravated Assault
Area	216.4	2.1	33.9	49.1	131.4
USA	432.8	4.7	34.7	111.6	285.6

Key Economic Data (Family income, unemployment)

	$25k-$75k	$75k-$150k	>$150k	Unemployment 03/2009	Unemployment 03/2010
Area	53.9%	25.1%	1.8%	8.5%	11.4%
USA	45.8%	29.5%	8.5%	9.0%	10.1

Key Household Data

	Population Age 0-17	Children w/Married Parents	Children w/Single Mother	Stay-at-home Mothers	Births to Single Women
Area	19.8%	62.2%	23.6%	29.9%	57.1%
USA	24.0%	65.6%	25.5%	27.9%	35.3%

Key Housing Data

	Owner Occupied	Median Year Built	Median Home Value	Home Value Growth, 2005-2010	Median List Price, 4-bedroom Home
Area	73.2%	1955	$84,700	2.8%	
USA	67.8%	1976	$187,045	3.1%	$288,846

Wichita Falls, TX
603,058

	Score	Rank
Overall	60.71	227
LDS Culture	37.98	56
Education	70.89	175
Crime	41.61	275
Economic	67.93	112
Health	22.23	361
Household	61.73	214
Housing	86.95	99

Key LDS Culture Data

	Positive	Negative	Ratio Pos:Neg	Commute>59 minutes	Commute<15 minutes
Area	2,980	236	12.6	2.0%	36.0%
USA	4,292	251	20.1	5.5%	34.1%

Key Education Data

	HS Grad	Some Coll.	College Degree	Free/Reduced Lunch	Students per Teacher
Area	88.9%	26.9%	34.9%	44.9%	16.3
USA	85.8%	22.6%	33.2%	41.2%	15.8

Key Property Crime Data (Rate per 100,000 residents)

	Rate	Burglary	Larceny, Theft	Vehicle Theft	
Area	5,287.4	1,233.3	3,667.6	386.5	
USA	3,413.6	806.6	2,388.0	262.7	

Key Violent Crime Data (Rate per 100,000 residents)

	Rate	Murder	Rape	Robbery	Aggravated Assault
Area	429.8	4.7	37.9	144.2	243.0
USA	432.8	4.7	34.7	111.6	285.6

Key Economic Data (Family income, unemployment)

	$25k-$75k	$75k-$150k	>$150k	Unemployment 03/2009	Unemployment 03/2010
Area	44.9%	31.6%	7.6%	6.9%	7.9%
USA	45.8%	29.5%	8.5%	9.0%	10.1

Key Household Data

	Population Age 0-17	Children w/Married Parents	Children w/Single Mother	Stay-at-home Mothers	Births to Single Women
Area	26.8%	63.2%	27.4%	27.5%	40.2%
USA	24.0%	65.6%	25.5%	27.9%	35.3%

Key Housing Data

	Owner Occupied	Median Year Built	Median Home Value	Home Value Growth, 2005-2010	Median List Price, 4-bedroom Home
Area	67.4%	1974	$118,300	3.3%	$169,900
USA	67.8%	1976	$187,045	3.1%	$288,846

Wichita, KS
148,091

	Score	Rank
Overall	58.68	272
LDS Culture	24.41	229
Education	68.64	200
Crime	38.00	302
Economic	64.42	159
Health	42.95	168
Household	58.64	238
Housing	79.23	223

Key LDS Culture Data

	Positive	Negative	Ratio Pos:Neg	Commute>59 minutes	Commute<15 minutes
Area	791	44	18.0	1.9%	48.8%
USA	4,292	251	20.1	5.5%	34.1%

Key Education Data

	HS Grad	Some Coll.	College Degree	Free/Reduced Lunch	Students per Teacher
Area	84.5%	23.1%	27.7%	48.4%	13.2
USA	85.8%	22.6%	33.2%	41.2%	15.8

Key Property Crime Data (Rate per 100,000 residents)

	Rate	Burglary	Larceny, Theft	Vehicle Theft
Area	4,322.8	899.6	3,058.5	364.7
USA	3,413.6	806.6	2,388.0	262.7

Key Violent Crime Data (Rate per 100,000 residents)

	Rate	Murder	Rape	Robbery	Aggravated Assault
Area	610.3	5.5	57.6	86.0	461.2
USA	432.8	4.7	34.7	111.6	285.6

Key Economic Data (Family income, unemployment)

	$25k-$75k	$75k-$150k	>$150k	Unemployment 03/2009	Unemployment 03/2010
Area	52.1%	25.3%	6.1%	7.0%	8.1%
USA	45.8%	29.5%	8.5%	9.0%	10.1

Key Household Data

	Population Age 0-17	Children w/Married Parents	Children w/Single Mother	Stay-at-home Mothers	Births to Single Women
Area	25.0%	63.8%	26.8%	26.2%	49.7%
USA	24.0%	65.6%	25.5%	27.9%	35.3%

Key Housing Data

	Owner Occupied	Median Year Built	Median Home Value	Home Value Growth, 2005-2010	Median List Price, 4-bedroom Home
Area	68.2%	1967	$86,000	2.8%	
USA	67.8%	1976	$187,045	3.1%	$288,846

Williamsport, PA
116,670

	Score	Rank
Overall	66.20	121
LDS Culture	29.35	151
Education	68.27	205
Crime	88.31	8
Economic	58.59	248
Health	47.33	99
Household	61.73	215
Housing	70.90	323

Key LDS Culture Data

	Positive	Negative	Ratio Pos:Neg	Commute>59 minutes	Commute<15 minutes
Area	1,480	112	13.2	3.6%	40.1%
USA	4,292	251	20.1	5.5%	34.1%

Key Education Data

	HS Grad	Some Coll.	College Degree	Free/Reduced Lunch	Students per Teacher
Area	87.8%	17.1%	29.2%	36.4%	13.7
USA	85.8%	22.6%	33.2%	41.2%	15.8

Key Property Crime Data (Rate per 100,000 residents)

	Rate	Burglary	Larceny, Theft	Vehicle Theft	
Area	2,063.3	460.6	1,527.9	74.8	
USA	3,413.6	806.6	2,388.0	262.7	

Key Violent Crime Data (Rate per 100,000 residents)

	Rate	Murder	Rape	Robbery	Aggravated Assault
Area	154.7	1.7	14.6	51.6	86.8
USA	432.8	4.7	34.7	111.6	285.6

Key Economic Data (Family income, unemployment)

	$25k-$75k	$75k-$150k	>$150k	Unemployment 03/2009	Unemployment 03/2010
Area	51.6%	24.5%	4.4%	9.0%	10.2%
USA	45.8%	29.5%	8.5%	9.0%	10.1

Key Household Data

	Population Age 0-17	Children w/Married Parents	Children w/Single Mother	Stay-at-home Mothers	Births to Single Women
Area	21.0%	63.7%	28.2%	27.3%	32.4%
USA	24.0%	65.6%	25.5%	27.9%	35.3%

Key Housing Data

	Owner Occupied	Median Year Built	Median Home Value	Home Value Growth, 2005-2010	Median List Price, 4-bedroom Home
Area	69.4%	1958	$125,200	4.1%	
USA	67.8%	1976	$187,045	3.1%	$288,846

Wilmington, NC
347,012

	Score	Rank
Overall	**61.32**	**213**
LDS Culture	24.93	216
Education	63.51	263
Crime	51.34	203
Economic	67.26	120
Health	34.66	288
Household	74.69	109
Housing	76.80	261

Key LDS Culture Data

	Positive	Negative	Ratio Pos:Neg	Commute>59 minutes	Commute<15 minutes
Area	1,730	95	18.2	4.3%	33.0%
USA	4,292	251	20.1	5.5%	34.1%

Key Education Data

	HS Grad	Some Coll.	College Degree	Free/Reduced Lunch	Students per Teacher
Area	86.3%	22.1%	37.9%	43.0%	15.1
USA	85.8%	22.6%	33.2%	41.2%	15.8

Key Property Crime Data (Rate per 100,000 residents)

	Rate	Burglary	Larceny, Theft	Vehicle Theft
Area	4,112.9	1,289.1	2,518.5	305.3
USA	3,413.6	806.6	2,388.0	262.7

Key Violent Crime Data (Rate per 100,000 residents)

	Rate	Murder	Rape	Robbery	Aggravated Assault
Area	384.0	4.6	34.3	127.6	217.5
USA	432.8	4.7	34.7	111.6	285.6

Key Economic Data (Family income, unemployment)

	$25k-$75k	$75k-$150k	>$150k	Unemployment 03/2009	Unemployment 03/2010
Area	51.1%	26.0%	9.2%	10.0%	10.5%
USA	45.8%	29.5%	8.5%	9.0%	10.1

Key Household Data

	Population Age 0-17	Children w/Married Parents	Children w/Single Mother	Stay-at-home Mothers	Births to Single Women
Area	21.2%	61.3%	28.7%	31.7%	18.4%
USA	24.0%	65.6%	25.5%	27.9%	35.3%

Key Housing Data

	Owner Occupied	Median Year Built	Median Home Value	Home Value Growth, 2005-2010	Median List Price, 4-bedroom Home
Area	69.7%	1989	$215,400	4.2%	$434,900
USA	67.8%	1976	$187,045	3.1%	$288,846

Winchester, VA-WV
119,512

	Score	Rank
Overall	60.91	221
LDS Culture	19.27	293
Education	65.15	242
Crime	78.28	37
Economic	68.37	102
Health	36.28	283
Household	49.38	304
Housing	73.87	299

Key LDS Culture Data

	Positive	Negative	Ratio Pos:Neg	Commute>59 minutes	Commute<15 minutes
Area	1,723	79	21.8	13.6%	26.4%
USA	4,292	251	20.1	5.5%	34.1%

Key Education Data

	HS Grad	Some Coll.	College Degree	Free/Reduced Lunch	Students per Teacher
Area	82.3%	16.5%	27.8%	31.9%	15.2
USA	85.8%	22.6%	33.2%	41.2%	15.8

Key Property Crime Data (Rate per 100,000 residents)

	Rate	Burglary	Larceny, Theft	Vehicle Theft	
Area	2,640.0	548.4	1,913.0	178.5	
USA	3,413.6	806.6	2,388.0	262.7	

Key Violent Crime Data (Rate per 100,000 residents)

	Rate	Murder	Rape	Robbery	Aggravated Assault
Area	202.8	1.6	48.7	43.8	108.7
USA	432.8	4.7	34.7	111.6	285.6

Key Economic Data (Family income, unemployment)

	$25k-$75k	$75k-$150k	>$150k	Unemployment 03/2009	Unemployment 03/2010
Area	45.0%	32.1%	7.1%	8.2%	8.6%
USA	45.8%	29.5%	8.5%	9.0%	10.1

Key Household Data

	Population Age 0-17	Children w/Married Parents	Children w/Single Mother	Stay-at-home Mothers	Births to Single Women
Area	23.6%	62.0%	25.9%	26.2%	43.9%
USA	24.0%	65.6%	25.5%	27.9%	35.3%

Key Housing Data

	Owner Occupied	Median Year Built	Median Home Value	Home Value Growth, 2005-2010	Median List Price, 4-bedroom Home
Area	69.1%	1984	$250,100	1.8%	
USA	67.8%	1976	$187,045	3.1%	$288,846

Winston-Salem, NC
468,124

	Score	Rank
Overall	64.34	154
LDS Culture	35.46	74
Education	68.90	198
Crime	35.83	314
Economic	62.42	195
Health	46.98	117
Household	76.54	89
Housing	86.44	111

Key LDS Culture Data

	Positive	Negative	Ratio Pos:Neg	Commute>59 minutes	Commute<15 minutes
Area	5,875	195	30.1	4.6%	32.0%
USA	4,292	251	20.1	5.5%	34.1%

Key Education Data

	HS Grad	Some Coll.	College Degree	Free/Reduced Lunch	Students per Teacher
Area	84.1%	19.7%	33.6%	43.5%	14.0
USA	85.8%	22.6%	33.2%	41.2%	15.8

Key Property Crime Data (Rate per 100,000 residents)

	Rate	Burglary	Larceny, Theft	Vehicle Theft
Area	4,850.4	1,426.0	3,102.5	321.9
USA	3,413.6	806.6	2,388.0	262.7

Key Violent Crime Data (Rate per 100,000 residents)

	Rate	Murder	Rape	Robbery	Aggravated Assault
Area	603.6	4.9	35.8	176.7	386.2
USA	432.8	4.7	34.7	111.6	285.6

Key Economic Data (Family income, unemployment)

	$25k-$75k	$75k-$150k	>$150k	Unemployment 03/2009	Unemployment 03/2010
Area	44.7%	28.6%	8.3%	9.9%	10.1%
USA	45.8%	29.5%	8.5%	9.0%	10.1

Key Household Data

	Population Age 0-17	Children w/Married Parents	Children w/Single Mother	Stay-at-home Mothers	Births to Single Women
Area	24.2%	67.0%	26.0%	25.8%	22.8%
USA	24.0%	65.6%	25.5%	27.9%	35.3%

Key Housing Data

	Owner Occupied	Median Year Built	Median Home Value	Home Value Growth, 2005-2010	Median List Price, 4-bedroom Home
Area	69.8%	1980	$148,200	2.5%	$246,900
USA	67.8%	1976	$187,045	3.1%	$288,846

Worcester, MA
783,806

	Score	Rank
Overall	62.65	186
LDS Culture	16.55	323
Education	79.71	70
Crime	63.98	116
Economic	74.49	48
Health	33.29	316
Household	75.31	103
Housing	58.42	355

Key LDS Culture Data

	Positive	Negative	Ratio Pos:Neg	Commute>59 minutes	Commute<15 minutes
Area	7,981	426	18.7	10.2%	28.2%
USA	4,292	251	20.1	5.5%	34.1%

Key Education Data

	HS Grad	Some Coll.	College Degree	Free/Reduced Lunch	Students per Teacher
Area	89.0%	16.8%	41.7%	27.7%	14.7
USA	85.8%	22.6%	33.2%	41.2%	15.8

Key Property Crime Data (Rate per 100,000 residents)

	Rate	Burglary	Larceny, Theft	Vehicle Theft
Area	2,093.9	552.4	1,369.4	172.0
USA	3,413.6	806.6	2,388.0	262.7

Key Violent Crime Data (Rate per 100,000 residents)

	Rate	Murder	Rape	Robbery	Aggravated Assault
Area	413.3	1.9	21.0	70.6	319.8
USA	432.8	4.7	34.7	111.6	285.6

Key Economic Data (Family income, unemployment)

	$25k-$75k	$75k-$150k	>$150k	Unemployment 03/2009	Unemployment 03/2010
Area	36.0%	38.6%	15.0%	8.6%	9.8%
USA	45.8%	29.5%	8.5%	9.0%	10.1

Key Household Data

	Population Age 0-17	Children w/Married Parents	Children w/Single Mother	Stay-at-home Mothers	Births to Single Women
Area	23.6%	70.4%	22.2%	23.3%	35.1%
USA	24.0%	65.6%	25.5%	27.9%	35.3%

Key Housing Data

	Owner Occupied	Median Year Built	Median Home Value	Home Value Growth, 2005-2010	Median List Price, 4-bedroom Home
Area	68.1%	1968	$282,800	-0.5%	$383,500
USA	67.8%	1976	$187,045	3.1%	$288,846

Yakima, WA
234,564

	Score	Rank
Overall	59.34	260
LDS Culture	33.97	92
Education	49.74	349
Crime	51.01	208
Economic	51.53	316
Health	52.40	31
Household	54.94	276
Housing	86.95	100

Key LDS Culture Data

	Positive	Negative	Ratio Pos:Neg	Commute>59 minutes	Commute<15 minutes
Area	959	52	18.4	2.5%	40.4%
USA	4,292	251	20.1	5.5%	34.1%

Key Education Data

	HS Grad	Some Coll.	College Degree	Free/Reduced Lunch	Students per Teacher
Area	71.3%	22.5%	21.3%	68.7%	19.2
USA	85.8%	22.6%	33.2%	41.2%	15.8

Key Property Crime Data (Rate per 100,000 residents)

	Rate	Burglary	Larceny, Theft	Vehicle Theft
Area	5,210.2	1,300.0	3,138.7	771.5
USA	3,413.6	806.6	2,388.0	262.7

Key Violent Crime Data (Rate per 100,000 residents)

	Rate	Murder	Rape	Robbery	Aggravated Assault
Area	332.5	8.1	42.6	104.0	177.7
USA	432.8	4.7	34.7	111.6	285.6

Key Economic Data (Family income, unemployment)

	$25k-$75k	$75k-$150k	>$150k	Unemployment 03/2009	Unemployment 03/2010
Area	50.7%	23.9%	4.5%	9.5%	10.6%
USA	45.8%	29.5%	8.5%	9.0%	10.1

Key Household Data

	Population Age 0-17	Children w/Married Parents	Children w/Single Mother	Stay-at-home Mothers	Births to Single Women
Area	30.3%	58.6%	27.0%	29.7%	41.3%
USA	24.0%	65.6%	25.5%	27.9%	35.3%

Key Housing Data

	Owner Occupied	Median Year Built	Median Home Value	Home Value Growth, 2005-2010	Median List Price, 4-bedroom Home
Area	66.0%	1973	$159,700	5.2%	$234,900
USA	67.8%	1976	$187,045	3.1%	$288,846

York-Hanover, PA
424,583

	Score	Rank
Overall	67.90	86
LDS Culture	18.82	303
Education	74.43	133
Crime	76.83	43
Economic	71.93	65
Health	47.33	100
Household	62.96	204
Housing	83.08	174

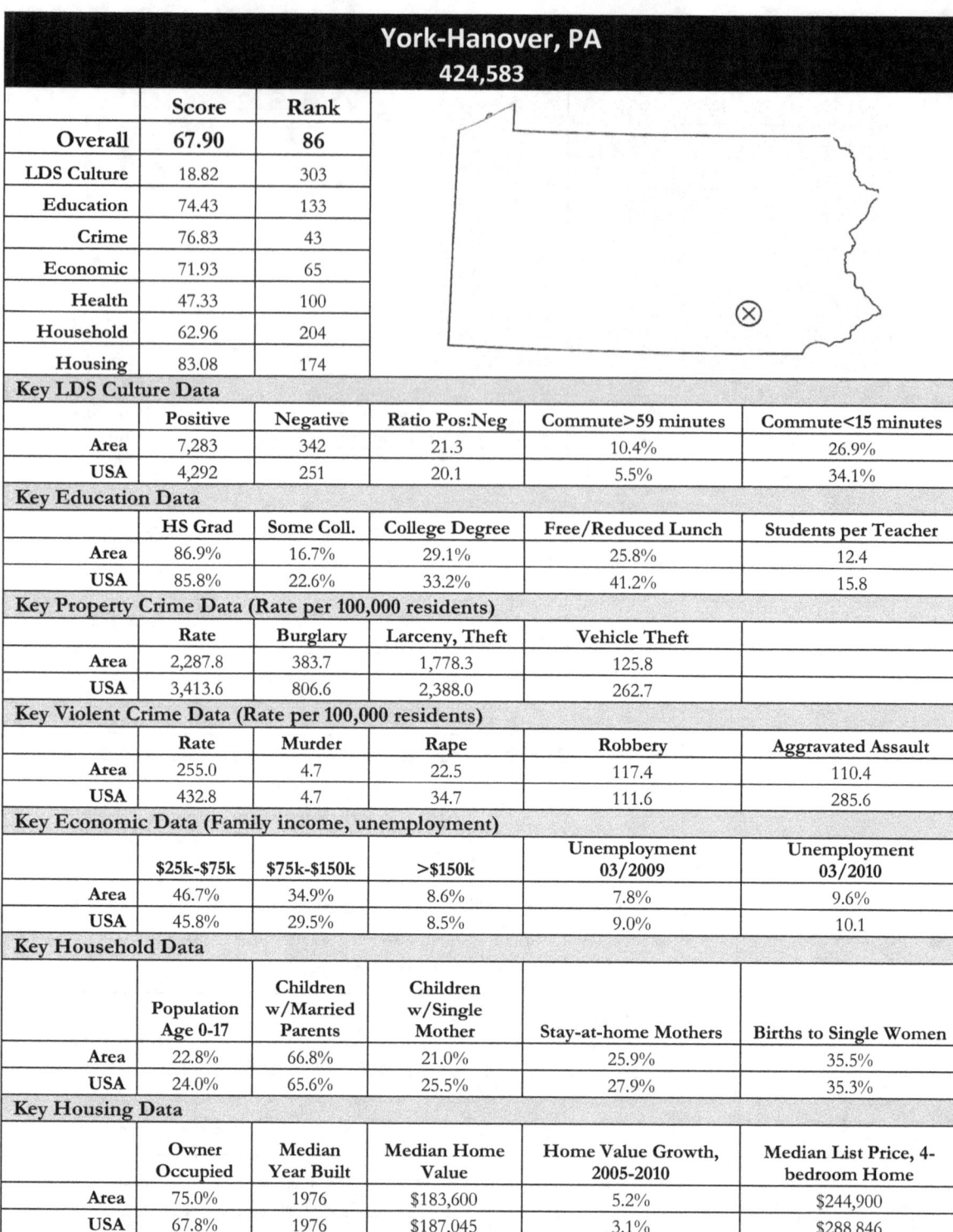

Key LDS Culture Data
	Positive	Negative	Ratio Pos:Neg	Commute>59 minutes	Commute<15 minutes
Area	7,283	342	21.3	10.4%	26.9%
USA	4,292	251	20.1	5.5%	34.1%

Key Education Data
	HS Grad	Some Coll.	College Degree	Free/Reduced Lunch	Students per Teacher
Area	86.9%	16.7%	29.1%	25.8%	12.4
USA	85.8%	22.6%	33.2%	41.2%	15.8

Key Property Crime Data (Rate per 100,000 residents)
	Rate	Burglary	Larceny, Theft	Vehicle Theft	
Area	2,287.8	383.7	1,778.3	125.8	
USA	3,413.6	806.6	2,388.0	262.7	

Key Violent Crime Data (Rate per 100,000 residents)
	Rate	Murder	Rape	Robbery	Aggravated Assault
Area	255.0	4.7	22.5	117.4	110.4
USA	432.8	4.7	34.7	111.6	285.6

Key Economic Data (Family income, unemployment)
	$25k-$75k	$75k-$150k	>$150k	Unemployment 03/2009	Unemployment 03/2010
Area	46.7%	34.9%	8.6%	7.8%	9.6%
USA	45.8%	29.5%	8.5%	9.0%	10.1

Key Household Data
	Population Age 0-17	Children w/Married Parents	Children w/Single Mother	Stay-at-home Mothers	Births to Single Women
Area	22.8%	66.8%	21.0%	25.9%	35.5%
USA	24.0%	65.6%	25.5%	27.9%	35.3%

Key Housing Data
	Owner Occupied	Median Year Built	Median Home Value	Home Value Growth, 2005-2010	Median List Price, 4-bedroom Home
Area	75.0%	1976	$183,600	5.2%	$244,900
USA	67.8%	1976	$187,045	3.1%	$288,846

Youngstown-Warren-Boardman, OH-PA
565,947

	Score	Rank
Overall	57.14	302
LDS Culture	26.86	183
Education	67.43	214
Crime	60.11	148
Economic	49.14	333
Health	39.63	220
Household	41.98	354
Housing	81.22	195

Key LDS Culture Data

	Positive	Negative	Ratio Pos:Neg	Commute>59 minutes	Commute<15 minutes
Area	4,942	321	15.4	6.4%	36.7%
USA	4,292	251	20.1	5.5%	34.1%

Key Education Data

	HS Grad	Some Coll.	College Degree	Free/Reduced Lunch	Students per Teacher
Area	87.0%	18.6%	24.8%	6.9%	16.7
USA	85.8%	22.6%	33.2%	41.2%	15.8

Key Property Crime Data (Rate per 100,000 residents)

	Rate	Burglary	Larceny, Theft	Vehicle Theft	
Area	3,294.6	925.9	2,127.1	241.7	
USA	3,413.6	806.6	2,388.0	262.7	

Key Violent Crime Data (Rate per 100,000 residents)

	Rate	Murder	Rape	Robbery	Aggravated Assault
Area	330.7	7.2	28.0	116.9	178.5
USA	432.8	4.7	34.7	111.6	285.6

Key Economic Data (Family income, unemployment)

	$25k-$75k	$75k-$150k	>$150k	Unemployment 03/2009	Unemployment 03/2010
Area	52.0%	23.9%	3.9%	12.6%	14.0%
USA	45.8%	29.5%	8.5%	9.0%	10.1

Key Household Data

	Population Age 0-17	Children w/Married Parents	Children w/Single Mother	Stay-at-home Mothers	Births to Single Women
Area	21.6%	59.3%	31.8%	26.8%	50.5%
USA	24.0%	65.6%	25.5%	27.9%	35.3%

Key Housing Data

	Owner Occupied	Median Year Built	Median Home Value	Home Value Growth, 2005-2010	Median List Price, 4-bedroom Home
Area	72.2%	1960	$101,500	0.7%	$139,900
USA	67.8%	1976	$187,045	3.1%	$288,846

Yuba City, CA
165,274

	Score	Rank
Overall	57.29	299
LDS Culture	12.02	351
Education	73.05	148
Crime	55.89	164
Economic	46.75	346
Health	48.59	78
Household	54.94	277
Housing	76.12	268

Key LDS Culture Data

	Positive	Negative	Ratio Pos:Neg	Commute>59 minutes	Commute<15 minutes
Area	1,451	78	18.6	12.0%	28.9%
USA	4,292	251	20.1	5.5%	34.1%

Key Education Data

	HS Grad	Some Coll.	College Degree	Free/Reduced Lunch	Students per Teacher
Area	78.1%	29.2%	26.0%	53.8%	17.1
USA	85.8%	22.6%	33.2%	41.2%	15.8

Key Property Crime Data (Rate per 100,000 residents)

	Rate	Burglary	Larceny, Theft	Vehicle Theft	
Area	2,898.0	791.8	1,754.6	351.5	
USA	3,413.6	806.6	2,388.0	262.7	

Key Violent Crime Data (Rate per 100,000 residents)

	Rate	Murder	Rape	Robbery	Aggravated Assault
Area	416.9	6.0	31.8	78.0	301.1
USA	432.8	4.7	34.7	111.6	285.6

Key Economic Data (Family income, unemployment)

	$25k-$75k	$75k-$150k	>$150k	Unemployment 03/2009	Unemployment 03/2010
Area	50.6%	23.1%	7.3%	18.3%	21.7%
USA	45.8%	29.5%	8.5%	9.0%	10.1

Key Household Data

	Population Age 0-17	Children w/Married Parents	Children w/Single Mother	Stay-at-home Mothers	Births to Single Women
Area	27.8%	62.9%	24.2%	29.2%	42.6%
USA	24.0%	65.6%	25.5%	27.9%	35.3%

Key Housing Data

	Owner Occupied	Median Year Built	Median Home Value	Home Value Growth, 2005-2010	Median List Price, 4-bedroom Home
Area	59.4%	1982	$246,600	-2.6%	
USA	67.8%	1976	$187,045	3.1%	$288,846

Yuma, AZ
194,322

	Score	Rank
Overall	59.53	256
LDS Culture	21.12	269
Education	66.04	234
Crime	61.64	137
Economic	36.13	361
Health	47.19	113
Household	56.79	256
Housing	92.84	26

Key LDS Culture Data

	Positive	Negative	Ratio Pos:Neg	Commute>59 minutes	Commute<15 minutes
Area	584	42	13.9	4.5%	38.4%
USA	4,292	251	20.1	5.5%	34.1%

Key Education Data

	HS Grad	Some Coll.	College Degree	Free/Reduced Lunch	Students per Teacher
Area	71.3%	25.9%	20.4%	72.6%	21.1
USA	85.8%	22.6%	33.2%	41.2%	15.8

Key Property Crime Data (Rate per 100,000 residents)

	Rate	Burglary	Larceny, Theft	Vehicle Theft
Area	2,758.0	676.1	1,759.4	322.5
USA	3,413.6	806.6	2,388.0	262.7

Key Violent Crime Data (Rate per 100,000 residents)

	Rate	Murder	Rape	Robbery	Aggravated Assault
Area	369.6	3.6	19.1	47.6	299.3
USA	432.8	4.7	34.7	111.6	285.6

Key Economic Data (Family income, unemployment)

	$25k-$75k	$75k-$150k	>$150k	Unemployment 03/2009	Unemployment 03/2010
Area	52.2%	17.8%	3.2%	15.8%	19.9%
USA	45.8%	29.5%	8.5%	9.0%	10.1

Key Household Data

	Population Age 0-17	Children w/Married Parents	Children w/Single Mother	Stay-at-home Mothers	Births to Single Women
Area	28.1%	60.2%	28.1%	34.8%	41.1%
USA	24.0%	65.6%	25.5%	27.9%	35.3%

Key Housing Data

	Owner Occupied	Median Year Built	Median Home Value	Home Value Growth, 2005-2010	Median List Price, 4-bedroom Home
Area	69.2%	1991	$152,800	6.2%	
USA	67.8%	1976	$187,045	3.1%	$288,846

Do you want to rate your community based on your own experience? Want to tell others about your school district, good places to shop, best neighborhoods, or travel times to the temple?

Visit www.BestLDSPlaces.com to post your own ratings and comments, and to see what others are saying about these 361 communities.

www.CivicusBooks.com

CIVICUS

www.CivicusBooks.com

BestLDSPlaces.Com

www.CivicusBooks.com

www.ingramcontent.com/pod-product-compliance
Lightning Source LLC
Chambersburg PA
CBHW080049190426
43201CB00035B/2145